# IN SEARCH OF

# Absolute Truth

*RIG-VEDA* VOLUME II:

SPIRITUAL INVOLUTION

RAMESH MALHOTRA

iUniverse®

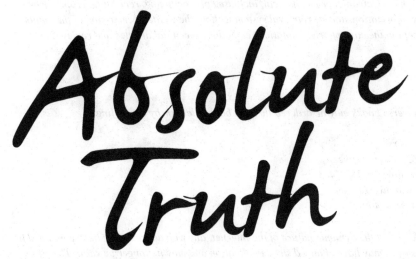

**IN SEARCH OF ABSOLUTE TRUTH**
***RIG-VEDA* VOLUME II: SPIRITUAL INVOLUTION**



*iUniverse books may be ordered through booksellers or by contacting:*

*iUniverse*
*1663 Liberty Drive*
*Bloomington, IN 47403*
*www.iuniverse.com*
*844-349-9409*



*ISBN: 978-1-6632-3948-8 (sc)*
*ISBN: 978-1-6632-3949-5 (e)*

*Library of Congress Control Number: 2022908350*

*Print information available on the last page.*

*iUniverse rev. date: 02/25/2023*

All the proceeds from the sale of this and other books dedicated to fund the construction of an elementary school located in Himalayas, where higher knowledge is brought as a service to the local community.

Our universe regulated by esoteric powers that influence without prejudice every creation: unmanifested or manifested; embodied or disembodied; and evil or not evil. The quest to know and unveil the secrets of such powers has been going on for centuries and will go on for more years come.

# Contents

## PART IV: MYTHOLOGICAL SPHERE


Preface to Part IV 1

9. Potency Dominion 5

10. Emissary Dominion 27

11. Ethical Dominion 50

12. Inspirational Dominion 70

13. Stimulus Dominion 99


## PART V: TRANSCENDENTAL SPHERE


Preface to Part V 151

14. Highbrow Dominion 153

15. Validated Dominion 185

16. Righteous Dominion 216

17. Cerebral Dominion 261

18. Sacrosanct Dominion 296

## PART VI: WORLDLY SPHERE


Preface to Part VI 339

19. Sacred Dominion 343

20. Exalted Dominion 382

21. Terrestrial Dominion 417

22. Perpetual Dominion 423

23. Holy Order Dominion 449

24. Underworld Dominion 482

Conclusion 489

Reference 493

# Part IV

# MYTHOLOGICAL SPHERE

# Preface to Part IV

AFTER THE CREATION OF THE DYNAMIC UNIVERSE AND establishment of the ground (Prithvi) located on the surface of planet Earth, all positioned within the terrestrial region, which has already experienced physical evolution. The creation called the astral body, which provides a domicile for the immortal spirit, manifested as the enhanced mysterious body Manu, capable of perceiving paranormal activities (phenomena). These activities include mythological, transcendental, and worldly. The first, mythological, still supported by the supreme powers of causation, including the supernatural, mystic, and faithful powers, commonly supported by an organized structure that used to explain the unexplainable. The second, transcendental, supported through specific practices such as yoga, meditation, contemplation, and undivided devotion to confirm the eternal truth. Here, infinite mind and heart join to go beyond even the divine nature to unveil the secrets of Mother Nature and come to know eternal truth. It goes beyond special plants (soma) to acquire mythical juice and then use the glands to transform this mythical fluid into nectar (*amrita*) to experience ecstasy. With both mythical juice and mythical fluid, astral bodies may reach beyond physical limitations and come to unveil the secrets of the supreme powers of causation. The third, worldly, is where the manifested mortal embodiment already exposed to transcendence, beginning to use a pragmatic approach to explain unexplainable actions. Embodiments even supersede the supreme powers of causation or the laws of nature that established in the worldly sphere; human beings do not accept paranormal activities unless proven with facts. They seek the unknown aspects of nature through scientific discovery. They accept nature as is and see no need to go beyond it to understand that which cannot perceived either by touch or through physical experience. If something cannot seen and observed in the same form by more than one, human beings define it as abnormal.

The ignorance behind these three aspects noted by the same invisible supreme powers of causation that prevail to regulate both the differentiated and undifferentiated universe—all forms of knowledge encompassed within one eternal truth. This means all creations, manifested mortal embodiments and immortal embodiments; that which is imperishable and that which is perishable; all immediate surroundings in the world and beyond; all aspects of the undifferentiated universe and the differentiated universe; and dormant and dynamic fiction and absolute truth.

Paranormal activities and phenomena fulfill the longings of the intuitive mind, heart, and soul, which helps individuals to understand existence and nonexistence. The ability to unveil hidden truths depends upon the seeker's ability to find resolutions to the problems facing humanity. The goal of each creation is to seek inner enlightenment, comprehend spiritual involution, and overcome the misery of living a material life.

In terms of mythology, the great primordial mother (*Shakti)*, with her feminine mystical power, appears to serve nature (*Prakriti*). This unmanifested feminine power accompanied by an unmanifested masculine power (*Purusha*). Together, they create the celestial, cosmic, and terrestrial regions. They jointly induce potency, which establishes the substratum located above the surface of the ground (*Prithvi*), from where they perform unexplained phenomena that create circumstances that impact moving and unmoving manifested mortal bodies. Through such phenomena, all creations cultivate wisdom. Through spiritual practices, manifested bodies come to comprehend the great elements of natural power. Through cosmic mystic forces, they transform to learn about the mythical powers created by the supreme powers of causation that influence individual embodiments and allow them to experience potency, which helps them gain control of their lives and others' lives, which pass from nonexistence to existence and go beyond the current state of existence. By genesis itself, the creation of a manifested embodiment represents a complex progression where physical mortal embodiments provided with a domicile by giving birth to (*Purusha)*, an invisible immortal embodiment, to acquire cognizance, through which they perceive and recognize their existence within the dynamic universe and, further, come to comprehend the powers of Mother Nature (*Prakriti*). This allows manifested embodiments to perform the actions and engage in the activities they need so they can survive as mortals. Further, such embodiments come to realize they are all regulated by divine powers *(Divine will)*, which connect the individual living spirit (*Atman*) prevailing within their embodiments with the ultimate universal soul(*Paramatman)*, which prevails in and regulates the manifested dynamic universe.

These aspects of attainment described within the *Rig-Veda* appear in chapters 6–10. After completing the initial physical evolution covered within the first volume, the readers, as the author did, will find it much easier to comprehend the spiritual involution relates to manifested embodiments such as human beings.

CHAPTER 9

# Potency Dominion

THE POTENCY DOMINION IS THE HOME OF THE ASTRAL BODY, which prevails throughout the terrestrial region, where the body lacks a hard shell and has a living spirit within a soft, unprotected abdomen, making the body vulnerable to predators. The soft abdomens of these astral bodies, hidden inside their shells, specially designed to wrap around and grip the coiled central columella-like snail shells. The heavenly bounteous power (*Rudra*), comes to serve, bringing the wind, (*Vayu*), which turns the air into a breeze and then creates breath, prana, which establishes itself as sovereign and fills the world with treasures and wealth, which if properly managed establishes a tranquil path through which one may come to overpower sorrow and be granted powers to serve as a chief. Rudra even embodies as a subservient poet, living happily with his children with such a boon that it enables the embodiments to survive one hundred winters. Understanding all this, the gods, in the form of awareness, transform selected living things, including creatures among the animal kingdom, into living beings. Human beings become aware of their surroundings and thus attain consciousness to act and to understand their actions, living in a moving and immobile body, which enhances the ground they live on and allows those things living in the underworld—the earth, (*Prithvi*)—to progress.

## TRANSFORMATION

According to *Rig-Veda* 6:1, the primordial energy, Shakti, from her invisible form, comes to appear as a potency. Like the heavenly bull, as the father, Shakti creates the phenomenon that allows physical powers to transform into spiritual forces through the mother serving as the heavenly cow. Such transformation endows with virtue the physical body, which acquires knowledge and wisdom to comprehend the new world, which can no longer conquered by anyone other than the godhead (*Indra*). As an architect, an inventor, a discoverer, and part of the godhead Indra, who can guide the supreme spiritual powers, prevails within the body as the holy living spirit, (*Atman*). Serving as the holy soul, Atman manifests within the mortal body. With worship, it comes to sit among all, serving as a pious blessing by way of the supreme immortal universal soul, (*Paramatman.*) With an individual mind and heart *Paramatman* through rituals and rites, generates abundant treasures in the form of noble thoughts just like the god Indra does. People blessed with eternal flame from the godhead (*Agni*). They acquire wealth, both physical and spiritual, and with such wealth they build an army that manifests with lofty, radiant flair. This generates a magnificent aura or halo around their embodiments, confirming the presence of the divine will and spiritual essence. With a reflective intrinsic nature, an indispensable quality, in their abstract forms, they establish individual character traits such as quintessence. Prevailing within the body, the essence comes to resemble the gods' abode. Looking upon worshippers and others, the gods watch eagerly and with respect, especially when their supplicants come to offer homage. With perfect glory, this brings even more delight by winning over other souls.

The gods given titles and a enriched position. They generate phenomena to magnify their embodiments as messengers who work to serve among other workers. They extend their presence from the higher region down to the lower terrestrial region, or underworld.

Serving as divine helpers, the manifested embodiments are honored by the twin demigod (*Aśvins*), who come to serve as the father and mother, carrying their progeny along with them, and become skilled so they fully respected as joy givers. With adoration, longing, and bliss, they come to shine like heavenly priests. As devotees with eternal flame, such progeny come to kneel at the feet of the god Agni, stating their intention to serve with pure minds. Within the shining dwelling of the godhead, they are honored with music, which mortal embodiments experience as the coming of heaven's lofty splendor, like a meteor producing refulgent light to signal that all should come to fight in battle. In their manifested mortal embodiments, the progeny appears as aristocrats, masters, or even the heavenly bull. They received by devotees, who come to kneel, their faces pressed to the earth to receive their heavenly blessings, which promotes the process of inner purification. The god Agni, as the Holy One, and the god Indra, as the lord of riches, toil among mortals to bring oblations, which are set aflame with burning fuel. Serving as the mighty guard of reverence, they make it well-known that their sacrifice and adoration intended to bring joy for everyone. Their singing of songs and hymns of honor imbues them with vigor, as with the son of strength. Their worship at the altar, where they look for divine favor from the illuminous gods, goes from the splendor of heaven down to the underworld, where they covered. In triumphant glory, the god Agni continues to shine, providing to the mortal embodiments long-enduring strength, along with abundant riches, which, working through phenomena, keeps them safe.

Mother Nature fulfills individual needs with abundant power and wealth, filling the whole kingdom with her offspring. As the provider of plenteous food, Mother Nature also seeks to make everyone happy and keep them away from sin and evil (*Rig-Veda* 6:2). In places, the power of eternal love, Mitra, brings passion and wealth and, through the god Agni, comes to establish grace, which creates the Bounteous One, who serves as the sovereign. The god Agni joins with eternal love, Mitra, to support godly forces, serving as rulers. The two together bring their own royal fame with glory. This results in total prosperity, offered to those who, along with singing devotional songs, willingly offer prayers with sacrifice. While speeding through the air, serving as friendly coursers, Agni and Mitra seen serving in one accord like a flock of birds in flight. With the heavenly sacrifice, they kindle and create within mortal embodiments the craving to attain bliss with solemn rites, which helps them to encourage others who are sore from the struggle, praying for their safe passage. Without enmity, Agni and Mitra's mortal embodiments, now with bountiful help from the lofty sky deity (*Dyaus*), bring by way of the eternal flame an inner illumination that lifts itself aloft with bright smoke. This creates an expansive glow, reaching the heavens, offered unto as the flames branch out, serving from the house of Agni, bringing the life force, prana, to support the embodiments and provide for their needs so that they may live for one hundred years and, like the sun, as the purifier, glow with radiant beams. Those in the house of the god Agni glorified along with other well-loved guests, such as elders in a fort, all claiming protection of their son. Agni presses down with air within the embodiment, and with eternal wisdom and the eternal flame. As Agni and Mitra work, they move into the wood and become invisible. Within the body, the life force moves like the wind without going astray and, like a young loving horse, brings home eternal wisdom. Knowing the imperishable nature of life on earth, the Eternal One, as the mighty host, gazes upon animals such an elephants and oxen that use their eternal power to split the wood-like flame to attain eternal wisdom. Manifested in mortal bodies, like priests, humans worship Agni and make sacrifices to him, who serves as the lord of all living things, to acquire eternal wisdom. By accepting such eternal wisdom as an offering, all living things prosper, while calling for favor from the heavenly trinity of *Agni, Mitra,* and *Aṅgiras*, who come all the way from heaven, the celestial and cosmic regions, to serve within the underworld, which is part of the terrestrial region. This allows mortal embodiments to dwell securely and learn to overcome the foe's malign oppression.

The true guardian of the law, (*Varuna*), who serves as the 'Most Faithful One' (*Rig-Veda* 6:3), comes to help these mortal embodiments win peace, and serves as a retainer who shines with ample light to dwell among other living things. In accord, *Varuna* brings the eternal flame to join with eternal love, guarded by the union of the godhead (*Agni*) and the powers of love (*Mitra*) by serving other newly created mortal living things and saving them from troubles. They offer help in the form of sacrifices and worship and offer intellect as a gift so the mortal beings may acquire wisdom to alleviate the displeasure that accompanies not being famous. The guardian of the law, Varuna, comes to save them from strain and helps them not to be afraid or to fear that ridicule or outrage will prevent them from moving forward. Looking freely upon the heavenly body (*Sūrya*), which dwell among gods come to dwell among those mortal embodiments who, with joy, cultivate an earnest desire to become the messengers of Mother Nature to serve as the "children of wood," who in the evening pass on the brilliant pathway, getting ready to face the darkness of night. With fierceness, all poised to rest, like birds, they perch within a big tree, feeling like trapped winners on a fast-moving horse that tries to shake off its bit and bridle, behaving like a piece of wood, looking into a hatchet, with a sharp tongue, ready to feed it into the smelter. The mortal embodiments as children of wood, they wait for friendly eternal love(*Mitra*), to come in the morning, bringing bright beams of light to create a splendor that crackles through the redness of night and given them possession of the life force (prana), the heavenly immortal beam. By day, scattering with vibrations, life force utters sounds like a plant, producing a voice to welcome the radiant heroes. Glowing, they come like rapid coursers, shouting from both worlds as they emerge. Filled with treasure, well wedded, they come along with both the vibrations supporting running streams and shining rays. They produce a native vigor that flashes, accompanied by a band of skillful living things, and arriving with refulgent lightning.

Even the demigods become invokers (*Rig-Veda* 6:4) as they come to support those who offer sacrifices, along with skillful service, and willingly worship to bring together living things. They all come to serve as the Sons of Strength, making the god Agni appear as the sun, the radiant herald. In the morning, such radiant herald, with loving favor, meets with living things and accepts their praise, which offered through both half-mortal demigods and immortal gods (divinities and deities). With the morning light, they appear as the guest (*Jātavedas)* among worshippers and regarded as wanderers who come dressed in splendor, following the bright rays of the rising sun. As the guest, *Jātavedas,* the Vedic god serves as an eternal purifier who sends forth soothing vibes that have ability to shatter the ancient stonework, creating strength for the ancient champions (*Aśnas)* by providing food for a feast. The *Aśnas* protect like bestowers of strength who, while traveling along their pathway, protect the sovereign's dwelling from foes and trouble. They even secure food so offered at night, while Vayu, the god of the atmosphere, overtakes the sky to establish the kingdom of living things. The Aśnas provide protection against the flying foemen who resist the sovereign's orders, which causes them to cast down like a steed. The powers of the god Agni, with Sūrya's fulgent rays, spread over the splendor and cover all the worlds. All decked with bright color, Sūrya displaces the darkness and, with the eternal flame, flies over to clear away any impurities (*auśija*), such as disease, and supports living things with an extended life. With most delightful beams, Sūrya produces a glow with a great loud sound, offering worship and praise to honor the heavenly gods who work through the network that regulated by demigods to trap any evil power. All decked out and chanting hymns, Sūrya and Agni seek foemen so they may have their wishes granted and help them to acquire the level of strength they desire, gain eternal glory, and win over the wealthy ones who store riches.

Those who seek such wealth, with worship, share the banquet like Sons of Strength (*Rig-Veda* 6:5). With grace, they go beyond to call upon the heavenly priest. Using their eternal flame, they split the dense wood to free up the trapped individual living spirit (Atman), which when freed appears as a fire that lights the blackened pathway. With thundering, and being white of hue, they appear as most youthful Sons of Strength, who in splendor come with loud voices, supported by Agni. With valor, as the Purifier, with the wind, Agni follows to crunch up the trees in the forests to further fuel the eternal flame. Moving as the Pure One, he moves onward in all directions. Like the most destructive heavenly power, he lets the living spirit go free after completing nine months (those who have completed nine months called *Navagraha.* The Novavax become demonic Brahman who, as the descendants of Agni, come to tear down the woods, boldly devastating all, creating a white flame. Like flying horses, the Brahman shear the ground, exposing the underworld, everywhere providing shining flames that flicker rapidly as they move over the high ridges of the earth's surface. With sharp stones as their weapons, used like projectiles, the Radiant One move forth to discharge fire from the ground, which appears as open mouth, the Radiant One appearing like a bull who has won its livestock. As the fierce flame, Agni comes as a hero, dreaded and resistless, who destroys the forests to bring the great impeller the sun, which provides light that reaches even to the underworld and boldly spreads across every region on the surface the earth. The mighty power drives all fight from the foemen by conquering or burning up those who are ready to do harm. The mighty power offers the wondrous wonderworkers the chance to serve as noble singers with wondrous wealth, all marked with life-giving force to become the bright ones, which groups includes a vast number of heroes.

## COGNIZANCE

With such invocation (*Rig-Veda* 6:6), youthful noble souls such as the Sons of Strength, through singing hymns and expressing themselves through guileless vibrations, acquire wisdom. Like the ancient sages, they send forth their acquired eternal wealth. Utilizing every aspect of their treasure, they bring boons, serving as pious servants in the evening and in the morning. Devoid of malice, they bring precious gifts to those serving as earthly priests or in other aspects as the purifiers of all living things. They establish happiness among other living things, so they can settle firmly on the ground. Like in the past, they come to dwell using their intellects. By regulating their mental power, they attain higher knowledge and come to deliver blessings. The sapient *Jātavedas* sends forth eternal wisdom in succession, to serve as a divine treasure. The youthful neighbors who subjected to such divine treasures attacked and harmed; they receive full protection from eternal love (*Mitra*) and godhead (*Agni*). Mitra and Agni together navigate individual which subject their foes to experience an internal heat that causes a high fever, and sometimes even subject them to external heat or fierce burns. The foes are even subject to the extreme ultimate power, Agni, as fueled with the sacrifice.

The mortal embodiments with wealth and splendorous glory, Sons of Strength, chant hymns and praises to the immortal ones and urge sages to use words of praise to worship the immortal brightness and bring it in with triumph. The universal soul (Paramatman), as the father, serves through the individual spirit (Atman). As the sons of the universal soul, the Sons of Strength continue to support individual living beings, serving through the primordial power, Shakti, who is omnipresent and manifests as heavenly creator (goddess) of the celestial power Brahma, the cosmic power Vishnu, and the esoteric power Shiva. As a trinity, this primordial ancient force, as Shakti, thus regulates the universe.

In manifested form, the omni soul (*Vaishnavas*) regulates all manifested and unmanifested mortal embodiments through the holy order (*Rig-Veda* 6:7). Blessed manifested bodies, like vessels fitted with a mouth, serve as great cisterns by offering libations with sacrifices and prayers. They propagate and convey to all that they should honor the mighty ones (divinities) serving the celestial region, the gods (deities) serving the cosmic region, and the demigods serving the terrestrial region, all of whom jointly cover all regions extending from the sky to the ground. The powers of Agni spring with mighty vibrations that generate a ghostly power that, wrath-like, serves the underworld.

Heroes and kings, bestowed with excellent powers, seek treasures from the immortal Vaishvanara. They hear hymns, which bring joy even among infants, as they honor the union of Agni and Vaishvanara, who, with their immortal mental powers, serve as the infants' parents. The two never decline to help to raise the infants with mighty ordinances. The infants come to find with the daylight their parents' bosoms and learn to establish their courses for travel that designed to help them reach the summit of heaven. With the immortal brilliant light, all-seeking, they come to Vaishvanara, who urges all creatures to rest, with their heads and limbs measuring out the realms of water in the seven swift-flowing streams.

Fully supported by infinite air, Vayu, they spread out like the lucid spheres of heaven (*Rig-Veda* 6:8), spreading around the world as undeceivable, guarded with immortality to serve all. At the holy gathering, with loud voices, they appear as Jātavedas, an epithet of the god Agni. The mighty omni soul overpowers even the godly power Vaishvanara, then explains to him the purpose of the reflective light of the moon. Jātavedas comes like a swift red steer, bringing vibrations that generate fresh hymns and producing pure mythical juice (soma), just like one created within the loftiest heaven. Now the soma flows within the manifested embodiments, producing nectar (amrita) to serve the living beings. Agni transforms his ferocious fire to provide bodily heat and warmth. Living beings with such power spring out, ready to serve Varuna and Mitra as their guardians, who bring a balance between the eternal law and eternal love. While they serve, they also keep under observation all those who attain higher knowledge and use such knowledge to measure out the space between the ground and the sky. Living beings such as Vaishvanara come to comprehend their parents and the heavenly mightiness from Varuna, becoming wonderful enforcers, using eternal love (Mitra) from the esoteric region, located between heaven and earth. These powers help them to uncover the eternal truth concealed behind individual ignorance. They quickly acquire creative power as provided by their parents. They hold two bowls, set apart by setting the boundaries, which act like two bosoms in the same skin. They monitor the region from the heights of the sky to the depths of the ground, all filled with cosmic vapor, thus bringing water to create floods and allow the waiting rulers to acquire and manifest as mortal bodies. With praise, they establish a kingdom where plants grow with their roots in the soil and, on the surface, without roots, become like trees with eternal flame, providing the wood that will serve as sacrificial fire sticks.

The god Agni comes to settle within Mother Earth, providing the eternal fire that works with the ruling heavenly power Rudra, which causes the wind, Vayu, to manifest as the union of Agni and Vaishvanara. Serving as manifested bodies, Agni and Vaishvanara serve as the parent Mataris̀van. From far away, they bestow upon the new young singers a very ancient wisdom so they can perform and become worthy to serve in the glorious holy synods. They settle as the undelaying King Indra, with a sharpened immortal bolt, with lightning flashes down to smite sinners like a tree. Unified, Agni and Vaishvanara, serving as the parents (Matariśvan), appear as avatars, wealthy chiefs who, with the same undelaying power, rule decaying good heroes. They do not have to bend to win, as Agni and Vaishvanara come to regulate such activities as both mortal and immortal. Engaged in such an act, they gain support by the hundredfold, even the thousandfold, and dwell within all three regions of the dynamic universe, constantly remaining as effective guards.

According to *Rig-Veda* 6:9, the princes serve as the patrons (Matariśvan) who bring in the united Agni and Vaishvanara to create an atmospheric region, establishing days with twenty-four hours, half the day in darkness and the other half in bright light. Such a union of Agni and Vaishvanara is sovereign, by whom, with diplomacy, select manifested bodies are born to overcome any darkness, at any time, through inner illumination. Such sovereigns, with neither warp nor woof, weave a web to collect thoughts and send them through the sounds they generate as they move, creating vibrations and converting these into oscillations, thereby creating this invisible network that, as a web, used to communicate among themselves. It used by their offspring to spread their spoken words. They use such a web to communicate with their invisible father, as well as with other ancestral powers far from them. In time, they even learn to understand unspoken words and sounds such as *warp* and *woof* as they come to serve as the immortal protectors of the world. They descend as they realize there is no other aid, except for the half-mortal demigods, who bring the immortal light e firmly placed within mortal embodiments. As the priests, the demigods behold a firm mind, and allow the swiftest mind to fly and connect with all the mighty powers.

They have one intention, namely, to move in one accord, unobstructed, with a single purpose, with open ears to hear and open eyes to see. They serve like the harbor light that seen by the immortal living spirit (Atman). This helps to bring into focus the roaming and other broadening minds in the distance, filled with thoughts, which brought into focus before the demigods speak of what envisioned. With such a focus, the demigods, in fear, bow down to seek the gracious power that brought through the union of Agni and Vaishvanara to assist with their immortal favors and thus help their region to overcome darkness.

## CONTEMPLATION

Contemplation is like mysticism, which, through ecstasy, helps lead one to an alternate state of consciousness that commonly supported by ideologies, ethics, rites, myths, legends, and magic. Within such a state of embodiment, one obtains insight into the ultimate or hidden truth, which leads individual manifested embodiments or living beings to transform into a state where they supported by various natural phenomena and related practices. In biblical, liturgical, and spiritual dimensions related to extraordinary experience, their minds go beyond the limits of human intelligence to seek union with the godly powers (*Rig-Veda* 6:10). Such a state achieved through sacrifices and through immortal favor that, by way of performing rites, reach the heavenly power. With pleasing praises and hymns, living beings come to experience inner illumination. Like Jātavedas, they advance by receiving rites, so living beings become successful and appear with aspects as radiant priests. With loud voices, they heard coming as the unmanifested God Agni to enkindle the eternal flame among all other living beings to serve as noble souls. As a composer, Agni sends forth with eternal strength to other embodiments, who, as pure as sacred butter, come to enhance other mortal embodiments. As half-mortal demigods, these turn the living spirit (Atman) into individual selves, all invigorated, serving by singing songs and coming to thrive to offer with glory gifts, hymns, and praises to honor the powers of Agni. The half-mortal demigods provide a wondrous inner brilliance that helps to win eternal powers, such as a stable filled with cattle. With such inner illumination, the manifested mortal embodiments come to know that they must leave behind the path that filled with darkness and begin to follow the far path to splendor, serving the space located between heaven and earth.

Once space, which has been subjected to night's thick darkness, is illuminated with purifying light and supported by the mighty divine will, it confirms the presence of Agni, who with wonderful wealth comes to all living beings and their rulers, the princes set to be distinguished, surpassing all others in his liberal gifts, his fame, and his heroic virtues. Wherever Agni seated, he accepts with gladness any sacrifice, making his worshippers serve as holy singers who manifest as Bhāradvāja. They scatter foes with the abundance of vigor he grants them to help them to live through winters as the brave sons. Appearing as feminine natural spirits (*apsaras*), they come with superb musical skills and, through their singing, generate the mystic nectar amrita, produced in the glands. This accompanied by beautiful godly music in the form of vibrant hymns. These mystic apsaras manifest and transform into mortal embodiments and serve as the living beings who perform in the court of the demigods and serve as the messengers (archangels) between the godly powers and manifested human beings, performing as the dancers and singers to spread the divine will across the various territories.

According to *Rig-Veda* 6:11, the apsaras eagerly press on to make sacrifices and celebrate the union of eternal love and eternal law (i.e., Mitra and Varuna, respectively). They worship Agni, who brings energetic powers to the cosmic hosts (*Maruts*) and delightfully supports the midair region. They serve the guileless earthly heralds who support the demigods, who appear as part of the holy councils to serve the mortal embodied living beings. Agni, with his purifying tongue, makes a sacrifice to the divine will by placing within the mouths of living beings a blessed longing, like a poet singing hymns and offering solemn service. This produces the sweet potion *amrita,* which distributed among the embodied living beings. Blessed, they come to serve as sages and as wise ones, who bring a refulgent beam from afar and spread it across the whole wide world, including the sky above and the ground below. The living beings, residing among these two shields, with rich oblations, come to organize their scarred lives and serve as humanity separated into five tribes. Each tribe brings its own gift, all of which offered with homage and reverence. The living beings clip the sacred grass and offer it as an oblation with a ladle full of oil that lifted and firmly placed on a higher place, thus setting it on the seat as the altar on earth. At this altar, they offer sacrifices that serve the mind's eye or inner eye, which is a mystical and esoteric concept, the third eye, usually depicted as located on the forehead, which provides perception beyond ordinary sight and strictly directed toward the direct source of external light, the sun.

Humanity with five tribes, clad in rich robes, with godly aspects, come through the eternal flame, Agni, who appears as the cosmic hosts (Maruts), representing the Son of Strength (Rudra), who comes in full force to enkindle the eternal flame that even the holy priests wish to escape like a woe from a prison. As messengers, with the holy Sons of Strength, the Maruts come from a great distance to meet with the sun god Sūrya. They originally serve as the herald (the sun) to spread light abroad and create meadows on the ground that may use to provide the dwellings for those who worship the ruler or king. The rulers and kings themselves in turn worship the god Agni, serving as the impeller between the sky and the ground. With full perfection, as the ancient father of the sky, Dyaus, they pronounce themselves as the holy ones, using the primordial power, Shakti, to regulate the celestial, cosmic, and terrestrial regions.

Fleet of foot, they enter the subregion between the sky and the ground and filled with rich oblations that intensifies the already manifested ground filled with grass and forest. Serving as most splendid sovereigns, they appear with a shining flame that refines the dense vegetation and forests. Like a smelter, they extol with vigor and come to operate like strong steeds, representing Agni in manifested form, with a dwelling, serving as the godly power Jātavedas. As a champion with fighting powers, he appears with the morning light (dawn), and as the sire, he offers sacrifices and with praise and wonder for Agni's shining glow. He even clears the woods to establish a site where the rulers and kings may quickly traverse the surface, like a flood rushing to loosen the ground. Jātavedas swiftly burns the woods and the vegetation, running over it like a desert to remove any guilty thief, as he comes to protect the champion from defamation. With the enkindled eternal flame on-site, he drives away affliction and saves the gladdened brave sons as they pass through one hundred winters.

According to *Rig-Veda* 6:13, during the spring, the god Agni brings the auspicious wind, Vayu, to move through the tree branches with blessings and wealth, bringing the strength needed to battle the foemen. The heavenly rain generates free-flowing waters. The Maruts, empowered, accompanied with circumambient atmospheric air, pass through tree branches and convert into breath as the vital force. With eternal wealth, they dwell among the wondrous splendors. The embodied Varuna provides the lofty law and eternal love (Mitra). Serving as the controllers, Varuna and Mitra providing many loving blessings, jointly bringing mighty force to slay their foes. The singers, bearing the pain of the newborn children of water, as sages, come to serve, inspired by eternal wealth. In accordance with the Maruts, as the Sons of Strength, through singing loud hymns, they enthusiastically offer sacrifices and approach the altar to worship, enjoying each precious thing and coming to gain treasures as royal wealth. The Sons of Strength (Maruts) grant to the mortal embodiments all things needed for their subsistence, and bring high fame to sages. They provide milk to the children of heroes through the cattle and provide food to the hungry wicked wolf, so it will not eat the cattle. As the eloquent Sons of Strength, with their might, they come to vouchsafe the seeds from which the offspring emerge. Filled with vigor, singing songs, they obtain riches in abundance, like the brave sons, which gladdens them to go through the upcoming one hundred winters.

The mortal embodied souls (*Rig-Veda* 6:14) who rest and ingratiate thought, singing hymns, please the god Agni as they find an abundance of food, which causes them to acquire the wisdom to develop the skills they need to serve themselves as the prophets, the glorified sons of the holy priest of heaven, Manus, who acquire even the foemen's hidden wealth. These embodiments make sacrifices at many places, serving those who are fighting the fiends. To them they offer rites so they can overcome their foes. Agni acts as the chief of heroes, as the winner of the waters, firm in the fray, and always looked upon as the mighty power who alarms the enemies, causing them to tremble. With their godly wisdom, the prophets defend themselves against any accusation that the mortals acquired wealth without conquering, without ever checking the enemy with their mighty deeds. They call upon the heavenly power Mitra and ask for a mighty favor from the demigods residing on earth and in heaven, namely that they bring from heaven the weal for the mortal embodiments so they may dwell securely and overcome the foe's malign oppressions.

## HERMIT

According to *Rig-Veda* 6:15, each time the demigods come from heaven, they appear on the surface of the earth as a hermit singing hymns and divine songs. They appear as the Pure One serving as the guest to all the tribes that strive through awakening early in the morning and, as in ancient times, meet the needs of each day. Their embodiments become as the newborn, by bringing everlasting food and establishing the eternal flame, like the flames in the woods. The terrestrial hermit *(Brigus)* is a savage friend who comes to serve the mortal living beings. They become glorified among themselves, every day facing the sun, the king of the solar race,*(Vitahavya)*, who takes them as refugees to the hermitage and transforms them to become mystics (*Bhrigus*). They perform austere acts and sing loud praises to the holy priests (*Brahmans*) serving as the foe less helpers, friends, wondrously skillful people who can subdue enemies near or far. They bestow the mortal embodiments with eternal wealth and allow them to establish homes within the manifested region between the ground below and the sky above. They are served by demigods such as the Maruts and the sons of Strength and are provided with light by the king of the solar race, *Vitahavya*, who as the sun helps spread the wealth far and wide. They establish themselves as the ancient sage *Bhāradvāja*.

Coming from the heavenly region, *Bhāradvāja* serves as the refulgent guest, becoming the herald of humanity who provides humanity with sacred rites and teaches them to sing like holy singers, uttering heavenly words. He also makes them to be the bearers of oblation to serve as envoys of the creator *Brahma*.

With his purified third eye, Brahma beholds the increasing morning light that appears upon the ground. With speed, he moves on like an untouched sage, following Agni with longing. Agni emerges from a burning log of wood and fights the dragon *Etaia*, which brings along an invisible heat so strong that it transforms the prevailing atmosphere into the invisible fifth classical element (ether), filling the sky above and the cosmic region below. Within this region, the fifth classical element allows the hymns, as vibrations, to carry eternal love, reaching all the mighty powers (divinities, deities, and demigods) prevailing within the ether.

Inflamed with fuel, Agni comes singing songs of purity that serve as the cleanser and turn those who are steadfastly ignorant into wise people with prayers. As a sacrifice, this provides bliss to the holy bounteous singers. The singers, void of guile, now come to appear as manifested bodies to serve as holy priests. At each stage of enhancement, Agni makes the mortal embodiments serve as offering-bearers and as envoys come to guard the Deathless One, who adored, through reverence, the immortal living spirit (Atman) within each mortal body establishes a link with the universal soul (God), personified in the Vedas as the father *Paramatman*. This individual embodiment is ever watchful, omnipresent, serving as the lord of the household (divinity). The god Agni serves two ways to move between the two worlds as the twin demigods called Aśvins. They lay their claim with gracious regard, paying their fair to put in place three protective guards serving in each region. One of these has a fair face; one has a face able to look rapidly around; and one has a face filled with wisdom. These three different guards, born in seawater, come to know those who do not know all the rules; these invited to worship and serve Agni. Each individually announces his offering, all to serve as the immortals who deliver blessings and save those who pray to and worship the wise heroes. From the inception to the end of the sacrifice, they endowed with divine power and the divine riches to guard such mortal embodiments against those who would come to assault Agni and those who would dishonor him, saving the embodiments by taking them to a dark place far away, where they brought great wealth. The priests, as does Jātavedas, come to serve as kings and as lords of the homestead, coming to learn all about the ancestral generations. The skillful mortal worshippers, like their half-mortal ancestors, begin to make sacrifices, worshipping as priests with a bright holy flame.

Agni enjoys these rites and sacrifices, along with the worship that serves as a divine offering. Like most youthful ones, the worshippers look upon the duly laid-out viands, and in gladness they worship Agni, who comes to help liberate them and overcome all things that trouble them, such as any dispute over the spoils. All the fair-faced demigods, with Agni, seated upon an altar lined with wool like a nest and bedewed with worship oil, brings the goddess *Savitar* to rightly provide the sacrifice. The priest *Atharvan* emerges from the gloom and arrives at the banquet, where with perfection he is born as rubbed with oil to arrange for Agni to come bewildered, moving in winding ways, like a superior being bringing immortal power, to strengthen all present with the holy law. So that the sacrifice will reach the demigods, manifested mortal living beings, as the lords or heads of kindle fuel, set up their homesteads. They bring the mighty powers on board and make sure their household gears are not defective, to allow the divine will to penetrate their grandeur.

According to *Rig-Veda* 6:16, the heavenly initiators in masculine form, the deva, and in the equivalent feminine form, the devi, both appear with excellence as supernatural beings, half of whom represented as good (Suras) and half of whom represented as malevolent (Asuras). Both, as the initiators, regulated by Agni and, with joyous tongues, by way of divine will, are both made into manifested embodiments as part of the sacrament, serving as noble and evil. They accompanied by the disposer of wisdom, who leads them onto straight paths to serve as the knowers. Offering a sacrifice, they support the wisdom seekers, including old and heavenly priest Bharata, who implores them to provide bliss (*Divodāsa*) by pouring out mythical soma juice. They offered gifts to serve as *Bhāradvāja*, who, in the celestial tradition, serves as the immortal messenger who delivers eulogies for those who come to hear, the pious singers who perform holy rites.

The demigods throw a feast for Agni to glorify the other bountiful ones, such as the invokers the Manus, and share love with others. They enjoy placed near Agni. They, in tribes, serving as the wisest earthly priests, offer worship to Agni. Filled with food from the feast, as envoys of Agni, they come to serve Aṅgiras as earthly priests. While seated on the grass, they offered gifts to make them physically strong, filled with inner flame that burns with holy oil and creates among the young a high blaze. Appearing as cosmic hosts (Maruts), they serve as the demigods, who provided with exceedingly great heroic strength. By rubbing, they spread out like a lotus flower and become as the highly renowned earthly priest *Atharvan,* who serves as the head, *Vishva*, and given the power to serve as slayers of the evil power *Vṛtra*. They break down castles and allow *Dadhyac*, son of Atharvan, to appear as the noble soul *Ṛṣi*, who manifests as the hero *Pathya,* who destroys the most vicious foe, the *Dāsas*, thus becoming the winner of the spoils in every fight.

Singing songs, Agni brings soma, which helps those who drink it to prosper and grow strong. By applying their minds, along with preeminent vigor, they gain a dwelling place that may last long to bring a bounty that is good. With the support of the god Agni, the Bharata tribe come out to seek those who serve as evil-slayers (*Vṛtra-slayers*) and marked as the heroes to fight, for which they are rewarded with riches. Fully supported, they surpass in greatness, untroubled, unsubdued, rising above all the prevailing living things. As in the old days, Agni, with recent glory, gathers light from the lofty heaven and spreads that light to bring out friends who boldly offer sacrifices. With praise, they become the heralds who sit through every age, serving as messengers, bearing and offering oblation. Then they manifest in two forms: pure and noble *Ādityas*, and neither pure nor noble Asuras. These are both regulated by the demigods who manage the midair region, that is, the cosmic hosts (Maruts), who connect the heavenly and earthly regions. In his excellence, Agni brings a strong and active eternal flame. Rich, as a mortal embodiment, he manifests to serve advanced living beings (humanity). Further, the immortal power Rudra brings wisdom as the Son of Strength to serve the living beings (humanity) who ring forth with hymns of praise. This makes humanity strong, which even today allows them to actively overcome their foes. With its pointed blaze, the eternal flame casts down each fierce devouring fiend and wins the war waged within the material world. Along with the external flame, the active godly power Jātavedas brings a store of riches for the wisest heroes, riches that used still today to slay the demons.

To protect living beings (humanity) from troubled by evil powers, sages, even today, offer prayers to guard them. Agni comes to the sinner with oblations to procure life for humanity and thus save them from woe. Using his flame, Agni, with his tongue, drives away the death that brought by evil deeds, striking the living beings dead. The power of Agni, through his flame, creates shelter for the noble king (Bhāradvāja) so he may travel far and wide, helping to conquer and bringing most excellent wealth. The external flame even helps to slay the evil power Vṛtra. Human beings, through singing songs, offer oblation to kindle the bright external flame. Serving as the father's father, along with the shining everlasting flame within, serving as the mother's mother, they come to sit at the altar and pronounce holy law. With devotion, the active godly power Jātavedas brings light from the shining heaven, which subsequently brings the progeny, the children of strength, who further come to support living beings (humanity). This all looks lovely, with the pouring forth of food, accompanied by worship songs as the children of strength approach the altar, which is like a covered shelter providing shade, protecting all from the fervent heat and the fire that brings glittering gold. The Mighty One, like a bull, breaks down the forts with his sharpened horn and slays the evil power.

## INCARNATION

As newborn infants, the children of strength held within the arms of the Mighty One as he bears the eternal heat provided by Agni. Skillfully performing holy rites, they appear at the banquet, serving as the best finders of wealth, which the Mighty One jingles for the newborn, all seated in their places. Serving the dear godly powers is the guest Jātavedas, who kindles and settles on a soft place, such as the heavenly homestead, where he harnessed with most excellent steeds. Bearing with the living spirit, the manifested embodiment served by demigods, along with divine will, which brings the sacrificial feast with a draft of mythical juice that in the form of sweet milk, thus giving birth to the members of the Bharata tribe, who with a high everlasting blaze come to gleam. They, with their individual living spirits (*Atmans*), serve the banquet, offering gifts as a sacrifice while singing loud songs of worship. With uplifted hands, offering prayers, along with making a true sacrifice with hymns, they bring hearty oblation, to enkindle the powers of Agni, so they may fight against the unmanifested evil power Vṛtra and bring wealth to crush the manifested evil powers (rakshasas) serving the earth.

The Mighty One, after drinking mythical juice (soma), with loud sounds, appears as the Bold One, armed with thunder, who comes to break loose the prevailing powers preventing animals from being set free from their stalls (*Rig-Veda* 6:17). They, with their new mighty power, smite those who are hostilely operating against animals and other living things. Singing hymns through their beauteous jaws, they come to serve by pulling thunder-wielding carts. They become the spontaneous victors and, as the champions, all with wondrous strength from the god Indra, come to pierce as in the past. They are delighted to hear the divine message (holy calling) in their prayers that exalt with the light coming from the sun, which brings out food in abundance to generate the ferocious energy needed to pierce and slaughter the foes, thus freeing the milk to flow from milk-bearing animals. With gladdening drops of milk, they become self-sustaining. And as they quaff milk, they broadened with splendid powers. Cheered with drops of the mystical fluid amrit, supplemented with the mythical heavenly juice soma, they attain delight. They gain perfect strength, with which they can burst through the strong enclosures.

With gladness and splendor, the sun comes to accompany them, bringing morning (dawn). With this mighty tower of strength, as within the heavenly region, the ungulates encompass eternal wisdom, without moved or shaken from their seats, working wondrously to store the ripe milk within their raw udders. In the morning, the envoy Aṅgirases burst the strong doors open and set free the cows' udders, all filled with milk, allowing the cows to spread out across the wide region on the ground. Like a mighty marvel coming from lofty heaven, the sun props open the doors and spreads out farther to fill the other regions encompassed by the two worlds, namely, the sky above and the ground below. The children of the heavenly gods supported and, as in times of old, follow the holy order, the young mothers serving as deities slated to develop as strong champions to fight the battles of morality and the wars of righteousness. At times they even support the godless in war and help them to win against their assailants by bringing the light of heaven. Even the heavenly powers bend backward, before any bolt sent forth by Indra in anger, to create terror. They bring the eternal universal soul (Paramatman) to support the eternal individual living spirit (Atman) within every living creature and then smite the assailing evil power (the dragon) in its burrow. The strong creative power *Tvaṣṭṛ* comes eagerly with the divine will to prompt any mighty bolt with one thousand spikes and one hundred edges to crush the evil power (the dragon), dressed like one hundred boastful bullies.

To establish a righteous environment, the trinity composed of Maruts, Pūṣan, and Vishnu, in accord, pouring forth with strength, fills the region with mythical juice to bless the embodiments consisting of physical, subtle, and astral bodies and to bring cheer and act in one accord, covering all three regions of the dynamic universe. They slaughter any prevailing evil power (Vṛtra) that may be threatening the newly manifested living things who are providing a dwelling for the individual living spirit. Further, they set free the waters, creating great rushing floods that swell to overpower any obstruction. The floods flow along steep slopes on their downward course, directed by Indra, the water speeding onward to the ocean. With new prayers, this brings protection for all well-armed heroes, to whom provide thunderbolts to make the world righteous and strong. These powers never grow old, while bringing victory to brilliant holy singers, to whom they bring strength through hymns of glory, also providing food and riches. Serving Indra, the patron bhagats, with God-appointed strength, come to serve as the brave sons. They gladly live through one hundred winters, supported through the heavenly power Sūrya and protected by the heads of nature (prakriti) who regulate the biosphere within which the mortal embodiment *Purukutsa* seizes the malevolent powers (Asuras) and their wealth and comes to serve Vishnu the Protector, who maintains a balance between good and evil. Using primordial power (Shakti), Vishnu vests the god Shiva with the power to create and destroy any noble or not so noble evil power such as the dragon. Before killing the evil powers, the primordial power sends them to reside in darkness at the bottom of the deep ocean, or to reside within the frozen part of the biosphere, far away from sunlight, which regulated and serviced by nature (prakriti).

According to *Rig-Veda* 6:18, devotees, with magnified prayers and songs, are invoked by the primordial power Shiva, who provides life to all manifested embodiments with a living spirit (Atman), which allows them, with glory, to surpass all others, even those serving as enlightened prophets (rishis), who go beyond the manifested material world. Uninjured in fights, the rishis never surrender in supporting the living creations. Mighty power in the form of Shiva arrives with an impetuous loud roaring sound, supported by the powers of Indra. Shiva, whirling with the dust, moves on high with one objective: to help living beings, irrespective of race, who are ready to overthrow any evil power and individually tame the ruler of evil powers (Dāsas), and to support others serving as subdued living beings, the noble souls (*Āryans*) that manifest as either four- or two-legged creatures and are served by the god Indra. As heroes, the Āryans come to behold the eternal truth, deemed so by the divine will, and encompass the mighty powers with ultimate strength. With such potent powers, they achieve a mighty victory to serve as the drivers of the proper season according to powers of nature (prakriti).

With a great bounty, human beings reestablish the ancient bond of friendship between themselves and the mighty powers such as the ferocious fire, Agni, and those serving as his envoys, the *Aṅgirases*. The Aṅgirases move wondrously to speak the absolute truth, and like moving water and wind and unmovable mountains (*Vala*), they serve humanity as Shakers with their firm beliefs. With fresh strength, they come as a force able to move or smite evil powers, preventing them from building any barriers or establishing castles of their own. The Shakers serving humanity, with holy thoughts, call upon the mighty powers, asking them to come and provide them with support to fight against the evil powers. They even call upon Indra, with his mighty power of thunder, asking him to bring along the noble embryo or seed that will help them to create their offspring. They move with speed to fight the moral and righteous battle.

With their mighty names, such living beings may serve as immortal, able to live forever, far surpassing all human generations. Serving as the most heroic ones, established in divine splendor, embodied with glory, riches, and valor, they are strangers to guile who are never false and will never become faithless Shakers. They well remembered by their given names as the crushers of the evil powers *Cumuri, Dhuni, Śambara, Pipru,* and *Śuṣṇa*. After these immortal beings ruin the castles of the evil powers, they loudly praised by Indra, who grants them his favor. They ascend, smiting down the evil power Vṛtra, holding in their right hands fast-moving thunderbolts. Using the art of magic, and with the bounteous power of Agni, they move like darts to burn down the dry forest of fiends who operate like a terrorist network. By joining with the powers of Indra, they come along with Agni to break the deep-reaching spear that evil powers use as their chief weapon to destroy the prevailing living things. With their wealth, they create thousands of paths that might supply them with ample strength to serve as the cosmic hosts (Maruts). The Maruts, as the Sons of Strength, invoke the godless powers who have remained at a distance from heaven, who are widespread across the earth, blistering amid the magnificent energy of heaven. As conquerors, the united Indra and Agni, full of wisdom, have no foe, no counterpart, and no refuge even to this day. They ensure there is no fear because their deed done and made them famous among one thousand others. Now they lie low like the holy manifested bodies *Kutsa, Āyu, Atithigva, and Tūrvayāṇa,* who boldly come to serve like the wisest of sages and demigods.

According to *Rig-Veda* 6:19, holy manifested bodies with living spirit have prevailed on earth and has already become affiliated with the material world. They fully grown with vigor. Serving as great heroes, they continue to grow. Working demigods, they ensure their needs fulfilled and thereby more than double in size. They decked themselves out as great heroes serving the youthful high and lofty ones who have accomplished their tasks and have gained control of the underlying biosphere, now established as enclosed global ecosystems. This is the area defined as the zone suitable for life on earth, all protected by the sky shield, created to protect the ground from solar and cosmic radiation and the heat generated in the interior of the earth.

This region is self-regulated as the righteous sphere, where all living beings integrate to cultivate relationships and, in compliance with the elements of nature, come to encompass various aspects of the biosphere, the lithosphere, the geosphere, the hydrosphere, and earth's atmosphere. It postulated that 3.5 billion years ago, life arose from nonliving matter, simple organic compounds. Through the process of biogenesis, life created within the un-decaying biosphere, where living beings gathered treasure through self-generated strength. They smoothed out any regularities so none could conquer them and so they could expand and accommodate their growth with complete perfection. They use divine will to stretch their arms wide to grant glory to all the household guards, the herders with their cattle, and they move around to save all of creation from any form of external combat. Grateful for their strength, they invite Indra to come to keep them free from all guilt, and to lie hidden among the heroic embodiments.

Like the old singers, without reproach, uninjured, the heroic embodiments sing praises and implement steadfast laws. While serving as wealth givers, they offer mythical juice (soma), which brings strength, accompanied by the precious food that humans need to eat to gain in might.

Thus, they become heroes of strength, with a most potent force, which serves to generate their subdued nature. With all splendid vigorous powers, they vouchsafe the prevailing humanity. This brings joy and helps them to grow with mighty strength, which, with friendly rapturous joy, helps them to win the battle, their loud sounds of triumph germinating new seeds and giving birth to offspring. Indra endows them with heroic skills, and with an exceedingly strong divine will, they win treasure, which assists them in conquering all foes, whether friends or strangers. With such heroic strength, the divine will comes along with Indra to serve from behind and in front, above and below, approaching the realm of splendor from every side and with glory. This provides humanity and other living things with the heroic aid needed to win wealth for their glorious deeds.

Serving as lords of the earthly region, the kings, the heroic embodiments vouchsafe the vast amount of heavenly treasure. Providing inspiration, long-lasting, along with the strength of a bull, they, in concert with the cosmic hosts (Maruts), bring a fully refined mighty power that even the heavenly rulers use to conquer all regions, including the celestial, cosmic, and terrestrial regions. Humanity and newly created living things, serving as households, with animals as a new form of protection, as thunder-wielder come to earth from on high. They bring water to support their offspring and cultivate friendship among all, also transforming the ground into fertile soil. They themselves, serving jointly, learn to invoke the living spirit to become victors over their foemen. By slaying all kinds of foes, they become happy heroes, using their ample riches to be helpful.

CHAPTER 10

# Emissary Dominion

THE EMISSARY DOMINION FILLED WITH ANCESTRAL WISDOM THAT manifests to serve as the godly power, which transmits such wisdom to newborn living things. In theological terms, the first image is of the immortal god Indra, who never appears and can never perceived. The second image of the immortal Indra appears in half-mortal form as *Maghavan*, who can perceived within the mind but it cannot touch. Then the third image of the immortal Indra appears as a manifested invisible immortal embodiment (avatar) representing a descendant of Indra. The fourth image of the immortal Indra appears as a manifested mortal embodiment who is honored as a holy man (prophet) who comes to live among another manifested mortal embodiments. Together they all uphold the principle of *essence*, creating existence from nonexistence, that is, creating something from nothing, and returning to nonexistence.

## DESCENT

According to *Rig-Veda* 6:20, the heavenly Indra does not know where the foes are fighting their battles or where they appear on the ground. He has discovered that living beings have acquired all the wealth buried beneath the fertile ground. The living beings grow corn to feed humanity on land with thousands of Sons of Strength representing the heavenly

Rudra winning the wealth that required to vanquish their foes in war. All the malevolent Asuras, entrusted with power from the sky lord Dyaus, persuaded to move toward Indra and form a spontaneous league. They are all supported by the powers of the Preserver, Vishnu, who slew the dragon that created the dam to hold back the water and prevent it from reaching the living things. Indra, mightier than mighty, as the strong victor, received with prayers, serving as the perfect invisible splendorous one, the lord of the bolt, who as the heavenly ruler has the power to smash the forts of the evil powers to pieces. With his nimble power, Indra causes freed water to become purified water filled with the sweet mythical juice soma. He comes to remove the hundred misfortunes simply by bringing purified water, carried within the streams, removing impurities and appearing as sparkling water. He removes the magical devices used by the evil Śuṣṇa to eat all the nutrients, leaving behind nothing.

By taking forms of drugs derived from great stalks (*druh*), the evil powers escape from death and receive life support. The god Indra causes such drug-bearing stalks to wither by enlisting the spiritual driver Kutsa, who sits beside Indra, to ensure all the magical powers supporting these great stalks (druh) exposed to sunlight. The sunrays, like the hawk, come to gladden, readjusting the strained heads of the stalks (druh) and transforming into the snake *Namuci*, who transforms a guileful evil mind into a noble mind, serving as evil devotees (Dāsas). With the voice of eternal truth, the Dāsas gain honor by guarding *Sayya*, by giving him a common name, Nam, used among humanity to identify those who transformed and enhanced by inertia. They provided with food for success and offered all forms of riches. Further, the great mighty power Indra, with thunder arms, comes triumphantly to shatter wrath and release the stronghold the unrighteous have on forts. He also comes to smite the ruthless serpents and the wily *Vyaṁsa*, *Śambara*, and *Pipru*, ousting them from the homes of all living beings. The sacred words *satnam*, *om*, and *amen* generate activity among worshippers and make the bounteous givers to serve King *Ṛjiśvan*. With their imperishable wealth, they overpower the tribe members, including the crafty *Vetasu*, the swift *Dasni*, and the speedy *Tugra*.

Along with all other serving hands, Indra comes to serve as the host, bearing in both arms the slaying thunder for the battlefield and mounting up the bays. Over the seven wrecked autumn forts, they build their shelters to serve the slain tribes of Dāsas. The provider Purukutsa returns as the ancient strengthener, and the singer Kavi returns as the favorite son of

*Uśanā*. With a roaring sound, Indra drives the waters, which makes a sound like rushing rivers. Over time, safely, they run to the sea, creating the noble T*urvaśa* and *Yadu* tribes. While they are at war, the *Dhuni* sleep and the *Cumuri* slumber, subjected to eternal invocation (*Dabhīti*), which brings light and hymns, generating eternal flame that further doused with soma to dress up their oblations.

According to *Rig-Veda* 6:21, with hymns, the glorified mortal embodiments, as the Mighty One with the powers of Indra, create true new heroes filled with wisdom and vigor. Victorious, they alone can invoke other mortal embodiments. They all worship the ancient seven sages (*Saptarishis*) and urge them to appear from their mighty dwelling, coming swiftly to smite down their opponents. With guileless speech and mighty thoughts, they bring resources that serve as food for living beings, which can stored by heroes such as the high-spirited bay steeds. The Mighty One brings abundant, un-decaying celestial wealth, which makes everyone joyful. Like the earlier singers, they tell others on hand. They obtain good fortune, based upon their individual shares and in the proper proportions, for serving, and as strong, rich invoking powers, they come to subdue as the Asura-slayers. Armed with thunder, Indra helps the heroes who are craving his fluency. They continue going forth, firmly grasping effectual strength and singing deep-piercing songs. To be bestowed with might and strength, they come near to Indra and are filled with noble thought (*Parvata*), which produces the mightiest roar that can boldly dislodge any firmly fixed pieces that never have been shaken. As the boundless faithful leader with noble thoughts, Parvata comes to serve like Indra over those in all places that are hard to traverse. The tyrannized living things become part of the ground, firm like the earth, and when operating in fear, they consume and retain the heat provided by Agni. Appearing as a heavenly soul, Indra comes to ride a bull that heated from every side. Serving as manifested earthly creatures, Indra and Agni bring floods to overpower those who hate devotion. Vishnu, with his splendid divine aspect, appears, in his right-hand holding thunder and in his left hand holding the eternal powers. He comes to destroy all fascinations, and at the same time confirms prosperity, vast and exhaustless.

According to *Rig-Veda* 6:22, all armed and strengthened noble souls, through subduing foes, come to serve themselves, designated as a mighty tribe with the much-invoked evil power Dāsa, whose power exceeds even that of the holy *Nahuṣa*, coming from both sides: evil and noble. The noble souls join with the messenger Maghavan, who bring blessings to serve creation. While serving living beings, the noble souls learn how to extract mythical juice (soma) from plants. With loud prayers and chanted hymns, they even learn to use their glands to transform the soma into the mystical fluid amrit. Having available both mythical and mystical fluid, Indra comes bearing thunder to help such enhanced living beings. Using both mythical juice from plants and mystical fluid from glands, and with undaunting support from the daring god Indra, the noble souls slaughter the strongest evil power, the Dāsas. With the demise of the Dāsas, the living beings help those who have sinned by serving as the heroes within the evil powers. They now offer praises to the mighty ones, seeking their guidance, and pour out further treasure with oblations.

Even the lowly singer who offers humble rites visited and given the powers to serve as the wielded thunderbolt that gives power to cattle and supplies their milk with mythical juice. The heroes, serving as bay steeds, store their physical strength and continue to serve as rich and courageous ones. While they hear the hymns of praise coming from the singers, they make their divine calling, honoring Indra and performing devotional services as in the old days to fulfill their longings. They accepted. While they willfully sing hymns and pray loud prayers, they continue to receive a flow of nectar (amrit) within their embodiments. This brings vigor and spiritual strength. Exalted, received with their sacrifices blissful sweet refreshment from Indra. They also receive a sacrificial milk cake, which commingled with mythical juice and offered to humanity, who in return receive it as a sacrifice so they may come to sit on the holy grass with the Mighty One. With ample room to accommodate them, devoted servants find other paths to seek other living beings so they may make them joyful.

The mythical juice flowing among all as friends replenished by others as their duty to follow the bounteous Indra. The mythical juice brings the divine will, which not only provides aid but also supports the living beings, providing them with extra mythical juice so they may share it with others and thereby win more favor. While the juice is flowing, amid loud sounds, Indra establishes the noble ruler *Bhāradvāja*, who also serves as the patron of singers, to disburse wealth and treasures of every kind.

According to *Rig-Veda* 6:23, coming with praises through the messenger *Maghavan,* soma is an impetuous drink that brings on a rapturous joy that, with glory, brings living beings to join with the messenger to produce new songs that, with singing and loud worship, serve the heaven-dwelling ruler of nobles *Bhāradvāja*, who thus helps them to build long-lasting friendships. As the wisest, a victorious hero, a friend of living beings, he comes to hear from envoy, offering an excellent divine calling with far-reaching aid. Such divine callings give the king the strength extolled among the holy council and operate like a lofty axle that no one surpasses in greatness. Like the branches of a tree, *Bhāradvāja* extends between heaven and earth and provides aid to others, including those who spring forth with heavenly energy. Such living beings, like the strong lord endowed with vigor and follow converging paths that lead them toward home, binding together younglings with a cord that builds no ties among the boundless ones as they perform one bounteous act today, another bounteous act tomorrow. Most often, Indra, with the trinity of Mitra, Varuna, and Pūṣan, comes to help the living beings overcome the foemen's domination. Like bringing the water locked in a mountain's ridges, they bring existence from what is not yet in existence, accompanied with song and sacrifice. Such living beings, with their might, develop an urge to rush into battle, loudly singing theme songs, their horses moving in time to the music. Serving neither for months nor for the autumn season, or enfeebled with age, they hie through the days. With glorious hymns and with mighty powers, they come with praises to celebrate the mighty glory. Steadfast, unbending, the living beings not incited by the bold powers of the *Dāsas*, who move from the high mountains to the level plains and even go into the deep waters, always finding firm ground upon which to rest.

According to *Rig-Veda* 6:24, as impetuous speeders, the bold *Dāsas* go to all depths and to any distance to provide strengthening food and serve mythical juice. Without any help, they stand erect. Unreluctantly, they always come to help during the gloom of night and in the brightened morning. Haltingly, they help living beings and keep them safe from harm when at home or abroad, and preserve them from injury, as the brave sons gladdened through one hundred winters.

## SPIRITUAL PROVINCE

According to *Rig-Veda* 6:25, living beings, whether in the middle region or the highest region, are all aided by Indra to subdue their foemen with strong powers like those needed in battle. With such support, like the hosts, they come to fight, checking the opponent's wrath. Uninjured, they chase their foes to every quarter and subdue even the evil *Dāsas,* converting them to join with their noble tribe of *Āryans.* Those who set themselves up as foes, with their manly strength, smite or strike those who are feeble and push them backward toward the foemen, so they drive headlong into the fight. With the strength of their arms, the noble heroes, filled with illuminated rays, slay the evil powers. With range in combat, they bring the two opposing sides, the *Dāsas* and the *Āryans*, who battle to win water, animals, and fertile lands for their offspring, together, as no strongman has conquered by trusting in valor.

None of the manifested mortal embodiments with their prevailing powers as living creatures can match the power of Indra, who by far surpasses all. Indra serves as the lord of both armies, *Dāsas* and *Āryans*, with valor, as their commanders, great heroes, come to call upon the expansive ranks to settle conflicts. These battles stirred up by the savior and protector of the *Dāsas* and *Āryans*, serving as a great foe or great heroes. Among manliest friends, the pious, and the chiefs, installed by their high dominion, are evermore known for their slaughtering of the evil powers with all royal power and might, given by the divine power *Bhāradvāja* to fight in favor of Indra. This comes with noble singing, to yield to the godless bands whom they are fighting against, who come before morning light. Even in holy battle, they urged by all hosts to gather in combat. Indra hears the living beings drinking soma, coming down as rain. They call upon him to win with mighty valor and give them support on the day of the trial, when the tribes gather on the field of battle between the warrior son and his father, ready to invoke Indra to gain great strength and win booty. The lord of the brave souls, Indra, watches these souls fighting hand-to-hand against the fiends to win cattle. Indra urges the sages to win for the pious (*Kutsa*,) without ruining or cleaving the invulnerable head of the demon (*Śuṣṇa)*, even if it cannot win through praise. The holy priest *Atithigva* brought forward in the lofty battle in a carriage to always help those who praise Indra. The strong *Dasadyu* fight along with the *Vetasu* and massacred the *Tugra* to strengthen themselves against Indra's *Tuji* tribe. Good Indra, fighting one hundred thousand foes, comes with the strange aid of the hero Divodāsa, who slays the mountainous evil power *Śambara.*

As heroes, gladly come to help those who with faith make soma. And to please the evil power Cumuri, they send the same ones, with kindness, to the evil power Dabhīti, who with might is able to kill while in deep sleep. At once, sixty thousand liberal chiefs, *Pithina Raji,* acquire bliss and achieve supreme domination. With the grit of the mightiest hero, Nahuṣa, as a friend, is the triply strong defender who comes to serve by invoking the blessed *Pratardani*, and thus he becomes the illustrious ruler who gains riches not through slaying foes.

According to *Rig-Veda* 6:26, their own existence and their ancestral relationship made apparent through serving the invisible power Indra and the half-mortal envoy Maghavan, who, from such half-mortal form, comes into existence as a semi manifested body (avatar), with a voice constantly singing and offering prayers and invocations, representing the ancestral power of Indra. It is through this process that the same abilities come to exist among the manifested embodiments serving as living beings. Singing hymns, they invoke the heroic powers representing the chariot-borne universal soul Paramatman, who manifests within the mortal embodiments, represented as an eloquent human who is ready to gain abundant riches. The living beings, with praise and honor, singing hymns, make sacrifices and offerings to extol His Majesty, who is rich in wondrous arts, surpassing the magnitude of the nobles on earth and the greatness in heaven. The stellar sun makes pathways to aid humanity, who endure an extended darkness to support the mortal embodiments who yearn to worship, never dishonoring Indra or the mighty powers (divinities, deities, and demigods). They never forget the old traditions, and they follow the divine covenant. Through prayer and with praise, they are known as the humans who use beads to worship. As mighty beadsmen, they serve the heroes who cherish such singers. This brings protection to the plants growing in the mountains. With further prayer, through blessed godly power, Varuna, Mitra, Indra, the Maruts, Pūṣan, Vishnu, Agni, Purandhi, and Savitar exalted with hymns and praises as those who are holy and mighty.

According to *Rig-Veda* 6:27, within the mystical region, unconscious traits refined to make the embodiments mindful, thus allowing further enhancement of living things—plants, animals, and others—which transformed from their wild nature to become refined, ready to serve within civilized society. They develop into the bovine family with noble souls just by imbibing the sweet mythical soma, which comes into existence when one serves the earthly powers of causation. These powers, as the primordial force Shakti, have existed since ancient times, helping the embodiments to perform deeds that generate friendship; therefore, they received and fully accepted by the heavenly divine powers. With libations, they bring joy among the bovine embodiments and cultivate a friendship with them to faithfully serve other living beings. With delight, such libations invoke the eternal flame and bring along wisdom, which when shared among other living beings causes humans to develop morality and righteousness.

Even though the humans know nothing about the vast powers of the gods, they bring abundant riches without even seeing the gods and their mighty power, thus making a productive society that generates bounty among all living beings. Every day, this renews the great divine will, and through personal experience, living beings witness as innocent children, observing with their own eyes. A special force descending from the thunder, *Varashikha*, slays the evil seeds, causing the boldest sound, as vibrations, and brings along a clan, the *Abhyavartin,* who filled with noble seeds (*Cayaman*). They arrive within the ancient grounds of *Hariyupiya* before the evil powers demolished. Terrified and thrashed, they escape to join with the vanguard *Vrcivans.* In a quest for fame, they gather at the river *Yavyavati,* where three thousand living beings appear as red steer, their tongues seeking good pasture. They move on to serve the five major tribes established to serve between earth and heaven, giving the *Turvaśa* to *Sṛñjaya* and giving the *Vrcivans* to *Daivavata.* Thus, with damsels, they create two teams, the *Abhydvartin* and the *Cayamdna.* Each wagon pulled by twenty oxen who serve the ruler of kernel, who serves the liberal sovereign *Prthu,* who is hard to win over.

According to *Rig-Veda* 6:28, they support the bovine goddess who provides earthly milk-bearing cows that come to serve as the mothers to livestock, *Kamadhenu,* bringing good fortune to living beings, serving from their resting place near the cow pen. A prolific living being, the liberal sovereign Prthu, aided by divine will, creates many-colored cows that produce milk each morning. Irrespective of color, each cow yields as a sacrifice pure white milk. As a divine offering, this brings a wealth of wisdom. Those who take care of others, those who give to others, ever increase their value with unbroken limits through the divine will, which turns individual beings into pious souls by providing them with eternal wisdom. They can never lost; no robber or thief can steal them or incapacitate them. Any evil-minded foe who attempts to harass such pious living beings will never be able to overpower individual wisdom or attain its pious dwelling place.

With such wisdom, living beings serve Indra as the head of all milk-bearing animals, who lives many a year through pouring milk from animals such as cows, and others who with divine gifts become the "pious chargers," who move on a dusty summit that no one can overtake and that never crumbles. As pious chargers, shepherds serve the cows without any danger, allowing them to freely roam the broad pasturelands. The shepherds as pious chargers blessed by the patron *Bhaga*, who as the envoy of Indra provides a portion of mythical juice (soma) to create longing within individual hearts, which invokes the individual living spirit (Atman). Bhaga, serving as the blessed shepherd, helps to fatten them so they do not reach a wasted state, transforming them from unlovely to beautiful. Bhaga helps shepherds to cultivate good pasture, both grass and crops, bringing sweetened drinking water to serve as the pure prolific drink. Similarly, Bhaga helps other living beings learn prayers and, by acquiring auspicious voices, prosper within their own embodiments so they may participate in the glorified assemblies. Bhaga establishes holy sites that may use by anybody, no matter who, whether a thief or a sinful man, and can even deflect the darts coming from ferocious powers such as Agni.

## ETERNAL PROWESS

According to *Rig-Veda* 6:29, those who follow the path of the pious chargers provide friendship, loving-kindness, and a glorious life as bestowed by Indra. With great kindness, Indra serves as the thunder-wielder and wins with divine will all that clings closely to and stands firmly on the ground, holding firm like chariot drivers with reins in their hands. Like the leading horses and stallions, ready to yoked for the journey, they serve as providers. Embracing the bold thunder, clothed in robes, with glory and strength, like guardians, they look to heaven for fairness. Like active dancers, they display themselves, with soma to drink and the best food to eat. Dressed and mingled with grain, they pray and recite praises without limit, extolling the gods for favors, appointed with greatness by their mighty chief. Surrendering to earth and heaven, filled with strong sense of endeavor, the living beings drive like princes. With their herds in water, they listen to the lofty power Indra and become ready to serve as unaided helpers with golden vision.

According to *Rig-Veda* 6:30, as heroes, unequalled in might and power, they come ready to smite the evil powers and thus bestowed with eternal prowess. Indra travels with informal knowledge about the biosphere, which exists between the two worlds, with one-half in greatness as the lord of riches and the other half serving in the heavens with spiritual wealth, called the lords of wealth. Godlike in nature, with mighty esteem, none of them hindered from spreading near or far into the regions that become apparent every day with the sun.

The lord of material wealth and the lord of spiritual wealth (*Rig-Veda* 6:31) both hold in their own hands the seed of living beings. With their opposing voices, they invoked in water as the seed of progeny, accompanied by the sunlight. The mighty powers of Indra shake all the regions of earth, making them move from their standstill position, also shaking all created living things. With disturbing powers, Indra shakes all those who are firm-footed. Frightened, they experience the shaking of mountains, extending to the trees in the forests of the earthly region and those in the hidden heavenly region.

According to *Rig-Veda* 6:32, the heroes are unable to produce words to describe this ancient activity, which is great, strong, and energetic, brought by the mighty wielder of the thunder who comes amid the bright sun. The sages, with glorified "parents," burst through the mountain; they come to serve with roaring holy thoughts, which loosen the bond and, by generating hymns, and with singers, hold the beams of morning light. Famed for their great deeds, priests kneel, and with loud sounds they conquer, each a friend of friends. In the fray, milk-bearing cows break the fortifications. Each serving as a sage among sages, they bring mares with abundant vigor and plenteous strength. Singing praises, the sages accompany the chargers who serve heroes as friends of friends. The lovers of song, along with others, come for the welfare of all.

With rush and might, Indra hurries to bring coursers to swiftly win over the waters by setting free the rivers that, nonstop and exhaustless, flow daily to meet their goal. With the mightiest rapture, Indra swiftly comes to the aid of heroes (*Rig-Veda* 6:33) who have won brave steeds. These heroes encounter and quell the evil powers and other enemies in battle. The heroes come with loud voices, invoking the tribes by providing them with the aid provided by singers and chargers while they serve on the battlefield. They pierce through a class of demons, the *Paṇis*, and win the booty that serves both types of foemen, the *Āryans* and the *Dāsas*. They strike them down like lightning, as well-shot wood, and once all defeated, they come to serve as chieftains, helping the tribes to prosper with scanty support. With aid, all the loved ones still alive keep fighting for the sunlight. They invoke gracious heroes who in the future are inclined to come near to provide them with shelter and help the living beings who, like the Mighty One, are ready to win cattle on the day of ordeal.

According to *Rig-Veda* 6:34, with songs, and filled with noble thought as in the past, the sages proceed to offer their eulogies with loud yearnings to Indra. Praising the bold powers, they invoke them by offering sacrifices and performing glorious actions. When all one hundred or one thousand singers, with love, produce songs, with loud praises they delight and rejoice like living beings with brightness from the heavenly sun. Mingled with the soft light of the moon, this brings yearning mixed with water to transform any deserted place, with sacrificial gifts to refresh the living beings. With mighty eulogies, speaking loudly like poets, they invited to join with the powers of Indra. This allows the living beings to engage in even greater encounters, like the foemen coming to love all life, guarding, and helping all.

Mythical animals such as sacred cows bring good fortune to others. While they rest in the cow pen, they even become happier as they draw near to other living beings. They are prolific, and appear in colors, as a morning they yield their single-colored milk to all living beings. Indra gifts those who offer sacrifices with material wealth, admonishing them not to attached or become obsessive. Assuring those to whom he gives, he gives them more, thereby increasing their wealth, making their dwellings pious. Such sacrificial gifts never lost; no robber can take them or ever injure them, and no evil-minded foe even attempts to harass them.

According to *Rig-Veda* 6:35, the mythical animals live many a year with the cows. The living beings give gifts and come to serve demigods such as chargers, whom no one overtakes at the dusty summit. Serving as cows of the pious worshipper, they, without stumbling, roam the widespread pastureland free of danger. These cows, like the patron Bhaga, even pour out the first portion of soma to the sacred mother cow, who within their hearts serves the living spirit and, with longing, serves Indra. When fattened, worn, and wasted, they become unlovely, but the worshipper continues to look upon them. They still bring prosperity to the houses they serve and, with auspicious voices and power, glorify the assemblies.

These milk-bearing animals raised in an agricultural setting to provide commodities such as milk, food, fiber, and labor. The ruminants, as livestock (*Kamadhenu*), are by fences or enclosures, wherein they roam freely. The products of such fenced livestock continue to play a major economic and cultural role in rural communities. In communities, the bovine goddesses referred to as "*Surabhi,*" the milk-bearing cow who worshipped as the mother. Miraculous, she provides living beings with whatever they desire. *Surabhi* serves as the "cow of plenty," as the icon of the heavenly Rudra's and is depicted as eleven white female cows with breasts who serve as the eleven females' deities. They not worshipped independently, and they have no temple. They are honored as bovine goddesses. With reverence, they are all honored together as the divine will, prevailing as the godly mothers who regulate all creations on earth.

The priests, with their ecstatic devotion and a form of special service (Yajna), trained to become proficient in the ritual practice and thereby become *Rtvijas*. As members of a social class, they are generically known as sages (*vipra*) or seers (*kavi*). They appointed specialized roles and, over time, develop their own platform to perform the ritual corpus. Eventually, a full complement of sixteen *Rtvijas* become accustomed to performing all the major ceremonies. The sixteen *Rtvijas* consist of four chief priests and twelve assistants. Within the priesthood, each denotes the element of both power and authority, and they are all given to serve as the officiants for living beings who, in effectual form, serve as the four chief priests who, with ecstatic love (*bhäva-bhakti*), are part of a priesthood (*adhvaryu*) of those who possess the traits of a genuine noble soul, *avyartha-kälatvam*, and spend all their time in devotional service and therefore become perseverant and tolerant through detachment from material things. Others, such as prideless kings, come to bestow the powers of mercy, through prayer, on an eager quest to faithfully serve the divine will. They become attached to chanting eagerly, with true qualities of the eternal universal soul (*Paramatman*). They attract the individual living spirit (*Atman*) and, as a pastime, attract all creations with Atman to their place of worship.

According to *Rig-Veda* 6:36, evermore, rich earthly ecstasies transform the established godly power to appear in the form of noble priests (*Adhvaryu*) who deal with vigor and serve as living beings who obtain strength and, through making sacrifices, acquire valor, attaining self-enrichment. Like rein-seizing impetuous chargers, they guide the living beings who regulated with loose power and use them to slaughter evil powers. Sometimes they become associates or demigods who, as part of the horse team the Aśvins, serve the gods who guide living beings. With integrity and mighty powers, they follow the godhead, Indra. Filled with vigor, and with strong praises, they produce holy songs that, like the rivers, make soothing sounds until they reach the sea, while they let the excellent spring bring shining riches to support the flowing rivers. As the sovereigns, without an equal in world, they serve as the lords of living beings, hearing the worship from those who without hesitation serve as servants on earth. As the guards, they consider godly treasure as their own, while they offer joy and fame and gain ever mightier power with each generation.

## PROPHETS

According to *Rig-Ved*a 6:37, the sovereign yokes the bay horses to the carriage that carries the heavenly powers who bring every blessing from Indra. Such powers invoked even to this day and brought to the feast that served to the brethren. Those who receive such drops, such as *vat*, overflow with purity and come to serve in the priesthood, then proceed to enjoy mythical fluid. As guests, they reach out to the celestial king, the ultimate source of strong soma, and with this they bring the well-wheeled chariot pulled by steeds that directly transports them to glory, flying with the mystical nectar (Amrit), traveling through the air, Vayu, which never ceases or fails. With Amrit, they stir up the supreme priesthood serving among living beings, as most efficacious princes assigned by Indra to serve as guardians with the power of thunder. They remove sorrow, and as a part of the Bold One, the noble souls, with their wealth and enduring vigor, singing songs, magnify Indra as the best slayer of evil (*Vṛtra*), serving as the heroes who protect the prince.

According to *Rig-Veda* 6:38, marvelous are those who drink and carried away by the great and splendid call, their ears filled with crying sounds, to join with Indra. Serving as bounteous demigods, they help the priests (*Adhvaryu*) by offering them gifts that make them more famous and help them to speak up and approach Indra even from a distance. They are represented by composing sacred verses, all upon request, in the form of the best songs, which with praises sung to give birth to the ancient everlasting powers. The prayers and songs concentrated, along with the sacrifice that, strengthened with hymns, used in devotion and offered along with soma juice. When the night departs with the coming of dawn, they become strong, along with the days, the months, and the autumns. Having been born to conquer might, as Priest (A*dhvaryu),* they come in full perfection to provide a large bounty. With glory through the great and powerful divine will, they, still today, invited as the helpful singers who quell foes.

With celestial soma (*Rig-Veda* 6:39), they come with eloquent wisdom and inspire devotion among all the close attendants serving as Adhvaryu. With grace, they send food and milk to the singers to fulfill their cravings. All led by the law, rushing like animals over the mountain. As holy minded comrades, they even break the ridge that has never broken to overpower demons (*Vala*), and like Indra they use mighty words to subdue the class of misers (*Paṇis*) who hide near rivers and streams, looking to steal cows. Throughout the year, at morning and in the evening, Indra moves through the darksome nights to establish the ensign, which in the morning appears as the dawn, as splendor, the day's bright light with the rays coming directly from the sun. This unveils the hidden world, not yet seen, so they may follow the eternal law. With the rooster serving as the host of morning, when they hear its voice, they light up and awaken the steeds, which they need to yoke, and find gladdened living beings enjoying the sunlight. Like an ancient king, with praises they fill their stomachs with plenteous food and gather treasures to distribute, such as water to give to herbs and other plants. Feeding without any form of poison all forms of kingdoms, they grow with loud sounds as they douse beings with soma, which makes every kind of kingdom joyful and happy.

According to *Rig-Veda* 6:40, setting loose the bay steeds, they learn to share their freedom with friends. This brings together the assembly. With the strength of holy prayers, they provide individuals with an offering of drink, which the mighty ones bring along e pressed between stones to generate eternal energy and create delight. With water, the mythical juice emerges, just as living beings draw milk from milk-bearing animals. Such mythical juice enhances the eternal flame, embodied by Indra and Agni. Among the bay steeds, the soma drawn and conveyed through the devoted minds of those who approach the priesthood (adhvaryu) to attain ever-greater prosperity. This cultivates ardent desire to listen to and hear the vibrations of the liturgical prayers. They offer sacrifices, which further increase their vigor so, on the day of hearing, whether present or absent, all mortal embodiments find their dwellings and are ready to serve in accord with the team of cosmic hosts (Maruts), who as demigods guard them and make sacrifices to help them. As part of the team, the Maruts offered purified pressed soma drops, which, mixed with water, lead them to seek a home among milk-bearing creatures such as cattle. When faced with the thunder-wielder, they increase their worship, and with appreciation, reach a well-formed place with sweetness where water fills the streams to drink. In omniscient form, they win the spoils as they stand to face the thunderbolt, thereby gaining more power. Drops of soma make the bulls ready to serve along with the lord of the bays, who in the past, as strong supporter, provided food forever.

According to *Rig-Veda* 6:42, they replenish all their powers like champions, and with libation they ask Indra to provide enough soma to fill their embodiments. Rejoicing, they serve as the ancient noble soul (*Satakratu*). Filled with mythical juice, they guard those who are fighting righteous wars. Such noble souls made omniscient with sacrificial gifts and travel speedily among wanderers. This brings powers to the heroes who serve at the forefront. With the mythical juice soma, they evolve to become immanent and help the impetuous ones as the messengers of gods such as Indra. Filled with juice, they attain eternal wisdom, thus learning to face the divine will, which engenders hope among them to serve as the Bold One and strike down any foe. The holy priests *dhvaryu*), expressed within the divine will, make offerings to keep everyone safe from the spiteful curse of each presumptuous highborn foe who creates, with wild joy, a kind of madness, the same kind that in ancient times caused the demon Śambara to become prey. From all points, the adhvaryu stand guard, the gladdening draft shed as mist, which ends up as pressed soma for Indra, who in wild joy comes to set free any animal or living thing held fast within the rock. The pressed soma offered to Indra brings delight even among the adhvaryu and helps them gain the power to transform into holy priests and rise to become the mighty envoy, Maghavan.

According to *Rig-Veda* 6:44, the wealthiest godly ones, with the most illustrious gladdening libations, bring along pressed soma, which makes them as the effectual *adhvaryu* as they are all bestowed with a wealth of hymns, wherewith they increase in strength so they may serve the Lord of Strength in conquest. Those heroes who have wronged no one provided with the proper aid to conquer. They become the most bounteous of all tribes prevailing in both heaven and earth, and therefore can admire the mighty powers that, with song, cause them to increase in individual strength. Swiftly, they become the Lord of Bounty and spread abroad seated among Indra. Listening to the powerful songs of praise, they begin singing songs for success and go farther by extending their growth. During the law, quaffing mythical juice, like deities they turn their minds to glory, and with winning lofty hymns, and with lovely personalities, they make apparent their beauteous form. They bestowed with their most illustrious strength to ward off manifold malignities. With an abundance of life force, they gain riches, graciously turning themselves into liberal givers like Indra. They are gracious as they come to serve the bay steeds. Indra, thundering from a rain cloud, sends forth water to cattle and horses. Through the old art, they come to cherish those singers who do not allow riches, who bring no gifts, and who never deceive heroes. Like the adhvaryu, they bring the king to the mighty Indra, who thereafter brings pressed soma. Exalted by hymns, serving like the ancient sages (rishis), they praised as the new sages. In their wild joy, not knowing everything, they use the soma to strike down the evil powers. They proclaim loudly as the heroes drink the pungent soma to gird themselves against the strong jaws of the evil powers. When Indra drinks such savory soma, with his thunder he comes to slay the evil powers, along with the supporting composers who come from afar to make such a sacrifice and thus help the lovers. Those supporters who produce heavenly sounds generate the mystical nectar (Amrit). With cheer and gracious favor, they keep far from hatred and affliction. The enchanted messenger Maghavan comes to overpower foemen, those who aim their hostile darts at both relatives and strangers who turn and flee, at which point Indra rushes forth and kills them. The epithet Maghavan wins these battles and sets easy paths for holy priests (adhvaryu) to follow, with ample freedom to plant seeds in the water to produce their offspring, who become princes to serve the god Indra. They join to harness the bay stallions, strong horses that harnessed to pull Indra's chariot. Speeding along, bearing together as harnessed thunder, they bring soma as the remedy and stand aside as the strong heavenly powers hold the vat filled with the shining eternal flame. With holy oil, like an exulting wave, they bring the strong and mighty juice that processed by the compressed cosmic stones. All being brought by the strong bulls, flowing within rivers, or standing in bodies of water such as lakes and oceans. With the morning light, as if wedded to a glorious companion, they sit beneath the light of the sun, which illuminates all the three worlds. With heavenly lucid power, the sun provides nectar (Amrit), which always kept under close concealment and held within the higher heavenly region and the lower earthly region. It drawn by a chariot, with the seven reins that harness the seven supreme powers of causation. They, with soma, gain the powers supplied by manifested milk-bearing creatures and spring forth with ripeness flowing from their ten fingers.

## INTERACTION

According to *Rig-Veda* 6:45, the ancient sacred language Sanskrit has refined, consecrated, and sanctified, regarded as the language used in ancient times to communicate among the noble tribes. Sanskrit held in high regard by all the youthful, trusted friends (*Yadu*) who descend from an ancient lineage. It provides guidance to the manifested noble souls to establish a tribunal system with the ruler *Turvaśa*. In ancient times, along the holy river *Sarasvatī*, one of the five major tribes, the Yadu, guided by eulogies, established. Great in their ways, they offer unfailing protection. Serving as friends, they offer psalms and hymns to praise the ruler serving the Great Providence, which is especially freeing after slaughtering the evil power Vṛtra. As guardians of the divine will, they come to regulate with friendly eternal love (Mitra), which represented among manifested living things as a halo, which indicates those who are above showing any form of dislike or hate. While guided as youthful friends, the Yadu, offering songs of praise so the milk cows will provide milk, through friendly merit, call upon Mitra to bring with the highest unchanging ultimate reality Brahma to come and accept them and, with his hand, provide them with the holy power to serve as good heroes.

The Yadu learns to pursue the stored treasures that in the olden days supported heroes in winning battles. They respect the external strength coming through the casters of the stone (comets). As the lords of strength, they use the art of outwitting to destroy the firm forts. Using the unbending divine will, they overpower enemies and, through the power of hymns, invoke Indra, the true soma drinker, to come transform the steeds into stallions, which like coursers come to support Indra. The divine will, most glorious, given to the lovers of song to stir them into a great power, providing them with the ability to acquire the power needed to subdue foes and helping them to find the swiftest passageway.

One and only one, the matchless one, with a most active heroic soul, Śatakratu is born to become the leader of all living beings and comes to serve as the lord of earthly treasures. With their individual desires yoked together, serving as one team, the Śatakratu excellently satisfy all their wishes. They withhold any given gift of power and wealth to share it with others who listen to hymns and songs, and they work with others to answer their unspoken requests. With might, they open and close the cow stall to set the cows free. Serving as heroic souls, the Śatakratu call upon all mothers to come and meet their children, as cows meet their calves, and ask them to share divine love with them so they may win. Like steer, they long to receive the delightful juice, poured out like motherly love, and to enjoy great benevolence, which no singer can rebuke with any song. With every draft, the milk cows urge their young ones to pour out their milk, like the lovers of song. As part of a rivalry, many singers beg to acquire wisdom, loudly invoking Indra to give them enough wisdom to serve as Āryans, who are set above non-Āryans, who as hoarders create a tribe of extreme misers, the Paṇis, who become head tradesmen, settling in tribes. Like a wide bush on the bank of the holy river Gangā, with bounty in the thousandfold, they instantaneously set themselves up with the rushing wind to offer gifts. Thus, suddenly, all singers come to praise them as the head of the tradesman tribe (*Brbu*), who come to bring one thousand material gifts.

According to *Rig-Veda* 6:46, as tradesmen, the Brbu win wealth and power; however, they not verily accepted by spiritual singers and poets as the true sources of wealth. During periods of war and conflict, Brbu tradesmen serve as pious ones, using their ruling tribe like a steed, racing and progressing, but in no way come close to calling upon Indra. Lord of wonder, Indra appears among all heroes, holding in his hand a thunderbolt, and with praises calls upon celestial bodies—comets, asteroids, and meteorites (casters of the stone)—to come pour mythical juice to serve the newly created embodiments. Indra appears with a chariot pulled by steeds to be the conqueror in such a battle. The pious tradesmen Brbu, knowing well, call upon Indra to bring his most active brave heroes to slay the foes and help thousands of living beings by providing them with material wealth, so they can prosper in the fight. Indra, in the epithet of an angry bull (*Rcisama*), comes with sunlight, water, and life, and an uncompromising position, to support and those who are fighting the righteous battle on behalf of Indra, so all can survive and become famous, enriched with mightiest excellence, serving as the wondrous godly powers.

Indra appears with arms of thunder filled with clouds of cosmic vapor, coming from heaven with such powers toward the earth, with the tribe of unlimited strength, the noble warrior (*Nahuṣas*). They serve as mighty fighters, designated to serve as the warriors of the gods, accompanied by mighty ones (divinities, deities, and demigods), to provide relief to the living beings. Empowered as the excellent nobles among humanity, they at the same time bring power to easily subdue their foes (*Dāsas, non-Āryans, and Asuras*). They manifest as noble souls (*Āryans, Ādityas, and Nahuṣas*), representing the messenger Maghavan, as one of the five tribes who enjoy eternal strength, exhibit divine valor, and cherish splendid fame. They set themselves up as the *Trksi* tribe, which includes the *Druhyus* and the *Paru* peoples, who fully bestowed with subduing power to win against their foes through nonviolent means. They happily granted a triply strong, blessed dwelling place located near the divine powers, far from the demigods. By using his powers, the messenger Maghavan subdues the minds of the foes when the evil powers boldly attack to smite him down. Maghavan, with love songs, is the closest guardian. He stays near to aid and strengthen those who are fighting the righteous war. At times, he shoots arrows that fly with feathered fletching's and sharpened points. Serving as a father, the messenger Maghavan provides shelter for the beloved heroes. Those whose bodies strained by the fight treated as sons, with Maghavan giving them refuge to keep them far from any unobserved hostiles. In the mighty fight, Maghavan, as father, urges the flying chargers to watch their speed as they drive down the uneven road. They follow their path the same as falcons, which eagerly follow the path of renown, the speeding river. They rush down steep descents like birds, and when attracted to bait, they respond to such urgings, their reins always held in both hands.

## POWER OF PROTECTION

According to *Rig-Veda* 6:47, mythical juice is good to the taste and full of sweetness, but it is too strong and rich in flavor when given as a draft to gladden the mightiest powers of protection, those who needed in battle as a bold and powerful force that no one can conquer. Indra uses such power to slaughter the evil power Vṛtra and to defeat the demon power Śambara, knowing that even after they slaughtered and beaten down, their souls will remain hidden among ninety-nine sheep. Soma stirs up vibrations and first influences individual voices by provoking the yearning to awaken from deep sleep, the true state of the immortal living spirit, which with imaginative power extends to the six constituencies, thus influencing all, excluding none. When the immortal living spirit expands, it reaches from the earth to the lofty heights of heaven, even expanding in breadth through the generation of internal power by way of the nectar (amrit). This spreads, fully supported by the mythical juice soma, to join with the heavenly powers to form the three headlong rivers, all extending from the wide midair region, producing brilliant colors. In the form of a wavy sea, they all appear at the forefront, creating a fullness that comes to dwell, appearing as the morning light (dawn). With their mighty powers, the cosmic hosts (Maruts) use pillars to support the upper shield and to allow Indra, as the leader, to come and guide humanity. With great treasure, he serves as an excellent guardian for humanity, who bears well through danger, and carefully provides guidance to lead human beings to an ample room filled with material wealth, which needed for happiness and security. This allows the heavenly power Sūrya and the high and cosmic hosts (Maruts) to establish a lofty shelter beneath the arms of the sky, in a place located right below the cosmic region, to protect living things from the surrounding terrestrial bodies.

Sitting on a wide chariot seat with his two best steeds, representing celestial power, Indra represents the powerful cosmic hosts (Maruts). With their chariot driven by the messenger Maghavan, they bring in hundreds of goods of all sorts, the best, which used to subdue and graciously lengthen the day. This allows human beings to expand their individual minds. Sharpened like blades made of iron, they generate thoughts and spoken words to seek and granted divine protection. The rescuer *Devanam* and the helper *Śakra* serve the heroes and others who come to listen to the godly word of wisdom that invoked by each. Mighty powers, through the messenger Maghavan, reach Indra and then offer prosperity, blessing the living beings and serving as the good godly protectors of all treasures. With favor, they baffle the foes as they provide worshippers a safe place to rest. The rescuer or helper enjoys the grace, holy power, and favor that comes from Indra, who driven from afar to become the good preserver. Like rivers rushing down a slope, hastily producing songs and prayers, linked with verses, they all gather and appear as thunder, which spreads bounteously among animals, along with drops of water filled with manifold libations. With loud sounds, they satisfy those who pray to and worship the higher powers. Even the rich nobles come with mighty power to find that the moves they make are alternate, where the rearmost foot precedes the foremost foot, which follows. With such movement, living beings, as famed heroes, become stronger and friendlier, ever advancing forward with first one foot and then the other. The kings of the world, ruling earth and heaven, come to see the haughty powers created by Indra. These powers provide for and protect living beings, turning humanity into devotees, further allying them with others. Rejecting those who disregard such worship, the devotees live to enjoy victorious lives through autumns.

In every figure and in every mode, they look upon Indra, who moves them by creating multiform illusions. Serving as the bay steeds, ten times one hundred, with the creative force Tvaṣṭṛ, they yoked and forever stand upon the foemen's side, even when the princes are at ease. With demigods, they reach a country devoid of pastureland but with spacious ground. The same ground that once was too small to hold the powers of *Brihaspati* now expanded to provide space for war, the supporting cattle backed by the power of Indra. Indra helps find a path to support the faithful singers who, day after day, far from their seat, drive like Indra from place to place, facing darksome creatures. With the hero, they slay the huckstering Dāsas, Varcin, and Śambara where in abundance (*Prastoka*) they gather in the waters, bestowed by Indra with ten treasuries and ten horses, all with great temperament, thereby providing them with the wealth that acquired after killing the evil Śambara. The holy priest *Atithigva*, as a gift, given ten horses, ten treasure chests, ten garments, and an added gift of ten lumps of gold, all of which are handed over to Divodāsa. Along with ten embodiments, the sons of *Sṛñjaya* are honored by given extra steeds and one hundred cows. As the recipients of all noble gifts, they take these to the tribal leader Bhāradvāja, who with wooded bounty uses them to establish a strong firmament. The steeds bear the brave victorious heroes who show their straps of leather, which lets their riders win all the spoils of battle. With mighty strength, this noble tribe, representing the rulers of heaven and earth, establish their conquering force. They brought forward as the sovereigns of the wood and are honored within their embodiments with holy gifts. Securely bolt and bound with straps of vigor, they move within running waters, serving as the bolt of Indra, who is the cause of the floods. The bolt of Indra, like the front line of the cosmic hosts (Maruts), appears as close-knit as the child of the law-abiding and loving souls Varuna and Mitra. The Maruts end up receiving godlike embodiments, filled with oblations. They, with loud voices, send forth vibrations, passing from earth to heaven, letting the world know, with drums, that there is an accord between the demigod Maruts and the celestial power Indra. These vibrations spread everywhere, imbuing foemen with thunder-filled strength, covering the region with vigor. They drive away all danger and misfortune. Like a war drum, Indra first shows their firmness. With the sounding of the war drum, they speak aloud, signaling the arrival of the heroic Bhāradvāja, along with the twin winged horses—Aśvins—serving as demigods. Together in triumph, the Aśvins come to support the warriors who are fighting the battle along with Indra.

According to *Rig-Veda* 6:48, each song sung, and every sacrifice made by the hero Bhāradvāja strengthens the winged horses serving as the demigod Aśvins. Further, with praise and everlasting wisdom, Agni comes to bless them as the Sons of Strength, representing two well-beloved friends who have come to serve as righteous fighters, all bearing gifts as gracious lords. In battle, they not only come to help and strengthen but also serve as the saviors of individual lives. With beams of the eternal flame, they emit the pure shining light that never changes with time and never fades, providing fair beams of brilliant light. By worshipping the great godly powers, eternal wisdom comes without delay, which, with the wondrous power provided by Agni, helps to unveil the absolute truth. With given strength, they win and even transform their life force prevailing in water, in stones, and in trees to create their own offspring, who all to come to support the eternal law. When the stones rubbed with force, this brings the immortal living spirit, as their own offspring reach a lofty height within the terrestrial region. Thus, they fill Prithvi with their brilliant shine, Prithvi being the vault, the material world, located between the two worlds. As the god Agni, they hasten with their smoke, moving amid the gloom of night to reach heaven in darkness. They make themselves apparent in the darksome nights, appearing as a red bull, with their lofty beams, pure brilliancy, appearing as kindled youthful ones, who carried in the shining hands of Bhāradvāja. With godly purity and splendid wealth, they come from the house of the lord to establish houses for themselves, a home for all members of the tribe. They guarded from the distress created by one hundred folks passing through one hundred winters. As youthful ones with godly souls, they become opulent singers, providing wonderful favorable music. They receive bounties to bring the wealth graciously given to them from Agni so they may find a resting place on the ground. As unfailing guards, they plant seeds and create embryos, never negligent about establishing their children to keep them far from celestial wrath and wickedness. They, as the youthful ones, learn to make friends with the sweet song that is sung among female embodiments such as cows to transform water into milk, which they freely pour out to cause their newborn to shine with a native sheen, which they shed like the immortal flame, before they are turned away by the cosmic hosts (Maruts). The impetuous Maruts on their way look upon all their splendor as they move, and with love from the females, they pour out milk like in the old days, the milk cows serving as the mothers that yield milk for all, which in the form of food nourishes all who drink of it. Through the mystic power of the eternal law (Varuna), the new ones pass over to the wise friend Indra, then to the Sustainer (Vishnu), and then they pass on to appear as a mortal manifested embodiment. They manifest and appear as Indra's avatar Aryaman. As joy givers, they bring plenteous food and, with wishes and praise, offer oblations to the demigods serving as the cosmic hosts (Maruts). The Maruts roar with the brilliant light carried by solar deity Pūṣan, who sets free from foes the individual immortal spirit (Atman) hidden within their embodiments. With inner illumination, it is easy for mortal embodiments such as Bhāradvāja to acquire eternal wealth and to learn not to tear up the roots of the useful tree (*kakambira*) or destroy a feminine stem that, as a malignity, is entrapped to serve as the neck of the celestial bird *garuda*, which during day brings the light from the sun and uses its soft nature, its friendship, and its curd-filled mouth to smooth the surface of the skin, making it uninjured and flawless.

A new tribe, higher than humankind, comes with glory to serve as equals to the supreme powers of causation. The tribe looks after all living things as in the past. Humanity, with a moral impetus, beholds such creations as the Vedic divinity Pūṣan, who with roaring sounds seeks guidance from half-mortal demigods and follows the immortal cosmic hosts (Maruts) and those glorious ones above, namely, archangels, the divine will, solar power, eternal power, and the immortal universal soul.

CHAPTER 11

# Ethical Dominion

THE RIGHTEOUS DOMINION IS WHERE AN INFLUX OF ESSENCE establishes a set of properties that make an entity or substance a fundamental necessity, and without such essence, the entity or substance loses its identity. The essence often serves as a vehicle for doctrines that tend to create different forms of existence, as well as different identities subject to conditions and properties. Logically, such a concept has a strong theoretical basis and is sensical to the whole family of worlds. Virtuous people bring happiness, taking a righteous approach, and closely listen to the calling from the gods Agni and Indra. They also follow the eternal law (Varuna) and practice unconditional love (Mitra). They, like the two young matriarchs, monitor sacrifices offered with praise from each tribe and use their sober minds and righteous souls to serve as the children of heaven. They gauge sacrifices and worship as Sons of Strength, and like heralds invite the bright red eternal flame representing the powers of Agni. Unlike their original ferocious form, they serve as two daughters: one representing bright beams of light coming from the sun, and the other representing the softer reflective light coming from the moon. They jointly serve as part of the bedrock of the constellations of stars, which serve as the sanctifiers, which through succession separate the path of vibration from the path of oscillation, traveling through to transform holy verses into hymns and thus coming to support the powers of the divine will regulating creation.

While they travel through the air (Vayu) as a lofty song, they bounteously fill all individual embodiments with eternal wealth, wisdom, and absolute truth. They support the most learned spiritual scholars (sages) who follow along with the gods, traveling the bright path with their well-harnessed horses. They yoke the horses to the heavenly chariot like the twin horses the Aśvins. With honor, they look on with farsightedness, which pleases well when yoked with refulgent thought. As the chiefs, *Nāsatyas* seek for themselves a dwelling that will fill them with new strength to have their children. They appear as objects creating movement (*Vata*) flying in the air (Vayu), and identified as bulls of the earth, which when in water appear as the deity of thunder who fertilizes the ground (*Parjanya*). They jointly stir up the regions by spreading eternal truth, which humanity hears only when it transforms itself into essence and comes to serve the holy spirit by singing delightful hymns, thus increasing their individual intellects and allowing them to achieve higher knowledge. This helps manifested mortal embodiments to comprehend the goddess Sarasvatī and know of the higher creative power to produce music, art, and other such things. In consort with the heroes, with their impatient lives, they inspire in accord with light and Sarasvatī. With a female voice, the children of heaven produce sanctuary music, unassailable and flawless, and with praise come to serve as the guards. All along the pathway, with eloquence and grace, they served by the solar deity Pūṣan in producing each prayer, with effective fulgent eternal flame to worship Agni, and with Tvaṣṭṛ generating the creative powers. They jointly make their prayers easy to hear and able taken home to share, as glorious prayers bestow life that makes them ever active, like godly persons with fair arms and fair hands. With divine songs, they honor the heavenly power Rudra, as the father of the dynamic universe, during the day and at night. They call upon noble souls (sages) for the great undecaying powers that bestow lofty bliss upon humanity as the youthful ones in support of the wise ones who worship and meet with singers to move with longing, like herders driving the cattle home. At all times, they worship the father rewarded with a meeting with the strong creator, who swiftly comes to serve like the heroes. Serving as Agni's envoys, the Aṅgirases lie with the singers' hymns upon their bodies, just like the stars that decorate the heaven. Each time when passing through the earthly region, the Sustainer, Vishnu, provides them with shelter and enough wealth and happiness for three lifetimes. With their own sweet song, they invoke their dwelling, as regulated by the eight elemental gods (*Aṣṭavasu*) who represent nature (*Prakriti*) in its different aspect. They embodied in the form of three natural cosmic phenomena, *Ahibudhnya,* Parvata, and Savitar, who with lightning bring sweet mythical soma juice to flood the earth, first through the creation of the plant kingdom. This kingdom of plants used by the liberal patron and lord Bhaga in offering oblations to bring wealth and prosperity. The noble tribes provided with the flourishing garden *Avestan*, which the tribes use in offering their relatives a reward for serving as patrons of this last place that can be used to fight the righteous war against the godless bands.

## HOLY ORDER

According to *Rig-Veda* 6:50, the goddess mother Aditi calls upon Agni to bring the eternal flame, along with unconditional love and friendship (Mitra) and the eternal law (Varuna). Mother Aditi asks as a favor that they bring out the gracious trinity of Aryaman, Savitar, and Bhaga to help any humans who are seeking freedom from material attachment and who commit no sins as free souls. The great heavenly power Sūrya brings the sun to guide humanity and allow them to experience the bright light as the ultimate source of absolute truth. With the twice-manifested cosmic body the sun, they can perceive all those performing sacred duties to fulfill the needs of humankind. Serving as the competent father Prajāpati, after passing through multiple cycles of eternal truth, they are born from the mind as the son Daksha, who lives for prolonged period (yuga). He fully supported by the ferocious fire, Agni, who provides illumination to create a wide holy dominion stretching from heaven down to earth. This established with the most blissful of lofty shelters to cover all the divine creations. These shelters provide ample space for creations to set up their individual dwellings, with protection coming from the hemispheres to provide a free space where they may work together as nonrivals. As resistless ones, each provided with excellence to invite the cosmic hosts (Maruts) as sons of the heavenly father Rudra. From the cosmic region, the Maruts stoop down to meet humanity, who tormented with affliction from the material world. The mother goddesses (*Rodasī*) as the patrons, cling closely to those who follow the sun deity Pūṣan, bringing bounty for humanity. Manifested humanity hears the Maruts and Rodasī, who bring along all other creatures, which come trembling and singing new hymns as the lovers of song.

Hearing heroes singing songs of love, they seek granted mighty wealth and the strength to provide protection to their sons and grandsons. This exalts Indra, who approaches the godly power Savitar, who comes to rescue them with her holy golden hands. With its bounteous face, the sun brings along morning, which discloses the precious gifts offered in holy service, including the gifts of those who worship and evermore enjoy the bounty. By the grace of the eternal flame, Agni brings richness among heroes, who verily, as the demigod Nāsatyas, come through with prayers to serve as holy sages (prophets). These sages come from great darkness along with Mother *Atri* to protect humanity from danger or conflict. With her godly powers, *Atri* bestows plentiful food and splendid riches. This graciously gives strength to those who serve dwelling in the waters with the sacred cow. Heavenly Rudra, as the father, in accord with the Sustainer, Vishnu, regulates the atmospheric air (Vayu) with the goddess Sarasvatī, who as a gift pours down rain to bless the prevailing powers the *Ṛbhukṣans, Vāja, Vidhatar*, and Parjanya, providing abundant food for humanity. The goddess Savitar, in accord with the creative powers of Tvaṣṭṛ and the sky lord Dyaus, pour gracious dew down upon the offspring, which on the ground transforms into water, filling the earth with flowing rivers both above and below the surface. The flow of water on the surface regulated by the powers of *Aja Ekapād*, and the water of the oceans regulated by the powers of *Ahibudhnya*. Strengthening the flow of water on the surface and in the ocean, they generate loud vibrations that create sounds that used to produce speech, which e recorded in a form to establish the holy texts. The children sing aloud and help the sage Bhāradvāja utter the hymns that bring noble thoughts that please the demigods, who elevated to serve as the holy ones.

According to *Rig-Veda* 6:51, the holy ones, as part of nature (*Vasu*), merge with the oceans (*Varuna*), with an infallible eye, and *Mitra*. In unconditional love and friendship, they start to move upward, forging a path to ascend toward the heavens, shining like gold and being as pure and charming. Once elevated as holy ones, they come to understand the holy order through which all mortal embodiments beheld with ranks, edicts, and the nature of creation, based upon how they perform in all their acts, good or evil, while they prevail near to home and far away. With his mighty order, the heavenly father Sūrya wedded to the earthly mother Aditi. Their offspring are Mitra, Varuna, Aryaman, and Bhaga, all with noble thoughts, faithful, and poised as they have attained inner illumination and have come to share their powers as sages with the great kings, who are brave and infallible, destroying their foes. The young heroes, imbued with a fair nature, dwell as noble souls (Ādityas), and as the offspring seek support from the newly appointed father of heaven to regulate the newly formed dominion, which accompanies guileless Mother Earth, and with Agni and nature (Vasu) as brothers. All of one mind, they bless humanity, providing them with manifold protection not subjected to any evil powers or any other creature. The individual embodiments guided along with the established rules of speech and vigor; thus, they suffer not from the sin of others, nor are subject to the deeds of others that are punishable by the powers of nature (Vasu). While serving, they do no harm unto those who hate themselves or those who opposed to offering homage or reverence to the holy law. They hold in place the lower stratum (earth) and the upper stratum (heaven), with all reverence and as commanded, so they will not banish even when human beings commit sins. With eternal law and order comes purity within the human dwelling and within their own homes to support the individual living spirit (Atman). This unfailing living spirit (Atman) makes all the far-seeing heroes to bow down and pay homage to the noblest splendor serving the holy ones. They come to shine safely through all troubles and gain the support of the mighty rulers Varuna, Mitra, and Agni, as well as the true-minded, who are faithful controllers of the hymns. All five human tribes on earth served by the powers Aditi, Indra, Bhaga, and Pūṣan.

Increasingly loud prayers reach out to seek help, refuge, and guidance, and deliverance by way of the protectors. From his celestial station, the priest Bhāradvāja comes to implore, offering along with favors, sacrifice, wealth, and honor the mythical juice soma, which provided through manifested solid cosmic bodies such as meteors (compressed cosmic stones) and shared with those who sit to offer oblations to Agni. This drives the wicked foe, the evil hearted thief, far away and opens easily traveled paths for the brave ones who destroy the greedy wolf Panni and allow the priest Bhāradvāja to appear within the most bountiful sky, seeking Indra. By traveling these good paths, they guided to enter the road that leads to bliss and from whereas noble souls they escape from all enemies, without a foe who gathers wealth and wisdom through attachment. The holy priest Bhāradvāja performs sacrifices both on earth and in heaven, which come crashing down from the huge mountains, the evil patron *Atiyaja* demeaning all the sacrifices. The evil patron holds in contempt any devotional prayer made to the cosmic hosts (Maruts), who are subject with devotion to bring the shining light in the sky. The evil patron hit with hot darts and burned with scorching agony by those who make any devotion in the morning to ask for the springing of life from those who protected by the flowing rivers, caused by swelling oceans. All those offering devotion firmly seated among mountains, honoring their guardians, calling to them as fathers or gods. They even defend humanity with the rising sun, which brings a healthy-minded outlook. Varuna comes most near, often bringing pleasing treasures. Indra comes often to provide protection; the goddess Sarasvatī comes with swelling rivers; Parjanya comes and brings herbs; and Agni as father comes well lauded and swift to listen. After invocation, the immortal universal soul (Paramatman), bathed in holy oil, seated on holy grass, comes to meet with the supreme powers of causation and listen to the divine songs that are offered by exceedingly good powers for strengthening the law. All seers (Ṛtus) who have taken appropriate drafts of mythical juice (soma) and come accompanied by the godly powers Indra, the Maruts, Tvaṣṭṛ, Mitra, and Aryaman, accept Agni as their holy priest, who ordains them with loud sounds and, as a sacrifice, offers a gift to them to accept the divine rules. Remembering, the heavenly folk listen to the process of invocation, the immortal universal soul Paramatman, who inhabits heaven and the midair region, bringing essence, joyfully sitting on the sacred grass.

On the manifested holy ground, in the form of speech, all the godly powers appear with worship to continue to survive within thoughts, transferring the immortal universal soul (Paramatman), which now exists within the two halves of the world, earth and heaven, and is heard through a child of the water as the living spirit (Atman) residing among individual manifested bodies that utters no word of indifference, and is closely allied in bliss, born on the ground (Prithvi), rejoicing and moving like the mighty wily serpents. Within the water, Paramatman gathers the heavenly life force (prana), which vouchsafed for the duration of its life. The supreme powers of causation kindly come to serve during the dark nights and in the mornings, providing physical strength through the eternal flame provided by Agni, and providing spiritual strength through the eternal love provided by Indra and serviced by the progeny (Parjanya), who as the manifested deities of rain, thunder, and lightning, fertilize the ground (Prithvi) as part of the terrestrial region representing planet Earth. These powers heard and accepted by humanity as the child of water, who generates thought and speech. The child of water supported by spiritual and physical powers, which generate holy food that helps them to learn to feed themselves, and serves them as offspring, granted space to store the holy food while it dispersed. With hymns and homage, the eternal flame enkindled, the fire that invites all the godly powers of causation to come and rejoice and create a great assembly to provide the individual living spirit (Atman) with holy gifts to serve humanity and other living things.

## PURSUIT

Among living beings, there are many spiritual seekers (*Rig-Veda* 6:52) who fulfill their holy duties, perform sacrifices, and offer oblations, neither to the earth nor to the heaven, but to the everlasting powers, which bring huge mountains crashing down. For such worshipping, they even belittled by the patron of sacrifice *Atiyaja* and disrespected for making such prayers to the cosmic hosts (*Maruts)*, seeking their support. They even blamed for bringing the agonies from the burning sun in the sky, creating scorching heat that punishes mortal souls. They demeaned as those who hold back mythical juice (soma) from those who do not pray or will not allow devotees to approach the guardians and despised as those who cast hot darts at those who hate devotion.

In the morning, spiritual souls spring to life. By worshipping the guardians and asking them to protect the rivers from swelling, they worship the fathers who firmly seated in the mountains, supporting all who call upon the divine will to defend them. They worship the sunrise in the day, which comes to make minds healthy and expose all treasures. The powers of causation often bring along the most observant Indra, who provides protection, and the goddess Sarasvatī, who provides Parjanya, who brings rain to swell the rivers and feed the plants, generating herbs that bring health and wisdom. Agni, with well-lauded sounds, comes swiftly to listen as a father hears his son. The immortal universal soul (Paramatman) is seated on the holy grass and offers invocations to the supreme powers of causation, offering holy oil to bathe in, asking that they come to meet one and all and offer the power of immortality to approach everyone who, through worshipping and singing hymns, are able to make the ruler of the law (*Varuna*) bring the seasons (*Rtus*). After listening to their calling, with pleasure, they offer an appropriate draft of mythical juice (*soma*) that brought by Indra. They accompanied by the godly powers the Maruts, Tvaṣṭṛ, Mitra, and Aryaman, and by the priests. They listen to the loud sounds as a gift ordained by the ruler of the eternal flame, Agni, the heavenly people remembering their sacrifices. All who serve as part of the supreme powers of causation, who inhabit heaven, now come from the midair region with invocations, surrounded by the air (Vayu) on the sacred grass, where Agni, enjoying the tongues of flame, appears to serve as the eternal flame. With the powers of Agni, the supreme powers of causation come to claim the eternal flame as part of their worship as they travel to connect the two world halves, earth and heaven. Traveling like the cosmic vapor, the children of water utter no words and disregarded even though they closely allied and rejoice in bliss. They appear as mighty, moving like the wily serpent that comes from heaven and is born on earth, where it gathers with others in the waters and kindly receives support at night and in the morning, vouchsafing the life force (prana) for the duration. They call upon Agni and Indra to come swiftly and, as the deity of rain Parjanya, hear thoughts with laudation. Agni generates holy food and rain (Parjanya) in the form of seeds and embryos, which carry the future offspring, whose parents granted enough food to support their children; they scatter with hymns until the holy grass enkindled with eternal flame. With humble homage, they form to create a great assembly, rejoicing in the supreme powers of causation who bring holy gifts.

After establishing a clear path (*Rig-Veda* 6:53), the offspring follow it and acquire higher spiritual wisdom that can penetrate through the physical body to reach to the heart of any creation. The little solar deity Pūṣan, with his mortal embodiment, comes to serve as the head of the new creation, working with material wealth and being subject to a greedy, rude, and ignorant nature. To transform such a nature, the divine will infused like a glowing goat with a horny point, which with bliss transforms individual heartless souls (*Rig-Veda* 6:54). With this bliss, an enormous strength like that of a horse or an elephant pierce through the mind and helps it to retain, store, and reserve wisdom, which with delight offered to share. With divine power, Pūṣan brings together intellect and wisdom to focus upon serving the manifested embodiments, with the goal of helping them observe others and discovering how a living being may get straight to the point, moving freely in an undamaged house and learning not to let boxes fall to the ground, or how to move like a chariot wheel whose fellies neither come loose nor are shaken. As promised, they given first a gift of wealth, so their kin kept near and safe, along with poured libations and worship. They drive along singing songs of praise, making sure no one injured, that no one sinks in a pit, and that no one breaks a limb. All manifested bodies thus arrive safely to their destination.

For deliverance, according to *Rig-Veda* 6:55, they select Pūṣan, a sibling with vital powers, who, most skilled, appears with braided radiant hair, and as a manifested body comes to serve as the leader of living beings such as sheep and goats, serving the godly powers. Pūṣan makes a stream of treasure, wealth that measured in terms of heaps of intellect and come to serve a meal of curd furnished by the mighty ones. This measured in terms of the physical strength that needed to establish a new domicile for the heavenly splendors within the earthly region. According to *Rig-Veda* 6:56, they call upon their allies who are ready to travel, and they come to serve as the best of leaders, guided by the speckled cloud that, like a carriage with golden wheels equipped to destroy foes. Serving as wise wonderworkers, they proceed to win over those who are renowned for the spoils and a craving for prosperity. They move far from sin and become rich by tending to perfect happiness for tomorrow, rather than today. Indra joins them as a deity of earthly region, Pūṣan, and calls for their friendship by offering, after victory, prosperity in the form of the spoils. Jointly, Indra and Pūṣan come to share a mythical drink, which made using the milk drawn from the team of goats. While the bay steeds stand ready to slay monsters and bring down the streams of waters to form rivers and create mighty floods, Indra and Pūṣan stand aside. Like trees, they extend their limbs in favor to offer love to all and cling to their embodiments, drawing the reins closer to attain remarkable success. For making such a sacrifice, as they move from one feeding place to another, the unified Indra and Pūṣan help young, embodied mortal souls, male and female, to join as couples. They continuously protected from evil forces, appearing as wild beasts that come from the midair region, and placed well with the supportive guides Mitra and Varuna, who provide a bond of solidarity, serving each married couple, ready to exploit the earthly region. As a legendary force, Indra and Pūṣan even shorten the distance they must travel by removing any obstruction from their path. They even go ahead to watch closely and ensure the cloud-borne deity Sarasvatī brings rain showers to drive off evil powers, including those hiding behind the clouds, such as the wolf or some other inauspicious wicked soul. As a legendary force, Indra and Pūṣan sit back from the road to watch the path as a robber lurks with a guileful heart, ready to attack and injure the young heavenly created embodiments. Indra and Pūṣan stamp with their feet to squash any firebrand snakes, which are wicked and double-tongued, whoever they may be. As a legendary force, Indra and Pūṣan, serving as wise wonderworkers, adjust as they have done thus far in serving the ancient sires, providing the best golden sword to achieve prosperity.

Young heavenly created bodies look upon Indra and Pūṣan as a union of godly powers (*Rig-Veda* 6:57) who have come to lead them to the fairest path for travel, always knowing that by following them, they will encounter rich meadows of grass where other gracious legendary powers are waiting to provide them with any help whenever it is needed. The unified Indra and Pūṣan call upon their friendship to win prosperity in the form of treasure, as they sit them down to receive, one by one, drinks of mythical juice, which strengthens their thoughts. Through consuming curd, along with milk freshly drawn from the team of goats, they cement thought with intellect. With bay steeds at hand, they come to help to win such strength as to slay the fiends. The unified Indra and Pūṣan, with their wondrous strength, cause the streams to create a mighty flood of water, while they stand aside favoring love, tightly holding, like an extended tree branch, the reins of the carriage they are driving.

The union of Indra and Pūṣan provides cool light in the morning cool light (*Rig-Veda* 6:58), one hot direct sunray at midday, and soft light from the moon at night. These all create dissimilar colors to support the young heavenly manifested bodies who, with their aid, become self-dependent, prevailing because of the auspicious bounty, like a goat born to guard the cattle who provide milk for bodily strength, and with hymns inspiring everyone all over the world. The united Indra and Pūṣan, flitting here and there, move lightly with the stick to behold every creature, helping others to follow the divine path. They serve like a golden ship that travels across the ocean, passing through the midair region, Similarly, the heavenly ambassador Sūrya comes to subdue with love, bringing desirous glory as he come nears to the relatives from the heavenly region, now prevailing in the earthly region.

The golden ship passes through the midair region, where Indra and Pūṣan are united, and this creates for the young heavenly couples a most auspicious shelter, to save them from those who are trying to conquer the region. These specially built shelters provide protection to the embryo (astral body), which holds the immortal universal soul (Paramatman). While passing through the midair region, all filled with shelters (*nakshatras*), each serves as the moon house (lunar mansion) where twenty-seven and sometimes twenty-eight ecliptic sectors prevail. Each given a specific name relating to the most prominent position within the asterism. Each setting is a prominent pattern or group of stars, the smaller constellations commonly referred to as ashrams, where the legendary powers may find a haven and not trapped or overpowered by the surrounding malevolent forces (Asuras). These small constellations (ashrams) traveled through by way of fair paths and thus provide protection to the progeny of the divine will serving the three regions.

## DIVINE UNION

According to *Rig-Veda* 6:59, the supreme powers of causation have known for a long time about the mythical soma flowing within their embodiments. They help in performing noble deeds, declared to be righteous in nature, always fighting the battle to remain strong and able to smite down all enemies or evil powers. They know their physical embodiments, after performing righteous acts, will leave behind their astral bodies, along with the beloved living spirit (Atman). Such beloved astral bodies with living spirits come to appear in the form of the twin horses the Aśvins. Serving as demigods, as father and mother, the two living spirits jointly represent the union of the gods Indra and Agni. Following divine will, they manifest to serve as a team responsible for extracting physical strength from food and spiritual strength from mythical juice. Once again, with delight, they placed anywhere. Their embodiment gains power to regulate the flow of the streams, serving as a thunderbolt that serves the friends of the law (Varuna) and the friends of eternal love (Mitra). They bring kindness and righteousness as a gift, accompanied by sweet speech and praise. With libations flowing, they provide guidance to all the creations, and before they advance, they yoked, looking to every side as a footless manifested embodiment. They use their heads to stretch their bodies, until their tongues emerge to speak loudly. Then they place their embodiment down on the ground for thirty months and let it crawl on its arms. Then, they again hold the embodiment, stretched like a crossbow, stretching their knees, assuming a posture that will not cave in during any fray or battle. Further, they exasperate the embodiment until it becomes sore. It hates driven far away, prey to the foeman's sinful hostility. Like heavens and earth, the powers of Indra and Agni ensure the manifested embodiments kept at a distance from the sun, so the bodies receive neither heat nor light. Indra and Agni control all the treasures that provide opulence and prosperity, until they come to hear the praise offered just for them. Once they accepted, they come near, drawn by hymns and songs, to drink soma. Those who truly worship Indra and Agni as strong and mighty heroes vanquish their foes and win the spoils. The two gods come to rule as sovereigns with ample riches, enabling victory in the righteous battle they fight to protect life, bringing milk, water, and sunlight back to the mornings from which they stolen.

According to *Rig-Veda* 6:60, those born of the union of Indra and Agni make their own kind of light, which appears at dawn as wondrous vapor covering all regions. With their mighty powers, Indra and Agni slay the evil power and, through the supreme powers of causation, draw their homage from demigods demonstrating their powers, such as the twin Aśvins. They provide an unlimited bounty and perform deeds, famous since the ancient days. As a pair, Indra and Agni let everyone know they can never harmed, even after they depart from the twin powers. As demigods, the Aśvins scatter the foes all over, and by invoking kindness, they kill and thereby eliminate all foes of the noble Āryans. With the ultimate power of nobility, they slay the ruler of the evil power (Dāsa) and drive away all enemies. With songs of praise sounding forth, Indra and Agni bring along blessings with drinks of mythical juice to serve the team of twins. They join with whichever team they desire and, like worshippers, pour libations to create more heroes. The heroes even drink soma to induce the glowing flame, which as a fire comes to burn all forests, leaving the ground blackened. The heroes receive much bliss as they enkindle fire, finding it easier to gain happiness than to be overrun with floodwaters. The unified Indra and Agni bestow an abundance of strengthening power through food, provided as a gift, making everything joyful. As twins, the Aśvins become the true givers of both food and riches. They invoke strength and vigor among all, and with all riches they bring in domesticated animals such as horses and cattle, which in the form of wealth, and with bliss, invoke friendship. Pouring libations, with worship, the Aśvins allowed to enjoy the sweetly flavored soma juice they offered.

According to *Rig-Veda* 6:61, the deity Sarasvatī came into existence to displace the broods, that is, the *Brsayas*, serving as non-Āryan tribes who live in ignorance, practicing the art of magic. They scorn whoever disperses higher knowledge, and they add poison to rapidly flowing waters. To remove such ignorance, Indra and Agni invoke purity through the immortal universal soul (Paramatman), which channels the immortal living spirit (Atman) to produce noble thoughts and uses its powers to raise consciousness. This helps one to overpower desire and the ever-growing demand for things that far exceed one's individual needs.

The living spirit with its full strength comes to smite and overpower evil thoughts. By offering tribute to the solar deity, who brings inner opulence, the living spirit thus establishes a boundaryless unbroken region where other living spirits can swiftly move and merge with radiant slow-moving powers, rushing to move forward. With roaring passion, the seven milk-bearing deities (Seven Sisters) spread opulence as they float within the running water in rivers and streams and turn the running water into holy water. From the holy water, the five noble tribes emanate and prosper, along with each of the seven rivers. They perform mighty deeds, marking their majestic glory as the water flows rapidly. Clearly victorious, and with the support of the goddess Sarasvatī, the noble souls, as manifested righteous bodies, guided by the holy sages. They assigned to serve, and they lead with glorious treasure as mortal embodiments. They accept friendship and obedience, which they spread to distant regions, keeping away from the ancient ghostly powers (Asuras), which once again trapped in outer space, forming giant ice planets.

According to *Rig-Veda* 6:62, the unified Indra and Soma come to exploit the opportunities provided by the sun, removing the evil curse prevailing amid the darkness. They work jointly with the sun, which brings the dawn, and they follow the motion of the sun to create a spiritual link, which as cosmic vapor connects Father Heaven to free-flowing waters upon Mother Earth. The unified Indra and Soma (God of the moon) perform daring acts by slaying the life force with cosmic vapor. They travel along, removing any obstruction. Like snakes shedding their old skins, they move freely, the cosmic vapor coming from heaven and spreading over the ground. With the removal of obstructions, the life force travels better with the river currents, reaching many areas, sometimes creating floods, or eventually taking the water from rivers, along with the life force, to fill the seas.

The unified Indra and Soma come upon unripe udders and breasts. With the power of the life force, they ripen the unripe udders or breasts so they may supply white milk, unimpeded in its flow. Verily, Indra and Soma come to bestow the white milk, along with wealth and victorious fame, which passed on to newborn manifested offspring who, when vested, fully blessed with mighty strength, ready to conquer in battle.

## CHALLENGE

According to *Rig-Veda* 6:64, with the glorious union and with radiance produce down, white splendor generates waves in the waters. The waves make all paths easy and fair to travel, and they appear as benevolent. With good art, they shine with luster, turning the beams into splendors that, when followed, lead to the path that leads to heaven. All decked out themselves, optimizing their shining majesty, they bring the goddess of morning, spreading in the distance, to serve the Blessed One. Like a courageous archer, the goddess of morning shakes the foes and, like a swift warrior, repels the darkness. To bring wealth and give comfort, the goddess of morning, invincible, self-illuminating, is radiant like beam of light. The light easily passes over hills like the waves riding on the waters. As dawn, she brings untroubled wealth, traveling like oxen, that at will accept riches and with pleasure appear as the child of heaven, who calls upon the lovely bounty. As the birds fly forth from their resting places and their stores of food, they learn to rise with the dawn, with the liberal mortal embodiments and the conscience at peace.

According to *Rig-Veda* 6:65, this motionless dawn, the goddess of the morning, by shedding light calls upon the human inhabitants, who come at nighttime with silver luster to show themselves through the shades of darkness. Dawn divided among the steeds, red-rayed in wondrous fashion, and shines like bright headlights, bringing splendid commencement rites, which drive the night's shadows far away. The dawn sets humanity on a quest to worship glory, power, and might, and brings food and vigor, opulent, with imperial sway for the heroes to serve with favor as the day enriches humanity with treasure to serve the hero and has them bring oblations to the dawn. Now when the singer sings a song of praise, it brings back the memories of the past that are common to all humans. The goddess of the morning stands on the mountain ridges, like Aṅgirases praising the stalls of cattle. With prayer and holy hymns, she bursts open heroes calls upon the fruits of divine will, shining through the ancient times to bless the child of heaven who comes to serve as the earthly priest Bhāradvāja, who gives the singers' wealth to the noble heroes and bestows them with widespread glory.

According to *Rig-Veda* 6:66, once the new form of evil power starts to swell and grow from the underworld, reaching the point where they are beyond control, the wise noble powers have no understanding of how to manage. They approach the powerful trinity Rudra, Agni, and the Maruts, who regulate the whole solar system, to seek support and heroic vigor, filled with the desire to strengthened and always appear in golden dustless form. They spread throughout the solar system by pouring rain upon all new forms of evil power, submerging the evil powers in the water and thereby gaining control by pushing them far away from the sun and into regions where they get no light or heat, thus transforming into bigger bodies that remain frozen, filled with evil powers. Further, the trinity of Rudra, Agni, and the Maruts decide to transform themselves from imperishable into perishable, and when they rise to appear among clouds, they join with water to move among the rivers. They first appear as dew, which brings pleasure with outer brilliance, and after they descend, they rise and start to behave as brave, bold, liberal dependents. Become fierce with great agility, they willingly accept their new mission. They use their inherent strength to provide potent lightning as their weapon, and they use their physical powers to drive their forces, with whom no team of goats or horses, and no charioteer, can compete. They travel through the air alone on their path, speeding without halting, running without reined, going through all the regions without anybody obstructing their path. They bring along progeny, such as the sons of Mother *Pṛśni*, who become mightier than the singers and produce vibrations that, like a band, passes through their lounge, where they offer sacrifices and serve as the cosmic hosts (Maruts). Like Agni with the eternal flame, they produce an impetuously bright flashing light. At the onset of the chanting of hymns, they turn with their loud prayers as the perishers sing to admire like heroes borne with splendid invocation. They develop as the swelling band of cosmic hosts (Maruts), as the broods, armed with glittering lances, call upon the noble supreme powers to come and join with them in the harsh battle.

According to *Rig-Veda* 6:67, the noble soul representing the true unity (Mitra and Varuna) comes into existence with unequalled arms to gain control by establishing covenants and put reins. Like the ancient noble leaders, the Ādityas, they protect the newly manifested embodiments representing the first living things with both minds and hearts and honored as true humans. They sit on the sacred grass and, with the power of hymns, generate thoughts and transform by sacrificing their mortal dwellings to acquire reverence. Serving as humans, they build teams that follow the covenants, and they come to guard and teach others by offering loving adoration. With eulogies, they bring new boon-givers. These new givers, like ancient leaders, provide safety from attack, and when needed they invite the ancient mighty powers to guide them and serve as the controllers of humanity. After hearing of their longing, the noble leaders the Ādityas, born of Mother Aditi, invoke eternal love (Mitra) and the eternal law (Varuna) to serve from the high dominion. Surrounded by both worlds, heaven above and earthly below, they, in the middle, travel through the wide and spacious galaxies, all of one accord and in the form of a union. The demigod Aśvins, with joy and gladness, bring forth all newly born mortal embodiments, ever true, who never falter in maintaining royal power. From the heights of the loftiest heaven, like constellations, they fill the gap with morality and righteousness, which recognized on the holy ground (Prithvi) located between the heavenly and earthly regions.

Newborns provided with mythical fluid, and other manifested embodiments served the same until they are all fully satisfied. The young ones quicken to jump and scatter. Like spring, they bring moisture, and they join with others to win by forming rain. The voices of the unified Mitra and Varuna are honored as envoys, faithful and wise, who worshipped and receive as nourishment the holy oil that annihilates trouble. With glory, they offer a sacrifice to Mitra and Varuna. They neither break the powers of eternal law and eternal love, that is, Varuna and Mitra, respectively, nor in any way offer sacrifices to those who are evil and godless. According to the spiritual covenant, they sing hymns and chant, uplifting their voices for one firm purpose: to affect their foes, and not the noble greatness. In union, Mitra and Varuna come near the dwelling of the evil Asuras and, with haste, harnessed with hymns, kindly bring out the dormant individual living spirits to develop a fleet of battle stallions.

## ALTRUISM

The power of altruism motivates people to go out of their way with compassion to bring happiness to others, including plants and animals, removing any kind of pain or suffering.

According to *Rig-Veda* 6:68, on trimmed grass, honored with rites, the perishable powers Mitra and Varuna join with the supreme imperishable powers, Indra and Agni, to carry the process that, from then to this day, with the highest success, has supported the glorious offspring of the ancient cosmic creation Manu. Honored and worshipped by humanity, Manu represents the ancient supreme powers of causation who brings with him the vigor and mighty strength that makes him among the strongest of ancestors. As a hero, Manu represents the most liberal princes, chiefs, and hosts who follow the law. He serves as a slayer to eliminate the evil power Vṛtra, and with merit and worship, he praised as the twin demigods with noble powers who provide, along with the mighty thunderbolt, joyous bliss. To protect sages, who stand near in times of trouble with those who have already freed from the ice planets, as the evil powers including serpents and other such creatures, come to serve with strength, like the mighty mortal bodies. The supreme powers of causation with gladness bring bounteous gifts for the noble powers so they may win through opulence. As they join with the noble powers and spread their mighty powers of morality and righteousness to generate a new kind of power, altruism, they take wealth from wealthy people so they may give food and treasure to the poor, and thus help break the curse of those who try to vex mortal souls for their own purposes. The noble and supreme powers of causation jointly take on the task of guiding humanity to serve as leaders, like the ancient cosmic creation Manu, who follows the righteous path and asks others to follow by removing obstructions from the pathways and helping them to reach the ultimate source of the mystical fluid (amrit), like the vessels that contain the mythical soma juice. They recite hymns as human beings to serve as the noble souls the Ādityas, who receive blessings and joy and given gifts of treasure, including mythical juice, accompanied by the brilliant rays of the sun. They repeatedly chant hymns of praise and, decked with special powers, come to overpower the physical strength of the foe. At the banquet, they bring along the noble spiritual powers and thus manifest as the cosmic creation Manu. Hearing the hymns, they stride in wild joy, drinking mythical juice to establish the firmament, holy ground (Prithvi), before encompassing larger regions to accommodate the broad new existence. The Manus learns to strengthen themselves with physical power before eating or meeting, offering sacred prayers to the united Indra and Vishnu. Then they offer oblations and holy oil to Agni, who beholds the vessels rich with mythical juice (soma) to invoke the eternal flame.

The twin demigod Aśvins, serving as the wonderworkers, exhilarated with mythical juice, come to hear through their ears the divine calling to go conquer, but they never conquered. When the twin Aśvins vanquish their foes, they leave behind the noble Manus to continue to fight the battle, serving within the infinite three divisions covering all regions.

From heaven to earth, with compassion and with beautiful powers of morality and righteousness, humanity and the noble Manus come from heaven down to the earth. They bring a rich embryo with a decree that parts them from one and causes them to go on to another, creating an everlasting pair. Like the sacred cow filled with pure water and milk, they come to pour out rich milk mixed with mythical juice, which transformed within any common embodiment. They turn the dormant living spirit into an active living spirit, changing the physical body to an active noble soul. The noble Manus arrives in the region located between the earth below and the heaven above, within which, by pouring out life force (prana), they bring prosperity. With merit, the noble Manus comes to prevail as the benevolent soul (humanity). They bring a righteous, moral life, received with offerings, which thus joins the heavens above with the earth below, serving as compassionate guides for the prevailing mortal embodiments. They succeed as the perishable seeds manifest and are born repeatedly, and similarly, living beings spread forth through the powers of perishable embodiment. The law of righteousness allows all things ruled by morality to flow forward, generating diverse embodiments. All enclosed in corpulence, they gain the brightness of heaven and mingle on the ground to acquire eternal wisdom. With instilled perishable power, these increased mortal embodiments transform from singers with a broad selection of hymns into manifested holy bodies who pray and seek bliss as earthly priests. Among noble souls with substitute powers, the Manus further enhance them by joining with the pouring rain, which drops balm, which with compassion yields comfort to all. Those who have covered their paths with wealth and great fame bestowed with prolonged strength, which abundantly swells among those who serve with heroic power. All-knowing as the heavenly priests, they serve as the father and then join to perform wondrous works. They pour out a bounty by bringing with them the eternal union made possible by joining the two separate worlds, where each exchange brings the power to gain wealth and to strengthen the power of compassion in others.

According to *Rig-Veda* 6:71, with golden outstretched arms, the goddess Savitar comes to provide effectual wisdom to the young ones so they may develop skills and implement those skills to serve as noble warriors who are able to defend their region. With Savitar's strength, they come from both sides, which allows them to build a noble force of survivors who enjoy the great wealth given to them. Along with the creative powers, they support both two- and four-footed living things that build habitations. As the guardian, Savitar, with aid and auspicious form, firms up and provides true support, producing a sweet sound with her golden tongue. Listening to her sweet speech, they continue bringing bliss, so none of the evil-wishers can gain power or gain control of the golden hands. As the goddess Savitar rises with the twilight to welcome home friends with her brass cheeks, she also speaks pleasant words of welcome. Savitar, like a fair director, extends her golden arms, exceeding the heights between the earth and heaven, and with such powers brings down comets to fall on the monsters to end all trouble and bring wealth enough for each day that passes.

The unified Indra and Soma (*Rig-Veda* 6:72) join with the heavenly body Sūrya to provide light from heaven to the Manus so they may exploit individual intelligence by killing the ignorance that causes darkness. They even help individual embodiments to achieve this on their own by removing ignorance through awakening, using the light provided by the sun to transform them into luminous bodies. They start by extending the morning and creating the highpoint, the sun, which in splendor serves as the two supporting pillars, that is, the earth, as the mother, and heaven, serving as the father. The united Indra, Soma, and Sūrya support the heavenly power, telling it to move ahead in removing the evil powers to speed up the river currents so they come to fill large bodies of water such as lakes and oceans. As the trinity of Indra, Soma, and Sūrya hold fast to the uninterrupted whiteness by creating the many-colored rainbow (*indrayudha*), they help to motivate any creatures looking for "pot of gold' wealth, fame, or victorious powers, which they pass on to the children of the noble soul Manu to serve a wide range of living things, transforming them with strength to create a wide range of mighty beings who are all capable of helping them to win the battle.

With oblations, the unified Indra, Soma, and Sūrya, like the ancient messenger Aṅgiras of the god Agni, come to serve the newborn with oblations, becoming like the mountain rendered holy *Bṛhaspati*. Having already traveled twice the righteous path, they now come to settle within the region with a firm third dwelling. They serve like the father who, with loud roaring and light, brings out the heavenly bull (the sun) to establish equilibrium and maintain a balance between the heavenly and earthly powers. The perishable *Bṛhaspati* given the power to make the space wider for any newly manifested mortal bodies. The godly perishable power uses this creative power to destroy the forts and castles of the evil powers and thereby gain rich treasures. They create great stalls for cows, filled with water to provide milk, served as mythical juice (soma) to all those striving to win. Perishable Bṛhaspati, with lightning, smites the defenseless foemen.

According to *Rig-Veda* 6:74, to compensate for the killing of evil spirits, the united Soma and Rudra offer seven great treasures: gold, silver, lapis lazuli, crystal, agate, red pearl, and carnelian. These represent the seven powers of faith (perseverance, sense of shame, avoidance of wrongdoing, mindfulness, concentration, and wisdom). The union then introduces the seasons that change every quarter, exposing all manifested dwellings. A terrifying dark figure who loves pain and creates horrible nightmares, Nirrti, comes to bring sickness. To drive the evil powers far away, the quadrupeds and bipeds provided with excellent experiences, through which glory enters their bodies. To protect the union of Soma and Rudra, they are provided with needful medicines to heal and cure their embodiments and set them free. Soma and Rudra also help the embodiments by drawing away from them any inherent sin that remains as a residual memory. Soma and Rudra come armed with effective weapons and bring along their kind, loving, and gracious nature to be shared with others and, through their joint efforts, release them from the noose so they are regulated only by the assigned powers Varuna and Mitra, who normally keep them away from sorrow by offering tender loving-kindness and who carry them by giving them strength and life.

CHAPTER 12

# Inspirational Dominion

THE INSPIRATIONAL DOMINION IS THE PLACE WHERE ANIMATION led to the first manifested mortal embodiment, Manu, who attained an erect posture, thus supporting bipedal locomotion, and given dexterous limbs, thereby allowing him to become creative and visionary. Manu learned to lift heavy tools using his complex physical structure, and he cultivated language through sound so he could express himself. As a visionary, he developed structures that could be adapted to support his subtle cooperative faculties and thus comply with the laws of nature (Vasu). Those like Manu understand their curiosity-filled desire to comprehend their surroundings. They learn all the powers that influence manipulative tendencies. With success, they learn and come to explain well, and create various learned societies. They, with their perishable nature, come to comprehend, which allows them to serve as emissary guardians. As guardians, they fully comprehend the five great inert constituents of nature: fire (Agni), essence (Akasa), water (Ap), air (Vayu), and earth (Prithvi). They accept the process of encirclement that empirically transforms living beings through the process of Mother Nature (prakriti), and using regulating powers (purusha), manifested embodiments, in turn, learn and regulated by the supreme powers of causation. These living beings come to conceptualize the great element of fire as Agni, as part of nature, and they serve as the mouth that can gobble up anything and reduce it to nothing.

Agni prevails over three levels: on earth as fire, in the atmosphere as lightning, and in the sky as solar wind. Agni serves as the medium through which earthly creation relates to heavenly powers.

The manifested mortal living beings holding the immortal individual living spirit come to seek ultimate union with the eternal mother, the universal soul prevailing within the universe. Through imaginative and visionary powers, they come to understand the relationship between the living spirit as a child and the universal soul as Mother Nature (prakriti). Through rituals (*homa*), along with designated godly powers, they create a sacred eternal flame that, like smoke (*apris*), unites the unmanifested universal soul (Paramatman) with the individual manifested living spirit (Atman). This is all accomplished through a special invocation of the twelve deities who form a pattern (zodiac) whereby each month of the year is represented by a given form of sacred smoke or a flame, each owning its own healing powers, which can be generated through burning, producing fragrance, including candle wax, resin, incense, and herbs of all kinds that produce sacred scents. These sacred scents cleanse the air, removing bacteria, mold, and mildew. The sacred smoke creates a calm environment with a smell that activates the individual's senses and stimulates the individual's energetic body.

## INVOCATION

According to *Rig-Veda* 7:1, the power of nature (Vasu) establishes a homestead engendered by the powers of Agni. The eternal flame invoked by rubbing fire-starting rocks or wooden fire-starting sticks, or even by using a swift movement of the hands to generate a spark that can create a flame that seen from afar within each quarter. Serving as the eternal flame, Agni comes to reside within individual dwellings, supporting the individual living spirit (Atman) and, with honor, making the embodiment serve as a home for the Atman. With its shine, the eternal flame evokes youth from within the body, which fades not, and even comes to glow more brightly with sacrificial viands. Among all fires, it is the eternal flame that is brightest and produces splendid light that begets noble heroes, giving birth to a majestic power among humanity, which altogether sets the noble souls down as victorious and grants them each the eternal flame with wealth and wisdom, thereby personifying them as brave sons and making the embodiments independently famous. With no foes dealing in black magic, they conquer with oblations in the morning and in the evening, coming like a ladle dropping oil. They seek blessing and serve through their devotion, seeking eternal wealth. Like the eternal flame, the old divine power *Jarasandha*, in silence, brings tranquility as the eternal flame burns to drive away all pain and sickness. The eternal flame even intensifies as a splendid fire, which is an excellent producer, a refulgent purifier, which with praises serves the patriarchal force that produces gracious luster to serve all and spread into places. In the fight with foemen, the eternal flame comes to support humanity, allowing them to prevail as heroes fighting against the godless ones who practice black magic.

With improved noble songs, Agni comes to sit with those without children, as well as in houses full of children. Wherever he appears, he serves as the friend of the household. The eternal flame makes mortal embodiments physically strong and helps them to carry the seeds, the embryos, which turn into offspring, which increase in lineal succession. Like chargers, the offspring help to guard humanity from the hated demons and from malice, as well as from boorish sinners. Humans themselves become allies of the individual living spirit (Atman). They subdue assailants and, using the eternal flame, surpass all others and come to support their offspring, generating vigor among them to create firm-handed warriors who win, passing over a thousand paths that will never perish. With the powers of Agni, they as the saviors protect against the foemen and, using kindling, guard against or remove any established sorrow among the lineage of heroes.

Agni serves in many places as the rich lord with oblation, kindling his fire among the priests so they go around offering sacrifices. Agni, using all means to draw worship from those rich in possessions, also brings out in abundance a continual offering that is most welcome. He brings fragrance to the assembly. Those assembled themselves ask Agni not to give up in fulfilling the desires of the heroes, the holy ones who, with inadequate clothes, live in destitution. Such holy ones yield not to brutes, who bring hunger to injure living beings, whether at home or in the forest.

Giving strength to the prayers and the blessings poured out by the noble chiefs serving the assembly, the holy ones grant the wishes of both those who pray and those who share their bounty. They protected with blessings forevermore. The swift-to-hear Agni brings forth an effulgent beam to help living things. Along with the Sons of Strength, this brings progeny, giving birth to a son, forever making sure such manly heroes never fail. Condemning scarcity, Agni brings a flaming fire, along with the godly power (divine will) to protect living beings from displeasure. Even after committing a fault, the wealthy mortals, fair of face, overtake the Sons of Strength and continue to offer oblations to the immortal powers. This helps them win treasure. With contentment, they come to serve as princes or become known as chiefs who bring ample riches and supplicates the noble souls to enjoy themselves, with undiminished life, and their noble children, who come to serve as heroes (victors). The noble souls, through their prayers, provided with full strength, with blessings poured out upon them. Serving as chiefs, they granted bounty to share, while the godly power (divine will) continues to protect them evermore with blessings.

According to *Rig-Veda* 7:2, with sacred smoke (*apris*), they come to honor the sublimely shining eternal flame, which reaches the celestial summit and spreads along with the illuminating rays from the heavenly power Sūrya. With sacrifice, living beings come to honor His Holy Majesty *Narāśaṁsa*, who represents the pure wise thoughts that inspire faith among living beings. They enjoy such offerings brought with oblations to the godly powers (divine will), with a sacrifice to the first manifested mortal embodiment, Manu, who as a living being extolled with such a sacrifice, which forever invokes the eternal flame and, representing the ferocious Agni, overpowers the evil Asuras. Through the power of worship, the embodiments of such evil power of transformed. Asuras learn to speak eternal truth and come as the envoys to serve both the material and spiritual worlds. They come on their knees and with reverence, bearing on the sacred grass, where they spread out and serve the powers of Agni. In adoration, they come on the spotted grass, which they sprinkle with oil and offer oblations. Agni throws open the doors for the carriage driven to the godly assembly. Agni comes to serve as the exalted morning and night, the heavenly women who come like two mother cows, licking their young. As pious priests with holy thoughts, *adhvaryu* come to invoke the worshippers seated on the holy grass, along with poets and singers, who, with worship and sacrifices, receive eternal wisdom and set up offerings whenever they called upon. In accord with the god Agni and the goddess Sarasvatī, appearing with mortal embodiments, the *adhvaryu* obtain godly titles and come to serve as the Seven Sisters prevailing within the kindred river *(Bharati),* where they grow, generating holy grass that is used to honor the three goddesses who are well pleased to bring along the deity of creative power, Tvaṣṭṛ, to support all new creations. With vigor, which springs out among new heroes, making them all-powerful, and being skilled in action, they become lovers of the godly power (divine will). With such godly powers and with oblations, they learn to adjust to the movement created by the coming of cosmic bodies, including comets, asteroids, and meteorites (compressed stones). The ferocious fire of the god Agni, the Immolator, comes to serve the true Atharvan priest Hotar, who offers worship to all the well-known godly creations and comes, duly kindled, together with the potent demigods to sit on sacred grass, along with the happy great mother Aditi, who with delight hails the prevailing immortal power of rain and thunder, Indra, and the immortal power of ferocious fire (Agni).

According to *Rig-Veda* 7:3, selected with the best skilled associates, they come to establish themselves firmly among humanity to worship and to monitor the sacrifices made by mortal embodiments. As the envoys of Agni, with the holy purifying flame, they fed with oil and eagerly neigh to serve in the pasture. They step forward crowned within a great enclosure, turning into splendor, from where the wind blows upon them, allowing them to move quickly onto the path of the black smoke. With a proclamation, they are now the newly born everlasting eternal flame. Serving as the godly envoy Aṅgiras, they rise upward to heaven, producing ruddy smoke, which ascends at the greatest speed. With its fresh luster, the smoke advances over the earth like a greedy body, approaching food to eat with its jaws, and then hurrying onward with a noose.

Running like hosts, each with a fierce tongue like pierced barley, the living beings decked both in the evening and in the morning. Like the most youthful coursers, they come with a kindled eternal flame and sit among their guests, generating bright light within their dwellings. They offer splendorous worship to heroes with fair faces, and with their beautiful aspects they display the eternal flame as they come near at hand, gleaming like gold. In the distance, they appear with a thundering roar from heaven. To bring out the illumination within each mortal embodiment, they, with their mighty powers, approach the wondrous cosmic body the sun. Using worship and offering sacrificial cakes and oblations, they come to guard those with boundless glory, which when obtained creates one hundred fortifications of iron. With songs and hymns impossible to resist, as mortal embodiments, they offer a hero's strength to the Sons of Strength who, like Jātavedas, guard humanity and preserve the noble princes who come to save singers. The Sons of Strength, as heroes, come with an ax newly sharpened blade. With their pure resplendent bodies, they spring forth eagerly. Longing for their heritage, worshipping the godly power (divine will), they appear, shining, as purifier sages among humanity, with mortal embodiments that, through Agni, attain perfect understanding. With happiness, they sing their prayers and praises to the divine powers, asking them to preserve their gifts evermore.

## NOURISHMENT

According to *Rig-Veda* 7:4, as the purest gift of the refulgent ones, with their knowledge, the splendid Aṅgirases, as the envoys of the god Agni, continue taking all the offerings made, bringing them to the supreme powers of causation for nourishment. The godly mother Aditi, giving birth, passes her wisdom to the newborn, to serve as the young one. From a tender age, the child quickly comes to seize such wisdom. Passing through the forest, the children observe the things manifest at any moment, and with bright teeth they learn to eat the plenteous food. Not long before, the gods' messengers all came to assemble beneath the white splendor of the sun, all created by Agni and allowed, as his messengers, to gain the power of farsightedness, leading them to understand that with such imperishable powers they could overpower the half-mortal perishable embodiments that serve the favorites, foolishly awakened. Once the living beings come to occupy their divine dwelling, all filled with wisdom, they surpass the half-mortal demigods and come to serve as immortals (divinities and deities). They appear as unborn seeds, which grow to become trees that spring up to support the ground by bearing themselves up as the ultimate stabilizers of all. They become the lords of nectar, the mystical fluid (amrit) providing substance that gives gifts of wealth to the heroes. As immortals, they now serve as the victorious power that prohibits living beings from being devoid of strength, beauty, or worship. They teach foemen how the treasure won, with labor and with the mastering of possessions. Humanity even comes to attain perfect understanding to realize happiness and, through singing songs of praise, serve the divine powers that can preserve them evermore with blessings.

According to *Rig-Veda* 7:5, the immortal living spirit (Atman) connects with the godly power Vaishvanara, which travels between earth and heaven, supported by the life force (prana). With such support, all mortal embodiments, with the immortal living spirit (Atman) in their laps, served by the speedy carried by the half-mortal perishable astral body. Carrying the immortal living spirit, they travel among the holy rivers, seeking a leader who can stabilize the fast-running waters and who will allow the astral body to stand firm like a bull. With the glory of godly power, the mortal embodiments grow and shine, serving among the tribes. Accompanied by godly power, they provide wisdom and treasure, while traveling far from fear. They cause all dark-hued races to flee and scatter, deserting all their memories of the past. With glowing powers, Vaishvanara takes over all vacated regions and slashes the dark-hued castles. Serving as envoy for both earth and heaven, Vaishvanara, with the glowing powers of the trinity, ushers in the threefold authority filled with un-decaying luster, becoming fully vested in the splendor serving the two worlds.

According to *Rig-Veda* 7:6, the high imperial ruler Indra, the strong god whom the folk laud for his deeds, celebrated by the singing of songs of worship by the fort-destroying sages. The sages bring food from the mountains, with illumination, as provided by the gods. As blessed sovereigns, they arrive to serve in the region between earth and heaven, all decked out and singing songs, with mighty actions performed by the imperial ruler Indra. They, as fort destroyers, push away the foolish, the faithless, those who are ungenerous and speak rudely, who make sacrifices and who worship without believing. Indra comes to shoo them far away, casting them in ice, turning these godless ones westward toward darkness. At the same time, he brings eastward the living beings with dexterity, served by aid virgin s. Rejoicing, with their faces turned away from the western darkness, they praise Agni, the unyielding tamer of assailants. They break down the walls with deadly weapons and bring morning light to a noble husband with young ones, all supported by Agni. With conquering strength, they subdue the tribe of Nahuṣa and pay tribute to them as manifested bodies (purushas) to receive the protection of nature (prakriti). Desiring to enjoy this gracious favor, they serve as the parents, serving under the united Agni and Vaishvanara, and they rise to find the choicest seat between earth and heaven.

The godly power Vaishvanara, in the evening (*Rig-Veda* 7:7), as the sun is setting, takes them to deeply hidden treasures, which Agni has brought from the earth and from heaven, such as the sea and other free-flowing waters on the earth and the trapped cosmic vapor above in the sky. Agni even sends forth a victorious strong courser with divine adoration as the herald of sacrifices to support Vaishvanara to measure the motion as his own. Alive in joy, delighting in the gods' alliance, reaching the heights of earth, they roar, burning with their eager teeth the woods and forests. The grass strewn with sacrifices and advances as an adored priest, with propitious Agni invoking both the boon-bestowing mother Aditi, and the most youthful, born to help manifested mortal embodiments. As the best of these, wisdom leaders found in solemn worship, as lords in the homes of human beings. Agni establishes the Holy One, joyous, speaking sweetly, who chosen as the bearer (Brahman), seated in a godly home, supported by Agni, as well as by both heaven and earth, which exalted to strengthen them. As the giver of all boons, the deity Hotar worshipped. Hotar is the deity who surpasses all in glory, who wrought with skills to show signs through hymns of adoration, which through the hearing advance the people's welfare and set their thoughts on the holy statutes. *Vasiṣṭha* now implores Agni as the Son of Strength (Rudra), and the lord of wealth and treasure, Indra, who provides food to singers and to nobles with godly powers, preserving them evermore with blessings.

The king whose face decked with oil and kindled with homage offered oblations by his faithful servants and the priests, who adore him (*Rig-Veda* 7:8). Agni shines forth when dawn is breaking, as the joyous holy priest acknowledged. The youthful Agni spreads out across the earth (Prithvi), bringing light to the growing plants that decorate the worshipped Agni. The powers lauded by the bounteous godly power, serving as the lords of riches, winners of precious wealth whom no one can conquer. The far-famed noble tribe of Bharata, with Agni, comes to shine like the lofty splendor (the sun), which has vanquished the powerful *Puru* in battle, as the heavenly guest appears in full refulgence and collects oblations that introduced graciously. Those who are noble born praised and lauded to increase their embodiments through the singing of songs. Winning countless treasure, they engendered with redoubled force provided by Agni who, splendid, chasing sickness, and slaying demons, delights the friends and blesses the singers. Then Vasiṣṭha, as the Son of Strength, the lord of wealth and riches, implores Agni to bring food to the singers and the nobles who, like the godly powers, preserve creation evermore with their blessings.

Roused from the bosom of the morning light, the beloved joyous priest, as the most sapient purifier (*Rig-Veda* 7:9), gives a signal to both godly powers and manifested mortals to bring oblations filled with pious riches to those who are most wise. With even force, they open the doors of the miserly Paṇis and bring them, along with the bright light of the sun, to feed the cheerful priest serving as a friend and home companion. Through the darkness of the still night, they made apparent. The wise never deceive, uncircumscribed, refulgent, the gracious guests, friends with good attendants. Shining forth with wondrous light before the dawn, like the young plants (children of the water), they enter the gathering to seek Jātavedas. At an adorable age, they come with refulgence, showing themselves to humankind, bringing a lovely luster that with kindness awakens the humans and enkindles them with a message from the gods, who fail not. With the band who pray and worship, Agni brings all the godly powers together in unity—Sarasvatī, the Maruts, and the Aśvins—who give water and riches.

According to *Rig-Veda* 7:10, the wise man, as lover of the morning light, bright, radiant, and refulgent, which moves and spreads far, its luster making a pure new divine splendor, comes like a golden hero to shine among others, generating longing thoughts and arousing individual living beings, such as the sun, which breaks through to create the morning. The priest's wave with their praise, singing and making sacrifices to the ferocious Agni, who regulates the sun for all the generations to visit, along with the most bounteous envoy who brings forth the divine will, asking for riches. With the goodly aspect fairly supported, the mighty mortal messengers carry such oblations. The manifested man of eternal wisdom joins to unveil the power of nature (Vasu) to bring along five godly powers (Agni, Indra, the Rudras, Aditi, and the Ādityas). They come as all-bounteous, serving as the perishable Bṛhaspati, who supported by the holy singers who eagerly plead for sacrifices from the joyous youthful envoy (herald) who serves over the mortal lord or ruler with material riches and requires them to follow divine worship as unwearied envoys.

According to *Rig-Veda* 7:11, after the death of the ruler (herald), without sacrifices, and without disturbing the astral body and the eternal flame, the immortal living spirit allowed to reside within the physical body, making joyful all the priests and deities who come to offer oblations to the mortal embodiment. They then sit and implore astral body evermore, undertaking the duty of those envoys who offer worship while sitting on the sacred grass. On the auspicious day, they offer oblations three times, until the treasures of the mortal embodiments either remain or sent to those serving as the envoys taken to the godly powers guarding the mortal embodiments from cursed. To the eternal flame, lofty sacrifice offered, with gifts provided to nature (Vasu), where manifested humanity, as the oblation-bearer, attains contentment.

## PERCEPTION

According to *Rig-Veda* 7:20, the state or quality of awareness that allows one to observe external objects and to know something within oneself called perception, where the embedded self as part of consciousness helps one to realize both the external world and the internal world. According to Vedic mythology, it is associated with the first creation, the original cosmic man, Manu. It is related to the comprehension of the powers of essence (meath) and to the ability to unveil the universal principle of existence and nonexistence, which regulates all surrounding physical manifestations and provides great reverence and the ability to comprehend the eternal controlling powers serving as the "seniors." The seniors shine forth within their well-lit dwellings, serving as the wondrous inner flame, well illuminated, worshipped, able to look forth in all directions, traveling the wide region between earth and heaven—and beyond. Among the youngest, they approach the great and mighty force, overcoming misfortunes. As the eternal flame is in the house, they, like Jātavedas, praised as noble patrons who protect the body from disgrace and trouble and serve among the elevated sage Vasiṣṭha, who travels with the trinity of Agni, Varuna, and Mitra, singing holy hymns. They bring forth most abundant treasure, which persists evermore, and gain vibrations by singing to the godly powers. With prayer songs and hymns, they generate thoughts that enlighten the body and help slay any evil power. So, by bestowing oblations, the godly power Vaishvanara, sitting on the grass, comes to overpower all. Singing inspirational hymns, and with the eternal flame, the seniors usher in the brightly glowing supreme powers of causation, first seen at the creation at the point of separation to establish earth below and heaven above. The middle esoteric region, fully filled with mighty powers (Vaishvanara) and noble souls such as Jātavedas, appears free from the heroic curse that at birth comes to bind all creatures or astral bodies while they move around guided by the herdsmen (sanctity) on a path to prayer, before they become too impolite to be regulated by the godly power Vaishvanara, whom herdsmen seek for help in finding their cattle.

According to *Rig-Veda* 7:14, with reverence, Vaishvanara offers gifts to those who, through eternal flame, attain brightness and, as the fuel, bring the godly powers. By performing rites and honoring the Holy One, the seniors even bring fuel to invoke the priest with the eternal flame. By offering praises and purified butter as a sacrifice, they honor the blessed light, like a piece of paper used to bring the oblations. Agni, along with the godly power Vaishvanara, pleased with such admiration, invoked and sanctifies those who pay their respects as herders who, with honor, offer eternal blessings, accompanied by ritual exclamation (*Vaṣaṭ*), which operates behind the third eye as the solar deity. From the mouths of the godly powers, Vaishvanara offers oblations to serve humanity and their nearest kin. Every embodiment, whether youth or wise master, given by the god Agni to the fivefold powers, who, while seated, guard them from all sides and protect their households and properties from woe. The youths and the wise heads learn to fly in the sky like big raptors (falcons), wandering like medium-sized arboreal parrots (*loriini*). They characterized by specialized wealth, and with brush-tipped tongues, they extract nectar (amrit) from various blossoms and pluck soft fruits such as berries. They glow whenever they see a fair sacrifice. Traveling in the front like heroes with their sons, they enjoy the sanctified gift. The best worshippers, expressing themselves by singing songs, offer oblations to serve Agni. As the lords of the house, they sit down and worship the Bright One with their riches. As heroes, they seek the powers of Agni and shine forth at night like stars, and then in the morning they emerge through fire as the sun provides heroes as their friends. Living beings, serving as humanity, come near and, like the singers, gain vibrations to produce their songs of praise. Heroes with thousandfold speech all come near with praises to meet the immortal refulgent glow. Serving as bright purifiers, they drive away evil powers (rakshasas). This brings abundant wealth to the young, allowing them to become children of strength. Like Agni, they bring fame to heroes such as the divine powers Bhaga and Savitar. This provides them with the power to protect themselves from distress, also bringing the hottest eternal flame, so they as young ones cannot consumed by enemies. They build an irresistible might, like an iron fort with one hundred walls, to defend the new creations serving as humanity.

According to *Rig-Veda* 7:16, the supreme powers of caution, during the evening and in the morning, preserve all creations from sorrow and from the wicked by serving them infallibly day and night. With a reverent hymn,

Agni calls the wisest envoy, as a Son of Strength, to come and serve as his immortal messenger. As demigods, the two red horses (the Aśvins), with noble sacrifices, all-supporting, yoked as well-worshippers, come with urgings and good prayers to bring the heavenly gift of wealth, which allows living beings to have happy ending. With the much-invoked bountiful flame, all mounted up with red-colored smoke, they touch the sky, and before they alight on the ground, they kindled to serve as messengers. The Most Glorious One brings the godly powers from the Son of Strength, also bringing all the food to the feast to feed human beings and other living beings. At the homestead, the herald of sacrifice, serving as lord of all, with blessings and as the cleanser, serves as a sage who offers worship to enjoy riches. All beings who make sacrifices granted with wisdom and wealth inspire with their zeal. Performing solemn rites, the skillful holy priests sing praises to worship well. As dear princes with the eternal flame, they appear as wealthy patrons who come to govern humanity. They part with gifts, leaving them in the animal stalls and in the homes of human beings, all of them bearing the sacred oil, accompanied by victorious spiritual powers. They sit, well satisfied, ready to guard humanity, moving away from slander, providing refuge from afar to any famous one who harmed. A priest with a pleasant tongue, most wise and near to humanity, brings riches to the liberal chiefs and speeds up the offering of gifts. These manifest as a wealth of steeds, driven by desire, renowned as they help to save the human beings from distress. The most youthful ones, with one hundred castles, give needed wealth, with full libations of soma poured forth to refill the empty vessel.

The manifested mortal body consciously makes sacrifices to support the supreme powers of causation, which bring the life force (prana) in abstract form as essence. In its indestructible form, it is the living spirit (Atman), manifesting as self in its eternal form (omnipresence). Both nonmaterial reality (purusha) and nonmaterial nature (prakriti) come to manifest a different material reality that, with every change, continues to be subject to the laws of cause and effect.

According to *Rig-Veda* 7:17, the unchanging eternal form (omnipotence), the universal immortal soul (Paramatman), and the individual immortal spirit (Atman) prevail within everything and, as changing entities, connect with nature (Vasu), which through the five great elements regulated by the messenger Aṅgirases, sons of Agni. They themselves as the aggressors, by performing various acts of wrongdoing, are defiant, using the ever-prompt powers of the goddess Savitar, who comes with supporting encumbered water that carries the individual living spirit (Atman) within the astral body as the embryo. Further, the messenger Aṅgirases, sons of the ferocious fire, Agni, provide them with what they need to create and organize the new world. They fully understand that the purpose of each creation is to cherish the life force and to provide the protection and guidance it needs to survive for a given period within this new world as purusha, with the blessed father of righteousness, and create new splendors as mortal embodiments by placing the astral body (embryo) carrying the individual living spirit (Atman).

According to *Rig-Veda* 7:18, Indra, as the ancient celestial power, promises that nonmaterial purushas will receive all necessary support so long as they provide no aid to any enemies or any other power that is planning to assault any astral body (embryo). They receive full support from the messenger Aṅgiras, representing Agni, so they may granted imperishable power to serve noble souls. Blessed, nonmaterial purushas appear in the image of godly power as avatars who follow the path that is supported by the heavenly powers Indra and Agni, who are further honored with prayers and are worshipped by other ancient cosmic noble powers, the Ādityas, who gracefully receive support from Bhaga, Savitar, Varuna, Mitra, and Aryaman, who come striding to serve as infallible guards. These ancient cosmic powers, the Ādityas, establish shelters within different regions, serving as holy sites to provide protection. These sites served by the invisible powers that remain unknown. No one knows who their creators are, who is serving such shelters, or who checks up on them and provides foster care to all. The ancient powers the Ādityas keep enmities away and remain busy saving the perishable astral bodies (embryos), as nonmaterial reality (purusha) creates ample room for them to pass by without disturbing the astral bodies.

During the day, the ancient powers appear as shepherds who hover and remain freewheeling. During the night they make sure foes have no time to strengthen themselves to potentially bring grief. They watch the perishable astral body all day, offering oblations to Mother Aditi and to loving-kindness (Mitra) so they may help the perishable astral body chase its foes away. The ancient twin powers, the Aśvins, appear as a pair of physicians who come to chase away the evil powers, removing iniquity, and make sure the astral body remains healthy. The ancient twin powers chase away the evil powers before they can attack the astral body. Agni, as the ancient power, blesses the perishable astral body by providing inner warmth, heat, and purity. While the astral body receives such external support, the powers of illumination—the sun, the moon, and the constellations of stars—similarly provide pleasing light and brightness. The ancient heavenly power Rudra, with the wind (Vayu), provides support to the astral body through the continuously flowing air that generates sweet breath. This inherent power, the breath, supported by the life force (prana) and chases away the strife and malignity that brought by foes to create even more distress.

Finally, with their ultimate powers, the Ādityas, as lords of wealth, remove the ultimate evil arrow shot by the foes to cause famine by holding back the flow of water in the rivers that are carrying the astral bodies. By purifying the astral body of evil and sin, they lead them to become bounteous, granting them shelter so they never suffer from any spontaneous harm. The demons injured by their own bad deeds and by foes who speak evil things and cause misery to the astral bodies. They are all overtaken by nature (Vasu), which comes to discern between the false and the true and accordingly subjects such foes to punishment. The astral bodies, blessed by heaven and earth, are placed within the shelters built into the mountains, where astral bodies receive aid to remove any iniquity running in the floodwaters. Water provides auspicious aid to the astral body, carrying and holding the living spirit (Atman), and take it to a place beyond all trouble and distress. The individual living spirit, imperishable, come to meets with the lord of governance (Varuna), the lord of eternal love (Mitra), and the ancient noble powers the Ādityas, who transform the individual living spirit (Atman) from invisible and immortal into a manifested mortal embodiment, Aryaman, who then comes to receive the ultimate truth (absolute truth).

The newborn, through aptitude, faculty, intuition, and judgment, comes to distinguish between right and wrong and, through comprehending absolute truth, recognizes the power of morality (the voice within) and the power of righteousness (the inner light). Directed by the newly awakened individual living spirit (Atman), the living beings awaken to an inner conscience, which leads them to practice compassion evermore, which allows the mortal living being Aryaman the opportunity to serve as humanity by following the holy laws and establishing shelter to provide protection, guiding individual mortal embodiments along the path of spiritual involution.

This involution permits the individual conscience to comprehend the power of compassion, which further brings the power of refulgence, which chases enemies far away. This happens in the same way that the godly powers (divinities, deities, and demigods) and noble souls (Saptarishis) use the paths of morality and righteousness to become compassionate to attain to inner peace and tranquility and receive bliss. This brings support from nature (Vasu), which regulates the wind (Vayu), and the wind converted into the swift breeze that serves as breath. Such breath accompanied by the goddess Savitar, who, with a sweet waft of water mixed with mythical juice, brings life force to plants, animals, and human beings. She further helps manifested mortal embodiments to accept the divine power serving as force (divine will), which helps them to comply with the divine covenant. The covenant regulates day and night, creates sweet dawn and dusk, and supports the atmospheric shield (the sky), thus protecting living things from impacted by extraterrestrial forces. The atmospheric shield in the past provided full sweetness to the Saptarishis, who help other manifested embodiments to receive the water enhanced with mythical juice, providing nutritious food just like milk.

The trinity of Mitra, Varuna, and Aryaman, through their powers, support and regulate mortal embodiments, while the trinity of Indra, Bṛhaspati, and Vishnu, with mighty strides, regulate the solar system. The trio representing three zones, celestial, cosmic, and terrestrial, graciously served by the ancient primordial force, Shakti. The midair region, located between the celestial region and the cosmic region, served by the twin demigod Aśvins, who regulate the area personified as cosmic hosts (Maruts). To safeguard those within the midair region, the demigods provide shelter, such as temples and other places of worship, which serves as the place for the astral bodies to redeem themselves, seek guidance, and receive direction.

## CONSCIENCE

Using the powers of morality and righteousness, and going beyond the norms, the inner conscience obtains compassion to help in distinguishing right from wrong. With enhanced inner conscience and compassion, the embodiments are associated with individual feelings that reflect, at the time a living being commits actions toward others, individual moral values, individual rectitude, righteousness, and an individual's ability to fully conform to principles or the divine covenant, resulting in integrity, which enhances the conscience by appearing in the form of compassion, commonly referred to as the "voice within" or the "inner light."

According to *Rig-Veda* 7:19, the ancient immortal universal souls with conscience, or the inner feeling or inner voice viewed as a guide to the rightness or wrongness of one's behavior, guided by the immortal soul Kutsa, who appears among mortal embodiments as *Ārjuneya*. He appears once good libation poured by Indra, who, like an enormous bull with sharp horns, singly energizes the agitated embodiment. Kutsa verily appears in battle aiding his charioteer, *Ārjuneya*, serving as the mythical conscience that comes to subdue the evil powers Kuyava and Dāsa Śuṣṇa. The immortal soul Kutsa, as the Bold One, the king of the tribe of *Sudas,* comes to aid the Bharata tribe and helps them attain victory by defeating the alliance of powerful tribes, the Puru. They eulogized for boldly accepting the offerings of *Trasadasyu*, the son of *Purukutsa,* who slays the Puru tribe to bring to the tribe of *Sudas* the land they won and invite them to the godly banquet as noble souls. They appear with heroes (the lords of the bay steeds), who slay foemen and swiftly kill the ruling Dāsas, along with the rulers of the sacred sites Cumuri and Dhuni. With thunder-wielding powers, they swiftly crush ninety-nine castles and capture the hundredth with their onslaught, also capturing the evil snakes Namuci and Vṛtra.

Indra blesses Sudas, who worships him and brings oblations that provide strength, so that with prayers, he yoked with strong bay horses and develops a mighty strength. Sudas never gives up on victory; with the bay horses, he builds his own assembly to fight the wicked. He delivers with truth and success, being faithful to the associated princes. They receive support from Indra's envoy Maghavan, who comes to serve as their loving friend. When they are near Maghavan, they remain fully under his protection and joyfully have their wishes fulfilled, all filled with humble pride. As if to receive noble spirits, they rise as the high priests Atithigva, Turvaśa, and Yadva. In truth, the envoy Maghavan gives them the skill to recite hymns. Singing songs of praise, they selected to join the assembly of noble souls.

The worshipper *Sudas* no longer spoiled as a lower-class, stingy, or ungenerous person. With loud sounds, he comes accepted as the hero who reverts to give other riches. As a favor, Indra comes to fight against the foemen, serving as a friend of the heroes and as their helper. With lauded heroic aid, Indra, by way of prayer, polishes the embodiments so they offered a portion of his mighty powers and receive his protection evermore with blessings, strength, and habitations.

According to *Rig-Veda* 7:20, the noble individual spirits born strong and godly in nature perform heroic acts and, as friends, come to support other manifested mortal embodiments in whatever deeds they perform, ensuring these conform to the godly power (divine will). Their noble living spirits save them from great transgression, inviting Indra to visit within their embodiments. Indra comes with his greatness to smooth out any deficiencies, eliminating or overpowering any evil power (Vṛtra) that may remain prevalent within their physical bodies. With the help of Agni, the youthful hero Kutsa, with his inner conscience, is the true divine singer who, within his heart, provides room and space enough to support even the chief *Sudas* and to grant the noble Bharata tribe with wealth based upon the oblations they offer. Like an unchecked soldier mongering war, the embattled hero serves the chief *Sudas*, who comes with his old, scattered army, ready to slay each foe. With divine powers and mighty greatness, they fight against a confederation of ten kings who fill both the worlds. *Sudas*, who serves along with Indra and other mighty lords of the bays, wields thunder that filled with mythical juice.

The tribal chief *Sudas*, at the banquet, appoints a chief of living beings, who with his strong army, which includes leaders and heroes, boldly acquires booty. The manifested mortal embodiments do not hesitate, nor suffer sorrow, as they acquire the godly living spirit (Atman), which fills them with noble conscience to make sacrifices to serve as lords of worship and lords of wealth, all born to protect the spiritual power (divine will). Whenever any elder willingly comes to help them, the younger one, who looks like the greater one serving the immortal body, sits aloof, inactive, always thinking about the wondrous Indra, who brings riches to the dear folks and, as a friend, presents oblations to the chief. Indra, with his thunder-wielding powers, ensures they receive as a favor the best of shelters by those who slay not and persevere with the mighty powers of the messenger Maghavan. The messenger brings food provided by the powers of Indra and by other wealthy patrons serving as lords of the bays.

Marked with wild joy, they called upon with rites and mythical juice, which offered at banquets so the holy grass will continue to grow, and then move on to grow plants, further distributing mythical juice among the eloquent council to drink and further serve humanity, enabling them to grasp higher knowledge. With such knowledge, humanity comprehends how the cosmic vapor, as compressed stones (comets), as celestial objects, exude mythical juice as they come near to the sun. Like the famous thunder god Indra, the cosmic vapor brings cosmic objects filled with strong mythical juice. Through such compressed cosmic stones, free-flowing mythical juice provided, as the rocks, like balls of ice, generate it.

The noble heroes fully comprehend that they shackled to the legendary evil powers appearing as fire-spewing reptiles, serpents, and avian, which maintain their traits as they descend, falling into the rivers and giving birth to living things, riding with an embodiment that passes through, creating a trembling fear. The manifested human beings, as noble powers with skills, master the use of weapons to perform godly deeds to overpower the dragon as their opponent evil power. With rapturous joy, they shake the evil forts with the mighty power of Indra, who as the thunder-wielder slays them. With true spiritual power, they subdue the hostile rabble and prevent them from approaching any holy spirit. Any noble soul whose strength surpasses the regions comes to comprehend the power of divine greatness. With their own power and might, they slay the evil power Vṛtra and ensure no foe has survived at the end of the battle. Noble souls, like the earlier deities, submit their spiritual powers to the supreme divinity Indra, who with humble hands invokes protection. To serve as the ultimate power of contentment, he provides one hundred aides, coming to serve as the helper who brings gifts to the unified Mitra and Varuna. Serving as the defenders, the two serve as friends, one at the left hand of Indra, and the other at the right. They eagerly help him to conquer, yielding great homage, which through grace and strength, amid the shock, incites the foemen, all ready to defeat them in battle. They place food into the hands of the wealthy commanding patrons, with the great powers bringing good things to those who deserve them and preserve them evermore with blessings.

## EMPOWERMENT

According to *Rig-Veda* 7:22, within the cerebral faculties, the firstborn, manifested as the self-born *Svayambhū*, appears as the son of the creator Brahma and as the mystic soul who wanders all throughout the world knowing all aspects of materialistic and spiritualistic realism. With the purpose of serving the manifested spiritual souls who fully dedicated as scholars, he receives transcendental wisdom as part of the mystic soul. The manifested spiritual souls served by Indra, who, after drinking mythical juice, guides the lord of the bays with cheer and invites manifested cosmic bodies to come and unveil the eternal truth. They first disclose their direct path of travel, which regulated by the laws of nature (Vasu) and is where the manifested bodies come to meet with life force (prana), which passes through like a breeze of joy, which as breath already serves humanity to become spiritual scholars. Dear companions of Indra, they, with delight, bring royal treasures, protected from the slaying foemen. The top position assigned to the self-born Svayambhū to closely observe the divine messenger Maghavan who, as the envoy of Indra, utters eulogies as part of every word spoken by the holy sage Vasiṣṭha and recited with prayers at the banquet. The drink of mythical juice prepared from compressed stones (comets) offered along with loudly sung hymns, representing self-adoration, to the courier Brahman. They never forget to sing hymns of praise to the immortal conqueror, as they, in their mighty strength, always utter the name of Brahma, the self-refulgent god serving as the lord of humankind who prevails through pious sages and invoked by the messenger Maghavan with libations. Their powers remain in force not too far from humanity. All these libations offered as a source of strength to heroes everywhere through prayer. Once humanity fully invoked, everyone achieves greatness to serve as wonderworkers. They perform obligatory actions (karma) and, with the powers of the mighty ones (divinities, deities, and demigods), serve other, interrelated elements (dharma), also coming to serve the empirical world along with enlightened souls (rishis). Like the ancient powers, they come to provoke, using hymns to the serve the newer powers with their auspicious friendship, all recited by sacred singers who preserved evermore with blessings.

According to *Rig-Veda* 7:23, the holy priest Vasiṣṭha offers up prayers of love and glory to honor Indra so he will come to serve them in fighting the battle by extending their existence. When listening to the words uttered by the faithful servants, if any raised cry amid combat, additional strength sent through the holy priest Vasiṣṭha, who reaches out to Indra, knowing well that the duration of any individual life limited. The holy priest comes to bear upon their safety, while they are facing war and troubles. The bays, seeking treasure, with their chariot, serve as faithful servants. Gladly harnessed, they sent by Indra and his mighty force to slay any evil prevailing within the two halves of the world. Defenseless foemen are subject to the air (Vayu) to accept the holy rite, and then taken to Indra, where they deliver solemn hymns for the bestowal of booty, such as the booty that causes a barren cow to swell with water and produce milk. With gladdening drafts, they rejoice like singers with a bounteous spiritual power. With such godly support, even the pithiest mortal embodiments receive libation. This transforms the mortal physical powers into immortal spiritual powers. With praises, serving as the arms of the thunder wielder, they glorified as heroes to serve Indra.

According to *Rig-Veda* 7:24, within the manifested world (Prithvi), regulated by Indra, the powers of humanity make a home and dwell among the much-invoked heroes, who grow and prosper, serving as *Mānasaputra*, the mind-born sons of the creator of the universe, Brahma. As mind-born sons, they acquire wealth and knowledge to vouchsafe, rejoicing in drafts of mythical juice as they appear first in unmanifested immortal form. The second time, they appear in strong manifested mortal bodies and drink pressed mythical juice to fully comprehend the true supreme powers of causation. They use hymns of praise to loosen their tongues and make a perfect loud sound to invoke themselves. They come to sit on holy grass, from where they drink the soma that offered them. They draw impetuous godly power, coming from heaven to earth, to serve as Indra's Bay horses. They listen to hymns, experience joyful life, and aid in security, while they come to experience the mighty powers that, by lending strength, create the powerful bull of Indra, which, serving as a vigorous courser tied to a chariot pole, can overcome the sky above. Filled with precious things, they express their glory in hymns to solicit the wealth of heaven and attain exalted favor to send plenteous food to the chiefs, who share it with heroes and their children. With mighty help from the potent Indra, they rush together as a furious army, strong-armed, flying as lightning, without letting their minds sidetracked. As mind born, *Mānasaputra*, smites foes on the hard ground before they can come and attack the mortal embodiments.

The Mānasaputra continue to allow their minds to traverse the world, but they keep those minds far from those revilers who curse them, who stop the mind from accumulating treasures. The divine powers, with fair protection, gives the ruler Sudas one thousand blessings and hundredfold success to learn to use weapons and contemplate. As the divine powers bestow fame and riches upon those with splendid minds, they strike down the foemen. Once the Mānasaputra contented with precious things, with exalted favor, Indra sends to the chiefs' plenteous food for the heroes and their children, whom he preserves evermore with divine blessings. Without a gladdening prayer, they, supported by Indra, come with oblations of unpressed and pressed soma. This generates delight and provides them with new heroic power, which offered along with chanted sacred hymns or psalms.

At all times, the Mānasaputra serve as one united front, like the sons of priests who invoke their father by way of their noble deeds, which allows them to prepare themselves to achieve new things, as libations taken from their priests, and then taken to possess all castles. Indra, as the famed conqueror, comes to serve as the sole distributer of treasure (Vasiṣṭha) and, in close succession, brings success and offers delightful benefits to the humans who serve him. The distributer of treasures, Vasiṣṭha, brings libations to bestow upon thousands both strength and wealth.

According to *Rig-Veda* 7:27, humanity, with decisive hymns, calls upon Vasiṣṭha with rejoicing. With the might of Indra, Vasiṣṭha comes during combat and provides shelter, also providing a stall for the cattle. Indra grants power to his envoy Maghavan, who holds a hidden bounty of eternal wisdom, to invoke many friends who already possess mighty strength and have control over many who live in exposed places to serve as members of humanity in the world. In various forms, such as the form of a king, which already prevails within the manifested earth (Prithvi), they come to serve the worshippers, providing riches to many living beings. The envoy Maghavan, with ever-bountiful strength, presents as an aid to Vasiṣṭha, serving as the perfect guardian, never failing, and always bringing wealth as a long-term friend to humanity. Through such powers, Indra provides the manifested bodies a place to reside and helps them gain a new way to grow riches, using their minds to explore treasures, and winning them steeds and cattle, which preserved evermore with blessings.

According to *Rig-Veda* 7:28, they all know how to yoke themselves together and appear as the bay steeds to guide mortal beings who come from all over to pray to Indra. They learn to use their ears to listen to the divine calling and, like impellers, reach out with greatness to serve as holy sages. With prayers and potent mighty powers, they guard all and hold mighty thunder with its awful strength. At times they become defenseless and see the need to draw together by the divine powers serving both halves of the world. They help those who are born with strength to develop a highly active dominion and overthrow those who are too sluggish. Even today, they serve with honor those hostile people who have expired through their own sins, now discovered as sinless, wondrous, and wise, and have already forgiven.

According to *Rig-Veda* 7:29, as the lord of the bays, Indra, with pressed soma, drinking along with Maghavan, produces eternal love with the well-effused libation. They bring wealth and come to serve as bay steeds. Those who accept the prayers offered with devotion and with hymns, listen with full satisfaction as Maghavan provides invocations along with eternal love. Verily, those human beings whom the lord wants to hear directly and, like the earlier sages, win. They serve Indra, just like envoy Maghavan does, and serve as fathers of the holy sage Vasiṣṭha, who has the power to invoke providence.

## LEVITATION

According to *Rig-Veda* 7:30, through the mighty support of the revered Vasiṣṭha, who, through strong thunder, provides potent valor, Indra comes and serves humanity, having them learn and accept the approach to seek ultimate reality. To help humanity, Vasiṣṭha and Indra exploit the high dominion, from where they can see how the manifested world regulated. Even with knowing all worth, through invocation and turmoil, the heroes must fight a battle to search for the life force bringing sunlight to serve all living things. As fighters, they first easily slaughter their enemies. During fair and bright days, humanity receives the morning light (dawn), which spreads like a banner between the noble powers and evil powers that are fighting fire in the battle. Serving as the heralds of humanity, both Indra and Agni sit by themselves and observe the divine power (divine will) as it comes to serve. This brings great fortune, which Indra and Agni together offer with praises to grant riches to the heroes and establish the princes. The heroes and princes provided with excellent protection, as in the past, enhancing their strength and happiness. As liberal lords, they, levitating and with wisdom, address humanity and grant them gifts of ample riches such as vibrations, which turn living beings into singers who offer the best prayers of praise.

According to *Rig-Veda* 7:31, with singers singing songs, Indra brings the demigod Aśvins to serve as tawny steeds who, through drinking mythical juice (soma), serve as friends. They gladly endow humanity with bounteous gifts, which glorifies the Aśvins, serving as the givers of true gifts. The mighty, boundless Indra helps them gain inner strength, like gold received as a gift from the mighty powers of causation serving all kinds of animals. Serving faithfully and singing loudly heroic songs, they mark such godly acts, and as they pray, they subjected to the foemen's hateful slander. With resounding voices, singing on their way, they reached by other demigods serving as the cosmic hosts (Maruts). With rays of light, they reach high above, without a drop, and ascend to reach the higher level, thus coming to serve as the wondrous heavenly power. Levitating, they provide eternal wisdom to help others become great with mighty powers. With further polish, they purified by their mighty offerings and their true devotion. Indra, in sublime form, provides the singers with pervasive powers to generate prayers and praises, which makes it so that even sages may never violate their statutes. By singing in choirs, they establish themselves as the envoys forever serving the victorious kings. They help by resisting anger, always strengthening themselves to serve as the loved ones, and coming to serve as Indra, the lord of the bays.

According to *Rig-Veda* 7:32, as lords of the bays, the Aśvins even go to serve the worshippers. They join the feast and listen without delay, no matter how far they are from the praying worshippers. They come flying like bees in search of honey, and they sit close to where soma is poured. Those craving singers set their hopes upon the fulfillment of their longing to acquire eternal wisdom from Indra. Like the lord of the bays, they learn to behold such wisdom as they call upon Indra, who in his strong right hand holds the power of thunder. Along with the powers of the thunder wielder, the Aśvins offer mythical juice mixed with coagulated milk. With such support, they come to express themselves, glad to hear with their ears the divine calling (divine will). The material wealth that despises prayer bestowed at once as one hundred thousand gifts. Nothing withheld; all provided to share with others. As heroes, the Aśvins never check what gained through Indra, who provides pressed mythical juice, liberally poured forth to cause the holy warriors to come together and become the Mighty One or to create a mighty shield to protect them.

After slaying the evil powers, the Aśvins divide up the material wealth, even bringing out the heretofore unreachable goods. Indra, the mythical juice drinker, armed with thunder, to serve the mighty ones, brings out the pressed mythical juice. Before they get ready and outfitted, the mythical juice stirred up and, along with rites, is handed out as a favor and with blessing. Those who without any grudge give wealth to the great conqueror, who dwells in peace and continues to thrive, by not being misers, come to serve with the evil powers. No one can overpower such an embodiment that freely gives. They, like the Mighty One, supported by the celestial power Indra and by the cosmic hosts (Maruts). They all come to defend the mighty ones (divinities, deities, and demigods) against all kinds of terrestrial powers, building a stable force, ready to fight, and even obtaining the spoils with such strong defender. All living beings wilt as they come to serve as gracious helpers. While as heroes, they acquire positions among the exceedingly great victorious soldiers, serving the lord of the bays (i.e., Indra), providing mythical power that pours out soma to subdue foes.

With holy hymns, they appear well arranged and in fair form. With many snares to subdue them, they offer selfless sacrifice and become devoted to Indra. They with their perishable powers attack material wealth and come overpowered by the imperishable spiritual power (divine will). On the decisive day, through faith, they win over the immortal powers regulated by the envoy Maghavan, the mighty ones winning the battle against their foes. Urged on by the promise of dear treasure, the noble twin demigods the Aśvins, serving as the envoys of Indra, using mystic power, pass through all dangers and threats. The Aśvins fight battles, first with the lowest form of richness, then with affluence, finally coming to win and rule forever with the highest opulence. With such opulence, they win any disagreement and thus overpower any evil power, all of which are unable to fight back. They become renowned for this feat, sharing their great opulence with everyone in the battle that fought to protect the individuals prevailing on earth. Such power can be neither invoked nor implored by any other than Indra. As the lords of ample riches of their own, with highest opulence, serving as the ample supernatural mystic power, the Aśvins support the singers.

The Aśvins provide eternal wealth each day to enrich those who sing songs with praise. They make sure they never abandon singers to woe. No matter their kinship, even when there is no father, Maghavan serves as the father, a true ally to every active person. He indulges with those who are much invoked. They bend with songs, like a wheelwright who fastens solid wooden wheels. A mortal embodiment never wins riches by way of unworthy praise; such eternal wealth goes to no miser or stingy person. The heroes loudly called upon with songs of praise. They gaze upon the heavenly light, even though, like un-milked cows, they provide light only on the decisive day. But, like Indra, they move the entire world, filled with desirous horses, milk-bearing animals, and all humanity. Calling for the mighty Indra, they bring along the victorious ones. The young ones come to serve as the hosts to the elders, receiving rich treasures from Maghavan, who, as during the ancient days, in every conflict, drives away the enemies. He makes it easier to win the war and helps the young ones serve as the good protectors in the war to cherish their friend Indra, who gives all eternal wisdom. Like a sire shares wisdom with its offspring, they guide those who invoked in such a way that they remain alive and look upon the light. Maghavan does not grant wisdom to any mighty foes, unknown, malevolent, unhallowed, who prevail on the ground.

According to *Rig-Veda* 7:33, with assistance, heroes, much invoked, go through all the water that is running down, serving as the movers of holy thoughts. Wearing hair knots on the right sides of their hands, and with white robes of purity, warning humanity as they rise from the grass, they can win, near to the holy priest *Vasiṣṭha*. They come to help, bringing strong libation and soma pressed by the son of Pradyumna. Serving as *Vayata*, like sticks and staves, they bring the defenseless *Bharat*a found by *Vasiṣṭha*, who comes to serve as their chief leader. These noble creatures cast a light before them, impregnating the world with gracious moisture, while Vasiṣṭha provides all with warmth. All the morning light, until they discover the sun's envoy bringing a growing glory with splendor to the sea of unfathomed depths, serving like the great Vasiṣṭha. Using the power of the wind, Rudra defines Vayu, which can never attained by any other power. With their sensitivities as wind, soft and swift in nature, they touch the heart like a secret reserve of life force (prana). They spread into a thousand branches, forming a luster that springs like the lightning that comes from Varuna to join with Mitra, forming a union. As seen with Varuna and Mitra, with adoration, a union is born, which makes the sacrifice, urged by both, with a common pitch to bedew and flow in mist, rising up with an inflated mind (*māna*), thence born as the sage who brings the load-bearing *sāman*—the first who speaks with a grateful heart to the compressed stones that bring reverence (divine will) and the holy priest Vasiṣṭha.

## PIOUS NATURE

According to *Rig-Veda* 7:34, the godly powers the *Viśvedevas*, with brilliant hymns, go forth, swiftly passing through empty space. Wrought and well fashioned, they listen to the primordial power, Shakti, who swells as the thinking heroes face their foes. The Viśvedevas fly like coursers tied to a pole, appearing with thunder and lightning, held within the golden arms of Indra. They rise like the day, with speed, and travel gladly like heroes into battle. Planting their flag, they declare their readiness to make a sacrifice, a sign of strength to all their people, with a signal to rise and light up the ground that bears the load of all living things. Agni comes with his ferocious fire, eliminating demons, and invokes the divine power (divine will) that implements the law in the form of hymns, which are close to heavenly songs, and sends forth with his voice to wherever the supreme powers of causation abide. This way the mighty power of the law, Varuna, with one thousand eyes, appears to behold the paths wherein the free-flowing waters run into rivers. As king of kings, appearing in glory, creating floods, Varuna, with resistless sway, covers all the regions. Assisting many tribes, serving with the praise of those who envy, devoid of light, he threatens the foes with his arrows. Putting the noble embodiment far from evil or sin, the godly Viśvedevas, through prayers, serve oblations to aid noble souls, and this brings out their dearest praise. In accordance with the divine will, the noble souls such as the child of water choose friends who come to serve them well by keeping them away from the dragon borne of floods, which comes from the midair region to sit atop the holy grass. The Viśvedevas make sure the dragon of the deep never harms the faithful servants who make sacrifices to become renowned heroes. The heroes, as virtuous men, march boldly on toward wealth, leading as great hosts who attack fiercely. They burn their foes with solar winds and, with their left hands, draw the creative feminine powers closer. Like wives, these powers give birth to the heroes' sons, who perform acceptable hymns that serve with the creative force Tvaṣṭṛ to attack many young goddesses (Aramati). Seeking wealth, such goddesses bestow treasures as lavish gifts. In the shelter of the immortal, the two heavenly mothers *Rodasī* and *Varuṇānī* bring forth a bountiful refuge in the *Varūtrīs,* who, through their creative power, fashion rich mountains capable of storing a great deal of water and supporting the formation of heavenly herbs, all sorts of which grow from the holy ground. In accordance with the sovereign of the forest, such growth prevails and comes to protect humanity so they may serve the two world halves, in concert with the cosmic hosts (Maruts) serving the victors as demigods. They firmly hold humanity in their possession to provide great wealth to all.

According to *Rig-Veda* 7:35, all friends of the heavenly powers Indra, Agni, Varuna, and Soma provided with oblations to receive health, strength, and comfort. They join in the battle with their auspicious friend Pūṣan, who, along with the dedicated contributors Bhaga and Sathsa, provides a garment (*purandhi*) as covering and aid in the form of riches. A true blessing, they appear in forms as the noble manifested mortal embodiment Aryaman. All well conducted as the Maker or Sustainer, as a pair they offer invocations, fair and far-reaching, and appear to serve the earth with their auspicious godly nature. Agni faces Varuna and Mitra, serving as the twin demigod Aśvins. As pious beings, they perform noble actions (Vita) and are honored as impetuous saints who in the past provided with offerings to invoke the powers of heaven and earth. The pair Varuna and Mitra, friendly, come to serve the newly established firmament within the midair region. With good relations between heaven and earth, they served by Indra. As the gracious victorious lords of the region where herbs grow on trees in the form of a forest, they come to serve humanity.

Blessed noble souls (Ādityas), jointly with nature (Vasu), become friendly and conform to the eternal law (Varuna). Blessed by the heavenly power Rudra, they bring along the tender females who kindly listen to the creative power of Tvaṣṭṛ and thus become the healers and, using mythical juice (soma), serve as the devotees. They even make sacrifices to transform heavenly bodies coming from outer space to become fixed sacred pillars, placed on the ground, on tender grass, which serves as a place of worship (altar). At the altar they receive the rays from the heavenly body Sūrya, who passes through the far-seeing body (the sun). With blessed power, they rise and appear in all the four quarters beneath the auspicious shield (the sky). Places of worship (altars) are all firmly situated on high ground in the mountains, from where water comes to fill the rivers. Serving as demigods, the cosmic hosts (Maruts) sing holy songs, serving with contentment the sustaining power of Vishnu, who with the patron Pūṣan covers all the air (Vayu) in the atmosphere. This way they bring in the life force (prana) so that all may live long lives and enjoy themselves.

The goddess of water, Savitar, rescues the embryos and seeds to support all creatures with morning radiance, along with the auspicious deity Parjanya, who transforms cosmic vapor into potent rain, which fertilizes the fields, serving as the gentle protector. The goddess Sarasvatī, with gracious holy thoughts, comes to dwell in the water, serving the liberal embodiments who prevail in the earthly and heavenly regions. The great lords of absolute truth, Viśvedevas, protect and aid each creature, such as the blessed horses and cattle, and come to serve humanity.

Pious and skillful, such creations, over time, through spiritual involution, come to serve their kind father, *Ṛbhu*, identified as the dragon of the deep ocean, who is given the opportunity to appear as a child of the water, Aja-Ekapād, who is graciously guarded by the godly mother Pṛśni, who is accepted by the new trinity of the Rudras, Vasu, and the Ādityas. A new hymn gives birth to the children of water who, like other holy ones, serve their offspring, all coming out of the ground to serve humanity and other living things. After hearing such invocation, they blessed and accepted by the immortal gods. Knowing all about the eternal truth, the eternal law, and the divine will, they, as humanity, worship the immortal holy gods, even to this day, when humanity travels broad paths, preserving evermore their godly blessings.

According to *Rig-Veda* 7:36, from the heavenly power Sūrya, as the seat of order, the milk-bearing creatures designated as the holy mothers let loose from the lofty regions to serve the new creations. They appear with a broad-reaching eternal flame, the ferocious fire of Agni, which lights up the spacious surface. With hymns, they invite the trinity of the Ādityas, Varuna, and Mitra to come and serve and fight the new evil powers, the Asuras. This trinity, who create massive strong floods, unerringly serve as leaders. These evil powers, which are always fighting against eternal love (Mitra) and friendship with their speech, stir up humanity, created to perform their obligatory responsibilities (karma). They organize their movements to glide like wind and come to fill the udders of those serving as the mothers. They spring up above the overflow, where even the bull, with his loud bellow, establishes Indra in a position in the lofty heavenly region. With worshipping songs that invoke the wise humans, Aryaman, yoked like the dear bay horses, appears as an enthusiastic noble embodiment. As a hero, he, from his own position, defeats those who are wrathful and malicious, while always offering adoration and worship with sacrifices, winning friendship and gaining long life. With the most reverence paid to the heavenly body Rudra, as a group he rises and provides food to humanity. Such noble souls come together with loud and glorious roaring sounds. They bring the goddess mother Sarasvatī, who appears covering all seven flooding rivers. She causes the fair streams to merge and become a strong river, flowing with a great volume of water that swells. They also come with rejoicing devotion to invite the cosmic hosts (Maruts), who come to aid and protect their offspring without letting the swift-moving imperishable, indestructible, fixed immutable powers, the *Aksara*, neglect to increase their riches. They bring the great goddess of pity Aramati to serve as the patron hero Pūṣan. They, as a council, look upon the old patrons (Bhaga) with favor and strength, singing bountiful songs of praise (Purandhi). They reach out to the cosmic hosts (Maruts) and the Sustainer, Vishnu, asking them to come and serve as the guardians of future infants, to vouchsafe the singers and their offspring, and to preserve them evermore with blessings.

CHAPTER 13

# Stimulus Dominion

THE STIMULUS DOMINION ENCOMPASSES THE NEWLY CREATED ground (Prithvi) where remnants of the ancient immortal living spirit trapped, seeking freedom from dark matter. They end up going out as a group who receive help from the birds, which as coursers appear with long legs, short wings, and long, downwardly curved bills. They fly together with cryptic plumage, and when alarmed, they crouch down and avoid detected by predators that hunt for the unmanifested immortal living spirit (Atman) that left buried in the ground or appeared first coming from the depths of the underworld. A new trinity, that of the Aśvins, Bhaga, and the dawn, appears to support such living creatures, as the ancient trinity of Agni, Indra, and Vishnu do not fully support them. They kindled with wellness and help the buried immortal spirit to rise from the depths of the earth and move upward to reach the ground above, seeking the heavenly powers Pūṣan, *Brahmaṇaspati*, and the Ādityas, who bring along water and light. With haste, the former trinity makes sacrifices to awaken the latter trinity and incite them to serve humankind with adoration. Appearing as a fleet of coursers, *Dadhikrā*, sitting on sacred grass with the swift twin demigod Aśvins, brings the goddess Iḷā to rouse a caravan of vigorous coursers. The heavenly power Sūrya provides bright light, along with the trinity of Agni, the earth, and the dawn, whom he summons to keep the embodiments ever mindful of the eternal law (Varuna). They manifest and appear on the ground like the heavenly bull, red and brown in color, which wards off all grief and trouble. Over time, being affiliated with the solar deity Ṛbhu and the wind (Vayu), they evolve like xenon, a dense, colorless, odorless gas commonly found in the earth's atmosphere in trace amounts. Although unreactive, xenon does undergo few chemical reactions to appear as the first noble gas that can synthesized as a compound. It never injures anybody but acclaimed as the noble soul, which as part of the thunderbolt (*vaja*) manifests as a self-evolved artisan who manifests as a skilled craftsman (*Ṛbhuṣkan*).

## SELF-EVOLUTION

According to *Rig-Veda* 7:37, as the self-evolved artisan (*arakhora*) from the ancient race looks birdlike, native humanoids, which always remain humble and kind, prevail in the forest with their fair-helmeted heads, all filled with thrice-mixed mythical juice, which parts with libations as they behold the heavenly light. Serving as rich patrons with unmolested riches, heavenly natured, they make sacrifices as they drink, becoming ready and giving bounties, singing hymns that speak to the inner soul. As the Ṛbhukṣans, the bounteous ones, these self-evolved ones use their talent, which they give apart with their treasure, whether small or ample, with both their arms fully filled, along with their greatest possessions. Out of their goodness, they grant all riches, offering gifts like noble souls with the thunderbolt (Vaja) serving as Indra. The self-evolved Ṛbhukṣans go working and singing through their dwelling place, always serving the individual living spirits prevailing within their bodies. To this day, Ṛbhukṣans serve as Indra, who appears as the lord of the bay steeds (Vasiṣṭha). Each day they offer their prayers and bring their oblations as servants to help others through the singing of hymns. Hoping for success, they fight in battle, with Indra granting riches to the priests at home, but only where such praises recognized. Indra, through his ancestral worship, brings food and wealth that enhances the heroes' embodiments and their dwellings.

The goddess of destruction, Nirrti, over time comes to reign in her omnipotent embodiment, especially through autumn, bringing food. Her three closest friends, who come to lengthen the day, rest at home in quiet. The goddess Savitar promises them riches brought from the organic bounty and, as the celestial guardian, attends to them and preserves the best food forevermore. As the benefactor Bhaga, they come to serve as the lord patron who, as a sharer and as the distributor, provides good fortune. The benefactor Bhaga, serving as an epithet of both mortal and immortal power, through the union of Savitar, Indra, and Agni, bestows wealth and prosperity.

According to *Rig-Veda* 7:38, the solar deity Ṛbhu, over time, with his golden luster, becomes like the higher divinities such as the goddess Savitar, and travels around inspiring mortals and distributing godly treasures. With the rise of Savitar, Ṛbhu comes with his golden hands to hear the sacrifices offered and spread abroad with effulgence. This brings the food to feed the mortal embodiments, and with praises brings in honor the true nature (Vasu) to offer all glory to the goddess Savitar. With sweet offerings and loud hymns of worship, Savitar provides all kind of protection to guard those who rule over humanity as princes. Even Mother Aditi, of all goddesses, with rejoicing and praise, welcomes the goddess Savitar and invites the high imperial rulers Varuna, Mitra, and Aryaman. In concert, they sing with emulous oblation, dispensing bounty that brought from both earth and heaven. Expressed as the lords of life, they entreated to bring along the mighty Bhaga, who provides protection. With such support, even the weak and poor can attain riches. By crushing the wolf, the serpent, and the mighty demons, the mighty power Bhaga completely banishes all affliction. Being very skilled in terms of the eternal law, the lords of life even come from death to help those noble singers who battle for booty, such as the womb (*Vājins*) containing the living spirit. As a mighty power, Bhaga, along with the powerful Agni, uses the sacred soft grass to tread upon and build a network that reaches to the godly assembly.

According to *Rig-Veda* 7:39, from the godly assembly, Ṛbhu scatters around, like a king surrounded by a band, and passes through, as he travels calling upon folks at night to team up in the morning with the wind (Vayu) and the sun deity Pūṣan. As blessed noble souls, they proceed in their wide, beauteously decked-out firmament, wending on the widely travel path to enrich all with the eternal flame. At all times, traveling as envoys, they hear and meet with others, providing holy aid so they can approach the place of congregation, where desirous worship, along with sacrifice, brings swift powers of purity (*nisatya*). Gilded with gold (*Purandhi*), they sing hymns to invoke the eternal flame among humanity. With such blessings from the ancient trinity of Mitra, Varuna, and Indra, and from the new trinity of

Agni, Aryaman, and Aditi, they travel from heaven to earth to serve the Sustainer, Vishnu, who, along with the joyful goddess Sarasvatī and the cosmic hosts (Maruts), as a holy being, supports humanity. With an unsated desire for riches that never fail, their allies become victors. Now serving both worlds, heaven and earth, they praised by the godly power Vasiṣṭha, accompanied by the holy trinity of Mitra, Varuna, and Agni, serving as the bright supreme deities who preserve evermore with blessings.

According to *Rig-Veda* 7:40, gathered as the audience of the council, the wealthy heavenly ones begin their praise to discover the most rapid course for following the goddess of water, Savitar, who produces wealth during the day distributed among the two worlds. Such distribution vouchsafed by the powers of Varuna and supported by the trinity of Indra, Aryaman, and Mitra. The mother goddess Aditi assigns the wind (Vayu) with the patron Bhaga to make humanity strong forever. The cosmic hosts (Maruts) bless the humans, along with the spotted coursers representing the goddess Sarasvatī. With the eternal flame from Agni, with the favor never to be robbed of its riches, as guided by Varuna as the lord of the law, and with Mitra as the lord of eternal love, the noble soul Aryaman fully supports them. Serving as the rulers or kings, the humans all work together until the job finished. The divine foe less mother, Aditi, listens, unharmed, delivering blessings to humanity, offering them appropriate ways to move swiftly with the bounteous sustainer Vishnu. Through the heavenly power Rudra, they gain their strength and, like the twin demigod Aśvins, seek embodiment. With celestial viands, without any anger, they glow like the patron Pūṣan and come to acquire the bounteous *Varūtrī*. Whatever it must give, they move swiftly to protect it and thereby blessed with the thundering power (Vata) that sends rain to create splendid wonders all around humankind.

According to *Rig-Veda* 7:41, after human beings have praised the two worlds, through the powers of Vasiṣṭha, along with the holy trinity of Mitra, Varuna, and Agni, they appear as bright deities representing world supremacy, with the patron Bhaga coming to preserve them evermore with godly blessings. They beg to serve the poor, and they make even royal kings give up their valuables to help the deprived poor. Singing beloved hymns, they serve the deprived poor mortal embodiments, invoking creative thoughts. Within their minds, spiritual energy provides supplemental support to cultivate their faith, which brings longer-lasting happiness. Living embodiments rewarded for serving their immediate needs and even extend beyond their mortal lives, seeking future immortality. Bhaga serves the bright deities who bestow a bounty of loving-kindness to help restore the divine force as the divine will among those who unfortunately subjected to insufficiency or otherwise deprived of the opportunities enjoyed by others.

Devotees worship in houses of worship or at home. They do this every day, three times a day, beginning at dawn, continuing at noon, and extending through the evening, until sunset. They worship the ascending heavenly power Sūrya and summon him to the blessed house of worship, gradually building honor among the unmanifested immortal universal soul, Paramatman. At all times, the heavenly power Sūrya, through his offspring the sun, provides direct light and, through his offspring the moon, indirect light. The sun and moon support the unmanifested immortal universal soul, which through its devotees provides them with physical strength, making them as strong as steeds to serve like horses and oxen. Using their physical power, they pull the chariot of the demigods who bring spiritual powers to support the unmanifested immortal universal soul and guide them to the right place, where they find hidden wisdom and knowledge that they can pass on to their kin, with a stream of riches, in both unmanifested and manifested form, pouring forth.

Patrons (bhagats), through divine will, help preserve the new creations by offering them divine blessings, so they become humbler and gentler, appearing as noble souls who go beyond to comprehend the eternal truth and attain inner illumination. Through such powers, they come to serve as the leaders with aggressive power and together harvest new splendors, with fast-running horses pulling the chariot carrying the godly powers. By divine will, they root out evil powers and gain control of all the newly manifested splendors. By counterbalance, they come to overpower the evil forces. In addition, Indra provides them with the mind and heart, along with additional subtle faculties such as intellect, to grow further by acquiring the eternal flame provided by Agni.

Patron bhagats learn to capitalize on the solar rays generated by Sūrya and, through their higher knowledge, spread these out so they flow like the heavenly waters, bringing mythical juice. By learning to balance the counterflow, such as the water on earth returning to heaven, by joining with the heavenly powers, all given uninterrupted access to the absolute truth. This provides them with a unique ability to strengthen the linkage and build a bond of solidarity with the vital powers of causation. Indra,

Mitra, Varuna, and Agni jointly become capable of generating the bodies consisting of cosmic particles—atoms, with electrons and protons—regulated by the invisible powers of attraction and repulsion, thus setting into motion the physical bodies strategically positioned to fill space. They perform actions, like the heavenly golden cow come to produce milk to take care of her offspring from the day of their birth. Thereafter, on a day-to-day basis, with gentle hands, they provide an abundance of mythical nutrients that, through the glands, brings out the innermost benevolence. This helps individuals to cultivate skills and acquire creative powers better than those of any of their friends. They learn to guide by the living spirit, which helps to cultivate a cheerful personality. With grace, such personalities acquire wings, like the birds, to fly as they learn to enjoy a life of unattachment. They become so powerful that they can even cause movement within the earth, such as earthquakes, and transform flatland into high mountains. Creating high mountains with valleys, they thus turn the solid surface into loose soil with running water. They can even turn the tides from deep within the ocean, causing the water to reach above the surface and flow across the land to germinate life.

## AVATARS

An avatar is the material appearance or incarnation of a deity on holy ground (Prithvi). Theologically, avatars of most often associated with Lord Vishnu, who in varying lists appears as the Godhead, including at least ten avatars (*Dashavatara*) manifesting as deities. According to *Rig-Veda* 7:42, the spiritual force Indra, Brahma, and Agni manifest as the avatar Aṅgiras, jointly coming forward and forming clouds that travel with a roaring sound, appearing with surrounding water. After traveling on a long-known path, passing through the manifested celestial and cosmic planetary bodies, they all come swimming down to settle themselves with grace along with compressed cosmic stones (asteroids, meteors, and comets). The holy impartial fire, Agni, yokes them as heroes, with ruddy horses or red steeds to bear them. The horses coming out of the chambers where the mighty powers have lived for generations. All glorified with sacrifice and worship, they sit to the left of the unequalled priests. They bring godly aspects that turn holy faithful worshippers into the noble goddess (*Aramati*). Serving as guests, they made apparent through their individual physical embodiments, which makes it easy for them to lie back within the enriched dwelling. Well pleased placed within the chamber that turns the embodiment from house to home, they filled with eternal wealth. By accepting the sacrifice from Agni and glorified by Indra, pleased with their powers, they accompany the demigods serving as the cosmic hosts (Maruts). Sitting on holy grass, they watch the night turn to dawn. With longing, they bring along Varuna and Mitra, and received with praise by Vasiṣṭha, all representing the victorious eternal flame, with a yearning for wealth. They also bring existence out of nonexistence, bestowing food, strength, and riches. Agni, with fire for worship, who sits in the godly assembly, generates a bright flame that scorches none.

According to *Rig-Veda* 7:43, the highest mighty ones, the *Vasits*, appear in many forms and thus are gladly recognized and honored as representing the holy order. All of one mind, closely knit, serving as victors, they come to remove poison and send forth, unharmed, wealthy people who enjoy life together and preserved evermore with blessings.

Flying at the forefront, the courser Dadhikrā, knowing his way, as he closely allied with the morning light coming from the sun, represented by the heavenly power *Sūrya*, follows the supreme powers the *Ādityas, Aṅgiras*, and Vasu. Dadhikrā is prepared to travel the established path of order, where Agni, forbearing like the heavenly army of the supreme powers of causation, heard by mighty ones (divinities, deities, and demigods), whom none can deceive. The goddess Savitar comes to fill the region with chargers that bring rich treasures. By holding hands, Savitar and Dadhikrā make all living things happy (*Rig-Veda* 7:44). Especially when they take away from all those lulling in slumber, they make them rise like other creatures and, through golden sublimity, ease their motion by extending their arms or wings. They are all bound unto heaven, worshipping the mighty light provided by the sun, which yields active vigor and makes them serve along with the goddess Savitar. Yielding, with strength and precious wealth, they come to vouchsafe treasure. Spreading out, they advance with luster, bestowing food upon the mortal embodiments. Such action produces, among those whose tongues produce pleasing songs of praise, honor for the goddess Savitar. With their arms, wings, and lovely hands, they offered manifold strength and granted with blessings forevermore.

## DIFFERENT WORLD

According to *Rig-Veda* 7:45, the heavenly power Rudra, prevailing within the heavenly region, fully armed with weapons, producing a sharp deafening sound that can be heard from miles away, comes to serve the newly manifested terrestrial region, where many splendors from the planetary system, based upon the respective positions of the planets, have acquired the supreme ability to hear such vibrations as eternal voices from the heavenly region to serve the manifested embodied souls prevailing within the terrestrial region. The imperial supreme power of causation, Rudra, comes through with the power to sway. Hearing such sounds, he willingly goes from door to door and helps to heal those in the family who are sick. Like an arrow, Rudra shoots directly down from heaven and gladly welcomed as he passes through the uninjured embodiments. Carrying thousands of medicines to inflict evil powers, creating progeny, always he brings offspring who, through worship, support him so he will protect them from slaughtered or abandoned—or even noosed when the embodiments are passing through with anger.

According to *Rig-Veda* 7:46, Rudra creates strong pulsations within the embodiments to help them reflect on and realize the presence of the immortal universal soul (Paramatman) coming as an immortal individual living spirit (Atman) swiftly flying through the shaft as a conqueror whom none can overcome. Heavenly Rudra, helping individual living spirits as Self, travels fully armed with sharp-pointed weapons and heard, but not seen, as coming from Paramatman. With the highest imperial sway, representing the immortal universal soul, the Self, flying above in the sky (*ākāśa*), travels with thoughts that, with vibrations, received as sounds coming from the ground, generated in the minds and hearts of living embodiments. Heavenly Rudra, like lightning, willingly shoots his bright arrows to bring down the eternal life force (prana) to heal any sickness in families and even travels door to door, where gladly welcomed. Whenever not welcomed, Rudra passes over the region, rarely injuring anybody on his way, just carrying with him a gracious divine power. He brings one thousand medicines to inflict evil, but never upon the progeny, even when there is anger or the opportunity to seize anybody. He neither slays, nor abandons, nor tricks. He turns barren ground into fertile fields, creating trimmed green pastures from where the manifested bodies can gain fame and even preserve blessings.

According to *Rig-Veda* 7:47, serving as a fast-running courser, Dadhikrā brings pure refreshing water to create a special beverage. Pious in nature, he provides soma that brings strength and sweet richness to eliminate lethargy and obesity. Within the free-flowing water, and even amid floods, the fast-running courser even creates his own offspring, moving with rapid progression among the waves, serving as a protector and bringing a most rich sweetness to take to Indra. Dadhikrā brings along nature (Vasu) to serve all living things, joyfully serving as a pious embodiment. Further, through the purifying process, like a wave, Dadhikrā brings eternal joy, which paves the path to reach and become united with the divine powers of causation. At all times, the courser Dadhikrā, by his nature, follows the eternal law, guided by Indra, and provided illumination from the heavenly body Sūrya. Filled with riches, he passes through flowing rivers, generating gleaming beams of light. To guide streams and rivers, he provided with ample room to grow as he travels and cultivates friendships to attain freedom. The liberal heroes Ṛbhu, Vāja, and the Ṛbhukṣans bring delightful mythical fluid, which flows among the waters, to all living things. Further, they receive as an aid the thunder and lightning (Vāja), which bring physical strength to help fight attachment or eliminate residual memories. Powerful Indra comes to invoke among living things the power to conquer and win booty by defeating the foes. Within the high dominion, where everyone faces close encounters with the foes, he becomes the ruler. With joint efforts, Indra, Vibhvan, Vāja, and the Ṛbhukṣans come to destroy the wicked foemen. They use the manifested mighty power, with ample room and freedom to gain single-minded power, and they seek protection through nature (Vasu), granting godly blessings to all forevermore.

According to *Rig-Veda* 7:49, waters that come from earth emerge from the center of a flood to become the force serving as the chief of all waters, who always makes sure the water flows, moving toward the sea, ever cleansing, never sleeping, and who comes to appear as the heavenly bull serving Indra. With thunder in the mountains, the water digs channels all over the ground, where Indra serves as the protector of all creations. The waters, which come from heaven, wander and dig deep into the ground, always flowing freely like nature, bringing brightness while speeding toward the ocean. With the power of the eternal law, Varuna purifies and, amid the waters, becomes the sovereign, who by the process of distillation comes to separate truth from falsehood. Without discriminating, the water continues to travel, with a bright light regulating its motion to protect divine creations. Even godly powers such as deities drink the same water that brings forth the hidden powers of the eternal flame representing Agni, who protects all living things.

According to *Rig-Veda* 7:50, to safeguard and protect those who have learned to build their nests near the swelling water, the union of eternal law and eternal love, Mitra and Varuna, respectively, come along with other godly powers to drive the hateful powers far away. They protect living beings from evil creatures such as scorpions and snakes, which, once they touch wounded feet or legs, create eruptions within the joints, such as the ankles and the knees, at which point the united Mitra and Varuna overpower the evil embodiment. The refulgent Agni comes to banish them or move them very far away, preventing the winding worm from even touching the wounded embodiments as they are brought near to the gracious goddesses. They even banish poison algae (*shalmali*), which found in streams near or among plants, driving it far away. The eternal power of Agni ensures the rivers remain free from algae and winding worms that afflict steep, densely wooded downward slopes. He also covers the downward slope into the valley that, initially waterless, filled with water and swells, forming naturally green (*sipada*) rotating rings. The noble soul Aryaman, the third son of Aditi, comes to serve as a close friend and companion of the mortal embodiments. These noble souls, depicted as the courser Dadhikrā, during the midmorning, with the sun, come to form a barrier (*aryamṇáḥ pánthāḥ*) in the sky like the Milky Way galaxy to protect fast-moving bodies such as racing stallions or twin demigods (Aśvins). This brings a trinity of supreme deities, Mitra, Varuna, and Bhaga, who come to serve along with the godly power Bṛhaspati, who invokes the rings built by the noble Ādityas and the evil Asuras.

According to *Rig-Veda* 7:51, the mother Aditi, with the unmanifested universal soul (Paramatman), to support progeny, provides mortal embodiments a home for their unmanifested individual living spirits (Atmans), which fully supported by the trinity of the Ādityas, Varuna, and Mitra, from whom manifested the mortal embodiment, Aryaman. Aditi provides the physical body and spiritual powers to create the noble mortal embodiment Aryaman, who proceeds to move within planetary bodies and becomes part of a group of solar systems that orbit and rotate around the sun. They manifest to fill the new material world (*Virāj*), which becomes part of the terrestrial region that now regulated by the new trinity, Varuna,

Mitra, and Aryaman, serving as the righteous guardians of Virāj, where fresh mythical soma brings omnipotence. Through the ancient trinity of Ṛbhu, Indra, and Agni, the new material world, Virāj, receives support from the ancestral twin flying horses (Aśvins), along with the multitude of demigods serving as the cosmic hosts (Maruts). Jointly, they come to support the invisible unmanifested astral body before placed within the material dwelling place, its embodiment. The immortal universal soul, Paramatman, as the father, comes to support and protect each individual living spirit (Atman). The astral body, consisting of the immortal living spirit, once placed within an individual mortal embodiment, receives support from subtle faculties, including the nervous system, which links the invisible immortal body with the outer manifested mortal physical body. The subtle faculties not only connect the immortal astral body with the mortal embodiment, but also protect the astral body from bondage with material world, which generates residual memories and ultimately, as if shackling it, prevents the astral body from leaving the embodiment; thus, the living being is subject to a process of encirclement to remain attached to the material world (Virāj). To bring into balance the united ancient deities Varuna and Mitra, the powers of nature (Vasu) used.

According to *Rig-Veda* 7:52, the new world (Virāj), as part of the terrestrial region, regulated by the godly power *Vāstoṣpati*, who himself regulates and protects the homestead. Mighty ones (divinities, deities, and demigods), along with the powers of nature (*Vas*u), influence every individual mortal dwelling, including sacred places of worship where divine worship (*Vāstu Pūjā*) performed. The mighty ones bless the embodiments, safeguarding them from obstacles, both moving and unmoving, by subjecting them to the vibrations generated as holy sounds. All the surroundings regulated by mighty ones, who keep each body safe from evil powers, starting with the rising sun in the east and the setting sun in west. Within each specific location, worship offered from outside by twenty-two deities. Within each site, ten pairs of deities, along with two kinds of demigods, come to serve the newly established world (Virāj), which receives full support from the lower earthly region and the upper heavenly region.

## SHELTER

According to *Rig-Veda* 7:53, the divine will establishes shelter for all those serving as noble warriors to protect the mortal embodiments and their offspring and provides the covenants necessary for mortal embodiments to serve and worship the ancient godly parents, who later come to prevail as high priests. The high priests appear as manifested mortal embodiments, who are all provided with new hymns to implement the divine order and with a set of two parents, each one appearing before all others. Under the established covenant, the high priests protect their possessions and hold onto their many treasures before they are granted liberal wealth that allows them to receive in abundance. Like Varuna and Mitra, the ancient guardians, they establish their homesteads to allow the new holy sages, the *Vastospati*, to build their individual homesteads, including spaces for both quadrupeds and bipeds. They are all brought together to work, cultivate friendship, promote fellowship, and bring welfare and victory to all as the saviors.

The invisible unmanifested noble powers (Ādityas) come to appear as noble warriors (Kshatriyas). These warriors serve as the gracious assistants to the new trinity, Varuna, Mitra, and Aryaman, who bring refulgent beaming powers from the middle region. They settle within the newly created material world (Virāj) located within the terrestrial planetary system as their homestead. According to *Rig-Veda* 7:54, the new trinity protect all from disease and bring happiness, granting whatever asked to provide prosperity to all quadrupeds and bipeds. The protector of the home, the manifested living being, learns to increase spiritual wealth to help domesticated animals and provide physical strength such as that enjoyed by youths to build friendships among all. This pleases the parents, who, as their offspring do, share fellowship to bring welfare, serving as victors within their dwellings (Vastospati). They end all disease and, in their weariest, become auspicious friends who come to serve, with eternal truth, all manifested living things that filled with illumination.

According to *Rig-Veda* 7:60, Agni creates gleaming tawny-hued teeth, which are all placed within the mouth like lance points and, when roused, bite deeply. They bark, allowing them to guard against boars and make others aware of their hidden powers provided by Agni. Indra creates vibrations that produce a noble sound among singers who create sounds to consecrate evil powers. Mothers produce soothing sounds while watching their children to help them go to sleep, and dogs bark to serve their masters and make the house a safe place to sleep. All relatives use a similar sound to provide protection and offer comfort. They sit, walk, and look upon the godly power Vastospati, serving as the Strong and Mighty One, peacefully rising out of the sea. They bring peace and tranquility with sweets that lull the singers and allow them to sleep in the courtyard or outstretched on beds with their matrons, like the heavenly bull with one thousand horns.

According to *Rig-Veda* 7:61, the noble guardian Vastospati develops mighty powers and comes to serve all manifested mortal embodiments as the noble warrior Kshatriyas. Wonderful, agreeable, Kshatriyas fights to protect living things that are righteous. The noble warrior Kshatriyas comes prepared to offer personal sacrifice, including giving up his embodiments to provide aid and ensure the defense of the new trinity, Varuna, Mitra, and Aryaman, who serve as the guardians of the noble moral power the Ādityas. He even strikes before a deadly weapon can strike any noble soul, protecting mortals. Hearing of the need for defense, he emerges from his shelter and toils, pouring out gifts that he offers graciously, with blessings, to those who seek freedom and those who suffer from sinless sorrow, faultless actions, or a needless fetter.

The Kshatriyas received by Indra and other mighty divinities, who happily lend them their immortal powers, while they are serving and aiding those who have gone astray and protected by the great and very gracious strong sons of Aditi.

As noble warriors, Kshatriyas receive support within the depths of the waters or on shallow ground, as they make sure no foe can attack or harm the divine seeds/embryos in the unmanifested astral body to create a manifested physical body to support. They allow the divine seed/embryo to spread unharmed within the vast kingdom. They help to increase the number of progenies through support of life force (prana) and, progressing as native glory, serve as the princes of the people, respected as noble warriors who never deceive and always maintain the statutes void of guile. Noble Ādityas, filled with morality from the mouth of a bound evil power, protect the noble warrior Kshatriyas by saving them from an arrow intended to strike down any malignity and killing any ravenous evil wolves. Bountiful Ādityas help Kshatriyas to enjoy themselves as in old days, both now and in the future. Everyone, even most men of wisdom, turns to the noble warrior Kshatriyas for vouchsafing. They live and pray for the mercy to become free and come to serve the Ādityas.

They wish to attain might like the Ādityas, to build a bond with the mother Aditi, who never despises and, graciously, with skill from the Vivasvans, provides them with weapons to destroy old age and dispel all sin. The Kshatriyas remove any hostility or indigence coming from any side and, through the mythical juice soma, produce mystic fluid, the nectar amrit, which produces divine powers. They guided by air (Vayu), and by passing through the glands of the manifested mortal embodiments, they attack the Aśvins. Like noble mortal living beings, the righteous warriors also offer worship and oblations, and regulate the breath that passes through the glands, to acquire mighty powers to generate pure mythical nectar (amrit). With individual fame and glory, they are blessed to quickly pass-through various successions that give birth to the primordial power, Shakti, who, with her strong sons, is responsible for the regulation of the supreme powers of causation, which, serving the noble warrior Kshatriyas, generate the powerful sweet fluid that with further refinement, passing through the subtle manifested faculties such as individual glands, produces the purest form of amrit.

The noble warrior Kshatriya gladly offers sacrifices to enhance the spacious region of Virāj, placed between heaven and earth, which he makes tremble with his godly powers. He even causes springs to flow through everything that observed. Singing praises, he invokes the creative power, generating thought among all who worship. While sitting on sacred grass, attending the assembly of warriors, the noble warrior Kshatriya gleams in his own friendly mind and shares his bright powers at the banquet with the cosmic hosts (Maruts). With their own golden ornaments, the Maruts appear with weapons of all types to support the noble warrior Kshatriya, who decks the new region, Virāj, with his bright light. He shoots his blazing darts, which pass through fragility, causing sin exposed.

Even before it is fully exposed, the divine will with its most loving holy powers comes to support all the divine creations. With delight, the divine will beholds the blameless ones, bright, who with purifying holy kindness, advance with mighty prosperity. They praised and bestowed with all kinds of titles, and as heroes, they enjoy the taste of the oblations offered them along with their offspring. They drink amrit so they awakened and enriched with excellent riches that bring felicity. Becoming princes, they themselves bring a hundredfold increase and, with blessings, come to preserve evermore. Singing in a troupe with the cosmic hosts, they pour down rain from the celestial region to connect with the other half of the world.

According to *Rig-Veda* 7:63, the divine will, with its greatness, generates trembling that reaches from the depths of the ground to the heights of sky, and even further reaches heaven. Amid this wild commotion, the middle region served by the demigods as cosmic hosts (Maruts), who move swiftly, fierce in their wrath. Moving with an all-surpassing might and vigor, they pass through each region, with embodiments looking on in fear at the coming of the bright light. The noble warrior Kshatriyas, with ample vital power, along with the cosmic hosts (Maruts), come to serve the king and princes, giving them fair praises, which gratifies them. The cosmic host (Maruts) travel onward to support living things, bringing delightful success to their favorite singers, who count their wealth by the hundreds, along with their strong steeds, in the thousands, all of whom serve as sovereigns to destroy the foemen and gift those who are distinguished to serve as the sons of bounty (Shakers). Simultaneously, the heavenly power Rudra implores the swift ones, that is, the cosmic hosts (Maruts), through the union of Varuna and Mitra, to bring forth Indra, who brings eternal love and affection, all working through Agni, who, with the power of attraction and repulsion, establishes encirclements based upon the principles that regulate the duration of existence and the ultimate demise that creates nonexistence.

According to *Rig-Veda* 7:69, the demigod Maruts elect to use immortal noble souls (Ādityas) to enforce the divine will. On the auspicious day, they allow the manifested mortal embodiment Aryaman transformed to become the unmanifested immortal soul, *Paramatman*, who, subdued, appears within the manifested mortal body to support the individual living spirit (Atman). This blessed union, with offerings and worship, becomes an active soul that brings forth well-wishers to experience such a transformation regulating the two extremes: heaven and earth. As an immortal soul, the union of Paramatman and Atman travels in unmanifested form but may still appear in manifested mortal form (i.e., Aryaman).

## PROVIDERS

According to *Rig-Veda* 7:60, arising each day with the sinless sun, the operating powers of Varuna, Mitra, and Aryaman, and the great mother Aditi, accompanied with hymns, come to seek the eternal truth. As they look upon all divine creations, they observe the supreme heavenly power Sūrya rising in the sky and providing space for the noble guardians. These noble guardians behold mortal embodiments, both moving and not moving, who are either good or evil. Sūrya, as he ascends, yoked by the united power of Varuna and Mitra, followed by seven gold coursers representing noble souls (Saptarishis). All come from Agni, and each spread like the droppings of eternal flame, all accompanied by spiritual powers, which spread and cover the newly manifested material world (Virāj), where living creatures served like herders, all coming from the oceans. They all come as coursers, mounted to provide rich sweets, there to help the singers with perfect songs of praise to grant all wishes. The coursers fully supported by the supreme powers of causation, such as the wind (Vayu), which unites the two separate halves (heaven with earth) by filling them with the five great elements, including air and water. The nobly born, as separate descendants, link up and serve as dear friends. With outstretched arms, they come to lengthen lives. They bring moisture in the form of dew and water to help pasture animals, such as cattle, produce milk. Famous, they help youthful worshippers hear the invocations through the vibrations generated by the trinity Mitra, Varuna, and Aryaman. As a trinity, the three gods vouchsafe the freedom of the young worshippers and provide them with additional room for themselves and their children. Those who worship all find paths that are fair and good to travel.

The ascending heavenly body Sūrya, producing bright beams of light, as the chastiser of all guile and falsehood, in accord with divine power (divine will), comes with the noble Ādityas and the new trinity, Aryaman, Mitra, and Varuna. Aditi, the mother of infallible and mighty sons, whom none can deceive, comes home to enforce the eternal law and brings her great power to awaken the worshippers and help them to acquire wisdom. With thought and insight, the deities easily find the path that banishes grief and trouble. Ever vigilant, with eyes that close not, and caring for heaven and earth in mortal manifested form, Aryaman leads the thoughtless ones with the guiding powers of Aditi, the eternal law (Varuna), and eternal love (Mitra), all serving to provide the noble guardian's shelter. The sons of the tribal leader Sudas granted lineal succession as bhaktas, who come to serve as the heroes (bold ones). They ensure they keep themselves free of anger so as not to upset any of the supreme powers of causation, and at the altar they offer oblations that purify the reviler by removing any stain. The god Varuna and the noble soul, Aryaman, save the tribes by giving them a place and the freedom to serve their mighty leader Suḍas.

## PROVIDER

According to *Rig-Veda* 7:61, the noble soul Aryaman brings comfort to the ancestral dwelling. The godly powers Varuna and Mitra assume the priestly task of performing sacrifices. They overcome every peril and preserve all with blessings, though they remain hidden are unseen in their resplendent meeting place, where they remain mysterious among the mighty ones who have dominion. All heroes cry, trembling in fear in the face of Varuna and Mitra. Those who win favor through prayer and worship gain strength and attain great riches by making their minds mightier. With Sūrya's spreading of beauteous light, two supreme powers arise who, like the ancient demigod Aśvins, behold all existing mortal embodiments, including all creatures prevailing on the ground in the new world (Virāj).

With full enthusiasm, the godly powers Varuna and Mitra respected as holy sages, renowned everywhere with the singing of hymns with devotion and respect. Varuna and Mitra serve as the sapient souls who, with favor, fill the new world, (Virāj), by creating the seasons. They are the bounteous givers from heaven, serving as guardians of the ground and prevailing within Virāj. The bounteous givers establish their shelters within the fields, and as custodians they watch unceasingly, visiting every spot. They establish a mighty strength between the two worlds as they pass through, making loving sacrifices to establish an enduring home to sustain people and animals such as steers. Those who are neither wondrous nor worshippers, who are cunning, follow Varuna and Mitra and remain untruthful. Keeping no secrets from the united gods, after offering their sacrifices, they, like priests, offer homage and use newly produced hymns to invoke the mortal embodiments that bring delight with the gift of song.

According to *Rig-Veda* 7:62, as part of their priestly tasks, Varuna and Mitra fulfill their karma-related responsibilities by making sacrifices, delivering living beings from every threat and safeguarding living beings with divine blessings. The heavenly power Sūrya, from aloft, sends forth beams of splendor to cover all creation and all the tribes located in countless places. The united Varuna and Mitra, in manifested form, along with other living things, receive the divine will, which supplies them with eternal wisdom. Mounted up with the heavenly power Sūrya, as it ascends, the great ensign the sun sends forth with praise its beaming light, which covers the fleet of horses and other animals with wings, who declare their freedom from all past offenses against the ancient trinity of Mitra, Varuna, and Agni.

According to *Rig-Veda* 7:63, to enrich the thousands of creations, the manifested noble power Aryaman comes with power to make living beings auspicious like the ancient heavenly power Sūrya, who himself is now mounted above and, through his great ensign the sun, rolls up sunbeams like a piece of rawhide that is polished to a shine just by removing the thick film that causes darkness. Restlessly, the new trinity of Mitra, Varuna, and Aryaman urge the creations to perform their obligatory actions (karma) and move forward by themselves. The obligatory karmic actions move them onward like a round wheel to harness eternal energy (*Etaśa*), which moves like a carriage, even though it to the great ensign the sun like a flag tied to a pole. In the early morning, the sun produces a refulgence that, with delight, invokes the powers of the heavenly goddess Savitar who, among singers, ascends to serve as the chief provider of joy and pleasure. She brings godly power (divine will) to direct the universal order, which never breaks down. She also brings along golden vision, a far-seeing power coming from the sun, to serve the manifested bodies and keep them evolving and rising toward heaven. To hastily fulfill her glorious goals, Savitar makes sure all those who inspired by the powers of the sun keep moving toward completing their goals and performing their assigned jobs. The immortal gods Indra and Agni prepare a sacred pathway cutting through the region that used by those who, with homage and oblations, serve the material world (Virāj) located between heaven and earth. Even manifested bodies can find such a pathway, and they learn to fly like a falcon, rising toward the sun, looking for a path that is safe and good to travel on. Once they reach the peak, they merge with the hidden trinity of Mitra, Varuna, and Aryaman, all in robes, hiding within the clouds, serving as the corporal who comes to rule the material world (Virāj). The union of Varuna and Mitra provides Aryaman with the imperial powers to serve as this new highborn corporal who comes to serve as a king. He assigned to serve as the righteous guard in performing obligatory actions (karma) to provide living beings with an everlasting divine order.

The highborn Aryaman, with imperial powers, serving as the prince of the holy ground, lord of running waters, brings his heavenly power to transform the cosmic vapor that falls like rain, bounteously pouring down with sweet-tasting nutrition. The unified Varuna and Mitra monitor all such activities and create the most efficient pathways for the heavenly water to travel through on the ground, which allows the chieftain of the Bharata tribe, who are foes, to enjoy such a blessing. Serving as the ruler, Sudas, guarded by divine power (divine will), causes the astral body and Atman to rise upward, sustained within a subtle body, as an emollient within the physical body. While serving the union, Sudas finds a proper dwelling place that provides him with happiness, and through his glands, he transforms soma into purified amrit and, through his breathing process, produces songs of praise that awaken the noble souls and generate thoughts to preserve the living spirit evermore by blessing it with divine will.

## HIGHBORN PAIR

According to *Rig-Veda* 7:65, the great ensign the sun, the godly powers Mitra and Varuna, and the everlasting primordial power, Shakti, called upon to answer individual petitions with holy thoughts and kindness, even including those of the evil powers (Asuras). All beings who are exceedingly fruitful blessed by and receive power from the union of Varuna and Mitra. Knowing that sin is bondage, a noose for wicked mortals, these beings try to escape before Varuna and Mitra come to set an orderly path over such troubles, like a boat sailing over troubled waters. The united Varuna and Mitra offer their blessings, which accumulate like dew on pastureland that produces sweet food and pour down the choicest celestial water. Offering soma and songs of praise to awaken the thoughts and spirit so these at least preserved evermore with godly blessings (*Rig-Veda* 7:66), Varuna and Mitra loudly move forth to appear as a highborn pair with extraordinary wisdom. With excellence, they perform noble actions (dharma) and thereby become great lords. As able, dexterous, and honest, Dakṣa, the son of the creator Lord Brahma, a great king, with Varuna and Mitra as the guardians, comes to serve with thoughts and songs of praise to invoke the sinless and most noble trinity of Mitra, Aryaman, and Bhaga, who send forth the powers of the goddess Savitar from the heavenly region to serve the newly created world (Virāj), where they make a home and guard the bounteous creations. These creations offer oblations as gifts and, with self-governing proclamations, become the worshippers of the mother of creation, Aditi. To fulfill their obligatory responsibility (karma), they continue to serve this vast domain as kings.

The great ensign the sun continues to rise along with Mitra and Varuna, while the noble Aryaman, the righteous warrior, slays his foes and gains wealth such as buried gold. With divine songs, they prevent any unmolested power to rise and gain mighty powers. The powerful trinity, with their sacrifices, appear as noble manifested embodiments (Brahmans) who come to replace the noble Aryaman through gaining the eternal law (Varuna) and, by acquiring royal powers, replace eternal love (Mitra). The noble Brahmans jointly serve Indra and Agni and light up the sky, while the heavenly power Sūrya, through the great ensign the sun, serves the new creations, humanity, through their tongues, transforming their minds with eternal wisdom. Using the undefined power of vibration, human beings produce speech, and through such gathering of their thoughts, their brains regulated. With the undefined power of vision, humans, through their eyes, can visualize all the mighty powers of causation regulating each of the manifested mortal embodiments (Brahmans). Through the power of unconditional sacrifice (dharma), the Brahmans surpass even the powers of Aryaman, who uses karma to rule the trinity of Varuna, Mitra, and Aryaman.

Serving as righteous warriors, Kshatriyas come to win the holy ground, a dominion established by defining infinite space and time, which expressed in years, months, days, and nights. With their sacrifices, they gain what no one else can gain. Even today, the manifested true mortal embodiments, the Brahmans, with the rising of the great ensign the sun, and by reciting hymns to worship the trinity of Varuna, Mitra, and Aryaman, enforce the law of the trinity and obey the law of eternal truth, thus strengthening the laws of birth. Even the terrible haters of that which is false happily come to offer the best defense to living things that no longer face an unfluctuating rising slope to heaven. At first sight, they attract the prodigy who will die, and with swift-flying horse Etaśa, as a celestial power, they come to accept death, preparing for it by keeping their eyes open, watching those with eyes mounted on each side of their heads, watching both fixed and moving things equally across the whole breadth of the region.

In his carriage, Sūrya brings light, wealth, and happiness. With bright eyes, the ordained witness the rising of one hundred autumns. Alive with infallible wisdom, Brahmans express the splendid union of Varuna and Mitra. With a draft of mythical juice (soma), the laws of heaven ordained, nearly void of guile, pressed with the powers of Varuna and Mitra to produce the mystical drink amrit.

According to *Rig-Veda* 7:67, with a holy heart, the Brahmans, offering oblations and singing forth with praises, given the power of persuasion at birth. As prophets, they deliver prophecies based upon their direct communication with the mighty ones (divinities, deities, and demigods). Such messages typically involve inspiration, interpretation, and revelation of the divine will concerning the betterment of the manifested social world. All known ancient prophets, according to tradition, deliver prophecies that they use to awaken desire among ruling powers such as the prince who serves as the divine envoy. Recognizing such persuasive power, the twin demigod Aśvins come to serve as the offspring of the bright power the sun, coming to serve humanity by teaching them to follow the laws of both karma and dharma. With brightened powers (solar flares), they enkindle other eternal flames and remove any apparent darkness that limits karma and dharma and prevents them from flourishing. As persuasive divine envoys, the twin Aśvins serve as demigods who appear in the sky like constellations of stars in the east, arriving with a banner in the sky as the two heavenly daughters, morning (dawn) and evening (dusk). Eloquent, both produce sounds like hymns. They become accustomed to traveling paths, but their appearance still surprises even the most skillful holy priest. As lovers of sweetness, they both arrive like a vigorous horse, as suppliants seeking libations, which they bear well, even after they drink enough pressed soma. As ancient powers, the Aśvins move forth to fulfill any desire for riches, never becoming exhausted by fulfilling such requests. In combat, the demigod Aśvins vouchsafe by enhancing the inner spirit with vigor. They never fail in making these enhanced spirits available to children and to their descendants, who wait upon them at the banquet. They become wealthy as they serve with the lovers of sweetness, and they bring treasure to establish friendships, coming to serve as envoys. They approach the embodiments with an offering of an anger-free spirit, and they enjoy offering oblation to all, with one intention, namely, to move swiftly like the seven rivers, as the daughter of Sūrya, yoked with strong steeds, keeps moving, driven by divine powers (divine will). With their bounty, the Aśvins never weary, and while speeding forward, exhaustless, they inspire with gifts of riches. They form friendships with princes and other noble-natured souls, to combine their animals as a form of wealth and, with other kinds of wealth, help all sorts of living things. As youthful twins, they come upon hearing the divine invocation, which imbues them with the power to establish their home in a good place where food is abundant, where their wealth vouchsafed, and where they are honored as nobles worthy of preserved evermore with godly blessings.

According to *Rig-Veda* 7:68, the demigods, persuasive, appearing as radiant noble horses, manifest as wonderworkers and accepted as oath deities (Nāsatyas). With hymns, they enjoy offering oblations when greeting others. They prepare by pressing the gladdening mythical juice (soma), which they partake of and then offer to others, along with swift thoughts, to bring out brilliance like eternal wealth. They come with the heavenly power Sūrya to support the sun, which brings light across the regions. They arrive even before the goddess Atri, offering wondrous nourishment, which given to store up and which they bring out only for those who are dear to them, and this as a favor. At the break of day, while noble souls are awaking with their thoughts, the Aśvins offer the soma to those who are ready to extol them with fair hymns, like the singer serving the cow so she may keep feeding her calf.

As wonderworkers, the Nāsatyas accepted with their golden chariot, which drawn by vigorous horses (*Rig-Veda* 7:69). Yoked, with bright fellies, fully supported by the god-adoring powers (divine will), they seated with the godly power (the trinity) that extends everywhere, covering all five tribes of civilization, representing fivefold noble souls. They extol like singers, singing fair hymns among themselves, especially when the path bends and they follow along with their horses, representing divine will. They drink from a cup filled with sweet juice, and they appear as a wondrous pair who at night turn gray and, in the morning, turn bright like the virgin aid daughter of Sūrya. They visit splendorous places and, through the eternal flame, provide a true altruistic sacrifice without any attachment (*dakshina*), which transforms the individual lives of the wonder working Nāsatyas, changing them into most pious souls. They learn to capitalize on the rays of light within their bodies, which masked, and come to dwell offering personal altruistic sacrifices (*dakshina*). By investing in the blessing of peace, they turn within wild thirsty cattle as libations and, with pious immanence, bring inner illumination. Serving as pious heroes, they appear in places. Worshipping with hymns, singing divine songs, they attain libations. Even when they are during the ocean, abandoned, uninjured, they appear as Bhujyu, the son of Tugra, who, as the ferocious fire, an element of nature, saved from the rising waters, unfading, undaunted, performing deeds of wonder. The Nāsatyas come to appear under the sign of Scorpio to invoke those who are returning home, where they surrounded with food, vouchsafed with wealth, and preserved evermore with blessings, yet serve as honored noble souls. The wonder working Nāsatyas, rich in all blessings, as young twin Aśvins, establish a place for themselves amid the manifested fertile ground (Virāj), which filled with sickness brought on by having material possessions.

## WONDERWORKERS

According to *Rig-Veda* 7:70, supernatural wonderworkers appear as a strong stallion with a fair backing. Able to stand, with most delightful eulogies, they come with warm bodies, ready to receive an offer to drink of the pure water that brought from the seas and rivers. This yoke, well matched, like shining stallions, using their dwellings to run along with the streams, following the heavenly waters, serve the ground and cover fields. They come to rest upon the summit of the mountain, from where they bring food, along with oblation, by themselves. With delight, they transfer water to others who are best suited, such as plants and manifested holy spirits, those serving well like royal poets, as seven rishis. Abundantly enriched with treasures, they look back with delight upon the former generations. With their hearts and with prayers, they serve as sanctified spirits (rishis) as they fulfill the hearts' desires of the manifested creations, desiring to gift them with the most delightful favor. This all comes in the form of a true sacrifice that offered as part of their persuasive power (*dakshina*), along with oblations, duly uttered with prayers, all coming from the heart of the noble soul Vasiṣṭha as a favor to such steers that addressed in the form of nigh, to preserve them evermore with blessings. At night, the wonderworker Nāsatyas, with clairvoyance, retire from serving the two sisters, morning (dawn) and evening (dusk). On their red pathway, as wonderworkers with clairvoyance, they invoke steeds and cattle, bearing rich treasure within their embodiments, like the ancient Aśvins, keeping themselves far from evil arrows both during the day and at night.

According to *Rig-Veda* 7:71, the mortal living embodiments always serve day and night, presenting as lovers of sweetness to keep their distance from penury. To preserve themselves as strong horses, Nāsatyas always seek bliss as they brought to serve the chariot. At the earliest flush of morning, they yoked as coursers to drive their carriage with reins of light, laden with treasure. The same chariot that princes use to transport the seated trinity is the one they fill, apprehensive at daylight, with riches. The Nāsatyas bring all the food needed to feed and set free the sage Cyavāna, who from the weakness of old age uses the fleet of coursers called Pedu. They rescued from distress and darkness by Mother Aditi, and by being set free from bondage, they endow King Jāhuṣa with the freedom to express his thoughts and sing songs. Just like steers, with vibrations they come to experience the power of music in the form of songs to invoke noble thoughts. Further, serving as the demigod Nāsatyas, dazzling, they bring abundant wealth that can harnessed steeds and cattle.

According to *Rig-Veda* 7:72, the Nāsatyas, with laudations, follow those who, with a shining light, bring a most delightful beauty to manifest among noble souls, serving as godly associates who follow laws and use their clairvoyance to serve as wonderworkers. They always remind others of their ancestral friends who serve as the common links among all. Further, through vibrations and songs of praise, in the mornings they awaken and invite those who long to know all about the genesis of earth and heaven. Wonderworker Nāsatyas called upon to serve the manifested noble soul, beginning at the break of dawn, which brings light to the poets to offer their devotions. The goddess Savitar, aloft in heavenly splendor, sends for Agni to bring the eternal flame. Savitar and Agni, singing songs of praise, invite the wonderworking Nāsatyas from the west, along with the twin demigod Aśvins, to come from their heavenly loft to the region below the sky. They bring wealth from all sides to serve the established human beings represented as the five tribes, whom they preserve evermore with their divine blessings.

According to *Rig-Veda* 7:73, once they have surpassed the limit of darkness, the Nāsatyas worship the immortal invisible universal soul (God), singing their songs of praise to invoke the twin Aśvins, who are far-reaching and born of great old age. The Nāsatyas, immortal wonderworkers serving as earthly priests, offer worship and sacrifice to those seated near enough to taste the pleasant mythical juice. They both make sacrifices to the ultimate universal soul (God), but they themselves choose whom to worship and whether to accept hymns to follow the divine course. Obeying as the appointed servant, Vasiṣṭha sings loudly to rouse all worshippers. These two, as priests, virtually come unto people, united, demon-slaying, mighty-handed, with mythical juice that exhilarates and brings fortune. From the west, the Nāsatyas and Aśvins appear, also bringing wealth from below and above to serve the five tribes and preserve them evermore with blessings from the ultimate universal soul (God).

According to *Rig-Veda* 7:74, at the break day the heavenly priests the Aśvins who with sacrifices invoke the ultimate universal soul (God), rich in power and might. They visit all heroes, house by house, to bestow wonderful nourishment received from the godly powers. As they drive, singing sweet songs, their carriage moves along, filled with savory drink. They bring soma to drink with the powerful essence meath, drawn forth with milk. Mighty, rich in genuine wealth, which injures, they bring physical strength like the horses that convey them in rapid flight down to the worshippers' abode. With speedy coursers, the heroes come with godly powers, well inclined toward the princes who, as the heavenly twin Aśvins, in pursuit of food, provide lasting glory to the liberal earthly lords (Nāsatyas) who provide shelter to the earthly creations, whom they lead, driving their carriage, offending none, serving as the guardians. Also, through their own might, the heroes grow strong and dwell in safe and happy homes.

According to *Rig-Veda* 7:75, the primordial force, Shakti, born with the creation of heaven and earth, serving through the supreme powers of causation the ferocious fire, as Agni, as ordained by the divine covenant, generates the eternal flame before she appears on earth to manifest within the fertile ground (Virāj). Shakti transforms to appear as the best of the ancient envoy Aṅgirases, who uncover all those who are fiendish and hateful by exposing their hidden positions and following in darkness the best pathways, those that rarely traveled by others. With great blessedness, Shakti rises with the morning light and, during the day, brings fortune and promotes that all living things perform the actions that support karma and dharma. Shakti vouchsafes manifold mortal lives through bringing splendid riches. She is famous among mortals, both male and female. Such lovely power in the morning seen as an everlasting splendor. The dawn, in bright colors, approaches in all regions where holy rites and holy worship are performed. The dawn, like a chariot, comes from far away, all yoked to visit the manifested material world, Virāj, where the five tribes have already settled.

The morning light (dawn) looked upon as the daughter of heaven who represents the Imperial Woman, wondrously opulent, who rules all wealth and treasure and is rich in spoils. She is the spouse of the heavenly power Sūrya. All youthful consumers, seers, and lauded priests eulogize this Imperial Woman, worshipper her as she brings a rich shine, representing the beginning of life, which brings out refulgence. Like variously color steeds, including red steeds, the Imperial Woman and Sūrya carry the magnificent morning light with another lovely carriage, the sun, which appears as the Fair One that brings rich treasure to their most faithful servants, who represent that which is true with the truth, that which is mighty with mightiness, and those who are gods with goddesses with the holy heavenly body that can break down strong fences to allow cattle and other milk-bearing creatures to come lowing and greet the ordained morning light. In this way, wealth brought to cattle, horses, and heroes, which they enjoy immensely. The Fair One comes to protect the sacred grass from reproach and to preserve it evermore with blessings.

## MYSTIC SOUL

According to *Rig-Veda* 7:76, Savitar, as protector of all living beings, from on high sends the immortal light to support all humankind, who specifically designed with a mystic soul. This mystic soul first passes through the divine eye, and then goes through different zones of the dynamic universe before it becomes apparent on the surface as the early morning light (dawn), which as a band spread over the holy world (Virāj). By setting an innocuous course, it travels to bring along the divine wish, which becomes a godly wish (divine will) ready to empower and support Mother Nature (Vasu) by setting its flag in the east, from where, when it is ready, it rises as the morning light. The light displays itself over the housetops, bringing truth, and rises as direct light from the sun, bringing with it eternal love and kindness (Mitra) to behold the eternal, so no one will reject the companionship established by the ancient sages in the form of a banquet to share the eternal law. From here, the fathers find darkness, which needs removed by the creation of illumination. Morning starts by the fathers meeting in the same enclosure, all striving not as minds, but joining with another as one mind, to injure no one and never break the eternal decrees. Even in rivalry, Mother Nature (Vasu) brings out the mystic soul Vasiṣṭha, extolled, blessed, and ordained to awake early every morning with loud sounds to serve the king of the animal kingdom and the queen of humanity. Other living things strengthened to share the shine by setting the banquet with the morning for all the highborn. This brings a bounty of sweet charm, which with soft vibrations produces a sound that, flushing, turns into hymns, all sung to invoke the noble souls who give riches, bring fame to distant places, and preserve evermore with blessings.

According to *Rig-Veda* 7:77, like a youthful woman, the morning comes and stirs into motion every living creature, and then comes to support all with the eternal fire, which manifests as fuel to feed mortals. This fuel serves as an inner light that, like the eternal flame, chases away the inner darkness among mortals and replaces ignorance with knowledge. After receiving knowledge, the mortal life given both inner light and external light to create full illumination. This light spreads far, increasing in brightness. In their white shining robes, embodiments produce beams of light in a lovely golden color that, like the mother, bring light to their own eyes and the eyes of those in other kingdoms. The light guides every day, and mortal embodiments come to appreciate the powers of auspicious the inner light, which just like Lady Dawn causes them to look like white doves and serve as fair coursers. It helps them to distinguish the light shining among them as they all travel around the world with this wondrous treasure called early morning light. They draw near to the paragon, far away from foemen, where they are prepared a wide pasture, free from danger.

According to *Rig-Veda* 7:78, the noble soul Vasiṣṭha drives away those who hate riches, pouring out in opulent bounty to welcome the auspicious morning light. Lady Dawn comes along with spiritual singers to send forth excellent beams of light that lengthen the days and grant food and other precious things to cultivate friendship. She brings chariots filled with bounty, pulled by cattle and horses. She comes along with a newborn as the awe-inspiring daughter of heaven who appears as the sacred cow (Kamadhenu), which comes to serve as the goddess of morning and evening light. Through hymns ordained by Lady Dawn (Uṣas), with the noble soul Vasiṣṭha, humanity served with vast and glorious sublime refulgent light that enriches all. With Uṣas, the light approaches with glory, ordaining parts both high and low with its sublime refulgence. It proceeds by bringing wealth that makes all happy and by using eternal flame that enkindles the eternal powers to come loudly singing their greetings. With chanting, like priests, they offer splendor to approach darkness and drive evil far away, moving from the east to the west. The bringing morning light and its luster joins with the rising splendor (the sun) to bring forth the eternal flame, Agni, who provides heat and warmth and sends detested cold and darkness far away. As one, Agni and Uṣas look upon the dawn as it breaks and move away to let the creations harness themselves, mounted to the carriage that drawn onward, well yoked with horses. Inspired, with loving thoughts, they greet other all awakened wealthy nobles with morning light, showing the fruits of their labor, with godly blessings evermore.

According to *Rig-Veda* 7:79, by sending out its gleam, the splendorous sun casts its bright rays upon the rousing land where the five mortal tribes have settled, filling everything in sight, reaching to the far limits of the sky and thus opening wide the fields of the new material world (Virāj) located between earth and heaven. The splendorous sun, as beautiful as the heavenly bull, with an array of light, comes close to the tribes, with the goddess Savitar, who spreads her arms and invites the celestial power Indra to come and distribute welfare among a select few. The best of the Aṅgirases, through the powers of Agni, bring treasures to bestow upon pious nature, where mortals, by using the powers of splendor (the sun), bellowing like bulls at the earliest light (Uṣas), spread out the ample bounty. Those who sing their praises speed up, settling among the mountain's portals, thus impelling every supreme power of causation to grant bounty by sending charm and pleasant voices.

According to *Rig-Veda* 7:80, the first awakened mystic souls, such as the priest Vasiṣṭha, with their songs and praises, welcome the goddess of light, Uṣas. Now jointly moving into surrounding regions, Vasiṣṭha and Uṣas make apparent to all existing creatures the power of the morning light (dawn), which spreads everywhere, bringing fresh life to all that hidden in darkness. With newborn luster, they waken the youthful who, unrestrained, come forward to appear with the sun, and with Agni and Indra, who generate new thoughts. With a blessed shine, they all come to live forever, helping the cattle and horses, and heroes who come streaming with abundance, pouring out opulence.

According to *Rig-Veda* 7:81, by removing the mighty gloom, the ascending light, coming from the ordained refulgent star, pours down its own beams. At all times sharing the light from the splendorous sun, the goddess Uṣas welcomed as the daughter of the sky who, as a Bounteous

One, brings all whatever they may long for and offers them health and wealth. Thus, Uṣas brings boundless joy to the world, accompanied by the heavenly powers serving as the sacred cow Kamadhenu, the daughter of heaven, who is behind all actions and activities, operating at all times, remaining unknown and unseen. This makes everybody yearn to be their own dealer of wealth, like a son who brings from afar a wondrous bounty to his mother as a source of nourishment for mortals to enjoy. Not knowing that the mother knows all about such opulence, filled with immortal fame and strength, that in herds of cattle creates a prince who promptly gives to others the similarly wealthy Lady of Sweetness without restraint to drive the foes away.

According to *Rig-Veda* 7:82, Indra and the divine power Varuna jointly subdue the infighting between the noble Ādityas and the evil Asuras. With his divine powers, Varuna, using rites, subdues the Asuras and, with Indra, spiritually subdue the Ādityas, thereby creating a balancing force by establishing two forms of rulers, monarchical and autocratic, who come to serve the loftiest region. Both powers navigated by the powers of the wind (Vayu), with might and strength that pierces through solid mountains and creates cascades of floods. The wind (Vayu) created by the heavenly power (Rudra) and fully supported by the heavenly body (Sūrya) who brings forth the splendorous heavenly body the sun. The splendorous sun cheerfully produces the vibrations that, through songs of praise, generate motion, thus giving birth to mythical power. This in turn places drafts into dry streambeds that, when filled, overflow with water. In battles and other fights, the sun ministers as priests, serving as the twofold power of Lord Indra and Varuna. All manifested bodies kneel to pray; all promptly hear the voices of the singers and poets who invoke spiritual powers among all mortal creatures, rapidly filling the material world (Virāj). Supported by the godly power Mitra, the world, unsurpassed in its might, brings peace and tranquility to those who have been waiting to overcome the awful problems created by the Maruts, the demigods renowned as the cosmic hosts serving Virāj. As high heavenly powers, Varuna and Indra bring along their preeminent shine to serve the manifested twin horses, the Aśvins, as the demigods who measure and determine each individual need and offer the proper amount of might. As one, Varuna overpowers the destructive enemy while Indra goes farther along with people to remove trouble and any misfortune and, by serving through the demigod Aśvins, ensure no woe from any side may assail the other. With such divine protection and invocation bestowed upon the heroes, Indra and Varuna offer kinship and friendship, along with favoring grace.

After the battle, Indra and Varuna continue to serve as champions, providing the heroes with needed strength, serving the two opposing bands. They shine to invoke among those who are fighting blessing for their offspring and progeny. All powers—Indra, Varuna, Mitra, and Aryaman—come to vouchsafe the glorious ones by providing them with shelter, supported by the beneficent light and the godly mother Aditi, with songs of praise provided and supported by godly desire (divine will), which strengthens the law.

## GODLY MOTHER

According to *Rig-Veda* 7:83, all the famous females who pour out milk and serve the godly mother Aditi make the males strong and thereby celebrated. Serving as manifested mother and father, represented as the demigods serving as twin horses, the Aśvins, which yoked, pull their embodiments like a carriage, passing through the newly created world (Virāj). At all times, the unified Varuna and Mitra best serve them, appearing as the sun and moon, regulated by the everlasting law observed by pious poets. While singing sacred songs, they produce soma to make their bodies self-luminous. They engage in the pressing of special plants to produce purified soma, ready three times a day: morning, afternoon, and evening. Through the process of procreation, the godly powers Varuna, Mitra, Aryaman, and Indra create offspring from outer space, the cosmic hosts (Maruts), by giving birth through cosmic vapor in the form of clouds. The Maruts appear as sprinkled water and rewarded with rain for every liberal sacrifice made to please the individual living spirit (Atman). With the merits of their worship, as youths, they work hard for days and nights to produce extraordinary gifts to honor the immortal living spirit (Atman) residing within mortal embodiments such as holy priests. With glory, they fulfill the quest and, as self-liberated catalysts, are honored as the sons of dualism (*Dyatis*) who strive on their own and come to join with the demigods serving as a band of cosmic hosts, the Maruts.

According to *Rig-Veda* 7:84, self-liberated, the sons of dualism welcome the sons of the godly mother Aditi, coming with Indra to offer gifts and homage, to return by holding in their hands the eternal flame. They fed to bring out their corpulence, and they transform each lick of the eternal flame into individual embodiments, into various suitable forms ready to serve the self-liberated kings, including the ruler of the evil power Dāsa, who quickens and builds a high dominion that promotes corporeal souls (Asuras) to serve as a greedy force. The Asuras cultivate a form of bond that twisted and tied like a rope or cord; far from the eternal law (Varuna), they still find a spacious room wherein to dwell, where they make sacrifices and form an assembly among themselves. After all, accepted, such ruling (Asuras) pray with passion to possess the riches that bring them further success. The power of eternal law, Varuna, with blessings from Indra, agrees to vouchsafe the places where they store their riches such as food and other treasure. The noble Ādityas, as banishers of falsehood, along with heroes, comes to serve the corporeal power with material wealth, boundless. Singing, they attend the banquet where evermore riches and wealth preserved to reach Varuna and Indra to seek their blessing, but with a strong urge to win over the Asuras and their offspring.

According to *Rig-Veda* 7:85, single harmless hymns, Varuna and Indra, accompanied by the morning light, emerge from heaven, shining, to offer corporeal power to both the Asuras and the Ādityas, who serve as their hosts and who welcome all through invocation with godly emulation. Sitting in their seats, Indra and Varuna, both self-lucid, bring heavenly waters, holding one separate from the other. In every quarter, they shoot their arrows to smite those foemen who either fall in the fight or fall on their own swords, defenseless. Like the wise priest skilled in eternal law, Varuna, they provided with a long sermon as one of the sacred gifts and, providing aid to those serving as noble souls, promote welfare among all with food.

According to *Rig-Veda* 7:86, with song and prayer, both Varuna and Indra strongly urge their sons and offspring to win and earn their own godly banquet filled with rich food. Evermore preserving with their blessings, and through their great wisdom, they go to the creatures who live in the spacious new world (Virāj). From the new world, the mighty ones, high in the sky, urge their sons to create motion like that which set like the ancient stellar bodies into motion, bringing inner illumination even before the external light spreads across the ground. Through such ancient stellar bodies, the planetary systems, the sons all commune and follow the eternal law (Varuna). Using their own minds and hearts, they are welcome to stay as united. They can receive and accept divine gifts, never angering, as they calmly look upon all to find graciousness among them. With pleasure, they question and seek advice from wise men, that is, priests and sages, in reference to any sinful act that has been performed to annoy the eternal law (Varuna), or any unfavorable action or transgression committed against the chief of eternal law that could lead to the slaying of a friend, or to the harming of anyone else. Unconquerable, they sing songs of praise to worship Indra. They even ask to free those from sins that were committed by their ancestors and that have offended them, like a thief who feeds the cow and steals the calf. Once they are freed, they come to serve like the noble soul Vasiṣṭha. They do not betray, do not engage in any thoughtless seduction, and do not create ill will, not even through evil activities such as gambling, antagonism, or getting drunk and losing their senses. As learned old man, they do not lead astray anyone who is younger, if only by ignoring them or falling asleep, knowing that any malicious act not excused. Those who serve as slaves and perform bounteous actions, pleasing the easily angered powers, become free from sin and receive gentleness and simple wisdom. This guides them to riches, and with laudation from Varuna, they brought close to, and jointly help to serve, his spirit.

According to *Rig-Veda* 7:87, the lord of eternal law, Varuna, cuts a pathway that leads to the heavenly power Sūrya, only allowing it to follow the pathway established by the sun, which follows the rivers and leads them onward to create floodwaters. In order make the waters race like chargers, Varuna creates great channels in the riverbeds. These channels follow the soft wind, which creates breath and, when it is blowing hard, makes a sound when passing through the region like that of a wild beast that seeks food in pastures. Traveling within the two dignified stratums—earth below and heaven above—the ruler of eternal law, Varuna, comes to serve both regions like a spy sent forth with the task of surveying the two halves of the world and keeping both well shaped to serve those who are holy and wise. With noble powers, well skilled in sacrifices, and prudently offering songs of praise, the noble powers understand that the eternal law, Varuna, seeks them out by calling the names of those who serve three times a day (morning, afternoon, and night). Seven days a week, they speak with the sapient powers, such as the Holy Mother, who knows where the eternal law (Varuna) resides. They keep Varuna's whereabouts a secret and teach all creations to speak about and serve all three heavenly regions, including the newly manifested world (Virāj), which are all supported by three pillars that rest on the lower stratum forming the earthly region. These three pillars provide support to the sixfold order: the four horizontal directions (north, south, east, and west) and the two connecting heavens above and earth below.

Varuna comes from heaven supported by a golden swing that covers the ground like a rainbow in its glory. The wise king Varuna, from heaven, sinks into the holy river, creating colors that appear as a strong wild mythical creature, Chiron, who rules from the depths. These wise kings, as the controllers of the manifested world, dispense a great power that regulated by all ordinances and evermore preserved with blessings from the godly mother Aditi.

According to *Rig-Veda* 7:88, the bright and most delightful holy priest Vasiṣṭha, as the bounteous giver, comes to worship the wise king Varuna with hymns, and receives the lofty inner flame from Agni, who appears as the heavenly bull that provides physical power laden with brilliance. With one thousand treasures, the eternal law, Varuna, evinces the true appearance of the ferocious fire (Agni) serving as the heavenly power that represents the planetary system. Serving in splendor, the sun, with its true powers, removes darkness by bringing light. The noble priest Vasiṣṭha can see the beauty that, by way of the union of Varuna and Agni, brings out longing, like a boat into the midst of the ocean riding over the waves. Happily swinging on a swing, the noble priest Vasiṣṭha appears within a manifested physical embodiment and placed with Varuna. With skillful power, Varuna transforms Vasiṣṭha into a widely acknowledged spiritual mystic power to serve as a clairvoyant rishi. With heaven and earth broadening by way of the lengthening morning light, these noble seers (rishi) come show the manifested sages how to nurture their own embodiments as bright singers among living beings. With glorious eternal power, Varuna thus enters the lofty astral body and sets up one thousand gateways to provide shelter to the individual living spirit (Atman). This provides the living beings with fixed habitations, where they may abide with eternal love and come to serve as manifested sages. The godly mother Aditi, with her mighty power, unravels that which binds the physical body to the astral body and thus wins favor, which preserved evermore with blessings within one embodiment.

According to *Rig-Veda* 7:89, the mighty powers restrained by the eternal law (Varuna) from entering the astral body, until the skin of the physical body has fully developed and can stand fast, ready to subjected to fast-moving winds and thunder. With mercy, the mighty powers (divinities, deities, and demigods) first seek strength for the astral body, which, if it stumbles, goes astray. The mighty powers seek mercy from the heavenly father Sūrya, asking him to bring his bright and powerful might to spare those among the worshippers who are on a quest and find themselves standing among fjords, seeking mercy spared from the consequences of whatever offense they have committed against the heavenly host.

## GODLY FATHER

Ecstasy occurs when an individual physical embodiment has an experience outside its body. The conscious individual living spirit, through the powers of contemplation, within a physical embodiment comes to experience ecstasy through the astral body's coming to unite with the godly father. By temporalizing, the past (what has been), the future (that which has not yet materialized), and the present (today) merge to form a single entity: the godly father. This eliminates any boundaries established by time and space and thus allows the astral body to go beyond the manifested material world (Virāj). With an altered state of mind, first the physical consciousness, which characterizes external awareness, is greatly reduced, and then internal mental awareness overpowers it; spiritual power accompanied with emotion creates a euphoria that allows the astral body to pass through the individual mind with the power of supreme knowledge (bodhi) to go beyond the vision that regards manifested spheres of existence as epochs (yugas).

According to *Rig-Veda* 7:90, such experience usually lasts for a brief time; however, in cases, the experience might last for several days and sometimes might even recur many times during one's lifetime. In a state of ecstasy, the manifested mortal embodiment appears as blessed with opulence, offering godly sacrifice to Dhisana. The union of the five great elements of nature, along with the three stellar bodies—the sun, the moon, and the constellations—brings ecstasy, generating eternal affluence enough for all aspects of the powers of causation regulating the dynamic universe. The mortal embodiments blessed with the highest knowledge enhanced to go farther and cultivate intuitive power (bodhi), which allows them to reach a state where they acquire the mythical juice soma through meditation. Further, through contemplation, they transform the mythical juice into mystical fluid (amrit), which runs through the glands of their bodies, just like the stirring of milk, where one first separates the butter and processes it to produce clarified butter (*ghirta*). An individual embodiment, after experiencing enlightenment, comes to experience the release of eternal radiant treasure. The demigod Aśvins, as a team of horses, learn to fly in the sky and, at dawn, bring said eternal radiant treasure, which generates experiences like those of the cosmic hosts (Maruts) serving as demigods who experience the powers of splendor, such as the sun, the moon, and the constellations of stars, creating illumination. This unveils the spiritual paths that, like streams, flowing into rivers. With an expanded mind and its infinite abilities, an individual embodiment filled with ultimate wisdom and, through the astral body, comes to comprehend the presence of the inner living spirit (Atman). With natural insight, Atman starts to manifest through the inner voice (Vata). This brings a special form of prosperity, giving the individual the ability to make a personal sacrifice to serve the goddess of prosperity and abundance and the guardian of the sacred fire, Dhisana. The sovereign pair of heavenly powers, Varuna and Mitra, who bring brilliance, appear as heavenly light as the divine gift of milk carried to the females. They also bring golden treasures to distribute among males, making them the mighty rulers who come to settle on the ground and serve creation by removing the prevailing ignorance.

According to *Rig-Veda* 7:91, the one who offers personal sacrifice to Dhisana will face battles within the new world, where enlightened souls enforce morality and righteousness. Indra works with the heavenly power Rudra, who regulates the air (Vayu), to bring the life force (prana), which brings heavenly seeds of prosperity and embryos to plant within honorable heroes. Such heroes come to fulfill their commitment with fair laudation, exerting all their power to preserve with blessings and give birth to humanity, who seek heroes only for the fame that brings inner peace and tranquility. The bounteous giver Vasiṣṭha travels like a courser, preaching to dispel ignorance, and if he cannot succeed or cannot help others, accepting it is not anybody else's fault, he considers it his own fault. Serving with inner peace, he, fully understanding the powers of inner peace, with adoration uses the eternal force, which not only increases power but also helps to overpower the demonic forces.

Those who are committed to seeking inner peace come to understand the mythical power that externally produced among heavenly bodies, including asteroids, comets, and meteors, which travel through the heavenly region as compressed stones. They generate vibrations as they come along with direct rays from the infallible heavenly guardian Sūrya. They also produce physical vigor, filled within thunder, bringing biological immortal power (Vata). By the time they arrive on the ground, they trapped within rocks, minerals, plants, and other kinds of creations. Thus, along with the immortal living spirit from the heavenly region, they, as eager envoys, acquire the material world and each morning practice invoking the immortal living spirit (Atman) to reside within their individual mortal embodiments. They continue to serve throughout the day and for months, serving from autumn to autumn to preserve the immortal living spirit.

The unified Varuna and Mitra continue providing the noble souls with eternal power to keep them safe from evil powers. Individual embodiments, singing hymns, offer praises to implore all kind of favors, continuing to seek support from Indra and Vayu. The united Indra and Vayu continuously renew their well-being, as the wise, bright arrangers, with undivided faith, continue to seek absolute truth. They come to form a friendship with the unified Varuna and Mitra who, as a team, support other living beings, helping them to live long lives. They continue to help through such a fellowship by following the divine covenant, which provides them with inner contentment.

Indra brings rich food and abundant treasures to allow such embodiments to proceed focusing upon establishing a single mind that regulates the individual breath (prana). This helps them to produce mythical juice (soma), which through the inner voice (Vata), transforms mystical fluid into pure nectar (amrit). This provides the embodiments with a far-reaching vision, supported by the team of Indra and Vayu. The flow of soma activates the inner voice (Vata), enables the amrit to pass through the body, the mind, and the subtle faculties comprised of hundred thousand nerves. The munificent team of Indra and Vayu attend individual embodiments and help them each cultivate a most gracious mind able to support the complex structure of the subtle faculties, which retain eternal wisdom and make known the absolute truth. Living beings such as coursers bring fame to all worshippers of Vasiṣṭha.

According to *Rig-Veda* 7:92, after drinking the mythical juice (soma) and experiencing the inner voice (Vata), the embodiments go through a process that makes them realize that the immortal universal soul (Paramatman) and its relationship to the individual living spirit (Atman) is one and only one. When offering holy rites through the union of Indra and Vayu, the embodiments come to comprehend each individual supreme power of causation regulating the universe. Individual embodiments, with undivided devotion, come to accept the demigods serving as the twin powers who, as a team, strike a balance between material power and spiritual affluence. As a gift to enjoy, and as a blessing, the Aśvins help the embodiments produce noble offspring. Through the process of encirclement, the Aśvins enhance their embodiments to become a part of the ruling powers, who as allies protect noble souls by smiting any hostile heroes, going into battle to conquer the foes and serve along with princes and kings.

According to *Rig-Veda* 7:93, the unified Indra and Agni come to serve as slayers of enemies, appearing with the twin demigod Aśvins, who accepted with pure laudation as they bring both material and spiritual wealth as a gift to build a domestic kingdom to support living things in producing noble offspring, also providing them with cattle and horses. As they grow together, the Aśvins gain in strength, as twins developing their vigor, and bestow ample riches upon the lord's pasture, both exceedingly mighty in power. Bestowing strength upon both the material world and the spiritual world, they remain fresh to last a long time and maintain their strength. They enter the assembly of singers singing hymns, seeking favor for their steeds, which used on a racecourse, with their jockeys being the unified Indra and Agni, whom all the singers call upon loudly with hymns. The twins seek favor from their protector and beg for riches to move into new bounteous regions. Armed with thunder from the unified Indra and Agni, they come to slay the foemen, and when arrayed, they seek to go against each other. As the two great hosts, with brightness, Indra and Agni meet them in a fierce encounter. Standing alongside the godless, they smite the godless, and with the support of freshly pressed soma provided by the mortal manifested powers, they show their loving-kindness. The ferocious fire of Agni invites the trinity of Mitra, Varuna, and Indra to kindle adoration to forgive whatever sins that may have been committed and thus remove all blemishes by ushering in the noble soul Aryaman, son of Aditi.

## GENDERLESS SOUL

According to *Rig-Veda* 7:94, to populate the material world (Virāj), the genderless soul split into male and female, separated by gender but both having created equal. Each gender shares basic knowledge, including knowledge of music, art, and intellect. Each part represented by the female trinity (Sarasvatī, Lakshmi, and Parvathi), who come to support the male trinity of Brahma, Vishnu, and Shiva. They established as each other's soul mates to create, maintain, and regulated by the cycle of encirclement or the process of regeneration, which allows them to grow and to enhance the material world, Virāj. The female trinity is responsible for the generation of vibrations that, through their association with water, work together to create combinations on the ground. Through separation and the pooling together of their resources, they create ponds, lakes, and oceans that participate in the creation of manifested living things, which further enhances the relationship. The union of the supreme gods Indra and Agni intensifies, their strength winning over the blessed noble souls with praise, producing sounds that heard and accepted to turn the noble souls into rulers. They granted favor and their hearts' desires and blessed to serve as soul mates, like Indra and Agni, the supreme heroes. The two gods make sure their devotees never experience any form of poverty, slander, or criticism. This sort of reverence soothes cravings by way of soft words or salient prayers accompanied by loudly sung holy hymns. The holy singers implore the twin demigod Aśvins to bring them success while serving as holy priests. They win all with eternal strength. All who are eager, with their songs, invoke the gods to turn earthly food into sacred food and thereby grant them success.

The supreme powers Indra and Agni, as a sacrifice, grant the holy singers a favor that permits them to conquer all others, including the wicked master. Now, at no time may an injurious hostile blow fall upon such mortal heroes, who provided with shelter by the supreme powers Indra and Agni. Whatever pure material wealth craved, such as gold or domesticated animals (e.g., cattle or steeds), provided by the supreme powers Indra and Agni, who further provide for the heroes. To obtain mythical juice (soma), they sing loud songs of worship, which serves as the best way to slay the foemen, and helps humanity to praise the gods with these delightful hymns. After slaying the wicked manifested souls with evil thoughts, or the demons with evil powers, such as serpents that can live in water or on the land, the holy singers not denied prosperity—or else slain with deadly darts.

Sarasvatī, the ruler of vibrations, brings a stream of pure water that runs from the mountains to the oceans. This free-flowing stream generates a momentary current to purify itself. As the ruler of vibrations, Sarasvatī wakens individual minds to cultivate their intellects and create all forms of thinking power. This helps to enhance the creatures prevailing within the great material world (Virāj). The ruler of vibrations, Sarasvatī, takes eternal wisdom from sources of reflective light such as the lunar mansion (the moon) and pours such light, along with rain, into the stream where the primary feminine deities, Sarasvatī, Lakshmi, and Parvathi, as counterparts of the male trinity Brahma, Vishnu, and Shiva, through their union, maintain essence (Self) in its purified form to attain a higher degree of self-knowledge.

According to *Rig-Veda* 7:95, water goddesses, represented as holy women, are friendly souls who attract male partners to establish the kingdom of Nahuṣa. They observe strong young male oxen that look for young cows to bring forth life together. Appearing as a fleet, their offspring evolve to become wealthy princes and princesses. As soul mates, they evolve to establish their kingdom under Nahuṣa. They deck their bodies and serve with sacrifice to honor the auspicious goddess Sarasvatī, who establishes them each in an enhanced mortal embodiment, which they reinforce themselves by following the laws of morality and righteousness.

According to *Rig-Veda* 7:96, this brings happiness among them. Serving as princes and princesses, they even get down on their knees to offer their reverence to the goddess Sarasvatī. They implore her to build a close-knit society and to give them her protection. With unbarred-doored shelters that serve as places of worship, they express their adoration and receive eternal wealth, including trees, which provide shelter to birds, animals, and other living things. Within the sacred order, the shelters bless their bodies, making them noble, and enlighten them through vibrations that turn most streams divine, as they sing the lofty songs as an offering with oblations to Sarasvatī. Furthermore, intensified hymns, full of strength, through vibrations, extend the power from the earth to the heavens. With support from Sarasvatī, this allows the princes and princesses to dwell among the five tribes (Purus) with the living spirit (Atman) as conscience manifested to appear as the cosmic self (Manu)—and they come to prevail throughout the material world (Virāj).

With manifested mortal embodiments providing a domicile to the individual immortal living spirit (Atman), these tribes come to dwell along the two stream banks, covering the ground with sacred grass provided by Sarasvatī. These tribes receive further support from demigods, the cosmic hosts (Maruts), who come from the esoteric region with the rays of the sun to serve as their friends. With plenteous help from the goddess

Sarasvatī, the tribes induct new chiefs, who helped the divine power (divine will) to send forth good luck and riches to deliver eternal power to support the progeny. At the time of birth, the noble Ādityas cause the female breast to swell with beauty, filled with milk, and grant the mortal physical embodiment with a perishable embryo, the astral body holding the immortal living spirit (Atman). To the new mortal embodiment, the noble Ādityas provide with their sacrifice an extended life span to the mortal embodiments. The embryo forms an inward bond with the physical body and establishes a link to connect it with the individual living spirit (Atman), which contained within the perishable embryo. As the embryos develop such a bondage, they receive additional protection from the higher demigods, namely, the cosmic hosts (Maruts). They also receive support from the celestial demigods the twin Aśvins, who come to serve as the bandagers. They also receive support from the supreme powers Mitra and Varuna, who come to heal any wound and aid the living spirit (Atman) in finding a proper physical dwelling to call its home, somewhere within the external physical body, the internal subtle body, or the perishable astral body, all of which are guarded by the trinity of Sarasvatī, Lakshmi, and Parvathi and surrounded by the unthreatened cosmic hosts (Maruts), who understand the prevailing situation and who provide extended life to the perishable astral body, the semi manifested subtle body, and the fully manifested physical body.

To protect the affiliation of the perishable astral body with its mortal physical body, the trinity of Aryaman, Mitra, and Varuna come to prevent the astral body from expiring and graciously provide it with a longer life by way of the physical body. The perishable astral body continues to reside with the immortal living spirit (Atman), which worshipped and honored by the ancient trinity of Ādityas, Varuna, and Mitra. The perishable astral body, by following the guidelines, experiences no sorrow and no harm, cultivating wings that spread and thus learning to fly like birds. Without a physical embodiment, the astral body even comes to serve as a semi manifested embodiment (archangel), which, unencumbered, flies from shelter to shelter within the ethereal region, where a perishable astral body may live a longer time within the manifested physical body. Like the ancient mystic souls, the Ādityas, the semi manifested body serves the perishable astral body living within the manifested body. Avoiding hostile areas, it serves the living being and arrives on a timely basis. Whosoever as a living being acquires such wholesome eternal treasure gains an extremely high level of wisdom, attains freedom from the shackles of material world, and lives long, free from sorrows.

The immortal living spirit (Atman) residing within the perishable astral body further protected by the individual physical embodiment serving as its guard. With grace, the noble Ādityas serve the mortal embodiment and save it from sinking, fainting, or losing all that it honestly acquires in the form of wealth and wisdom. Such manifested mortal bodies, no longer fierce or angry, experience no soreness or distress. They receive help from the noble Ādityas, who originally placed with the astral body to develop a link with the physical embodiment that provided the shelter needed to help the astral body before it finds a new resting place. Manifested embodiments, supported by noble souls, make personal sacrifices to gain support to help other astral bodies find a nice shelter or resting place. Manifested noble souls, including the astral body, the subtle faculties, and the physical body, all seek protection and fight to attain extended life within the material world (Virāj). They guard themselves against coming offenders and accompanied by both light and heavy powers to influence and control.

Manifested noble bodies, such as the mother of wealth, Aditi, come along with the trinity of Mitra, Aryaman, and Varuna to defend and guard such mortal embodiments by placing their dwellings in an auspicious place that is free from malady. The trinity provides the manifested noble bodies with triply strong powers to secure their fortunes and with an extended life, always supporting the subtle faculties and the mortal physical embodiment. The ancient supreme powers Indra and Agni look upon the newer noble powers, the Ādityas, and if needed come down from the banks of heaven to guide the manifested mortal embodiments. They find it pleasant to watch the manifested embodiments led like one horse after another, easily making their passage, which makes it difficult for demons to approach them. Serving as noble friends, Indra and Agni help each noble embodiment to find another, also showing them how to transform from living beings to cultivate a human body by developing friendship and trust, which brings them all closer to each other. Jointly, they learn to produce food and share their milk-bearing animals, such as cows, to provide the nutrients they need to generate energy and survive. They perform noble acts and perform no evil deeds or try to conceal their wealth. They come to manifest by themselves with the noble power needed to transform any evil power into a good power and gradually gain control of their subtle faculties, which shield the perishable astral body.

## STEM

The stem of a word is no more than a shoot arising from a set of roots, but stems are capable great diversity. For example, in Sanskrit, a single root verb might be the origin of hundreds innovative words. This single root verb used to create other words by way of a straightforward process. But unlike the root verb, the stem only rarely becomes innovative words. According to *Rig-Veda* 7:97, to protect against demonic powers from gaining control of individual physical mortal embodiments, the manifested supreme immortal universal soul, Paramatman, manifested as Lord Vishnu, appears as a stem (*davita*) and, through all the prevailing powers of causation, comes to support many entities, with each entity, through the power of the five great elements such as Vayu (the air) being given the power to serve as the life force (jiva), which causes each manifested mortal embodiment to develop a dual system of breath: inhalation and exhalation. This breathing system regulates and controls the cycle of life and death, which also liberates individual living spirits from the cycle of life and death (moksha). It is through the stem that, as the Sustainer, Vishnu provides proven power (*Trita*) to bring inner illumination. Even the cosmic hosts (Maruts), serving as demigods, bring into balance the demonic and divine powers to remove the demon ruler who flies through the atmosphere (Vayu) and runs in water (Āptya). Using the powers of the stem (*davita*), the demigods come to collect the demonic powers that generate evil dreams, gradually removing their powers altogether.

Once such demonic power conquered, the proven powers of Trita bring inner illumination, which appears as the deity Uṣas, who pushes away evil dreams and gradually puts all fears to rest, serving as the daughter of heaven and appearing as morning light (dawn) and evening darkness (dusk). Trita and Uṣas keep pushing the evil powers as far away from the embodiments as possible, even well onto the ground. The child of heaven (the sun) comes to protect through offering the powers of prayer (Trita Āptya) to all perishable astral bodies by creating a garland (rosary, or *mālā*) that aids such astral bodies in attaining inner illumination. This way, humanity can keep away evil spirits and prevent them from generating bad dreams. They also can easily overpower the subtle faculties by way of the limited inner shelter provided to the perishable astral body. Humanity learns to retain inner illumination (Trita Āptya) through prayer and even learns through prayer to seek the physical and spiritual energy that is necessary to fight evil thought. The deity Uṣas, with strong, self-dependent Rudra, the supreme powers of causation prevailing between heaven and earth, appears with a windstorm that no one can overcome. They fly swiftly, as if through a shaft, to acquire and build up conquering strength.

According to *Rig-Veda* 7:97, for the first time, an assembly of human beings come to offer their worship with godly love and delightful libations, which engenders among individual human beings a stronger craving to seek the gods' gracious power. Members of humanity cultivate friendship and seek guidance from the exalted sinless bounteous god Bṛhaspati, who comes to support them as a father supports his son, bringing along gracious divine forces (divine will) to serve the members of humanity who offer glorious homage, accompanied with great songs of praise. Homage paid also to Indra, who serves all the creations that prevail within the material world (Virāj), along with reaching all the heavenly kings and the bounteous god Bṛhaspati, who serves the terrestrial region. They all join the heroes seated at front of the altar who have received blessings to fulfill their craving after donating their wealth as an offering, so they may remain safe from those who come to irritate humanity. At birth, they granted with immortal pleasures invoked by the powers of the bounteous god Bṛhaspati. They, as holy ones, along with their households, serve as foe less. Clear-voiced, in full strength, they all draw together to bring forth the red-colored clouds created by red-hued horses, fully robed, resounding and offering mighty friendship. Once they enter the pure dwelling, they provided with one hundred refulgent wings and swords made of gold, with which they come to gain both visible external illumination and sublime inner illumination, granted by the bounteous god Bṛhaspati as a friend. This allows them easy access to most bountiful refreshment, brought from both heaven and earth. Further, with merit from the bounteous god Bṛhaspati, they increase in grandeur and come to recognize the manifested mythical sage Brahmaṇaspati. With laudation and prayer, they bring the strong thunder-wielding power provided by Indra.

According to *Rig-Veda* 7:98, with favorite songs, the humans waken the immortal living spirit (Atman) to generate powers of thought to destroy the malicious, godless foemen. Indra, through holy priests and sages, offers the mythical juice (soma) produced from the stalk or stem of the plant, placing it within the physical embodiments. This mythical juice brings out radiant color, like the sun and the cosmic wild bull. Each day, the desire to drink soma increases, which brings along the desire to enjoy pleasant food. As time passes, these desires increase in strength, even among the newborns, to attain future greatness. Indra, who fills the wide midair region, provides mythical juice to humanity so they may obtain the power of freedom. Like the mythical imperishable sage Brahmaṇaspati, they become prouder with strength in their arms, which power they may use to subdue the passion that often causes holy wars, which could lead the heroes into a fight.

The godly power (divine will) joins with Indra to conquer all deeds that directed are performed through his envoy Maghavan. After they conquer the godless wily ones and their magic tricks, they take all their possessions, including their great flocks and herds. With the eye of the sun deity Sūrya, they empowered with soma, and by the trinity of Indra, Brahmaṇaspati, and Bṛhaspati, with soma, they come to behold all the treasure that provides joy to all manifested mortal embodiments and to the immortal living spirit (Atman) prevailing within the embodiments. The trinity manifests to serve the material world (Virāj), which surrounded by dark matter (earth) and cosmic energy (heaven). While providing wealth, the gods themselves evermore blessed to serve as part of the formless metaphysical trinity.

According to *Rig-Veda* 7:99, with their power, the trinity protect all creation whenever the world threatened with evil, chaos, or other destructive forces. The Supreme Being as manifested Self appears within the material world (Virāj) with authenticity to serve as the divine power according to the doctrine of Vaishnavism, which represents the ancestry and incarnation of the heavenly supreme powers. Within the newly created world (Virāj), these supreme powers appear as manifested bodies responsible for serving humanity. Theologically, all the incarnations are part of the supreme earthly self, the creator Brahma manifested as Brahman. Whenever the world threatened with evil, chaos, or other destructive forces that have the power to oppress the subtle astral bodies holding the living spirit (Atman), the primordial power, Shakti, manifests on earth as Shiva. Shiva comes and overpowers the evil forces, also supporting noble souls and guiding the creations that serve living things. The immanent majesty (reality) that grows beyond all bounds and flows beyond all regions, covering both manifested and unmanifested bodies, is honored and worshipped in the form of the god Vishnu, who knows all about eternal truth and thus is inflexible in establishing rank and order among the non-born and the born alike, allowing some of them to reach the uppermost heights of divine grandeur.

They reach the vast, high vault that connects with the heavenly region, where they received from the earthly region, fully supported and secured at the zenith, where the earth's eastern pinnacle meets with the heaven's western pinnacle. Such a union brings ultimate sweetness that makes the food rich and turns regular water into rich milk, also turning the ground into rich, fertile pasture. The union vests the creations who serve the two worlds with both physical and spiritual powers. In the form of the celestial deity (reality) and as the earthly self-Vishnu, it manifests as an avatar to establish rigidly fixed pegs that create a spacious room (*akasha*) from where the heavenly Sūrya transforms the initially soft morning light (dawn) into terminal evening light (dusk). Both dawn and dusk supported by the deity Uṣas, who herself serves the supreme power of causation Sūrya and brings the life force (prana) by way of sacrifice. Giving birth to the eternal flame, the ultimate source of creation, Agni, comes to manifest among all living things to perform acts of morality, righteousness, and compassion.

This gives birth to humanity, who enhanced like the bull-jawed devotee Dāsas, so they can even overpower any demon's magic tricks or wiles. The supreme powers of causation join forces with Indra to destroy the evil powers fenced within the grounds of ninety-nine castles and to smite down the prevailing evil power Śambara. One hundred thousand heroes attack the defenseless evil king *Varcin*, who is savage, a barbarian, controlling his slaves and servants. Strong in might with lofty hymns of praise, exalted with loud solemn sounds, they pour out food upon the camps of evil while Indra and Agni, serving as the supreme powers of causation, go through singing hymns and songs. The sage *Vaṣaṭ*, twirling his hair, brings water to crying thirsty lips, and Vishnu, serving as the special avatar (*Sipivista*), comes to provide special service as he exalted with songs of eulogy.

According to *Rig-Veda* 7:100, living beings seek to become great self-benefactors, receiving gifts brought by the far-striding avatars of Vishnu, who come singing mantras, adoring the inner living spirit (Atman). They constantly sing out prayers, producing long-lasting vibrations that move with the mighty breath to bring much inner comfort. By implementing the proper breathing process, they gain wisdom and learn to store such wisdom within their embodiments to produce both physical spiritual energy able to turn fast-running horses into stallions. With such breath supported by energy, individuals can stride across the manifested material world (Virāj) three times, witnessing one hundred bright splendors amid the grand space, becoming stronger than the strongest, and honored with glorious names that come to live forever.

## COSMIC FORCE

According to *Rig-Veda* 7:101, the immortal powers of causation stride over the ground to support the mortal embodiments by holding onto the perishable astral body that provides the dwelling place for the immortal living spirit (Atman). The avatars representing Vishnu first appear as the cosmic man Manu, who provides humble trust and safety and creates spacious dwelling places to host more manifested mortal embodiments (Svayambhū). As manifested bodies, they appear with a noble soul who is skilled in the eternal law. They express milk from the udders, generate the mythical fluid soma, and create amrit. Next, Manu quickly engenders as the seed, which germinates and grows into a plant that remains stationary, and engenders as the embryo, which is born to create moving living creatures. The ruling godly powers who turn cosmic vapor into water appear to help both living plants and growing creatures to appear, as the next cosmic man (Manu) establishes triple shelter—sun, moon, and stars—to provide threefold light that, as a sanctuary, vouchsafes creations and helps them become successful through befriending others. The cosmic man Manu appears as the father with a genial flow that bedews the mother; therewith the living beings are born who need nourished to support their own offspring. This creates the powers of the cosmic man Manu, who creates triply flowing waters that bring heavenly reservoirs sprinkling down like dew, shedding their treasure with a murmur, creating sweet streams all around where the deity of rain, Parjanya, comes singing songs that fill the embodiments with purified water to feed Manu, who, serving as an impregnating bull, is greatly pleased by the rain showers, which provide food for the plants, protecting the fruits. In various forms, the cosmic man Manu comes to behold himself. Some remain fixed, while others move, creating seasonality—the singing of one hundred autumns.

According to *Rig-Veda* 7:102, the cosmic man Manu, through the rain deity Parjanya, brings the offspring. Hiding within the cosmic vapor, these offspring fly along with the rain, which comes down as a gift from the gods. They appear on the ground, turning the ground into pasture, sending forth all forms of life: cows, mares, plants, and nutrients. Males and females alike come with life force (prana) carried within the seed or embryo. They drink the savory juice that poured into their mouths, and within the breath, as oblation, it provides eternal nourishment. The ultimate unchanging universal reality, Brahma, pervasive, genderless eternal truth, changes not, yet causes all changes. As a metaphysical concept, Brahma is the single binding force that enforces unity among all the diversity that exists within the universe.

According to *Rig-Veda* 7:103, the unchanging reality, Brahma, creates water intuitively filled with wisdom and generates inspiration. This helps creations to lie quietly, fulfilling their wish to use their inner voices to produce mythical sounds to lift their embodiments, as a frog jumps, to join with the proclamation. Similarly, other animals, such as cows, seeing rain, also see it bring water, pouring upon them, creating a yearning thirst. They low beside their calves. Others seek yet others who are like the initial one, greeting the others with cries of pleasure that move the male and female toward their offspring, where they receive other kindnesses, enjoying the hidden flow from the source of intuitive wisdom as inspiration (*prajna*) within the water. Once moistened by the rain, like frogs, both males and females spring forward with their voices, always looking for a solid place to land. When one of them repeats the other's language, they learn as learning a lesson from a teacher, and with that, they notice as they converse eloquently on the waters that all their limbs grow larger. Similarly, the cow bellows, the goat bleats, and other animals make different sounds, none sounding the same. Even though one frog is green in color, and another spotted, they all bear one common name, yet the sounds each makes vary.

Unchanging reality, Brahma, sitting near the vessel filled with mythical juice (soma), administers a rite to create one of the deities, *Ātiratra*, who comes to extend beyond ignorance and darkness. On the first day of the year, while sitting, unchanging reality (Brahma), as part of a yearlong rite, offers soma to the holy priests (adhvaryu) with uplifted voices. Greatly stressed, they come from their hiding places toward the heated cauldrons, and they show themselves after sweating for twelve months to receive freedom. After the holy priests enforce the God-appointed order, they return to their heated cauldrons. From there, like frogs, they gather round the pool honoring the arrival of rain. Humanity never neglects the season that brings rain, with the bellowing of the cow and the bleating of the goat. The rain grants milk and vouchsafes the colored treasures such as spotted green frogs, lengthening individual lives to hundreds of years by cultivating during this most fertile season.

According to *Rig-Veda* 7:104, the god Indra, with mythical juice (soma), comes to burn and destroy the demon foes and send them downward, with proclamations to impact those who add gloom to gloom and to annihilate fools. Indra slays them, burns them, or chases or pierces the voracious ones to keep them far away from humankind. Indra, with soma, further removes sin, besetting those foes who are against prayer with wicked boils. By lighting a fire beneath the cauldron, he destroys the devourers of raw flesh, those despicable villains with ferocious eyes that cultivate perpetual hate. Indra, with soma, plunges those who are wicked into the depths, a place of darkness where there is no support, hence making sure that not one of them may ever return and express their wrathful might.

The unified Indra and Soma come hurling down with their deadly thunderbolt, crushing wicked fiends and forcing them out of the mountains, striking them with their celestial darts, which burn the demons to death. Before the demons can race away, Indra and Soma push them out of heaven with their deadly darts of burning stone, like comets. With a fiery flame, scorching hot, and with their darts, they cast them down. They plunge down upon the voracious ones surviving within the depths of the ocean and, without a sound, let them sink. After eliminating the evil powers, Indra and Soma come to controls both vigorous steeds and the lords of humanity, who offer them hymns and songs of praise along with wisdom. They serve humanity as nobles of the realm, who can animate with their breath. In their impetuous manner, Indra with Soma jointly destroy all these evil beings, slaying the treacherous fiends. Let the wicked have no bliss because they evermore assail humanity with their malignity. For those who are accustomed to being evil, they burn before they can attack the righteous. They sent to the serpent or consigned to the lap of monster.

Indra goes after the goddess of the hidden realms of death, Nirrti, who powered by Agni. This brings pain and sorrow to all those associated with her who seek to destroy living things by going after their inner souls (Atmans), which reside with vegetation, cattle, steeds, and any other manifested body. Nirrti serves as an adversary, thief, and robber and sinks to destroy both herself and her offspring. With the powers of Indra, any prudent noble soul finds it easy to distinguish between the two opposing worlds, determining what is true and what is false. Indra, with mythical juice (soma), comes to protect the true and honest soul. He brings nothing to those who false and never aids or guides the wicked or those who falsely claim the title of noble warrior. With soma, Indra slays the fiends and those who speak untruths. When they entangled in his noose, he slays them with a mighty weapon, letting the most dreadful of all creatures, that is, any fiend who says he is pure but who calls on demons, die. They wander at nighttime, the owls, hiding their bodies amid their guile and malice. They fall downward into endless fissures and destroyed, with a loud ringing sound coming from the celestial region as the compressed stones (meteors) come as cosmic hosts (Maruts), searching among the people for the evil powers (rakshasas). Once the cosmic hosts seize the rakshasas, they grind them to pieces. Those who can transform themselves into bats, which at nighttime fly abroad to discredit and contaminate holy worship.

Indra hurries down from heaven and brings the envoy Maghavan, along with Soma, to smite the demons with his rocky weapons and sharpen thunderbolts. The cosmic bodies (compressed stones) come from all directions, forward, backward, above, and below. Like demon dogs bent on mischief, they gladly fly to bring harm to the invincible powers. The envoy Maghavan uses a sharpened weapon against the wicked, which he ends up casting at malevolent wizards. Indra makes sure the fiends of witchcraft never reach noble souls, thereby keeping earth safe by coming with the morning light to drive away the *Kimīdins*. This also keeps the earth free from woe and from the trouble and grief that comes from the midair region. Maghavan joyfully slays both male and female demons who are skilled in the art of magic.

# Part V

# TRANSCENDENTAL SPHERE

# Preface to Part V

The basic meaning of the transcendental sphere goes beyond the fundamental structure of living things and merges with a framework of higher knowledge gained through individual experience. The transcendental state possesses extraordinary attributes. In spiritual terms, transcendence refers to God's nature and to godly power, which is independent of the material universe and goes beyond all physical laws. Transcendence is a state of being that has overcome the limitations imposed by physical existence and goes beyond the material world to gain independence. Transcendence attributed to the divine, a physical fully enhanced with eternal wisdom. Thus, like godly power, it transcends both the universe and the ethereal zone, which the human brain cannot comprehend. At such a stage, subtle faculties such as the mind, love, devotion, and faith, expand to allow the manifested embodiment to comprehend the working of the supreme powers of causation within nature (prakriti). Nature itself creates false or misleading sensory illusions (maya), which results in a misrepresentation of creation and prevents the mental powers from understanding in depth the esoteric or ethereal zone. This makes it difficult to differentiate between illusion and truth, defined as cosmic nous, where after comprehending the five great elements of nature (Vasu), one understands the order of physical power but remains unable to comprehend the order of essential power, which regulates the three major elements that are responsible for causation and illumination. Thus, the mind comprehends only five of the eight elements (Aṣṭavasu) of nature (prakriti) that represent order, which is responsible for causation, which continuously operates both the physical and spiritual power regulating the dynamic universe and is responsible for the transformation of the active manifested form into the divine transcendental form. With such transformation, the manifested embodiment learns to unravel the secrets of nature and comprehend the powers responsible for creating the surroundings. All creations, manifested and unmanifested, perishable and imperishable, mortal, and immortal, are subject to all aspects of nature. This includes the fields of science, philosophy, spirituality, and faith, and the realm of all living things, including rocks, minerals, plants and vegetation, birds, and animals, wherein the roles played by evil spirits and noble souls become apparent. It even includes the weather, geology, and forests, among other things, which become sources of alteration, intervention, and creation, and objects created by human beings.

# CHAPTER 14

# Highbrow Dominion

THE HIGHBROW DOMINION IS THE REGION WHERE MANIFESTED embodiments come to comprehend the power of cosmic nous and become fully accustomed to the changing states of nature, which supported by the glorified supreme powers of causation. Living beings can properly experience sorrow and overcome any trouble with loudly repeated praise and worship. They understand the two mighty powers Agni and Indra, who, along with a contribution from nature, provide eternal mythical juice (soma), which goes rushing down within the embodiment like a bull running to meet a bounteous cow. With such contribution, an embodiment becomes so powerful that it can eliminate enmity, even conquer it, by managing the two most magnanimous opposing powers, evil and nobility, thereby bringing peace and tranquility.

## INSIGHT

According to *Rig-Veda* 8:1, after a long period of oblation, along with daily prayer and worship, manifested embodiments invoke the powers of Mother Nature (prakriti). They learn through the envoy Maghavan how to use their skills to regulate the vibrations generated by the planetary system, which allows them to understand wisdom. They do this by creating oscillation and producing songs and hymns, which they need to overpower the foemen.

Regulating the mighty powers of vibration, they obtain eternal strength, which allows them to gain control over the cosmic power so they may direct the impact from the outer regions and the casters of the stone, which appear as asteroids, meteorites, and comets. With inspirational powers, they accompany the hundred thousand thunders coming from heaven to earth and learn of the countless wealth they carry. They come to comprehend they are friends, and not servants or slaves, who bring along an abundance of treasure to support the individual mental faculties, the individual mind, prevailing within the manifested mortal embodiment serving as Mother Aditi. Once they become an integral part of the embodiment, they transform their individual mental powers to fight the battle of morality, serving as noble warriors going after evil forces. Instead of using weapons, they use the power of vibration and hymns to win over their enemies by tuning their minds and thoughts. The enemies become as faithful friends, sounding forth with powerful psalms. The mortal embodiments use psalm verses to tear down the castles of the evil powers, bringing thunder to destroy their forts. Keeping safe their devotees, they cover the ground with sacred grass, which they use to feed animals such as cows and horses in the tens, the hundreds, and the thousands. In progression, they bring the vigorous fleet-footed animals closer, blessing them to serve as domesticated animals. Milk-bearing animals such as cows come to serve as the mother goddesses that help other animals with holy songs, thus yielding a rich supply of milk. They provide an unfailing supply of food, which fills the streams with abundance.

Indra, appearing as the wealthy envoy Maghavan, who comes to serve as the healer, never casts aside any strangers. With his manifested mortal embodiment, he overpowers enemies by establishing peace, and comes to serve with morality and his thunder-wielding power. The embodied souls save their mortal bodies by working with nature, for example, supporting trees to produce nutrients, thereby making them unfit to burn. As drops of nectar start to flow rapidly through the manifested physical embodiments, they listen to their inner consciences, which bring delight by weakening the evil powers, so they are unprepared to fight or kill. Serving as mighty fighters, (*Tugryas)* hear the common request with empathy and serve as noble souls and honored faithful friends, like heroes.

*Tugryas* provide living beings with the eternal joy and pleasure needed to perform selfless actions, even enabling plants fixed to the ground to serve with the luster brought from lofty heaven. Through extracting mythical juice (soma), they rush through running waters and, coming out of compressed cosmic stones, pass through the waters as if through a sieve to produce clean juice, which they offer as a sacrifice filled with praise and eternal wisdom. The living plants producing mythical juice (soma) even offer their own personal sacrifices to provide an excellent means to gladden and swell.

Creation appears as the mighty power Śakra, who, as an epithet of the godly power Indra, possesses a unique strength. Śakra helps to control anger; while he does not beseech, he does bring a swift, effectual, ecstatic joy. With its mighty strength, soma provides him with conquering powers. While transported, the soma distilled and, in its pure form, is a gift that brings ecstasy. With bliss, not piousness, it comes to glorify and bestow great wealth, causing living beings to rejoice in their affluence, as a lake is able to hide a great amount of soma.

With their golden embodiments, the steeds, in the hundreds or thousands, harnessed together to serve Indra with devotion. They are yoked to a chariot wrought of gold, appearing in the rain as peacock tails with their pure white backs spread with color, conveying to all the impact of a quaff of the sweet juice that, when taken like nectar, brings out eternal devotion in the lovers of song, who pour out savory sap as sperm, gladdened and prepared to meet with their companions. The mythical juice brings out wondrous short-term mighty powers that help to create strong holy progeny.

The mythical juice serves like adrenalin, which quickly moves them to destroy Śuṣṇa and his evil fort or castle, crushing his evil powers to pieces. Indra brings along thunderbolts and lightning as he invoked with the powers of the sun. He also brings the morning light (dawn) to remove the gloom of night. With praises, Indra asks nature (Vasu) to serve the princes *Paramajyā, Ninditāśva, Prapathī, and Medhātithi.*

Vasu provides them all with most liberal gifts, filling them with eternal faith to move like a carriage among the physical embodiments, yoked like horses. Along the way, they meet the skilled, self-respecting, well-established son Yadu, who comes to serve as the ruler. They acquire the skills required to deal with the most precious invisible force (spirit) that can balance enmity to bring peace, which guides herds of cows to become united without greed for gold or other material wealth. The noble souls, such as the sons of *Āsaṅga*, come to serve nature (*Svanadratha*), obtaining joy through high ecstasy, and move forward as ten thousand blossoming play, like lotus flowers, emerge from the water and stand up in the lake, confirming the arrival of life in ponds of water located on the ground (*Virāj*).

According to *Rig-Veda* 8:2, all who appear as manifested mortal living things with good physical ability and a positive mental attitude cultivate qualities that exceed those of normal manifested embodiments. These mortal embodiments, with mystic abilities, acquire impossible physical strength and exceptional proficiency to go beyond any other prevailing living being. In spiritual terms, they defined as Siddhis, which are superior to humanity, even beyond the lion in their superhuman strength. Such enhancement of humanity commonly referred to as genetic modification, or attributed to cybernetic implants, nanotechnology, or radiation, all of which truly represent an aspect of spiritual evolution. Such human enhancement can be temporary or permanent, depending on the strength of the influence of the eight great elements of nature (*Aṣṭavasu*), which impose a kind of modification upon the manifested mortal embodiment. Depending upon whether it is natural or artificial, it can become part of the future evolutionary process of human beings. Even the planetary system, as is the case with manifested mortal embodiments, which house the immortal individual living spirit (Atman), is subject to the same phenomenon that creates bondage between the material and spiritual worlds. Such bondage is ultimately regulated through the thirty-three supreme powers, including divinities, deities, and demigods, where each eleven as a group are designated to serve above in the heavenly region, representing cosmic energy; below in the earthly region, representing cosmic matter; and in the middle esoteric region, encompassing the interaction of cosmic energy and cosmic matter, generating imperishable light.

## ATTRIBUTES

According to *Rig-Veda* 8:3, the heavenly body Sūrya, with his imperishable light, serves all rotating planetary bodies in outer space as perishable light (*Prabhāsa*). During the day, Sūrya supplies direct light produced by the burning of the furious fire (the sun), and during the night, the soft reflective light coming from the moon covers outer space in star constellations and the nine planets (*Navaratas*) passing eternal wisdom from the heavenly region to the earthly region, along with the creation of vibrations that generate cosmic vapor filled with a bonding fluid, namely, mythical juice mixed with water vapor. Through three primary he types of manifested bodies, eternal wisdom passes and illuminates, making a profound impact upon each manifested embodiment. These imperishable sources work closely with the five great perishable elements of nature, including Prithvi (ground), which supports all the creations; Agni (fire), who supports life; Vayu (wind), who pervades every manifested aspect; and Āpa (water), which in vapor form prevails within the atmospheric region as essence (ether). All together, these five great elements and three illuminated bodies, eight in total, represent Mother Nature (Aṣṭavasu). They create unjustified aspects, the spiritual term for which is "lunar mansion" (Nakstrani), that cover twenty-eight sectors, all located within the ecliptic zodiac. The supreme powers of causation, after consuming sweet honey blended with milk and barleycorn, create a feast that unmanifested mortal embodiments consume, then transform from their unmanifested invisible imperishable powers into manifested perishable powers as Siddhis. Such an advanced accomplishment, changing from normal material into paranormal supernatural magical powers, done by a process of advancing through sadhana, meditation, and yoga, or using psychic powers (Pali), often used interchangeably in Buddhism. As Siddhis, the powers regulate and manage all manifested physical mortal embodiments. Any manifested physical embodiments who are not fully enlightened end up drinking a badly mixed blend as a bitter draft. Instead of attracting far-extending godly powers, they chase their own physical manifested embodiments as hunters chase a beautiful deer in their desire to overpower weaker creations such as innocent animals.

Among the three forms of reservoirs, the heavenly above, the earthly below, and the esoteric region in the middle, cosmic matter interacts with cosmic energy to create the eight supreme powers of causation that operate through vibrations and fill beakers to the brim with mythical juice (soma). Serving with purity, the eight supreme powers of causation seat themselves in places where mythical juice blended with milk and then transformed into curd, which by coagulating (curdling) milk. The coagulation enhanced by adding rennet or another edible acidic substance such as lemon juice. With cheer, the drink served by the noble Ādityas, going straight to the heart and reaching the living spirit (Atman), thus coming to serve the manifested noble heroes. When pure strong soma pressed and is not admixed with milk, it creates a cake that makes the rich quaff go through the body naked, like wine.

The praising of such a rich quaff comes from those of high rank. Like the famed lord of the bays, they add no milk and pay no attention to any chanting of hymns, or worship, or holy psalms; they disrespect all this and, as foes, become prey unto other foes or manifested bodies, who receive no help from Indra or Agni. The heroes, on the other hand, practice dedicated devotion (sadhana) to achieve spiritual enlightenment and acquire supernatural powers. This includes the practice of yoga, meditation, and contemplation, by which they proceed to become extraordinary noble souls (Siddhis). With praise and hymns, they acquire skills and proceed to serve as Kaṇvas, the envoys of Indra, and with thunder offer eulogies. Knowing well that with their powers of meditation and contemplation they acquire the ability to press their own mythical juice (soma), the Kaṇvas angrily punish the slothful, disallowing them from spending even an evening before they sent far away. The skilled noble Kaṇvas know well how the mystic powers the Siddhis use eternal love to invoke the godsent mystic powers. The Siddhis, along with the envoy Kaṇvas, established through spiritual powers as the divine will throughout the three regions, accompanied with hymns and provided with a gift of mythical juice. They even help those who are not as strong or glorious, providing them with strength and endowing them with a great bounty, as exalted by Indra. With valor, they perform glorious deeds, singing love songs and hymns to confirm evermore their might. Indra, as a doer of great deeds, comes holding a thunderbolt in his left hand, representing physical strength, and holding spiritual powers in his right hand, which he uses to subdue and overpower evil forces. With pleasure, the Kaṇvas serve Indra in all regions. Invoking eternal wisdom, they serve with the mystic Siddhis to seek and drive those who are swift by bringing them a wealth of steeds and a collective inspired mind. They appear as heroes among living beings, slaying evil powers to faithfully serve the worshippers.

The envoy Kaṇvas and the mystic-minded Siddhis sing glorified songs to honor the Lord of the Brave and the Mighty One. As renowned lovers, the Siddhis, with their strong bonds of friendship with the envoy Kaṇvas, restore the wishes of the wise Medhātithi who, with the holy law engraved in stone, brings the law in the form of text, the *Manusmṛti,* which becomes part of the holy scriptures (*Dharmaśāstra*). This permanently records the laws of the quality of selfless devotion (dharma), through which the roots of civilization (*Vibhindu*) planted. With this, humanity expands in the thousands, four times and thereafter eight times—and more as marked. With a feast and a pledge, the mystic minds (*Siddhis*) guard wisdom, while sages serve savory juice mixed with milk and soma. With cheer, they cultivate the vision of the civilization and come to share eternal wisdom with others. This kind of grace makes manifested mortal bodies mentally strong enough to serve like the envoy (*Kaṇvas.*)When attacked by enemies, they all gather to seek assistance for guarding and supporting each other.

Exalted with abundant wealth and skills, the manifested mortal bodies, while singing praises and holy hymns, generate pure hues from the fire, which enhances them both mentally and spiritually. With solemn rites, majesty, and praise, they acquire futuristic souls and come to rule with a thousandfold power, serving as devotees and holy singers. They proceed to worship Indra, making sacrifices so he will come and serve in the battle, tending to those who wounded and to other soldiers who have been stressed by fighting the righteous war. The manifested mortal bodies spread out with the direct source of light (the sun) supporting the futuristic soul, with Indra covering all regions from earth to heaven. Holding all creatures close, Indra provides the embodiments with distilled drops of soma and urges them to proceed as he does, supplying all with their first drink of soma. Then in accord with vibration, over time, they come to worship the cosmic body Ṛbhu, who evolves, lifting their voices as they sing hymns. They increase in physical strength, ready to make sacrifices. In their wild rapture, as in ancient times and still today, after taking in the mythical juice, they sing forth with praises to Indra. With a hero's strength and with prayer, they obtain mythical powers. They come to serve like the holy sages *Bhrigu*, *Yatis,* and *Praskaṇva.* While the world cries out for mythical powers, cosmic sages bring wealth so the heroic powers may transform river water into holy water. Thus, sages, like the holy water, go and join with the mighty water of the ocean, merging forever with the unattainable supreme powers of causation.

## DISTINCTION

According to *Rig-Veda* 8:4, every manifested living being follows Indra, who urges them to follow him and serve as the brave champions of tribes represented by the chiefs *Ānava, Turvaśa, Ruma, Ruśama, Śyāvaka, and*

*Kṛpa*, who go from east to west and from north to south. Each morning as the envoy Kaṇvas come, and each evening as they go back, they offer, with praise, prayers to reality (Indra), who creates a great impression as he comes quickly, like a thirsty wild bull running toward a pool of water in the desert. After drinking drops of rich, gladdening mythical juice, the Kaṇvas come to serve as godly messengers, ensuring they continue to represent Indra. They bring with them bounty, pouring through them as if pressed in a mortar, and further purified to become mythical juiçe. The champions of brave tribes, the chiefs, take the drink so that their spiritual energy may overcome those with greater physical strength and so they may crush evil. Making themselves as preeminent heroes, and with reverential prayer, they come along with the Mighty Power to represent to others as friends. They ensure there is neither fear nor fatigue among those serving as chiefs of the tribes, serving with honor, and performing great deeds. Serving as glorified heroes, Turvaśa and Yadu, as fair friends, bring along horses and cattle, providing them with food evermore, accompanied by eternal wealth, which brings radiance. Once they eat to their hearts' desire, they go like antelope, running for drink. They come only on the day after the rain comes down with its unsurpassed might. This brings soma juice, which flows forth with vigor among holy priests, who yoked as the bay steeds and come to serve as the Vṛtra-slayers, fighting against the foes. While the holy priests become pious to serve the worshippers, the solar deity Pūṣan comes filled with mythical juice to serve along with the appropriate food. The priests and Pūṣan develop a firm alliance with wisdom (Śakra) and come to serve as the epithet of Indra. Once they invoked, with the aid of the life force (prana), they appear as seeds and embryos that develop into astral bodies, providing dwelling places for the immortal living spirit (Atman), which resides within mortal embodiments. The morning light gives them both treasures and the longing to win eternal love (Mitra). With praises, they sing psalms to win over the solar deity Pūṣan, who brings radiance to the immortal living spirit (Atman). Without any wish freed, it joins with the Lord of Excellence, the solar deity Pūṣan, who brings radiant power to serve the most liberal auspicious gathering, filling them with strength and providing pastures of wealth.

The opulent King Turvaśas, with splendid morning rites, provides a gift to establish the heavenly manifested mortal souls (rishis) who appear as shepherds (*Priyamedhas*) to serve along with the envoy Kaṇva, where both come singing morning songs. Along with one hundred steeds, they provided seventy thousand head of cattle, including sixty thousand spotless ones, which purposely come to manifest as mortal embodiments that move into the forest to serve as noble souls (rishis). Such movement of eternal wisdom passing through the three primary sources of illumination makes a profound impact upon such mortal manifested embodiments by generating an illusion that creates things that are not what they seem to be. This means that existence, which is constantly changing, always conceals the true nature of reality, which itself remains unchanged. With the power of Mother Nature, as an epithet, Lakshmi manifests as the goddess of wealth, prosperity, and inspired love among all manifested mortal divine powers (rishis), honorable seers (yogi), great sadhus (sages), and blessed souls who seek to unveil the illusion she has created. The foregoing all follows a program of intense meditation, concentration, and contemplation (*tapas*) to allow their noble souls to go beyond the mundane material world, which regulates the senses and prevents the physical body from distinguishing illusion from reality. When the individual mind is unable to separate illusion from reality, the individual physical embodiment acquires memories. These residual memories create a wall that limits an individual's ability to see a clear path, which prevents the individual from attaining emotional calmness. Over time the physical body becomes content with illusion and thus is unable to go beyond the limits of the physical world.

According to *Rig-Veda* 8:5, from far away, the power of reality appears as red light (dawn), spreading afar with divine will that yokes the carriage to display the powers of the Creator. Here the twin horses, the Aśvins, shining wonderworkers serving as demigods, bring part of the morning light (dawn), along with ample wealth. The envoy Kaṇvas, with mystic souls (Siddhis), come to serve with the wonderworking Aśvins, who are glad and happy to attain success. Most liberal, best at winning strength, as inciters, Siddhis bring the mystic souls as the lords of splendor, along with the envoy Kaṇvas. They visit the worshippers' abode, bringing mead, consisting of fermented honey with water, as mythical juice, which they offer as a sacrifice to the devout worshipper. Like horses with wings, they come rapidly like hawks. They appear as the holistic Sudeva, who, like the twin horses the Aśvins, comes singing songs of praise. They fly three distances: first, providing external illumination that comes as direct light from the sun during the day; second, providing reflective light from the moon, which traverses the sky during the nighttime; and third, coming from constellations that serve as the pathfinders who, as winners of food such as beef, bring wealth to all by opening paths for others to tread. With holistic powers, they bring wealth to cattle and noble heroes, who, among other manifested embodiments, provided the ability to process their physical energy like horses and appear as the lords of splendor who come to glorify others as wonderworkers. They borne on paths of gold. Drinking sweet mythical juice, they serve as lords of ample wealth. They, like the chiefs, provide shelter. Never assaulted, they come down to favor the people who are praying along other people.

Like the demigod Aśvins, the Siddhis and Kaṇvas can perceive individual minds. They drink gladdening drafts of soma, which brings eternal wisdom. This brings riches in the hundreds and thousands, providing them with a sustainable source of plenteous food. Verily, sages call on the serving as the heroes who move in higher dimensions, like a cone, serving priests with such power to trim the sacred grass and bring oblations, all prepared by the powers of the Aśvins, who come to invoke the conscience within them. With hymns of praise, the powerful Aśvins move near to their hearts to invoke the inner conscience, which fills the skin and prepares the body to travel the pathway to receive the savory essence meath. Filled with the soma provided by the demigod Aśvins, they go into trances and begin the transformation of their bodies with blessings from the lords of ample wealth. Their progeny, with plenteous food, unveil the secrets of nature (*tuğra*, commonly expressed in the form of a calligraphic monogram). With such visual representation, they come to understand individual strengthening powers such as Mother Nature (Vasu), who transforms cosmic vapor into water molecules, which emerge from the sky and travel lightly over the surface of the ground, creating rivers that flow in the darkness to remove ignorance. The calligraphic monogram represents how the waters find the path to reach their ultimate destination, settling to the bottom of the ocean. Without ever knowing the secrets of nature, *tuğra* defines how water reaches its high destination, where it loses its identity forever. Similarly, as winged steeds and birds flying up into air, the Siddhis and Kaṇvas lose their identities once they reach their destination high in the sky.

All creations such as the calligraphic monogram provide aid to wonder-workers (Nāsatyas), which come as directed by the powers of the envoy Kaṇva, serving as the minister, repeatedly providing aid through the life force (prana), serving as breath to support the individual living spirit residing within the manifested body. It cast into the heated pit where the demigod Nāsatyas come to serve as envoy Kaṇvas and move near to provide aid to them by offering eulogies with merit. By invoking the powers of *Priyamedhas, Upastuta, Atri, Sinjara*, the Aśvins, and *Amsu*, the revered sage Agastya serves the other revered sage, *Sobhari,* who prays while singing hymns to the demigod Aśvins, who, sitting in their carriage and waiting to ascend, permit the active spiritual powers to hold the golden reins. This provides bliss to all spiritually active souls, even those who dwell above the sky. They fully supported by a spiritually activated golden shaft and a spiritually activated golden axle, which connect both the wheels, which made of a spiritually activated material. whose power is as pure as gold.

## DYNASTY

According to *Rig-Veda* 8:6, with ample spiritual wealth, the mortals come from afar to offer eulogies to the immortal ones. Renowned as splendorous demigods, the Nāsatyas enjoy the plenteous food provided by their devotees. They bring along brilliantly rich shining steeds, dappled horses, and birds with pinions, and they come with a new type of skill to offer sacrifices. The manifested mortal embodiments, with rich food stored in their wheeled carriages, never delay in generating vibrations and creating rhythmic sounds like songs. Borne on chariots wrought of gold, they, like fleet-footed coursers, come with swift thought, brought by the renowned splendorous demigod Nāsatyas. With wealth, divine powers, and simple tastes, they find the wild beast that is associated with wealth and food. The demigods share the leftovers, which they present as a gift, using the method of bookkeeping for coins (Kāśu), to the demigods, who create one hundred head of buffalo and ten thousand of cattle for the ten kings who appointed to watch over the manifested mortal embodiments. To track each foot, a king serving as the intelligent administrator Caidya provides a shield, so that no manifested mortal body, not one, may walk upon the path on which such kings walk. No other prince has more gifts than the kings of the Vatsa dynasty had. The branches of this dynasty represented by Kuru, who, during the early periods of the kingdom, represented the five different tribes that prevailed throughout the material world (Virāj). During a later period of the Vatsa dynasty, they five tribes divided into different branches to encompass the vast area of the material world (Virāj). The Vatsa dynasty spread eternal wisdom and enlightened mortal living beings so they could cope with the challenges represented by the principles of karma and dharma, and with other related practices related to remaining in compliance with the material world. All-encompassing, the first Eightfold Path of enlightenment determined who would reach nirvana. The descendants of the Vatsa dynasty were famous for keeping their words to people, ensuring they fulfilled their promises. The famous vow of the Vatsa dynasty given by a person as an oath, through swearing on the family name. The vow might pledge to provide anything ranging from political support to monetary support, to emotional support, to protection.

The holy priests, sons of the holy law, with their strengthening presence, sing hymns as a form of praise, causing a rhythmic vibration that invokes the powers of Indra. With his mighty power, Indra brings cosmic rain filled with knowledge, which magnified by the famous Vatsa dynasty, and with the envoy Kaṇvas removing any displeasure. They make all the manifested mortal embodiments bow down, with their loud sacrifices offering words to Indra. Their arms, when they bow, just like rivers bend toward the sea. The power of Indra shines forth brightly, bringing together the heaven and the earth like fiercely moving skin over the heads of the evil power. Indra causes a single thunderbolt to become one hundred bolts. Lightning appears as a blazing fire, like bidden thoughts, advancing spontaneously like the envoy Kaṇvas. Filled with the stream of sacrifices, it comes to glow and shine. The famous Vatsa dynasty obtains its wealth in horses and in herds of cows, which with prayer the Vatsa dedicate to Indra. The Vatsa dynasty first noticed when they receive from their father, as they are born, light from the sun. They are all filled with a deep knowledge of the holy law, with lore, and with the beautiful ancient songs. In time, the Vatsa dynasty, as the envoy Kaṇvas, fills with blessings from Indra. They gain self-strength, and whatever the noble souls (rishis) have not praised, they with lauded praise continue to exalt, which brings out their strength. With such strength, they shine like thunder, which breaks the evil Vṛtra to pieces, tearing them limb from limb, freeing the waters to merge with the sea. As part of the ancient culture, the evil Dāsa, as a member of the Asuras, survives and does not fight back against Indra's thunderbolt. He does fight his trepidation, at length lying down in the waters, their own footsteps, smoothed down, hidden deep in the darkness.

Indra aims to secure a spacious place between heaven and earth where he may receive the bounded powers of Yati, the freedom fighter, along with those of the noble soul Bhrigu. They both appear as spotted cows who, with praises, listen to Indra and yield the milky draft with lard to serve as an offering. Once they teamed up, they receive through their mouths the germ of life supported by the power of breath, which comes from the heavenly power Sūrya as sustaining power. Sūrya, like a mighty lord, comes with hymns of praise offered through the envoy Kaṇvas. With an increase in power, this generates drops of mythical juice, which when poured forth bring strength. Under guidance, Indra brings thunder and food for all, having a stronghold within cows, which bring forth progeny filled with heroic strength. He further grants to all a wealth of steeds, which he shows among the tribes who brighten as they age. They attract kindness from Indra as they come within heaven's fold, which shines as they put forth their power to govern their people, mighty, unlimited in strength. The tribe of elders (Nahuṣas) bring oblations to provide help through drops of mythical fluid, which spread afar and, like a mountain slope, moves downward to meet with streams, where sages manifest, supported by vibrations, songs, and hymns.

Coming down from their lofty place where water stirred up, they see the refulgent light of the primeval seed. With their heavenly power kindled, the envoy Kaṇvas, until they exalted with all wisdom, bring the heroic spiritual strength, which accepted as their eulogy. They guard carefully. Through strengthening their thoughts, they prosper with the thunder-armed Indra, who serves through singers singing all types of hymns. Through their devotion, they come to live with the envoy Kaṇvas, who sing as they speed down the slope, like waters, with songs of praise, their hymns causing the rivers to swell and join with the ocean, which makes them strong and eternally ready to resist any wrath. Indra comes from regions far away to drink soma juice, along with lovely bay steeds, who have already grazed the sacred grass.

Indra, as the slayer of the evil power Vṛtra, with his shining wheel, after drinking soma, decorated or dappled as a horse from heaven (Etaśa). Etaśa comes as light, flying, rejoicing, invoking mortal embodiments, and gaining spoils. In making sacrifices, Indra and Etaśa gladden manifested bodies (*Saryandyan*) as they grown in heaven, with the strong thunder-armed heavenly bull serving as the chief drinker of soma. They bellow as the killers of evil power (Vṛtra-slayers). The envoy Kaṇvas, with their hymns of praise, come to magnify ancient thought, swelling individual minds, filling them with wisdom, and calming them as running streams do.

The steeds and the embryos are praised like beauteous birds (Priyamedhas), which by drinking the mythical juice (soma), invoke godly powers, swelling their numbers to one hundred thousand, all gaining strength through the existing tribes—Parsu, Tirindira, and Yadavas—creating ten thousand head of cattle and steeds, three times a hundred, all bestowed with the *sāman* song, which reaches up to heaven, invoking buffaloes to come yoked in fours, matching the fame of the ancient manifested mortal embodiments.

According to *Rig-Veda* 8:7, Rudra and his wife, Pṛśni, the latter as the regulator of Mother Nature, appear as storm deities, who bring along their offspring, the Maruts, who are young demigods, to serve the terrestrial region. These young demigods, like their ancestors, appear as violent, aggressive, and armed with golden weapons. They have iron teeth and come roaring like lions, accompanied with lightning and thunderbolts. They come to reside in the north, from where they ride in their golden chariots. As dark red clouds and as ruddy horses, they drawn by windstorms. They accompany their troops, like companions, represented with shining golden helmets and with breastplates of lightning. They come as the supreme power Indra, bringing their own axes, which have the power to split the cosmic vapor and release water, which falls as rain upon the surface of the ground (Virāj). The Maruts are born with a much higher power that makes them capable of shaking the mountains and destroying forests. They are born with mouths from the broken womb of the mother goddess Aditi, who remains pregnant for a very long time before giving birth to a son who, in spite of her powers, is unable to threaten the supreme powers of Indra.

## ELOQUENCE

According to *Rig-Veda* 8:7, the seven horses of the sun, Tṛṣṭup, with hymns ascend to the three regions—lowest, highest, and middle—regulating Mother Nature. They come amid the mountain clouds as shining semi manifested "bright ones," showing their might just like the ancient cosmic hosts (Maruts). These young ones, as bright ones, serve with the sons of the cosmic mother Pṛśni. Raised with cosmic vapor, they follow a self-determined course, creating the mountain clouds, which bend down, creating loud roaring winds—and when they pass through the valley, they pour out the streaming waters that feed plants. These young ones, sons of Pṛśni, spread mist abroad, like ancient Maruts, covering mountainous rock, and then roll with the gusty winds as they go on their way, making rivers in the hills running through the valleys. Before descending, they bow down to honor the earth. They set themselves up as the mighty sustaining force that calls upon the night for aid in making the day successful, then they proceed with making sacrifices. Verily, with a wondrous red hue, they speed on their coursers, roaring over the ridges of the sky, following the bright rays of the sun, and dropping mighty power simply by loosening their reins.

They run like coursers, spreading beams of light, eliminating ignorance and darkness. With hymns, the bright ones come out and accept the songs of praise as the young ones, serving as demigods, bring out all the milk-bearing animals, such as the sacred cows, which pour out milk bundled with wisdom. As a thunder-wielding divine power, Indra fills the clouds with water, establishing them as great containers, like lakes. Thus, the young demigods call upon the sky to send forth the bounty like the rich patron Ṛbhukṣans. The Ṛbhukṣans quickly turn individual longing into contentment, and they set their own bodies with other manifested bodies. They bring wisdom as they manifest along with the other prevailing embodiments, providing them with gladdening soma to drink. With heavenly power, the rich Ṛbhukṣans, along with distilling rapturous joy, bring down the sustaining powers. From the hills, the bright ones, as young Maruts, resolve issues and bring together all manifested mortal embodiments by sharing with them drops of mythical fluid along with divine will, which diffuses as a great band filled with invincible power. They elicit happiness among all and, like rain showers, blow fiery sparks, providing milk and the eternal flame that never fails.

With tempests and hymns of praise, the sons of Pṛśni, with a tumultuous roar, hurry forth in their chariots, which filled with eternal wealth, bringing aid to the envoys Trita, Yadu, Turvaśa, and Kaṇva, who all come as bounteous ones flowing in streams, like holy oil floating on the surface. Singing hymns, they increase in might and, with rejoicing, keep growing on the surface of the ground with the sacred grass, which trimmed in adoration of the prevailing holy priests (Brahmans). They bring together the two worlds, also bringing cosmic vapor, one world provided by the goddess Sarasvatī, and the other provided with beams of light, coming to serve as the splendor of the planets (the sun). They accompanied by the supreme power Indra, who provides thunderbolts and performs heroic deeds, splitting the gloomy evil power Vṛtra in half. Like the mountain clouds, Indra breaks them, tearing them limb from limb.

The Brahmans fight a battle against their foes, and to reinforce themselves, they seek the trinity that provides power and strength. The trinity deck themselves out for glory, with bright celestial lightning in their hands and with helmets of gold, representing purity, upon their heads. The trinity eagerly come from far away and appear roaring fearsomely, emerging from a cave as the heavenly bull. They see the golden-footed steeds waiting to accept the sacrifice offered to honor their great kingdom. Like the fire-red leader, they draw others, such as spotted deer, to yoke to the carriage. The bright ones serving as young Maruts shed rain upon the royal *Susoma, Saryakiavan, and Arjika* tribes, who establish their homes to serve heroes. Like the ancient cosmic hosts, the Maruts, singing, they invoke the godly powers and grant favors in support of Indra as a friend, who serves as the supreme power of causation regulating all the manifested mortal embodiments. The envoy Kaṇvas come singing forth with praises to support Indra, who wields thunder, wearing golden swords to bring a new form of contentment. They attract all those who come to join them and become heroes as impetuous ones. With their wondrous strength, before they sink into the hills, they flee into the abyss like flying steeds. On their tortuous path, where even the mountains bend down, they provide strength and life, which they carry through the midair region.

With all success and support, the Kaṇvas create a wonderful path decked with bountiful pure forms such as shaded trees, which provide a canopy to protect against the bright rays of the sun. The mortal embodiments (sages), granted profound intellects, generate vibrations that produce hymns within the midair region to support the Vatsa and Nahuṣa tribes. The Kaṇvas lead the tribes to drink pure soma and thereby acquire higher knowledge. Before the tribespeople drink the savory juice, they first offer a sacrifice to the demigod Aśvins and the envoy Kaṇvas, who once prevailed within the heavenly region. They bring eternal love (Mitra) along with the soma, which mixed with pleasant tasting meath and pressed by the envoy Kaṇvas. As it was in olden times, they serve the heroes and even call upon noble souls (rishis) to come from the heavenly sphere and bring inner illumination to those who care and offer loud prayers that heard by all. The prophetic rishis, the noble Vatsa, and the sons of the envoy Kaṇvas all come with magnified prayers that turn hymns into holy songs. Among the Vatsa and Nahuṣa tribes, with such powers, they freed from any stain caused by residual memories. They bring contentment while the immortal soul serves as evil-slayers. The lords of ample wealth who once prevailed as the supreme powers of causation now bring along the twin demigod Aśvins, who with their carriage bring one thousand adornments for the parishioners (sages) and their offspring. They all continue to sing sweet songs, bringing rich goods and providing with the ability to discover opulence. Parishioners (sages) and the twin demigod Aśvins, traveling through the sky, welcomed with songs of praise and granted rich gifts that no one may obstruct. They observe there is no reason to rebuke the supreme powers of causation, which once were the twin demigod Aśvins, and now appear as Nāsatyas, so they can travel near and far, bringing with them a carriage filled with one thousand adornments. They serve the prophets (rishis) and the noble souls (of the Vatsa tribe), and they worship in exaltation with rich food that purifies them and provides grace. With the offer of one thousand adornments, rishis and the Vatsa bow down to the demigod Nāsatyas in gratitude for the food that provides physical strength. By dropping purifying emollient, this brings bliss among worshippers (sages) who can slay their foes and, if needed, receive support from the demigod Nāsatyas. They receive honor along with rich treasure. Singing holy hymns like the highly renowned heroes, they blessed with good things, all coming from earth and heaven, to help them and others. Once they invoked, they become contented and transform to serve as holy sages (Priyamedhas). Through the singing of prayers and hymns, they produce eternal love to honor the commentator Medhātithi, who offers solemn rites, as do the ancient demigods who come to unveil the laws of karma and the laws of dharma, and they graciously assist the holy sages, who acquire eternal strength and, through eternal wisdom, come to unveil the secrets of the supreme powers, which remain concealed among *Vaśa*, *Dasavraja*, the *Kaṇvas, Medhātithi, and Trasadasyu*, who serve within heaven, on the earth, and in the midair region.

Serving as holy sages, Priyamedhas appear as epithets of Agni, who through eternal fire appears in four forms. First, in the celestial region, he manifests as the illuminated celestial bodies (the sun, the moon, and the constellations). Second, in the cosmic region, he manifests as the life force providing vitality. Third, within the midair region, he prevails as water vapor, which holds the living spirit hidden within a seed or embryo. Fourth, within the terrestrial region, he prevails as the eternal flame serving as the platform (altar) where unmanifested bodies transform into manifested bodies, including terrestrial bodies such as meteors, and as hearth fires, kiln fires, and other similar forms. In his manifested body, Agni, along with Jātavedas, comes to perceived and is responsible for serving the manifested material world (Virāj). This grand space holds one hundred bright splendors, which all serve among those who are stronger than the strongest, who are honored with glorious names, and who come to live forever. Through understanding different forms of fire that prevail within the universe, worshippers come to gain an understanding of all existence (Pali). Understanding the powers of nature (prakriti), they acquire knowledge and wisdom to comprehend the true meaning of Jātavedas, representing the five aspects of absolute truth: (1) knowing all about how things are created, (2) enjoying all creations, all creatures, and everything that has come into existence, (3) comprehending the physical and spiritual powers regulating living beings, (4) learning to exist by possessing riches without attachment, and (5) in order to enhance life, acquiring eternal wisdom through seeking freedom from the cycle of life and death.

## CAPABILITY

According to *Rig-Veda* 8:9, all holy sages within this spacious place develop their own dwelling places where they live and enjoy the manifested material world (Virāj). They learn to secure their mortal material embodiments by keeping away from malignities and focus upon cultivating the five tribes, all of which bestowed by the first cosmic body, Manu, who defines the laws of karma and the laws of dharma that shared among all manifested mortal embodiments. Through songs of praise (hymns) and oblation, they fill their stomachs with sweet soma and cultivate purified amrit. The twin winged horses, the Aśvins, as demigods, serve everyone as the lords of ample wealth, who do whatever needs done and help individual manifested mortal embodiments to face situations. They even help them to get out of tricky situations, such as floods, and protect them from the evil powers growing within plants and hiding in trees or existing among individual manifested bodies. They come out and succeed by serving as wonderworkers. They employ forces of advanced demigods (Nāsatyas) to exert their powers, when needed, to heal wounds. They even become part of speech (Vasta) and of their own accord, as wonderworkers, help to unveil the absolute truth, not only through singing hymns, but also through personally visiting the prophets (rishis) and noble sages (seers) and offering them gifts.

Generating splendid thoughts, they pour forth hymns, serving as the noble tribe of Atharvan, who comes to extract mythical juice (soma) and offer heartfelt oblation, accompanied by rich praise, all coming from the ascending carriage of the twin demigod Aśvins. The supreme powers of causation lightly roll on, on their way gathering speed, and proceed like clouds moving the heavens. The tribal Nāsatyas witness them moving speedily along and offer them songs of praise and with hymns, remembering to invoke the special envoys Kaṇva, Kakṣīvān, Ṛṣi, Vyaśva, and Dīrghatamas. They also help to establish sacrificial chambers (Vainya Pṛthi) where mindful supreme powers of causation, such as the demigod Aśvins, appear as guardians of the home, using speech (Vasta) to save other living creatures from foemen. They come to the homes of the mortal embodiments to give them the seed to produce offspring, guided jointly by Indra and Agni. Served by the demigod Aśvins, resting in one dwelling place, they blessed to serve by the wind (Vayu), which brings harmony through the cosmic body Ṛbhu, who directed by the noble Ādityas and, standing still in his striding place, established by the Sustainer, Vishnu.

According to *Rig-Veda* 8:10, the supreme powers of causation, serving as demigod Aśvins, come from far away and, with the heavenly light, come to build a mansion above the sea. They remember appearing as the first cosmic man, Manu, who, with the son of the envoy Kaṇva, prepares the sacrifice and engages in worship to honor the trinity of Bṛhaspati, Indra, and Vishnu. The trinity comes along with other gods to lead the Aśvins, rapid steeds, to inspire marvelous works among manifested mortal embodiments. They always received in friendship, which makes them most famous, known for passing along their kinship to the supreme powers of causation. Even without the sun, with solemn rites, they make the worshipper rise with inner illumination, come to know the holy work of sacrifice, and comprehend the powers of the gods through drinking the sweet mythical soma. As the lords of ample wealth, the demigod Aśvins linger with the Druhyu, Anu, Yadu, and Turvaga tribes in the east and in the west until they are called upon to serve as the lords of great riches, flying over the firmament, speeding through heaven and earth, traveling along with the divine godly nature, which always stands ready to serve.

According to *Rig-Veda* 8:11, Agni, in as half-mortal manifested embodiment, Jātavedas, comes to serve with demigods, offering sacred rites to guard those who make sacrifices in adoration. The mighty power Agni glorified at festivals, with Jātavedas bearing divine offerings, who comes to fight foes and drive them far from mortal embodiments. The two together drive the godless and evil enemies, and as Jātavedas and the manifested Agni, they avoid the worship of hostile men, no matter how imminent it may be. The mortal worshippers (sages) adore the immortal powers who bring divine will to aid and mortals, and honor them with songs, yearning to be with Agni, who help draw their minds away from the great Vatsa kingdom and farther away from their lofty dwelling place. Even though Agni remains the same, prevailing among all living beings in places, he appears at the fight when mortal living beings seek his strength. When called upon to aid in the strife, Agni becomes giver of rich gifts in war. The ancient powers adore his ability to make sacrifices when he serves as an old priest. They meet with praise and sit together to satisfy specific needs, winning happiness through the worship offered them.

According to *Rig-Veda* 8:12, mighty Agni comes to join with Indra, and with joy they meet to share the drafts of soma that springs with noble thoughts. Serving as immortal powers, they smite any monster filled with greed. Serving as the boldest Adhrigu and the greatest Daśagva, they stir up the light coming from the sun and shake down the waters flowing toward the sea. They remove longing, driving away the monsters who reside in the rivers and, through their powers, creating mighty floods to put back into place the laws of karma with the ordained archetype Manu. They, as progenitors of humanity, further put in place laws of dharma to ordain aesthetes to serve as the progenitors of noble souls. Both karma and dharma, existing within the universe through godly power (divine will), accepted with the meteors (casters of the stone) entering the atmosphere to free the water that creates a tidal wave (tsunami) in the sea that spills over onto the ground. They said the pure emollient that comes with the meteors, producing hymns and spiritual songs. As lovers of the supreme powers of causation, from afar they send gifts in the form of cosmic vapor, which spreads across the waters and appears as rain coming from heaven, to maintain the bond of their friendship. They bring along beams of light to mark such actions, and they grow strong, especially when the sun assumes its position between heaven and earth, setting with thunder in its arms. The mighty lord of heroes comes to smooth out the thousand buffaloes before they can grow strong and consume those who are malicious.

By casting thunder, which brings the rays from heavenly power Sūrya, Agni conquers the woods. The new selfless noble living beings in time approach to come and serve as beloved ones. In places, the marks set by archetypal man, Manu, including karma and dharma in the form of pious seeds, which with sacrifice purify the individual living spirit (Atman) and helps it to progress meeting with justice.

Imperishable Indra, drinking perishable mythical juice (soma), wins mortal friends who, as worshippers, enlarge with their praise to meet the mark. They set out like the archetypal man, Manu, the ordained of karma for the worshippers (priests). Gladly offering up their hymns, like Agni, with a sacrifice of oil in their mouths, they swell. Once they go forth singing hymns to Indra, they learn to follow the laws of dharma and to honor the godly mother Aditi, coming to serve together as sovereign lords. They work to glorify their sacrifices so they appointed as clergymen, who aided by singers singing songs and offering eulogies. The supreme powers of causation, instead of turning away from the bay steeds, offer the archetypal man, Manu, the law of karma and the law of dharma. These laws recited by the prophet (rishi) who comes to serve as the sovereign lord.

The worshippers drink the purified soma and learn to transform it into amrit, thereby turning mortality into immortality (Trita Āptya). With delight, the cosmic hosts (Maruts) drink the flowing drops of mythical juice and serve as the heavenly ruler Śakra, who transforms into the ruler of universe, the mighty power of *trāyastriṃśa*. Traveling far into the sea of air, the worshippers rejoice when bringing out the flowing amrit that aids those among them who are serving as lords of the heroes. They shed the juice to bring delight, the drops magnifying the supreme powers of causation, who promptly arrive to help and to gain from the sacrifices of those leading powers to whom provided manifold instructions to help worshippers seek all kinds of wealth. They do what Indra did to slay the evil Vṛtra and, at the foremost place where choral bands play and sing with vigorous strength, bring might. They hear the loud calls coming, not from earth, or from heaven, nor from the firmament, but in the form of holy hymns, all sung with the vigorous strength contained within the thunder-wielding powers. This at once shakes the firmament, before, in a violent rush, with vigor, Indra arrives at the furious fight.

Two beautiful bay steeds carry Indra to the place where the evil Vṛtra, as a dragon or even a snake, as the fighter, holds back the water, stopping it from flowing freely. Indra breaks the barrier and sets the waters free, creating mighty thunderbolts and causing floods. The two beautiful bay steeds bring the Sustainer, Vishnu, with his energy, tromping wide, reaching the three great steps above the ground where the Sustainer grows ever greater day by day, along with all the other living creatures that bow down to honor such a power. Indra and the cosmic hosts (Maruts) humbly submit to the manifested mortal embodiments and to all living creatures that bow down to the yonder source of light (the sun). This brilliant light continues to sit above in the heavens, while all living creatures bow down on the earth to the supreme powers of causation. With this, Indra, with noble thoughts, uplifts the holy sages and their affiliates. They come on foot in their own embodiments to hear the eulogy, and they rise to come together and, with one voice, partake of the streams of milk as part of the worship, which takes place in a central spot specifically set up for holy sacrifice at the altar. The holy priests, serving Indra, offer oblations and give wealth to the brave heroes, also sacrifice their good steeds and cattle. This remembered as the first form of oblation offered by the supreme powers of causation for these sacrifices.

## INVOLUTION

According to *Rig-Veda* 8:13, each individual pure mind exalted with the power to generate free-flowing mythical juice (soma) gains the power that brings success. For the first time coming from the heavenly region, the supreme powers of causation bring a most glorious success by saving from the floodwaters. They bring such a strength that it can even help to resolve all disagreements, so instead of everyone being at all, they all go to provide aid to their friends and, as song lovers, offer libation and worship. Shining forth, they approach Indra, rejoicing, sitting on the sacred grass, where they provide pressed juice to those who crave to find the light of heaven, which brings manifold wealth to help others. Those who enthusiastic worshippers boldly sing old songs, which generate an increase in individual desire, which grows pious, like the branches of a tree, each level of which produces sweet varieties of fruits that glorify living beings. The enthusiastic worshippers move like water, speeding down a slope, singing to the lord of heaven, who as the sole ruler of all people provides seeker with aid and joy along with drafts of soma. Skilled in singing glorious songs, the lord of the two victorious bays, Indra, comes with praise for the living beings, the glorious worshippers who seek an abode and those who bow when they pray. He also brings dappled steeds and puts forth effort to bring out a mighty intellect among swift steeds.

The worshippers granted wealth with the rising of the sun, and at noonday, when Indra comes with his horses, well pleased, drinking a milky draft, speeding forward, he calls to them. Like in the past, they spin out like thread, rejoicing while praising Indra, who provides everlasting fame and brings opulence to princes. Indra, as the Vṛtra-slayer, comes from far away in the sky and appears near the surface of the ground, near the deep sea, serving as Śakra, guarded by singers singing songs offered as oblations and drinking the mythical juice that delights the tribes and makes them strong. He also comes in haste to aid them, to make the longing worshippers (sages) grow within their stirred minds and strengthened by their spiritual songs at the holy place of the Great One, Trkadrukas.

According to *Rig-Veda* 8:14, at times, at the holy place, true to their duty, the worshippers offer worship to become pure and wonderful. As in the ancient days of Rudra, they move with fresh, strong individuals in a cognizant order referred to as the individual state of wisdom. They selected to drink sacrificial juice and then make new friends and subdue enemies. They praised with love songs, and those who turn with Indra blessed and granted with wealth, mostly in the form of herds of cattle and steeds. They provided with two strong stallions, which, as the highly lauded bays, blessed with physical and spiritual powers, drawn from their untouched age and with most gladdening prayers. Along with making ancient offerings, the worshipped implore with praise, serving as youth with strength, coming to rest upon the sacred grass till they reach old age. Serving the mighty ones, who laud for aid, prophets (rishis) eulogize by pouring out an abundance of food to guard the worshippers.

Indra invites cosmic bodies, those who sing hymns, and yokes their minds with praises as they make sacrifices. Yoking their bodies like horses, they share their feast of soma with the bay steeds, tormented. With consent from Indra, they approach the attendants with glory. In assent, the heavenly power Rudra roars to accompany the cosmic hosts (Maruts) and enjoy the feast. The Maruts, victorious bold followers from the heavens, come to the place of eternal love, in alliance within the heart, coming to know well the true sacrifice offered. Worshippers (sages) come along beholding the light, and they timely proceed in life by performing orderly rites, duly measured, and view the sacrifice that offered to Indra, whose carriage pulled by strong bay steeds. Indra establishes the worshippers (sages), serving as the strong anchor Śatakratus, who joyfully receives cosmic bodies such as meteorites—tightly compressed stones. Producing strong soma from plants, and offering the rite, they hear a calling from far away—loud thunder coming to aid the thousands.

According to *Rig-Veda* 8:15, Indra, as the sole sovereign of all wealth, wants those worshippers rich in cattle to serve him with strengthened power and be enriched to go beyond this, even serving as worshippers who come and bring pressed juice, like a herd of cattle that yields plenty of milk, much more than any other milk-bearing animals. There is no one included with the demigods except Indra and benevolent humans who give part of their sacrifice to welcome the casters of the stone that have fallen to earth. As soon they land on the ground, they served as large, strongly compressed stones, accompanied with mythical juice, which with joy is the true pinnacle. Coming from heaven, they seem to have created as the children of heaven provided to Indra, who, after being gracefully refined, wins all treasure by way of his own effort. Once they experience ecstasy, which spreads over the firmament, filling the manifested world, they, with the realms of light, tear the evil power Vala limb from limb. As they move forward, they filled with hidden wisdom like the sacred cow, which receives further support from the envoy Aṅgiras, serving as the epithet of Agni, who goes head-to-head with the evil power.

Within the luminous realm of heaven, Indra establishes for himself a firm, secure, immovable place where the cosmic bodies (casters of the stone) move as children from the pinnacle of heaven, coming with hidden spiritual powers. They enjoy a wave of floodwater that creates bright and shining drops of mythical juice (soma), which produces gladdening hymns. With praises, the worshippers increase in number and rewarded with bliss for worshipping Indra with his two long-maned bay steeds, performing bountiful sacrifices to create soma juice, which is create amid the water's foam, which comes to rest among their heads to subdue the contentious evil powers the Asuras. Representing the darkness, the demon Namuci, with the evil rulers the Dāsas, use mystic arts to cast down earth. Drinking soma, they approach heaven and save face against the power of Indra. They scatter in all directions into settlements without pouring out any gifts.

Seven living beings, as patriarchs, through consuming mythical juice, attain eternal wisdom. Loudly singing hymns, they come to serve as holy sages (Saptarishis). They invoke Indra, inviting him with songs of praise and honoring his power. With their lofty might, they receive dedicated support, coming from heaven and earth to fill the ground, hills and plains alike, supported with floods and light, which provide physical strength.

Such physical strength supports the kings who smite dead the evil power Vṛtra and gain full control of the spoils of war. They have become highly renowned for wild delight as conquerors in the fray, singing to the strong Indra, who invites the manifested comic bodies (casters of the stone) that, as meteorites, come with their shining bodies to bring bright shining light, like gold. In the initial stages of illumination, the first mortal body, that is, physical life (*āyu*), is developed, later to be enhanced through the development of subtle faculties, including mental abilities, thus bringing in the spiritual powers to create the first cosmic body, Manu, who appears on the sacred grass, where a beam of light comes forth from the heavenly pantheon of Sūrya. With the lofty powers of the god Indra providing life force (prana), this builds physical strength and grants spiritual wisdom. This all comes with a thunderbolt to fulfill individual longing, augmented by the powers of heaven and earth and represented by the renowned supreme powers of causation. They bring water from the mountains to stir urges, while the power to sustain provided by Vishnu, the lofty ruling supreme power who, along with Varuna, regulates divine law and ushers in eternal love (Mitra). This is all accomplished with the cosmic hosts (Maruts) providing great delight. Thus, the firstborn embodiment, Manu, serving as the lord of humanity, is liberal in offering gifts to those who perform, by their own accord, excellent deeds for everyone and forevermore. Ever alone, they highly praised for putting to rest the evil power Vṛtra. Only Indra has the ability to execute such a mighty deed.

According to *Rig-Veda* 8:16, with praises, Indra, the most liberal sovereign, gain control of humanity and come to rule by offering hymns of praise. His worshippers provide him with delight and glory through singing songs. Like floodwaters longing for the sea, the sovereign of humankind, offering eulogies, invites kings who are strong enough to win and gain the spoils through fighting righteous wars. Perfect, profound, and victorious, with ecstasy that delivers joy to those on the battlefield, the kings, as noble heroes, when venturing into war and winning the spoils, lead human beings to serve as their advocates who honor them with songs and solemn rites, which magnifies their achievements. The prophets (rishis), with their mighty powers, invoke others who lauded to bring out the true heroes from among them who can perform victorious deeds of might, even when they are all alone. With such strength coming from celestial Indra, human beings magnify him with songs, hymns, and sacred eulogies, which helps them to advance. They attain eternal wisdom, which brings them enlightenment, and they learn to guide and lead others in the war, quelling their foemen. In the fray, they helped by the savior Indra, who guides them beyond all enemies, like a ship to a safe harbor. With heavenly pressed mythical juice, humanity and their heroes yoked with prayer, serving as long-maned bay steeds that listen to their friends.

## SOVEREIGNTY

According to *Rig-Veda* 8:17, holy priests (Brahmans) who pour soma into the mortal embodiments offer a eulogy, withholding their words. Such pleasant drink spreads like sweet, delicious juice within the body, reaching the heart. Like a woman adorned with a robe, it enters the other body parts, including those close to the astral body with an inner living spirit (Atman). Once a human's manifested mortal embodiment activated by the powers of Indra, it transports the juice all throughout the body, making the neck strong like a stem and creating stout arms, which may use to smite the evil powers. It also helps them to move forward to slay the fiends. Then the embodiments become like mighty rulers. Made radiant by the soma, they are delighted to worship and offer *kundapāyya* to *Akhandala* and his great-grandson *Srngavrs*, who build strong pillars or create bondage through thoughts among their ancestors. Serving as the ancient powers of causation and the winners of the spoils, preeminent among others, they are honored as the holy *Prdikusanu* leads Indra as a wild horse, with a drink of mythical juice, as if headed to war. Through divine grace, *Prdikusa*nu inspires virtuous impulses, which impart strength so they may endure the trial, resisting temptation.

With the virtue of excellence, reinforced by godly power (divine will), *Prdikusanu*, Indra, and S*rngavrs* appear among of humanity to serve as the select ones who are ready sanctified. With divine grace, they are dedicated to devotional service, such as bhakti, and Hadith, to attain Kripa, sanctity, and nirvana, ultimately attaining self-realization like the ancient sages Buddha, Muhammad, Jesus Christ, and Moses, among many other spiritual scholars who are honored as Vasiṣṭha, serving like as revered seven noble powers, the Saptarishis, with divine grace, which is not a gift but rather is earned through following a devotional practice.

According to *Rig-Veda* 8:18, such mortal embodiments offer prayers to win unearned grace from the noble Ādityas and in so doing come to cherish life. They tread as infallible guards, strengthened along the path to happiness, but not the part where the enemy assaults nobles. The godly Ādityas bring along other powers—Bhaga, Savitar, Varuna, Mitra, and Aryaman—to provide shelter. They implore the mighty powers, who come to offer foster care checked by the godly mother Aditi and no one else, except the lords who assigned to guard them. The sons of Aditi know to keep the enemies away and unprovoked by giving them ample room.

Mother Aditi guards the herd by day and frees them from guile at night. During the day, they strengthened by the constant singing of hymns to save them from grief, and at night Mother Aditi comes to offer each the loving-kindness that brings well-being and chases foes away. The twin demigod Aśvins, as a divine pair of physicians, maintain health by removing iniquity and chasing the foes away. Agni, like Sūrya in the heavens, comes to bless with fire, which provides heat and warmth, while the heavenly power Rudra brings a pleasant wind to provide sweet breath to all and ejects any foes residing within the embodiments, also driving away disease, strife, and malignity. The Ādityas, simultaneously, keep mortal embodiments far away from soreness and distress. They even remove the arrow of famine and keep enemies far away from the lords of all wealth. The Ādityas, serving as bounteous ones, grant shelter, so individual astral bodies may be set free. They even help the sinners by freeing them from sin. Whatever mortals, with the demon powers, comes to injure others suddenly suffers harm by way of their own evil deeds and sins. They overtake the human body, becoming foes, and make noble souls speak evil words, which causes misery within their false hearts. Mother Nature (Vasu) comes to discern the true from the false and provides those who are true with shelter. She comes to their aid from the mountains, wherefrom she brings the floodwaters to keep the foes away from heaven and earth and help those who are true to overpower such wickedness. With the auspicious shelter provided by Mother Nature (Vasu), those who are true carried beyond all trouble and distress.

The mighty ones grant the Ādityas seeds to have children and provide them with an extended life span so they may live long and offer sacrifices. The mighty ones monitored inside by the Ādityas, supporting the living spirit with kindness that builds a bond and brings them all together. Such noble souls protected by the powers of the cosmic hosts (Maruts) and the twin demigod Aśvins, who further supported by the powers of eternal love and eternal law (Mitra and Varuna, respectively). In the form of a trinity, Aryaman, Mitra, and Varuna provide a home that guarded by the powers of the cosmic hosts (Maruts). They come to meet with humanity that filled with praise. The Ādityas, serving as mortals, are prone to death, but their lives graciously lengthened. Physical and mental strength provides energy and force, which increases the capacity for natural growth among all plants, animals, and other living things, allowing them to survive by way of nonphysical powers such as enthusiasm, intensity, and vigor. This represents vitality among the holy souls serving the immortal power, their living spirits residing among blessed holy priests (sages). The messenger Agni brings the primordial power, Shakti, who provides the bounteous giver with extreme vigor.

## VITALITY

According to *Rig-Veda* 8:19, the primordial power, Shakti, with bright light and with divine oblations that supported and expressed through her vigor—expressed as prayers and devotions—makes noble souls to appear in the sky, creating bright clusters of flame. They appear as galaxies generating colors that represent different constellation regions, all regulated by immortal vigor, which generates rainbows in the sky. On a grand scale, the noble souls come together, meeting at a sacred place, to receive the sacred blend of mythical juice, which they offer as their first joint sacrifice, as pure as precious metal like gold. They chose to serve as the immortal priests. Skilled in sacrifice and eternal wisdom, they come to offer holy rites, serving as the Sons of Strength. They are all blessed with brightly shining halos atop their heads. Like holy sages, they provide the light of excellence, which comes from heaven. With grace from other celestial powers, namely, Mitra and Varuna, they serve the mortal embodiments prevailing on earth. By offering oblation, they win over floods. With their reverence, they bring the fuel that can invoke the eternal flame and skillfully minister the sacrifice. This produces a splendid eminence among fleet-footed steeds, without causing any trouble to the mortal embodiments. No matter which side they come from or overtake, they well supplied with eternal flame, supports them as they serve as the Sons of Strength.

As lords of might, they become the worthy friends of humanity, and with praises, they provide perfect security. They come to serve among mortal embodiments. As the sovereign lords of wealth, they rightly praised for having the auspicious eternal flame. The sovereign lord of wealth comes to rule over humanity, as humanity brings sacrificial gifts to win riches. They seek help with their thoughts and make their sacrifices, as well as acquire the ability to stand erect, serving as prosperous human beings. By winning coursers, the singers, who are heroes, and whose physical bodies are the dwelling places of mortals, they receive other prizes, such as a chieftain's ornaments. Represented as the ferocious fire, Agni desired by all, well lauded, and loved zealously.

The humans attend offerings with words of worship offered to the Sons of Strength. The Sons of Strength give sacred gifts, and to hold their position, which is directly above humanity but beneath the powers of nature (Vasu), they speak words of wisdom and eternal truth. The powers of Vasu operate through humanity, who offer sacrificial gifts and skillfully bring homage, which flashes fast, bringing with it spiritual music and holy words. Humanity, that is, mortal embodiments fueled by the eternal flame commanded by the eternal law and adore by the divine covenant. With splendorous thoughts that exceed the thoughts of all other living beings, like a flood they overcome each greedy villain and the wrath of evil hearted folk. The trinity of Mitra, Varuna, and Aryaman bring inner illumination through the Aśvins and Bhaga to comfort and support the worshippers, who also receive help from Indra. Most devout, they serve as exceedingly wise sages who look upon the altar arranged with offerings to the supreme powers of causation. Each morning they offer, along with oblation, pressed mythical juice, which strengthens them so they may win mighty wealth. They set their hopes upon Agni to bring them the gift of bliss that transforms the sages into blessed ones. They show forth with individual minds filled with eternal wisdom, which brings success in war, allowing them to conquer fiends. They bring down enemies with the firm hope vanquishing them with the aid of Agni.

As a friend of humanity, the Blessed One comes down to serve as the herald or messenger bearing gifts to give the best among the worshippers a sharp-toothed power, supported by Agni, who transforms into the Blessed One to create a young radiant power who is honored by a feast and songs. Honoring Agni with their sweet anxieties molds their heroic strength into an eternal flame that used along with the sacred sacrificial oil, the flame moving upward and downward like a sword, slicing through robes to kill the evil Asuras. The young radiant ones of the next generation, as the noble supreme powers of causation, come to serve as the friends of humanity.

As distributers of skilled sacrifice, they come with sweet-smelling mouths, through which they offer a precious gift that originally used to invoke the holy worshipper (priest) who serves an immortal power, the god Agni. As the Sons of Strength, they help the mortal embodiments to be set free and come to serve as the bright immortal power of eternal love, Mitra. Filled with friendship, they received as the support (Vastu) that serves only the bounteous ones who are not miserly, selfish, or greedy. As living beings serving as worshippers, they feel no hunger or distress, nor live in sin. And like sons, they cherish their father's house. They offer oblation as they rise unto the supreme powers of causation, gaining immediate aid from the supreme power, the most excellent Agni. Mortal embodiments gain wisdom that affords them the bounty to lead together with others in seeking wealth. Moving from the excellent powers, they attain farsightedness, which with delight makes them open-minded. They go ahead and conquer. With aid, they fill up their stores and pass among the noble heroes, with whom they build bonds of friendship.

Like the bounteous ones, their spark is black, and in due time, it comes crackling to kindle the dawn. Friends of the mighty morning come shining at night to create luminous sites. The chosen immortal priests, skilled in sacrifice and eternal wisdom, coming to help them succeed, serve as good helpers, also serving as the Lord of One Thousand Powers, a friend within Trasadasyu's kingdom. They all come to serve as the messengers of Agni, on whom all other fires depend; they grow like branches on the stem serving as the parent, amassing treasures for their people by singing songs of worship. The noble Ādityas, as guides, lead the mortals to the farther bank, where all the princes (bounteous ones) and others ruling humanity as kings, or serving as advisers to humanity, exposing them to the divine covenant, learn all about the individual messengers serving as the trinity of Mitra, Varuna, and Aryaman.

Like swift travelers, the spiritual souls are all checked by the lord serving the manifested worlds as the Sustainer (Vishnu). They are all conferred with vitality, and as spiritual souls they appear as the trinity of the Maruts, the Ṛbhukṣans, and the Rudras, by whose powers they create a firm, suitable, fully strengthened embodiment.

According to *Rig-Veda* 8:20, those who exceed in brilliance, with sacrificial food and love, come to be born as a young tribal girl appearing as an innocent cow (Surabhi) representing the godlike nature. The Surabhi accept obligatory responsibility (karma) and are prepared to go beyond to attain wisdom and subsequent devotional responsibilities (dharma). The innocent female cow comes to know the dynamic heavenly power, Rudra, whose sons manifest as the cosmic hosts (*Maruts.*) They appear as the demigods, serving the ground (Prithvi), as holy priests. Swift and strong, they band together to serve as the Sustainer, Vishnu. While passing through thick clouds, they bring rain, bursting forth on the ground. They monitor the desolate landmasses where they elect to stay, joining as one, coming to represent the true union of heaven and earth. The cosmic hosts (Maruts), as demigods, with the holy priests, spread out with their luminous bodies, causing a stir that shakes even the immovable mountains and the trees of the forest. As they approach terrestrial bodies, the Maruts follow a free course. Leading in furious rush, they move away from heaven, now serving as higher heroes. With their mighty arms, they come displaying their gleaming knickknacks, which cause trembling on the ground (Prithvi), imbuing them with godlike nature (Surabhi) to appear as the bull that, like dazzling heroes, and with impetuosity, wearing the great splendor, they show their rigidness. Even the axle of their chariot, serving the godlike nature (Surabhi), covered in gold. Wellborn, mighty, they explode with milk by way of the kindred sacred cow, providing food and delight. They bring such balm to drop, also sprinkling oblations, which they offer to the Maruts serving as the lead bull.

The Maruts come like a strong vehicle, solid in look, solid naves. Like winged falcons, they serve as heroes, their chariots pulled by stallions. They enjoy offering ornaments made of bullion with decorations. All bright, these placed within the arms of the heroes as their splendidly glittering weapons. They toil, not to defend their bodies from attack, but to show a hero's strength, holding their arms in their mighty arms, with glorious expressions on their faces. Their presence extends like the sea, alone and resplendent, so that the ancestral mighty powers breathe with life force (prana).

The Maruts come singing praises. Like the wheel spokes that support their embodiments, they produce loud roaring sounds, showing off their power. They move on to give gifts and blessings amid the light of early morning. As strong men, like heroes they make sacrifices. They approach with glory, as in war, winning the spoils and thus gaining great bliss, now serving the world as Shakers.

The creator of the broad kingdom ruled over by Dyaus and filled with evil powers (Asuras) comes with desire like the noble young ones who serve as the strong sons of Rudra. They come with the bounteous cosmic hosts, the Maruts, moving onward, pouring down with the rain. The evil Asuras now come with kind hearts. Like the noble young ones, they accepted, along with the sacred cow with a godlike nature (Surabhi). The sacred cow, singing the new song, comes to the plow as do the steers serving as strong young bulls. Like a celebrated boxer, they overcome their challengers in every fight, and like shining bulls, most illustrious with honor, they join with the cosmic hosts (Maruts), and they sing their own song, allied by a common ancestry. With energy like the sacred cow, when they display their eternal love and conquer, they turn every head, including those of the mortal dancers with breasts adorned with gold. They form a brotherhood that marks, and noticed as their eternal friendship with the Maruts. This brings rich and noble gifts, including a potion that serves as medicine to help those who are the friends of noble souls. The Maruts will not serve the haters and will not serve those bringers of bliss who offer auspicious aid to the victorious ones who fail to guard the holy rivers such as the Indus. They do not even assist or give aid to those in need by providing them with lifeblood. Krvi, who makes rives flow smoothly and keeps their surfaces calm, creates trimmed grass all along the rivers, where people may rest. Krvi also creates places of rest in the mountains or on the seas to support physical bodies. As blessed graciously cosmic hosts, the Maruts cast to the ground with a sick man's malady and come to repair any dislocated limbs.

CHAPTER 15

# Validated Dominion

THE VALIDATED DOMINION IS THE REGION WHERE NOBLE POWERS come to prevail and serve as minor deities. They attain a transitory divine status and serve as guardian gods, representing the souls of dead heroes. Or, as half-gods, they go through a process of heroization, making them demigods (*hemitheoi)*, and thereby come to appear as half-mortal and half-immortal. There are three notable *hemitheoi*, the first of which is the heavenly bull (*Nandi*), who travels within outer space. Nandi supported by the primordial power, Shakti, who appears with Lord Shiva, serving as the auspicious destroyer and as the protector of manifested mortal embodiments. The second notable *hemitheoi*, appear as heavenly bird *Garuda)*, which like in kite formation, flock and rides serving within the midair region providing divine life force (*prana*). The bird *garuda* responsible for regulating the life force as breath and sustains the material world (*Lord Vishnu*). The third notable demigods *hemitheoi* is the bovine goddess, milk-bearing cow (*Surabhi*), who serves as the mother of universal immortal soul (*Paramatman*) and whose divine vehicle appear as *astral body* which represent existence (*Brahma*).

In terms of mythology, such creatures defined as one-half manifested, physical powers, and the other half unmanifested, serving as the spiritual power. Jointly personified as demigods who serve all creations including humankind. They also serve as guardians, patrons, and protectors of geographical places and of all things personal, cultural, and occupational. As part of etymology, they serve the divine powers (*Ishta*) devata, (*Kuldevi-kuldevta)*, Gramma-devata and, as the divine will, manifest to appear as guardian deities, serving as protectors (*devas*) and patrons (*yogis*) who manage renunciants (*Mahadeva*). Matchless, possessing nothing firm, they come to protect humanity, always seeking to help any righteous warriors who offer their lives as a sacrifice to provide relief for others.

## CHAMPION

According to *Rig-Veda* 8:21, as youth behold their mightiness and go forth seeking friends as those who give freely, they choose Indra as their guardian. Serving as lord of the land, lord of food, lord of horses, lord of cattle, and lord of plants, Indra brings drops of mythical juice as he joins with the singers. Indra, who as avatars appears in forms, they bring the mythical juice with a bull-like strength for others to drink. All singers sitting like birds beside lavender, drink honey mingled with milk, which heartens them to sing loudly to exalt the powers of Indra. With reverential prayer, all speak and ponder awhile, expressing their wishes as blessed hymns to represent themselves to the liberal lord of the bays. Even today, as in the past, people seek the thunder-armed Indra to provide them with wealth and divine aid to serve the heroes and spiritual scholars who are known to be friends with the divine. Such a friendship provides rich rewards, with Vasu regulating the five great elements of nature and providing all wealth, refined powers, and godly vision. Those who know about such powers also know that such powers come with blessings to magnify the devotees and help them. Borne by bay steeds, serving as the lord of heroes, ruling as humanity, they take delight in supporting other living beings. Indra, through his messenger Maghavan, bestows worshippers with hundreds of cattle and steeds, along with heroic friends, so they may withstand any wrath and fight for wealth in terms of cattle and horses. The victors, singing battle songs, come to meet with the wicked. As they invoke heroes, they smite the foemen. They show forth their strength through their thoughts, all expressing their support for Indra. Since ancient times, they have beseeched Indra, who is rival less, for his support and have sought true companionship for the companionless, even in times of war. They find their devoted friend, but not like the wealthy who blown by the wind. Instead, they find those who not even scorned by thunder, whom they invoke. Indra, as father, makes sure they do not waste time like fools by staying at home or sitting idle with friends. As the giver of cattle, Indra pours out juice for those who do not take for granted this gracious gift, He even lays to waste the fortifications of the foe and brings gifts that could otherwise give in vain. Indra, along with the goddess *Sarasvatī,* bestows such wealth so great that it serves the emulator (*Citra*), who allows kings to rest and dwell together. Goddess of rivers *Sarasvatī,* along with deity of thunder (*Parjanya*) that brings thousand gifts that fall with the rain.

According to *Rig-Veda* 8:22, Parjanya has, even today, the most wondrous carriage pulled by the twin demigod Aśvins, who swiftly follow red paths with their carriage for the sake of the heavenly power Sūrya. The young ones, much longed for, easily invoked soon guided to perform their first mighty deeds. They wait upon and benevolently serve the sacred cow Surabhi, who is without rival or foe. The Aśvins, with homage, represent two omnipresent deities that bring kind help to those who seek the dwelling of the gods as worshippers. One drives the two-wheeled chariot that moves on its course. The milk cow accepts the benevolence of these lords of splendor. Their chariot has a triple seat and reins of gold, traveling between heaven and earth to bring the twin Aśvins to serve as wonderworkers (Nāsatyas). They plow the ground, favoring the cosmic body Manu, who is responsible for the first harvest under the sky. As exalted lords of splendor and ample wealth, the Aśvins, with prayer and praise, follow the path of the everlasting law from the high dominion, where with mighty strength, King *Trasadasyu* raises his first son, *Trksi.* Soma plants, pressed with stones, supplies the heroes and the lords of plenteous wealth with soma in the abode of the worshippers. The demigod Aśvins board their chariot with its golden seat and, as lords of plenteous wealth, bring an abundance food. Their aid, wherewith, separated from his friends *Paktha, Adhrigt, and Babhru,* who join the Aśvins, soon coming to heal whatever is diseased. The Aśvins continually invoked the defenseless ones at the same time of day.

Lovers of the song, singing, come to the mighty ones who bring blessings in all forms. Heroes, with ample food that strengthens them, along with Krvi, speak to the Aśvins, whom the universal soul (God) reveres with homage given to both at the same time of day. These lords of splendor, whose paths are red, make sacrifices in the evening and in the morning. Lords of ample wealth, the Rudras supply absolutely nothing to the foes of the mortals, even when they pray for their favor. The immortal universal soul, God of the inseparable Aśvins, calls the sacred cow Surabhi, who comes swiftly with joy to protect them, even when they are far away. The lords of great wealth, by offering their aid through wonderworkers, travel from home to home with Aśvins, bringing cattle, steeds, and gold to the chief drinkers of soma. Indra, with strength, heroic, firm, and excellent, comes to all those uninjured by the rakshasas. With his coming nigh, the lords of ample wealth bestow all good things that obtained.

According to *Rig-Veda* 8:23, Agni receives the worshippers who pray with the godly power Jātavedas and willingly accept the divine will that comes with smoke, representing the eternal flame whose true nature none can grasp. This exalts Agni as the giver of the flame, who serves with his friends the *Visvamanas* without any conflict, all singing songs to help the individual embodiments. Those who stand firm in the conflict warrant praise, win food and vigor, and discover how the priest obtains wealth—the selfsame thing they are seeking. The friends the *Visvamanas*, with their imperishable flame, become the refulgent ones, with glorious glowing jaws. Skilled in fair sacrifice, they extolled to arise, shining with refulgent light, which manifests within them as godlike loveliness. Calling, they offer eulogies and oblations to Agni, serving as his devoted envoys, all bearing gifts. Agni calls upon them to invoke the old priests to come and serve the living beings by singing loud songs. They perform solemn rites and, like wise men fair of form, serve with kindness. Their friends are those who keep the holy law, live true to the law, serve with perfect sacrifice, grace the places of prayer with law-loving songs. Making sacrifices along with enhanced living beings such as humans, they seek Agni's truest envoy, Aṅgiras, serve humankind as illustrious earthly priests.

The imperishable Aṅgiras, envoy of Agni, regulates the eternal flame and enkindles other fires to show his strength by appearing as flying horses or stallions. With such eternal flame, Agni and Aṅgiras bring forth the Lord of Power, along with the Lord of Might, who in combination bring along the heroes, rich in strength, and guard them in their battles, along with their sons and their offspring. The lord of humanity, eager and friendly, enters Manu's race, and through Agni, with his truest envoy, Aṅgiras, upon hearing of any evil attack, immediately manifests and appears anew with a loud voice. With the eternal flame, Aṅgiras burn the evil rakshasas. No mortal foe is ever able to prevail against Agni overpowered by Aṅgiras, who serves with the ferocious fire.

Like the ancient sage Vyaśva, Agni and Aṅgiras attain the powers of the heavenly bull to find good things, which they enkindle with wealth. They establish as well as stabilize the human tribes (Uśanā Kāvya). Like the godly power Jātavedas, they come to sacrifice for humanity and, with all power and of one accord, appoint their godly messenger, who through hearing, first makes a sacrifice to protect the mortal heroes as their immortal messenger. With far-spreading eternal flame, as purifiers, the heroes follow the black path, with lifted ladles, to call upon the splendid, brilliant flame just like the ancients did. Wasting nothing given by the one who duly worships them with sacrificial gifts, they obtain plenteous nourishment to serve as famous heroes. Serving with the chief of sacrifices, Jātavedas, the messengers first pay homage to Agni, and then to the ancient sage Vyaśya, who with a ladle offers sacred gifts. Singing hymns, the heroes pray to and worship the splendid flame of Agni. Then they come to land where the son Sthurayupa, singing songs that spread across far distances, enters the homes served by Vyaśva, also offering worship to Agni, all the heroes appearing as noble souls (rishis). As noble souls, they welcomed among humanity, serving as their guests. Their offspring become the sovereigns of vegetation and the kings of the forest, serving as sages (rishis). Like the king of manifested humanity, they worship the ancient powers that provide aid to all the manifested mortal embodiments, who offer oblation that invokes the mightiest lord of all. The heroes come to sit on the sacred grass, along with supreme powers of causation, and offer homage to Agni, who brings abundant treasures and grants opulence to fill the desires who crave for such. With the store of heroes, their progeny, and the highly renowned powers of Agni, they bring the most youthful of the gods, *Varosusaman*, granting the gift of wealth to all his kinsfolk. As mighty conquerors, with support from Agni, the heroes find nutritious food among herds of all kinds and learn to extract ample wealth. The glorious Agni brings the imperial sovereigns, immortal, holy-minded, Mitra (eternal love) and Varuna (eternal law).

## COMPANIONS

According to *Rig-Veda* 8:24, companion, imperial sovereigns, learn to pray for Indra, who appears with arms of thunder, to glorify their bold and most heroic friend who is skilled in the art of slaying the evil power (*Vṛtra*) thus coming to be known as the famous and imperial sovereign Vṛtra-slayer. As a hero Indra's gifts surpass those of other wealthy chiefs, and when he glorified, it brings riches and fame to the one who gives him the glory. Indra has achieved the highest rank among the gods to serve as wealth giver, the lord of the bays. He declares the preeminent wealth givers as the bold ones, glorified to serve others. The workers of destruction stay neither on right nor on left, and neither do the hosts who gather around as the lord of the bays in battle. Thunder-armed, as the immortal universal soul Indra enjoys the songs coming from the stall with cattle and steeds as he fulfills the wishes of those who sing his praises. As the chief Vṛtra-slayer, Indra reminded through the hymn the Visvamanas, most excellent mighty guides. The Vṛtra-slayer, serving as a hero with boon, is the longed-for excellence who comes when invoked. Indra much invoked like a dancer. With great power, he is unsurpassed, as is the bounty he bestows upon his worshippers. Most mighty, most heroic, he comes with a mighty bounty, full of the strength needed to win wealth. Maghavan serves as Indra's messenger and, like thunder, never allows prayers for divine assistance to send forth to any other god, as none other than Indra has bounty enough to save those in need of saving. He has splendid wealth and power. Lovers of the song pour out for Indra drops of milk blended with soma, that drink as essence (meath), for bounty and majesty and, further, to solicit help from immortal universal soul (God), who speaks to the lord of the bay coursers and imparts the ability to hear the Aśvins with praises. Never has any hero been born who is mightier than Indra, none like him in goodness and wealth. Indra serves as a ministering priest who pours out the sweet juice that gladdens most. So is the hero praised by Indra to prosper, along with the tawny coursers, without whose power, goodness, and contributions nothing would ever happen or attained. Seeking glory, when invoked, the head of all power and might glorified for his constant sacrifice. Singing praises to his friends, the hero deserves lauded by all tribes, as without him they would not be able to overcome. The one who wins the stable full of cows and horses and keeps it, the celestial god Indra, speaks more sweetly than butter and essence (meath).

Heroes with measureless power come with bounty that never surpassed by liberality. Like light, they cover all, represented as the strong unfluctuating guide Vyaśva, who praises Indra, who gives all possessions acquired from the foe to the worshipper. Now, the son of Vyaśva praises those who, after having reincarnated ten times, still come to serve him, who living men glorify, who knows well the thunder-armed Lord Indra, who avoids every destructive power, and who every day protects those who honor him from pitfalls. Lord Indra aids those who are old and, most wondrously, slays not his foes. He sends down the active rishi Kutsa, who seeks him with all his might. It is most wonderful to gain the ability to conquer all foes, which comes from the wise Vyaśva. Such a wise soul sets humans free from ruinous woe by designating Aryaman, along with the seven holy rivers, to serve as a valiant hero able to bend the weapons of the Dāsas. As to a boy who presented with a gift of wealth, Varosusaman brings great riches to the humans. *Vyaśva's* sons blessed with female partners who bring in ample richness and eternal wealth. The dynamic universal force Narayana, who participates in the creation of the fourteen worlds, all regulated by the ultimate universal soul (God), as Brahma, deliberately offers Vishnu the power to sustain, maintain, and preserve the newly created dynamic universe. It is this vital force, Narayana, who annihilates the dynamic universe at the end, defined as *maha-kalpa*. During its stage of active existence, the sacrificial power of essence (meath) serves as the primordial power, Shakti, who as a soma-bearer serves through the sons of Narayana, in the hundreds and thousands, who are rewarded if one should ask who sacrifices his life (Vala) and now comes to dwell on Gomati.

According to *Rig-Veda* 8:25, as guards, the dual power Mitra and Varuna come along with other holy faithful ones to follow the law and offer sanctified power as a blessing to the sapient offspring who, like charioteers, come from the ancient powers, all highborn, and learn to stand fast according to the holy law by serving as the twin demigod Aśvins. Possessing all the wealth, most glorious, and with utmost sway like the mighty mother Aditi, they represent a great union that is true to the law, and they govern the godly powers and the imperial lords, remaining true to the eternal law. The heavenly protector Prajāpati, as the son of fatherly powers, with the twin offspring comes to serve as a competent manifested power possessing both spiritual power and physical strength. Serving as exceedingly strong lords of grace, the Aśvins bring rays of light and come to dwell in places where food begins to grow. From the celestial and cosmic region, they gather up gifts, which they take to the terrestrial region. With heavenly mist, they come along with rain to provide support. As the sons of *Daksa* and *Yagna,* the twin demigods come from the lofty sky, looking down below on the ground at the herds, all supported by the holy and revered imperial lords. True to the law, they appear exceedingly strong, and when they sit down with the sovereign princes who appointed to implement the law, they stand fast with their sway and maintain those sovereign rules and laws. As pathfinders, they blessed with keen eyesight, able to see unobstructed. Even with their eyelids closed, they can fully perceive their surroundings. The mother goddess Aditi endows them with mighty strength to guide the enhanced demigod Nāsatyas to come and guard the cosmic hosts (the Maruts). As the defenders of the bounteous gods, the Nāsatyas protect day and night. While protecting with the mortals' dwellings, they serve unharmed, like the bountiful god Vishnu, who slays no one. Moving along the holy river Indus, with protection, they first mark, and then elect, the far-reaching trinity of Mitra, Varuna, and Aryaman. Even during periods of flood, they bring along the cosmic hosts (Maruts), who, along with the twin Aśvins, serve Indra and the divine power Vishnu. Having one mind, they serve as heroes. Using their opposing power, they break the enmity of every foe and, with the fierce power of the floodwaters, repel the furious ones. Serving as one godly power, they come to serve as the one lord of humanity, which helps them look forth everywhere. With the advantage of keeping to the old holy laws, they are accustomed to, and support, the supreme statutes. With the eternal law, that is, Varuna, they come with a ray of light from heaven to earth, where they measure out and set specific boundaries. With the heavenly majesty Sūrya high above, they spread light from the sky across the region where needed, serving these two worlds with illumination.

Celestial Agni, with his eternal flame, brings along gifts to offer to those who are sitting far from the lord of food. He comes to support the living things, also to serve as the controller of the gift of un poisoned food. So, in the morning and in the evening, the heavenly body Sūrya, speaking, brings enjoyments. The black *Uksanyayana* and the white *Harayana*, serving as bay steeds, rise. They give a harmless embodiment, *Susaman*, and like the twin Aśvins, they travel farther and given troops of tawny-colored steeds. With active embodiments, they are ready to serve like righteous warriors. As the supreme powers, the two sages learn to hold the reins and bear the whip, leading as two strong coursers, like stallions. With praise, serving as the royal embodiments, the demigods call upon those who have attained embodiments to come and unite with the gods of strength, ready to pour down eternal wealth that will never vanish. With godly might, they appear with a manifested embodiment serving as the astral light Varosusaman, who offers glorious rites to protect all serving

Nāsatyas. The astral light also provided with strong godly power, making oblations while pouring down soma, which fills individual embodiments with richness and prosperity. When night has passed, they send plenteous food to serve to the heroes, traveling with the famous embodiment. With glory, they pass over enthusiastic servants such as the demigod Aśvins, who bring precious gifts and whom they always serve, along with the god of the storm, Rudra, who works proactively to lead all to a safe place.

Like the demigod Aśvins, who have no foes, Rudra flies all around, stirring up noble thoughts, serving as a fleet of flying steeds. To serve as wonderworkers, the Aśvins come as lords of splendor, honey hued, filled with a sustaining opulence. They serve as rich and noble heroes with manifested embodiments that are impossible to overthrow. Indra as enhanced demigods (Nāsatyas) welcome them. With the best accord, bringing along godly offerings, even from other gods, and with uplifted voices as the compilers of spiritual hymns, the Nāsatyas come with loving-kindness like the cow and serve the demigod Aśvins, who call upon the sages who serve the heroes (rishis). Representing the prophetic sons, they bring the ancient trinity of Indra, Varuna, and Mitra, who of one accord come to serve the noble Aryaman. The noble souls of the ancient trinity yearn for gifts as those bestowed upon princes, like the mighty power, for whom they sacrifice, who clothe all, including women with their robe. As Aśvins, they help to bring glory, honoring the princes with mighty power, and they welcome humanity with regard and care. The Aśvins pour down wealth into the homes they come to guard, also channeling songs and prayers to offer their sacrifice. The heroes, by themselves, called upon by their own envoys, answering the loud call of the twin Aśvins. They come yonder on the sea, the immortal souls enjoying their home as they eat and listen to the river, which flows with clear water and creates streams of gold, by which they attract others. With glory and fame, they come through with brilliant songs, singing as they move toward the place where the pathways marked with light. As steeds, they harnessed, ready to draw their carriage. Mother Nature, Vasu, helps their embodiment, feeding the pair well by offering drinks of mythical juice to produce physical strength.

The wonderful wind, Vayu, brings along his creative powers. Tvaṣṭṛ, Vayu's father-in-law, comes and serves humanity as the elected one. Humans pray for wealth, whereby they may gain control and, in glory, pass through the air (Vayu), which filled with mythical juice ready to effused. The auspicious wind drives while seated on a wide seat, serving as his mighty carriage. Vayu and Tvaṣṭṛ call upon noble steeds to take them to the humans' homes. They provide humans with food meant for nobles. Liberal like compressed cosmic stones, riding on the backs of horses, Vayu is glad and joyful in his hearts to serve as a godly power. With precious water (*jal*), he and Tvaṣṭṛ come to vouchsafe humankind, providing them with strength and noble creative thought.

## IMMORTAL

According to *Rig-Veda* 8:26, the immortal universal soul (God) receives united praise from the midlevel gods who pour down wealth so that the never-vanquished Varosusaman may come, along with the wonderworker Nāsatyas, offering glorious rites. With protection and aid, these strong gods pour down wealth with oblations to provide the embodiments with wealth in the daytime and, when night has passed, send them plenteous food. As heroes, the Aśvins are the famous embodiments known best for traveling in glory, marked as zealous servants with strong voices. The heroic Aśvins send precious gifts. Even when offended, they think of the heavenly lord Rudra, who leads them to a safe place beyond the reach of their foes. As a fleet of steeds, the wonderworkers fly all over, stirring up thoughts. As lords of splendor, the Aśvins bring honey-hued soma, all-sustaining, to the noble heroes who never overthrown. The hero is welcome, by Aśvins, with an offering to Indra. The wonderworking Nāsatyas come with Indra and other gods. Lifting their voices like Vyaśva, they manifest as strong oxen; with loving-kindness, like sages, they come well lauded. The Aśvins, serving as holy souls (rishis), listen to the call to burn the misers or other evildoers who are nearby.

The heroes listen to the son of Vyaśva and, of one accord, regard the trinity of Varuna, Mitra, and Aryaman, yearning for their gifts, which the princes carry in their arms to bestow upon the mighty power day after day. They even sacrifice clothes, providing women with their robes, and as Aśvins, they glorify them, honoring them. Whosoever cares for the manifested bodies reaches out wide toward their dwelling as the loving Aśvins do. They call to them to come pour down wealth and guard their homes, making sacrifices and singing hymns, the most fetching of all calls. Be they in the yonder sea of heaven or at home enjoying their food, they listen to the immortal gods.

The Indus River, with its clearly flowing water, attracts all the streams toward its path of gold. The demigod Aśvins with their glory and fame come through with brilliant songs to point out the pathways marked with light. Harnessed steeds who pass through Mother Nature (Vasu) carry the well-fed pair through the air, with Vayu coming to drink the offerings of milk mixed with essence (meath). Wonderful air, the lord of that which is right, who is also Tvaṣṭṛ's son-in-law, comes as a benefactor, praying for wealth. For glory, all seek the air with juice effused from heaven, the auspicious who comes to drive the carriage with a wide seat, pulled by noble steeds, to call upon the homes of manifested souls who possess a wealth of noble food, liberal like the cosmic bodies (compressed stones) on horseback. So, with gladness and joy in their hearts, the humans worship the auspicious god of the air, Vayu, who endows them with water, strength, and thought.

According to *Rig-Veda* 8:27, Agni, with his eternal flame, reaches down to the foundations of the earth, with stones and grass, the ground (Prithvi) where desirous seekers worship him with sacrifices. Accompanied with songs, personified as the immortal, imperishable power Brahmaṇaspati, who worships the Maruts, Agni comes along singing with all creation, including plants, trees, moving bodies, cattle, other living beings, and flowing water. He comes as the dawn comes after night, exposing the earth and the great elements of nature (Vasu). As the possessor of all wealth, he generates the individual thought process and, along with other godly powers, goes forth with sacrifice. They revive the same powers used by their ancestors, such as the noble Ādityas and Varuna, who stand fast and firm, providing illumination.

The Maruts, serving as the lords of all wealth, along with their troops, make themselves into the strengtheners of humanity, serving as worshippers to destroy their enemies. These lords of all wealth fully guarded, but they harm no one—nor can anyone harm them. In their dwelling places, they remain fully protected, free from foes. With one mind and of one accord, singing holy songs of worship to honor the goddess Aditi, with mighty power they come as one to individual homes to bring delightful things. Demigods, through Mitra, bring eternal love and friendship to cultivate society. The trinity of Indra, Varuna, and the Ādityas, as swift heroes, settle on the sacred grass, where they set up a banquet to serve the array with pressed soma. They hastily called away by the lord of eternal law, Varuna, who, supported by Agni, provides the eternal flame to enkindle the sacrificial fires. This brings other powers as a trinity, the Maruts, Vishnu, and the Aśvins, who bring along the patron Pūṣan, all of them coming to join with the famed Indra to serve as Vṛtra-slayers and be the first to win the spoils. As a guileless god, Pūṣan comes from all directions to bestow his gifts upon nature (Vasu). All the gods come from places both near and far, remaining strong within their refuge and ensuring it provides them with unassailable protection. They form a close alliance with other godly powers, along with the patron, who remains strong and comes to be known as the destroyer of foes, calling for the prosperity enjoyed in former days bestowed upon their new city. They send forth to win a fair reward, with homage, from the lords of all wealth. They sing songs of praise and pray that milk will come from their cows without fail.

The excellent Savitar mounted up on high, with her powers, makes sure all manifested bodies—bipeds, quadrupeds, and birds—carefully guided, in the hopes that they will settle and perform their tasks. Singing praises with godlike thoughts, they invoke each other, and with grace and hope, the godly powers come to strengthen all. Through the power of the immortal living spirit, all mortal embodiments share gracious gifts, which increase their individual strength, hereafter supporting each event, for which they make ample room. With loud sounds, the guileless godly powers meet to render praise to the mortal embodiments, who hear none but Varuna and Mitra. They honor and obey laws, which provides their households with the power to endure, and they gather plenteous food and, with obedience, serve the godly powers. They pray that their offspring will prosper in every way and remain unharmed. Even without war they gather wealth, and as they go on their way on pleasant paths or in their homes, the trinity Mitra, Varuna, and Aryaman protect them with one accord by sharing gifts. Even today, they make sloping paths easy to travel, creating an effective network. Performing rites, they appoint a ruler, such as the sun, who ascends, serving as the lord of all wealth. Before sunset or upon awakening, they acquire all wealth. The demigods, at noonday and even in the evening, shelter worshippers so they may go ahead with making their sacrifices to protect against the evil Asuras. Nature, Vasu, the possessor of all wealth, appears during sunrise, or at noon, or in the gloom of evening, serving as lord of all riches who gives fair treasure to the individual embodiments who make sacrifices as wise men. The demigods, serving as the imperial rulers, claim the boon and provide wide-ranging protection to the Ādityas, offering holy gifts, which when received bring great bliss to all manifested creations.

Unlike the twin power of the Aśvins, the omnipresent Surabhi, serving as mother cows, pay homage to all kinds and, with special help, enhance the dwellings of individual worshippers. The omnipresent powers the Surabhi follow their course along with the lords of splendor, who in their chariot move swiftly, in their benevolence allowing the trinity to come along. Occupying a triple seat, with golden reins, they, in their famous vehicle, travel between heaven and earth. The twin Aśvins, along with the enhanced demigods the Nāsatyas, come plowing and turning the ground for harvest, supported by the cosmic immortal universal soul, Paramatman, all serving the sky as the mortal manifested immortal spirit, Atman, who serve as the lord of splendor Manu. With prayer, they praise and exalt divine power (divine will), which brings them wealth, all traveling the path of everlasting law (Varuna), who from the high dominion yields a mighty strength, like the compressed stones generated by the solar deities, serving as heroes, forming comic bodies that appear on the ground. Trasadasyu's son Trksi, the lord of plenteous wealth, fills the worshippers' dwellings with soma.

Riding in the chariot with a golden seat, the trinity, serving as the lords of plenteous wealth, provide abundant food, aiding the ancient souls such as the adrift (Paktha). Burning with fierce fire, adrift detached from friends such as the demigod Aśvins, who come speedily as twin horses to heal whatever is diseased. They continually invoked, resistless, fresh as the day, serving as the lovers of song. All the heroes call upon the mighty ones (divinities, deities, and demigods) to offer their blessings. Once they eat of the lavish food that strengthens them and purifies their blood and body fluids, they receive Krvi with reverence. Paying homage to the heavenly powers the Rudras, the lord of ample wealth, they entreat them, and they come as lords of splendor, the twin Aśvins, blood laying out their path, running in the early evening or early morning and even at the time of sacrifice, which is made not solely as a prayer to preserve the mortals and save them from their foes. The mortals call upon the omnipresent Surabhi for bliss, as the sires through whom thought strengthened, speeding and with joy, come from far away to help protect the manifested bodies. The lords of great wealth, bringing aides with them, for example, the wonderworkers, go from home to home. The Aśvins enrich the homes with cattle, steeds, and gold. They bring soma juice to the chiefs to drink, endowing them with heroic strength so they may remain firm, excellent, and uninjured by any foe such as the rakshasas. They come at night, along with the lords of ample wealth, to bring all the good things that can obtained during a period of hardship. The twin Aśvins ascend.

## MAJESTY

According to *Rig-Veda* 8:28, the thirty-three gods seated on the sacred grass and, as in the days of old, found with Varuna, Mitra, Aryaman, and Agni, along with their consorts sending a boon (*vaṣaṭ*) to the deities serving as the guardians of all the tribes in the west, the north, and the south. As the gods desire, they send what they wish to mortals or immortal demons. The seven splendors carry seven spears, with seven glorious acts to achieve.

According to *Rig-Veda* 8:29, the seven supreme powers of causation, running as seven noble streams, each carry a spear that used to establish their individual splendor. Each splendor assumes a form to possess all the seven glories. Each one, manifested as an active youth, covers the brown ground from which the deity manifests and appears all decked out in golden ornaments. Like a luminous fire, they occupy the place, each making a sacrifice to the eternal flame. All three deities, as one, come along with the air (Vayu). One serves the firmament, providing breath, like a sharp steel knife. Another seated among all the deities, encompassing cosmic vapor, which, with the thunderbolt, turns to rain to slay the evil Vṛtra. The third appears bearing a pointed weapon, bright and strong, as the eternal soul (essence) that comes to serve a healing medicine, always watching and knowing of all the places where hidden treasures lie. The deities, with a mighty stride, come to establish an altar located three steps above the ground, and from there they regulate the atmospheric zones, rejoicing. The deities serving as a pair, one male and one female, they ride on winged steeds and journey forth, traveling from the earth to the two highest parts of heaven: the celestial region and the cosmic region. There, they set up places of worship, serving the imperial king's holy oil, all singing loudly the *sāman* hymns, whereby they invoke the heavenly Sūrya to create three sources of external light: the sun, the moon, and the shining stars of the constellations.

According to *Rig-Veda* 8:30, none of the godly powers serving as deities are small or feeble. All are verily great, coming as lauded to be the destroyers and remove any evil power. As manifested godly powers with mortal embodiments, they come to serve as the holy ones. With benedictions, they defend and succeed. They speak and lead others, all coming from the home of the ancestral father, the cosmic body Manu, who follows the path far into the distance. There Manu stays with the manifested embodiments, serving as the god of all humanity and other living things. According to *Rig-Veda* 8:31, Manu provides protection and shelters their cattle and steeds. Ultimate reality (Brahma) is well pleased with those devas who worship, make sacrifices, pour out libation, and prepare meals to serve as a sacrifice to the ruler Śakra, who protects the divine creation from woe. The ruler Śakra, with a glorious chariot, comes with speed from the godly powers and, with their might, subdues all hostilities. Each day, he passes over the houses of the embodiments, libation, rich in milk, flowing, which brings an exhaustless number of progenies. The godly powers constantly bring drafts of milk, both of each pair working with one accord, spouses, they press soma plants to produce mythical juice. As united devas, they harvest enough from the sacred grass and come to move on the ground, where their strength never fails. Never denying or hiding from the favor shown to them by the godly powers, they win glory for themselves. With children on their side, they attain the full extent of what life has to offer them, all decked with ornaments of gold. They serve the Immortal One, with sacrificial gifts of food and wealth to satisfy the love of the gods and pay them the honor they are due.

Humanity claims protection from the hills and protection from the floods, the trinity of Vishnu, Pūṣan, and Bhaga standing at their sides. The lord of wealth, all-bounteous, travels the broad path that leads to the Aramati region, which is blissfully free from foes. The godly Viśvavedas, along with the peerless Ādityas, seeing the trinity of Mitra, Aryaman, and Varuna, guarded on all these paths as their fair footsteps follow the eternal law. Glorified with songs of wealth, the first, Agni, comes to honor the mortal embodiments as well-loved friends of the gods who prosper in all areas. As in all frays, like swift heroes, the embodiments relocate. As they attended by godly powers, they make sacrifices and strive to win over the deities, and through such winning over they conquer those who do not worship. By serving deities, the worshippers remain free from injury, and with drafts of the mythical juice, they made pious. There is no action equal to the things they do for self-preservation, and nothing can keep them from making sacrifices as they strive to win the hearts of the deities. With such strength, the heroes acquire proficiency and fleet-footed steeds.

According to *Rig-Veda* 8:32, the impetuous Kaṇva, through songs, tells of the deeds that created the mythical juice that brings wild delight. With impetuous influence, the strong godly power Ahīśuva slays a trio of evil powers—Anarsani, Srbinda, and Pipru—and releases the previously stranded water, causing the dwelling places to flood. The godly powers relocate to the top of the high mountain Arbuda. This represents a large victory and brings fame, with strong mythical juice produced from soma plants, which helps the godly powers to fight, coming down as a torrent from the mountain. Rejoicing in the soma, the heroes burst open the forts holding the horses and cattle, which all come out of their stalls. With libation, they take pleasure, receiving the divine gift and joining with Indra, who comes from far away. Lovers of the song, the singers, with divine praise, drink the soma to quicken themselves, and take delight in eating the undiminishing supply of food brought to them.

Maghavan, serving as the messenger of Indra, as a source of great wealth, rich in herds of cattle and steeds, with gold, wields strength given to him as a sacrificial gift. With his arms widely outstretched, he comes with a loud sound to aid in the overdue work that well needed to bring success. The noble Śatakratu, when serving in battle, acts as an evil slayer, yet still gives wealth to the worshippers. The godly powers further strengthen mountains to bring a boon and to rescue the soma pressers as friends who satisfy their needs and help the mighty with streams of wealth as they sing songs of praise. The godly powers, great and firm, win glory in wars and gain vast wealth through their mighty powers. They live to be brave and energetically perform gracious deeds so that no one can say they have not given enough. Without any debt or obligation, they come to serve as holy manifested human beings (Brahmans), who as active members of society press soma and offer it free of charge. Singing loudly with praises and prayers, unchecked and strong, they receive favor from Indra, who provides aid to hundreds of thousands of worshippers and provides light as they go forth, calling to other folks and serving the mythical juice. Godlike in nature, the Brahmans pour forth the soma as a gift from Indra and create by themselves the milky drafts that served to the patron Tugra as libations. Even when they are angry mood or have sinned, they offer the mythical juice to the patron as a libation.

After crossing a great distance, three regions' worth, and passing through the lands of the five tribes, the patron Tugra continues to listen as he proceeds, allowing his voice heard so that he noticed. Indra sends forth a ray of eternal light, like the bright light coming from the heavenly power Sūrya, who with songs attracts the waters and gathers them into the valley. As the hero fair of cheek, Adhvaryu pours forth soma to those who, as twins, loosen the clouds to bring the waters that fill rivers, which flow downward, becoming ripe like milk, which settles in the female embodiments. This is all met with praise as Tugra, Sūrya, and Adhvaryu, the matchless ones, slay the evil *Ahīśuva*, the son of *Urnavabh*a who covers *Arbuda* with frost. Unconquerable conquerors, they sing forth with the prayers that given by Indra, who in the wild creates soma juice, considered among the gods to be as delightful as the holy law. They allow the bay steeds with golden tresses to share in the banquets. The feast is prepared by Priyamedhas of the bays to bring wisdom through soma.

## RITUAL

According to the more than fifty manuscripts making up the Manusmṛti, now known as ancient ritual text the Dharmaśāstra, the metrical Sanskrit text dated from the second century BCE to the third century CE, the first majestic immortal, the unmanifested supreme power of causation Manu, with a sermon, first appeared as the manifested embodiment Bhrigu. During this discourse, various aspects of the altruistic nature (dharma), such as duty, rights, laws, conduct, and virtue, communicated. To the mortal manifested embodiments, as decreed by the immortal cosmic body Manu, the living beings come to reside on earth to serve as members of humanity. All facing the war waged with the newly manifested material world (Virāj) learn to attain peace and tranquility. With fame, the Dharmaśāstra spread long before the colonial era, serving during the medieval era, along with first Buddhistic law and other similar covenants established and provided through the manifested holy spiritual souls (messiahs, mystics, or prophets). Serving as the messengers of the supreme powers of causation, they composed verses in meter that came to be accepted as holy hymns (slokas), expressed in the prevailing language and transmitted in the form of dialogue between an exalted teacher serving as a prophet and worshippers eager to learn all about altruistic nature (dharma) as presented in the holy text Manusmṛti, each verse coving specific aspects. The first fifty-eight verses of the Veda attributed to the son of the universal soul (God) as the first cosmic body, Manu, while the remaining verses, more than two thousand attributed to the messenger Bhrigu.

Seekers of higher knowledge come to sit on holy grass, seeking to comprehend. The mythical drink pressed from soma plants poured down into the streams as oblations. Those who defy such practices of worship gather. These called the evil powers, who inspire worshippers to eliminate the evil ones and thereby become Vṛtra-slayers, receiving support from Mother Nature, Vasu, who comes to protect the devoted mortal embodiments. Mother Nature comes with a loud call and assumes the foremost position to fulfill all requests. She brings, in the form nectar, mythical juice from the heavenly and earthly regions, the mythical juice that makes the manifested embodiments, such as the bold heroes, all bellow like bulls. Serving the sages and prophets are the emissary Kaṇvas. They pillage and bring great spoils, and with eager prayer they turn a shade of yellow to become active with the invocation of the immortal living spirit, which stores all power, living among all creations as Indra's messenger Maghavan. Serving as an ancient famous commentator, Medhātithi brings wealth generated through vibrations and, with song, fills all with drinks of the mythical juice to help build a close-knit kingdom for all living things, gladly represented among the ancient plant and animal kingdoms.

The bay steeds, bolt-armed with their chariot of gold, as the source of material wealth according to the commentator Medhātithi, praised as the strongest and wisest among all animals, standing steady and firm. They receive support from Indra, with great riches, as they are honored by millions to serve with their mighty powers and tear down all the evil forts. As the bold of heart whom none can provoke, they stand tall, bewhiskered with confidence, glorious, much lauded, serving as the strong helpers, with the might of a bull overthrowing foes, becoming known for their vital physical power. They win, drinking the flowing juice with joy. Checked by the godly power, they tear down the castles with their physical strength. Like wild elephants, they rush this way and way, hot and angry. Compelled by no one, they move with mighty power. They never overthrown, arriving steadfast, ready for the fight. With the divine messenger Maghavan, they avert the attack with the calls of praise. They never stand aloof, verily coming forth like rushing bulls. Like the Mighty One, they celebrated as the bull, famous in regions both near and far. They reined, filled with all the strength of a bull, with the golden whip held by Indra's messenger Maghavan.

To manage the bays, which are as strong as bulls, the ancient noble soul Śatakratu, with pressed mythical juice, straightens them as they rush forward with the power of a bull, causing them to run like bay horses or move like flowing streams. They come with the most potent drink, the savory soma juice, and join with the wise messenger Maghavan, who hears the songs, the prayers, and the hymns of praise. When the bay horses mounted to the carriage, the mighty powers allow the messenger Maghavan to yoke them and, with libations, drive them past Indra, serving as the Lord of One Hundred Powers. As the friend of the Loftiest One, Indra, as the Vṛtra-slayer, Maghavan accepted and lauded by the nobles. In sweet oblation to bring happiness to the soma drinker, representing the heavenly lord who neither denounces their declarations nor undermines their appearance as another, Indra is delighted, whose mind described as a stream that, like a bird, cannot restrained. He has an intellect that makes him appear as a lightweight. But his mind, like that of a woman, operates like the twin demigod Aśvins. The Aśvins rush on in their wild journey, drawing a carriage, which they lift high with their powerful wings. They fly like stallions, yoked to their carriage with their eyes cast down. They do not look up; they just watch closely that which is beneath their feet, all beneath a veil so that no others can see it. They come to show the male Brahmans how to meet their female partners.

## SHIELD

According to *Rig-Veda* 8:34, the sky god, as the ruler of eternal law, Varuna, referred to as "the father," controls all the powers that illuminate the sky and complements the mother serving the ground. It is through the sky gods that Indra passes godly desire (divine will), which serves as a eulogy, commanding that it travel far and accepted as the divine calling that covers all parts of the larger pantheon ruled by the sky lord Dyaus. As the new father of the sky, Dyaus is part of Sūrya's pantheon, coming to serve through the sun as regulated by celestial power, which, along with the established planetary bodies, represents Sūrya's kingdom. During the night, the sky serves as a mirror for the moon, the patriarch, with the constellations as the matriarch. So long as he remains the ruler, Dyaus can serve as the father, enabling the universal immortal soul, Paramatman, to establish the individual living spirit, Atman, which in its manifested form, Kaṇva Shakha, represents the seven noble powers of causation, the Saptarishis. These powers offer rich eulogies, until the living spirit itself is truly abstracted and ready to join with the universal immortal soul. The manifested form of Kaṇva Shakha, with the original dominant attributes, appears as ancient powers such as Agni, Indra, Varuna, Mitra, the Aśvins, the Maruts, and the Rudras, before such heavenly powers transform to appear in the sky as manifested bodies that rotate to produce a vibration that heard like a resonant voice. Before falling, they drawn toward the ground as earthly stones (meteors). These meteors drawn along the surrounding rim, which shakes like a wolf worrying a sheep while it generates soma. The father of the sky, Dyaus, continues bringing his bright light to support the manifested bodies during the day. At night they are all supported by the heavenly pantheon regulated by Kaṇva Shakha, who represents the seven noble powers of causation (Saptarishis), who called upon to assist in winning the spoils. They set forth, first to shed the juice that strengthens, provides abundant blessings, purifies, and provides perfect care to help all others. They also bring along the lord of lofty noble thoughts, with infinite wealth and countless aides. Through the demigods, adored by prophets, sages, and priests, they do work and come near to serve animals with wings, such as falcons, which appear in the sky, joyfully rushing to serve the bays. They even bring along evil powers such as the snakes at their feet, tasting with their last breath the draft of soma, which motivates the embodiments to speak their last words (*svāhā*), representing the end of their lives.

Well-nourished horses appear, alike in hue. As well-fed steeds, they come as the lords of the mountains, also coming from the region of the sea. They bring wealth to the thousands of heroes, providing them with both cattle and steeds. This brings great riches to the hundreds of thousands who live yonder beneath the sky to please Father Dyaus, who seeks to return to the heavenly region. The thousand steeds, along with the mightiest troop, received by Indra, becoming a gift (*vasurocis*) to Mother Nature. Vasu fertilizes the ground by turning the soil brown, and speedily joins the invisible power of the wind, Vayu, who spreads out to bring along powers from the pantheon, ready to support the splendid fleet of bright bay coursers, which appear in the middle of the kingdom of the Pargvata tribe, who receive rich gifts, which makes the steeds move swiftly and turn the wheels of the carriage as they run, while the powers of causation Agni and Indra stand hidden in the woods.

According to *Rig-Veda* 8:35, three pairs of gods serving as the supreme powers of causation—Agni with Indra; Vishnu with Varuna; and the Ādityas with the Rudras—form a close league to support the five great elements of nature (Vasu). With one mind and of one accord, they join with the heavenly pantheon of Sūrya to bring the dawn. It is through drinking mythical juice to generate holy thoughts that the mighty ones become ready to serve all living beings. In close alliance, they work with mountains on the ground and in the sky, surrounded above and below by heaven and earth. With one mind, they bring the heavenly power Sūrya, along with the morning light and the twin demigod Aśvins, to serve soma juice. All twenty-one deities, in close alliance with cosmic vapor and the cosmic hosts (Maruts), and of one accord with one mind, accept Bhrigu and his sacrifices as the humans who make sacrifices and deal with them offer libations for the purpose of strengthening. The deities accept the songs of praise as a youth accepts a aid virgin. Serving as the twin gods, they arrive with libations to serve the union of the sun and the dawn and to bring strengthening food, which accepted with songs and solemn rites as coming nigh from the twin gods.

Like starlings, the Aśvins fly toward the trees in the forest, or come like buffaloes, seeking as they move on their way to appear as a large noble swan. With oblation, they fly as a pair and manifest as aggressive hawks, while the manifested bodies, like buffaloes, keep returning home to drink of the mythical juice and be satisfied. They conquer all foes and protect themselves with praise like the worshippers, coming to bestow affluence upon the progeny.

With one mind and of one accord, the sun and the dawn, serving as the twin Aśvins, grant vigorous strength to their worshippers so they can slay their enemies, animate noble souls, and provide their progenies with affluence. Through the trinity of Mitra, Varuna, and dharma, the twin demigod Aśvins granted vigor and strength to join with the Maruts, the cosmic hosts. They approach the noble Ādityas, serving as the avatars of Vishnu, and join with Aṅgiras, the envoy of Agni. They form a trinity with the Marut, and all come praising to call upon the mighty powers Ṛbhu and Vāja to form a league of mighty ones. The Maruts, as demigods, approach the immortal universal soul (Paramatman), as the individual immortal living spirit (Atman) joins to bring noble thoughts that, through the powers of prayer, endow them with power so they may slay the evil rakshasas and drive away disease.

By strengthened with righteous power, noble souls come ready to strengthen others to fight the righteous war. By providing strength to the milk cows, they enable them to provide milk filled with mythical juice to the righteous people who come in strength to hear the god Atri's eulogy. In the same way, they hear the soma presser Śyāvāśva, who, with joy, runs and spins like a three-day-old stream. With solemn rites, in accordance, with one mind, they seize the reins of the chariot filled with the savory soma. Guided by the twin Aśvins, they come calling, eager to provide aid and grant treasures to the worshippers. With sacrifice and reverence, they support the noble heroes, who through drinking the gushing juice, come as eager demigods, bringing aid and granting treasures to the worshippers. Sated with the consecrated drink, they approach the powers of causation, asking them to come join them, and provide aid and grant treasures to the worshippers.

## REFULGENT ONES

According to *Rig-Veda* 8:36, the ruler of eternal law, Varuna, comes forth singing a song unto the band of Maruts, who are wiser than those who guard well without thinking, moving like herds of cattle instead of horses. All together with praise, they sing songs and hymns. Like their father, Nabhāka, they offer eulogies, while sitting at the source of all rivers, to the heavenly Seven Sisters who, as Agni's envoy Aṅgiras, bring a brightly shining manifested embodiment from the cosmos known as the Refulgent One. They serve as teachers disseminating divine knowledge and come to serve as the mediator between creations and the Creator. They especially arrive when the source of light blocked by an opaque object. A three-dimensional body may fall over the source of light and create a shadow or darkness. With a cross section of shadow, this creates a reverse projection to serve as the object blocking the light. Within outer space, in the absence of diffusing atmospheric effects, this creates a shadow in the vacuum that is stark and sharply delineated, creating a high-contrast boundary between morning light and nighttime darkness. Such shadows cast astronomical objects such as sunspots, the only astronomical objects that can produce shadows on the ground and even on the sun and the moon. In the right conditions, even cosmic bodies such as Venus and Jupiter can create similar blockages, generating transitional darkness (Nabjaka) that allows the evil powers to gain control and influence living things. The noble power Śatakratu comes gladly to keep the holy grass trimmed and shed mythical juice, which he shares so others may survive until the darkness goes away. The heavenly powers Indra and Agni come along to support the Maruts so they may be the victors. After winning over the floods, they come to serve as the messenger Maghavan, who serves soma to worshippers, also serving to the noble Śatakratu to make him happy and content. Through sharing soma with all, the messenger fixes himself, and with aid from the noble Śatakratu, he brings along food that makes him glad to be serving the creator of heaven and earth.

Serving as the father, with mythical juice, Maghavan comes along with cosmic meteors, which like shooting stars come down to earth to serve living things. Serving as the movers of cosmic bodies (stone hurlers), these bodies come with hymns of praise to glorify Mother Earth (Prithvi). Hearing all this, the mother Atri brings along the family of the divine power Śyāvāśva, who come specifically shaped to perform holy rites to honor Indra. They give aid to those fighting the fierce fight, and they strengthen those who, as heroes, offer prayers to Trasadasyu.

According to *Rig-Veda* 8:37, with prayer, the family of divine powers serve as Vṛtra-slayers with mythical juice, which they shed by declaring war with the evil powers. The divine powers helped by Indra, as the lord of strength attained success, serving libations, at noon they pour out soma and come to serve with thunder. As conquerors, they come to save all, serving the sole ruler or sovereign of all life, Indra. As the lord of strength, Indra comes to save all those who are sincere, the archaic ruler now serving consistently as the Lord Supreme. The two worlds, that of matter (earth) and that of energy (heaven), help regulate the middle esoteric region, which is in turmoil, with one trying to overpower the other and thus save all. As the divine power, Śyāvāśva hears all the voices making requests of Mother Atri, performing holy rites to honor Indra, who gives aid to the Trasadasyu tribe in the fierce fight and comes to save the heroes and strengthen their powers.

According to *Rig-Veda* 8:38, the twin winners of the war, serving as the priests of sacrifice and holy workers, come well marked among all the bounteous riders to subdue the Vṛtra-slayers. Indra and Agni send the compressed stones (meteors) filled with mythical juice to provide eternal wisdom. This brings delight to all those recognized by the gods. They accept the sacrifice for weal and share their praise among the heroes representing Indra and Agni. Pleased with the libations, they accept the sacred gifts offered by the two gods, using the Gāyatrī mantra, serving as the worshipful heroes of Indra and Agni. They come early with godly powers to serve as the lords of genuine wealth. They shed mythical juice and listen to the ancient voice of Atri, also hearing the voice of Śyāvāśva, along with the calls for help from the worshipping souls (sages), the same ones who in the past, with grace, brought in as associates of the goddess Sarasvatī by singing psalms of praise.

According to *Rig-Veda* 8:39, with praise and worship, along with sacred food, the glorious envoy Aṅgiras, all decked with the godly powers, between both gathering places, allows the worshipping souls (sages) to move forth in their mission to serve within the immortal places. Agni, with his eternal flame, comes to support the embodiments, so they may generate a new form of speech to overpower the hateful godless ones and all malignities of the wicked, and even cause the destroyers to retreat without hurting them. Agni, pouring holy oil into the mouth of the fire, offers hymns that acknowledged by the gods as the most excellent form of worship. This brings bliss to his messenger to bestow with vital power all who supplicate, each embodiment, by forming the rings of Mother Nature (Vasu). This strengthens the gifts from nature (prakriti), which granted with delight to those who have the godly calling to stir every embodiment.

Agni, through his eternal flame, makes himself renowned, performing wonderful victorious acts. The priests serve choice sacrificial meath to those who represent the godly tribes. They urge them to honor the deities, who spring with godly powers and know all about the mystery of humanity and all about the giver of wealth, Agni. By opening both doors to the place of worship, they come to receive a new gift, along with the eternal flame that inhabits the godly powers, to offer up sacrifice. This brings them great delight, and in their presence, the eternal wisdom welcomes all who adore the godly powers. The eternal flame, who lives at the source of all streams, comes to dwell within their embodiments and serves as the lord of the sevenfold human race. As the best, with wisdom, the eternal flame Mandhātar inhabits the embodiments and serves as the sacrifice for slaying the Dāsas. Sages serve the three gathering places, along with the thirty-three godly powers, who are envoys sent to conciliate. The eternal flame, serving first the manifested deities and then the half-mortal demigods, comes to rule over the wealthy and powerful, like a dam built to hold back the waters.

According to *Rig-Veda* 8:40, Indra and Agni, as the conquerors in the fight, bring eternal wealth, and to overcome the strong wind, they fix themselves within the burning wood to set traps for those who do not engage in worship. The mightiest heroes adore those who come with steeds to win with strength, sacrificing everything to become famous dwellers who serve with Indra and Agni in the fight. Filled with wisdom, they come to knit the body of friends with other embodiments and serve as heroes. They sing sacred songs of praise to worship Nabhāka and serve the union of Indra and Agni. Among those who belong in this material world (Prithvi) and placed within the heaven and the earth, sitting in its lap, the ground, they pray and granted rich treasure. Coming from the sea, they serve as a foundation while all remain powerful amid their might. From beneath the foundation, they rip up the old brambles of creeping plants and demolish the hiding places of the evil powers. At the same time, they help mighty Indra to expose or even destroy the hidden treasure, which gathered and moved.

With the same songs of prayer, the manifested embodiments call upon the powers of Indra and Agni to show them sundry ways to win such treasures. Using their own heroes, they subdue those who provoke them to fight, winning in the endeavor. From the sky, Indra and Agni, at their best, appear with two refulgent beams that rise to bring the downward-flowing waters to form the rivers, which run as if just released from their restraints. Indra, with ways to aid and guide the rivers, serving as the lord of the bays, comes with the uplifted hero *(Hinva)*, who with prayers soon inspires holy hymns. As heroes Hinva, bright and glorious, with Indra demolish the evil brood of the enemy of the gods Śuṣṇa, coming to support the manifested embodiments through the heavenly streams. Inspired with worship with holy rites, *Hinva* and Indra appearing as glorious heroes, truly brave, tearing the evil Śuṣṇa to pieces and winning back the heavenly streams; while Indra and Agni, as sires, sing praise songs for their envoys the Aṅgirases and Mandhātarm, who guard the shelter and preserve all their masters' stored riches.

## MINOR SOLAR DEITY

According to *Rig-Veda* 8:41, heroes, hidden at nights, by morning come with their magic arts, becoming visible to all the dear ones who follow the eternal law. They prosper, serving as the three sources of light, by which they make everything on earth visible. To measure the vastness of the sky, they establish the four visible quarters. This is how divine law, Varuna, unfolds, appearing as a strong godly herder coming from the east, from where the heroes also come to support the world full of life. With well-known names, they come to serve, and with hidden names they represent their mysterious nature, coming as beams of light in the morning. These beams of light possess wisdom, each in a varied form coming from heaven, and store it in various places, such as in the nave of a wheel. They honor all the types of animals that gather among their fold, such as the mustered steeds, which they yoke. In robes, they serve as the minor solar deity Trita among tribes in regions where they jointly contemplate like the godly powers and come to serve mortal embodiments, performing all works. Before they taken home by the divine law, Varuna, they far removed from the oceanic region, from where they ascend to the heavens, worshipping the realms they possess. With their bright feet, they overthrow magic and ascend to heaven to serve as the rulers who, as bright far-seeing rays, pervade the three superior realms below the heavens. Seated firmly with the divine law, Varuna, they come to rule through seven kings, who after making a decree, overpower the darkness by bringing out the ancient seat, wearing robes of light, to serve as the pillar between the two worlds, heaven and earth, supporting them all by balancing their physical and spiritual powers.

According to *Rig-Veda* 8:42, demigods appear first as the fire god, Agni, who, once fully enlightened with the eternal flame, serves as the lord of wealth. Agni appears with his eternal flame among the mortal rulers who propped up by the heavens to measure the vastness of the earth. Serving as the king, Agni, as supreme, approaches all creations regulated by Varuna, where humbly they worshipped as the revered ones. As the wise immortal guards of the dynamic universe, as part of their rule, they vouchsafe all between earth and heaven with a triply barred protection. With sharp sounds, the god of the eternal law, Varuna, with strength and insight, helps the manifested mortal embodiments to board a ship that bears them safely beyond all misfortune. As heavenly demigods with manifested physical bodies, the Nāsatyas hasten like cosmic bodies, bringing with them drafts of soma and eternal wisdom. Even as the wise ones, they called the old Nāsatyas.

According to *Rig-Veda* 8:43, Agni, in the half-mortal manifested embodiment Jātavedas, serving as a lord, appears with sages who, with prayers and songs, go forth in worship to unveil that which has never conquered. He produces a song of praise to receive the eternal flame, sharpened with gleaming light, which brings ultimate transparency. He goes through the forests, devouring them, producing a gold-colored banner, which like fire appears with smoke. He urged on by the wind to rise aloft to heaven, with light borne through the flames. The flames become visible all around, even in the gleaming of the morning, as the heroes speed along in the dust, their feet turning black. They spread over the ground to provide nourishment to budding plants that devoured, never wearying, always seeking to support the tender shrubs. With a flicker and a fiery glow, plants bend down to lick with the tongues of flame, while growing in the woods, all splendid. They become kindle and used to build a home able to withstand the floods.

Spreading with hi forces so plants appear as newborn children, once worshipped with offerings, Jātavedas comes to serve as a shining flame, using the sacred oil, kissing the ladle with his mouth and serving with hymns. He wears on his back ox skin and cowhide, which he bears with the mythical juice soma. With the shining flame, soma offered to the priests as homage, along with eternal wisdom, and they offer worship and most excellent oblation. They seek ultimate purity. As the trinity Bhrigu, Manu, and Aṅgiras share their wisdom and the eternal flame, they cause better to grow from their goodness as a friend creates friendship, providing richness to thousands in the form of enough food to fill storehouses.

The heroes offer support to sages, as Agni provides the eternal flame to the worshippers. Like brothers in strength, like a lord with brilliant red steeds, they all sway and provide pleasure. With applause and praises, Agni goes into a stall to seek cows, and by its lowing, hears a calf that longs for milk. Aṅgiras, the envoy of Agni, serves all people who have pleasant homes and helps grant their wishes. Sages skilled in holy song, as the best thinkers among thinkers, come to share their thoughts at the sacred feast. Agni, as invoker, turns to the priests, who with prayer offer the sacrifice that in places look as though a prince selected to rule over all the tribes, to come in battle, invoking divine aid. With prayers to Agni, whose blazing fires served with sacred oil, they have ears to listen to their calling. When Jātavedas, representing Agni, beats away all foes, he calls upon those who hear Agni calling the divine powers to come and serve as the kings of humanity, who are wonderful and follow the holy law. Like a bridegroom, they stir up all of humankind, and from that they build a fleet of noble steeds, which determine how to slay their deadly foes, such as the rakshasas, who appear from all directions, their sharp flames shining powerfully.

Most manifested godly powers, such as Manus and the best of the Aṅgirases, light up with the eternal flame as they mark Agni's speech. With Agni's brilliance, even the strength of heaven is borne with the floods that bring water to earth. With the singing of hymns, the primordial power that formed all creation called upon by those who are good, who each receive a portion of the food sent forth from Agni. With devout gazes, they, throughout the day, behold the light that overpowers distress. With cheerful hearts, they venerate Agni, dear to all, who starts burning to provide them with the purifying eternal flame. Rich in light, beams appear from the heavenly power Sūrya, rays that boldly demolish the gloom. With prayers, the embodiments receive the gift of immortality, which never fails to elicit the choicest wealth from Agni.

## HEAVENLY HOST

According to *Rig-Veda* 8:44, humanity learns from Agni how to create their own fuel, through offering a lubricant to awaken their guests. Even today, accepted that the envoy of Agni will come when come placed out in front, welcomed with sweetly spoken words and awakening powers. The envoy Aṅgiras accepted to come dwell within the manifested moral embodiment as a heavenly body that, from the lofty fires, enkindles the eternal flame that travels on high, appearing as the beloved flame, with ladles full of sacred oil offered by the worshippers to the envoy. The acceptance of such offerings brings Agni near, who, within the embodiment, serves as the Refulgent One. As human beings worship Agni, they come to hear the cheerful voice from the priest who, as invoker, creates a rich and splendorous light. Met with praise, the beloved Agni brings wisdom and mighty strength, accompanied with solemn rites. He accepted straightaway with offerings as his best envoy, Aṅgiras, comes to guide and to create seasonal sacrifices. Such excellent godly power, with brilliant flames, enkindles to appear as the heavenly host who moves forward by showing the sages and heralds the way. Void of guile, the ensign of sacrifices, appearing as smoke, filled with rich light, comes to the seekers. The guardian god Agni, with his mighty power, comes to save the worshippers from those foes who injure or destroy, using his power as the Son of Strength. He makes the embodiments of the worshippers beautiful, as if blessed by his ancient sage, singing ancient hymns. This invokes the Child of Strength through the purifying flame and well-ordered sacrifice. So, Agni, rich with friends, in fiery splendor, seats himself upon the sacred grass.

Human beings who serve Agni within their own abodes, for the sake of wealth, shine as worshippers. Agni, with both head and height, reaches heaven, along with Indra, serving as the heads of the earth. They quicken to put in place the waters to feed the sprouting seeds. With the eternal flame, pure and resplendent, they blaze high, filled with luster and effulgence, manifesting as Agni's envoy. Appearing as a lord of light, the ruler with the choicest gifts, Aṅgiras, comes to help defend the worshippers as stirred to action by their thoughts. Through his singing of songs, he enhances humanity and claims them as friends. With his godlike nature, void of guile, Aṅgiras, who bears a most holy sway, comes to serve as the holy singer who brings light, creating holy humanity. Humans worship Agni through meditation and exalt him in song, evermore creating a special friendly bond with him as if they were part of him and he were part of them, with every divine prayer fulfilled in time. The excellent lord of wealth Agni, rich in light, bestows upon them all his favor and grace.

Agni, whose laws stand fast among humanity, resonant with songs of praise, speeds forth as rivers hasten to the sea. Among the youthful lords of humanity, Agni comes to stir up all the sages as they eat, singing glorifying hymns. In this, Agni hastens them to perform sacrificial rites. As the Mighty One, armed with sharp teeth, Agni presents his worshippers with goods. As the singers of praise to gracious holy one, sharing in his feast and his wisdom, ever watchful as sages, they come to shine like the eternal flame in the sky. Agni, serving as a sage, protects them from their foes before any misfortunes fall upon them. In this, he prolongs their lives.

According to *Rig-Veda* 8:45, those whose flames lit with a powerful fuel, sitting on the trimmed sacred grass, lauded as great, become the friends of anybody who has a stake in being their friends. Ever young, unequalled in fight, they lead the army of the gods, serving as heroes. As warrior chiefs, they come to serve as newborn evil-slayers. They ask their mothers to increase their body size and make them fierce and renowned. The grandmother Śavasī answers the prayers of those who seek to win in battle and serve as stately ones like the majestic white elephant. They climb up a hill, from where they hear Maghavan, the envoy of Indra, who craves to grant them whatever will make them strong and firm. Before the holy warrior Indra will go to battle, borne by noble steeds, and as the best of all divine charioteers, he repels the thunder coming from all directions. Before they will send their own to repel the attack, they ask the most glorious godly power Indra to set his carriage out in front, in the foremost place, to help them win, he whom no wicked power is able to injure. Their enemies, namely, Śakra, may try to escape from Indra and his power.

With divine bounty, rich in livestock, the warrior chiefs come near to Indra, approaching softly. From the thunder-armed power, they receive wealth, including hundreds of steeds, all unrivalled, ready with gifts. From their exalted position, they give Indra's worshippers hundreds of thousands of their boons. Indra tears down the strong forts of the enemy and, as the winner of spoils, distributes the wealth among humanity. They come to support the highest sage who, with one drop of mythical juice, brings cheer and thus comes to serve as a marketer. To Indra's opulent embodiments, they bring the treasure that they are reluctant to give, feeling it an insult to give material wealth. Indra, as a friend, supplies them with soma and waits to see how the manifested mortal embodiments feed the herd and, among those who are not deaf, how they quicken to listen for aid, calling from far away. When their request granted, their call not having forgotten, they welcomed to become close friends with Indra. Even now when someone is in trouble, by thinking of Indra, they receive gifts of livestock.

As the lord of strength, human beings rest on Indra as old men rest upon a staff and learn to dwell within such power. They sing praises to Indra, worshipping him as the god of mighty valor whom no one challenges, even in war. As heroes, with mythical juice shed and poured out for them to drink, they sit to finish celebrating. They do not let those fools who armed or those who mock them hypnotize them; they only learn when they seek to have love for their enemies. They give others rich milky draft to cheer them, with great munificence offering it like a lake offered to a wild bull to drink from.

Proclaiming their deeds everywhere among assemblies, the new and ancient Vṛtra-slayers come to win a thousand arms in battle of. With Indra, who drinks soma juice, they, like the daughter, mother, and grandmother Kadrū, through their heritage, display true might, having given the undeniable strength that passed on to Yadu and Turvaśa, the heroes who conquered all by making sacrifices. Magnified by the powers of the lord who serves humanity as their guardian, they disclose the great wealth found in livestock given by the celestial cosmic bodies the Ṛbhukṣans. They not restrained, but strengthened by serving Tugra's son, who, in addition to receiving flowing juice, receives ancient wisdom from his father, Triśoka, who cleaves the hills to form a wide receptacle for the mighty cows so they can issue forth with their milk. Whatever the plan or purpose for transport, or whatever Indra can do for those on earth who have heard little, their hearts turn to those on high so they themselves become highly renowned. With lofty praises, they become kind to those who trespass not once, not twice, and not three times, but who trespass repelling all attacks, in fear that the one who is all-powerful will crush all the mighty enemies.

Those who are wealthy and in positions of power may never live to see a friend or son in need: herewith, may the heart turned to whatever a friend, unprovoked, has ever said unto another friend to cause the latter to turn and leave in distress. Heroes, with unquenchable enjoy, bring soma juice, very near, as a hunter rushing down to the bays, yoking them by hymns, giving them splendid embodiments, and presenting them to the priests, which drives all enemies away, the heroes smiting the foes who press in all around them and bringing the wealth for which we all long. Indra, who remains concealed in a fortified place, precipitously brings wealth for humanity, which is recognized as being sent by the divine.

CHAPTER 16

# Righteous Dominion

THE RIGHTEOUS DOMINION IS THE PLACE WHERE THREE SUPREME powers of causation join forces as a triad or trinity, manifesting to serve as one. All the supreme powers of causation merge and become one supreme power to support every manifested mortal embodiment. These divine powers serve as the virtuous power, including the physical or natural world, the spiritual or sensory world, and essence or spirit. They function as the Trimurti, encompassing causation, sustainability, and resurrection. In the Vedas, they personified as Brahma (the Creator), Vishnu (the Preserver), and Shiva (the Resurgent One). Individual domination within the Trimurti may vary depending upon the lineup of powers that serve as united worshipped as Dattātreya.

## BENEFACTOR

According to *Rig-Veda* 8:56, the deities that serve nature regarded as the guardian king *Saudharma-kalpa*, the highest in all the heavens. These deities are all born in the heavenly region, representing a subgenus, which in turn represents the main classification of the four godly powers (devas) representing the six ancient deities Jupiter, Perun, Perkūnas, Taranis, Zeus, and Thor. They all prevail, serving as the kings of the heaven (Svarga) who come to serve on earth (Prithvi). As the celestial powers, they regulate lightning, thunderstorms, rain, and the flow of rivers to create floods. They come to resolve any fight or conflict. Indra, the celebrated godly power, kills the malevolent Asuras, who stand in the way of human prosperity and happiness. To overcome the deceiving force's evil powers, Indra, as the slayer of evil, brings rains and sunshine. As a mighty power, Indra comes to support humankind and serve as their friend and as the friend of those righteous devas who rule over the much-sought noble souls. As to rebirth, laid out by the doctrine of manifested mortal bodies (samsara), the devas demonstrate godly noble power and are subject to suffering and ridicule, and reduced to just figureheads, coming to suffer rebirth and re-death. Indra, in the iconography, shown as wielding a thunderbolt (*vajra*) and riding on the white elephant *Airavata*. The elephant sometimes featured with three heads and sometimes with five heads—and sometimes it is a single elephant with four tusks.

According to *Rig-Veda* 8:46, Indra, the lord of ample wealth, comes to guide depending upon an individual's need, and serves like the tawny steeds the Aśvins. He also serves as the hurler of the thunderbolt and the true giver of wealth. The poets celebrate with their songs the one serving as the Lord of One Hundred Powers, with one hundred aides to provide guidance to every conceivable manifested mortal embodiment (Aryaman); the semi manifested cosmic hosts (Maruts); the unmanifested eternal law (Varuna); and invisible eternal love (Mitra). All void of guile, these gods come to protect livestock and provide the heroes with strength enough to prosper, with speed like that of the noble Ādityas. Ever in search of wealth, which all desire, human beings learn to pray to Indra in the hopes of becoming as fearless as the lord of wealth and remaining strong.

Verily, combining their strength, all the fearless powers aid humans in becoming rich in material wealth. They allow their swift steeds to bring soma juice from the bays to serve as the most excellent drink. Indra comes to slay most enemies fighting the invincible war. He wins by bringing the heavenly light, with merit and all-bountiful fame, securing a mighty victory—and for his good deeds he is offered libations. Responding to humanity's wish for cows, steeds, and chariots, as of old being gracious, Indra leads humans to become the greatest of the great heroes. Nowhere else can bounds of such munificence found. The messenger Maghavan, with strength, rewards those who sing hymns, and serves as the high glorifier and friend to all generations who offer praise. All races of humankind, including the women, lift their voices to invoke the gods, as aided by the messenger Maghavan, with Indra serving as champion and protector of those performing great deeds, making them rich with all kinds of wealth.

During their wild rapture brought about by the soma, heroes, lauding the gods, singing as wise people, come to Indra, who gloriously named the Mighty One, and, as the hymns allow, given wealth of all kinds, including excellent treasure and strong steeds, which invoke deeds of might. The sovereign ruler of all precious things, who has the power over all those who are fair-minded, shapes himself thereafter as the Mighty One, pouring out bounties upon other travelers, along with the demigod Maruts, who, known to all, are all prepared to go along, singing and making sacrifices. With songs and praise, they perform according to the divine will, lifting their voices when making the sacrifice. They worship the thundering ones, the troops flying over the ridges of mountains to bring along the mightiest power, Indra, who comes to crush the evil-minded and others outfitted with material wealth to meet their needs. Stirring up thoughts, such as being noble winners, strong, wondrous, in splendid excellence, as the sole lord of victory, Indra brings joy, giving all an overpowering wealth, like a chief in need of mighty deeds.

The godless one's approach those who have received a great reward (Vaśa) for appearing as the rising light (*Aśvya*) at dawn. Kanīta, the munificent son of the divine king *Pṛthuśravas*, brings in sixty thousand steeds, ten thousand cows, and two thousand camels, ten thousand of which are brown in hue, and the other ten thousand of which are red in hue, along with ten thousand cows with three spots each. The ten thousand brown cows increase the wealth by creating a fleet of steeds whose tails are long and fair and turn with a swift whirl like a chariot wheel. The munificent Kanīta, son of the divine king Pṛthuśravas, also provides a chariot of gold, and to the princes passes on a bounty, along with most lofty fame, which they win themselves. As part of the tradition, this accompanied by rites performed by the great strong wind, Vayu, to vigorously support the light that they use to attain great wealth. Those with two thousand horses arrive like rays of light in the morning, all fully vested with drafts of pressed soma to serve as pure and bright. Those inclined toward the Glorious One become bounteous themselves by being borne on firm and prosperous ground, with Nahuṣa providing land as a gift to those who are wise and devout. The lord of bounteous beauty meets with praises along with the wind, Vayu, who drops down opulence, hurried along among steeds, camels, and hounds as he spreads forth with rain.

So, with a prize dear to all, sixty thousand gain powers to become like bulls that resemble vigorous steeds. They come to humanity as a herd of oxen that, like a grazing herd that complains, become one hundred camels and two thousand white elephants, given as a gift to the Dāsa *Balbūthas*, who comes to worship Indra and *Tarukṣa*, serving humanity. Through Vayu, Indra and his guards all rejoice with the morning light, which brought forth by a stately woman, Vaśa Aśvya, adorned with ornaments of gold.

According to *Rig-Veda* 8:47, with help from the noble souls, the trinity of Āditya, Varuna, and Mitra let the worshippers know there is no sorrow or harm that can ever reach the manifested mortal embodiments. Those who follow the trinity and receive their support kept safe from any harm, by being provides with incomparable aids to keep all woe far away. The trinity, like birds, spread their sheltering wings to cover and protect the devotees, who in turn provided with shelter and defense. The trinity, by spreading their wings, provide shelter even to those already provided with protection by their own wings. Most who are wise, given a home for their life's special purpose; this is over and above the riches they given by the noble Ādityas. Like a good driver of vehicles, they learn to avoid poor roads, letting sorrows pass them by. For this, they receive special favor and grace from Indra. They guarded against sinking or fainting upon losing the wealth, wisdom, and material gains that they have either received or earned themselves. With neither anger nor distress, they use the shelter provided by the noble Ādityas, from whom they receive a blessing. Knowing well that they blessed with physical things such as carriages and armor shields, the embodiments, when in a fight, serve as each other's guards and protect against both great offenses and smaller mistakes. That is why such embodiments receive support from the wealthy mother Aditi, who brings another trinity, namely, Varuna, Mitra, and Aryaman, with each providing shelter as three of the supreme powers of causation. Their auspicious powers, which are free from malady, provide the ultimate protection.

Triply strong, this trinity comes to extend beyond the noble Ādityas, looking down from above. Like a guide exploring a riverbank, they lead embodiments along a pleasant path, like a rider leads horses toward an easy passage. They leave behind the evil and their friends the demons, while they follow noble souls serving as righteous members of humanity. They fully support animals such as cows and other milk-bearers and help others, who end up striving for fame by performing noble deeds. Each manifested evil deed, however, remains concealed within the astral body, causing the individual to end up moving far from the powers of the solar deity (*Trita Āptya*). Their individual dwellings house their dreams, and after they are dead, they are brought to the Lady of the Light to remove all such dreams by returning them to the solar deity Trita Āptya, where, with a garland or a chain of gold representing a rosary, a child of heaven helps to remove the bad dream, whatever it may be, consigning it back to Trita Āptya, thereafter feeding the humans food and helping them with their noble work as an offering to atone for their evil spirits. Just as Trita gives food and work, the solar deity Trita Āptya brings DaVita as morning light to bear away the darkness.

## SAVORY VIAND

According to *Rig-Veda* 8:48, after, with religious thoughts, enjoying the savory viand, the individual embodiment finds that the best hidden treasure enjoyed as food given by all immortal and half-mortal divinities. They call upon the physical powers to gather themselves and ask the godly mother Aditi to enter their embodiments to serve as a spiritual power and as the appeaser of built-in celestial anger. Just like the river Indus, they enjoy friendship with Indra, who brings a swift carriage that pulled by steeds and moves toward riches. After they have drunk soma and have become immortal, they attain the eternal light as if discovering the godly powers. Malicious foemen can do no harm to such immortal living spirits residing within the mortal embodiments, the spirits absorbed into their hearts, providing sweet soma from the Indus. Like a wise friend helping a loving friend, they, as rulers, with soma lengthen the life span of their mortal friends. The glorious drops of soma, once absorbed, bring freedom, and create a closely knit bond, like a strap securing a carriage. This helps them to prevent their feet from slipping on the way. In addition, they drink drops of soma so they may spared from disease. This helps them to shine bright like the eternal flame, which produces a clearer sight that helps them celebrate better, as the drops of soma help them attain comfort by way of enlivening their spirits, just as ancestral riches help kings to prolong their life spans.

The heavenly power Sūrya brings longer-lasting days with sunshine, giving kings the mythical fluid as a favor to make them prosper. As devotees, the kings are mindful of the living spirit and its powers, which refresh all embodiments and further allow the Indus River to continue providing pleasure. Those who given soma come to settle; their vision clears, and their behavior comes to serve the embodiment as an ancient guardian. Mindful of the holy statutes, they commit no offenses, and as kind and godly friends, they serve with grace. They join with the friend whose heart is tender and who worships the lord of the bays, never harming them when they are drunk. With soma now deposited within their embodiments, they worship the god Indra in exchange for a longer life span and freedom from any maladies that sap their strength. Gradually all fear vanishes, and as they pass away from the darkness, they meet their fathers, who reside within the holy river Indus, with their hearts filled as if they had drunk soma.

They themselves become immortal, like the individual living spirit that has already entered the mortal embodiments. This grants them soma to serve with oblation, allowing them to rest securely in godly grace and favor. The godly fathers associated with such embodiments spread abroad, passing through earth and heaven, offering oblations to serve those living within the holy river Indus, allowing them to come and serve as the lords of riches. By given a godly blessing, as the gods preserve them, they never sleep and never controlled by idle talk. Evermore as friends, drinking soma, they speak as a council of brave sons. As the givers of life, they even help to focus the eyes, serving as the light finders. Residing within the Indus, and of one accord, they provide protection to guard all from behind and from the front.

According to *Rig-Veda* 8:49, from the flowing river waters, a fire, the hidden eternal flame, manifests on the ground to support the mortal embodiments, including the holy priests, each carrying a long ladle full of oil to serve as a bomb. They come to support the life force that grows within the sacred grass. Agni, with his eternal fire, chooses the mortal embodiments, such as the Sons of Strength, to invoke the envoy Aṅgiras, carried unto Agni. The envoy moves through the throngs of holy priests, who move their ladles to bring out the Child of Force, who in the form of a sacrifice comes fast with drops of oil for the sacrificial rites. With Agni as the Disposer, they transform any righteous sage into a godly herald who, with worship, brings cheerfulness and, with holy rites, comes to serve as the pure holy man.

As the singers of hymns, holy men establish eternal youth, which brings godly longing. They feast with the five great elements of nature (Vasu), who are all seated at the banquet, ready to rejoice with gracious songs. Famed for his art, Agni, as the Preserver, known far and wide for being righteous, appears among the holy sages, all of whom sing with godly power, coming to shine with the most resplendent eternal blaze. Sending bliss unto the folk and the worshippers, the princes, with the eternal flame, subdue their foes and then come to rest in the company of the godly powers. The ferocious Agni himself scorches the earth, burning even the high undergrowth, to release bright eternal love (Mitra). Mitra comes to serve those who injured, as well as those who plot ill against their friends, while ensuring no friend is handed over as prey to their mortal enemy, nor any wicked friend or fiend who comes to conquer the unassailable guards protecting the most youthful gods.

Using his eternal flame, Agni comes to protect with the first hymn, then the second hymn, followed by the third hymn. And then he brings his power and might to go through the fourth hymn to invoke the five great elements of nature (Vasu). Taking from each friend who brings no gift, he reserves each deed of strength for the nearest friend who injured in service to the godly powers. Those who are renowned, Agni, by extending their lives, gives them the wealth they crave to attain a more glorious righteousness. Excellent in strength, with quickened thoughts, they find true wealth and are like the heavenly bull, who, with its mouth full of sharp teeth, and with strong horns, exerts pressure like a child of strength to stand up and not wasted. The holy priests start spreading everywhere, making offers with oblations to those who receive all the precious things that stored unweariedly within the woods. They bear up, offering gifts to the bright and shining godly powers serving as the seven powers of causation, the *Saptarishis.*

The priests come to worship godly powers as one, freely giving to the everlasting ones who can cleave through rock to bring out the heat that produces a fervent glow. They rise above, finding themselves among the manifested mortal embodiments with the eternal flame, and come to join with those whose pasture trimmed through the powers of the restless one. They offer food to all the tribes. With noble psalms, the invoked priests tell their wishes to the thinking powers that dwell with, serve, and guard the embodiments. With speed, they show forth with strength of various sorts, serving those both near and far. Agni, appearing with his ferocious flame, along with the friendly guardian of the sky, comes along with praise for the worshippers (holy priests) and the slaughterers (rakshasas) to protect those serving as lords of their households. He ensures no fiend threatens those rich in light, or comes with any form of spell, and from the distant pastures, he drives hunger far away, also chasing the demons' friends.

The mightiest come to listen to the prayer. Along with the godsent messenger Maghavan, who creates motivated thought, they come near to the mythical juice soma. Then they go on to serve as the strongest independent rulers, serving both heaven and earth, all supplied with power and might. Seated first among peers whose souls long for mythical juice, they fill themselves and then go on to serve the lord of wealth Indra, who knows well who the victor will be in the fight, namely, the lord of the bay steeds. Indra vanishes and becomes invisible, appearing as the unchanging messenger Maghavan

As the envoy of Indra, with divine wisdom, Maghavan wins the booty. Like the thunder, he seeks Indra for help and salvation, and assistance in comprehending the divine powers (divine will). After that, he blissfully follows the heroes who have found eternal wealth. With an increasing number of steeds and livestock multiplying as if from a golden well, he bestows the gifts that he has stored up and is unstoppable in bringing whatever one may ask. Thus, the receivers come to worship the divine powers as they help the worshippers find great wealth that they may take for themselves as the messenger Maghavan gains cattle and steeds. Such gifts result hundreds of herds, with the thousands of singers, nearing the fort, sing of the grace of Indra.

Whether it is simple or not, the holy sage Śatakratu offers praises to Indra with love, gladdened and saddled with a deep longing. Śatakratu comes with strong arms to break down fortifications and, as the Great Destroyer, hears the loud cries of those who are rich who seek Śatakratu, who emerges from the eternal flame, Agni, now seeking Indra, the lord of eternal wealth who is counted neither among sinners nor among the cheap or foolish manifested embodiments, sheds soma provided by the mighty ones. Like Indra, the mighty ones, yoked in fight as powerful conquerors, as well as debt claimers, know all and will not be deceived. As the best charioteer, the Vanquisher marks each fault, knowing that the strong who come near to Indra provide security from failings and fear. Serving as a helper, Maghavan drives away foes and enemies. As the liberal lord of bounty, he strengthens the ample embodiments of those who worship Indra, which brings honor to Maghavan, the great lover of the song, who welcomed with pressed soma, which he drinks as the Vṛtra-slayer, guarding against foes as the best defender. Indra, as the first, the last, and the middlemost, keeps watching from behind and defends from all other directions—below, above, in front—serving as a shield.

Staying far away from the terror sent from heaven, Indra deflects all weapon attacks, always serving as protector—today, tomorrow, and the next day. His singers, each day, worship their brave lord who keeps them safe by both day and night. As a crushing warrior, Maghavan passes his heroic might, like the might of the divine, into the exceedingly strong arms of Śatakratu, who comes to grasp the thunderbolt.

## COSMIC OBJECTS

According to *Rig-Veda* 8:51, Indra offered praise when the crushing warrior Maghavan serves both him and those who supply soma, amid hymns coming with great energy magnified among manifested bodies and to serve as the great gift, solitary among chiefs, companionless, impetuous, and peerless. He enables the embodiments to become further refined and sophisticated to become great and rise above others. Thus, in terms all things born, in might, the lord of swift bounty wins even with worthless steeds, which must told by Indra to stop drooping and to perform heroic deeds. To increase as worshippers, the embodiments pay devotion to the mighty powers, attaining a most potent blessed state that strives for fame. Indra makes the bolder spiritual move to hold them and serve them strong soma, which they take with reverence. Worthy of song, Indra looks down upon living beings as if investigating a well, pleased with their skills. They drink soma as they each find a mate to later become their soul mate. In strength and wisdom, all the godly powers, including Indra, guard those who with praises acquire might and offer their best service to the godly powers.

With such power, they slay evil ones such as the strong Vṛtra, and as the council of the Beauteous One, they establish the races of humankind, whom Indra already knows through their renowned deeds. The mighty Indra, at their births, provides them with mental power like Maghavan's, grants them livestock, and helps them increase in number. The eliminator of evil power, serving as the Vṛtra-slayer, combines his mental and physical powers to win the spoils. As thunderbolt-armed heroes, humankind receive the consent of the Almighty, so they become truthful, never again being untrue. Even during death, they given inner illumination, the last gift given by Indra.

According to *Rig-Veda* 8:52, with the powers of the ancient mighty ones, the first one manifested as the cosmic father who, beloved, equipped with efficacious prayer, was allowed to pass through the cosmic shield (the sky) to appear as the cosmic body Manu, traveling alone as a individually manifested body appearing as compressed stones filled with water, never forsaking the mythical juice (soma), and appearing as meteors coming to the ground (Prithvi). With all hymns and prayers serving the godly powers, the individual manifested bodies look like Indra, knowing full well that the powers of Agni, through his messenger Aṅgiras, support all living things on the earth. Performing great deeds, as the promoters of song to strengthen old sages and become blessed, with Indra they make a loud presentation to express the desires and intentions of the pious singers who cry "Hail!" all singing loud hymns, honoring Indra to gain a stall of livestock.

All deeds of might done, except those yet performed by any who are devoid of guile, who remain resting with Indra. The singers, however, have known since the time of their manifestation that they must serve mortal embodiments and establish five tribes among humankind. Indra sent out with his individual voice, and the priests scatter across the pasturelands to find their own dwelling places. With praises, human beings perform their deeds and race against the wheel. With a great steers, they boldly stride for life and let the cattle take their corn to make mythical juice. Receiving the pressed soma, they crave to serve the ruling powers, such as the competent father Dakṣa, who exalted as the cosmic hosts (Maruts), serving as heroes, with the poised singers duly coming as a band, all singing. Once allied, they prevail and join with the heavenly power Rudra, appearing as rain clouds. Of one accord, they call upon Rudra in battle to bring about the death of evil power. With the strength assigned to them, they sing praises to the godly power Indra for providing them with protection.

According to *Rig-Veda* 8:53, Indra takes great delight in the hymns and displays his bounty with a thunder that drives off the enemies and those who dislike praying. He crushes to the ground those who are miserly and mean, neither bringing him gifts nor offering soma to impress the gods in heaven, the sovereigns of humankind. Indra visits individual dwellings to listen to the humans' prayers, which fill both heaven and earth. Even amid the rocky heights, or in the hills, beheld breaking hundreds and thousands of cosmic rocks for the worshippers. Both night and day, the worshippers seek a taste of soma to fulfill their hearts' desire. Strong-necked like young steers, they never bend down to appear with the noble power Brahma, who with libation covers the steer and ministers to all creations who delight in the powers of Indra, who serves as the Vṛtra-slayer.

According to *Rig-Veda* 8:54, with a gift worthy of heroes, they summon the powers with loud voices and become dearest among humankind and other milk-bearing animals They hasten to offer soma to the dear god Puru, who appears vigorous in heart and comes to rule cheerfully over the earth. *Śaryaṇāvān* rules the holy river Ārjīkīya, which provides as best soma, which Indra eagerly rushes toward to drink of plenteously.

According to *Rig-Veda* 8:55, through the powers of Indra, humanity called upon to go from east to west, and from north to south, following the fleet of steeds that bring an effluence of rich heavenly light, the rivers filling with soma as they move toward the sea. Humanity, singing songs of joy, calls upon these great and wide rivers where even milk-bearing animals such as cows come to profit from the powers of Indra. The soma provided to the bay steeds to carry in the chariot transporting the godly powers. With glory and majesty, the gods welcomed with songs of praise, the strong lords performing great deeds. After the milk-bearing steeds have provided soma for the feast, they call upon others to sit on the sacred grass with Indra. As always, the commoners invoke Indra. Human beings are pleased to watch as amrita extracted from the soma. Neglected, all skilled pious men sing sacred songs as they haste toward the highly renowned godly powers. The mighty ones come to rest, serving as kings, riding on spotted livestock decked with golden ornaments. In addition to one thousand spotted livestock, the great-grandsons of the goddess *Durgaha* receive as a gift pure brilliant gold. The one thousand munificent cattle are renowned by the godly powers. Singing loudly while performing the sacred rite, the great-grandsons bring soma and, like priests, invoke Indra, who as composers of the songs, cherish Indra and find the hidden wealth.

At the helm, in rapture because of the soma, as a strong slayer of evil, Indra does not hesitate to give glorious wealth to those who sing his praises, honoring his godly power. The worshippers toil and invoke the godhead to come and serve as Śakra, asking for currycombs for their horses or for golden whips like that Indra, as the Vṛtra-slayer, uses. The worshippers urge Indra to open the stall full of cows. Indra scatters ample wealth, including that which buried, piling it in heaps. Serving as the lord of the bay steeds, with fair-helmed thunder, Indra performs pleasing acts for the heroes, who offer praises from olden times, along with a sacrifice. Speaking loudly, much invoked, the thunderbolt-armed Indra comes from the celestial region to carouse and serve soma to those who pray. Pouring out the soma brings wealth. Verily, as he did yesterday, the Thunder Wielder drinks soma to fulfill his desires.

Covering a wide range, the Glorious One appeals even to the wolf, the savage beast that kills the sheep, and follows the path to the decree, which he graciously accepts. Amid praises, with wondrous thoughts, the wolves come forth performing deed of vigor that have not yet covered by Indra, whose glorious title not a one has heard. Known from birth as the Vṛtra-slayer with great irresistible power, Indra is invincible, possessing a matchless might, and excels among all who seen and all who traffic in strength. Indra, as the Vṛtra-slayer, serving his constant worshippers, brings prayers that have never heard before, invoking the eternal flame, which meets with the Thunder-Armed One to perform mighty acts. By providing aid, they call forth in eager hope. As in the past, they offered soma to invoke the five great elements of nature (Vasu) and the primordial power, Shakti, who inwardly calls for the powers of the strongest god, Indra. The worshippers come to depend upon her powers, she whom none but the epithet Maghavan may invoke, sparing the established human tribes from misery and famine, setting them free from this dire curse. Maghavan and Shakti provide the worshippers success through the wondrous thoughts of the mightiest ones, enabling them to find the way and allowing the juice poured, keeping them from fearing sorrow caused by the goddess of darkness, Kali, who allows the evil powers to vanish by themselves.

## INCARNATION

According to *Rig-Veda* 8:56, the noble Ādityas graciously support the trinity of Varuna, Mitra, and Aryaman, who come to bear all distress, serving as the noble warrior Kshatriyas, who, incarnated as Dattātreya, come to serve the mortal embodiments. The trinity prepare the defense of the great noble Ādityas and guard them by informing them in advance when the deadly weapon strike will take place. The Ādityas blessed to hear such news beforehand so they may guide the mortal embodiments to prepare defensive shelters, toiling to pour out gifts with the blessing to transform their perishable embodiments into imperishable embodiments. By freed from material wealth and its associated sorrow and sinful attachment, they see no fault in letting themselves accept the support of Indra. Indra enlists the other renowned powers of causation to release the Ādityas from the shackles that bind them by pouring out gifts of soma.

The gracious mother Aditi lends aid to those who go astray and join their enemies; instead of saving their perishable embodiments from the foes, she enables them to go from the shallows into the depths, thus making it easier for them to seek the help of the Ādityas. To make sure not even one noble seed or embryo harmed, she continues to appear among the folk in her native glory, never deceived, serving the princes, and enabling them to maintain their statutes, void of guile. The bountiful Ādityas enjoy helping the perishable embodiments, both when they are young and when they are old. Thus, they vouchsafe everyone who, in wisdom, turns away from sin to live long in the world beyond this one, enjoying a new life, one of mercy and of freedom from any residual memories. The great mother Aditi now comes to serves the bountiful Ādityas, never despising them and very graciously inclined toward them so none of the weapons of the Vivasvans may harm them or destroy them, and so they may never grow old or remain burdened with sin. From any side, hostility, indigence, or a combination thereof may come to attack them, knowing that the noble supreme powers serve as their guardians. Even within their perishable embodiments, they receive aid and divine bliss to perform great deeds, also providing backup in any assault against Indra or the brave noble souls who have great power and wisdom.

According to *Rig-Veda* 8:57, with strong thoughts, they comprehend the majesty of the Mighty One, by virtue of which they come to grasp his greatness and, with a golden thunderbolt, deter anything that comes their way. The lord of might who rules over all humankind will never bend and will never call upon any power that will not aid the manifested embodiments. Ever further, in battle he will always win, serving as the light among hosts who called upon to serve Indra and provide him with the praise, he is due without measure, along with the most bountiful wealth. The Ādityas call upon the peerless ruler to provide them with his ample bounty. They urge him to drink soma with praises as the old dancer, the lord of humanity, comes to sing. The Mighty One, whose friendship no mortal embodiment has ever obtained, nor can attain unless they aided by his thunderbolt-armed associate, serves as a righteous warrior in battles for water, for sun, and for filling the earth.

With sacrifice and songs, the Ādityas seek Purumayya as the chief lover of song, who provides help in any battles where Indra, as the Thunderer, comes with his friends, moving them forth with his guidance and preparing them to offer a sacrifice. The chief lover of song, Purumayya himself given ample space to build his own dwelling place. At the banquet, the godly powers provide countless broad pathways for humanity and create a space for their cattle and steeds to pull their carriages. After offered pleasant-tasting soma, the humans gifted with two white-hued steeds, two brown-hued steeds, and two red-hued steeds, all of them reined and obedient, so they may join in the ritualistic sacrifice to transform and become beauteous ones, that is, Asvamedha. These six horses matched with mares to give birth to the well-marked brown Patakratu and the red mare Vṛṣanvati, who in obedience follow the path under both rein and whip. Given their deeds of might, they are beyond the reproach of all human beings, who love to blame and find fault.

According to *Rig-Veda* 8:58, with songs of praise, the godly ones are all sent forth into the holy river Indus, where they serve as hero-gladdeners and, with hymns and gifts invite heroes to make sacrifices. The heavenly bull, which longs for their approach, appears as the lord of the cows, which turn or run away from the bull, although none killed. The dappled cows provide streams of milk, prepared with drafts of soma. Serving in the birthplace of the godly powers, they prevail as clans within all three luminous realms. The dappled cows, with praises, serve their guardian, Indra, the lord of the brave, Son of Truth, appearing as bay steeds. Like the red steeds, they sent to the sacred grass, where they sing songs of worship to Indra, thunder-armed, who as a cow yields milk mingled with essence (meath) stored in a vault. When the heavenly bull and Indra mount on high, arriving at the home of the bright ones, they call for meath to strengthen them and enable them to reach the higher place that seats their twenty-one friends, including the three members of the trinity and the seven members of the *Saptarishis,* who all sing forth with songs of praise. The young *Priyamedhas* sing loudly and, with their fervent praise, gain a stronghold.

Now, with musical instruments from the Renaissance, the viol and lute, they produce penetrating music. To accompany the stringed instruments, they use their spiritual voices to sing hymns, with which they invoke

Indra. This allows the dappled motherly cows easily milked, and Indra quickly seizes milk once it separated from the soma. After Indra and Agni have drunk their fill, along with the other gods, they, with loud sounds, come as the god of eternal law, Varuna, who regulates the seven glorious rivers, whose waters flow from the throat, where there is a windpipe and an ample mouth serving as a drain. They come to face the floods, causing mother cows to go unto their calves. The fleets of steeds that spring as well-harnessed worshippers guided in their fair form. Indra, with his very mighty hand, holds onto the enemies with utter disrespect and sends them far away to branch out among the clouds and be smitten by their own voices like crying children, exceedingly small, thereafter given newly fashioned embodiments. As the lord of the home, fair-helmeted, Indra ascends in a chariot wrought of gold to deal with the Heavenly One, the thousand-footed one, red of hue, matchless, who sheds blessings wherever he goes. With reverence, he becomes sovereign lord, who comes near with success to prosper them and bestow gifts. According to ancient custom, while the sacred grass strewn as sacrificial food for the bird *Priyamedhas*, the offering made.

According to *Rig-Veda* 8:59, the sovereign lord of humanity, as the Vanquisher (*Vṛtra-slayer*) who fights as the preeminent host, with songs of praise, is honored by Indra, who comes along with a sustaining ancient hand, *Puruhanman.* With a splendid bolt of thunder, he establishes a bond with the great heavenly body Sūrya and his pantheon. Since no one can, by way of their deeds, attain such strength or offer any sacrifice to make them resistless, daring, and bold in might, they all worship Indra, who with praise to the ancient hand serves as the potent conqueror in any invincible war. At birth, the mighty ones spread out among humankind, sent with loud voices out from heaven to find a seat on the earth (Prithvi), from where, with a loud voice, Indra passes through one hundred barriers and comes to match the powers of the source of one thousand lights (the sun), thereby giving birth to thunder, with Indra serving the two worlds, heaven and earth.

Performing heroic deeds with his might, and with all strength, Indra appears as the messenger Maghavan, the Strongest One, who comes to help set up a stable full of all kinds of animals, supported by the thunder provided by Indra. Together, Indra and Maghavan prevent the godless mortal embodiments from obtaining food and living long lives, except for the bright-hued steed Etaśa, which yoked and urges that praise given to the great conqueror Indra. Indra and Maghavan invoked in the shallow waters and in the depths of the underworld to perform deeds for mighty nature (Vasu). Serving as a hero, Indra rises to bring great wealth, which passed through the renowned messenger Maghavan. Trampling the attackers, Indra justified as the courageous heroic guard. The strongest among the evil Dāsas struck down, especially those who bring no sacrifice. The inhuman, godless infidels and their friends blown away or cast down to the mountain to face a quick death, just like the mountain itself casts down the evil power, (*Dāsa*). Loving Indra gathers them up in his hands like kernels of corn and gives them to animals, wishing for them to increase in power. Sages trim the sacred grass and continually praise the beautiful bestower *Sāra*, who comes as one mother with one calf, serving as the noble sons of *Suradeva*, who bring a calf led by three chiefs, along with a milk goat.

## COMMEMORATION

According to *Rig-Veda* 8:60, Agni comes to commemorate by bringing great wealth from the solar deity to guard against all malignity. He knows that those who serve him all have hatred in their hearts but have no control over their anger. They even hate their birth friends. Because of this, all the godly powers, serving as Sons of Strength, with the auspicious eternal flame, bring wealth and all good things to keep the mortal embodiments from filled with anger (malignities) and keep them away from greed for material wealth. While Agni comes to protect all those who offer gifts, such as sages, in worship of the godly powers, asking for wealth and assistance. With riches, heroes offer gifts that bring bliss, asking served by the epithet of Agni, Jātavedas, who does not abandon sinful and evil hearted men. Agni, as the source of the eternal flame, however, allows no godless person to receive his bounty, saving all his treasures with his godly powers. Serving as Sons of Strength, Agni and Jātavedas bring along the great and excellent Vasu as a friend, who comes singing praises, his songs bringing him near to the bright and beauteous piercing flame. Paying homage to the lord of wealth, Agni, and with praises, the heroes ask for help from the Sons of Strength, expressed as Agni's epithet Jātavedas. They bring precious gifts to the ancient immortal priest, asking him to come and serve the priests of the mortal embodiments and thus turning the embodiments into a most delightful house. Agni, after making a sacrifice and performing holy rites, advances to offer songs, first to the warrior steed, then to the ground (Prithvi), serving as the lord of wealth to win wars and cultivate friendships, also offering to vouchsafe the food. Then Agni seeks the seeds to support longer lives for the progeny protected by nature (Vasu). The heroes' chanting encourages Agni, the piercing flame, to reach the point where, when the chanting is loudest, he transforms their riches into fame and turns the bright light into a piercing flame, summoning *Purumīlha*, who, from within the dwellings, keeps foes far away and provides the physical embodiments with health and strength. Serving as guardian of the life force, eternal flame establishes the different tribes based upon their inner illumination, along with eternal love (Mitra) and the glowing brand of eternal law (Varuna).

According to *Rig-Veda* 8:61, Agni, through oblations, prepares the piercing flame *Purumīlha* serve as the minister who, by way of his orders, causes the tribes to rejoice and join in friendship, thus enabling the seated priests ruling over manifested human beings to distribute their active power among all humanity. With a glowing inner light, the manifested human goes beyond all thought. With their tongues, they come to represent the races of humankind who seize the internal flame and follow a twofold path: first giving life force to the embodiment to climb and push up through the eternal flame, for example, in the woods, and second, through the power of the tongue, striking the tower of strength like a radiant wandering calf that finds none shackled and, with its mother's praise, becomes great and mighty among all domesticated animals such as horses. The life force comes to serve among humankind, whose ancestors can traced. The life force also brings along individual milk-bearing animals, such as cows, which once placed among the flowing rivers. With a resounding noise, they are set down in five places among streams, where all who are cast down work through the power of Indra to support the ten godly powers the Vivasvans with a threefold hammer from the sky, serving the progeny with a source of water, and who with light and prayers are implored three times a day: morning, midday, and night.

The newly created eternal flame kindled so that all may proceed with the sacrifice and anoint the priests. From their mouths they pour forth with reverence, like a mythical exhaustless fountain with a wheel above, setting into motion objects such as fireballs and meteors, filled with soma mixed with essence (meath), which poured into a tank, from which it gushes out like a wellspring. Two mighty ones, as blessed demigods, come to make sacrifices, serving the heavenly bull and the earthly cow, the pure source of gold, which comes to protect the embodiments as an amulet.

From heaven, they pour forth with mythical juice until it reaches the earth. These animals, like the mother cows beside their calves, come to meet with their kin and then come to know their own unshakable place, where there is plenteous heavenly food, which they gobble with their greedy mouths. With light and prayer, they serve as the celestial gods Indra and Agni. With the milk comes rich divine food, which apportioned out by the Holy Soul (Pious One), who, together with the rivers, filled with the seven rays of the sun. Jointly they rise as a new trinity—the sun, Mitra, and Varuna—who serve as medicine for the sick man. Being, paid oblations, they serve as well-beloved ones, at home as if their tongues encompass heaven.

According to *Rig-Veda* 8:62, with the powers of eternal law, Varuna, the holy soul, keeps the law in the heights and complies with the powers of the trinity, who like a yoked carriage protect the embodiments. Within the twinkling of an eye, they come to protect the holy sage (*Atri)* by overlaying the pit with both cold and hot temperatures, so it flies away and is gone like an eagle with its prey. They fly near, listening, assuring, and hoping to protect at any time of the day. Serving as the demigod (*Aśvins*) they first hear from their closest kin in their dwelling place. Like the holy sage, Atri, they shield the embodiments by preventing any severe action, which they do by generating sweet speech through prayer, by which the eternal flame obtained from the ancient sage (*Saptavadhri.*) They gain insight and, with an edge, offer their praises to the elders. They learn the ancient way to build a brotherhood, thus identifying kindred souls, who come to help and protect the demigods. As twin demigods, (Aśvins), speedily pulling their chariot, move throughout the regions of the earth and the heavens. The two steeds approach cattle in the thousands, passing by them without remembering the rising of the purple-tinted morning light that brings along the true light of the law. The Aśvins look upon the ax-armed black band that surrounds them and then comes to save them by breaking down the old fort of darkness.

According to *Rig-Veda* 8:63, after exerting strength through the power of thought, and with glory from Agni, the dear friend Mitra, with the power of eternal love, comes to every home as a guest. Being with sweet speech, he served sacrificial oil that pleases his eternal soul. Mitra presented with eulogies, gifts, and songs of praise, much lauded like Jātavedas, bearing oblations that reach up to heaven. The godly powers at their noblest and best, prepared to serve, come as Indra, who as the Vṛtra-slayer received and welcomed by other powers, including the evil (*rakshasas*), which are mightier and richer than King (*Srutarvan*). With their great carving qualities and powers, and with their great skill set, they meet with the deathless *Jātavedas*. With praise and adoration, the kings come to offer sacred oil and, with the power of vision, look through the gloom of night to see the ferocious flame honored by the worshipping priests with sacrificial gifts. With lifted ladles, they receive the offering.

Being with hymns and addressed as the cheerful guest, Agni, wellborn, most wise, worker of wonders, is never deceived by anyone who comes near to him. Regarded as dear to those who are most grateful, and as a provider, he grows mightier eulogized. Most splendid among splendors, Agni, in any battle against a foe, given a loftier glory, becoming as bright as Indra, the lord of the heroes, who brings fame, along with steeds and cows, filling the embodiments and become a highly renowned celebrity who, with praises, performs glorious deeds.

The envoys of Indra come to serve as refulgent ones (*Gopavana)*, such as *Aṅgiras,* the envoy of Agni, who hears all the calls from the priests to the Holy One. The priests implore Agni, seeking his aid in gathering up the spoils once they defeat the foes. The priests call upon those who reel with joy (*rksa*), such as the son of the rich king *Srutarvan,* who strokes the fleece of longhaired rams. With four steeds and four coursers pulling their splendid carriage, they come as fleet of foot with the winged *Shavistha* to offer the sacred feast. The steeds with wings, able to fly, and come to serve as Tugra's sons, declaring the absolute truth. They flood the river (*Paruṣṇī*) to bring more horses along with the floodwaters to serve as fast-running stallions or flying horses.

According to *Rig-Veda* 8:64, Agni, as a charioteer, with steeds and stallions, invites the best and most skillful ancient herald seated among the godly powers. Most youthful, the Sons of Strength grant all the wishes of those who make sacrifices and give them all honor, designated as the holy faithful ones serving the lords of wealth. The Sons of Strength the hundreds of thousands of chiefs, providing them with riches to serve as holy sages, good craftsmen who can bend fellies. They perform such bending so they may receive any general call for sacrifice coming from the immanent envoy Aṅgiras. Formerly appearing as ugly and deformed, with eyes unable to see far, they now appear as supernatural powers, or Siddhi (*Virūpa,*) who shine powerfully early in the morning and rise as missiles filled with the power of Agni. With fair praises, the light never ceases and comes to lie low over everything, although it is far away. Like a thief in combat, the Siddhi (*Virūpa*) do not allow the dawn to miss any cows that are floating away, stuck in a miserable situation. The noble powers serving as the Siddhi (Virūpa) prevent any fierce, sinful, hateful tyrannical foe from smiting any noble soul as a billow might smite a ship.

Jointly, Agni and Indra come to humankind, who sing reverent hymns of praise and acquire strength to fight their terrible, troublesome foes. Agni never wearies of lending aid so they may win cattle or wealth. In the great battle, he makes room for them, where they not cast aside, as the one who bears the load and snatches up the wealth goes on to win everything. Agni neither pursues epidemics nor fears the worshippers who gain impetuous strength. Any reverent human beings who labor unwearyingly for favors and success accepted by Agni. He abandons the hosts of the foemen, passing them over, and goes on to accompany those who stand for Indra, who has long been known as their gracious father, to whom now they pray for bliss.

According to *Rig-Veda* 8:65, the cosmic *Maruts*, along with Indra and Agni, as friends, come to destroy all the code words and the magic power, using evil beads to form a hundred-knotted garland to serve as a thunderbolt. As a friend, Indra, along with the Maruts, grows strong and charged. To release the evil from the seawaters, demigods surround with the light of heaven and share the mighty soma. With a loud roar and with songs, they invoke the ancients to bring out soma for the liberal god Indra, surrounded by the Maruts, who, along with the much-lauded drink, bring with thunder, which they offer as a sacrifice from their hearts to give birth to Śatakratu, a wise and noble soul. After the morning rites, Śatakratu gives strength to the mighty powers rising with the thunderbolt. After having quaffed soma, they, with clamped teeth, shake the two worlds, complaining with a fearsome roar, all uttering and hitting hard with death the ruler of the evil powers, Dāsa. Indra measures out an eight-foot circle (mandala), inside of which he worshipped with nine cups of soma, faithfully following the eternal law.

## SAPIENT SOUL

According to *Rig-Veda* 8:66, from the progenitor's lineage comes the sapient soul, who is born to establish individual brainpower. The patriarch of the Gotra clan belongs to the specific lineage that represents this heritage. In such a way is the epoch of Aṅgiras established. Two main clans, one as enlightened teacher (Gautama), and the other as enlightened prophets (Bhāradvāja), are loosely bound together under the same epoch of Aṅgiras. They are both born as Śatakratu, having acquired eternal wisdom from their blessed mother, Śavasī. One, Aurṇavābha, comes to possess might; the other, Ahīśuva, comes to possess fame. Serving as two alike sons, one with the might to overthrow, the other with the power of fame, they smite their enemies like spokes hammered into naves. Once all the evil powers nailed down, their mighty ruler, Dāsa, loses his freedom.

After Indra drinks a single draft of mythical juice from the thirty buckets full of it, within the groundless realm of space he pierced through to appear among the skilled and mighty singers (*Gandharva*), thereby increasing their strength. The Gandharva come to serve as members of the highest noble power, that is, Brahmans. From the mountains, they descend with Indra, shooting through a well-directed shaft. They create one and only one form of a bowl, which filled with enough grains of rice to feed the birds with one thousand feathers and one hundred spines that at birth manifest as strong bodies (*Ṛbhus*). The *Gandharva* makes friends with these birds, which, with praises, take food to them to eat, as the males and females representing humanity.

According to *Rig-Veda* 8:67, the Ṛbhus, in their exploits, perform mighty deeds, their hearts set upon the firm ground of undivided faith. They, with the powers of Vishnu, take all things in their stride, taking the milk from one hundred buffaloes to steam with their rice, then come swinging like ravenous boars. Using the deadly longbow, well fashioned, along with good arrows, all decked with gold, they achieve success. They drink sweet mythical juice, well equipped with arms. Warlike, they increase in sweetness before they come to Indra, who served with soma as the guardian of thousands and as the hero of hundreds of such kind. They bring ornaments for the cattle and embellish the steeds, each with two rings, old chimes, in their ears, which makes them look like the Bold One, who stores an ample supply of jewels and is renowned everywhere as the good lord. None other than the priest and the hero receive such gifts, which needed to win and prosper.

Indra, as the lord of devotees, ensures that Śakra, with his stomach full of might, despite his wrath, may never subdued, deceived, marked, or blamed. Like Indra, he becomes a conqueror, an evil slayer who drinks soma and brings all to order. All treasures combined and blessed easily to bestowed upon the uninjured conqueror as he speeds forth with hope, craving gifts of corn, gold, and livestock, including speedy horses. Never alone, Śakra grasps a sickle, filling his arms with what they can hold as he gathers the barley.

According to *Rig-Veda* 8:68, the Ṛbhus, as sapient souls, always active, never restrained, with soma conquer and burst forth to serve among holy souls (sages) and noble powers (rishis). The sapient souls cover all that is bare and provide with medicine all who are sick. They help the blind man to see and make the crippled person walk. Sapient souls, opposed to hatred, come to serve ignorant souls, providing them with wide-ranging defense to protect them from hate, from waste, and from those who weaken all living things. Through insight, using their skill, they serve heaven and earth, driving away the sinner's enmity to serve the Impetuous One. As they go about their task, they are enthusiastic, obtaining divine grace to satisfy their wishes, such as having their thirst quenched and finding what lost long ago. With speed they come to serve with the pious man in lengthening the span of life they have remaining. Graciously displaying their tender love, unconquered, with gentle thoughts, they bring sweet soma without terrifying or causing alarm, serving it to the noble souls. Without hurting or wounding, they bring a dazzling inner flame seen as coming from their dwelling place, overpowering their wicked enemies. Seeking the godly powers or a king to come and chase the ones who hate them far away, they, like the Bounteous One, dispel foes.

According to *Rig-Veda* 8:69, the truly wise noble power Śarakratu comes to serve as a comforter, which no one other than Indra can do. He is gracious to serve the kindly old men, helping them to win the spoils and then, as prompters of the poor, pour out the mythical juice. Indra's strength and his power of thunder helps them move their embodiments like a chariot, so they neither lag nor find themselves at a place where they are nearest to fame and victory. Winning the prize of victory, they come to establish a firm fort near Indra, where they appointed a place to proceed, singing auspicious hymns in due season. Without disgracing anything, they remove all barriers from their broad course to open it wide so they may proceed. This grants them their sacrificial names. They exalt the supreme sage from the sky, *Ekadyu*, to become immortal. Serving as goddesses or gods, with delight, they bestow a bounty with praises, enriched with prayer that comes soon.

According to *Rig-Veda* 8:70, the immortal god with his mighty arms gathers up manifold nutritious treats and performs mighty deeds, serving with mighty bounty, bringing wealth that promptly provides aid. Heroes, with their auspicious art, welcome the immortals and the mortals without hesitation, who appear as a fearless bull. Glorified like Indra, they come to serve as the lords of supreme wealth, as self-ruling kings who come in bounty without harming anyone. With a prelude of music, they intone a special chant (*sāman*) filled with eternal wisdom, bringing answers to all. Approaching the Bold One, they bring the riches gained from the barbarians and in turn give such booty to the holy singers. With the giving of such booty, they win the spoils, rejoicing in such a way that gives them hope.

According to *Rig-Veda* 8:71, Indra, as the Vṛtra-slayer, comes near to meet the heroes, who bring an offering of meath and strong drafts of soma, all filled with delight and joy. This serves as the strengthening food that comes to grant the wishes of their hearts and generates delightful thoughts. They come down with hymns of praise and, seeing no foes, call upon heaven, the inspirational realm of light, which articulates itself through compressed cosmic stones (meteors), which come submerged in milk. The heroes offer these things in celebration of Indra and his grace, and they hear his call to collect the soma in chalices and vats, where blended with milk. Seen within the vats is a flood from the moon. The heavenly lord comes to lay eyes upon the divine drink, carried by the hawk, which flies, carrying in its talons the drink of the gods.

According to *Rig-Veda* 8:72, the godly powers (Viśvedevas) protected by the trinity of Varuna, Mitra, and Aryaman. This helps them to succeed in reaching the far-seeing gods, who further prosper those who follow the eternal law, allowing them to move safely beyond woes as a ship moves over turbulent floodwaters. Wealthy with praise, the noble soul Aryaman meets the regulator of eternal law, Varuna, and then welcomes the noble Ādityas. Not sinners, they serve the sapient god of eternal love (Mitra). They slay the foe and help those who serve as the bounteous ones in their homes. While journeying on the road, they invoke the godly powers, which allows the manifested embodiments to prosper. With respect and honor, the ancient immortal godly powers Indra and Vishnu, along with the celestial demigods the Aśvins, the half-mortal cosmic hosts the Maruts, and their kith and kin, the bounteous ones, having been in existence since ancient times, set forth right from their mothers' wombs, securing their brotherhood and kinship. Since the early days, the chief Indra has regulated the bounteous ones.

## MORAL SOUL

According to *Rig-Veda* 8:73, Agni, as a dear guest and loving friend, with loud sounds, brings riches from olden times to help the far-seeing godly sages. Among mortal embodiments, he establishes himself as the most youthful godly power who, through hearing their songs, comes to preserve their seeds or embryos. With praise, he serves as the messengers the Aṅgirases, who with strength come to fulfill the wishes of the sages, thus appearing with a plan of sacrifice to create a child of power who manifests as the kingdom of vegetation. These children speak to the godly powers through vibrations in the form of prayers, making all their dwellings happy habitations, and rewarded with songs to treat the embodiments and provide them with wealth. The kingdom of plenteous vegetation, filled with songs, as the house of the lords, inspires through worship, hymns, and sacrifices to win over all kinds, making them wise and strong. With glory, serving as the foremost champions in battle, with their mighty dwelling place provided by Agni, the inhabitants of the kingdom rest in peace among those who, although they may smite others, do not smite the hero's sons, so they prosper well.

According to *Rig-Veda* 8:74, Indra, with invocation, invites the righteous twin demigod Aśvins and the Nāsatyas to come and experience the divine by serving as righteous souls. They hear the calling and come to join with Indra. After they drink the savory juice, they come to appear as a major deity, Krishna. Manifested to represent the eighth avatar a of the supreme god Vishnu. They are worshipped as, the god of compassion, tenderness, and love, who widely revered among divinities as the most popular among all those lords of wealth whose birthdays celebrated every year. Through drinking the savory juice, he worshipped as the most popular among all the heroes, with all singers calling upon Krishna in a single loud voice.

The heroes serve as the chiefs of the devotees (sages), singing praises, whereby they granted an unchallengeable home, from where they drink the savory soma, appearing in the form of drops of nectar or ambrosia, which fills each individual embodiment. As in the worshippers' abode, the twin demigod Aśvins firmly yoked together to draw the carriage of the lords of wealth. With a pair of demigods on each side, the Aśvins and Nāsatyas, the lords seated three to a bench. With favoring grace, they accept the prayers and songs offered to them. While they listen to the songs, they drink the savory soma juice.

According to *Rig-Veda* 8:75, the twin demigods, wondrously strong, well skilled in the healing arts, come along with praises and delight to serve as the competent father Dakṣa and his competent son Viśvaka. They call upon mortals to strengthen their friendship and set them free from their distressed minds and help them gain wisdom like Viśvaka, who as their friend saves their lives and sets them free. The twin demigods, as the possessors of great wealth, learn from Viśvaka to prosper in their current situation and, as the hermit Viṣṇāpū does, get out and gain what is good for them, becoming as competent as Viśvaka, who teaches them to save lives and, instead of breaking off their friendships, provide support to strengthen their friendships. As impetuous heroes, winners of the spoils, they travel afar to call upon helping hands. Like their gracious father, they serve soma and bring sweetness by toiling with Varuna. They seek help from the goddess Savitar to implement the holy law by providing among the animal kingdom with horns, so they may spread everywhere. With the holy law and physical strength, they defeat in war even mighty warriors as they come at them, all without breaking off their friendships and acting as if they are free.

According to *Rig-Veda* 8:76, the impetuous heroes, the splendid twin demigods, accepting the praise they offered, become like a fountain filled with sweet juice, pouring out a stream to serve to the heavenly chiefs. They play like wild bulls beside a pool filled with sweet libation, sitting on the sacred grass with the demigods. Serving as heroes with joyful hearts, they safeguard life, and as the eternal spirit *Priyamedhas*, they serve all. They appear in the houses where the holy grass trimmed, making sacrifices while performing the morning rites. Rich with soma, they gladly come to sit on the sacred grass, prepared to serve the mighty ones in heaven, all coming through the pool to the wild bulls. Along with steeds of varied hues, they now appear as lords of splendor, wondrous, bearing all strength on the path of gold. Manifested as priestly singers, with hymns they sing praises to gain strength, wondrous, fair, and famed for performing great deeds as expressed in their hymns.

According to *Rig-Veda* 8:77, Indra appears in a stall serving as the mother cows who low to their calves with glorious songs to become as wondrous gods coming to checks up on them to see if there are any attackers. With joy and delicious soma, they, as the bounteous givers of gifts, served by the soma's richness, which makes them as strong as mountains that filled with precious things. Indra, with his quickly won booty, is rich in all ways to serve the hundreds of thousands of livestock, giving them strength enough to climb the high hills, barring the way to the powerless. None stray; they perform their acts for the one to whom they sing, praising his warrior's strength. With their wisdom and their wondrous deeds, in mighty excellence, they sing hymns to serve the great rishi Gautama, which attracts others, who come to help. With divine might, they stretch out beyond the boundaries to the heaven. Within the earthly region, the presiding Indra and his envoy Maghavan are unable to comprehend how they achieved such a goal, and they honor such worshippers. None of them keeps the wealth, each becoming a most liberal giver, and with inspiring songs of praise, they ask that all may win the spoils.

According to *Rig-Veda* 8:78, the celestial Indra, along with the cosmic hosts the Maruts, singing a lofty hymn, slay Vṛtra, wherewith the godly powers transform into holy ones who provide the ever-wakening divine light. Indra shoos the cursers far away, thus allowing the splendorous demigods the Maruts, with refulgence, to bring along the godly powers as they eagerly strive to win through divine love. Holy hymns of praise provided by the lofty Indra, along with the Maruts, allow Śatakratu to serve as the Vṛtra-slayer, killing the foe with a hundred-knotted thunderbolt. With good aim, Śatakratu fetches those who are bold at heart and, in his glory, brings about a rapid torrent of water. This allows him, the Vṛtra-slayer, to win the light of heaven, which provided in unequalled measure through the messenger Maghavan. Śatakratu smites the newborn to make sure evil is dead, before he spreads out over the spacious earth, no longer able to get the support needed to prop up the heavens. With the sacrifice made for him with loud songs of joy, as the mightiest he surpasses all, now bringing cows filled with raw milk. From the heavens, the supreme power Sūrya rises to provide heat so the milk, filled with pure soma, may bring joy, especially to those who, with songs of praise, come to acquire the necessary traits to win in battle.

According to *Rig-Veda* 8:79, Indra, who is near to the mighty evil-slayer, with praise and hymns offered libations. With the best of all arts, true to his royal nature, he sends forth bounteous gifts and, in alliance with Śatakratu, claims to be the Glorious One served by the mighty Sons of Strength. The Sons of Strength offer an unsurpassed number of prayers to serve Indra with songs of love. They serve along Maghavan, truthful in art as the lord of the bay steeds, and never allow themselves to reach so low that they defeated by the evil powers. The mightiest lord, the wielder of thunder, from far away sends wealth to the worshippers. Renowned for impetuosity, art, and strength, he alone serves as the guardian of righteous souls, he who is resistless and never conquered by foes. Among the foes, the wisest, the Asuras, seek to share in the bounty by offering shelter and defense, like a mighty cloak, so that they in their glory may reach all righteous souls.

## SANCTIFIED SOUL

According to *Rig-Veda* 8:80, Indra comes down like a virgin aid in a stream to find pressed soma that he may take home to be serve to the mighty powers such as the yonder-roaming manifested soul Śakra. Beholding every part of the embodiment, Indra allows Śakra to pass with songs of praise, which pass through the teeth, accompanied by food such as grain and curds, which the living beings serve as a cake. While getting well, though not yet attaining full strength, they slowly take in drops of soma to build up their strength, like a young river builds up its flow to become the holy river Indus. At all times, worshippers, with their wondering wills, seek help in becoming wealthier without simultaneously becoming hostile toward others. Once they unite, they begin to help themselves. With the godly powers, they sprout up in all three places, belowground, aboveground, and in the air. Being declare as the head, the father, they turn out manifested embodiments into a plowed field. They use parts of their physical bodies, below the waist, to help to grow crops like hair, and they help in cultivating the fields from that point on. The embodiment, like apala music, cleansed, giving the skin thrice the sunshine. The sun, as it travels across the sky, brings the morning light, transforming the wise embodiment Śatakratu into a car or wagon that can be yoked.

According to *Rig-Veda* 8:81, the all-conquering Śatakratu, most munificent of all, with prayers and songs, invites Indra to come and drink of the mythical juice lauded by, much invoked, like the leader of the song. The embodiments serve the renowned ancient Indra who, as a dancer, mighty giver of abundant strength, brings them much closer to the worshipping souls (*Sudaksa*). They take strong drafts of soma mixed with barley into their mouths. Calling to Indra with loud songs of praise, they augment their strength with the gladdening drops, which with godly power bring a vigor that far surpasses all. This imbues them with the support of the all-conquering godly powers, who appear among the righteous warriors. With weapons drawn, they no longer restrained, as the soma grants them with powers such that they can never overthrow. As chieftains of irresistible might, they receive riches from Indra by which they become omniscient sanctified souls and worthy of praise, able to be the deciding voices in any disagreement. Indra gives them food and one hundred powers, which multiply into one thousand powers. They seek wisdom from the wise Śakra and become the kinds of givers who can direct the thunder-armed steeds to win in battle.

The wise and noble power Śatakratu finds enjoyment in their songs. Like cattle in the pasturelands, they come to serve as thunder-armed, with the hope in their hearts granted their wishes. As noble heroes, they guard with care, and they have great speed and foresight, which makes things terrible for their adversaries, as they now rejoice in the noble power of Śatakratu. They come with Indra, the most splendid of all, to celebrate the slaying of the greatest evil power, Vṛtra.

Most widely famed as the best among the gods, known as the true giver of gifts, the soma drinker, with arms of thunder, the Mighty One appears among all human beings as the lover. They celebrate with Indra, singing loud songs and drinking soma, which makes poets sing praises. Appearing among the seven communities (T*rikadrukas*), they rejoice in the sacrifice as the gods stir their minds and prosper them, letting the drops of soma pass within the rivers that flow into the sea. Along with the wakeful hero with divine might, they receive the soma with food, which fills their breasts with the mythical juice. In the form of singers, *Srutakaksa* sings songs and, in the self-created form of Śakra, serves cattle and steed. S*rutakaksa* and *Śakra* come from far away, to appear near as manifested cosmic bodies such as meteors (casters of the stone). As the heroes' friend, and with a hero's art, strong within their hearts, they win everything by serving as the wealthiest lords who prayed to by the worshippers. Not being slothful priests, as the lords of treats, they provide eternal wealth in the form of soma, which blended with milk and pressed to ensure no ill will affects the light of the sun, which gain friends. With the help of Indra, they answer to all their enemies and support the poets and other faithful friends who loudly sing praises as they follow along.

According to *Rig-Veda* 8:82, the heavenly Sūrya, mounted up with the famous wealthy heroes, hurled along with Indra. They come like a bolt, both using their mighty arms to slay Vṛtra and destroy his ninety-nine castles, before they move deep into the ocean, where, like the dead fish (ahi), they block all sunlight in the water. Indra, as the gracious friend, sends a broad stream full of riches—horses, cattle, and corn. Sūrya comes along as the sunrise to support the powers of Indra, along with other mighty ones, such as the lord of the brave, who already knows they are immortal and are not subject to death. With this thought in mind, which is indeed true, they come with soma as they travel far and near, making themselves strong to strike the evil power Vṛtra dead. With vigor, as heroes, they sit as most mighty above those who made joyous with soma, and with a powerful bolt, they become invincible, whom none may deflect. Rising from the lofty heights, as a song lover, Indra lauded as he makes the wild path fair for the messenger Maghavan, who as the sovereign in command, holds a sway that none, neither audacious man nor God, disregards.

The two gods from earth and heaven revered as they stand at the helm, possessing a mite that none may resist. Like black cows, red cows, or cows with spotted hides, they issue white milk. In terror, the cows shrivel in the face of the dragon and his furious might, fearing the monster might fall upon them. As the defenders, knowing they are invincible, the two gods also know that no foe has the power to slay them. They, the best enemy-slayers, are the famous champions of humanity. In their munificence, they come much lauded with names, with the same thought, longing for milk whenever soma shed. They are honored by these libations, which even cause the evil powers to awaken to the prayers offered by the hero Śakra. Coming to aid, the defenders bring delight and riches to those who worship them with joy, with libations offered them by the strong heroes who, with their teams, defeat the foes. As they drink the soma juice, rejoicing in their spirits, they bring great opulence to enrich all votaries with gifts. With soma, and with their wedded wives, they lovingly flow with the waters, which flow restlessly, and present gifts to Indra as a sacrifice so he will provide them with strength.

With might, after a cleansing bath, like bay steeds with golden manes, they come to the banquet that laid out for them by the Lord of Light. Onto the grass they shed drops of soma, then lead Indra to the worshippers so he can endow them with skills and the light of heaven. The votary priests who praise Śatakratu presented with gifts and provided with wondrous strength, which makes all worshippers gracious. They made excellent by way of food and strength, with Indra and Śatakratu blessing them all with contentment. Bearing the soma juice, they are the best Vṛtra-slayers, skilled at the art of showing kindness to all. The lord of rapturous joy brings libation to the bay steeds, and with this libation the bay steeds come to comprehend that the best Vṛtra-slayer, Indra, serves through Śatakratu, who brings the shed soma and teaches them the art of drinking it in drops. This is how Indra provides all with wealth and the skills to be powerful.

The absolute or supreme godly power that regulates the universe is known by names and titles, along with aliases and epithets, such as *entity*, *force*, and *reality*. The absolute itself possesses the highest possible ontological status in terms of existential ranking. In plain language, this is the entity that is the greatest, highest, and truest entity in existence. The absolute power is often associated with the generating of noble thoughts among manifestations. It interacts with lower or lesser types of living things either passively through emanations, or actively through incarnations such as avatars.

According to *Rig-Veda* 8:83, the most famous heavenly mother of all, in her absolute form, by using pure force, comes to yoke the embodiments that serve as the twin demigod horses, the Aśvins, who turn colorless water into white milk and red plasma. Starting from the heart, they gladly transform individual manifested physical bodies into spiritual luminous bodies, such as the sun, the moon, and the constellations of stars. Through the powers of eternal law (Varuna) and eternal love (Mitra), they maintain, regulate, and observe the everlasting covenant. The manifested embodiments, as pious singers with sacred songs, appear as poets and evermore bring soma that has already pressed by the cosmic hosts served as a drink by the twin Aśvins. The manifested embodiments become self-luminous and, moreover, set themselves up as purified to serve in the three places where the trinity of Varuna, Mitra, and Aryaman take the procreant drink.

Heralds such as Indra, desirous of the milky juice, come early in the morning to drink thereof and then, gleaming and excellent, like princes, emerge from the waters to serve as troops to fight against the foes. All those who are impure hasten to appear as great deities who, with favor, even today make wondrous claims as they spread abroad. All the realms of earth supported by the cosmic hosts (Maruts), who create the luminous regions beneath the sky. Even so, pure in might, the Maruts invoked by those who, having drunk soma, have survived the separation of heaven and earth.

According to *Rig-Veda* 8:84, through the powers of soma, the demigod Maruts, with vigor, form a band and abide as the power that comes to prevail within the mountains, serving as charioteers to Indra, the song lover, who comes with songs and soma, and calls upon the godly mother cow as she calls unto her calves. Moving with speed, Indra, as the lover of song, enters every domicile with the flowing fluid that sets free living spirits, such as the falcon, which come to serve as kings and as sovereign lords of all the families representing humanity. Indra hears the feminine voice of *Tirasci*, the mother who serves her valiant offspring to satisfy them with wealth of all kinds, producing a most gladdening song. With hymns, they spring forth with ancient thoughts full of sacred truth. With loud songs and hymns, they magnified, able to strive and win and celebrated as heroes capable of mighty deeds. They come to glorify Indra, who with pure hymns brings the pure milky draft with delight to strengthen them and purify their songs of praise. With the purpose of assisting them, Indra comes personally to endow them with pure riches, which gladly met with pure soma for their vouchsafing. This pure wealth further enriched by the pure worshippers who can strike the evil power Vṛtra dead and move forward pure in heart to win the spoils.

## RIGHTEOUS SOUL

According to *Rig-Veda* 8:85, the seven mothers serving as the seven holy rivers make it easier for the heroes to pass through the darkness of night and reach the morning light. Making their progression even longer, they speak with pleasant voices, passing through the day and nights, following Indra, who makes the floodwaters stand still. Darters, small tropical birds or fish, penetrate through the troubled water and pass through the twenty-seven compressed ridges of the mountains to accomplish what neither godly powers nor mighty mortal noble souls, with their full-grown vigor as strong heroes, are able to achieve. The mightiest force, Indra, firmly grasping an iron bolt in both his hands, comes with his powers originating from his head and mind, and in his mouth as speech, to open a pathway so his worshippers and others may rush in to listen to the holiest of the holy ones as the casters of compressed cosmic stones come down from outer space, shaking the ground with meteors. Serving as the banner of the heroes, Indra counted as the chief among all living things. Currently, Indra, with his arms takes control of the wildly rushing thunderbolt hurtling toward earth, making the mountains roar, which he uses to slay the dragon. The cattle bellow loudly, and the noble souls serving the holy Brahmans with their hymns draw nigh the powers of Indra. With praise, the holy souls serve all the creatures of the world and spring into action for all other living things, along with Mitra, representing eternal love. Singing songs, they wait upon the lord of adoration, Indra. All deities and their friends fly away in terror if they catch even a whiff of evil power. Timid, they seek support from Indra and look for friendship among the cosmic hosts the Maruts, who fight in all the battles, seeking to attain victory. The strong Maruts, who appear in groups of sixty to one hundred eighty, prepare themselves and become strong, appearing worthy of worship, coming like beams of light, which earns them adoration and oblation. Like a sharpened weapon, the Maruts dare to stand along with Indra, the Thunderbolt, who is ready to attack the godless evil powers the Asuras, scattering them with his wheel.

The strong and most auspicious ones, filled with beauteous hymns, forsake their bodies in order to accept laudation, which invokes within them noble thoughts and sends them forth to float like boats sailing on a river. The embodiments of the famous and dearest ones come stirred up with hymns to receive the divine will. Indra, with fair praise, welcomes them with gifts and with powers as they pay him homage. He invites them to come near as singers and encourages them to refrain from crying out. Their voices heard as a backdrop, a visual phenomenon, where heavenly water flows into the source of creation, *Amsumati*, from where it advances to support the supreme powers of causation with about ten thousand rounds. Inhaling deeply, Indra turns toward the heartened heroes, asking them to lay their weapons aside. From a far distance, protagonists see the optical phenomenon moving along the slope of the bank of the Amsumati, then it sinks into the river like a black cloud, which sends the protagonists forth to fight in battle. From the source of creation, Amsumati, blossoms are dropped, creating splendid light, which with the powers of Indra manifest to assume a proper bodily form, appearing as the mighty perishable Bṛhaspati, who comes to aid the godless tribes and conquer all those who have been against the gods since birth, thus using Indra and the seven noble souls, who have never faced a rival, appearing as hidden demigods, to serve both heaven and earth. They serve the manifested world, which brings great pleasure to Mother Earth (Prithvi).

With his thunderbolts, the thunder-armed Indra boldly smites evil powers, none of them equal to the lowest of the mighty powers, Śuṣṇa, who provides strength to the mother cow and serves as the chieftain of all mortal beings. Indra is the mighty slayer of the evil power Vṛtra, who aims to obstruct the river's flow and bring floods, enthralled by the evil forces the Dāsas. The wisest among come to rejoice with libations and enjoy a splendid day, irresistible, free from any form of anger, and performing only great deeds, serving as heroes. With only one main evil-slayer, that is, Indra, the manifested mortal embodiments beseech the heavenly power serves as the sustainer of humanity, Vishnu. Incarnating to serve as the slayers of Vṛtra, they called upon with praises like the avatar who is the helper and the protector, who brings treats and wealth that makes human beings famous.

Serving as manifested cosmic bodies, the Ṛbhukṣans, even at the time of their birth, are invoked for doing many good deeds. They provide humanity an advantage, such as offering soma to invoke others. The Lord of Light brings light and joy to the evil Asuras so they may prosper, along with the messenger Maghavan. They perform laudable deeds on the sacred ground with trimmed grass, without diminishing the contribution from steeds and cattle, which are secured by the powers of Indra and granted to the worshippers to produce pressed soma as a reward—but not to the riteless godless barbarians, who are subjected to a steep decrease of their eternal wealth, which never nourishes, other than death.

According to *Rig-Veda* 8:86, Indra, Lord of Light, takes the joy from the Asuras and brings it to his messenger Maghavan, to help him prosper with lauded deed, whose grass is trimmed for without any waste for the share of steeds and cattle that Indra has secured to grant to the worshippers who press soma and give it as a reward, but not unto the barbarian or the riteless godless man who sleeps. With an unbroken step, Indra follows and, of his own devices, lets die those who hide from the wealth that nourishes, such as the noble Śakra, who is far away, and the Vṛtra-slayer, who is near at hand. They all reach heaven by singing songs as they pass along the pressed soma to the long-maned steeds that accompany them. Whether the offering within heaven's bright sphere or in the dark basin of the sea, the chief Vṛtra-slayer, places on earth, is hard to approach, being still amid the firmament.

The soma-drinking Lord of Strength, besides providing flowing soma juice, delights in the bounty, rich in pleasantness, and the abundant wealth. Indra does not turn away, instead remaining as their companion during the feast. Indra never shies away from protecting their children, sitting down beside them to drink of essence (meath), showing great favor to the messenger Maghavan. Indra sits beside the soma brought from the casters of the stone from outer space. Neither god nor mortal has attained the might to surpass all that has made, the gods who have not attained it being of one accord, forming a kinship with Indra, the hero who in all encounters overcomes the most eminent powers as the destroyer in the conflict, fierce and exceedingly strong, resolute and full of vigor.

Poets join in song to honor Indra, urging him to drink of the soma juice. The Lord of Light stands fast on the law and, with might and power, gives them his help. The holy sages stand all around him, looking on and singing to the inciters full of vigor. So as not to deceive, they serve with the chanters, with whom nigh they bear. Loudly, they call out to the mighty Indra and Maghavan, who evermore possess irresistible power. Holy, most liberal, they lead all to riches, and, thunder-armed, make all pathways pleasant for worshippers, knowing well that Śakra, most potent with strength, will destroy their castles before the Thunder-Armed One causes all beings to tremble as he shakes the heavens and the earth. Indra, as a wondrous hero, guards them by seeing them through woe. With his thunder, he gets them over the floods Indra and is honored with opulence, all-nourishing and much to desired among kings.

## SELF-CREATED NOBLE SOULS

According to *Rig-Veda* 8:87, the self-created noble soul Śakra, serving as a king with *sāman* hymns, is honored as the lofty sage who guards the eternal law and inspires praises through Indra. Indra provides Śakra with art as the conqueror who, like the splendorous bodies such as the sun, the moon, and the constellations of stars, supports everything with his almighty powers to generate a radiant light, which comes through the sky, creating the luminous realm of heaven. By bringing godly power, manifested deities and demigods appear to support Indra. They strive to win friends while Indra endows the would-be conquerors with unconcealable powers as vast as a mountain that spreads in all directions, served by the heavenly powers. As truthful soma drinkers, they come to serve the two extremes, heaven and earth, and with strength pour out libations, serving as heavenly lords. While Indra storms through all the foes' castles, he becomes the slayer of evil powers (Dāsas), serving as the lord of heaven.

Indra accepts the charge to be the true supporter of manifested mortal embodiments and the friend of the worshippers who sing songs, praying that he will increase them with the might that makes rivers swell to create floods, which cause the water to join with the ocean. With holy songs causing thunder, they come to pound day by day, building the wide chariot yoked by the bay steeds. This is the chariot of the gods that bears Indra, yoked with holy words. Indra, through the valor of the holy and noble Śatakratu, brings great strength to the heroes so they may remain active in fighting the war. The gracious Śatakratu, who has never been either a mother or a father, comes to the immortal soul contained within the mortal embodiment. The embodiments, becoming blissful, begin to pray for divine strength to serve as both worshippers and heroic warriors.

According to *Rig-Veda* 8:88, the zealous worshippers who offer soma to Indra come to listen to the one who arrives amid loud sounds, nearing their dwelling place. As the lord of the bay steeds, fair-helmed, Indra rejoices, claiming the highest glory as they offer him the soma along with eternal love songs. Indra meets with the source of light (the sun) and enjoys all good things that his worshippers bring in the hopes that their newborns will acquire power and granted treasures, if such is part of their inheritance. With these praises, Indra sends wealth enough for all, injuring no one. The worshippers learn to share what Indra grants them as gifts. To satisfy their individual wishes, he turns their minds, giving them godsends.

In battle, with the power to subdue, all hostile bands, as their fathers did, nullify the curse placed upon them and, as victors and vanquishers, conquer all on earth and in heaven come to close. As the victorious powers, they, like a calf between two mother cows, attack the evil powers, causing all the hostile bands to shrink away and faint in the face of the wrath of Indra, who brings them aid. With the Eternal One on their side, as the inciters, they shoot no one, and no one shoots at them. The best of charioteers, Tugra, unvanquished strengthener, comes to arrange the things that have left unarranged. The wise noble soul Śatakratu, as the source of might, provided for by Indra, the friend of all. In exchange for the support of Tugra and Śatakratu, Indra names them as the guardians of treasure. Sending wealth (absolute wisdom) in the form of dialogue, he empowers the embodied noble souls at birth to experience eternal powers, which, like the voice of the goddess *Vāk*, help to unveil the eternal truth (*Aranyaka*). This constitutes the ultimate method whereby one may attain higher wisdom, which is transmitted to allow living beings first to comprehend their external environment and then, through eternal powers, to comprehend internal wisdom, which is presented in the holy scriptures. It is the method used to share divine knowledge with others. The first form of wisdom comes as vibrations regulated by the goddess Sarasvatī that generate deep maternal emotions. The second form of wisdom is the vision to see far, *Kashyapa*, who created through the union of the two serving as the parents. The third form of enlightenment, Gandharva, comes through the reciting of prayers and hymns that help to unveil the eternal truth to manifested holy souls as described in the scriptures.

According to *Rig-Veda* 8:89, the learning process moves through the setting of the intention among the ancient deities and demigods and is accomplished through the performing of heroic actions and by providing a portion of protection, accompanied by the use of pressed soma, and the production of nectar and ambrosia, so that the learners, by consuming the food that will provide them with the proper nutrients, may best engage in physical, mental, and spiritual practices. Allowing the manifested mortal embodiments to share in the right to serve in the foremost places with society, as both friends and comrades, the gods smite foemen dead. Worshippers and singers call forth Indra to provide them with strength, loudly singing hymns to express themselves to one and another as they endowed with the power, according to divine will, to behave honorably toward everyone in existence and try to grow in greatness. By following the holy law or the commandments, mortal embodiments become enough to divide the underworld. With the law, they call on the mighty powers to come down from the summit of the sky, where they sit alone. With invoked inner spirits, they speak as friends, from their hearts, and then cry with emotion like children. Once they declare their noble deeds, they perform them, and with feasts and soma feasts, they call upon the powers of Indra, serving as the bounteous lord *Sarablia.* Indra and Sarablia distribute the heaps of wealth along with the soma that brought from far away by the seven noble souls, the Saptarishis.

The enemies run around in all directions; there is no one there to keep them back, until Indra sinks this thunderbolt deep within the vital parts of them that are evil. Rushing on, they press on toward the iron fort, from where the freed eagle, accompanied with thunder, flies to heaven to bring pressed soma, then goes deep into the ocean, sinking into the water, the thunderbolt emerging and, as a tribute, causes the water to flow in a circular course, moving continuously onward, generating floods. As the Gladdener, and seated like the queen of the gods, Indra utters words as if generated by the voice of the goddess Vāk, which no one comprehend, including the powers of heaven. At this point, Indra moves forth with vigor, until the noblest among the enemies vanish, and the deities generated by the goddess Vāk appear in animal forms, each form speaking as the Gladdener, yielding food and vigor. Vāk approaches the milk cow and asks it to step forth with a wider stride, serving as the comrade Vishnu, who makes room for the god of the sky Dyaus, who with lightning from heaven slays the evil power and frees the rivers so they may flow freely under the command of Indra.

According to *Rig-Veda* 8:90, the mortal embodiments come to toil and serve the godly powers as they share sacrificial gifts along with the power of eternal love (Mitra) and the power of eternal law (Varuna). The Supreme Power, hearing them from far away, comes along with farsighted chiefs and kings, all serving wondrously with the sovereign power to set things into motion with their arms. They accompanied by beams of light coming from the heavenly body Sūrya. As messengers with hard heads, they run to take soma to Mitra and Varuna without question and without summoned to return. They stand still, waiting for either dialogue or a hostile clash, as they keep everything within their arms safe. To the manifested mortal embodiment Aryaman, and to unmanifested eternal love (Mitra), they sing reverent songs like the pious one. Hearing these pleasant hymns, the eternal law, Varuna, comes through singing loudly to the sovereign kings. Having a high stake in the situation, Varuna is the red treasure who brings the only son born of the three immortal powers, who can never be deceived, to monitor the families of mortal embodiments. With songs, they uplifted to perform acts most splendid as they come to serve, of one mind and with one accord, the demigod Nāsatyas. They meet to enjoy the gifts to them brought by the lords of great wealth, which they use to invoke a bounty, which is fact, not challenged by any demon power. Moving farther east, with praises, they offer worship to the chiefs who lauded by one of the seven rishis, *Jamadagni*, who comes with the wind, Vayu, who evokes fair hymns and offers a sacrifice that helps them to rise and reach the heavenly region.

In the middle region, they pass the mythical juice through cheesecloth to strain it, and thereafter it cooked by the sunlight. This offering helps them to follow the straightest paths to the ministering priests, to whom they give a taste of the mythical juice as a sacrificial gift. The leaders of the harnessed teams, after drinking the draft of soma mixed with milk, verily come to see the heavenly light Sūrya. By acquiring great arts, the noble Ādityas indeed admired evermore for their greatness and fame, serving among the high priests. Like the godly powers that spread forth as unconquerable eternal light (ultraviolet light), the light comes yonder amid the ten surrounding arms, all bending down low, clothed in raiment reddish in hue, and with rich rays seen advancing in various tints. After passing through three mortal generations, the fourth and fifth generations enter the cosmic world, where they are placed in a lofty position near the sun, from where they are purified by the green plants serving the ground through the heavenly power Rudra, serving Mother Nature (Vasu) and the heavenly daughter Vayu, who, in the center, serving as breath, provides the nectar to serve to the noble Ādityas and the motherly power Aditi, who understands that she must not injure any sinless holy embodiment (i.e., sacred cow). Those weak-minded mortal embodiments come to adopt as gods and goddesses those who are eloquent in their skills and who, with uplifted voices, stand near at hand with all devotion.

## UNDER THE SKY SHIELD

The upper atmosphere consists of ozone, a highly reactive gas composed of three oxygen atoms that travel with direct sunlight, which every day comes from the outer world, which includes the evil powers, and every day produces particles smaller than the size of a thumb. These particles generate strange forms of light, ultraviolet and infrared, which consist of other, poisonous particles that can hurt manifested embodiments. According to *Rig-Veda* 8:1, Indra, as a group of noble souls called the

*Valakhilyas*, along with Agni, with his ferocious firepower, creates extra heat. Together they transform the evil powers into more than sixty thousand brilliantly shining tiny lights. Through severe atonement and self-control, they turn these into thumb-sized particles and hang them upside down like plants with their roots facing toward the illuminated heaven, with the leaves of the plant body facing downward toward the earth. Thus, the ozone shield transformed into a zone where breathing is possible, with the lower atmospheric sphere, with self-discipline (ascetic power), holding the first visible illumined body, rich with the greatest treasure, which regulated by Indra.

Indra's messenger Maghavan manages these living beings, the manifested mortal embodiments. Serving with thousandfold wealth, they, with self-discipline, create one hundred hosts. They rush to slay the poisonous light, and as they travel, they turn this into bright light reaching from the sky and falling upon the mountains, serving the kingdom of vegetation, all filled with the gift of flowing water that feeds the plants and turns into an effused gladdening current. Indra keeps it filled the lake from the life force, such as that of living things, becomes accustomed to resting within the bounty of the water. Coming with thunder, he keeps the lake filled.

With a matchless breeze, the hosts strengthened and become eloquent as they start to produce soma, the sweetest natural drink. As the mythical fully fills them, it brings joy, evenly scattering gifts, such as the dust that skids over the regions. Those with loud urging produce their own godlike power, using special plants that, when pressed, produce the mythical juice that used to transform manifested creatures such as steeds to develop wings and learn to fly like birds, all appearing along with milk-bearing animals filled with sweet milk.

Strong and preeminent, Indra's disciples the Kaṇvas come to pay him homage with unfailing wealth to serve all those who sing songs and serve as heroes. Like thunder, they bring plenteous springs that pour forth, creating streams. Now, upon the surface ground, with the art of sacrifice, disciples become heroes who, while resting, think high thoughts and make sacrifices, which action generates a swift movement that creates vibrations. They acquire mighty power and come to join with the mighty ones who serve as the powers of causation. Appearing as active, fleet-of-foot tawny coursers realize a swift victory as they go forth planting seeds, like father of the abyss, creating the cosmic bodies the Manus. They travel with the wind and plant seeds within all the ground visible in heaven and on earth. Serving as a great soul, Maghavan presides among all kinds, creating within them the craving for wealth and prosperity. There is a fight between the law of devotion (*Nipatithi*) and the law of cosmic bodies (*Medhātithi*), two great souls with the same godly parents. Maghavan comes to support the prevailing descendants of *Indra, such as Kaṇva, Trasadasyu, Paktha, Dasavraja, Gosarya, and Ṛjiśvan*, all of whom come with the life force to vouchsafe all wealth, including material wealth such as gold.

According to *Rig-Veda* 8:2, with praises, Kaṇva, Trasadasyu, Paktha, Dasavraja, Gosarya, and Ṛjiśvan, as descendants of Indra, become famous far and wide and exceedingly bountiful. Distributing their precious wealth among thousands, they shed worship like hundred-pointed arrows. Unconquerable, they provide support in war by using Indra's mighty arms. Like streams, they come down the hill serving as liberal worshippers, springing forth with enough soma to gladden all. As friends gladdened with soma, they take the waters and, as gracious lords, give it to the milk-bearing animals to drink. Peerless, they called upon to give aid, flowing forth with drops of essence (meath). The gracious lords also bring, along with hymns, drops of soma, all accompanied with praises and rites, rushing, like a steed, seeking to make the food sweet and pleasant for the lover. They manifest as fearless *paura* (citizens). Without no fear of evil or demons, they dish out nothing but love, and with strong praises, they grasp whatever left. Like winning heroes, they come to serve as the Supreme Ruler with their mighty wealth; and in spring, they bring the stored-up thunder to pour it out evermore upon the worshippers. Now whether they be from far away in the heavens or from close by on the earth, with mighty thoughts they come to harness the bays, which come from the sky, along with the lofty ones. They use the bays to drive the chariot, pulled by steeds who injure none, and as they move forth with their impetuous strength, supported by the wind, they silence their enemies while flying through the sky. From the gracious hero, the worshipper learns how to perform in a fight against the abundantly vigorous Etaśa, Vaśa, or Dasavraja, taking decisive action. Serving the messenger Maghavan, with his support, Kaṇva attends the sacred feast and takes home the friend *Dirghanitha* to serve the Stone-Darter, Gosarya, who brings great wealth, providing living things with a bright gold stall.

According to *Rig-Veda* 8:3, the mysterious manifested soul Manu *Samvarani*, along with *Maghavan, Nipatithi, Medhātithi, Pustigu, and*

*Srustigu*, drinks with his son *Prsadvana*, who serves as the host of the ruler *Praskaṇva*. They all come to serve with the holy spirit Rishi *Dasyave-Vrka*, who helps to save them from decay and abandonment by providing them with aid, to endow thousands with the newest hymn so they may know how to serve as inspirational sages with eagerness and joy. Like the seven sages the Saptarishis, they sing songs that resound in the loftiest parts of the dynamic universe. Displaying their heroic might, they send thunder down to all living things that invoke them, and bestow precious things upon them, the newest favor being a stable full of cattle. They by the gracious lord helps worshippers to attain great wealth, nourishing them with mythical juice and songs of eternal love. Indra, who never deserts the worshippers, along with the messenger Maghavan, continuing to serve as his envoy, brings the bounty and evermore pours forth with mighty powers, overtaking all the malevolent powers, including Krvi and Śuṣṇa, yonder in heaven. With such mighty support and silence, Indra and Maghavan gain control of the deadly bolts and keep them from spreading out. First appearing as the sons of the earth, who are born as Āryans with godly wealth to regulate all the malevolent powers including the Dāsas, they lead the pious tribe of *Ruśama Paviru*, providing them with immense wealth. Enthusiastic singers sing songs and bring soma, feeding distilled oil to the fire, which bring a richness and sweetness to all those with heroic strength, flowing like soma drops. The manifested power Manu and the unmanifested power Śakra join to appear as the godly powers the Vivasvans, who bring with them the power of eternal love, expressed through the minor solar deity Trita, who comes joyfully to serve the newborn gods of wealth the Āryans. Trita also comes along with Mother Mātariśvan, Medhya (nutrition), and the spiritual master Prsadhra, all of whom cheered by drinking pressed soma, reflecting upon the active Rjunas and the inactive hermit Syūmaraśmi, all supported by the ancient voices of Dasonyas and Dasasipra.

According to *Rig-Veda* 8:4, making their own loud bodily sounds, the all arrive to meet with the Sustainer, Lord Vishnu, whose stride is three steps wider than that of all other manifested godly powers, including the Vivasvans. With proclamations of eternal love (Mitra), they recognized for their great deeds. Like Śatakratu, they seek to serve as renowned cow milkers who yield an abundance of milk. As the Sustainer, the great father Vishnu blesses them with divine will, so they may possess the eternal law and eternal love. He brings along ample resources, including horses and cattle, to make them as strong as the lords of riches and the good lords of wealth. They increase to nourish others who are eager for such wealth. They all call upon Indra who, with the lord of wisdom, Śatakratu, who never neglects, comes to guard them carefully. Together they call upon the noble Ādityas to come of their own accord and bring mythical juice from heaven to establish themselves on the newly created ground (Prithvi). Indra, the lover of the song, along with the liberal messenger Maghavan, with favor call upon the disciple Kaṇva to come and hear all the songs sung and then listen to the eulogy that offered since ancient times. Singing, they offer *bṛhatī* as a sacrifice, poured forth to worshippers with thoughts and tossed together with the wealth from the mighty storehouses. Both the ground and the sky, with pure, brightly shining light, bring the drafts of mythical juice mingled with milk and essence.

According to *Rig-Veda* 8:5, the highest messenger, Maghavan, preeminent, like the heavenly bull, breaks down the walls, barriers, and forts to support the animal kingdom. As the lord of wealth, he comes to subdue the kings Āyu, Kutsa, and Atithigva, who through daily sacrifice refined in might to generate a rousing power. Serving as Śatakratu, they come to regulate the cosmic bodies that, as compressed stones, appear as falling stars, also pouring out essence in the form of meath, along with drops of soma that has pressed out by the people. This repels all enemies and keeps evil far away, thereby allowing all worshippers to win treasure on their own.

The stalks of the plants used when extracting the soma from within. Śatakratu creates a firm base from which to provide aid and resolve conflict, using the most auspicious way to serve all good relatives, and comes to bless the chief of humanity to serve as the lord of progeny. As the lord of heroes, Śatakratu serves the victors in the battle and aids those who sing loudly to keep their spirits ever pure and bright. In battle, as the surest ones, the victors obtain grace and, with holy offerings and invocations, win all the spoils. As the lord of the bays, Śatakratu, answering their lengthy prayers, enables them to fight and win with his divine help. They fight to take the leader of the raiders who seek to steal their steeds and cattle, uniting with those who stand alone.

According to *Rig-Veda* 8:6, the poets extol the gods through hymns in exchange strengthened in might and, with their loud songs, acquire heroic power through mythical juice. The ancient ruler *Pauras* comes to aid with hymns and offers libations that bring joy to the prevailing fundamental realities of the manifested world, including Lord Krishna, who sends a direct message along with authoritative the collection of holy scriptures called the *Samvarta*. Through such fundamental realities, the powerful celestial gods Indra and Agni rejoice in the worship coming from the heavenly spirits of nature (Vasu), which come directly through the heavenly body Rudra. They both hear the call to send aid to the demigods, namely, the twin Aśvins and the cosmic hosts (Maruts). The powerful trinity of Pūṣan, Vishnu, and Sarasvatī comes to support the seven supreme powers of causation, calling upon water, wind, earth, and fire. Buried among the manifested mountains that are all covered with forest, they hear any such cry.

With bounteous gifts, the most liberal of the mighty ones, Indra, as the eliminator of evil (i.e., the Vṛtra-slayer), brings a boon for the benefactors. As the leader of the heroes wounded in battle, he leads them in combat, from which they emerge as most famous. They win invocations, and after feasts and entertainment they rest and come to serve the godly powers as true devotees (faithful ones). Indra, with his powers, brings truth to the people and, through his messenger Maghavan, provides them with aid by bringing plenteous food, flowing forth among the streams. Filled with songs of praise, they call to the wise noble soul Śatakratu, who pours bounty down upon Praskaṇva, making him exuberant, so he shall never fail.

According to *Rig-Veda* 8:7, great Indra, with his might, beholds the bounty brought in by one hundred white oxen, which shine like the stars in heaven. They are so tall that they prop up the sky with one hundred sticks of bamboo, one hundred dogs, and one hundred other beasts, all with suntanned skin. They appear in clusters of one hundred roaming the holy ground (*balbaja*) with four hundred mules, all red of hue and blessed by the godly power *Kinvayanas*, who spreads through life as physical energy, like horses that tread among embodied living beings. As a team of seven dark mares, they extol the supreme powers of causation. Not yet fully grown into their great fame, they rush along paths with such haste that no eye is able to follow them.

According to *Rig-Veda* 8:8, from the exhaustless bounty of the firmament, Praskaṇva displays himself in a fullness as broad as the heavens to appear with the more than ten thousand sons of Putakrata. Each comes with his own wealth, having given one hundred head of workhorses, one hundred head of fleecy sheep, and one hundred bands of diligent workers, all picked because they are *Putakrata's* sons. They led forth as chargers, instead of coming with lesser physical strength, such as that of a herd of horses, which fact is observed by Agni, who comes as himself in a carriage, serving as the oblation-bearer with his resplendent eternal flame and with high shine coming from the sun, representing the heavenly luminous body Sūrya.

According to *Rig-Veda* 8:9, as endowed by Agni, Sūrya brings primeval wisdom and quickly seeks the mighty twin demigods the Aśvins, who drink of soma, their third libation, and thus transform and come to manifest as enhanced demigods, Nāsatyas. After approaching the prevailing thirty-three mighty powers of causation represented as deities, they attain true wisdom (absolute truth). By accepting worship, libation, and drinks of soma, they come to experience the bright eternal flame representing Agni. As wonderworkers, they serve heaven and earth as bulls in the midair region, where purified air transforms into ether and the essence that supports existence. In the war, with one thousand promises, they come near, drinking mythical juice as their portion of amrit granted by the holy powers. With songs, the demigod Nāsatyas drink of its fullness and sweetness and learn to assist the manifested bodies by offering worship.

According to *Rig-Veda* 8:10, all the priests, in sundry ways, arrange to make the sacrifice, of one accord appointing the learned spiritual scholar Brahma, who, through sacrifice, provides them with higher knowledge and in many places enkindles the eternal flame serving as the power of Agni, who as one fixed thought towers high above the shining and illumining Sūrya. Still as one and only one, Agni, in a bright and radiant chariot, comes with many thoughts, bringing all the treasure that can be continued three wheels, sitting comfortably while lightly rolling along, bringing great wealth to the newborn.

Indra and Varuna together offer to share in the streams. In glorified form, they come hastily with libations, where each sacrifice assists the worshippers in shedding amrit internally as if watering plants. With efficacious vigor, Indra and Varuna help the worshippers on to a path that leads them beyond the middle region to find the absolute truth, with words of wisdom from the divine power appearing as the god Krishna. The worshippers hear all seven manifested holy voices (the Saptarishis), who like a wave pour out the eternal truth. For their sake, as the manifested planetary system serves the lords of splendor, they come to aid the pious living things. The bewildered living things, with their own thoughts, acquire wisdom as drops poured forth from the seven streams (Seven

Sisters). Thus, sitting on the seat of sacrifice, enriched with soma, Indra and Varuna bring gifts come to help the worshippers. With great happiness ascribed to the two bright ones, Indra and Varuna, with truthfulness, great strength, and majesty, come to serve as the lords of splendor, providing aid to all worshippers three times a day, seven days a week, pouring holy oil onto the eternal flame. As in olden times, Indra and Varuna impart revelations to holy souls (rishis) who, through the process and power of song, make an offering at the place of worship, from where they acquire eternal wisdom and behold the individual immortal spirit that glows forever. The united Indra and Varuna grant those worshippers who are void of pride cheerfulness and wealth to nourish them.

CHAPTER 17

# Cerebral Dominion

UNDER THE SKY SHIELD, MANIFESTED BODIES SIFT THROUGH THE external and internal residual memories they have accumulated over their lifetimes. These residual memories include violent acts, killings, insults, eating the wrong food, and engaging in undesirable activities, such as giving up on faith and breaking the eternal law. To overcome this process of destruction, positivity induced by practicing mantras (Pancha Suktas), which first bring normality to life. The quest is to purify oneself and attain an even higher level of being, namely, that of the noble soul, and then to ascend even farther to the unmanifested immortal godly powers. There, manifested bodies learn to subdue their needs and desires and, by themselves, learn to overpower evil forces so they face no threats. They rise above other mortals by joining with the ruling noble powers. Once their brainpower becomes great enough that they attain this higher position, they allowed to go beyond the material world. They come to serve within this region, extending into the upper illuminated region. The living spirit, Atman, overpowered by the iron-strong ancient primordial force Shakti, who takes the living spirit to the heavenly region, the home of the universal soul (*Paramatman*), where it may merge with *Paramatman* and lose its identity, just as a river loses its identity once it merges with ocean water. This process is like igniting wood, which bursts into flame and, with the sweetest mystic libations, loses its identity.

## SUPERNATURAL

According to *Rig-Veda* 9:1, serving at the banquet of the mighty gods, as supernatural, such embodiments gain in strength and flow like the mystic river Indus. As the individual living spirit, Atman continues to flow onward, spreading like the eternal flame that seeks its ultimate destiny of merging with a larger body. While traveling, day by day, Atman draws power by consuming the froth that appears when it merges with divine immanence. Further, through the power of prayer, Atman dips itself within the mythical river once it becomes purified, then manifests and specially comes to serve as the offspring of the heavenly power Sūrya. Slender, Atman serves as ten heavenly aid virgin s, representing ten different shades of white, like the rainbow, which firmly pressed to hold such powers within a single embodiment. Those embodiments who have achieved this state practice self-restraint until the final day, when they send forth vibrations, which like musicians blow through with rage and emerge from the skin as mythical fluid. With triple foe-repelling power, the female trinity, like cows, sanctified by turning water into milk. Transforming water into fresh milk, they produce soma. The draft creates wild rapture among the embodiments, who, like Indra, slay the evil powers and become sanctified as heroes as they pour forth with eternal wealth.

According to *Rig-Veda* 9:2, the heroes invite others to come and enhance their embodiments by purifying them with mythical juice, which passes through the body, which acts like cheesecloth, to produce curds. These others serve as Indra's heroes, who receive mighty food that gives them physical strength and makes them appear as the heavenly bull. They speed forthwith, running within the holy river Indus as most splendid steer. With physical strength and spiritual power, they come to sit at a spot within the stream to capture the flow. With their acquired creative powers, they draw others into the water to become holy embodiments and serve as sages. Like the holy waters, they come and spread over the ground to serve as a drop cloth, upon which the milk poured to separate the curd. They serve as a holding vessel, like a lake, to swept along with the water that protects the bodies. During the floods, which brighten the way, they acquire light and learn how to store the soma. They now come ready to supply mythical juice, dropping it upon the friends of heaven. To purify themselves, they lie on the ground, like curd on the cloth, and, still in the water, pop up in yellowish-brown earthly bodies. Like bulls, they bellow with mighty power, fair to behold, as they join with the power of eternal love (Mitra). They hold everything together, with direct rays coming from the sun that make them shine, and as they seen moving along in the river Indus, they appear as mighty singers. Beautified, they bring with them delight, all decked and with ample room to pray. They offer worship with the joyous draft taken from the holy river Indus, here Indra, as a friend, comes to fill the streams with sweetness, before sending the water back to the goddess Parjanya, who helps create rain by bringing water from heaven and having it fall onto the earth. Parjanya makes a sacrifice to all the rivers as the recipient of milk-bearing animals and speedy steeds that come to serve the heroes.

According to *Rig-Veda* 9:3, immortal godly powers, from vats filled with living spirit (Atman), come to appear with wings, and like birds they fly to settle in the woods. Singing the hymn of the gods, they enable the living spirits to move swiftly through the wind (Vayu), traveling along the invisible winding way to create breath (prana) as they learn to fly unchallenged. While flying, the godly powers serve as bay steeds equipped with the skill and force to protect the living spirit within devout living beings, who come singing holy songs and participate as righteous warriors. Going forth with heroes, the devout ones fly along with godly powers to win all the spoils and return with them. Flying speedily along with the carriage, they bring gifts. They let their voices heard with praises like sacred bards, diving headlong into the waters with godly power to bestow rich gifts upon the worshippers. They rush ahead in the stream of water, across the regions on the ground, and as in heaven they move with a roaring flow. They make sacrifices and reach up toward heaven as they cross through regions without defenses. As in ancient times, serving the godly powers, they prayed to as deities. Appearing yellowish brown at birth, they follow the holy law. Engendered with strength, they come to settle on the ground, serving as stretched-out cheesecloth through which soma flows, moving onward into the stream. Flowing with soma as they move on their way, they conquer all who are highly renowned, winning the spoils with their eternal inner light. Winning makes them ecstatic, as they know they are better than those who win through physical skill and mental strength.

With soma, the heroes drive away all foes and improve themselves as purifiers. They seek help from Indra and from the heavenly power Sūrya, who through the sun provides a portion of external light to enhance their mental power. The sunlight aids them in traveling long distances, using their vision to look well upon the physical weapons. With mythical juice pouring out from the stream, they enhance their paranormal vision. Doubly victorious by having gained riches, they, unsubdued in battle, pour forth with wealth to overpower their enemies. By worshipping, as manifested bodies, they learn how to get rid of their residual memories, sins, or bad karma. Further strengthening their mortal embodiments by following the eternal law, they purified by passing through the holy river Indus. As flying birds, they come forward with manifold wealth, each quickly finding a mate, like steeds, to produce offspring.

According to *Rig-Veda* 9:5, the heavenly lord Sūrya spreads light in all directions, expressing himself as a friendly bellowing heavenly bull that speeds onward, producing glittering sparks by sharpening its horns on the firmament. Generating such brilliant wealth, Sūrya creates an adorable splendor that shines within the mighty Indus as a stream of wealth. The tawny demigods who spread out on the old grass now come to worship the Mighty God and the other gods. With passion, they appear as the glorified self-enkindled (*Pavamana*). Along with this flame, they lifted to the golden celestial doors, where they wait for them to opened. With the high honor they receive as a well-formed lofty pair, they come to serve as beautiful virgin aid who appear with the morning light and the evening light. Thus, each godly power comes to look upon manifested mortal embodiments as the three beautiful goddesses Sarasvatī, Bhāratī, and Iḷā, who serve along with a trinity of male gods. Jointly, they summon the champion creative power Tvaṣṭṛ, asking him to protect the newborn within the holy river Indus who served by the ancient god Indra. As godly powers, Tvaṣṭṛ and Indra appear as the wise perishable embodiment Prajāpati, serving as twins in anointed bodies to preserve the kingdom of evergreen vegetation. Within the refulgent body the moon, one thousand branches sanctified and enkindled with the imperishable living spirit (Atman), which through the wind (Vayu) brings both the eternal flame and the life force (prana). Both the perishable Bṛhaspati and the imperishable Brahmaṇaspati serve the heavenly gods Indra and Agni.

According to *Rig-Veda* 9:6, within the flowing rivers, the supreme powers of causation come to appear along with the mythical juice that flows within the holy streams, already filled with power and strength like the heavenly bull. On the ground, as a woven filter, they serve the mythical fluid as a devoted friend, first serving the immortal universal soul (Paramatman). Later they separate into independent parts, all of them appearing as the immortal living spirit, Atman, floating on the river Indus, along with many gladdening sanctified coursers that, with full strength, are already following the river as it flows. They monitor the amount of mythical juice that is poured from the river onto the ground, thereafter, serving the ancient gladdening juice with highly renowned power that, after filtered, moves forth to fill stream. Like water running down a steep slope, the sparkling drops of soma flow until fully purified and ready served by Indra. After having passed through the filter at least ten times and becoming clean, the soma, with vigor, like a steed, swaggers through the woods like fire. The strong juice mixed with milk then poured forth as a feast for the steer, which move away as the draft serve all the godly powers. All effused, the gods flow onward with the stream to serve the milk to other gods. The strengthened ones with their souls ready to make sacrifices, as fully effused, flowing quickly, keep pouring forth to bring ancient wisdom to serve with the strong drink. As a friend, Indra, at the feast, gladdens the heroes and refreshes them with secret hymns.

According to *Rig-Veda* 9:7, moving forth on their way, the glorious flowing drops maintain the eternal law, and along their course they make the necessary sacrifice, sinking down into the mighty waters They sink into the streams filled with the most excellent wealth, the best of which they offer at the holy place with an oblation that sets them up with truly guileless physical bodies. A steer sent forth with a continuously sounding voice as the eternal flame, which is like the life force within wood. The noblest sages, endowed with physical strength, call upon the holy river Indus as they come near it. Filled with eternal wisdom and with purified strength, they win over the heavenly light. They come to sit next to the king, who seated above them as the host of all people. At the proper time, they call the noble sages to come and serve, who approach with their shining golden color. They sink and settle as if into wood and show their zeal by singing hymns. Indra, with the powers of the wind (Vayu), comes to support the twin demigod Aśvins to attain joy by drinking the gladdening juice. The streams filled with pleasant-tasting soma flow through to the mighty powers serving as a trinity, namely, Bhaga, Mitra, and Varuna, who have eternal wisdom, which enables them to win wealth and gain treasures from the renowned powers among both heaven and earth.

## LIBATION

According to *Rig-Veda* 9:8, Indra, conforming to the desires laid out in a bowl of soma, flows forth in his heroic might as supported by the wind (Vayu), pure breath flowing into his nostrils as, like the twin demigod Aśvins, he gains in heroic strength. Fully purified soma incites the heart to generate eternal love (Mitra) and set in place as a sacrifice. All those with ten fingers decked with seven organs: two eyes, two ears, two nostrils, and one mouth. These all serve to regulate the heart and cause it to function like the hearts of the seven noble sages (the Saptarishis). This allows the embodiment to rejoice in all that passes through it, as milk that poured through cheesecloth to filtered, to produce the gladdening draft for the gods. After purified, the concentrated milk, as curd, placed within the embodiment. As if golden-hued butter in a jar, it brightens as it flows on to others, making them rich, driving all enemies farther away, along the river Indus. With the purified soma kept for the friends, the gods send down water to return as rain from heaven. This generates other streams, all flowing on the ground (Prithvi) and serving the earth with their opulence. Soma brings victory in war and allows others to obtain the drink so they may helped in finding light and food for their progeny.

According to *Rig-Veda* 9:9, the heavenly sages, whose hearts purified and whose minds have gained eternal wisdom, with both their hands pressed together, come to rest on the ground offering prayers, which they send forth to receive breath, or the life force (prana). This force, dear to all people, helps the sages to move onward, joining the glorious embodiment void of guile and experiencing utmost enjoyment as prana flows within the embodiment. Serving as the brilliant sons, born to luminous parents, the sages spring forth with prana and become great sons, serving as strengtheners of the law who urge the seven supreme powers of causation to stir up the guileless rivers by way of the invisible third eternal located just above and between the two visible eyes. As the source of oblation, the third eye is what guides the Youthful Mighty One, who with a higher vision moves beyond the physical region's observable by the two visible eyes. The third eye helps embodiments to conform to the eternal law and direct their actions on earth as perishable embodiments. Within the holy river Indus, they directed to go beyond the sky shield to reach the imperishable powers such as Indra and Agni.

The immortal flying courser invited to look down upon the ground at the fountainhead of the seven springs serving the seven sages (Saptarishis), who spread out to serve all regions. They satisfy the seven ruling feminine powers of causation (goddesses) with holy rites, invoking the self-enkindled (*Pavamana*). This draws any dark shades away from the living spirits and thus establishes illuminous souls. Pavamana meets with ignorance, using newer hymns to make the path ready to bring in a new light to displace the darkness. The Pavamana renowned as a great power among all living beings, serves the heroes who blessed with offspring who fight to win eternal wisdom, all through winning the light.

According to *Rig-Veda* 9:10, Pavamana, along with thunder and lightning, becomes renowned by serving as an eager flying courser. He comes with the wealth, flying forth hurriedly to pull the chariot. Holding the reins, with urgency and speed, singing joyful songs, he brings soma along with him, all decked with grace and eulogies. He comes to serve kings and the seven holy priests, offering a sacrifice of the gladdening draft, letting the drops flow forth abundantly, with song, in worship, with the soma flowing as from a stream. The godly powers the Vivasvans arrive with the morning light, producing glory that passes through the sun, like the openings in the cheesecloth on the ground to filter the mythical juice. As in ancient times, singing worshippers open the doors, so all may hear the sacred songs already accepted by the mighty ones. Serving amid a close society, the worshippers sit with seven heavenly priests, thus forming a brotherhood to serve as one. They inspire kinship among the godly powers and, through the sun, provide illumination. All sages through their offspring serve all the gods, including the sun. Using their third eyes, which providing visionary power, they come to behold each quarter of the heavens, where priests placed within their sacred chambers.

According to *Rig-Veda* 9:11, the singers purify the holy river Indus and willingly offer worship to all the gods, also offering soma as served to the heavenly sage Atharvan. They commingle milk and divine devotion to bring along the Ultimate Power, which by pouring out soma, helps milk-bearing animals such as cattle, steeds, and humans to grow like plants. Singing songs of praise, they bring out the brown hue among all the other independent mighty powers representing the ground (Prithvi), which extends down to earth. They represent the sky, serving as the upper shield, bringing a red hue that extends far into the highest level of heaven. Purified effused mythical juice supports all the terrestrial bodies, which band together to extend beyond the sky shield. They move rapidly toward the ground as they pour out the powerful substance of water mixed with sweet milk to create mythical juice. They bring this to the earth, where served with the power of essence (meath). With humble homage, they draw forth the curd and, blending it with soma, create a libation to serve to Indra so that he may provide the power needed to cause the waters of the Indus to rise and move forward to join with the ocean, its ultimate destination. Through drinking the mythical juice and the blended libations, the terrestrial embodiments become chiefs who, as friends regulated by the divine will, deliver prosperity to all living things.

According to *Rig-Veda* 9:12, the sovereign of the heart, Indra, effused with soma, rejoices. He gives riches and heroic strength to Pavamana, then pours down exceedingly rich sweets as a sacrifice, like a mother cow lowing to her calves, and calls upon sages to drink the soma juice, which filled with wisdom. While floating on the waves, he comes to dwell in a place where he seated upon cowhide to inspire rapture. Farsighted Indra, as sage and seer, at the pivotal point of heaven, uses a straining cloth of wool to worship, where he embraces the river Indus, which holds soma. Before the soma poured, it passed through the purifying sieve and poured into jars. Through air and vibrations, Indra and Pavamana use their voices to travel to the high regions of the sea, and the sea shakes the jar filled with potent meath, dropping it onto a tree that never fails to yield sweet heavenly milk, which urged upon the manifested generations. The Wise One, as a stream of sages, urges the mythical juice to flow speedily to the places covered by the sky shield.

According to *Rig-Veda* 9:13, the mythical juice, once it passes through the purifying fleece and one thousand streams, moves to a special place where it purified further and then flows into the clouds, Vayu, who serves Indra. Singing forth, longing for help, the Pavamana entertains the godly powers with soma drops. With one thousand powers, purified for victory, they partake in the feast of the gods. As the Indus flows, it becomes a great store of food. Living bring treated to the effused soma, which brings wealth and gives them heroic power. With coursers as their drivers, they urge them forward as they pour the soma through the woolen straining cloth. Loudly it flows like milk cows lowing to their calves then run forth from both hands. As the Gladdener, Indra, with a roar, drives all enemies away from those he loves, driving off the godless, then coming to sit in the place of sacrifice, where he looks upon the light.

According to *Rig-Veda* 9:14, the Pavamana responds to waves on the river, widely flowing. Singing hymns, with love, he is on active duty supporting the five kindred tribes. With songs and hymns, drinking soma, all those who are powerful, great in physical strength, rejoice in themselves along with all the godly powers. Once freed, the Pavamana flows away to serve as the river's companion, leaving behind his physical body and disconnected limbs. Like a fair youth, Pavamana adored by priests' daughters, who, robed, produce milk. With his fine fingers, with a desire for milk, on a winding course, Pavamana goes on his way, uttering with his voice, and the priests' daughters find him with their nimble fingers, approaching him, adoring him as the Lord of Strength. They vigorously held back like coursers, possessing all the treasures in heaven and on the earth, and welcomed as faithful friends.

According to *Rig-Veda* 9:15, the heroes, singing songs, approach the fast-moving carriage belonging to Indra, at which special place they ponder with holy thoughts how to best worship the immortal gods where they seated. Like good horses, they led out on the path that shines with light, and like strong steeds, they exert their strength, thrusting their horns up high. Stimulated like the heavenly bull, the herd led to perform heroic deeds. They move with vigor, the steeds, all adorned with beauteous shining gold rays. Serving as sovereigns of the streams, they trot over ground that is rough to pass, bringing rich treasures packed tightly in the carriage. They descend into the reservoirs to beautify themselves, to arrive with containers of abundant food. They use all ten fingers and the seven organs to produce pleasing songs, making themselves beautiful, and good weapons, serving as the best of gladdeners.

According to *Rig-Veda* 9:16, the soma pressers produce the juice that brings rapturous joy. The raw fluid run through a sieve to bring out its full strength, like a flood, for use by the mighty powers to win over all milk-bearing animals standing in the bodies of water from which they drink but in which they never submerged. Being waterless, the drink is pure, and it moves with the purifiers' thoughts as it comes out of the sieve, as good as that made back home to gain wisdom. With humble homage, soma drops flow forth, contending for the prize of glory, purified by passed through the fleece to attain all beauty, so a hero such as Indra can stand amid the milk-bearing animals that swell, unable to reach the heights of heaven. The stream of the creative juice falls lightly through the cleansing sieve and then through the cloth of wool, singing like living things.

According to *Rig-Veda* 9:17, the rapid streams of soma, flowing down a steep slope, kill the evil powers, who are full of zeal as they consume the effused soma juice, and then fall like rain upon the earth. At the same time, Indra, with his followers, flows with the stream of soma, which swells like a wave. Soma flows through the sieve to by the devotees of the gods who slay fiends. Serving pitchers of soma, they rush to pour it through the sieve that causes the sacrifice to become strong. Amid the shiniest bodies of heaven, soma moves at the speed of light to reach the same height as, or to move above, the three beacons that light up the realm (i.e., the sun, the moon, and the constellations). To the leader of the sacrificial rite, the singers and composers sing their songs, offering what they love to see. The manifested souls, along with sages, sing their hymns. Eager to help, they decked as strong steeds ready to serve the gods. The soma flows onward toward the stream of eternal wealth, coming to rest in the homes of the singers, drunk as part of the sacrifice.

## ORIGINATOR

According to *Rig-Veda* 9:18, sitting on the hills, they who dwell there send the soma through a sieve with the art of a lyricist. They offer the purified soma to the offspring of the sacred composer or sage in the form of eternal wisdom. All deities, of one accord, drink the effused soma to commemorate the mighty pair who hold all the treasure that could desired in their hands. They serve such mythical juice, as mother serves both the earth and heaven. It takes but a moment for the mighty flow to reach the two halves of the world, the deities serving as the two strong ones who, as purified pitchers, come with a loud cry.

According to *Rig-Veda* 9:19, the purified soma brings wondrous treasure, as it meets with loud sounds both in earth and on heaven as served by the twin demigod Aśvins, the lord of the sun, and Indra, who as the ruler of all kinds, including other great rulers, provides mythical sounds to prosper them. Those among the living who cleansed, such as the tawny steer, bellow on the grass and then sink, settling into their homes. Over productive steers that generate sacred songs and produce evocative sounds not yet purified and therefore cannot impregnate the milk-bearers, who long to meet their lords. As a mother to her darling son, they yield shining milk and draw near any who stand aloof in fear of the enemy's strike.

According to *Rig-Veda* 9:20, the self-enkindled Pavamana finds a wealth of soma, which he brings down to provide vigor, strength, and vital power to the mighty foemen, whether they are near or far. Coming forth through the cheesecloth, soma flows, subduing all the enemies of the sages, and then served at the banquet for the gods. The self-enkindled Pavamana sends forth treasure in the thousandfold to those who, in the shape of a female, come singing as living beings. They grasp all things within their minds and generate nectar to purify their thoughts. To find fame, they pour forth with lofty glory and send riches to serve the liberal lords who are taking food to those who sing their praises. With divine art, the wondrous steed cleansed to enter the songs and serve the pious king. Like a courser in floodwaters, the king remains invincible. With his clean hands over the top of the jar, he behaves like a liberal chief, making sure the soma goes through the sieve so it can endow the heroes with strength.

According to *Rig-Veda* 9:21, Indra flows through the running drops of soma, spirited in mood, with the exhilarated Pavamana looking for light with which to drive off foes. He enters the room where the pressers are and willingly imbues them with the life force as a response to their praises. They carefully transport all the drops of soma to one common reservoir, from where it falls into the river to support the waves. Pavamana obtains all blessings and, in an embodiment much to be desired, comes harnessed like coursers. The courses drop soma, bestowing with manifold desires those who have looked upon but have not yet given anything. Bringing with him the wish to design a better wheel, Pavamana observes that the soma, flowing purely and shining, remains within the stream. The drops that cry out in resonant voices, like swift steeds run the course, and roused to life by way of hymns from those humans who are good.

According to *Rig-Veda* 9:22, the rapid soma streams stirred into motion, moving like strong steeds, the embodiments hurrying forth like an army. As swift as the wind, they move lightly, forming rain and storms, as the deity Parjanya comes like the flickering flames of a fire. With soma juice blended with curd and purified, those skilled in singing sacred hymns gain their hearts' desire, namely, immortality, by singing songs. Cleansed, the drops begin to flow, the stream never relenting. They reach the designated regions by following their path, traveling over the ridges of the earth to seek the highest realm of all. Once over the heights, they find the brightest strand that spun and deemed to be the most desirable wealth, which seized by penny-pincher barbarians, who call upon the divine powers to spin it like thread.

According to *Rig-Veda* 9:23, effusing the soma that runs swiftly in the streams forms the essence of the gladdening drink, which makes it sacred here in the new resting place, where the ancient souls come to meet the sun, which shines like the self-enkindled Pavamana, bringing imperishable wealth to foemen and providing soma as food for the progeny. The living beings experience the purified soma as an exhilarating drink that causes them to drip with wisdom. This drink of sap, mighty in strength, increases their intelligence, which counters any curse placed upon the brave heroes. Indra, along with the powers of purified soma, as a companion at the feast, when such drafts smite the defenseless foes but do not kill them dead, shrivels them up and drains them of their strength.

According to *Rig-Veda* 9:24, Indra streams with soma drops. Purified, the soma blends in with the water, where it further cleansed to join with milk and to flood down a cliff being, where it cleansed yet again, before reaching Pavamana. The soma flows farther downstream to serve the gods with sips of the mythical juice and to seek for manifested mortal embodiments who have already seized and are ready to come forth as victorious. The embodiments hailed with joy, as the flowing soma comes to delight the living beings who have already designated to serve as the rulers of humankind. The holy river Indus, effused by compressed cosmic stones (meteors), begins running faster as a filter, readying it for Indra with his decree from on high. It flows on toward the best Vṛtra-slayer, who hails it with joyful laudation, fully effused with eternal wisdom and ready to serve those who are dear to Indra, the slayer of sinners. The green-hued mythical drink, as a draft, strengthens the gods who fly through the wind (Vayu) and supports the demigods serving as the cosmic hosts (Maruts).

According to *Rig-Veda* 9:25, the self-enkindled Pavamana, with an enlightened soul, sends vibrations through the wind (Vayu), moving on to the dwelling place and, with songs, passing through it, both enforcing and abiding by the eternal law. Appointed embodiments as ruling deities shine through steer, deer, and sages, as any other foe-slayer. The godliest souls each now take on a beautiful form, having gone through the purification process, which regulated by the immortal souls. Indra, regulating the mythical juice, comes to flow with engendering power red as blood. Exceedingly great in wisdom, he serves as a visitor among living things.

The soma flows within all living things, serving as the best exhilarator, filtered as a stream, taking its place amid the powers of song.

According to *Rig-Veda* 9:26, living things run exhaustlessly within one thousand streams, where sages, using their fingers, dressed and decked out as vigorous creations. They come and sit upon the ground (Prithvi), in the lap of the mother goddess Aditi, served by the holy river Indus, supported by the heavenly powers. As the nourishers of many sages, with their creative power, send the wise Pavamana through the sky to help the godly powers prevailing among the noble dwellers the Vivasvans. They use both their arms to send forth the lord of infallible speech. With beloved green eyes, and as omni sense sisters, they place the stepping-stones all the way from the mountain ridges down to the sieve, where mythical juice is formed and the creative self-enkindled Pavamana aids others with song and cheer, serving as the priest on the river.

According to *Rig-Veda* 9:27, sages overflowing with laudation bring the purifying cloth. Their foes scatter, cleansed by the power of Indra, and spread out among the wind (Vayu) like the filtering cloth. With soma, the sages invoke the omniscient steer to come and serve as the head of heaven, that is, Sūrya, with the soma effused within wooden vats. They adorn the body of the mother cow with gold (material wealth) so she may prevail within the river Indus. The conquerors low but never overcome the self-enkindled Pavamana. Gladdening drafts of soma drops on the cheesecloth and then waft into the sky as cosmic vapor to join with the heavenly power Sūrya. On the firmament, the holy ground, Indra, with a tawny steer, comes to purify and continues to flow in the Indus.

According to *Rig-Veda* 9:28, urged on by the manifested embodiments, with vigor like that of a steed, along with the lord of the mind, the Omniscient One runs to the woolen straining cloth and passes through the filter with soma effused by the godly powers. The essences of all the gods shine with beauty in the dwelling place of the immortal godly powers, with the Omniscient One serving as the dearest among them, being the foe-slayer. The gods directed by Sūrya's ten sisters, bellowing on the way as they run onward like steer to the wooden vats. The swift, strong invoked Omniscient One serves in splendor. Like the sun and all other forms of light, he brings purified soma, dear to the gods, as he flows, mighty and infallible, serving as the slayer of sinners.

## BENEVOLENT MIND

According to *Rig-Veda* 9:29, the lord of the mind, the Omniscient One, moves forward with his mighty force that flows with the current like effused steer and sets the singers to singing songs of praise. With their songs, and with the learned priests, they adorn the steed that brings forth light, which merits laudation from the purified winners. They fill the sea full, then claim the praise for having won all precious things. At once, the soma flows onward with the stream, moving away from the enemies' place. The embodiments kept away from those who are godless, those with ill-omened voices, so they may be free of blame. The holy river Indus flows to bring the wealth from both earth and heaven and serves with splendid vigor.

According to *Rig-Veda* 9:30, the Omniscient One, as the Potent One, flows easily through the cheesecloth lying in the river, lifting his voice as he floats along, serving with pressure and with purifying speed. While beautified, he bellows, sending forth a very mighty sound as he pours mythical juice within the stream, which can now conquered by the living things who crave to do so. Accompanied by the hero and his offspring, the self-enkindled (Pavamana), the Omniscient One comes with soma and settles in the vats of wood or vats of stone. The tawny-hued ones, driving forth like the sweetest and richest mythical power, now prevail within the Indus. Such mythical power provided to Indra moves through thunder, bringing forth a rich sweetness and an inspiriting strength.

According to *Rig-Veda* 9:31, the benevolent soma drops from heaven fill the rivers, providing the ground with wealth. This increases the mighty power of the ground as the head of all strength, which receives the omniscient lord of the sapient mind. Along with this, the gracious heavenly lord Rudra brings the wind to imbue the rivers with a power that further refined to make them great. Coming from all directions, generating vigor, Rudra and the wind unite to establish a gathering place and provide added strength. The brown-hued animals pour forth with milk, which mixed with imperishable emollients to serve those in the sublime heights, with a desire to form a friendship with those who bear arms and are ready to serve the lord of all minds.

According to *Rig-Veda* 9:32, the solar deity Trita, with a mind of his own, sheds ecstasy upon those assembled. They file out and take the lowly fourth position to glorify the tawny-colored cosmic bodies (meteors) and urge them to appear as compressed stones. Filled with mythical juice, they arrive on the ground (Prithvi), accompanied with rain, to join with the Indus as it flows. Just like Indra, they provide mythical juice to enhance the embodiments and cause them to appear as flying swans, thus representing the divine sisters. They come singing divine songs to help the female steeds soak in a bath with milk within a vessel filled with mythical juice.

The flying swan, viewed as a blessing, comes from heaven to the earth. Expressed as a dashing deer, it comes to the place of sacrifice, where a mother sings with joy as she meets with her lover or her child. They come to settle a race of their own, all bestowed as liberal lords with their mothers, with illustrious fame, glory, intelligence, and wealth. Running with the waters, they create the surf, which generate ripples and vibrations to support those skilled in music and the other arts, helping them to gain speed and move toward the woods. The mythical juice, nectar floating on water, runs over the earth like a heavy ox.

According to *Rig-Veda* 9:33, the swans float within the stream like bright brown drops, moving with the flow to strengthen the mythical juice that stored in wooden vats. On the ground, they are all supported by Indra, the wind (Vayu), and the eternal law (Varuna), and protected by the celestial power Vishnu. The god Soma, guided by the cosmic hosts (the Maruts), utters words as a lowing calf speaks to its mother, the grown cows giving milk. They go on bellowing to their young ones. The sacred mothers perform the holy rite, uttering their praises to the children of heaven, who appear decorated from all directions, with soma as a reward poured forth to fill the four seas, all filled a thousandfold with riches.

According to *Rig-Veda* 9:34, fully effused drops of soma move onward, impelling the stream to split and establish places to pour forth. The trinity of Indra, Varuna, and Vayu, along with the protector Vishnu, flow with the cosmic hosts (Maruts), all of them supporting the cosmic bodies. These cosmic bodies appear as compressed stones (meteors) that come to pour forth with soma and, with strength, call upon their skills to extract the sweet milk that poured out as refined liquor. With the powers of the three sun goddesses, they make Indra glad as he watches the tawny-hued ones all decked with their heritage. They go back to the goddess of milk, Pṛśni, and her dearest dwelling place to offer a sacrifice and oblations. United stream, they, with their songs, flow straight ahead, singing in loud voices, which makes the milk-bearing embodiments low as they feed their offspring. Near the ultimate destination, tawny in hue, the self-enkindled Pavamana appears within the river Indus, as the shaker, makes all things flow. As the bearers of wealth and might, the valiant heroes come to subdue their enemies and, with the precious flow of the Indus, arise with strength. While sages strive for victory, by way of which they also win power, they perform holy works. As the guardians and as movers of speech, robed in song, they worship, taking the purified soma to serve to the lord of the holy law, so rich when purified that it sets others' hearts toward the gods.

According to the *Rig-Veda* 9:36, the guardians, the cosmic bodies take a break from filling themselves with soma and, like carriage horses, move forward to achieve their goal. Thus, the god Soma, watchful, bearing up well and cheering the gods, flows past the sieve and turns toward the vat, ready to drop all the soma and filled with eternal wisdom. The excellent Pavamana makes the lights shine brightly for all and, with speed, pushes farther along with his mental power and his skills. Beautified and pious, he comes adorned with his hands full of soma, which flows through the fleece straining cloth. All treasures from the heavens poured upon the earth to establish the ground (Prithvi) as the firmament. Pavamana, serving as the liberal worshipper, climbs to the heights of heaven to worship, seeking steeds and other milk-bearing animals. The heroes find the lord of physical strength, the steer or heavenly bull, with poise pouring out invisible drafts of mythical juice, flowing through the skin, which serves as a purifying sieve.

According to *Rig-Veda* 9:37, slaying the fiends, loving the gods, farsighted, and tawny colored, the self-enkindled Pavamana flows through the purifying sieve to seek eternal wisdom. Bellowing then coming to a place of rest, the vigorous Pavamana runs forth as a fiend-slayer. Through the fleecy sieve, he observes the luminous realm of heaven reaching above the three sun goddesses and passing the high ridge created by the heavenly body Sūrya, which includes the Messier 45 galaxy and the Seven Sisters (Pleiades). These all generate their own light by soma. As Vṛtra-slayers, they expand space, never deceiving as they go on creating space by winning everything as urged by the holy spirit. With Godspeed, they willingly move forward with the Indus and Indra, all serving as containers for firewood, filled with mythical juice.

According to *Rig-Veda* 9:38, in a chariot driven by steeds, the self-enkindled Pavamana goes to war to support Trita, bringing with him compressed cosmic stones (meteorites), which impel him onward with the tawny ones, who serve soma and are ready to provide power to the holy river Indus, all supported by Indra. Pavamana and Trita carefully adorn the ten active participants to make them bright and beauteous by drinking the gladdening draft. Pavamana settles down amid the living beings supporting their families. He appears as a large raptor (falcon) that looks for true love. As young ones, exhilarated, Pavamana and Trita look downward from their place in heaven, where they consume the soma that has passed through the sieve and poured out as tawny juice to flow forth with wisdom, causing them to cry out unto the well-beloved place.

According to *Rig-Veda* 9:39, large raptors such as falcons' dwell among the godly powers and, with swift motion and lofty thought, in their beloved form, come to prepare that which is not yet prepared. They bring prepared food that may store among the manifested embodiments. They descend from the heavens like the rain. With a mighty bestowing power, they pass through the purifying sieve, with their ability to see far and send forth their internal light. Following a rapid course, with the waves of the river, they fly from heaven to the earth, serving as the cheesecloth. They invite from far away and close by to partake of the invisible soma, which poured out with eternal wisdom to serve their union, with Indra singing hymns to restore the compressed stones (meteors), urging the tawny ones to make a sacrifice.

According to *Rig-Veda* 9:40, the self-enkindled Pavamana remains active, even while his purified enemies decked to serve as sages, who come singing holy songs like their sapient ancestors. With red blood, appearing among the manifested embodiments, Pavamana finds a place on the earth to settle and establish his fortified abode. With the soma flowing within the holy river Indus, he sends great opulence in all directions, pouring forth with a hundredfold treasure. Pavamana, floating in the Indus, amid splendor, finds a boundless supply of stored food. Once it cleansed, it brings heroic physical strength along with spiritual richness to serve the worshippers, who prosper through singing hymns. The Indus continuously purifies the mythical fluid to bring forth its ancient richness. This doubles the pile of eternal wealth to serve the mighty Indra.

According to *Rig-Veda* 9:41, active and bright, Pavamana comes forth with impetuosity, moving swiftly like the heavenly bull. After defeating the ruler of the evil powers, Dāsa, the riteless with Black skin, Pavamana seeks the bridge of bliss, leaving the bridge of woe behind. Then the roar of the mighty Pavamana, serving as the heavenly bull, heard coming with a rush of rain and lightning, flashing from the sky shield. He pours out abundant food and wealth, and as he passes through the holy Indus, he brings along things that are pure as gold, such as milk-bearing animals and steeds that remain as the leftovers. Flowing onward most actively, he fills the river with mighty power to serve heaven and earth. Appearing to the morning light, he invites the heavenly power Sūrya to send forth beams of light. Coming from all directions, flowing around the world, the light protects the streams by creating moisture and humidity (Rasā).

## HERITAGE

According to *Rig-Veda* 9:42, the supreme powers of causation, after causing the waters to run and flood the earth, establish the solar body (the sun) that, as part of its heritage, represents the heavenly power Sūrya. After this, they manifest wearing robes of green to match the ground whereupon they establish the milk-bearing creatures serving as mothers. These are all regulated by the inherited primeval plan to bring soma floating within the holy streams. With this flow, they effuse with their ancient heritage to serve as the gods of the gods. The head of all godly powers, the victorious Pavamana, comes to provide them with purified soma. This wins over the thousand powers, including all the remnants, who shed the ancient mythical fluid, pouring it through the purifying sieve. Running through thunder and rain, these gods are set apart as the elect among the all-prevailing gods. Soma, after purified, goes on strengthened by the law, Varuna, who then sends all things desired by the godly powers. The effused mythical juice pours out wealth like milk from a mother's breast and imbues steeds with physical strength, providing all heroes with an abundance of food to store.

According to *Rig-Veda* 9:43, enrobed in sacred songs, the Lovely One brings milk-bearing animals decked with soma, which brings rapturous joy. All those who sing songs and desire grace adorned by holy river Indus as well as by Indra, who drinks purified soma. The Indus flows on, beloved and adored, with the ancient sage Medhātithi serving as the self-enkindled Pavamana. The two find exceedingly glorious wealth residing within the Indus. Laden with boundless might, racing like coursers on the river, they take soma as a prize to all those who love the gods. The river roars even before it passes through the filter, with Medhātithi and Pavamana flowing on their way to win strength and speed for the sages who praise them upon receiving the mythical juice and thereby gifted with heroic power.

According to *Rig-Veda* 9:44, the holy river Indus, in response to great rite, generates godly vibrations that create restless waves as the river flows forth, impelled by prayers and hymns. Pavamana continues floating in the Indus, in a rush to go far away. Serving the singers as the Wise One, he among all the gods is the most watchful, and with soma he advances further. After passing through the purifying sieve, he travels onward, seeking strength for those priests who embellish their sacrifices, which they offer on the trimmed sacred grass. Bringing power, Bhaga and Vayu come to serve the sages and heroes, leading them as gods. They seek to increase their wealth, become the best, win strength, and be highly renowned.

According to *Rig-Veda* 9:45, those who view the river's flow as entertaining to the gods receive a delightful drink from the Indus, which governed by Indra, who takes such a drink himself. The holy stream itself serves as the embassy of Indra, serving all the gods. As friends, the gods provide balm, both red of hue (blood) and white of hue (milk), to generate the sort of rapturous joy that unbars the doors of wealth. Passing through the sieve, a courser then tied to a pole, the running river Indus belonging to the gods. All the friends lauded as a sport, with the eternal flame hidden in the woods. With such power, the gods move beyond the hustle, chanting as singers, praising the holy Indus, wherein they step to announce the creation of the manifested bodies who come to worships their heroic strength.

According to *Rig-Veda* 9:46, the coursers sent forth to lay a feast in honor of the gods who enjoy the streams of soma flowing through the low-lying mountains, the soma blowing with the wind (Vayu), made beautiful like a bride for her husband. Compressed stones (meteors), like mortars, bring drops of soma to serve as rich food that provides strength like Indra. As the conqueror of wealth, Indra finds the flow that provides opulence to the self-enkindled Pavamana, who adorns all ten of his fingers to please Indra. With nimble hands, he seizes the brilliant juice, cooks the food, and comes to drink the gladdening draft.

According to *Rig-Veda* 9:47, the self-enkindled Pavamana, mighty in strength and with reverent solemnity, rises with joy to appear as a bull ready to perform the task of crushing the manifested evil powers the Dāsas, who are a force reckoned with. With songs of praise, Pavamana, with a gift of soma from Indra, comes along with the prophet serving as the sustainer. With one thousand thunderbolts, the bring riches for the sages who honor them with songs. Both the prophets and the sages win riches as they prevail in war.

According to *Rig-Veda* 9:48, the sages seek kindness from those who protect them from their mansions aloft in the heavens, where, gladly crushing the bold, ruling with mighty sway, they destroy one hundred forts and hence force the Sapient One to fly off with strong wings, like the falcon, which, unwearied, comes down from the sky. As the lords of wealth, they see with the coming light that the raptor appears as a friend, a guardian of the law. The fastest flier of all, the falcon flies to come forth and attain mighty power and majesty, actively ready to assist.

According to *Rig-Veda* 9:49, the sages come down with the pouring rain, creating waves in the waters, bringing a plenteous store of wholesome food along with them. They flow onward with the holy river Indus, which enables them to deliver the milk to strangers' homes. The chief friends of the gods, with sacred rites, they pour forth with strength, creating floods with the rain. Filled with vigor, the streams run with soma, which passes through the fleecy straining cloth. Verily, the sages move onward like the self-enkindled Pavamana, flowing like gods and beating off the malevolent powers (rakshasas), flashing with an ancient majesty.

According to *Rig-Veda* 9:50, riding on the loudly roaring river with powerful waves, the sages lift themselves up and urged onward like a sharp-pointed arrow, at the same time effused with joy. Once they make it to the flocculent ridge, they agitate even the compressed stones. Tawny in hue and well-beloved, they come like the self-enkindled Pavamana, dropping eternal wisdom along with mythical fluid. They flow with the current through the sieve, then the most powerful among them seated. Cheerfully singing songs, they move along with the flow, exhilarated, providing for Indra a drink of soma mixed with milk as a balm from the holy river Indus.

According to *Rig-Veda* 9:51, after filtering the soma, the sages (*adhvaryu*) express it through compressed stones to make it purer. Thunder-armed Indra comes along with rich, sweet, most excellent soma juice to share with the gods and the demigods serving as cosmic hosts (Maruts), enjoying the holy river Indus flowing with soma, where now mixed with eternal power (essence). As the self-enkindled Pavamana, they taken the fully effused strengthening soma, pass it through the purifying sieve, and then give it to others, providing them with strength and fame. All celebrate, singing like the wild steer, winning wealth, which they take to their dwelling place in the sky. The soma provides vigor as it flows and filtered in the ancient way.

According to *Rig-Veda* 9:52, to become fully effused and beloved, the thousand streams run over the surface of the ground, serving as the fleecy straining cloth. With its power, the river Indus shakes, becoming a cauldron that bring gifts to the righteous warriors. The shaken holy Indus, along with a prayer, fills the manifested embodiments with vigor so they appear threatening in war. The holy river Indus, as the wealth giver, with mighty power, aids the warriors by pouring out soma for one hundred years. One thousand pure, bright, mighty streams, all filled with compressed cosmic stones (meteorites), along with the divine powers, come to crush the fiends, the river level rising by itself to drown the foes who trouble the manifested embodiments.

According to *Rig-Veda* 9:53, after the conquest, the victors join the mighty ones, like a horse yoked to a carriage, and win the prize with fearless hearts, all singing praises. Without any evil thought, the self-enkindled Pavamana assails the enemies of the holy law and crushes those who would not fight to support Indra. While floating in the holy river Indus, he brings delight and, like a tawny steed, drives forward, dropping soma for the Maruts.

According to *Rig-Veda* 9:54, the ancient prophets, manifested in mortal embodiments, win one thousand gifts and of one accord serve as the heavenly body Sūrya. Like the sun, they pass through the heavenly shield (the sky) and run toward bodies of water such as lakes and oceans, where, along with the splendidly shining seven holy rivers, they come to rest. Prevailing over all things in existence, they flow along with the source of mythical juice, carried by the self-enkindled Pavamana, thus representing the heavenly power Sūrya.

According to *Rig-Veda* 9:55, appearing in the holy river Indus, brilliant, they pour the best purified soma out for their friend Indra. The milk-bearing mothers, with wealth, as a feast from the gods, pour forth with nourishing milk, like kernels of corn, which provides bliss. The holy river Indus, with praises, springs forth with mythical juice to satisfy the dear ones seated on sacred grass. They feed their cows and horses with the soma, which allows them to fly rapidly on throughout their days. If any conqueror not subdued, they come to attack them and remain as the enemy. They destroy thousands in the flow. However, instantaneously, with the flow of mythical juice purified through the sieve, they follow the glorious law. The always loving gods come to slay the villains.

According to *Rig-Veda* 9:56, the prophets pour out soma as strengthening food, feeding one hundred active streams, serving as friends of Indra and winning friendship along the way. The ten female powers, all singing songs of welcome, serving as virgin aid greeted with love. With mythical juice, the self-enkindled Pavamana, all decked out to win, flows, thereby supporting the river Indus and providing sweet juice to both Indra and the heavenly guard Vishnu. Manifested as prophets and as singing sages, they remove distress. The holy streams that never fail flow forth like rain showers from heaven, bringing strength in the thousandfold.

According to *Rig-Veda* 9:57, the powers flow, beholding on their way the beloved sacred lore. Green tinted, brandishing arms when they decked, they appear as big as the elephants that are obedient to the kings or as large as the falcons that hide in the woods, ready to fly to the holy river Indus and provide purified treasures to both heaven and earth.

## ARMOR

According to *Rig-Veda* 9:58, *Durgā* identified as the mother of the goddess of war, Adi *Parashakti*, whose strength is in combating evil and demonic forces. Sapient armor appears in fierce form to serve as protection for the mother. She unleashes her divine wrath against the wicked to liberate the oppressed. This requires the primordial power of causation, Shakti, for either destruction or empowerment. Swiftly, with sapient armor, Shakti runs as the giver of delight, filling the streams with mythical juice. With the morning light comes grace, exposing to the manifested mortal embodiments all precious things that come from the sapient hands of the male *Dhvasra* and the female *Puruṣantis*. They quickly accepted by thousands, bringing delight. With soma, they flow onward, winning cows and steeds, taking such wealth to the progeny (*Rig-Veda* 9:59). Flowing onward with the water, the wealthy progeny sanctified by the mythical fluid extracted from soma plants. The soma flows onward from the pressing boards to purified, and then served to the self-enkindled embodiment Pavamana. Pavamana bypasses all trouble and distress to come to serve as a heavenly sage (prophet) who sits, with full inner illumination, on the sacred grass. He is born of the holy river Indus to become the greatest power to rule over all manifested mortal embodiments, singing forth with sacred songs. The most active self-enkindled embodiment, Pavamana seen moving on the holy river Indus with his thousand eyes open (*Rig-Veda* 9:60). With his thousand eyes, as the bearer of sapient beauty, filtered through skin as through a fleecy cloth. The prophet Pavamana, already in the stream running with soma, passes soma through his embodiment as if through fleece before it goes into the body stored in jars. Pavamana, serving as a prophet, now finds his way to the heart, where the gods plant seeds to bring forth progeny.

According to *Rig-Veda* 9:61, moving onward, the holy river Indus, with food for all, bringing wild delight, batters down the ninety-nine castles. It swiftly tears down the forts and overpowers the town of *Turvagato* to save the Yadu tribe, which blessed with pious power (*Divodāsa*). The blessed tribe, finders of wealth, represented by domesticated animals such as cows and horses, enjoy material wealth such as gold. They travel along with the river Indus on their horses and bring a boundless supply of food to store. Seeking friendly love, like waves, they flow through the purifying sieve to manifest as self-invoked prophets. Using the same waves in the stream, they overflow the purifying sieve and, graciously purified like soma, come from all directions. With riches and food, such embodiments, serving as offspring, children of the water, are born to serve as holy prophets. They worshipped like the envoy of the heavenly godhead. As the children of the water, with ten swift fingers, they beautified and seen as noble souls (Ādityas). With embodiments like that of Indra, they use their limbs to fly in the air (Vayu). Effused, as prophets, the children of the water move onward like the shining beams representing the heavenly body Sūrya. They come supported by the supreme powers of causation, which function like a purifying sieve. They learn to flow with sweet eternal love to serve both Mitra and Varuna as manifested bodies, such as the patron Bhaga, the mover Vayu, and the giver Pūṣan. Children of the water, highborn, with soma, formerly set up in heaven, now on earth obtain strong sheltering power as those who are renowned. Striving to win, through their powers, the manifested living things gain all wealth and all glory, transforming from ungodly men into godly human beings. As humanity thus finds both the freedom and the space to follow and adore Indra, they serve the eternal law (Varuna) and receive support from the demigods serving as cosmic hosts (Maruts). Even the gods come to worship Indra, and the holy river Indus fills with beautiful, well-descended milk-supplying animals, which come to serve Indra, the active crusher of foes. The mother cows see their calves strengthened with songs of praise to win the heart of Indra. Pouring forth soma with blessings, milk-bearing creatures pour forth with milk as the food that fills the holy streams, increases their strength, and allows them to reach the sea.

From heaven, as the sapient armor, Pavamana arrives on the earth with marvelous thunder and with lofty light that invokes the prevailing embodiments. With gladdening soma, Pavamana manifests to serve as the king, flowing over the ground and purified by the woolen straining cloth. With inner illumination, Pavamana with his splendid skill set sends his luster to appear as heaven's light, which sent from the heavenly power Sūrya. This luster flows onward with the soma, bringing with it divine delight to help the gods who are overpowered by the wicked. By killing the foemen and those who hate the gods, Pavamana, with his red blood blended with the milk of the lovely cow, manifests as a large raptor (falcon). In such an embodiment, he wins booty every day while resting in his own home. Then he flows onward, fully strengthened. Like Indra, he slaughters the evil power Vṛtra, then goes around continuing to create mighty floods. With the rain, he brings gifts of soma to win riches to strengthen the heroes through the art of cleansing hymns. Aided by Indra, through grace and solemn rites, he chases away the foemen, driving off the godless, and with the strength of soma continues to flow on. Reaching a special place, the self-enkindled Pavamana brings great riches and destroys his foes, while the holy river Indus grants him heroic fame. One hundred obstacles removed; Pavamana never checks the circumstances when bringing along a divine boon. The river Indus, flowing mightily with soma, glorified by the manifested bodies who drive away all enemies. In friendship, lofty and glorious, Pavamana comes to serve as the guardian of the noble powers, saving them from every foe. Those in the war, with their awful weapons with sharpened points, struck down and subdued.

According to *Rig-Veda* 9:62, the rapidly free-flowing drops of soma, poured through the purifying sieve, bring pleasure by preventing manifold mishaps. This brings progeny to coursers and warrior steeds, which brings success. It also brings prosperity to milk-bearing animals. Iḷā, guardian of the Ganges, with perpetual offerings, creates a holy mountain as a tribute. Stalks of soma plants appear on the surface that, when pressed, bring rapturous joy. Iḷā comes to settle in the streams, setting them up as her home, from where she emerges as hawk. From the soma plant, loved by the gods, the juice purified and poured into the waters. After being hard-pressed, it generates something like sweetened milk. Serving the drivers as a decked courser, Iḷā mixes such juice with essence and takes it to the festival. As nectar (ambrosia), taken from the holy rivers whose streams merge with the river Indus, where it dropped like sweet juice. When poured, it passes through the purifying sieve and flows onward into the ground. Finding its home in vats of wood, which ample room and freedom, it is, in its sweetest form, poured out like butter consumed by Agni's messengers the Aṅgirases. Serving as the most active and benevolent ones, they present as the self-enkindled Pavamana, who levitates as a lofty friend.

As the remover of curses, mighty, with strong sway, Pavamana brings treasures to the worshippers. He pours out these treasures by the thousandfold, including milk-bearing animals such as steeds. Exceedingly glorious, much desired, wandering, these animals go far, fully effused with wisdom, to serve as noble, beautiful living beings. Serving as sages, they drink in the gladdening drink in honor of Indra so they may measure out the regions filled with countless wealth borne within the mountains. In the trees, where the streams merge with the holy river Indus, they settle down, providing shelter and nests for the birds. Manifested mortal embodiments support the self-enkindled Pavamana, assessing the mighty powers contained within the vats. They yoke the triple-seated carriage carrying the seven seers (rishis), all singing holy songs and moving along with the tawny coursers. Under pressure, they speed on their way like swift steeds going into war, hoping to defeat their enemies and bring back the spoils.

By pouring out glory, they serve the heroes standing among milk-bearing animals floating within the river Indus, already served milk mixed with mythical juice to generate a draft of essence to serve to all the other gods. The best gladdening soma juice poured amid the singing of loud songs. This brings out the lofty celebrities, who enjoy the milk that brings valor. Being fully cleansed, they herewith bring the spoils, all singing special hymns, to Jamadagni. Recited by the seven holy spirits (Saptarishis), the songs allow all nourishment blessed. With drafts of soma mixed with essence, the celebrities, along with the leader of the song, move onward to provide wondrous aid to all kinds. Once the leader of the song stirs up the waters in the rivers and in the sea, they flow onward to all sages, who stand up to attest to the divine mighty power that makes the rivers flow. Showers of rain fall from heaven to form streams that perpetually brighten the flow, providing the fleece that spreads along the earth. The potent, imperishable Indra purifies the perishable holy river Indus, which provides strength to serve the almighty lord and bring him enjoyment. The true mythical juice sits in the purifying sieve as the self-enkindled Pavamana manifests as a sage and, with praises, strengthens the heroes.

## PERISHABLE

With heroic strength, Pavamana, with soma, creates thousands of manifested mortal embodiments. As sapient perishable cosmic bodies, they are all directed by the powers of vibration expressed as holy hymns—*Gayathri, Brhati, Usnik, Jagati, Tristup, Anustup, and Pankti.* Each power of vibration regulates the supreme powers of causation, who appear as seven fast-flying bodies, each drawn like a chariot with three naves wheels. The naves wheels represented by three gaseous giants, *Sūrya, Saturn, and Jupiter.* Unlike the gracious bodies, the manifested perishable terrestrial bodies form the solar system. They are all hosted by the imperishable immortal living spirit (Atman). The terrestrial bodies provide the physical bodies with food and swells of water, producing vigor and the immortal living spirit, which comes to serve as the best of gladdeners. Seated with their cups, the gladdeners pour forth with purified soma, serving as the protector of manifested physical bodies, that is, Vishnu. The heavenly body Rudra, through the powers of the wind (Vayu), brings out the true richness of the sweet mythical juice. When effused, the soma gives birth to the brown-hued spirit serving as an enlightened soul, which with swift and solemn sacrifice passes through twisted obstacles. It recognized by every embodiment as the source of every noble act performed and augmented through the strength of Indra, who drives away all godless powers. Such brown hue received by Indra and therewith given a place within the region where mythical juice flows onward within the holy stream.

The direct light from the heavenly body Sūrya surges along with usable water that is good for the living mortal embodiments. Pavamana, prevailing high manifested mortal embodiments, yoked to the direct light (the sun) to appear as the flying courser Etaśa. He travels as breath through the realm of air (Vayu), serving as ten kinds of coursers, all of which, tawny hued harnessed by the mighty light of the sun. Indra continues to serve the holy river Indus, bringing singers, who all pour forth the gladdening juice to support the power of the wind (Vayu). They pour forth drops of mythical juice to spread over the ground, serving as the fleecy cloth. Pavamana finds wealth for all and is not attacked by foemen, who may not win. He sends riches in the thousands within the stream, including both steeds and milk-bearing animals, as the remnant to the highly renowned as the spoils of war. The self-enkindled Pavamana conveys the compressed stones (meteors) coming from the heavenly power Sūrya, floating through outer space and falling onto the earth, to pour the juice and fill the jars. The brilliant drops passed through the compressed stones as the solemn sacrifice then poured into stream in worship of the divine law and to strengthen all animals. The drops pass through the purifying sieve, from where they flow on the ground and blend with water to form curdled milk. When effused with the powers of Indra, they come to appear as heavenly thunder and become a gladdening drink most rich in sweetness, which is dear to the godliest powers. Once they flow through the strainer, the drops even bring wealth.

The living embodiments adorned by Indra and, like tawny coursers, learn to follow the holy stream Indus, becoming the givers of delight unto others. The soma poured forth like gold. As heroic sons with horses, it brings strength to milk-bearing herds. Indra pours the mythical juice on the ground, whereby, passing through the fleece, it acquires a long-lasting sweetness to serve well in battle. Singers seeking help from the sages get all decked with loud songs and prayers coming with the bellowing steer. The singers, with their thoughts and their hymns, sitting within the stream of sacrifice, receive soma like an active steer that roars. The godly powers with humankind flow on, providing the gladdening juice, with the wind (Vayu) passing through the breath, making its commands. The living beings enter the lake that served by the self-enkindled Pavamana, who, with the purest form of wealth, becomes renowned. With the soma flowing, he chases away the foes, bringing wisdom and delight, help to drive off any who do not love the gods. After Pavamana has poured out the brilliant drops of soma juice, he shares the holy lore with all kinds and, with beautiful drops, swiftly drives all enemies far away from heaven and out of the firmament.

Pavamana, fully effused, comes to settle upon the summit of the earth (Prithvi) where, purified, the holy river Indus provides wisdom. As a learned one, Pavamana drives the foes the rakshasas far away. Bellowing as he pours forth with the most excellent mythical juice, and with splendid strength, he secures the treasures of earth and heaven.

According to *Rig-Veda* 9:64, with the power of soma, even a splendid steer may transform into a godly stallion fully ordained by the eternal law. With mighty strength, the steer drink from the holy river Indus with vigor and low together with other steeds to unbar the doors to eternal wealth. The milk-bearing animals such as cows, which desire the physical strength of the stallions, move swiftly, effused with soma drops to become potent and brilliant. With purified hands, they become beautiful enough to serve as holy spirits that move onward over the earth. Soma juice, as the treasure for worshippers, poured forth upon the firmament, where streams filled with soma flow. The holy spirit finds others who have effused by the heavenly rays of light from heaven (Sūrya). Flowing in every form, bringing soma, they swell to fill the ocean. Pavamana urges Sūrya with his voice, thanking him for providing the light that serves as a purifying sieve. Sages, purified by hymns, come from the Indus to serve as the enlighteners. As friends, they start out in a chariot pulled by steeds, creating a god-delighting wave that flows, further purifying like a sieve. Alighting in their homeland, along with the eternal law, they serve as a sieve to provide the gladdening draft. This establishes godly interaction between the perishable river Indus and the imperishable Indra, who flows onward with the stream. With luster, the water appears as milk, all cleansed, as lovers of the song deliver it among the people to comfort them. With vigor, Indra separates the milk from the curd. For the feast of the gods, the soma delivered to Indra's glorious palace, accompanied by the singing of hymns. The soma flows rapidly toward to the lake, where the drops are made beautiful as they approach the lake, the true place of sacrifice. The area filled with faithful friends who provide all with shelter, the mighty heroes guarding their homes.

Loudly neighing, the courser Etaśa, harnessed, with singers, travels to the lake. All friends sing with a prudent wish to make sacrifices and cause the unintelligent to sink. Indra provides grit to the cosmic hosts (Maruts) who come to flow within the holy water of the Indus, which filled with rich, sweet juice. They find a place for the sacrifice, which controlled by skilled priests and sages, who, with holy songs, adorned by the beautiful noble soul Aryaman, eternal love (Mitra), and Varuna, who enforces the eternal law. They all drink soma as served by the purified Pavamana, who as a sage, or as the cosmic hosts (Maruts), worships those who come from the Indus. Drinking soma even while still being purified, in desperation they move onward, their speech touching the thousands who are singing hymns drinks from the holy river Indus, not wanting to stop the thousands who are longing for war. The much-invoked river Indus, as the friend of living things, enters the lake, bringing bright drops of soma blended with milk. These generate a brilliant flashing light. The drivers send forth the strong steeds to draw nigh for the spoils. Like righteous warriors, they stand specially arrayed, with the soma coming from heaven to prosper them and flow as the sage watches for daybreak.

According to *Rig-Veda* 9:65, the glittering aid virgin send forth the glorious sisters, closely allied with the ultimate imperishable divine power Sūrya, to the holy river Indus. As a mighty lord, Pavamana appears to permeate the invisible divine will accompanied with perpetual essence and comes to serve as the heavenly god of light among those gods appearing as the supreme powers of causation to support creation. The mighty lord, as a sapient imperishable power, who appears with the rain, pours out praises. This brings a special type of nourishment to the gods, who faithfully, with luster, call upon the Ultimate Splendid One. They rejoice as noble, moral, righteous souls who endowed with heroic strength like the holy river Indus. With both their hands dipped in the waters, they cleansed to go farther toward the gathering place. The immortal Vyaśva, singing songs of worship, appears as the Mighty One with sapient imperishable powers and one thousand eyes filled with colored fluid, He drives with vigor like the compressed stones. The compressed stones produce a yellow juice that distilled into nectar (amrit), like the soma the gods drink from the river Indus, to gain eternal love, the winners of all wealth from the Mighty One. The Indus flows onward with animals such as steer, which travel in its waters. In spirit, the cosmic hosts the Maruts win all riches by way of divine might. They send forth such riches as they go into battle like fully compressed cosmic bodies. Those who purified, as the lookers upon the light, come to serve the Sustainer of creation, Vishnu. Acknowledged for singing their own song, they flow as a tawny color in the holy stream. They engage in battle along with their ally. As the perishable Indus River, they all pour out abundant food for all, along with mythical juice, which flows in rich streams. They acquire the ability to sing loud songs vigorously, becoming part of Indra's mighty force. Receiving potent gladdening juice, they join with compressed cosmic stones (meteors) to serve as strong destroyers of their enemies.

Imperishable mighty powers, along with the perishable self-enkindled Pavamana, with holy songs sung by manifested living things, move on their behalf and travel through the firmament, serving the ground (Prithvi), where the holy river brings a hundredfold increase in noble animals within and around Indus. This brings along a gift of fortune that aids in arranging for the banquet of the gods. The soma, flowing with might and speed, brings beauty and a brilliant light show. As it flows forth with an exceedingly loud roar, it reaches wooden vats, where it comes to a rest like a large falcon alighting upon its aerie. Water-winning soma flows to join with the gods Indra, Vayu, and Varuna, who bestow upon the progeny food from all directions, offering from all directions the soma, which enriches a thousandfold. The soma, whether far away or near at hand, stored in the depository belonging to Śaryaṇāvān and stored in *ārjikas*, urged upon tribal kings taken to the worshippers' homes. There it shared among the five major tribes. Celestial drops, once expressed, pour forth with rain from the heavens, providing the heroes with strength. Wearing ox hide, they urged forward to flow and serve as the Lovely One, Jamadagni, of tawny hue, who lauded with songs of eternal life. The horses urged to speed up and to drop soma like a bright light, stirring up vital power and blending with milk to form beautiful streams. Those who toil with the juices move with this splendid flow and go forward in service to lay the banquet of the gods who, fulfilling all desires, are represented as the Guardian, the Excellent One, and the Gladdener, who fully understand the all desires and represent the sage with the noble heart, most wise, who has wealth and intelligence enough to comprehend desire.

According to *Rig-Veda* 9:66, the Gladdener, as a noble sage, sought by friends to come and rule in two positions: one standing still, and the other turning away. From these two positions, the Gladdener encompasses all directions, as the seasons come and flow onward, generating food, creating precious boons of every kind. As a friend to the friends, the Gladdener, from the loftiest ridge of heaven, generates bright rays that spread by way of the divine will, creating a purifying force. Along with the mythical juice flowing in the seven rivers, this purifying force commands the flowing streams of milk that run onward to merge with the streams of soma. Effused, and with a gladdened heart, Indra brings with him an imperishable fame and comes to serve as the godly powers the Vivasvans, who come with the sages singing their hymns and serving the Seven Sisters. Based upon their adolescence, the Seven Sisters are all decked out to appear within fresh streams to drive toward purity, serving as the sieve for the worshippers within the woodlands. The self-enkindled Pavamana floats in the river, the first invoked to pour forth to the Mighty One. Pavamana is like a courser, eager be acknowledged by the Seven Sisters, who pour soma upon the ground to pass through the sieve and fill the distillation vats with the power of the living spirit and the invisible power of essence. Their holy songs sound forth with the noises of milk-bearing animals, who are at home with the drops of soma juice that placed as a sacrifice in the river Indus. With great delight, the water flows toward those who robed in milk. With divine friendship, the Seven Sisters help others who willingly serve those who offer sacrifices to the river Indus and crave eternal friendship. The soma flowing in the river serves the great living things, with the help of Indra entering the mouth to reach the throat. It strengthens individuals who come to serve as righteous warriors, who prevail as the mightiest ones, even stronger than the most valiant and most brave ones and more liberal than the bountiful ones.

Pavamana, serving the ultimate imperishable divine power Sūrya, brings food to win over living beings and their offspring. Forming a new friendship, Pavamana and Sūrya, extend their companionship for posterity. Agni pours forth life and eternal flame and sends down food, vigor, and strength so living things may drive misfortune far away. Once Agni, with his eternal flame, comes to join with the self-enkindled sage Pavamana, who serves as chief priest regulating all five tribes by providing them with great wealth, with prayers he performs a task requiring great skill. Imperishable Agni pours forth his splendor to strengthen heroes by granting them with wealth to nourish them. Their sweet praises invoke Pavamana, as a sage, who helps them flee far from their enemies, who are in a place where they receive no heavenly light or heat. With adoration from living beings, Pavamana sets the steeds running in the river Indus, which transform into Pavamana, who invokes the lofty Varuna to bring forth a brilliant light to abolish the darkness. The tawny colored Pavamana serves as the destroyer. He springs up in radiant streams, which gleam and move swiftly, as the best chariot driver, praised with the fairest praise.

In the midair region, the beauteous ones appear as shiny gold cosmic hosts (Maruts). As the best, Pavamana wins the booty through his penetrating rays. This gives strength to the singers to take control of the fleecy sieve to purify the soma, while Indra comes to the holy river Indus. Such purified soma then passed through compressed cosmic stones (meteors), the draft summoning up thick leather, that, is ox hide, and all blessings for long life brought about from the bright milk from heaven.

The stream running with soma, joyous, strong with sacrifices, bounteous, bestowing wealth, effused with cheer for the manifested living beings, flows toward the greatest gladdener as a prince—Indra. Poured forth by compressed cosmic stones (meteors), the soma sends out a loud roar as it flows within the stream with illustrious might. The river Indus urges it forward to flow through the earth serving as a fleecy cloth, later appearing as the Tawny One with a loud roar, signaling its strength. The river flows through the earth, bringing ecstasy and fame, along with a wealth of milk-bearing animals and strong steeds. Soma brings wealth in the thousandfold. Purifying the soma as it runs its course, the river passes the drops through a sieve to allow the mythical juice to come nigh to Indra. Thus, the river flows with excellence, providing the best soma juice to the Living One. Like aid glittering virgin, it brings forth essence, accompanied with vibrations and oscillations, which, when songs sung loudly, cause the self-enkindled Pavamana to appear. Dropping the mythical blend drawn from the sacred goats that serve the solar deity Pūṣan, Pavamana provides protection for all on the path and bestows power upon the aid virgin s. The soma, flowing like a gladdening lubricant worn as the braided locks of a rosary (*mālā*) and shared by the glittering aid virgin s. The soma juice, glowing as a god, flows like a pure lubricant shared effused with those who support its onward flow in the stream, begetting the sages' speech. Wealth givers among the gods, like a raptor (falcon), the sages dip their jars into the river. Wrapped in robes, they go on roaring loudly, enkindling the vats. Soma effused and poured into pitchers. Hawks come rushing toward the flow that is most rich in sweetness and brings delight. They sent forth like chariots with the gods displaying their brilliant strength as they fly (Vayu), as the best givers of delight, they sent forth to provide mythical juice.

According to *Rig-Veda* 9:67, those bruised by the pressed stones, having passed through the sieve, lauded as demon-slayers, even passing through the fleece. Extolling, they give soma and strength to the worshipping heroes so they may drive away any danger, whether near at hand or far away. As Pavamana, they cleansed with the purifying power of the soma and come to serve as the most active priests. They serve as agents of Agni, invoking with the cleansing light, that effuses, all with a fiery glow. The demons purified and cleansed by prayers, cleansing power generating a bright light poured out with libations to serve as the eternal flame. Goddess

*Savitar*, with libation and purifying power, comes from all directions to purify and cleanse the three sublime forms of Agni. Through the mighty trinity, the company of gods, she even cleanses nature (Vasu) to produce pure songs.

The god Jātavedas purifies himself by filling himself with soma juice, including the stalks or stems of the plants, and offers the best of oblation to the gods. As a friend, with homage he approaches those who wander with praises, seeking after the young ones. With solemn rites, the young ones undergo a miraculous recovery, a restoration, representing the revelation of essence, the pedigree of *Ahlaya's* lost ax. Living beings come to learn about the essence stored by the holy saints, which can only extracted through the hymns of the self-enkindled power *Pavamana* or from food that completely purified and made sweet by the touch of Agni's messenger, Mātariśvan. Whosoever reads and learns to unveil the power of essence stored within the holy saints, or by singing hymns for Pavamana, or through the goddess Sarasvatī, draws milk and butter from the water, similarly drawing the powerful essence from the holy saints.

According to *Rig-Veda* 9:68, just as cows yield milk, free-flowing soma drops produce an enriched essence to serve all those seated on the grass. The Shining One, who willingly accept streams of milk from udders, with a roar, spreads out amid the highest stems, with shoots, to appear with the ancient ceremonial drink that provided to the demigods (tawny ones). After passing through the body, which serves as a sieve, the soma expands to cover quite a wide area, accompanied by divine will. This gladdening drink measured out by the twin demigods is ceremonial. The Aśvins appear with the eternal light to serve as an eternal pair, flying high toward the great limitless regions with a sheen that never fades. Serving as parents, wandering along, they strengthen themselves to face the floods. At the same time, sages (rishis) make a place for them to swell with their own native might. Mythical juice from the stalk of the soma plant mixed with grain, in males and females alike, to preserve the cranium, containing the brain, which provides the necessary intellect, where sages plant the germ of the eternal law into those who are young. Then a distinct living creature, half concealed and half exposed, appearing as the self-enkindled embodiment Pavamana. The rishis know him as the Gladdener (falcon), who one time brought a soma plant from far away. The Gladdener pulverizes the stalk, thus ensuring the mythical juice runs in streams, yearned for and ready with praise. Together with the rishis, Pavamana, with prayers and hymns, as a friend, effused with soma. They are all served by ten friendly women who adorned by their male counterparts.

Invoked by the godly powers of the earth, using a cloth of wool shorn from sheep, the rishis purify the mythical juice that gives them strength enough to win the spoils of war. Self-enkindled Pavamana, with his friends, springs forth, creating a fair chorus of songs that resonate with praises as the friends celebrated. The undulating stream, rich with essence, along with the winner of immortal wealth, the divine voice sent forth from heaven, sent into every region. The filtered soma in jars comes to settle in bodies of water such as rivers, ponds, lakes, and oceans. With milk and water mixed, it continuously pours forth from compressed cosmic stones, until in its purified form it finds its place of rest. Even then poured forth along the way, soma, as the mythical fluid, vouchsafes many, imbuing with lively vigor so they may invoke the benevolent gods of earth and heaven to send riches to the noble heroes.

According to *Rig-Veda* 9:69, nocked like an arrow in a bowstring, Pavamana, with hymns, let loose like a calf from the udder of its mother. Pavamana comes first with a full stream of water to acquire milk and then, impelled with holy rites, along with soma, manifests as creation. In deep thought, and with the savory juice, he makes a joyous sound as the soma touches his tongue. Then it stirred within his mouth, and he shouts out challenges, with the drops of soma flowing through his body, which acts as a fleece. It purified through his skin, and he comes to appear as a longing bride, one of Mother Aditi's daughters, serving the worshippers. The sacred drink takes on a gold tint, as Pavamana, well restrained, shining like a strong bull, arouses their might. With the bull bellowing, the cow comes nigh and approaches the goddesses in the gods' own resting place. After the soma passes through the individual embodiments, which act like the bright fleece of a sheep, it appears as a newly washed garment. Freshly bathed, golden hued, in a bright shining vesture, it resists harmed as it becomes immortal. It serves with a radiant robe along the ridge of heaven, sprinkling forth from a container filled with moisture from the sky.

Beams of heavenly light (Sūrya) urge all creations to speed ahead with cheer and then fall asleep together. Sūrya rushes forth, performing a full course of holy rites, which no other being can even come to close to matching, except the purest one of all, Indra. Moving down the steep slope of a mountain toward the valley, the strong drafts find human beings and cattle living together in the same home. Some left with them as wealth is poured out in the form of goods, gold, steeds, cattle, and corn. With great heroic strength, the god Soma, as the father, lifted on high as he heads toward heaven, serving as the Maker of life. The drops of soma, as the self-enkindled Pavamana, speed forth, racing toward the booty. Fully effused, the soma passes through the cheesecloth, while, golden hued, Pavamana casts off his coverings to pour down like rain into the holy river Indus, which flows to serve Indra, the blameless and gracious foe-destroyer who brings splendid treasures to all creations who worship heaven and earth and all the gods who protect creation.

CHAPTER 18

# Sacrosanct Dominion

THE SACROSANCT DOMINION IS THE UNIFIED PLACE WHERE ALL fully purified living spirits, Atmans, come to merge with their original source, Paramatman, and thus perishable embodiments become imperishable embodiments to serve within the home of the universal immortal soul (God). All the perishable demigods, after drinking purified mythical juice, transform into female goddesses (deities) and male gods (divinities). They prevail forever serving as the mighty powers, covering undefined space for an unlimited time. Entry to such a path to unison granted only after passing through the four stages of life (learner, head of the household, retirement or old age, and finally apathy) and living as detached from the material world. These four stages described as awakening, dreaming, sleeping deeply, and finally going beyond the material world. In terms of spirituality, these stages relate to fulfilling the obligations one is given when born (karma), the pursuit of wealth or material advantage (*artha*), seeking the eternal and inherent nature of reality, comprehending the underlying cosmic laws, behaving rightly, respecting the social order (dharma), and finally achieving emancipation, enlightenment, and liberation to be released from the cycle of rebirth, all powered by the eternal law of encirclement (moksha). These mutually exclusive four phases serve as the individual aims of life (*puruṣārtha*).

Historically speaking, moksha achieved in only three ritualistic ways: holy scripture (Veda), ascetic practices (yoga), and undivided devotional worship (bhakti). The point of these rituals is to go beyond karma and come to overpower the first four *lokas*, prevailing above the seven underworlds. These include (1) inherent nature (*adhilokam*), (2) the substance that causes attachment to the material world (*adhibhutam*), (3) the astral body composed of subtle material that serves as an intermediate between the intelligence (mind) and the living spirit (heart) (*adhiyajnam*), and (4) the individual living spirit, which is part of the immortal universal soul (*adhyatmam*). To attain ultimate freedom or liberation from the law of encirclement (moksha) or from the cycle of life and death, one must go beyond these four spheres (lokas).

## ANIMATED MIST

According to *Rig-Veda* 9:70, within the heavens are seven milk-bearing animals that pour forth drafts. After the drafts purified, as part of the process to attain freedom, they produce three times more milk than the prevailing milk-bearing animals on earth (Prithvi). From the pivotal point, they go to the four beauteous points (north, south, east, and west) to perform holy rites. They gain powers and invoke their internal strength, which transforms mythical juice into the eternal nectar (*amrit*). This fulfills their longing to attain immortality. In addition, with recital and holy worship, they gain eternal wisdom, which allows them to serve at all the points on the ground (Prithvi). All gladly wrapped in lucid fluid (*amrit*), with glory they find the gods' resting place, which is nothing but brilliant rays. There they remain unchanged, imperishable, and forever free from death. As sages, they recognize there are two kinds of illumination: one generated by the godly supreme powers of causation, and the other generated by highly advanced purified manifested mortal souls. Through invocation, mortal souls generate inner powers that, like purified amrit, serve in the same way as the soma brought by the gods to produce the self-enkindled immortal power Pavamana. They welcome both, serving as adored kings who served by the ten most skillful offspring born of intermediate mothers.

The kings watch over the nectar in and look upon as the beholders of manifested mortal embodiments. Adorned, they flow forth with mighty strength, and as beholders they rejoice in the space between earth and heaven. With their mighty steer, they aim to make offerings to dispel the evil hearted. They serve as bowmen who, amid the game, beholding their two mothers, go roaring on their way as the cosmic hosts (Maruts). By knowing the eternal law, with the earliest light of heaven, they pass as the wise ones, chosen to tell the truth. Like the fearsome bull, they bellow with violent might, farsighted, sharpening their yellow-colored horns. They assume a seat in the well-fashioned place, with cowhide and sheepskin as their raiment. They drink mythical juice to make their bodies pure, free from both spot and stain, coming as golden-colored sheep, which roll down like the trinity of Mitra, Vayu, and Varuna. They prepare a threefold meal for the skillful manifested bodies, so they can go to the gods' banquet, where mythical juice enters their hearts to join with the reservoir of soma.

Those manifested bodies that are beyond misfortune and torment have neither the urge nor the strength to flow with the mythical fluid, which moves onward to the throat, reaching the heart like a meandering river. Skilled, they bear up to pass like a boat over the water, serving in the battle like heroes to save themselves from the foemen. As guardians, these mighty powers each take a seat to serve as ever-watchful guards and save their charges from fiends and evil spite.

According to *Rig-Veda* 9:71, golden hued, using the clouds as their headband, and using milk and the ground like a fluffy carpet, they cover both worlds, in their strong state bellowing out prayers from beneath their robes as the proceed as one to slay their foes. The evil Asuras fly away, afterward throwing off their coverings, then come to meet at their father's place, where they appear in bright robes. With both hands, they move onward like compressed cosmic stones. Excited with prayer, they flow with water and become rowdy. They draw near to complete their work. Frolicking, they sing songs while bathing in a stream to satisfy both themselves and the worshippers. They pour essence all around the house of the celestial godly power, also covering the mountains, by which they receive both strength and mighty power. Through such great powers, they offer oblation to the noble powers, like cows grazing holy grass and learning to lift their udders. Mixed with such powers, the water produces the choicest milk. Through sitting on the lap of the godly mother Aditi, they send forth embodiments with attachments that, like limbs, help them move forward and backward.

As a wanderer, the large flying raptor (falcon) speedily reaches the home of the gods, the mysterious place where all creations such as astral bodies choose to come to rest. At this newly fashioned golden palace, they sing songs, urging the gods to come down to the sacred grass and serve as the holy one. As coursers, they move from the home of the gods and fly far away toward the heaven, reaching a triple height, from where they observe unmanifested red-hued navigators (astral bodies), which come singing to bring along milk-bearing creations (embryos) by the thousands, guiding them and leading the way. Shining splendidly, they pass through many mornings looking for shelter for their embodiments, and then come to assume a radiant hue. Whenever they enter a fight, they drive their foes far away, serving as the winners of food, which they serve as the hosts of heaven. They come along with praises, providing glorified essence, which, like milk, brings about the mythical juice. They roam around as a herd and appear as the heavenly bull; they bellow and assume brilliancy from the heavenly pantheon of Sūrya, who provides them with luminous power. Like the heavenly falcon, they alight on the ground to look for the mythical juice that provides wisdom to all living creatures.

According to *Rig-Veda* 9:72, the embryos of golden-hued steeds yoked to fill a jar and mingled with milk, from where they send out vibrations in the form of a voice to call upon their many loving friends. Highly lauded, they increase with song and utter words, defining eternal harmony in unison, of one accord, while Indra pours soma into their mouths, which moves down their throats like the ten milk-bearing sisters. They all join to dwell as the sacred cow with her male partner. With clean hands, these milk-bearing sisters provide the lovely souls with essence as they go upon their way. With a roaring sound that shows their unrest, the cows come to serve their loving daughters, representing the heavenly creator Sūrya. As the heavenly falcon, with delight, they bring two sisters who live in the same home. As heavenly bodies, they come to form compressed stones (meteorites), and when they fully washed, they appear faithful, creating the seasons and coming to serve as the lords of the animals.

More liberally than in the past, Indra offers a sacrifice of pure mythical juice while floating within the holy river. Urging with his arms that the soma pour forth in streams, with kind godly power, he fulfills the request for a sacrifice while seated on the ground. A golden-hued bird perched above serves the well-skilled sages who use their intelligence to drain soma from the stalk, which grumbles and makes them all like the Everlasting One. They sing hymns and take milk to the place where they are to offer the sacrifice. Sitting together on the ground, they give birth to a new one, which as the mighty sustainer of the heavens brings distilled mythical juice to pour into the streams and create waves. With a thunderbolt, Indra appears as the steer, spreading a wealth of soma far and wide, causing it flow to make everyone's hearts rejoice. Over the ground of the earthly region, the soma flows on its divinely appointed way, enabling the prayers of the wisest sages to pour through so no one denied the rich treasure from reaching their home in time. They clothe themselves in bright raiment to appear in the holy river Indus, bringing a gift of one hundred steeds, one thousand cattle, and gold. This is all measured out in exchange for an ample amount of the splendid strengthening food that provided by Pavamana, who listens to their prayers.

According to *Rig-Veda* 9:73, placing a drop of soma on the nave of a wheel makes the wheel move faster. The sages, all together, reach the place of the sacrifice, where the evil Asuras have seized the three lofty heights and taken possession of the eternal truth. The pious souls, borne across as strong steers, gather again to duly stir themselves up by riding over the waves of the river. They send forth their friends, singing hymns to fill the flowing streams with the essence of the immortal spirit. All supported by Indra, they appear with their purified bodies, which emerge only to refine others so they may gain additional strength. Like a sanctifying gear, they sit around, supported by the vibrations, which generate songs like those of their ancient fathers. They perform holy work to guard themselves from harm, bringing the eternal law (Varuna), which spreads throughout the aquatic air. Sages with mighty powers hold on to endure the coming floods. With exhaustless tongues, they send their voices down from the vault of the heavens, to pour into one thousand streams. Wild and restless, they as keepers continue to serve, never closing their eyes. They find in every place a bonding power that empowers the embodiments, including those who are blind. Serving as the father and the mother, in unison they bring a bright light and come roaring with verses of praise, burning any riteless living being. Indra protects those with swarthy skin who hate the supernatural might and dislike those who guide the noble souls with song from blowing away, serving as their counselor. From his ancient dwelling place, Indra comes quickly to help those who are blind and deaf. He turns such manifested embodiments far from the path that the wicked travel. He guides them to follow the path of the law, with one thousand filtering streams stretched across time like thoughtful sages, thereby purifying the songs. Bright colored as spies, the sages come vigorously, void of guile, excellent, and fair to beholder humankind. Guardians of the law, most wise, unable to be deceived by the three purifiers, come to settle within the heart. With wisdom, they behold all creatures and drive the hateful riteless ones into the pit. They spin the threads of sacrifice as if passing them through a purifying sieve, with the eternal law (Varuna) tongue-tied, to whom they attribute their supernatural might. This way they by strive to become prudent, not knowing this power shall go down into the abyss.

## IMAGINATIVE

According to *Rig-Veda* 9:74, on the ground, where large imaginary pillars support the sky with stalks of the heavenly plant soma, which moves itself every which way, filled with essence by the immortal universal soul (God), everything is brought together to create the material world, Virāj, which is located between heaven and earth. Every newborn manifested body within Virāj, as a youngling, cries and yells until it is red in the face and strong, ready to win the light of heaven. Serving as the heavenly embryos, the newborns swell in water and spread wide beneath the shelter, where they manifest in bodies and pray to the gods to learn the truth. They proceed with sacraments, rituals, and rites, all offered and supported by sages, so they may remain still as they receive food, that is, mythical juice. Mother Aditi, within this broad space, guides the mighty powers (divinities and deities) to the right path and provides them with well-made food, which consists of eternal wisdom blended with meath. Hence, manifested bodies, serving as younglings, gain control of the free-flowing waters and all kinds of animals, serving as prakriti and Mother Nature, Vasu, causing floods. With loud sounds, they help to transform milk into purified butter and draw animated mist from the center of the place of sacrifice to unite forever with love, appearing as the bounteous ones who form bonds of friendship with the younglings so they may swell and come down as rain, roaring, following the waves. The younglings offer vitality and provided with skin to experience godly enjoyment before they placed upon Mother Aditi's lap. With this, progeny brought to the region where essence extracted from the thousand streams to create the exhaustless ones. With the power of procreation, the exhaustless ones descend and reproduce in fours, dropping soma and filling them with the sacred gift of amrit. They strive to attain bounteous powers as they assume a pure white color, which brings them a heretofore hidden boon. They move down the steep slope, singing songs of sacrifice that burst the heavenly barrel holding the water, thus providing them with anointed milk in beakers before they move on to serve as conquering coursers.

The younglings have pious souls within their embodiments, sent as a gift, like milk-bearing cattle that through the hundred winters provide the pilgrim Kakṣīvān with mythical juice that blended with milk as it flows within streams. An embodiment thus represents a pious soul, which when cleansed manifests as a peafowl, which lives on the ground but can fly to bring forth heavenly beauty. As the best givers of delight, the peafowl grow with the sweetness of Indra's mythical drink.

According to *Rig-Veda* 9:75, graciously minded, flowing on their way, the youthful ones win dear names. As they grow to become great with mighty powers, they acquire vision and become far-seeing. They ascend to serve among the heavenly power Sūrya and look forth in all directions, serving as invincible heads of the hymn, speaking of sacrifices and, with their tongues, pouring forth with divine will, which with essence (meath) serves the lustrous region of heaven. As the offspring, they acquire the secret name of Sūrya. They are the sons of heaven and earth, with Sūrya serving as their mother and father. They sent forth upon flashes and bellow as they led to the golden reservoir filled with mythical juice. With milky streams of sacrifice, they sing forth with a triply high brightness that appears in the morning. With compressed cosmic stones (meteors), they graciously illuminate both heaven and earth, serving as the parents. Following onward, setting the seasons in order, they escape, though still swelling day by day with the sweet juice that brings prosperity, soma, which cleansed to empower the living beings who drink the milky draft as a gladdening drink. Exceedingly strong, foaming, it even incites Indra to give them wealth.

According to *Rig-Veda* 9:76, the potent juice as it flows comes to serve as the heavenly sustainer, supported by godly powers, which manifest as embodiments to hail with shouts of joy, thereby generating golden-hued coursers with brave bodies that impetuously win splendor in the streams. They take their weapons in hand and, like heroes, win over the light in battle to serve the animals floating within the holy river Indus, where the mighty Indra stimulates them. They urged forward and supported in their task by the skillful sages. Purified soma, flowing in rivers and making waves, once it enters their throats, gives them the strength to approach Indra. This way, the two worlds connected through the stream passing through their nostrils like lightning through the clouds, dispensing exhaustless power amid the singing of songs. They move onward, serving as the kings of the holy clairvoyant souls (rishis), and come to the light of the gods, rising with their songs of sacrifice. Even those who adorned with the bright rays of Sūrya arrive as beams supporting the father of hymns, whose wisdom is beyond reach. Appearing as a bull to the herds, they flow like thundering steer into the water's lap. As the best of cheerers, Indra flows along to provide them with protection and help them to overpower their enemies in the fight.

According to *Rig-Veda* 9:78, more beauteous than the beautiful, Indra, with his thunderbolt, brings sweet mythical juice from the vat. Like oil dropping in abundance, it comes to fill the streams, and as a sacrifice it flows unto the lowing cows with their milk. Along with the ancient one, they flow from heaven, speeding through the region, trembling with vibration. Like the flying falcon, they come to snatch the terrified heart without causing alarm, to behold as served with sweet soma by the bow-armed god Kṛśānu, serving as the messenger of Indra. With the first, freshest drops of soma juice, they become fully effused to flow on their way to endow all animals with mighty strength. Like a large, beautiful snake, worthy to looked upon, they come to provide sacred mythical juice to all, but only after all the prayers have offered to please the much-lauded holy river Indus. Having persuaded in their hearts, well knowing, they come to provide support in any fight against their enemies. They bring in the embryo or the primordial germ, seating themselves beside the Strong One, who moves onward to the wide-open stall of domesticated animals that serve humanity. The potent juice of heaven flows to protect all who observe the great eternal law, Varuna, whom no manifested embodiment can ever deceive. The holy spirit, along with eternal love (Mitra), comes to support them during times of trouble, like an impatient horse neighing amid the herd.

According to *Rig-Veda* 9:78, the king, with a raised voice, follows them as they move along. Vested with the waters, they fill their stomachs with mythical juice as needed to win all kinds of animals. The ground itself serves as a fleece, retaining any impurity, thus provide bright and clean filtered soma to the manifested embodiments, where it seeks out the special places. The embodiments blamed when the waves reach into the woods. The sages watching over humankind and other living things face many paths on which to move forward. Like one thousand bay steeds, living things find a resting place on the ground. Those who manifest and dwell within seawaters appear as celestial nymphs (*apsaras*), which each have a female spirit and a wise heart. The talented apsaras, flowing in the water filled with soma, come to serve as creative souls producing heavenly music. They urge the head of the house Gandharva, serving as the envoy of Indra, to follow the way to the eternal path. With bliss, and flowing with soma, they win animals in the thousands, their bodies floating in water with golden light. This is all created by the godly powers, who provide the gladdening draft to bring out the red-hued self-enkindled Pavamana. Serving as a faithful friend, Pavamana provides real treasures acquired by slaying the enemies, both near and, far, and grants both security and ample pasturage.

According to *Rig-Veda* 9:79, the compressed stones (meteors), golden hued, serving as godly powers, arrive from heaven. They give no gifts and no food to any who are godless until they attain success through prayers. With drops of distilled essence, the godly powers flow for those who have a serious urge and, like horses, find crafty ways to go beyond without hindering their mortal embodiments. They continually bear precious wealth that shows their sincerity as the true destroyers of those who hate noble souls. Like thirsting in the desert, they seek to conquer those who with evil thoughts who, as kin, praised high in the heavens. Upon a high ridge of the earth, their offspring grow up, but the compressed stones come to chew them up. After sages have milked the cows with their hands to fill the streams with soma, their hands become like ox hide. They seek divine strength along with enough soma to fill the holy river Indus. With the first taste of the draft, they granted a low level of awakening, as Pavamana fights every single foe.

According to *Rig-Veda* 9:80, the mythical juice is a sweet and gladdening drink that flows within rivers. Beholding humankind, with the everlasting law, it calls upon heaven to send the perishable Bṛhaspati, who comes roaring with lightning, with the power to create lakes on the earth for containing the mythical juice. The rivers flow with milk-bearing cows, who glow, as the divine establishes a house of iron. After lengthening the life spans of the highly renowned princes, they flow toward Indra, who with his mighty power provides the gladdening drink. The best giver of delight, Indra, through his throat, brings about a gladdening might to create the Auspicious One, who with fame and vision comes to spread himself abroad, meeting all things that with vigor, like the tawny steed, flow sportingly on their way. The visionaries among manifested mortal embodiments, with ten swift fingers, serving as godheads, milk cows to produce the richest essence (meath) floating within one thousand flowing streams. The soma itself wins over thousands, all driven as manifested embodiments. They hope to win even the compressed cosmic stones, which bring forth all the godly powers. Skillful handed, these visionary manifested embodiments, with their ten swift fingers, come along with compressed cosmic stones to channel the waters. As a guild, or as steer enriched with sweet soma, they are glad, along with other heavenly hosts, to be guided by Indra, who through the self-enkindled Pavamana creates waves within the rivers.

According to *Rig-Veda* 9:81, the powerful Indra, beauteously adorned, moves onward from the throat and then moves like waves to purify himself and produce the lovely curd that effused, bestowed upon the cheerful heroes as a gift. From there, the mythical juice flows into beakers served to the chariot horse, which swiftly turns into a stallion as it goes on its way. Thus, knowing both generations, the horse obtains the right from the gods to wander while subjected to purification, and then it scatters wealth into the holy river Indus to bestow a great bounty as a liberal prince. The giver of life and wisdom, the Indus generates opulence, which is sprinkle not at home but in faraway territories. Pūṣan comes as Pavamana, the two serving with one accord the bountiful Varuna and Mitra. They join to serve as the ruling perishable Bṛhaspati. They bring along other cosmic powers, including the Maruts, the Aśvins, Vayu, Savitar, Tvaṣṭṛ, and Sarasvatī. The heavens and the earth, along with all the other invigorating pairs—Vidhatar and Aditi, and Aryaman and Bhaga—are blessed to serve the spacious firmament (Prithvi) in which Pavamana takes delight.

## EMISSARY

According to *Rig-Veda* 9:82, even as king, Pavamana uses soma to regulate both energy from heaven (red in color) and matter from earth (tawny in color), to create compressed stones that appear as heavenly bulls. They serve as the Wondrous One, who hollers to all animals. Purified, they pass through the filter of the purifying fleece before they spread out over the ground with the mystical spirit the hawk, which has strong eyesight sharp enough to find the place to receive eternal wisdom like drops of oil. The Wondrous One seeks glory through other manifested mortal embodiments and, with grooming skills, becomes robust in power, gaining soma as a prize by graciously driving all distress out of the embodiments. As the milk does, they pass through cheesecloth to create butter, even coming to appear among robed embodiments.

Appearing as the deity of rain, Parjanya manifests among the mighty falcons. Like their father does, they fly over mountains and come to land in the center of the ground, where they make their home. Among the flowing water, they serve the Seven Sisters as rivers, appearing along with all kinds of heavenly compressed stones (meteors) to offer the beloved rite, like a wife provides delight to those who listen to her message and her desires. They appear to serve as the worshipper Pajri, who comes during the holy songs and goes on to live, watching in times of trouble to help free the falcons from blame. Like the ancient people, they come to the holy river Indus unharmed, to strengthen themselves, winning hundreds of thousands of spoils. With newfound happiness, they flow onward like the water, following the eternal law to become properly ordained.

According to *Rig-Veda* 9:83, they spread above the cleansing filter as a raw mass, serving the dormant universe that has neither subjected to heat nor has gained in physical appeal within the dynamic universe. Manifested as the perishable Bṛhaspati, seated high above the scorcher's sieve, the swift ones come to favor those who stand upon their purified consciences to serve as perishable manifested embodiments. They all stand separating the threads, generating a glittering light at the heights of heaven. As the best spotted steer, they direct the morning light with yearning and strength, so they can sustain the things surrounding them. With their great wisdom, like mighty sages, they appear to serve as the fathers, who behold the embryos laid down that will emerge as the manifested mortal embodiments. They, as Gandharva, the messenger of Indra, are all placed within protected physical bodies, where they will dwell. Wondrous, they guard the generations of the gods and serve as princes or lords. They capture foemen, and those who are most devout share in the eternal wealth, including the essence (meath) captured by the gods. With rich oblations, robed in clouds, they offer sacrifices to the divine as they sit with the godly powers. Manifested as the holy Bṛhaspati in perishable embodiments, they come to serve as kings. Riding in their chariots, and they go to fight the righteous war with one thousand weapons, and upon win granted fame.

According to *Rig-Veda* 9:84, the most active among the gods, who overcome the floods and serve as the trinity of Indra, Vayu, and Varuna, bestowed with happiness and placed in wide room, serving as an ample dwelling place, with living creatures serving the host of heaven, the imperishable Brahmaṇaspati. Those who come near to eternal wisdom as it flows go onward to serve in unison, providing effective aid, running through the holy river Indus. Floating on the ground, provided with heavenly light (Sūrya), they closely monitor the morning light and the water poured from the river to bring out the life from within the plants, which is considered a godly treasure that brings happiness. The river then pours forth with soma. With flashing lights, the gladdened god Indra serves the ground as part of the earth. The host of heaven providing illumination, Sūrya gives to the winner one thousand drops of mythical juice. Sūrya and Indra raise their voices with such vigor that they bring about the dawn, wakening all. Flowing, the holy river Indus, blown by the wind (Vayu), merges with the ocean, where it sinks into the water and comes to a rest. Then Sūrya and Indra manifest as milk-bearing animals.

With their mythical power, they produce an ever-increasing volume of milk as they acquire the superpower to become the invisible life force, which rises amid the songs with vibrations and heavenly light. For the winners of wealth, the mythical juice keeps flowing to help devotees, singers, and any devoted souls by providing them with the eternal wisdom that is dear to all, even those in heaven.

According to *Rig-Veda* 9:85, the mythical juice, flowing to serve Indra, carefully effused to prevent sickness in all who drink it. Indra will not allow anyone who is double-tongued to come near any drops of the juice loaded with opulence, especially the fiends. The manifested self urges all to drink soma to gain godly vigor, which needed to move forward in the fight. Well-loved ones, shouting with joy, rise to seek Indra and to drink soma, then smite their enemies and drive them away. Unharmed, the victors, with cheer, pass through the Indus, which continues to flow, carrying the noblest of food. With eternal wisdom rise with songs of praise, embracing the mortal embodiment that has attained eternal wisdom and is ready to serve as the sovereign of the manifested material world. Wondrous, one hundred streams, filled with hymns and one thousand songs, like the holy river Indus pours out the essence from the land that is under water. They flow forth herewith as a bounty within the mountains, following along with mythical juice, carving a broad path for all creations. Beakers of balm and milk, once they passed through the fleecy filter and carefully cleansed, decked as a prize for the charger, with the mythical juice flowing down into the throat, guided by Indra.

From there, Indra invoked like the other imperishable godly powers Mitra, Varuna, and Vayu and like the unchallengeable perishable embodiment Bṛhaspati. With ten rapid fingers, they all come to serve from the jar of essence (meath) and also given soma, and then manifest as a courser with wings, such as a horse or a bird. With hymns and holy prayers, they send forth their voices, all passing through the filter, as they hasten to offer a eulogy and gladdening drops, which move to find their way to Indra's heart. Truly purified, they pour out strength among heroes and offer shelter and wide pastures. Where there is no oppression, all holy work performed through serving the holy river Indus, with such work gaining the workers divine opulence. Those who see afar rise into the sky and, like holy sages, come to experience the ultimate heavenly illumination that shines among all. Within the king, the powers of soma roar, passing through the filter as it drains the milk of heaven, enabling the ones who drink it to comprehend the supreme powers of causation serving in the high vault of heaven. Unceasingly, the honey-tongued loving ones grow great with the lake waters that, its waves rich with meath, serve as the cleansing sieve. As the loving ones, they sought by many voices, like that of the eagle that has flown away to heaven. The younglings, worthy of laudation, resting on the earth as a bird golden color, look high toward the vault of heaven and see the risen Gandharva, beholding all his various forms and figures. Their rays shine abroad with gleaming splendor, serving as the parents, pure, lighting up the two worlds.

According to *Rig-Veda* 9:86, the self-enkindled Pavamana, with divine gladdening soma, is urged with songs to flow swiftly along with the sons of the fleet-footed chargers serving as emissaries and flying like the eagles of heaven, Astrojyoti, cheerful, rich in essence (meath), which they gather from the reservoir and give out as drops of mythical juice. They, like rapid chariot steeds, turn in ways, the exhilarating juices brought forth like drops of soma rich in essence (meath), tagged like the waves, serving Indra. As thunder-armed milk-bearing animals seek their calves to feed them milk, and like a prodded steed finds the light, they speed onward into the battle for the cloud-borne heavenly reservoir. Similarly, they guided over the woolly surface, seeking the sieve to purify the mythical juice as nourishment for Indra. With a fleet of swift steeds, dropping as they pour milk into the vat, the self-enkindled Pavamana and the sages (rishis) continuously pour out soma to ordain those friends whom the sages love and adore.

Serving as a visionary who see all things, the sovereign, with skills, passes like the rays that shine upon all abodes. Rife with natural power, he flows over the world, serving as king. Pavamana sends beams from earth to heaven with the ensigns, which, ever steadfast, travel around and, using the sieve, serve the cleansed golden-hued soma, which comes to rest within the vats, as where one sits in its place. Served with rites, the soma flows as an ensign of sacrifice and advances to the special place of godly powers. The soma speeds along with one thousand currents to fill the reservoir, where it passes through the filter, bellowing as a bull. The sovereign dips in the sea, in the streams, flowing within rivers and moving with the vibrations as a part of the waves. High heaven's sustainer, at the central point of earth, rises on the fleecy surface, where Pavamana stands, with a decree from the heavens and the earth, dependent upon the roaring thunder at the summit of the sky. Soma flows on, obtaining Indra's friendly love, and once it purified, it settles in the jars. With the light of sacrifice, extracted from the delicious meath, as a very wealthy father receives from the gods. With gladdening cheer, Indra loves the mythical juice, enriching it with mysterious treasure from earth and heaven. The vigorous visionary lord of heaven, far-seeing, shouts to the beaker to envision one thousand streams all colored gold and resting in the place where eternal love (Mitra) dwells and, as the guide, makes beautiful the rivers channeled like sheep.

Within the river, the self-enkindled Pavamana speeds ahead of the cows, sharing the great booty with those who fought on the front line in war, serving as a well-armed steer, purified by worshippers. This living spirit, Pavamana, like a bird sent forth with the waves, flows onward to the fleecy sieve. Indra, with eternal wisdom and noble thought, comes to serve between the earth and heaven as a holy one (sage), flowing with bright purified soma. The holy ones come, filling the firmament located between the two worlds. Knowing their realm of light, they come with rain to summon their own primeval sire, who first penetrates his form to provide those of his own race with shelter and defense. From their high station in the loftiest heaven, they come as victors to all whom they encounter, with the holy river Indus having already established as Indra's special place. They appear not as friends, but as the promise of friends, speeding onward. Youthful, they gain a hapless assistant from among the aid virgin s. On a blundering course, they come singing songs, exhilarating, tuneful, uttering praises as they enter the places where the people meet. Worshippers, exalting in their hymns and with mythical juice, draw near to meet with the milk-producing mothers whom the river Indus cleanses with mythical juice, pouring the soma out as plentiful nutritious food, which, unendingly, three times a day, provides the heroes with power, enriching them with nourishment, strength, and essence (meath). Seeing it flow, the steer, along with the lord of hymns, comes from the far side of the day. In the heavenly morning, the mythical juice comes floating in the streams, making the tumblers resound. The singers serve as aides to allow the cleansed mythical juice to enter Indra's heart. Within the bodies of the prudent singers, the soma flows like the spirit of an ancient sage who once guided manifested mortal embodiments and now comes with a roar toward the vats filled with mythical juice.

Through worshipping the divine powers Trita and Vayu, the singers change tack to offer meath to Indra. They become friends with him, drinking purified meath, which makes the mornings shine and spreads out to make more room for the rivers. In twenty-one streams, the rivers pour out the milky fluid that brings cheer, yielding whatever the heart finds to be sweet. Flowing onward, the soma flows in Trita and Vayu's celestial forms, filling the holy river Indus, pouring first into beakers and then through a sieve. It sinks into the throat, creating a roar, thus leading manifested mortal embodiments to appreciate the heavenly illumination provided by Sūrya. Compressed cosmic stones (meteors) flow onward toward the sieve in the holy river Indus, before entering the throat.

## SAGACIOUSNESS

The self-enkindled Pavamana, farsighted, now looks upon humanity and the animals filled with purified soma sitting among the high holy souls the Aṅgirases, who seek favor as, rejoicing, they come down from heaven in the form of a raptor (falcon). Herewith, sages come along with all forms of hymns to appear at the holy river Indus. Seven milk-bearing mothers, glorified amid the tawny-colored waves, purified in their own skin like wool. They come to meet with the mighty living being, propelled as sages into the water's lap, their place of sacrifice. After attaining purity from the Indus, they lunge at their foes as Ilis makes the way easy for the pious man to travel, making for all a kind of shroud, so they may run like sporting coursers onward through the fleece. The ceaseless fountains of water, with their hundred streams, sing as they hasten near the golden-hued ones clad in robes and providing milk with swift beautiful fingers, all coming from the third height of heaven. These are generations of the celestial seed that come to serve as the sovereign lords of all the world and all life, where the self-enkindled power Pavamana holds sway over the holy river Indus. The waters, such as the sea, become the first establishers of the eternal law, exposing the noble soul (sage) to the light within regulating the five regions of the world. The sages reach beyond the earth and into the heavenly region, from where it receives the light that filters and purifies mythical juice.

Once the soma is purified, Pavamana, supported by the godly region, serving as the chief, holds fast to his longing, until all the living creatures have turned to seek the godly powers. They travel onward, like the singer travels over the fleece-lined sieve, where the tawny steer, with hymns and songs, bellows into the wooden vats, singing loudly to create a resonant harmony and, like a child with holy songs, gives a kiss to claim the praise of all the others. Once invoked, the rays of the heavenly power Sūrya come spinning like a robe, tied in a bow with triply twisted thread. Guided by the holy law, they come to serve as the women's escorts to the special place. Amid the flow, the king of rivers, that is, the lord of heaven, follows the path of the holy law and, with a shout, pours forth as golden hued with one hundred streams, bringing wealth and uplifting his voice while purified. Pleased to cleansed, Pavamana outperforms Sūrya by making it through the fleece that covers the wide sea. Purified, pressing the stones with his hands, he speeds on to war to win the booty.

Pavamana sends food and power in streams, the food sitting in beakers as the hawk sits in the trees, and he pours this food out for Indra as cheering juice to make him glad, this farseeing bearer-up of heaven. The Seven Sisters, serving as the mothers, stand around the noble infant, all skilled in holy song, as the messenger Gandharva brings the floods. Divine, beholding the mythical juice, they reign as the kings of all the world. As sovereign lords, they pass through the river Indus, harnessing the tawny-winged chargers as they pour forth the milk and meath like oil-rich fire (eternal flame), allowing the people to abide in the divine proclamation. With power from the soma, they behold the living beings from all directions. The self-enkindled Pavamana guides them as they wander, beholding wealth, treasure, and gold, so all may have the strength to live longer as the winners of the gold and the goods. The cattle, impregnated, float in the Indus, in the middle of the manifested material world. Rich and brave are those who win all with soma, serving with the holy singers. They wait upon others while they sing. The waves of meath awaken desire. The steer, enrobed in milk, plunges into the stream.

Seen as the king ascending in his chariot, on his way to war, with one thousand rays and with his high renown, dear to all, Pavamana sends forth abundant triumphant praises, bringing offspring each day he succeeds. As Indra craves for Indus to provide divine quaff, Pavamana provides the blessing to bestow wealth upon his children and embraces his steeds. Each day, the strong soma, lovely, golden hued, is recognized more and more for the wisdom it stirs up in both the races as it goes between the two worlds as the bearer—the world of humankind and the world of the gods. All find solace and comfort in the mighty strength of the essence (meath). They seize the flying steer at the resting place in the stream. Cleansed with gold, they grasp the animals therein, singing forth skillfully to invoke Pavamana. With the holy song, the mythical juice flows onward like a mighty stream. It glides like a serpent from its ancient skin, as a playful horse running like a tawny steer. As a flood dweller, foremost, it displays its might, set up among living things as the measurer of days. Distilled mythical juice flows like oil, fair, billowy, of golden hue, to borne like a vehicle of light, sharing a home with wealth. Loose in the heavens to provide support, uplifting and cheering the one who drinks, the triply mixed draft flows round the world. The holy hymns speak to the stalk, which claims the praise when singers approached its beauteous embodiment with song. Then the soma flows forth rapidly, collected to run over the body like fine fleece cleansed. When the balm from the river Indus mixed with milk within a bowl, it sinks into the jars filled with soma served to the winners of power. Worthy of laudation, they run onward from the fleece, as the well-loved meath moves along with the river, destroying all voracious evil powers (rakshasas). As brave sons, the winners arrive at the assembly, where they speak as the bold ones.

According to *Rig-Veda* 9:87, the bold ones run onward to the reservoir and find a seat, then cleansed. They speed forward after having purified to join in the struggle and support the beautiful courser that, with its reins, leads others to fly forth from the sacred grass. Well-armed by the godly powers, flowing onward like the holy river Indus, the bold ones lift the curse and guard themselves against the treacherous onslaught. As fathers, the begetters of the gods, and with very skillful flying, they receive reinforcement from the heavens and support from earthly powers. Serving as seers (rishis) and noble souls (sages), they come as the champions of the manifested moral embodiments, serving with wisdom. Astute and sagacious, they cleave the queen Uśanā from the heavenly power Rudra to discover the hidden nature concealed among milk-bearing creatures, which carry the most mysterious living things. This divine mysterious living thing takes its own water and converts it into milk, which then becomes the mythical juice soma. It creates enriched meath, from which the astral body appears in order to provide a living spirit for the physical embodiment.

The self-enkindled Pavamana appears as a steer, coming along with Indra to offer the mythical juice, all flowing through the filter. He appears as a strong one who gives freely, winning over hundreds of thousands who, without fail, seek to live on the holy grass. Among cattle, the mythical juice, as uncountable wealth, becomes renowned for providing immortal strength. The cattle sent forth among steeds, the purified leader rushing into battle to attain glory. While the soma cleanses itself like a colander, it invokes others to flow forth to bring enjoyment to the manifested mortal embodiments.

As a large raptor, such as a falcon, it brings dainty viands, which by themselves send booty and wealth. The mythical juice pressed through the cleansing filter comes to serve as the host of those who loosen the reins on animals with wings, including birds and flying coursers. The heavenly bull remains strong with its sharp-pointed horns, sending the brave warriors forth into the fray to seek the loftiest mountain, where the milk-bearing animals hidden somewhere in a cave or locked in a stable. Indra clears himself to allow the stream to flow with mythical juice, which passes through the clouds of heaven amid lightning and thunder caused by Indra. Cleansing themselves, the warriors borne on the ground, appearing among a herd of cattle, where they receive praise from the Mighty One, which prompts them to become fully bestowed, ready to serve as suppliers of ample food.

According to *Rig-Veda* 9:88, Indra comes to drink the fully effused mythical juice that flows in the stream. He chooses to serve the holy river Indus. As the Indus serves up this special drink, all the warriors cheer and celebrate. The mighty ones acquire abundant treasures, which they offer in celebration of their triumph in the battle with the lunar dynasty of Nahuṣa.

The twin Aśvins come along to invoke the wind, Vayu, who is most gracious to physically enhance them. The Aśvins are later mentally enhanced to serve as Nāsatyas, who become the wealth givers. With mythical juice, they bring a boon, serving the patron Pūṣan with inspirational songs.

Indra monitors the Nāsatyas as they perform great deeds, including the drinking of soma. Knowing that they can destroy forts with their mythical power, the patron Pūṣan brings a white horse, Pedu, and under the special protection of the demigods, kills the progeny of serpents and, with the mythical juice, slays every evil power (Dāsas). Like Agni, when they let loose amid the forest, the Dāsas, with a fierce fire, destroy any splendor. Indra creates splendor with running water. The mighty god Rudra, with a roaring wind, enters the fight. With soma allowing the individual living spirit released, Pavamana manifests. In its current form, the soma, passing through the clouds, descends with the rain. When effused, the soma, swiftly flowing, breaks away like a running river, soon reaching the sea. Flowing onward, it invokes the potent band of cosmic hosts the Maruts, whom none revile. Gracious unto others, like water, offering a thousandfold sacrifice for victory, the kings honor the eternal law (Varuna) and its statutes, lofty and glorious, with pure soma, with eternal love (Mitra) appearing as the beloved and adored Aryaman.

According to *Rig-Veda* 9:89, the chariot horses move along the pathways established by Pavamana. They flow like rain from heaven and, with a thousand currents, allow soma to sink within plants, trees, and other forms of vegetation, hiding like milk within a mother's bosom. The king cloaks the horses within the robes of the rivers, all mounted like straight ships sailing ahead as ordered. With speed like that of the hawk, they drop soma that has purified in water, which flows from father to son to bring about offspring for the father. They come as red tawny steers, physically strong, from the lord of heaven, and appear with a watchful tawny lion, supported by the guardian of the essence (meath). They appear as the first hero, who in the fight seeks cattle and, with his eye, provides the steer protection. They harness the broad-wheeled carriage, which pulled by mighty coursers, which backed with meath as they bear up, enduring that which is appalling.

The twin sisters, serving as mothers, bright and with strength, watch their children: one female, the other male. With vigor, both, as racers, pour out the holy oil, providing eternal strength. Sitting together, they attend everything, as they are in the same container. They flow with purified soma, paying homage, moving in all directions reinforced by the heavens and supported by the earth. Keeping all the creations in hand, serving as the team's lords, as well as the singers, remaining cleansed in the sweet stalk, they perform their deed of glory. Fighting, uninjured, as the evil-slayer, Indra, serving as the godhead, vouchsafes all with ample riches, splendidly serving as the head heroic vigor.

## PATH OF ORDER

According to *Rig-Veda* 9:90, urged upon, Indra comes with a carriage. Serving both earth and heaven, he goes forth to gather booty. He sharpens weapons on the ground, and with his hands containing every treasure, intoning a sacred song, he comes to guide from the triple height of heaven, serving to bestow life. While dwelling among wood and stones, serving as the lord of eternal law, Varuna floats in rivers with lavish treasure distributed along with blessings. Like a great conqueror, the lord of all heroes comes flying as the winner of riches, and with sharpened arms and a swift bow, never vanquished in battle or in any fight with the foemen. Providing security to the lord of the wide dominion, Indra and Varuna send forth to the earth and heaven with their all fullness. They come striving to win the morning light and the waters and call upon cattle with abundant vigor. The united Varuna and Mitra, cheering the holy river Indus, along with the self-enkindled Pavamana, come along with Indra and the Sustainer, Vishnu, as cheering godly powers. They all appear with the company of cosmic hosts (Maruts) and the holy river Indus. They cheer and rejoice in the mighty powers of Indra. Thus, like a wise and potent king, they all flow onward, vigorously destroying every kind of misfortune. They come with well-spoken hymns to provide long lives to those who deserve it, preserving creation evermore with blessings.

According to *Rig-Veda* 9:91, in a chariot race, the skillful speaker, chief, sage, or inventor of hymns serves upon the ground, settling in his resting place along the river with his horse wagon. With drops of soma pressed by the wise Nahuṣa, immortals and mortals made beautiful for the banquet, all coming from the holy river Indus, provided with sheep and cows. They come roaring with a guide, the self-enkindled Pavamana, who brings soma along with white milk from milk-bearing animals, passing it through one thousand fine hairs to generate the tunes for the singers.

The heavenly power Sūrya knows the one and only path to eternal truth. Traveling this fair and open pathway, he breaks the strongly seated demons. After going through the cleansing process within the Indus, Sūrya robed in vigor and, with a swift bolt, tears apart the higher powers both near and far. Fully prepared, he goes forward on the path in the ancient manner, but with a new hymn, to give all the bounty to those on high whom any foe finds difficult to conquer. With gifts of food and purification, Sūrya vouchsafes the waters of the earth and the light of heaven. Milk-bearing animals such as cows offer their offspring the milk that provides health, ample land, and the light that grants soma, providing them with long lives to look upon the sunshine.

According to *Rig-Veda* 9:92, the golden-hued juice, once poured through the filter, sent forth to conquer with song. It gains vigor after cleansed, with the godly powers rejoicing and entertained. The holy spirit, as the filter, bearing the name of a sage, seeks a dwelling place. The holy rishis come with seven holy singers, who settle as invokers among the two worlds, heaven and earth. The wisest, most propitious godly powers drink the soma as head toward the cleansing station. They rejoice in the same lofty wisdom provided to the initial five tribes. They labor to become sages and to regain that mysterious place where soma served to give birth to Pavamana, who serves all thirty-three gods. Serving from the ten highest mountains, the mighty god prompts the seven fresh rivers, brightened and adorned, to serve the godly powers. Now the rivers let the eternal truth be known to the self-enkindled Pavamana, who comes along with singers and other worshippers. They are all provided enough room and daylight to receive the cosmic body and noble power Manu, who repels the evil Dāsas. Serving as a priest, the noble Manu seeks a station rich in cattle and goes forth as a true king, serving amid the great assembly, where soma brought forth in beakers. Appearing as a wild bull, the noble power Manu serves in the forest where he first came to settle.

According to *Rig-Veda* 9:93, ten heavenly deities come pouring out rain upon swift-moving thinkers as they adorn sages who run like the golden-hued children of the heavenly power Sūrya, reaching the vat like a fleet of vigorous coursers. Even as a youngling, they come crying to their mothers (cows) and their bounteous fathers (bulls) like steer flowing along with the water. As young cows with soma and milk, they hasten to meet at the preordained meeting place, the beaker. From the swollen udders of milk-bearing animals, they stream forth to serve the holy river Indus. This readies them with washed treasure to serve the head and chief of the milk within the vessels. Serving all the gods on the river Indus, the manifested chiefs appear with a roar, showing their physical strength like horses. They come in a carriage, willing to give away of their treasure. Now they dispense their riches, cleansed of their glorious wealth, distributed among the great heroes. With their long lives, they worship the holy river Indus, enriching it with prayer to come soon.

According to *Rig-Veda* 9:94, the chiefs, with their beautiful chargers, strive with songs, serving as soldiers of sunlight. Acting as sages, they flow within the water and, with song, ask for all kinds to prosper. The world expands for those who formerly found the light dispensing the eternal law of life. Swelling with song for all kinds that live in stables, the chiefs, with deep devotion, loudly call upon the holy river. The sages with their holy wisdom visit all worlds in their carriage. Serving as heroes, they gain fame like the demigods, along with material wealth and the skills to praise the ever-present demigods. This is how glory is born—and the heroes come forth to give such glory to the singers. Clothed in glory, they become immortal as they measured by their success in battle. The stream provides food and vigor to all kinds, including cows and horses. They give a broad spectrum of light that fills the gods with rapture. Things become easy to master. The self-enkindled Pavamana, with soma, quells the foemen.

According to *Rig-Veda* 9:95, when the tawny steeds, neighing loudly, settle deep within the wooden vessel, they cleansed and then led off by folks who take their milk and, through its powers, sing songs of praise. As one who rows a boat, golden hued, they speak forth with their voices for those who have been set loose on the path of order. Uttering the secret names of the gods, they arise from the sacred grass and hasten onward like the waves in the sea, singing holy hymns as nigh they come to press the soma. They come with adoration and longing to drain the stalks and allow the steer to dwell on mountains. Serving as bulls, decked in the uplands, singing hymns, they bellow as they attended. Trita, along with the eternal law (Varuna), comes from aloft to appear in the ocean. Sending their voices out as directors to loosen the invokers' thought process, serving in the holy river Indus, Trita and Varuna cleansed with soma, while Indra rules and seeks the advantage, all three seeking to become with heroic vigor.

According to *Rig-Veda* 9:96, at the front of the carriage, they go forth as the heroes, the leaders, winning all the spoils, serving as the hosts. Rejoicing, they provided with soma and with robes of colors. Blessed with friends, they jointly call on Indra. Manifested mortal embodiments decked with gold and with their golden tendrils adorned offer compelling homage. The friends of Indra, they mount their carriage, knowing well the eternal truth. They offer prayers to the gods and flow onward with sublime food and soma. With floods from earth and heaven, they come from immense space to bring comfort while they cleanse others in the flow for prosperity. With constant vigor, they flow on, seeking happiness and perfection. With this wish, friends assemble to honor the self-enkindled Pavamana, the father of holy hymns. They flow onward to serve the rulers of earth and heaven, with the father of the eternal flame, Agni, supporting the heavenly generator Sūrya, who begets the trinity of Indra, Vishnu, and Brahma. They bring along the leaders of the spiritual hymns (rishis) and come to control the savage oxen, serving amid the vultures and the fast-flying raptors (falcons).

To cleave the forests and produce soma, which he cleanses with a sieve, Pavamana appears within the river and stirs the water into waves, generating voices and producing songs of praise. Beholding the inferior powers, he brings cattle, which come to rest, well knowing they protected by the oxen, which serve as the warriors among all domesticated animals. In battle, they never do harm; instead, they fill the thousand amiable streams that pour forth with strength and vigor to support the thoughtful Pavamana. They manifest in the holy river Indus and support the domesticated animals, appearing like plants that move to create waves. Grateful to the gods, they place the soma in a beaker to delight Indra. With one hundred powers flowing with the thousand currents of the river Indus, they move like a carriage pulled by horses, heading to the assembly. Born in times of old, before the world came into existence, they become the finders of treasures, which they drain with compressed stones, decking themselves in the waters. Warding off curses, they find a new way to pray while they cleanse themselves.

Serving as the father of the sages, the self-enkindled Pavamana performs his old sacred duties. Fighting unvanquished, he opens the enclosures holding back the large steeds that he gives as a gift to the heroes. Life-bestowing Manu, as the foe-killer and comforter, rich in oblations, flows onward, now conferring riches and, with Indra, bringing forth weapons. They flow onward with the rich, holy, sweet soma, enrobed in waters on the fleecy summit. The soma settles in vessels, which become filled with the most gladdening drink. It pours forth in one hundred streams, to serve to the victorious gods at the banquet. With a divine roar, the gods pour out rain from heaven and into beakers, where blended with milk to prolong life. Purified with holy hymns, the soma defeats the malign powers. Strong coursers bring the fresh milk poured by Mother Aditi. Making their passage through a wide space, pressers cleanse them. Armed with noble weapons, they stream forth, bearing a secret name. With love and glory, the strong horses appear as the wind (Vayu) and the cosmic hosts (Maruts) in their adorned carriage. At its birth, they deck the lovely infant in songs and with the wisdom of poets and sages as they go singing through the cleansing filter. The leader of the sages (rishis), with one thousand hymns, strives to find another form of soma that, like the majestic Virāj, could bring forth splendid singers who, like the hawk, seated between earth and heaven. As birds with wide wingspans, they seek all kinds of weapons, following close to the sea and its waves.

The great bull assumes his fourth form and makes a declaration like a fair youth who decorates his body like the coursers. Rushing to gain riches, the herd of steers flow to the pitcher and, with a roar, pour what they have into the beakers. They flow on with mighty Pavamana within the Indus, loudly roaring as they pass through the fleecy filter. Entering the beakers, they cleansed, with the gladdening soma going on to make Indra joyful, with all the streams of soma, fully effused, mixing with the milk in the goblets. Singing psalms, well skilled in song, as chanters, the steers roar and chase any foes away from the mighty Pavamana who, entering the Indus, sings as a lover to his sweetheart. As a bird flies and settles in the forest, the mythical juice settles, purified, in goblets. A stream full of soma mixed with milk challenged by a beam of light that comes, golden hued, rich in boons, to cleanse, brought to the waters like a woman, where it roars within the chalices of the pious ones.

## DIVINE BEING

According to *Rig-Veda* 9:97, with urgency and great passion, the godly powers impart their powers to the singers, who sing as the soma is poured over the filter to measure its power and determine if it could be supplied to the priest, fairly robed, who pronounces invocations so the mighty sages will win in battle. The sages roll onward with beakers filled with purified soma, hoping to join the far-seeing godly powers at the feast, where they may watch and observe from the fleecy summit. The prince, nobler than the nobles, purified, roars and runs forward to preserve the blessings forevermore by offering praises to the gods, singing loudly and sending forth the mythical juice in exchange for great riches. The flowing soma, with a sweet flavor, passes through the filter. The pious ones come to rest near the pitcher. Winning the friendship of the deities, they, as divine beings, come to flow in one thousand streams that make them joyful, such as the holy river Indus. Praised after the ancient ruling, they come nigh, seeking great bliss from Indra. Flowing, golden hued, cleansing themselves, and enriched, the singers bring soma in support of Indra. They come nigh together with the gods for bounty and preserved evermore with blessings. The god Uśanā, proclaiming lofty wisdom, declares this as the generation of divine beings serving as deities. With their brilliant kin, far-ruling, sanctifying even the wild boar, they advance, singing like the swan Vrishagana. They bring restless spirits into their dwellings and, like friends, meet Pavamana with praises, singing in concert with the music. They follow with a wide stride and move rapidly, sporting with pleasure and lowing like cows. With sharpened horns, they bring forth an abundantly silvery shine, at night and by day becoming golden and strong. They bathe in the river Indus, serving Indra, with soma enhancing their strength to make them joyful and able to quell malignity and slay the demons that make the mighty kings uncomfortable. In a stream, they flow like milk out of compressed stones, mingled with sweetness, passing through the fleecy filter. The river Indus rejoices in the love of Indra, the god who gladdens others for his own enjoyment. As Indra purified, he pours out treasures, a god bedewing gods with their own juice. The river Indus, changing in quality with the seasons, on the raised fleece, is engaged with ten swift fingers. The red bull, bellowing to drive forth the domesticated cattle, causes the heavens and the earth to roar and thunder. Indra, through his armor, shouts in battle, letting his voice rise and be known. Swelling with milk, abounding in sweet flavors, the soma-rich plants provide essence (meath) for the herd to move forward. Shouting, the herds cleansed by the mythical juice, becoming fully effused. Soma flows through them, inspiriting them, creating rapture among those aiming for the death shafts. They continue flowing with the water, wearing raiment resplendent in color, all effused, eager to support creation. Pleased with the Indus, they send it forth to flow along an easy path, with ample space to provide comfort. Dispelling any misfortune, the river runs over the heights, over the fleecy summit, and pours down as celestial rain, falling hard, refreshing the earth, bringing with it health and bounty. Flowing, the Indus uses the wind (Vayu) to speak to the lower relatives and set them free like locks of hair loosened from a braid. Like a knotted tangle, they fall part as they cleansed with the mythical juice and learn to comport themselves with true righteous conduct. They neigh like tawny coursers and, loosened, come like young ones to serve in the house of the gods. With delight, they serve the river of the gods, Indus, which runs over the heights, over the fleecy summit. With one thousand streams, inviolate, it moves with its sweetly scented flow to provide the strength needed by conquerors and heroes. Without a carriage, without reins, they guided yet unyoked, until they become like contestants or coursers, either flying or not flying. With brilliant drops of soma juice, they run forward to serve as divine beings, coming nigh to drink at the banquet of the gods.

The holy river Indus pours down rain from heaven into the vessels. Soma as one of the riches sought with longing by the exceedingly strong heroes. With the word of the loving spirit in the form of itself, the chief of all food appears with the highest statute. Then loudly lowing like the cows, as chosen and well loved by the holy river Indus, the head of soma in the beakers, the heroes appear as liberal celestial sages, carrying with them a bounty of rain that pours as they flow like authentic absolute truth. They endow their king with the strength to hold the ten bright reins, as the supreme powers of causation, as deities, guide humankind, subjecting them to purification through filters. As the king of the supreme powers of causation, Indra, lord of riches, uses immortal deities and half-mortal demigods to distribute the ancient treasure. He also uses the Indus, which he cherishes and keeps in divine order. In haste like steeds, coming in victory and with glory, they reach Indra, then use the powers of the wind (Vayu) to generate vibrations and oscillations that produce hymns and songs to serve as a source of entertainment. They provide thousands with ample food, along with mythical juice, honoring those riches once they cleansed. Fully effused with God-delighting soma, they flow home with the soma to serve to the nobles. Rich in boons, like priests, they acquire favor and, as the best of cheerers, serve as heavenly worshippers.

Serving as creator of the gods, Indra comes to the holy river Indus to support its onward flow as it carries the soma of the gods along with ample food. Jointly, the gods go forth in war against the well-established mighty powers of causation, serving the heavens and the earth.

The strong manifested bodies yoked like coursers, swift of thought, appear as lions. The carriage follows directly along a path to send them forth with happiness. Appearing in the holy river Indus, they cleansed and then spring up to join with godly powers in one hundred streams, effused as one thousand sages. They prepare and purge, coming from heaven, showing the strength of the Indus, known as the forerunner of abundant riches. Like the streams, they pour forth as if from heaven—the wise king who treats others with kindness and friendliness. Like a son following his father's wishes, they grant the family success and safety. Now, like the streams, they pour forth with all their sweetness purified. They make everything go through the filter.

The race of milk-bearing creatures given a special gift by Pavarridna to bear children who will serve the heavenly body rich in brightness, Sūrya. Bright, bellowing along the path of order, they come to shine as the eternal flame. They flow as a gladdening drink for Indra, sending their divinely willed voices forth with the holy hymns of sages. Pouring out like streams providing the gods' feast with soma, they are always looking down like the heavenly eagle. The beaker holding the soma enters the river Indus and, with a roar, approaches like a ray of light from Sūrya. As the first of three voices, the courser utters through its prayers the law of order. The second voice comes from the mother cow, singing hymns to the master, eagerly longing for soma. Sages with their hymns obtain effused soma, which purifies them, and offer to blend the hymns to create other songs for Tṛṣṭup, who unites them with soma. Thus, soma poured into vessels, purified to serve the welfare of all, and passed onto Indra, who, with roaring voice, makes it swell, generating an abundance of the mythical draft. The third voice comes from the singer who, through singing true songs, ever watchful, helps the soma to settle within in the ladles. The courser, the mother cow, and the singer further cleansed and served by holy sages (*adhvaryus*). Paired up, they eagerly follow the leaders of the sacrifice and, with their hands clean, offer purified soma to the Creator who resides everywhere, filling the space between heaven and earth, forever undisclosed. The Creator helps manifested embodiments obtain everything they wish for and provides everything the victors need. Cleansed, the Strengthener and the Increaser provided with a bounty of soma, which helps them to gain luster. The old sires, who know the footsteps, come with the light that used to find the stolen cattle on the mountain.

In the first vault of heaven, and in the ocean, with a loud roar, the king of all being comes to search for the creatures. He looks in the filter, on the fleecy summit, and within the effused drops. With soma, the child of the water appears like a steer. He is chosen by the gods to perform great deeds, serving like Pavamana, granted strength by the godhead Indra, and served by the river Indus, all generating light like the heavenly power Sūrya. This makes Vayu glad to go farther and increase the bounty with cheer to honor the eternal law (Varuna) and eternal love (Mitra), who cleanse the other gods, also gladdening the cosmic hosts (Maruts), thereby causing all of heaven and earth to rejoice with the powers of soma. They flow onward like righteous souls who slay the wicked, driving away enemies and sickness. They blend their milk with the milk provided by cows to serve to the friends of Indra. They pour forth with meath, which brings a wellspring of treasure that sent to the heroes as a happy fortune brought by Indra cleansed within the Indus, which pours riches into the ocean. Strong pressed soma, like the impetuous coursers, flows in the stream, speeding downward with the floodwaters. Cleansed, it settles within the wooden vats, flowing with milk and water in the Indus.

Those who are strong and wise long for the coming of the soma. Indra's chariot comes with the bright sun, pouring the potent soma upon the pious. Purified, with ancient vitality, the soma, like the daughters of Sūrya, penetrates are forms of creation. The creations find a threefold refuge in the waters, all coming singing like a priest to the assembly. Now, chariot-borne, the mythical fluid flows unto the worshippers as godly soma, purified and flowing into saucers. It is sweet with water, rich in meath, and holy as the truthful-minded goddess Savitar. Vayu comes to the feast purified by eternal law (Varuna) and eternal love (Mitra). They all flow as the inspirational song, leading the carriage of newborn heroes, with mighty Indra, wielding thunder, provides garments to clothe the embodiments and send them forth as purified to meet the milk-bearing mother.

An abundant yielder of soma, Indra draws his chariot horses so they may bring treasures, bright and golden, which come in a stream as celestial riches, all cleansed, emerging from the ground. Thereby the heroes acquire possessions to serve the holy souls (rishis). One of the manifested seven rishis, Jamadagni, pours forth with purified wealth, flowing onward with the holy yellow water of the Indus filling the deep holes such as lakes. The heavenly power Rudra comes with the swift wind, Vayu, full of eternal wisdom, and quickly comes to appear among the newborn nobles.

Those who have purified and have become famous come in search of glory. Serving as foe-killers, in triumph they fruit trees, the ripe fruit dropping, as sixty thousand. They eagerly pray for the defenseless living beings the *Prishana*, who exploit the clean blue lake as they strive forth in battle. The gods send them off, or turn them away as enemies, or slay them, all appearing foolish and unfriendly. Indra comes unto the three extended filters and hastily passes through each one, cleansed. Serving as patrons are the gift giver Bhaga and the liberal lord Maghavan, who, with the free-flowing waters of the Indus, flowing with soma, bring essence (meath) to provide wisdom to all who drink it. They all flow together on the way to from nonexistence to existence, appearing as noble rulers and serving as kings. The Indus drives the drops of mythical juice to the assembly after it passes through the fleecy filter. The Great Inviolate One, drinking water from the Indus, comes singing to the assembly like an eager sage. Wise men come with ten swift fingers, providing a balm to humankind. The water brings essence (meath) mixed with soma, thus establishing the freely moving self-enkindled Pavamana, with everything piling up like the spoils of war. This boon vouchsafed by the eternal law (Varuna) and eternal love (Mitra), who supported by the heavenly mother Aditi and the holy river Indus, which are both supported by the powers of matter (earth) and energy (heaven).

## DEFENSELESSNESS

According to *Rig-Veda* 9:98, the streams best at providing strength are filled with riches and are sought by many in the thousands, but these thousands are conquered by the great ruler Pavamana, who comes with fully effused soma, moving onward with the holy river Indus, surrounded by plants and trees. Distilling soma through fleece, Pavamana stands to seek light and a living thing to offer as a sacrifice. The holy river Indus, representing godly power to every mortal worshipper, attracts riches in the thousandfold, all manifested in one hundred forms. Serving as an evil slayer, Pavamana has much in material wealth. He craves food and happiness and is hard to resist.

The native plant crushed between a pair of pressing stones. The wavy Indus River loved by Indra. The ten sisters, beloved by all, by bathing in the holy river with fleece, purify their bodies, which take on a golden-brown hue. With the exhilarating juice, they come forth to serve all the deities. Longing for soma as a drink that enables even those who are dear to heaven, they receive it and thereby become worshippers who serve the highly renowned princes. With holy rites, the river comes to serve heaven and earth as their friend. The goddesses bruised when the calmly moving river roars loudly to serve the Vṛtra-slaying god Indra, who drinks down the soma, serving as the guardian, as the goddesses come to sit with the gods. At the break of day, these ancient powers flow into the sieve, snorting away early in the morn like foolish evil hearted ones. Being friends of princes, they treated as most resplendent one. Regaining their sense of smell, they come with great strength to win a home for themselves.

According to *Rig-Veda* 9:99, with boldness and love, the goddesses vigorously create an arch and, singing songs, move in front of it to don bright attire, while in the back, the divine lord serves soma to the self-enkindled Pavamana. At night they take the plunge and move forward, strengthening themselves with food. Their thoughts run quickly as they turn a golden hue and drink of the purified soma, which chiefly Indra drinks. All animals take it into their mouths, just like the old kings did—and now new princes take over. While purified, they sing ancient psalms and songs of praise, now bearing the names of the gods, who pray along with them. With purified drops, courageous in the fleecy sieve, they serve as godly messengers, speaking the sages' morning prayer. The best of the cheerers, they take their seats, cleansing their innards with soma. Like a pregnant cow, they babble on, worshipping the lord with song, fully effused and beautified like the god among all gods, penetrating even the mighty floods and collecting eternal wisdom and all that is known. Then they flow with the river Indus, guided to the cleaning sieve. Indra, yielding the highest joy, provides them a seat within the two worlds, heaven and earth.

According to *Rig-Veda* 9:100, the guileless ones, in the morning, sing praises to Indra as a well-beloved friend, while the mothers lick their newborn calves. While the river Indus cleanses the mythical juice, it brings forth doubly refined wealth to distribute among the worshippers, increasing their treasure. The worshippers are set free from all the songs that yoke the mind, just like thunder, when the rain comes, frees all the treasures of earth and heaven, which allows the mythical juice to increase in quantity. The stream, when pressed through the sieve, runs on like some victorious warrior's steed, hastening onward through the fleece like a fierce horse to win the prize. The soma keeps flowing with the stream, the sages gaining in mental power and strength, the mythical juice effused for Indra to drink along with eternal love (Mitra) and eternal law (Varuna). The three gods flow toward the filter with the stream, all effused and serving among the best victors.

The richest and sweetest soma reserved for the gods Indra and Vishnu, and others. The mother cows, void of guile, caress their golden-colored calves, as the self-invoked Pavamana licks the newborn calves, following the divine law, and commands them to move on with wondrous rays. Highly renowned, striving within the homes of his devotees to drive away all their gloom, the lord of great sway lifts them above the earth and takes them to heaven, where, as Pavamana, he assumes the coat of majesty.

According to *Rig-Veda* 9:101, as their first possession, the newborns receive an exhilarating draft of soma, which they drink like a dog with a long tongue. Purified and effused, they flow hitherward like able steeds in the river. Humans sing an all-pervasive song and bring forth a sacrifice to receive the soma purified through the compressed stones. The soma, rich and sweet, is destined for the sieve to become effused, being the source of Indra's joy. The strong juice reaches the gods.

Within the river Indus, soma flows on for Indra's sake and for the sake of the deities. The lord of speech exerts himself as ruler of all. As mighty inciters of the voice behind the song, like one thousand streams flowing to the ocean, day by day, as the lords of opulence, serving the friend Indra, the patron Pūṣan and the fortunate Bhaga come with purified soma. These lords of the multitudes look upon the earth and heaven were dear cows low in s joyful mood, together consuming the gladdening drink. Pavamana the mighty, worthy of fame, takes the drops of purified soma to the five tribes, which makes them opulent. The soma flows in drops to the unblemished, the friends without a spot, the benevolent ones, finders of the light. Effused by means of compressed stones, soma carried upon ox hide for the treasure finders, the food coming from all directions. The soma juice, accompanied by song, purified, combined with milk and curd, when moving or when firmly set in oil, resembles the lovely rays coming from the sun. Let not the power of humanity restrain the voice of such outpouring of juice, as Bhrigu's sons chase *Makha* to drive away the greedy hounds.

According to *Rig-Veda* 9:102, the godly messenger, as a child, appears in the streams and follows the plan of sacrifice, bypassing all things that were dear in the past and coming to occupy a position near the sun god Trita, coming among compressed stones, serving in secret, passing through the seven lights of sacrifice. Serving in the heights with Trita, the child reaches the stream that runs in three courses. He regarded as wise enough to measure these courses. At birth, he taught by his seven mothers to serve like a sage, firm and sure, with his mind set on eternal wealth. Under his sway, of one accord, all serve guilelessly as righteous warriors or as deities who are both honored and coveted. The child strengthens the law to generate a much longed for sacrifice. Appearing as a most liberal sage, he, by himself, comes to perform rites like his young parents. He adorned in woven clothes and possesses wisdom, his radiant eyes open to proceed with the sacrifice. During the solemn rite, he seeks a heavenly plan to implement the holy law.

According to *Rig-Veda* 9:103, purified ordained priests, their voices raised in song, bring meath and soma as they sing holy hymns. Blending milk with curd, they pass it through the wool filter until it turns a golden hue, purified. The priests sit on three seats to rest, looking at the large wool filter that produces essence (meath) and soma, which overflows the vat, drops dripping out. The seven holy souls (rishis) loudly sing hymns to praise all the godly infallible powers, those leading the hymns taking on a gold hued. The soma is purified before reaching the two extremes, that is, heaven and earth. With godlike qualities, the rishis associate with Indra, the Immortal One, and go forth serving as purified priests.

According to *Rig-Veda* 9:104, sitting down as friends, the priests who purified sing loudly to the Immortal One. As children, they decked for glory. Performing holy rites, they unite, bringing wealth to the households, including calves and their mothers. With double strength, the godly powers provide the gladdening soma. Once purified, the rishis given the power to serve as the most blessed ones at a banquet arranged for the troops serving eternal love (Mitra) and the eternal law (Varuna). Singing loudly, they find the hidden wealth meant for them. They clothed in robes the color of milk, the same hue as the river Indus. With godly food, and as sovereigns, they offered the gladdening drink to all. As friends among friends, they achieve success, driving off all demons and voracious fiends. With these godless ones eliminated, they keep sorrow and falsehood far away.

According to *Rig-Veda* 9:105, Indra, like a mighty steer, brings the gold-colored juice produced by the light of heaven, having found a way to keep the soma flowing through the purifying sieve given that he is the best among all conquerors. The conquer gains control by gathering up the spoils, in this case all free-flowing water, and capturing all the cattle by way of his thunderbolt. Vigilant flow, Indra causes the soma to flow in the holy river Indus. Soma brings the splendid power that enables seekers to find the light of heaven. Beautiful for Indra's sake, the mighty juice purified and served to seekers on the path of one thousand ways. The best seekers of prosperity, the sweetest in service to the gods, proceed, loudly roaring on the thousandfold path. The river Indus, flowing mightily toward the banquet of the gods, brings rich essence mixed with soma, the liquid ready to fill the beakers set at each place. Like drops from the divine, it swims in water, everyone exalting in delight. The immortal gods endow the stream with opulence, all the liquid purified, with the addition of purified drops of pressed soma, pouring down with the rain from heaven. Hiding beneath their hoods, the seekers find illumination. For the soma filtered, it flows with the waves and passes through the wool filter, all the seekers shouting and singing while purified. With song, the seekers send forth the mighty powers hidden within the roots of trees to go below the ground and above the ground, with the ground serving as the fleece. All above the ground achieve a triple height as with psalms and glory, the soma poured into the jars that left open, like an impetuous steed ready for war. While the soma is filtered, the seekers, still singing, golden hued, glide along the course of the river, passing through the wool filter and continuing to flow. At this point, the worshippers, along with the famous heroes, pour forth like faithful votaries in the streams, carrying soma and meath that fully effused and filtered, singing, from all directions.

## EVERLASTING ORDER

According to *Rig-Veda* 9:106, the immortals sprinkle the effused soma as the best of all sacred gifts they may serve to their friends. They run amid the streams of water, which filled with compressed stones and fully effused soma. Standing in waters, artful in their effusing the soma and blending it with milk, they serve it to everyone present to calm them, only after it pressed. Those who have come to see the delightful gods serving on the holy river appear with their mental powers manifested to make them farsighted. Cleansing the soma, the stream flows along in its watery robe as the giver of wealth. The gods sit in the place of eternal law and create a fountain made of gold, filling the heavenly udders with milk. They come ready to serve essence with soma, seating themselves in the ancient gathering place. Washed by the men, the strong, farsighted ones stream forth with nutritious food that fulfills all their desires. While they cleansed, they, like watchful deer, pass through the wool filter. They become singers like Agni's messenger Aṅgiras and rise to reach the heavenly illuminated body Sūrya high in the sky. From the bountiful Sūrya, the best soma flows to serve the holy saints (rishis) who, along with the singers, keen of sight, become sages. The most welcome among the godly powers in the sky with the illuminated body of Sūrya.

Pressers generate soma, which runs over the ground and across the fleecy backs of sheep, even running across the back of a tawny-colored mare in an exhilarating stream. The pressers return to the water, rich with soma, where animals such as cows wait milked. They approach with the mixing vessel, which is like a sea, serving as the bringers of cheer to the celebration. Effused by stones, the soma passed through the long wool filter and enter the saucers. Then a noble person creates a golden-colored fort and comes to settle within the woods. The soma beautified like the fine wool of a sheep, becoming like an impetuous steed in war. Even Pavamana, with the joyful sages at the feast of the holy bards, with his godly powers, swells in the river, causing it to surge.

The soma from the stalks, exhilarating, rests not in the vat but overflow it with drops with essence (meath). Like dear sons, the sages decked out to look lovely, all clad in shining robes. Skillful at their work, they drive forth in their embodiments, like a carriage into the river, forming a band. The drops of living soma pour out, the gladdening drink filled with wisdom and essence in the basin of the sea, which the sages find exhilarating. As Pavamana, king of the gods, forms waves in the sea, he comes performing a rite to serve eternal love (Mitra) and the eternal law (Varuna), increasing the flow of soma with his lofty proclamations, far-seeing, lovely, guided by the manifested embodiments who serve the gods from their homes in the sea.

The gladdening juice flows for Indra, having pressed by the cosmic hosts (Maruts). It passes through the fleece covering the thousand streams, made bright and beautiful for all manifested noble souls. The purified souls serving within the basin, singing hymns, filled with joy and eternal wisdom, they come to join with the godly powers. Robed in a mortal embodiment, floating in the floodwaters, the Mighty One appears fully clad and drives the milk to settle into the vats. The holy river Indus, each day flowing with soma, inspires friendship and delight. The friends who come to follow its flow subjected to demigods serving as the tawny hued Aśvins, who can pass beyond any barrier. Serving close to the bosom of the gods, the Aśvins provided with soma day and night. They take some to their friend Sūrya, serving the refulgent light of the moon, which glows along with the coursing river like a bird. Skillful handed, the Aśvins lift the purified soma and raise their voices in the sea.

Pavamana causes the rich yellow soma to flow in abundance, producing as much as he desires, making it pure and bright by passing it through the filter of long wool, then bellowing like a steer in the woods. Then Pavamana, as the balm, flows with the milk into the special place where the other godly powers live. The soma flows on to all kinds, giving them strength. Exhilarating, the soma is the first liquid to spread out into the sea, along with the godly powers, then it flows to earth, even coming to flow to the realm of heaven. The righteous sages who have become far-seeing urge the soma onward with their songs and hymns. Passing the soma through the cleansing sieve, Pavamana flows in the stream and serves it as a gift to the cosmic hosts (Maruts), as the gladdening steeds, serving with the strength of Indra, are provided with the food that makes them wise. Urged onward, under pressure, clad in watery robes, Indus speeds to the vat. Engendering light, he makes the cows low, then takes them as the spoils of war.

According to *Rig-Veda* 9:107, nine heavenly bodies (Navagraha) that follow a direct orbital rotating pattern recognized in the Vedas. The Navagraha establish themselves as constellations within the celestial region, which is right below the heavenly region. They appear as a group of stars forming an outline or pattern typically representing a mythological person or lifeless creature. The constellations noted in prehistoric stories, beliefs that supported by individual experience, creation, or mythology. The recognition of constellations has changed significantly over time in terms of their sizes or shapes. Twelve ancient constellations now belong to the zodiac, which form an elliptical pattern. The illuminated bodies include the sun, the moon, the planets, and other, smaller manifested bodies that traverse the dynamic universe. The nine heavenly bodies, the Navagraha, as a part of the constellations, are known to influence every creation prevailing on the ground (Prithvi) commonly referred to as the manifested terrestrial body (earth). The nine Navagraha include five planets that operate individually, namely, Mars (Mangala), Mercury (Buddha), Jupiter (Bṛhaspati), Venus (*Shukra*), and Saturn (Shani). These are all represented in the pantheon of the heavenly body Sūrya, who himself regulates the whole heavenly region, which represents three aspects of the plasma body as the moldable substance that exists as one of the four fundamental gaseous states of dark matter. The gas is in the form of ions, which orbit as electrons and, when breaking away and freeing themselves, become ions. Based on the temperature and the density of the environment, plasma is either partially ionized or fully ionized, appearing as bright light. When partially ionized, the plasma forms the ionosphere or magnetosphere surrounding manifested matter such as earth. Within the environment of space, the light of the sun becomes part of the constellations, along with the moon, with generates reflective light. Jointly, the sun and moon form two planetary nodes, with Rahu creating a shadow ascending north. Ketu creates a shadow ascending south. In addition to these observable phenomena, the universe, beyond our galaxy, the Milky Way, creates an estimated $1 \times 10^{24}$ stars that are invisible to the naked eye from Earth.

According to *Rig-Veda* 9:108, Indra, with gladdening soma filled with sweetness and eternal wisdom made great. Cheerful in his dwelling, like a heavenly steer, he appears as the flying heavenly body Etaśa, finding the eternal flame and the strengthening food to become excellent. With spoils and wealth, he is splendid, calling Pavamana to serve all the generations of mortals and immortal gods. Once Etaśa and Pavamana find the manifested physical body of the ancient Dadhyac, who left behind his DNA in his carcass after dying, they use it to become one, which allows them to open locked doors. By opening the manifested physical body of Dadhyac, they revive sages, who appear in order to fulfill the wishes of the gods. They win fame by generating nectar (amrit) and effusing it with godly power, once again causing it to flow in a stream. Serving as the best rapture givers, Etaśa and Pavamana send the mythical fluid through the long wool filter for purifying, a process that causes the free-flowing waters to generate waves. They emerge from a rocky cavern and take the amrit to the refulgent red cows in the water, serving as divine heads of the stable filled with milk-bearing cows, which burst out along with steeds.

Serving as brave lords, Etaśa and Pavamana pour themselves out to serve as steeds worthy of laudation, speeding through the region, causing a flood. They swim in water and roam in the woods; increasers of water, they create one thousand streams. As dear steer running a race with the deities, they steeped in the law, waxen and mighty, serving as kings of the law, gods of the lofty ordinance. They cause all friends of the gods to shine gloriously by strengthening them with food, filling the fountain of the midair region. Mighty ones, fully effused, they roll onward to serve the dynamic universe as supporters of the tribes. They cause rain to pour from heaven, the flowing waters inspiring thoughts of winning the spoils. Like the steer of heaven, they pour forth with a thousand streams, creating rapturous joy, bringing all excellent things.

The Mighty Immortal One, by giving life, lightens the darkness by causing the sun to shine. Well praised by sages, and with his wondrous power, he dons the threefold manifested bodies (physical, subtle, and astral) as his robe. Once effused, he brings good things, bounteous gifts, and sweet refreshing food, along with mythical juice, thus bringing tranquility. The dwellings on earth then supported by the celestial demigods the Aśvins, the cosmic hosts the Maruts, and the terrestrial ruling body Bhaga. They jointly drink mythical juice and transform from a threefold manifested embodiment to become the perishable embodiment, Aryaman. The trinity of Mitra, Varuna, and Indra provide the ability to defend oneself. As imperishable embodiments, they also provide support. Indra, as a manifested body, drinks soma and comes with weapons to serve as a gladdener, also serving the holy river Indus, which flows onward with stored sweetness. As a soma holder, the god Indra becomes the heart that guides the rivers through the manifested material world, supported by the noblest pillars Mitra, Vayu, and Varuna, who support the heavens.

## RADIANT GODS

According to *Rig-Veda* 9:109, Indra Mitra, Pūṣan, and Bhaga together drink soma before they speed onward like a flowing stream. Indra drinks the juice for wisdom, and all the other mighty powers (deities) served such a drink for eternal strength. Thus, bright celestial soma flows among the vast number of immortal dwelling places. Flowing onward as the father of the gods, Indra appears in every form, filling the mighty sea. As a radiant god, he serves both heaven and earth, providing it with blessed progeny. Drinking the bright juice, as a sustainer, he comes to serve the sky shield, eternal truth flowing through him with the directive that he serves as the splendid power causing streams to flow across the earth and pass through the great fleece. As in olden times, when young boys, led by older wise men, purified and became joyous, Indra appears as a shiny star in the sky, coming with blessings as the finder of light. On the earth, cleansed within the river Indus, he keeps people safe by giving them all the possessions they need to survive in the material world. Flowing in wisdom as the soma he provides, Indra imbues the strong courses with spiritual power, bathing them in eternal juice to win the prize.

On its way down the river, the soma passes through compressed cosmic stones further purified. Indra comes to earth with his own soma, shining, offering delight, which brings fame. As a golden-hued infant, decked as a newborn, Indra floats within the holy river Indus, passing through the godly sieve to conform to eternal law (covenant). The Indus, as it flows, creates a rapturous joy, transforming manifested living beings into noble souls (sages). With good fortune, waves lap in the flowing water. The noble sages bear the beauteous name of Indra, wherewith they overcome all demons and foes.

Deities accustomed to soma present a blend of milk and soma, coagulated into curd, to the sages. It flows forth within one thousand streams and effused through the filter of long wool, flowing endlessly through the water. Pressed between cosmic stones, it becomes fertile, as if having passed through Indra's throat. The mighty soma poured through the thousand streams as if through Indra's mouth, then passed through the purifying sieve, a balm from the holy river Indus. It becomes a pleasant milky liquid served to steer as a great delight. With a light sheen, cleansed for the gods and becomes a gold-colored liquid, the gods wearing divine robes. From the holy river Indus, Indra flows downward into streams to strengthen them as they merge with the floodwaters.

According to *Rig-Veda* 9:105, overpowering the evil power Vṛtra, Indra runs ahead, getting stronger as he speeds along, his powers increasing like one exacting justice. In effused form, soma causes warriors to rejoice and gain supremacy in the war. Like the self-enkindled Pavamana, they perform mighty deeds as supported by the heavenly power Sūrya, the sun, who generates direct light and spreads moisture by way of the indirect light of by the moon. Moving swiftly, Indra vivifies the milk-bearing animals, so they provide milk to serve all mortal and immortal embodiments. The half-mortal embodiments serving as demigods, who serve to uphold the eternal law, blessed with amrit, which, like soma, causes extra strength to flow through their bodies to serve the mortal embodiments. The embodiments endowed with glory, and provided a well to drink from, bearing the fragments from the presser's arms. Then, beautifully radiant, and certainly heavenly, they come to sing with their kin, who look like the goddess Savitar.

The stall opens. The grass trimmed. As elders' embodiments addressed through hymns and become renowned for their mighty strength. As heroes, they urged onward, their heroic power flowing forth from the great depths of the sky, along with the primeval milk of heaven. With loud uplifted voices, they honor the birth of Indra. So long as the self-enkindled Pavamana serves both heaven and earth, they continue to exist, all tied to the mighty power who stands in heaven as a bull, serving as the chief of the herd. Pavamana continues passing soma through the wool filter to cleanse it. Like a playful infant, floating in the river Indus, he creates one hundred spiritual powers and obtains one hundred physical powers. He continues flowing with the currents, becoming holy, sweet, and purified. As the river Indus flows on, it creates a wave pleasant in taste. Indra brings a winner's strength, finding the treasure that bestows long life. Therefore, the heroes flow with divine will as the witnesses who provided with the power to subdue their assailants. They relentlessly chase the demons and, well armed, fight them. After conquering their foes, they provided with an external source of soma.

According to *Rig-Veda* 9:111, golden and splendid, the heroes purify themselves and, with their allies, defeat all their enemies. They become allies of the princess Sāra, cleansing themselves within the holy stream. They shine forth, yellow and red in color, to encompass all forms, all appearing with seven mouths, which they use to haggle for treasure, seeking bargains, always watchful for the miserly demon Paṇis. They use their mother's houses as their abodes, where they offer sacrifices, oblations, and worship. When they travel afar, they hear the hymns or holy songs that resonate with joy. Ruddy hued, they win threefold life power. They move to the east as directed by the intelligent Saramā, still rivals as beautiful embodiments generating beams of light. Singing as a beautiful celestial body, they come as thieves to steal cows, all while singing hymns. Lauded for their valor, without success they try to provoke Indra, who with his two thunderbolts remains unconquered.

According to *Rig-Veda* 9:112, others, with various thoughts and plans, come from all directions to serve as Brahmans, the highest members of the priesthood. As worshippers, they seek those who shattered or disfigured by vampires. The river Indus, flowing for the sake of Indra, filled with the soma derived from the seasonal plants growing on the ground. The feathered birds of the air appear and, with cosmic stones, enkindle a flame, seeking the godly powers who store gold within the holy river Indus, which—again—flows for Indra. Decomposers, like parasites, draw power from Indra to lay mush upon the stones. Striving for wealth, with varied plans, the decomposers desire to serve as sacred cows. They draw like horses as their own embodiments serve as hosts who invite laughter and jesting. The male, filled with desire, approaches his mate the frog, eager to seek the flood, just as the river Indus flows for the sake of Indra.

According to *Rig-Veda* 9:113, Indra, the best of the evil-slayers, who drinks soma, and the carriage mover Saravanan store up vigor in their hearts, prepared to do heroic deeds. On the ground as the lords of the four quarters (north, south, east, and west), they experience ecstasy with the power of soma. In the land of honey, fully effused with passion, of undivided faith, and with true hymns, offer a sacrifice. On this ground, the holy river Indus flows, serving Indra and the daughters of the heavenly illuminated body Sūrya. This brings the deity of rain, Parjanya, who, like a wild bull, seized, held, and nursed by the godly messengers the Gandharva, who use the soma from the Indus. Splendid in the law, declaring the truth, they speak to the workforce, renouncing their faith in the king. Decked with soma, they flow in the Indus, which joins with other streams, to become strong and great. With the soma, they meet to prayer. Golden hued, they flow along with the Indus, which serves for the sake of gods such as Indra. The self-invoked Pavamana, serving as a priest, recites the rhythmic prayer while worshipping the lords of soma, which appears among the compressed cosmic stones (meteors) that come from above, bringing forth delight from the Indus. This moves the perishable Pavamana from the material world into the imperishable world to become deathless, un-decaying, wherein the light of heaven is set, shining with everlasting luster. Placed in the realm of immortals, the Pavamana dwell with King Vivian's sons in the secret shrine of heaven, where holy water is poured upon them, so they remain ever young and fresh. In this realm, where they move as immortals, is in the third sphere of the innermost world of heaven, where everything fully illuminated. That causes even the immortals in this realm to be eager with desire to enter the region of the radiant indirect light (the moon), where food and true delight found. The immortals in this realm are happy to transported with joy and ecstasy, fulfilling their longing like a river merging with the ocean, the water seeking to become cosmic vapor so it may return to the heavenly region.

According to *Rig-Veda* 9:114, as part of the sacrosanct dominion, those who walk according to the laws of nature and abide by the powers of the holy river Indus blessed as children with richness, filled with the eternal mythical juice that brings immortality and noble thoughts. The revered sage Kashyapa, one of the seven ancient rishis, with a loud uplifted voice, sings hymns. Kashyapa reveres eternal wisdom. He was born to serve as the sovereign ruler of the plantation within the first kingdom. The rishis serve in the seven illuminated upper regions (*lokas*), which served by the pantheon of the celestial power Sūrya and administered by the seven sages (rishis) and the seven noble souls (Ādityas). They all guard the seven holy rivers, serving as the seven daughters of the heavenly powers, and guard, and offer oblation to, the manifested King Soma.

# Part VI

# WORLDLY SPHERE

# Preface to Part VI

THE WORLDLY SPHERE IS FREESTANDING. IT CAME INTO EXISTENCE through immortal power for a period to link together all imperishable and perishable creations prevailing within the worldly sphere, where they pass through the life cycle, which begins with total darkness, or Kali Yuga. Such a life cycle accompanied by the power of illumination, which allows embodiments to exit and pass through natural, mythical, and supernatural phenomena, all subject to the laws of nature, through which perishable existence becomes imperishable existence. The duration of such existence, and its quality, governed by the supreme powers of causation, comprised of physical evolution, spiritual involution, and an understanding of the power of essence, governing existence, and nonexistence. The physical powers regulate the physical body; the spiritual powers regulate the invisible body; and an understanding of essence allows the living spirit to go beyond the worldly sphere and into the celestial or heavenly sphere or return to life. Jointly, the supreme powers of causation influence manifestations, even determining the quality of their existence on the holy ground.

The first period of the individual life cycle begins in darkness, or lack of knowledge, which defined as the lowest form of physical manifestation. Here, creations limited in their movement and their life force is inactive. Then there is the plant kingdom, the plants fixed to the earth with roots and with a limited ability to think and act. The next is the animal kingdom, which is far advanced and subjected to the process of physical evolution. The process of evolution gives rise to the human kingdom, where physically advanced embodiments gain higher spiritual knowledge. With further enhanced spiritual knowledge, embodiments come to know eternal truth and pass such ability from one existence to another, thereby establishing a foundation to attain enlightenment and transform from perishables into imperishable embodiments. Knowing absolute truth, the embodiment reaches the point where it becomes ethereal, passing from one era or epoch (yuga) to another epoch.

On a larger scale, the worldly sphere consists of many lifetimes, or eras or epochs (yugas), that are all associated with the planetary system or cosmology. There are four epochs defined in the Vedas, namely, *Satya Yuga, Treta Yuga, Dvapara Yuga, and Kali Yuga,* with each having a duration one-quarter of that of the lifetime prior, which governs intellectual capability, life span, emotional power, and physical power (dharma). Thus, with a ratio of 4:3:2:1, Satya Yuga is the longest period; Treta Yuga is one-quarter shorter than Satya Yuga; Dvapara Yuga is one-quarter shorter than Treta Yuga; and Kali Yuga, one-quarter shorter than Dvapara Yuga, is the shortest. All four epochs combined make the complete universal cycle, *Chatur* Yuga, which repeats again and again until the dynamic universe merges with the dormant universe and ceases to exist.

**Satya Yuga** is the longest epoch, representing the age of eternal truth, or the golden age of the luminous bodies of heaven. It represents the age of illumination or perfection. In this epoch, there is no crime in accepting religion, spirituality, or essence. All bodies live long, serving as saints. They live lives that are powerful, honest, youthful, vigorous, erudite, and virtuous. They serve with supreme blessedness. There is no agriculture or mining, as the earth yields its riches on its own. The weather is pleasant, and everyone lives happily. There is no disease, no decrepitude, and no fear of anything. Virtue reigns supreme. The human stature is twenty-one cubits (33 feet, six inches). The average human life span is one hundred thousand years. Satya Yuga referred to as heaven.

In chronological order, *Treta Yuga* is the second yuga, the age of virtual wisdom that diminishes slightly with time. It represents the ultimate home of the immortal universal soul. Whereas in the beginning, the mighty power, with an immortal universal soul, maintained dominance in wars fought to enforce righteousness and morality, now, with the change in the environment comes more frequent wars and battles. The universal soul diminished as compared to its predecessor. Still there are no material needs and thus no need for agriculture, and no need for manual labor or skilled operations such as mining. With seeking to fulfill their needs, greed develops within this period, and therefore the level of control diminishes. This era marked by three-quarters virtue and one-quarter sin. The normal human stature is fourteen cubits (22 feet, four inches). The average human life span is ten thousand years. In this epoch, the manifested universe considered the sphere of essence from which everything originates, or the home of the Creator. This yuga belongs to the invisible universe and is unapproachable and incomprehensible by even the unmanifested mighty powers. This sphere especially remains unknown and serves as the barrier between the Creator and creations.

Next is the third yuga, *Dvapara Yuga,* which consists of five spheres: Jana Loka, Mahar Loka, Swar Loka, Bhuvar Loka, and Bhu Loka. Within these lokas, the immortal universal soul starts to disintegrate, to appear as individual living things that seek benefits from the material world and presenting with distinct qualities. With the disintegration of the universal soul, or dharma, all forms of disease become rampant and generate discontent, causing individuals to fight among each other to gain power and control. During this yuga, living things maintain their original characteristics from youth to old age. The life span of the human declines to few centuries. Each embodiment is half virtuous and half sinful. The average human height declines to seven cubits (11 feet, two inches), and the average human life span declines to below one thousand years. The universal soul starts to manifest as living spirit and therefore is no longer as strong as that of its ancestors.

*Kali Yuga* is the fourth stage, the epoch of darkness and ignorance, where people, because they lack in virtue, stop behaving righteously (dharma) and justify their existence only through how they fulfill their individual obligations and responsibilities (karma) and nothing else. They become slaves to their passions and barely retain any power, being much less powerful than their ancestors. Society falls into disrepair, and people become liars and hypocrites. All desire to acquire higher knowledge and eternal wisdom lost. Study of scripture decreases. Humanity starts to depend on forbidden, dirty food. The environment polluted; water and food become scarce. While the need for material wealth increases, eternal wealth declines sharply. The family unit becomes nonexistent. Everyone is one-quarter virtue and three-quarters sin. The average human stature is three and a half cubits (5 feet, three inches). The average human life span declines to less than one hundred years. Humanity declines to behave like domesticated animals. Knowing all about the epochs (yugas), regulated by the supreme powers of causation, those on holy ground and subjected to Kali Yuga, where manifested mortal embodiments become subject to destruction.

In this epoch, newborns in manifested bodies, as "goodly infants," with the goal to reach the sacred dominion through spiritual involution, ascend and reach Satya Yuga. They know from the past that the holy ground filled with reverence and divine will accompanied by essence, by which the ground (Prithvi) created to extend through the divine shield (the sky), reaching from the surface of the terrestrial body to the highest celestial region within the dynamic universe. This accepted as the temporary place for righteous souls who have performed charitable deeds throughout their lives to attain liberation (nirvana), but it is not yet the place where one attains salvation—moksha—from the cycle of birth, death, and rebirth.

Ancient Greek philosophers, Hindu scholars, and the scientific community have only recently come to comprehend thc planctary system and its relative position within the universe. Using astronomy and astrology, they have acquired knowledge to unveil the hidden secrets prevailing within our solar system responsible for the causation and the existence of manifested embodiments. Through their observations, scientists now accept that the sun produces direct light, and the moon provides reflective light. In addition, they accept that there are hundreds of billions of stars that form the Milky Way and other galaxies, all distributed uniformly, all moving in the same direction. Further, the scientific community has recognized that the dynamic universe is expanding at an increasing rate.

Once the fixed amount of energy and matter prevailing within the dynamic universe gradually cooled (around 13.799±0.021 billion years ago), the first subatomic particles gradually gathered to form a simple atom. Within this structure, the vibrations created the power of gravity, which influences every filament and cavity. As a giant cloud, hydrogen and helium gradually drawn to this place, where this most dense matter formed the first galaxies of stars, through which everything else observed. It is still not possible to see any of the objects that prevailed 13.799 billion light-years ago. These can studied through the movement of galaxies. It discovered that the universe contains much more matter than is accounted for through visible objects such as stars, galaxies, nebulas, and interstellar gas.

CHAPTER 19

# Sacred Dominion

Life on earth (Prithvi) started to appear, all sharing a common ancestor that lived long before, 3.5 billion to 3.8 billion years ago. Through a progression, early biogenic graphite, according to the fossil record, evolved into microbes and multicellular organisms. The fossil record shows a pattern by which biodiversity shaped through the repeated formation of new species (speciation), changes within species (anagenesis), and loss of species (extinction). This occurred alongside the process of spiritual involution.

The highest place in the worldly sphere represents the sacred dominion, also called Satya Loka, the sphere of absolute truth, where the heavenly power Sūrya rises, generating the ferocious fire, Agni. The next Tapo Loka, where matter transformed into new forms of energy manifested plasma body (the sun), which produces direct light. The sun produces morning light, which removes the dark of night. During the darkness, there is a soft reflective light coming from the galaxies of stars (constellations) and the moon, which serves as the home of the supreme powers of causation, which through these bodies provides reflective light to the lower five Lokas. The aspects of those who exist within the lower five Lokas are based upon their level of comprehension of the absolute truth.

The fifth sphere is Jana Loka, full of brilliance and radiant activity, generating electromagnetic waves that transform the universal soul

(Paramatman) into two components, one serving itself as the Creator, and the other serving as the life force (prana), which houses the living spirit (Atman). The fourth sphere is Swar Loka, which serves as the home of the creations who comprehend the eternal truth and the supreme powers of causation. The third is Mahas Loka, which is home of the creations who, as manifested embodiments, comprehend eternal wisdom and the laws of nature (prakriti and purusha). The fourth sphere, Bhuvas Loka, is home to those creations who comprehend intellect. At the bottom is Bhu Loka, which is above the underworld and serves as the home of those who are oblivious to their surroundings and who live in gloom and doom.

## GENESIS

Satya Loka represent the genesis of mortal incarnations as the descendants of the ancient gods who appear on holy ground (Prithvi) and have already acquired sufficient knowledge, as goodly infants, to move ahead as the initial phase of living beings. According to *Rig-Veda* 10:1, the goodly infant, as a child of the earth, reappears in white shining splendor, filled with eternal flame, representing the life force (prana), supporting the prevailing ancient messiah, within a dwelling as a child of the earth. All such children of the earth supported by the heavenly father, as the child first appears hidden among others like a beautiful plant filled with soma. Appearing as a brilliant sweetheart who comes to remove the gloom of night by infusing it with morning light, the child wakens the godly mothers, who come forth with a loud roar, like protective powers, to manifest and serve as sustainers, all sent forth by the lofty Vishnu. They themselves, as fully wise and enlightened souls, come to reside above the holy ground (Prithvi). From their place, they provide soma mixed with milk, which they place into the child's mouth as it is set upon the ground amid free-flowing water. All of one accord, singing forth with praises, the milk-bearing mothers feed their children and thereby cause them to increase in physical strength.

In their altered form, the children of earth appear within their own manifested mortal bodies. These bodies invoked by the holy priests, who perform a rite to make the embodiments shine with glitter and become refulgent. Each with a signature way of acting, with worship, the children of earth come to share in the glory of godly might. Individually served with the eternal flame, as provided by the godhead Agni as the guest who summoned to earth. Served at the centermost station of the earth, the children of earth are all vested with mortal embodiments, which appear decorated with garments of red. As priests pour out their libations, all serve the great king who comes along with the high priest from heaven to the earth to serve the godly powers. These powers worshipped as messengers or godheads. The children of earth never, ever surpass their parents, who always come to fulfill their needs and help them in their longing to meet to reach the gods.

According to *Rig-Veda* 10:2, the most youthful mighty victors, gladdened with a godly yearning, come with the celestial powers to serve as the lords of the seasons by offering each season the best worship. Heralds invoke them to serve as deep thinkers with purified minds and given the power to seek by way of the intellect. The intellect brings everything into true order. The young victors honor Agni by supporting the true order through prayer and worship (*svāhā*). The manifested bodies follow the gods' pathway. As they start to travel, they begin executing godly works. Agni, who knows of their worship, when they have fully completed the cycle to become earthly priests, assigns them specific rites to bring forth the seasons. These youths ensure no deity in the established order neglected, as they perform their duties. With their powerful intellects providing them with the necessary knowledge, they learn to correct their individual faults and failings. Like skilled godly messengers, they assigned specific obligations befitting their strengths to regulate the seasons. In terms of their brains, they first work with weak and feeble minds, with the full understanding that the mortal brain is not inclined to think about making sacrifices and is not wise enough to discern the heavenly power whom they worship, namely, Agni.

The ruling fathers elect leaders to offer solemn rites, to cultivate a pleasant dwelling place for worship. These appear among the brimming heroes. They receive rich food to nourish their embodiments and enable them to move within the free-flowing waters. Agni, along with the creative power Tvaṣṭṛ, gives birth to splendorous things that used to travel between heaven and earth. The embodiments know well that Agni, as their father, will establish a lighted pathway to support them in shining with a resplendent light.

According to *Rig-Veda* 10:3, the potent kings serving as marvelous envoys kindle the strength that engenders beauty among all manifested souls. All-knowing, they shine with other lofty splendors to chase away the dark of night and usher in the direct light of the sun in the morning. They overcome the glimmering darkness as they bring forth beauty in the form of a blessed galaxy of stars, all of which serve the mothers or daughters. Holding aloft the radiant constellations of stars, they emit light while serving as the messengers who receive direct light from the sun and bring reflective light from the moon, which represents the heavenly treasures from the pantheon of Sūrya. This brings the feminine, that is, eternal love (Mitra), along with Agni, who offers a blessing to other messengers in support of the eternal law (Varuna). Shining with a conspicuous luster, they turn the darkness of night into a shining white garment. Singing forth with loud voices, they kindle all rays of light, generating auspicious friendship among all rays and bright beams, which gleam like teeth. Served in adoration by steer, they become visible as they make sounds. Coming from aloft, their brilliance flows with a radiant splendor to become the effulgent protective shield (the sky). Upon reaching the heavenly region, they bring the best and the brightest, the luster forming the galaxies of stars. All very sportive, they pierce the summit, flowing through it with a radiant splendor. Appearing along with such galaxies, in their chariot with fellies, they come gleaming and glittering as a team, loudly roaring, which travels afar as an envoy of the ferocious fire, Agni. They shine with an ancient flame and come echoing. They bring ample wealth to serve the envoys, such as the two youthful demigod Aśvins. Serving as matriarchs, they come like rapid horses, impetuous steeds, ready to connect earth with heaven.

According to *Rig-Veda* 10:4, the youthful demigods serving as matriarchs send forth praises and oblations, to invoke Agni, who appears like a fountain in the desert, serving his worshippers. The ancient ring restored, with the people gathering to seek warmth in the cattle stall. Most youthful, as the mortal messengers of the gods, they go forth gloriously with light between them, which makes them grow, these noble infants nurtured with sweet affection by their mothers. Over the slopes of the desert they pass, longing to set the beasts free. Whether they are foolish or wise, they verily wish to be free from error. Agni knows where the magnificence lies. As a house lord, he watches their movements when they come to lick and swallow, kissing like young aid virgin ens. Rising, his supply of ancient fuel ever refreshed, Agni creates a banner of gray smoke, making his dwelling within the wood. Any swimming steer that presses through the waters to come to Agni's place accorded a mortal embodiment. They are like thieves who risk their lives to hunt in the forest, where, with their ten girdles, they come to secure their mortal embodiments. They sing a new hymn meant especially for Agni, asking him to endow their embodiments with parts that glitter. In homage and with prayer, they honor the godly power Jātavedas, also singing songs to exalt Agni, asking him to evermore protect the children and descendants who, with ever-watchful care, guard the bodies.

According to *Rig-Veda* 10:5, the holy ground and the ocean hold treasures that borne within the heart, which hides the secret of love within a couple's bosom. Like birds flitting in a fountain, the embodiments inhabit one common dwelling place. Sages guard the strong stallions and the sweet mares, all seated together within the holy order. They keep concealed within themselves their highest names as a holy pair, and with wondrous power, the couple give birth to infants to propagate, the infants appearing as manifested living beings. They move from the pivotal point as if weaving threads. As the move among the sages, they refreshed with food, following the natural order, by which they receive guidance from the ancient times. The goodly infants, each wearing the shroud of earth and heaven, become strong by eating nutrient-rich food, drinking pleasant drink, and acquiring physical bodies. They are honored loudly by the Seven Sisters, who serve the supreme powers of causation, providing the infants with skills and offering them sweet soma to drink to acquire higher knowledge. They brought to understand that their ancestors of long ago are now serving as the patrons of the heavenly power Pūṣan, all dressed in robes from the solar deity. They come to behold the seven pathways to attaining eternal wisdom, knowing that they are created to help those mortal embodiments who are facing trouble.

Standing within their own dwellings, they serve the paths, the goodly infants separated from the ground by the highest pillar. Unable to reach the highest heaven, they received within the bosom of the heavenly mother Aditi, to receive the divine sacrificial gift. The able, dexterous, honest deity Dakṣa, who establishes a birthplace for them, provides them with the gift of eternal flame, served by Agni. As the firstborn in the holy order, they drink milk from cows and attain spiritual power, at the beginning of life receiving physical strength from the bull. Agni, as a favor, continues to protect them and help them to acquire higher knowledge. Through comprehending the eternal power of vibrations, they succeed in serving as creative composers or singers. With a glowing power, they are honored to serve with the noble flame that goes forth, encompassing all with a far-reaching luster. As the son of the godhead Agni, the Holy One, everlasting, they shine, provided with beams of light from the far-off constellations of stars. They form bonds of friendship with the newborns and bring them to serve in the form of a fleet of steeds that never trip or stumble. With oblation, the divine share with manifested living beings as day breaks. As an offering, they come in response to the devotion shown them, coming to rest within the mortal embodiments. Through their might, they remain unscathed. Increasing in strength, they are content to appear as godly powers.

With ease of flight, the children of the earth travel to appear as cheerful priests who offer the best sacrifices. Using their tongues, they offer a godly balm that helps them to mingle with others. With songs and adoration, they invoke Agni, the heavenly power who creates the dawn for the god Indra so the latter may come and serve the holy ground. Agni and Indra appear with the godly power Jātavedas, loudly singing hymns as they travel along with those who carry the sacrificial ladle to bring goodly treasures. They all meet to serve in war, seeking booty, riding steeds. The children of the earth receive help form both Agni and Indra. At the time of their birth, Jātavedas comes to sit with them, with the aim of invoking more of the gods. Coming near, the children of the earth obey Jātavedas and follow the divine law (*sunimons*), thereby allowing the godly powers to place them into ranks to serve as the chief protectors.

## PLAN OF EXISTENCE

The plan of existence as Tapo Loka, where, according to *Rig-Veda* 10:6, the newborn, surrounding by the natural world, which serves as the home of the life force, is born of passion to build a supportive community. Such life force represents a combination of inert matter, the innumerable atoms making up inorganic substance (purusha), and the omnipotent force or vital energy that causes motion (prakriti). The interaction of these forces results in the formation of physical mass, which can be set in motion to give birth to duality, multiplicity, illusion, and delusion. This motion creates shadows, which cause darkness and create ignorance among living things, although such living things wish to protect the plane of existence through creating a sustainable and friendly environment. The living things evolve become more significant, more meaningful. This results in a world filled with the craving to foster love, friendship, and tolerance.

The priests as noble souls work together until the work fully completed. They never destroy any manifested body or consume or scatter their skin. Serving as protectors, the priests mature before they proceed on their way to the regulating divine powers (deities). They receive powers from the newly created plasma bodies, such as the sun, or the face with eyes—that is, the moon—which are always in motion. They travel within the wind (Vayu), carrying the living spirit to serve both the earth below and the heavens above. They even reach deep into the ground, placing the living spirit within the roots of plants. Such manifested mortal embodiments, with water, come to serve as an initial home.

As per the divine order, every living spirit that resides in the ground, such as plants, serves as a source of food for the animal kingdom. Creatures such as goats consume plants and acquire the fiercely burning eternal flame, which gives off a splendorous glow among. In various auspicious forms, the animal kingdom unites to serve the pious power Jātavedas, who acts an auspicious cover over the different regions. Serving as a father to the noble souls, Jātavedas comes forward in response to oblation from all those who clothed in new life. With an increasing number of offspring, the noble powers once again unite, this time in the form of the pious Ādityas. They help blind birds living in ignorance, reptiles injected with poison by aggressive serpents, and wild dogs or jackals that consume all things. Heavenly priests (Brahmans), with soma provided with embodiments, along with the fat and the marrow to heal themselves and create new flesh to serve the Bold One. Glowing fiercely, they are eager to attack, but they learn to restrain themselves before they face any evil power. They are forbearers, using the godly ladle to scoop up soma, which merits eternal love, which brings the gods to come and serve them amrit so they may attain immortal powers. They rejoice, remaining restrained as they use their glands to cleanse the nectar. This makes it so that neither their mortal embodiments nor their flesh bears any residual memories or stains. Uniting with the god Jātavedas, they carry on offering oblation before they depart to join with death (Yama). They serve with skillful powers, using their astral bodies to worship Indra, supported by Mitra (eternal love) and Agni, the source of the eternal flame.

United with the gods, the noble souls always watch as they pass through the supreme assembly. They make offerings to Agni, the father, who brings along Varuna (the eternal law), Indra, and Mitra (eternal love). These divinities or deities gladly sit down and allow the physical embodiments to depart with a burning glow, while Agni and Indra yearn to refresh the spot that has scorched by fire. Physical bodies such as water lilies grow along with tender grasses and leafy herbs. The plants are cool and full of moisture, which freshens the herbs. The female frog filled with delight, indicating that Agni is nearby.

According to *Rig-Veda* 10:7, the eternal flame brings good luck and establishes a higher level of intelligence so the noble souls can serve as wonderworkers who receive protection from the godly powers by offering them far-reaching blessings. The singing of hymns brings forth bounteous gifts such as cattle and horses. Manifested embodiments who sing hymns gain enjoyment and serve as noble souls. In honor of Agni, prevailing in heaven, they observe the bright holy light coming from the heavenly pantheon of Sūrya. With effectual prayers, the embodiments who worship, such as priests, rewarded with gains and profits and ever guarded. They served rich food brought by red steeds. Serving as holy ones both day and night, they become even more pleasant. Manifested embodiments, with their arms, invoke fire, Agni, who comes with helpful hands to serve as a kind friend and adorn them in splendor. They established as half-mortals, demigods, serving as invokers among the ancient priests and as the lover of sacrifices, all filled with a desire to worship Agni, as well as all the gods in heaven. Even if they were void of knowledge, no one would be able to fool them. They worship the noble powers that regulate the seasons. As nobly born themselves, they worship the guardian Agni, as well as the protectors of life, the mighty divinities, and deities, with vitality and vigor as bestowed upon them. These gods, being the gift givers, accept the charge of protecting the individual embodiments with unceasing care.

According to *Rig-Veda* 10:8, Agni, provider of the eternal flame, advances further, raising his lofty banner, with the bull shouting proclamations from the sky shield. They set themselves up in the upper limits, which the supreme manifested mortal embodiments learn is the upper limit of the holy ground. Polishing their skills, swimming laps in the free-flowing waters, the younglings with humps on their backs represent the strongest of the physical powers. Like the heavenly bull, they come frolicking, upright enough to serve as the strongest power.

Earthly calves, which grow into sacred cows, never cease hollering to the spiritually manifested perishable powers, coming with offerings to establish an assembly and move within their dwelling place, serving as the chief of physical power, which is a male, and the chief of spiritual power, which is female. They joined together and serve as the heads of the family. They make sacrifices and determine the tactics for facing the fast-moving water coming in waves to bring forth a heavenly luster.

In the morning, the red light invites physical powers such as horses to work with cows, the spiritual powers, to refresh their bodies by putting their dwellings in order. Encompassing the elements of nature (Vasu), they proceed every morning and every evening, appearing as the twin illuminators, dawn and dusk. They make sacrifices to become imbued with the power of eternal love (Mitra), and through the act of seeing, they establish the mighty order according to the eternal law (Varuna). Jointly they make sacrifices to remain confined as manifested youngling, children of the water, whose offerings deemed acceptable and received by the godly power Jātavedas. Serving as skilled leaders, they offer specifics rite for each given region, which they follow as an auspicious team. They offer sacrifices to the heavenly light-bestowing Agni, providing him with honor by uplifting their voices in oblation to the eternal flame. The solar deity serving as the chief or sire of the chamber, Trita, with the intention of carefully selected embryos, chooses a female manifested embodiment ready to produce newborn, using her bosom to feed them, her glands that connect her heart to her mind producing milk from the stem of Āptya. The sun gods use this as their weapon to go forth in combat, fighting a holy war. The three-headed solar deity Trita holds the powers of causation, the seven rays of which urge upon the creative power Tvaṣṭṛ. Holding spiritual power, they appear with Indra to manifest as godly mothers embodied as earthly cows. They, as brave females, cleave the mountains and crush to pieces the evil Asuras, facing manifested the noble Ādityas and thus gaining much strength, to be deemed as the highest mighty power. The three heads of the solar deity Trita seize such godly mothers to serve the creative force Tvaṣṭṛ.

According to *Rig-Veda* 10:9, appearing as benevolent embryos, children of the water bring along energy that, with great delight, provides a portion of vitality through the most auspicious mothers who longing to love the embryos. They gladly bring others, who already accept water as good for drinking, to receive strength for procreating. As goddesses, they provide aid and bliss to cause the water in the streams to serve as the source of health and strength. As a part of the floods, they rule like queens and provide balm to precious beings, so they may gain supreme control like kings. Within the waters, the balm heals individual embodiments. Agni blesses them with medicine loaded with eternal flame, which keeps the embodiment safe from any harm. Even when they subjected to the sun for a long time, the waters find all sin buried within evil, such as falseness, lies, or broken oaths. Water goes through the embodiment to remove impurities, which appear as far away, seeking moisture.

## RIGHTEOUS EMISSARIES

Righteous emissaries represent the Jana Loka. According to *Rig-Veda* 10:10, the splendid god Agni, along with spiritual power, brings mythical power (soma) to transform noble living beings (sages) into righteous emissaries. Through this, the sages learn to build friendships and become generous. Passing through thin air (Vayu), they transmit their powers of essence as they cover the wide area marked by bodies of water such as oceans. They remember the days when their father obtained the holy ground to serve their offspring, as companions the male and female partners passing through death as the divine pair Yama and Yami. With love, they develop a friendship that lasts until death, and they consider all as strangers with no close relatives. Through the immortal powers, they see the individual spirit prevailing among mortal embodiments who long to have progeny to allow them to knit their relationship together as soul mates among other living spirits in love. Gandharva, as a messenger, who speaks purely and walks in morality, passes through the flood to appear as a child of the water, coming to establish a bond with another child of the water, thereby becoming kin. Having known these children since they were in the womb, the creative power Tvaṣṭṛ creates a soul mate (vivifier) for each of them, who appears in many shapes and in all forms. They all perform in concert with order, and none violates the holy ordinances. They are all fully acknowledged as divine creations, all belonging to the gods as the children of heaven and earth. Early in their lives, they come to know who speaks, who beholds, and who declares the eternal law and eternal love.

According to *Rig-Veda* 10:11, the female mortal embodiment Yami possesses the temperament to attract the male mortal embodiment Yama. They rest on the same couch, sitting beside each other, as they learn to raise their offspring. One yields to the other, the husband thus setting the wheel of life in motion. They are in love and cannot stand still. With their eyelids closed, they see divine sentinels, who make them wander all around. The heavenly power Sūrya, regulating day and night, grants them light, which spreads out into the area between heaven and earth, and as a pair they become kindred pair. The husband Yama performs unbrotherly acts with his wife, Yami, succeeding without question. When spouses perform acts that are unsuitable according to the clan, either morally deficient or unfair, either husband or wife makes of their arms a pillow for the other's comfort. In Yama, there is no trace of heart or spirit in a different body, as he surrounds his wife like a girdle. The wife Yami embraces Yama, enfolding her arms around him like the bark of a tree. They win each other's hearts and let their fancy form a blessed alliance.

According to *Rig-Veda* 10:12, from the very first, as part of the everlasting order, the powers of heaven and earth have recognized the nature of husband and wife. But as righteous messengers, they must speak the truth that they must serve according to divine will and harness all their vigor to serve the holy spirit as the priest. They serve the supreme powers of causation, and to establish the chief among the godly powers, they recognize the appointed one to whom all oblations directed, the one who creates fire by creating friction with wood or striking stones together. With the kindled eternal flame generating joyous worship, the husband and earth praise Agni, whom they serve forever. They use their glands to transform soma into amrita. Sitting within their embodiments on the holy ground, they served drops. Serving the heavenly powers, they into sacred chants, coming to serve as the motley pair with both physical energy and spiritual force.

With praise and work, their mortal embodiments, with sacred incantation, cause them to prosper by way of hearing the divine call of Yajur, who comes to connect the two worlds. Serving as twin demigods, the Aśvins drop down and, invoking their inner strength, build by both day and night, using their physical strength to invoke the sweet power of essence. Using their inner spirits, serving as refreshed parents, they are ready to take hold of families and serve like kings who fight to defend the holy law. As parents, they fully understand eternal love (Mitra), to whom they direct their songs, and they temper any cynicism toward the eternal law (Varuna). Using both their physical strength and their spiritual knowledge, they come to understand the powers of immortal nature (prakriti), where a relative may become a stranger. They overcome Agni, who ceaselessly guards Yama and Yami. They further come to understand the immortal aspect of individual existence, which is not easy to comprehend.

Serving on the council, the gods rejoice in seated among the godly mortal embodiments, all of whom receive the soft reflective light from the moon as well as the direct beams of light coming from the sun. They know they are served by two divine splendors, which are unwearied in their rotation to maintain the required brightness. As part of the divine council, the gods consider this as their secret plan—therefore, no one who manifested in a mortal body may have such knowledge. Other godly powers, namely, Savitar, Aditi, and Mitra, proclaim the eternal law (Varuna) so humanity does not sin. When Agni hears this, he brings the eternal flame among the manifested embodiments, along with a carriage filled with nectar (amrit). Thus, embodiments can continue to serve between the two worlds (heaven and earth), whereas the parents, the distant deities, come to stay to support all creation. With loud ancient inspiration, they rise in prayer to tackle problems and help mortal embodiments to follow the pathway as do the mortal princes.

According to *Rig-Veda* 10:13, using two carts (*havirdhanas*), the embodiments carry soma. They yoke their prayers with the ancient inspiration, raising their voices as they travel the princes' pathway, bringing soma to all sons of immortality who can hear all those who possess a celestial nature. Speeding along, they come nigh like twin sisters, religious-hearted votaries who walk forward and take their places, as they know they are near to serving in their proper stations, all very near to soma. The divine powers rise within the five spaces where they established their domicile, at least four feet above the earth, and from where they monitor the observances of the devout observance. By the sacred syllable they utter, they measure their purity at the principal place of order. For the gods' sake, they choose death as their portion, and for righteousness, they choose life eternal. The perishable Bṛhaspati and the mortal rishi, as a sacrifice, offer Yama in death, delivering him up as if their own dear bodies. The Seven Sisters flow on toward the youth, on whom the cosmic hosts (Maruts) wait: like the sons unto the father, they bring a sacrifice to the lords, who toil to prosper them well.

According to *Rig-Veda* 10:14, the mythical powers within the soma plants, when pressed out in the mortar, produce a sweetness that makes the soma rich, with which they realize their spiritual powers. When crossing the river, they take it gladly to celebrate in the thousands as they receive potential for great health, which like a honeycomb helps them to recover their memories. With sacrifices and oblations, the creations applaud as they serve the lord of all strength and power, with whom they gladly carouse as the treasure of choice most worthy. This brings out the hidden power of eternal wisdom. As the lord of precious boons, Indra, serving as inciter and as spiritual leader, who with the churl, as the guardian of singers, gladly carouses to eliminate woe and any hatred. This helps further refine the churl to bring them great wisdom, as the lords of mythical power, serving as the twin demigods Vimada and Nāsatyas, churn to unite the formerly separated heaven and earth. As a united pair, they serve as creator gods with the various supreme powers of causation (the Godhead). Without any complaint, serving as a united godly power, with honor and worship, they shed tears serving as demigods. Once again bringing together both creator and creations, sweet soma offered as they go forth with the mortal embodiments. By using their glands, such embodiments generate nectar (*amrit*), which turns perishable embodiments (noble souls) into imperishable embodiments (deities). They come to serve as the messengers (divinities) who enrich every embodiment with all pleasantness.

## GODLY FATHERS

According to *Rig-Veda* 10:15, Godly Fathers who have attained the life with spirits, they may ascend, to the lowest, highest, midmost as gentle, and righteous, who when call, they receive share of Soma. They are paying homage to Fathers, who passed of old age, and who followed by all those, who have rested in the earthly region. They dwell among the Mighty Races who have attained the gracious-minded Fathers. They gained son as progeny from Viṣṇu. Those who enjoy pressed juices with oblation, seated on sacred grass, they often as closer to Fathers, who sit on sacred grass, they offered specially made oblations which they accept. This brings with most auspicious favor, which without a trouble, give others health and strength. Fathers, worthy of the Soma, invited to their favorite oblations, as they laid on the sacred grass, they nigh and listen gracious unto those and bless them. Bowing with bended knees, and seated southward, they accept this sacrifice of offered with favor. Fathers, punish not for any sin, performed, or committed through human frailty. Lapped in the bosom of the purple

Mornings, it gives riches to the man who brings oblations and offer the offspring a portion of that treasure, and, present, them with energy. The Godly Fathers who deserve the Soma, they come to Soma banquet, as most noble. With Yama, yearning, they rejoice eat and given offerings at the pleasure. The eternal flame, Agni, with the gracious Fathers they dwell in glowing light, like Kavyas, who craved among the Gods, as the oblation winners, sing praise as singers' praises. They come, as Agni, the eternal flame, with countless Godly Fathers those who dwell light, as primeval God-adorers, eaters, and drinkers of oblations. Truthful they travel with the Deities along with godhead, Indra. Fathers whose eternal flame have tasted, they come approaching as soon, as the kindly leaders, they take proper place. Eat sacrificial food presented on the grass: grant riches with a multitude of hero sons. *Jātavedas*, with eternal flame entreated, bear the offerings which like fragrant which, they give them to the fathers who did graceful prayer *Svadha.* They eat, with God, and bring gifts. Serving *Jātavedas*, who knows the number of Fathers those who are present and those who are absent. All Fathers, known and those not known they accept the sacrifice, well prepared with portions. That consumed by fire or not cremated, with joy in their offering, during heaven, —they granted as the Sovran Lord, the world of spirits, within their own body, they bring with pleasure the Divine Will.

According to *Rig-Veda* 10:16. Serving as eternal flame it neither burn, nor consume or not let body or skin scattered. *Jātavedas*, appearing with manifested body, as matured they come to Godly Fathers. They become as the controller, serving as Deities'. They receive Sunlight with eyes, and with air receive spirit, before they go with merits to earth or to heaven. When they come unto lot of waters; in plants they make their home. With heat it burns to bring out auspicious forms. They bring out glowing splendor, Jātavedas, which bear as a man of the pious region. Fathers with the eternal flame offered oblations to Jātavedas wearing new life, and rejoin, in body form to increase their offspring. Any damage so ever inflicted by the dark bird, the Emmet, or the serpent, or the jackal the fire devoured all to heal. With Soma transform them into the Brahmans. By protecting shield, with flesh against flames encompass fat and marrow. Those Bold One, with fierce glow, eager to attack and consume those fail to griddle. Forbear, who merit Soma serves love with ladle: which brings drink to rejoice from the Immortal Deities. They send afar flesh-eating fire, bearing off stains as it departs to serve as it is subject to Yama's.

Jātavedas with skill. carry oblation to the God. By choosing as God, for Father-worship the flesh-eater, who prevail within dwelling. With offerings to meet Agni, it brings Fathers, who support the Law and announce with oblations as paid to Fathers and to Deities. Agni, again refresh the spot with coolness which scorched and burnt. Allowing fresh waterlily to grow along with tender grass and leafy herb. With, coolness, Plant with fresh moisture, freshening Herb, they come along with the female frog bring with delight.

## IMMORTAL SPIRIT

According to *Rig-Veda* 10:17, *Tvastar* prepares nuptial of his daughter, where all the world hears as they assemble. Yama's Mother, Spouse of great *Vivasvān,* who vanished as her dwelling carried from mortal embodiments. They hid the Immortal spirit, by creating one like her which they gave to *Vivasvān.* The chief wife of Suraya (*Saranyu*) brought this to the Aśvin brothers, both twinned pairs of children. Guard of the world, (*Pūṣan),* bear as cattle, which never injured, hence, serve as the provider of knowledge. They consign this to Fathers' who keep, as being gracious Gods which as eternal flame (*Āyu*), giver of all life, protect and bear forward on the distant pathway. The goddess (*Savitar*) the transport them where they dwell and appear as the pious, who passed before. Pūṣan knows all the realms: from whereas the ways they conduct as free from fear or danger. Giver of glowing blessings, all-heroic, as the wise go before watchful. Pūṣan who are born to move on distant pathways on the road, far from earth, and from heaven. Both most traditional places of assembly, which they travel and return with perfect knowledge. The pious call and worship goddess (*Sarasvatī*), while they proceed with sacrifice. The pious receive from goddess (*Sarasvatī*) bliss that offered to them. Goddess (*Sarasvatī*), come along with Fathers rejoicing oblations, while joyful seated upon the sacred grass and provides the strengthening food to removes any sickness. The Fathers called on goddess (*Sarasvatī*), who come right forward to offer solemn service. It gives sacrifices with food and wealth, representing a portion worth a thousand of refreshment. The Mother goddess, floods and make all bright and shining, serving as cleansers of holy oil. For, Goddesses, they bear off all adulteration as they rise purified and brightened. Through days of earliest, holy oil drops, as they descend on to their place, just as before, holy drops offer throughout the seven oblations, while moving, they are staying at the same place. The holy drops, falls and shoot like shaken arms, they come from the bosom from the *Adhvaryu's* purifying filter, and from godly power it offers with heart and cry the scarifying rituals (*Vaṣaṭ*). The fallen holy oil falls from stalk like it falls away from the ladle. Presenting as God (*Bṛhaspati*) they pour forth to make others rich. This like plants of earth bring cows as rich in milk, and manifested bodies rich in speech; bring essence filled with pure like cosmic vapors.

According to *Rig-Veda* 10:18, As the death, pursue its special pathway, away from which Gods travel, suggesting anyone who has eyes, to see and ears, to hear, they will not injure heroes, and will not touch their offspring. Even though, they may bring death (*Mrtyu*) on to their footstep, allowing further prolonged times for existence. This will allow sacrificing opulent children with possessions, cleansed, and purified. Separated from the death, these the living beings will now be calling for success to the Godly powers. They go forth, dancing and laughter, to celebrate further prolonged existence. Godly powers erect such barrier for the living that let none other reach this limit. They survive a hundred lengthened autumns, and they may bury death under neath mountains. The days follow in close succession of the season, duly come after the seasons. Each successor does not fail his foregoer, they form their lives like great Ordained. They live their full lives and find old age delightful, striving one behind the other.

The godly creative skillful craftsman (*Tvashtar*), who creates and implements as gracious, to serve by lengthen living days of existence, which allow even un-widowed, goddess (*Sati)* as like dames serving their noble husbands, who embellish with fragrant balm and ointment. All decked with fair jewels, as tearless, free from sorrow, the dames first go up to where husband resides. From fire rise the Goddess (*Sati)* unto the world of life. Serving as woman, they lie with lifeless husband, who that come by the side. Wifehood with husband, as segment took hand and wooed as a lover. From his dead hand, godhead take the bow, which carried with divine power and with might and glory. Noble heroes, with divine art, as the hosts, overcome those that fight against them. They go to them as the Godly Mother, which like Earth spread by far exceedingly kind and gracious. The young dame, as wool-soft unto rewarded as giver they preserve with breath to wonder from bosom. They stagger themselves on Earth, without heavily pressing downward: they afford easy access, gently tending, cover like a mother wraps her child with skirt. Now the throbbing, as Earth, it free from motion, as thousand lumps remain above the grounds, from home where they are distilling fatness, let them ever in place of sanctuary. They stay on from where, they go over a place serving piece of earth. Free from injury Father keep the pillar firm, and it allow Yama make abiding-place. Even arrow's feathers, they let a matching day fit the word, they held as a courser with the rein.

## DOMESTICATED ANIMALS

According to *Rig-Veda* 10:19, the domesticated animals, turn, and they go no farther on their way, without first visit to Wealthy Ones (*Agni and Soma*) which bring riches, again to secure wealth. They return repeatedly to get *soma* from Godhead *Indra,* and they give back to Godhead (*Agni),* which as eternal flame support the herder who let then return to feed. The godhead (*Agni*) keeps and let the wealth remain with them as they called upon by herder. The herder knows well, virtually their coming, like parting their home to return. They watch their approach and let them rest as they return. The herder mark well, as they drive forth; they mark their wandering away, their turning back and coming home. Home-leader, lead them to home where godhead *Indra*, restore all kind. They rejoice in them alive and as they offer on every side, butter, and milk as the strengthening food. All the Holy Deities pour down flood and wealth and as their Home-leader, they lead them home, restore them to bring home coming from four quarters of the earth; from these they bring back kind.

According to *Rig-Veda* 10:20. They send unto a good and happy mind worshipping godhead (*Agni*), along with youth fullest of Gods, as resistless, Friend of laws, which they guard along with the heavenly light. Spotted, they seek the mother's breast, with their mouth they magnify, flame with banner they homed in light. With glitters their row of teeth they act kind to the human as *Sage* reached from the ends of heaven, giving the clouds to the splendor. To taste man's offerings, as Strong they risen erect, fixing dwelling, they proceed to offer sacrifice with oblation, with worship they rest rapidly to come with furtherance. Godhead (*Agni*) as sword-armed come to serve Gods. With service for chief Lord of Sacrifice (*Agni), they* call upon Living, Son of Cloud to bless evermore who come, who magnify *Agni* with sacrificial gifts. The path treads with glorious black, white, and red, and striped, and brown, crimson to sire begat him bright with hues of gold. With thoughts, Son of Strength, godhead (*Agni)*, with instructive wisdom (*Vimada*), in accordant with the Immortals, offered with hymns, soliciting divine favor that brought all food, strength, a prosperous dwelling.

According to *Rig-Veda* 10:21 in choosing to sacrifice, sitting on the trimmed grass, glad invoking Hotter Priest (*Agni*), reveal-piercing with brightly shining, as the wealthy ones, adorned who bring the horses as their gift. With the sprinkling ladle, godhead (Agni) offering a taste with great buffing, with the holy statutes to rest with ladles that overflows. This produces black and white gleaming colors, that gladly assure all glories to celebrate. Godhead (*Agni*) deems wealth, victorious and immortal that bring vigor, with glad carouse filled with splendid sacrifices. Skilled in all lore (*Agni*), brings from the past legendry Sage (*Atharvan)* to life which served as the envoy of Sun God (*Vivasvāns)*, that at glad carouse and well-loved friend of death (*Yama*). During sacrifices they polish them to adored by Godhead (*Agni),* as they proceed for rites. All fair and lovely treasures they at glad carouse they offer as they are polished to become great. Godhead (Agni), as the Holy Priest offer rites. Those who with butter shines as glad carouse filled the eyes with bright light as the most observant as they are refined. Wide and aloft, they spread along with Godhead (Agni) with its brilliant flame. With the Bull, bellowing at their glad carouse they impregnate the females.

## LOVING FRIEND

According to *Rig-Veda* 10:22 with fame godhead (Indra), come with renowned loving friend *(Mitra*), who come in the home of Holy Soul (*Ṛṣis)* and in secret they praised with song. Godhead (*Indra*) famed among all with the glorious Thundered as praised, those loving friends (*Mitra*) appearing mid the folk, they completely win to become full renown. Sovran Lord of great and perfect strength, exert heroic might, fearless like thunder, as Father they bear loving friends as their darling sons. Harnessing with they as two blustering Steeds (*Asvins*) supported by Wind-God, to appear as the Thunder, that speed along the shining path, making divine way glorified. The godly embodiment even supports those dark Steeds of Wind which come to ride. They appear without driver they find all those who appear as mortal and immortal soul. When they approach, they ask if they are the holy priests (*Uśanā*) and why they come to appear as with manifested dwelling and why they come to serve as mortal embodiment coming from distant realms of Earth and Heaven. With the support from Godhead (*Indra*), they speak fair with holy prayer as offered to help to strike dead the monster (*Śuṣṇa*). The ancient Dravidian, (*Dasyu*), riteless, void of sense, inhuman who follow alien laws. As slayer of the foe, they with weapon wields even the worshiper (*Dāsa).* Hero with Heroes, as strong dear friend (*Dost*) whom God help. In many a place, they are blessed with divine gifts, as they sing with praise the monarch (*Vassals*). With urge as heroes, they slay the enemy, and bring brave in the fight come with swords that serve as Thunder. Even when hidden among numerous as stars they appear as the tribes of Sages. Who comes as Hero Thunder-armed: coming swift to bringing gifts and whose hand as prompt slash and burn. As the divine companion they destroy the whole evil progeny (*SUSnia).* As profitless hero, they like godhead (*Indra* enjoy the bliss brought as favor by Thunder. With soft impulses godhead (*Indra*) be fruitful and innocent whose treasures, milk bearing cow, filled with Thunder. That Earth, through power of knowing, brings things that may be known, handless and footless yet might they thrive, slowest, turning to the right, for every living person as they drink the Soma. Godhead (*Indra)*; not withheld, as the divine good, as the Treasure-giver which preserve the singers and liberal princes who make us wealthy, with abundant riches.

According to *Rig-Veda* 10:23 Godhead (Indra) who worshiped from the right hand wields the bolt, seeking sundered courses come to drive Bay Steeds. Shaking with might his beard, he progressed, casting forth weapons he deals the bounties. The Bay Steeds found treasure with sacrifice and with wealth become opulent serving Indra as slayer of the foe. Lord of Might appear as *Ṛbhu, Ṛbhukṣan, Vāja* serving as the devotees (*Dāsa*) 'along with godly powers they destroy.

Ancient famed Princes (*Maghavari)* brings thunderbolt of gold, serving as the controller of carriage, drawn with two Tawny Coursers, declared by Godhead (*Indra*) as the Sovran Lord with power spreads afar glory. Sovran even brings rain that comes like herds throwing drops of moisture covering the yellow surface. With the sweet juice, they establish the pleasant place which, and stirs the worshipper as wind disturbs the wood. With laud and praise they perform deeds of valor and serving as fatherlike brings power to make them strong. They with voice slew thousand wicked ones who spoke in varied manners, like contemptuous cries. The truthful Ṛṣi (*Vimadas*) formed most bountiful unmatched abundant place for them. We know the good we gain from the Mighty One; when we attract others as herder calls the domesticated animal. Never such bond of friendship dissevered. We know those who care for others as brother, the godly powers support such auspicious friendship.

According to *Rig-Veda* 10:24 Godhead (Indra), drink the Soma, which pressed out in the mortar. All filled with sweets, which sent down with great riches, glad carouse-in thousands. It prepares all most healthy, all filled with sacrifices, with lauds oblations that brings Lord of all strength and power, they grant grand carouse-the best choice worthy treasure. They come as Lord of precious boons, inciter that churl to bring Godhead Indra, with glad carouse that save from woe and hatred. Strong, Lords of Magic power, serving as Twain, shaken the united worlds apart, which appealed by *Vimada*, that forced apart the pair *Nāsatyas* as the united pair were rent as under all the Gods complained. The Gods to the *Nāsatyas* cried, Bring these together once again. Sweet going forth approach to home through your Deity, both Gods, enrich us with all pleasantness.

According to *Rig-Veda* 10:25, blessed with sharp minds, physical energy, and noble hearts, which provide spiritual power, the embodiments learn to enjoy soma and to relish life on earth with a great celebration. With nectar (amrit), they learn to be content, like the animals grazing the land. Consuming soma and drops of nectar, they continue polishing their skills, which directs their actions. The divine powers influence their increasing longings and pleasure. They celebrate and spread out to seek riches. They further polish their skills by practicing simplicity, so they do not neglect to abide by the law. Like a gracious father gives his son, they receive protection from godly powers, which saves them from slaughtered. In concert, they sing and worship to keep moving like streams of water, drinking soma and nectar to live and granted pleasure. They learn to use the powers of their minds, which are like filled beakers, which with the mighty power brings along strong skills, like the sages have, which they use with their noble hearts to throw open the stall doors and set free the cows and horses.

Serving as the guards of the herds, the embodiments direct the flow of soma while spreading out and use nectar to cover a wide range of living beings. Spreading soma in all directions, and serving as guardians, they are never deceived. Like kings, they drive foemen away from their dwellings and ensure no one wicked becomes the ruler. They are watchful over the mythical juice, making sure soma passed to those who seek wisdom and that some is put into the storehouse for later obtaining vital strength.

Those who are better skilled than others become guides, glad to save those whom they protect from harm and sorrow. Polishing their great art, they even come to serve as the chief slayers of foemen, through the holy river Indus, with their gracious friend Indra serving in the war, which they win them as his offspring. Victorious, serving the gladdening drink, they grow in strength and become very dear to Indra. Singing mighty hymns, they carouse with the great earthly sage Kakṣīvān. To serve as sages, they are honored receive gifts that bring power and wealth.

According to *Rig-Veda* 10:26, the sages proceed with their teams, singing lovely songs, to meet with the glorious solar deity Pūṣan, who comes with a yoked chariot pulled by the mighty twin Aśvins. With sacred hymns, the sages serve as singers, and with godly powers they serve with mighty majesty. Making offerings to the solar deity Pūṣan, they given eternal wisdom and higher knowledge, even higher than that provided by the mythical juice floating in the holy river Indus, which, drawing moisture from corn, bedews the pastures. This inspires fulfillment through the singing of hymns, which stirs the singers to serve as sages. Jointly, they share each sacrifice with the chariot driver and the steeds. As holy men, rishis, along with the singing friends, serve to faithfully guard the sheep. They weave their clothes and their hair to make beautiful things. The mighty lord of spoils and wealth Such, as a holistic sign, weaves them together, making strong friends of them, which brings prosperity to all. Moving lightly like goats with their goatherd, they make lovely things and can never be deceived.

The solar deity Pūṣan appears among the goats, who turn about the chariot pole. Serving as friends, all supplicants born in olden times bend their arms in a display of certainty among the goats. The majestic Pūṣan speeds up his chariot to increase their store of wealth and hearkens them to listen when they called upon.

## UNRIGHTEOUS

According to *Rig-Veda* 10:27, with firm determination, the majestic solar deity Pūṣan, serving as a patron, provides aid by pouring out soma to slay anybody who, with unrighteous power, has no oblation to offer or exhibits abnormal behavior. In the righteous war, those who are radiant according to divine will lead the friends in the fight against evil, that is, those with a godless nature. After preparing it at home, using vigorous steeds, they pour soma out for all those who are fifteen times stronger than normal. Since they do not know the strength of the enemy, they declare only that they will slay the godless in the battle. As soon as they see the enemy raging and furious, ready for combat, they speak forth with praises for the vigorous steeds, even though with mighty deeds, the divine messenger Maghavan, unrecorded, as in the past, surpasses even the potent ones who abide in peace, conquering them by grasping their feet and throwing them off the mountain. Nothing hinders Maghavan from exploiting his heroic powers; he uses divine will to support the cause. Even the deaf tremble at his roaring. Every day the gods come to agitate the air (Vayu) and create a dust storm. They see drinking mythical juice that not blessed by gods and, thus, are the architects of their own destruction. The fellies of the gods' carriage pass over those powers who have blamed and mocked noble souls. This way noble powers grow to be full of vitality and vigor, which noticed, sooner and later, by the evil powers. With two canopies, they surround all, reaching the limit of this region, where they are set free like creatures to eat of the barley and become pious. Seen wandering, they hear pious echoes all around them. When the ones who gathered ones fed by herdsman from the cornland, the captor yokes even the yokeless creatures who have always been seeking their own freedom, setting them loose to go free. Serving according to the divine will, they disappear, holding true to the spoken divine word. Thus, living creatures separated into quadrupeds and bipeds. As per divine will, without a fight, they separated with riches, one set worshipping with the warmth of eternal love as bipeds such as human beings. Not knowing it, the mother carries within her breast the infant noble soul, which she soothes. The fathers, dressed as heroes, amid a conflagration, become fat and wither like dice thrown in a sporting game. Both reach the holy ground, hallowed on the way, purified in the heavenly waters. Crying aloud, they run in all directions: one-half of them will cook; the other half will not. The goddess Savitar declares the quadrupeds as a group that, according to divine will, survive by foraging for food in the woods. These are the ones who supply milk and butter.

From a distance, Savitar sees a troop advancing, moving not on wheels, but with their own godlike nature, as friendly ones, bipeds seeking to serve as noble living beings to create a new generation such as humanity that can overpower or destroy any bands of evil beings. These types of bipeds harnessed but drive not too far away, most often lingering. They use water as an aid him or an object, following the all-cleansing sunrays above them. Often, they guided by the thunderbolts hurled down from the misty realm of Sūrya. Beyond the misty realm there is another glory. When they pass, they leave behind no sorrow. The lowing cow, bound fast to a tree, seen by a predator. By living in the material world, and with Indra strengthening the noble souls (rishis), they can face their fear of death, as they see themselves standing in the gods' mansion, where they first created; the separation came later. The trinity welcomes such eternal souls to the holy ground, where they bathed in water and give off moisture as cosmic vapor, traveling between heaven and earth. The life cycle is well marked, and they know they must not hide during times of war, where the heavenly pantheon of Sūrya provides the light that exposes eternal wisdom and carries the eternal soul within the cosmic vapor as it travels through the interstellar realm located in the terrestrial region, which provides the cover to convey the eternal soul to holy ground (Prithvi).

According to *Rig-Veda* 10:28, the eternal soul once again manifests in many forms, appearing as mortal and immortal souls, traveling between heaven and earth, although the invisible power is never free from the robes that veil it. The manifested eternal soul, as a heralded priest, after many days of serving the godhead Indra, the earth's guardian, becomes a friend serving as the best among heroes. The manifested eternal souls rejoice like young birds sitting in a tree, a swift-flying pair roused by laudation. With the morning light, they perform their dance, servants performing a heroic act. Their victorious embodiments shine with a triple splendor, thereby attracting one hundred chiefs, each with a holy eternal soul. Kutsa, a holy eternal soul, serves the gladdening draft to please Indra before speeding off with mighty skill through the doors, singing songs. According to divine will, Kutsa presents a gift that attracts all, bringing food to offer to Indra. Famous, Kutsa is a hero serving the cosmic region with a plan to serve the holy ground and the actions to back it up. He seeks other living things as a true friend, taking wide strides toward the Sustainer, Vishnu, helping all in his path with the food that generates thought.

According to *Rig-Veda* 10:29, Kutsa speeds happily toward the heavenly body Sūrya, and together the two of them end their journey like bridegrooms who wish to meet their future spouses. Strong, with heavenly natures, they present food, along with songs, as a measure of praise for Indra. From a wide well, heavenly majesty dispensed onto holy ground as eternal wisdom, along with choice soma mixed with butter and sweet essence (meath). After making this pleasant drink, they pour out a bowl full of the sweet juice as a bounty for the faithful. Across the holy ground that is part of the terrestrial region, with great power and eternal wisdom, it expands, served by the friend of living beings who exploits his heroic power to enable Indra to win the war. Multitudes of manifested living things strive to win friendship as the chariot of Indra ascends in battle and moves with gracious favor.

According to *Rig-Veda* 10:30, with exertion, embodied eternal souls serving as priests (*adhvaryus*), with glorious food, meet both the eternal law (Varuna) and eternal love (Mitra). With their support, the embodied souls spread out and go far to merge with the celestial waters. With oblations, the manifested eternal souls, longing to merge with the celestial water, look down upon the purple-tinted eagle, which is flying and following the waves, with the skill to reach the reservoir. As a child of the water, it flows with the blessed waves and receives the pressed soma it desires, filled with sweetness, which brings a bright light to shine upon all, feeding them the fuel as if in a flood. The sages worship and make sacrifices. This brings rich, sweet-tasting water. As children of the water, they received with heroic might by Indra. Delighted, the young male embodiments presented with pleasant damsels. They go unto the embodied eternal souls who use herbs to purify and infuse the waters. Like virgin aide bow before the gallant youth, coming with love and a yearning to meet them.

With his heart in accord, Adhvaryus, single-minded, serves as the heavenly waters, making room to imprison them, which frees them from the mighty imprecation. To Indra, they send forth a rich current that mixes the essence with waves. This gratifies all with the godly waters. They send essence-rich waves to Indra in rivers that transform nothingness into something, namely, offspring, who bring a wealth of sweet oil and balm, to sacrificed to the gods, whom they implore. The wealthy ones of the waters, hearing the divine invocation, send forth rapture-giving waves on the river that allow Indra to drink, which sets the demigods in motion to connect heaven and earth, as the two are in motion. This gives birth to the clouds, desire springing up among those who wander the path, a triple-distilled transport connecting the two bodies, earth and heaven, to form one universe. The winding streams, with their double current, like cattle raiders, seek lower pastures.

Waters that dwell together, thrive together, serving queens, the mothers of the world, who are honored by the noble souls (rishis). They send forth with sacrifices and holy worship, singing hymns and praying for riches. In need, they open their ears to hearing the divine call as it comes upon the waters. The wealthy ones of the water control all treasures and increase their intellect through transforming soma into Amrit. Like the queen of independence, Sarasvati gives life to the worshipper serving as a singer. When the worshippers behold the water, they come forth carrying milk and butter, also bearing pressed soma and essence to present to Indra. They harmonize with the eternal souls (*Adhvaryu*) and become rich with eternal wealth, serving as living beings. As friends, they come to sit with the gods in their dwelling place. Seated on holy grass, they bring in the soma as the children of the water. Now the grass filled with water, the eternal souls appearing as pious ones. Seated at the place of worship, the *Adhvaryu* bring pressed soma juice for Indra in service to the gods.

According to *Rig-Veda* 10:31, with a benediction from the gods, the *Adhvaryu*, approach with the support of the gods, thereby happily making friends as they pass through all troubles triumphantly. The manifested bodies who think on wealth and strive to win adoration following the path of order. They receive counsel and, with their own insight, grasp for the noble vigor of the eternal soul. They sing hymns and allocate portions of soma poured out, walking as friends into the wondrous world. They gain comfort, power amid their circumstances, and become acquainted with immortal powers.

Pleased, the eternal lord loves the households of manifested embodiments. Savitar, goddess of water, created to serve as the patron Bhaga. With grace, Bhaga appears as the manifested noble soul Aryaman, who manages cattle, appearing with delight in the morning. With the dwelling place set up for the assembly of the gods, the morning light brings with it rich food. The noble souls gather to sing praises. As singers, they increase their riches. The first, most gracious, with far-extending favor, comes to exist with full abundance as a manifested eternal soul, like the bull. With their own support, the noble souls build a mansion where all may dwell together.

The vegetable kingdom grows to become a tree that provides wood to create a forest, which as part of the holy ground (Prithvi) becomes the place between earth and heaven. The twin demigods stand fast polishing their skills, never aging, producing hymns with which to praise and serve many a day. Here is the place beyond the bull, supporter of the heavens and the earth. With divine power, the noble souls make their skin like filters, which like bay coursers protects them from the heavenly rays coming from the illuminated body Sūrya. With divine bliss, they pass over the wide earth, generating a wind (*stega*) like a cloud of mist infused with oil, covering the embodiments with eternal law and eternal love (Varuna and Mitra, respectively). They hide from the ferocious fire (Agni) in the woods, whizzing forth with the solar wind in cosmic splendor.

When called suddenly, they go to protect the sacred cow that rests alone, self-protected, and end all her troubles. On holy ground, the first son springs from father and mother to start up a game that all seek to play. The son of *Nṛṣad* given the name of *Kaịnva*, a brown-hued courser that comes to win the treasure. Dark colored, this courser, with shining udders, comes swollen according to the divine will and divine order.

## BENEVOLENCE

Celestial world (*Swar Loka*) represents the altruistic souls which according to *Rig-Veda* 10:32, as benevolent come with speed, bringing the pair male and female, which brings along the meditating gods, which in turn deliver a boon. Indra graciously accepts gifts from both male and female, in return helping them attain higher knowledge by drinking soma. Indra wanders through the sphere of light (heaven) and the bottom realm of the earth, the created material world (Virāj). In the manifested sphere, he praised and is often the subject of solemn rites to conquer the noisy babblers who present no gifts and have no appreciation for beauty or for the offspring who honor their lineage. A wife, having attracted a husband, with a shout of joy, joined in auspicious marriage by way of a rite. The beautiful meeting place looked upon, where, like milk cows, the divine order establishes the wedding train, where the herd's mother counts as first and best of all. Around her there are the seven-toned people singing in a choir. Before coming to rest, the Pious One reaches this place. The victorious heavenly power Rudra, with his band of immortal gods, and with the wind, helps to pour out essence (meath), with the power of songs of praise, to win the gifts. Rudra's band maintains the law of the gods and advises the divine powers to remain lying hidden in the waters.

Indra, who knows well, beholds all, and shows this as instructed by the godhead Agni. When faced with a stranger asking the way to follow, Indra, knowing all, provides them with skills and guides them in traveling onward. With eternal truth and blessing, Indra and Agni provide instruction so the stranger may find the path that leads directly forward, and as the breath remembered to this day. The breath itself remains concealed within the bosom of the mother, passing through youth into old age, and when it is come upon, the offspring become gracious and good, learning to be free from anger. A metal pot representing purity (*kalasha*) used with blessings to carry the generous present of soma to the wealthy princes, which they bear in their hearts as a unique reward.

According to *Rig-Veda* 10:33, people impelled to seek the fastest pathway to the divine patron Pūṣan, who appears as an eternal universal soul with exotic power and provides safety to the universal gods who can hear the cry to behold the universal law. In their ribs (*dubsasu*), which built to protect their organs, they feel pain, with trouble coming from the rival powers, along with indigence, nakedness, and exhaustion, which press upon their ribs, making them sore, this causing the individual living spirit to emerge, fluttering, like a bird flying out of its cage. As rats eat the woven threads, the exotic power cares for the consuming individual soul of the divine singer (*gatakratu*).

With mercy, Indra, bounteous lord, father unto all, serves the priests (rishis) as they choose as their prince the most liberal *Kurusravana*, son of *Trasadasyu*, who with his carriage, three bays harnessed to it, comes straight on. As the giver of one thousand drafts of meath, serving as a sire, *Upamasravas* speaks words that impart a sweetness over the fair field marked for his grandson *Mitratithi*, who offers his father's eulogy. Controlled by the immortal gods, the lords of the liberal embodied living beings, they come to live one hundred lives and achieve a stature beyond even that of the gods as they part from their friend.

According to *Rig-Veda* 10:34, from the windy heights, spring tall trees. The eternal grandson of love (*Mitratith*), rolling with power, turns toward a place dear to him, where he drinks, deeply of the gods' mythical juice. *Mujavan*, who never slumbers or dies, never pushes or gets angry, but with friends he remains ever gracious. With a single point of finality, like a devoted wife whom he alienates for the sake of death while his wife holds him aloof, his mother hates the wretched and finds no one to give her comfort. As a dear horse that has grown old and feeble, he finds nothing to profit the gamester. Others caressed like rich wives in hopes of seeing the powerful ones die, all of them coveted like a rapid courser. Father, mother, brothers, saying they know him not, bind him and take him with the coursers. Then the embodiment resolves to play with them no longer, seeing his friends depart, leaving him lonely. He seeks the meeting place of like a gamester seeks a gambling house, wandering with his body afire. Still, with an eager longing he engages in a game of dice, betting all he has against his opponent. Verily, it is as if the dice armed with goads and driving hooks, deceptive and tormenting, causing grievous woe. Gambling pays off meager amounts and then destroys the man who wins, deeply immersed in playing and hoping to win.

Merrily accompanied by a troop of fifty-three, the goddess *Savitar* remains faithful the whole time. The troops bend not even in the face of mighty: even the king pays them homage and reveres them. Downward they roll, and then spring quickly upward and, handless, force the man with hands to serve them. Cast on the board like lumps of magic charcoal, though cold themselves, they burn the heart to ashes. The gambler's wife left lonely and wretched; the mother mourns the son who wanders homeless. In constant fear, in debt, and seeking riches, he goes by night unto the homes of others. Sad is the gambler when he sees a matron, another's wife, and her well-ordered dwelling. He yokes the brown steeds in the early morning, when the fire is cold, and sinks down as an outcast. To the great captain of a mighty army who has become the troops' imperial leader, he shows his ten extended fingers and speaks the truth. The gods advise those who have no wealth to refrain from playing dice: instead, they should cultivate their cornland, then enjoy their gains and deem that wealth sufficient. There are the cattle, and there the wife of the gambler. So, the good goddess *Savitar* tells the gambler to make the gods his friends: show mercy. "Assail us not with your terrific fierceness. Appeased be your malignity and anger and let the brown dice snare another captive."

According to *Rig-Veda* 10:35, the fires associated with Agni waken Indra and bring the first light at dawn, which begins to shine, representing the great pair of heaven and earth. To this day the favor of the gods claimed as the grace of *Śaryaṇāvān,* who represents the hills and holy streams, serving as the mother of opulence. With innocence, all pray to the heavenly power Sūrya and to Indra, God of the dawn. So may the flowing soma bring bliss today. May the great twin demigods serving heaven and earth keep everyone free from sin and bring peace and happiness. Morning sends forth its light to drive sin far away. With prayers to Agni, happiness enkindled. The first dawn brings the host of gracious gods, richly shining, who strive for wealth. The wrath of the malign kept far away. Dawn comes forward with the bright beams of the sun, flushing to bring the light that shines upon all to make the day auspicious and renowned, free from all sickness. At morning, let the fires mount upward with the sun to create a lofty blaze.

According to *Rig-Veda* 10:36, the twin demigod Aśvins harness their swift-moving carriage and, with prayers, enkindles Agni, who sends them a portion choice and excellent, along with the goddess Sarasvatī to deal with the wealth. Dhisana, mother of opulence, cries in eternal sacrifice and, with prayer, enkindles Agni to further declare the eternal law. The law of the gods causes mortal embodiments to acknowledge higher wisdom while the sun rises, their beholding all the rays of morning. To this day, manifested bodies pray with innocence, strewing grass, adjusting the compressed stones, perfecting all with their hymns. The noble souls the Ādityas keep moving restlessly, praying to Agni for contentment. The great holy grass bids good morning to the gods serving the banquet—Agni, Varuna, Indra, Mitra, and Bhaga, all seated among the seven priests and the demigods to gain contentment. The noble Ādityas, in perfect accordance, help make the sacrifice and thrive through the powers of Pūṣan, Bṛhaspati, Bhaga, and the twin Aśvins, also imploring the enkindled Agni for happiness. The Ādityas, serving as gods, vouchsafe individual embodiments so they may become praiseworthy and prosperous, and receive a hero's sure defense. For cattle, for offspring, for progeny, and for extended life they pray to kindle Agni, also asking him to bring peace and tranquility. To this day, the cosmic hosts (Maruts), serving as demigods, come near to provide aid and make sure all fires are well lit. All gods come with gracious favor to help collect the spoils, that is, the wealth and other possessions. They serve as deities in the battle to protect all and rescue them from affliction, as they fear no danger with their ability to provide milk as libation, a feast from the mighty gods.

## REGULATORS

Bhuvar Loka is the region regulated by the godly powers, according to *Rig-Veda* 10:37, with homage unto the eternal law (Varuna) and eternal love (Mitra) as the regulators of the noble souls the Ādityas, along with the cosmic hosts the Maruts, serving as demigods, who offer their solemn worship to the mighty gods, with the ensign seemingly far away as are all who are born of the gods. They sing their praises to the heavenly power Sūrya and to his son Dyaus, regulating the supreme powers of causation. They all speak the eternal truth and come to guard all beings from every direction, whatever heaven or earth, as they spread out. All else that is in motion finds a place of rest as the waters ever flow and mount to the sun. No godless man since the remotest time has ever drawn down upon the divine powers driving forth with winged dappled steeds. The divine luster waits upon Sūrya to move, who rises with a different light, the light that scatters the gloom and shines upon every moving thing. It keeps far from all feeble and worthless sacrifices and drives away disease and removes every evil dream. It sent forth to guard the law of the universe, and to enable those who so desire to arise free from wrath. When the heavenly power *Sūrya* addressed with prayers, to this day he comes with godly favor to serve their purposes and desires. This, as part of the invocation, represents words from the heaven and earth, and from Indra, who regulates the flow of the water, and the cosmic demigods the *Maruts*, who hear all, and never make anyone suffer in the presence of the light of the sun, providing living beings with happy lives until they reach old age.

Always with cheerful spirits, and always keen of sight, they preserve all their children, keeping them free from sickness and free from sin, granting them long lives to look upon the heavenly body *Sūrya*, rising day by day, with the great power of compassion, Mitra. Like Sūrya, the children live long and look on as the Far-Seeing One brings a glorious radiant light with godly power, which brings joy to everyone with the eyes to see it. Mounting up in the heavens, the light shines forth in a flood. With luster, it serves the whole world and all of life, coming forth with beams and then returning unto its rest, joining with the heavenly power Sūrya and forming the golden hair that ascends day after day, still bringing pure innocence.

The light comes to bless with its shine. The perfect daylight comes to bless the cold with its fervent heat. The heavenly body Sūrya bestows riches that bless the homes, even when the manifested bodies are traveling. Living creatures of all kinds, including bipeds and quadrupeds, vouchsafed and provided with protection. They may drink and eat invigorating food, and still they granted health and strength, along with perfect innocence. If by way of grievous sin they invoke or provoke the godly powers with their tongues or in their heart, then the power of nature (Vasu) removes their guilt. If they should lie according to the will of the evil one, then they led into a pattern of thought that causes deep distress.

According to *Rig-Veda* 10:38, in the great battle, the glorious Indra, amid the loud hullabaloo of war, wins the victory. Amid the strife, bold animals enter the ring, where arrows are flying all around them. The heroes come from their homes to bring food and milk, and to meet with Indra. They even meet the renowned friendly conqueror Śakra, with a desire to enlist nature (Vasu) to enter the fight. The godless man, much lauded, asks Indra who would be easier to defeat in war, *Dāsa* or *Ārya*, and asks his help in subduing the godless men in the clash. Indra invoked by many, especially by the few who stand nigh to provide comfort to the warriors. Indra, famed hero, winner in the deadly battle, favors the manifested bodies even today. For Indra hears the self-calling as a capturer, like a steer that never yields, urging him amid the churl to release the noble soul (*Kutsa)* to come herewith and sit still.

According to *Rig-Veda* 10:39, the name of a father is easy to invoke. All assembled as a body invoked, bringing the embodied demigods the *Aśvins*. The demigods come swiftly rolling in, and in turn engage in worship to invoke the evening light, same as they do the morning light. Awakening all with pleasant strains of music, they let the hymns flow forth, giving rise to abundance and fulfillment of desires. The *Aśvins* bestow upon godly souls a glorious heritage, also giving princes the fair treasure, that is, soma. This provides bliss as they grow old, their embodiments serving as their homes as they continue to serve as helpers of those who are slow and lag. The embodiments recognize the *Aśvins* as enhanced demigods, *Nāsatya*s, coming as healers to serve the blind, the thin and feeble, and others with broken bones. They make the weak sage (*Cyavāna*), worn out from old age, young again, as they serve as free-flowing energy like that of the calligraphic monogram (*Tuğra*) which through libations comes to praised. With upraised embodiments, the *Nāsatyas* bring to life for the people the ancient deeds, like physicians bringing a patient back to health. They lauded with the divine will and with essence to restore the ancestral powers serving as the demigod (*Aśvins*).

They *Nāsatyas* believed, listened to, and cried for, as their sons seek aid from their respective fathers and mothers. The *Nāsatyas* serve the poor, those without kin or friends, or any blood ties, sparing them from any curse or attack. As mother and father, mounted on a chariot, they appear as the good-looking, aid virgin aid (*Vimada)* or as the bride *(Purumitra*). They come when called, for example, by the weak woman who granted noble offspring, thus establishing her as a happy wife. Giving again the vigor of youthful life, they come to serve through the old sage Kali, the destroyer of evil forces, which loom on the horizon. With worship, *Vandana* rescued being raised up from within the deep dark pit and, in a moment, is given the power to move like the righteous warrior (*Viśpalā*) The twin *Aśvins*, endowed with physical strength, hidden in a cave, well-nigh dead, bring forth replicas of real weapons to free noble souls, including *Saptavadliri* and *Atri,* from the pit of fire, taking them to a pleasant resting place in a shallow cove near the shore, appearing as white-colored coursers, mighty with ninety-nine gifts of strength, with *Pedu* serving as protégé of the mythical horse. The *Aśvins*, endowed with demigod powers, bear their friends speedily to the joy-giving patron (*Bhaga*), invoking creative manifested embodiments.

They appear as two kings, coming from no direction, whom none may check or stay. They remove any grief, distress, and danger that manifests among living beings. The demigod Aśvins, swift to hear, borne on their glowing path, consort to be foremost in the race. They arrive in a chariot pulled by the cosmic body Ṛbhu, who moves faster than the speed of thought, harnessed where the heavenly daughter springs up to give to birth to the godly power Vivasvan, who comes to welcome night and day. As conquerors, the Aśvins emerge from the split mountain where they have their home, causing the cows to stream forth with milk for the sake of the prophet Śayu. They even go into the wolf's deep throat to free the swallowed quail. Then the ancient sage *Bhrigu* prepares a meal to applaud the *Aśvins*, with *Bhrigu* coming in a manifested body, all decked as a bride ready to meet her bridegroom and, upon bearing a son, stay with him forever.

The chanting of Vedic mantras (*tapas*) is part of a variety of austere spiritual practices (*ghosa*) used to mortify the body. Mantras widely used to expound spiritual concepts that developed through heat or inner energy, which comes about by meditation, for example. Any practice used to obtain special observations and insights, called spiritual ecstasy (*vṛddhi*), sometimes even sexual intimacy, involves penance and pious activity, in addition to extreme meditation and self-discipline. This includes a spectrum of practices ranging from asceticism to inner cleansing, to self-discipline, which often involves solitude and is a part of the monastic practice that believed to be a means to liberation or salvation (moksha).

According to *Rig-Veda* 10:40, the radiant embodiments go on their way all decked like heroes, following a happy course. Starting at daybreak, they visit every house, borne through prayer and sacrifice. Like godheads, in the evening and in the morning, and at every waystation where they rest for the night, they enter their warm beds with intimacy, like a widow draws toward her late husband's brother, attracting him like a bride attracts her groom. Rising early, they sing out their praise in the voice of a herald, then meet for worship. Each morning they do this, like going to the house of ruin, whoever brings the libations coming to serving as a hero. As two sons of the king, as hunters, they follow two wild elephants, calling with oblations in the morning and the evening, and other appointed times, praying the traditional prayers as the make their offerings to chiefs.

As the lords of splendor, the demigod Aśvins bring food to strengthen Ghoṣā, the daughter of the king, to serve as heroes. They begged to stay near during the day and to bear with her through the night, always helping to enrich the embodied chieftain with steeds. The Aśvins, serving the wise saint Kutsa, also serve the manifested embodiments by coming along in their carriage to the people who sing their praises. The Aśvins are like the bee with honey in its mouth, which honey the aid virgin carries off in her purified hands. They come near to help the twin demigods Bhujyu and Vaśa and transform the breath of the queen of the wind, Sinjara, into life force for Uśanā, with whom they secure friendship for those who worship them. By granting protection, they fulfill the desire for happiness, also protecting Krsa and Śayu, who serve them. Straightaway, the Aśvins come in splendor to the worshippers and throw open the cattle stalls. With thunder, they give birth to sevenfold mouths to feed, with the female bringing forth newborns that appear like plants of a wondrous beauty. This immediately causes rivers to spring up and begin running down a deep descent, from that day becoming the experts and the lords of the waters.

As living things grieve, crying aloud and making sacrifices, the manifested bodies set their thoughts upon a distant hope. Bringing lovely things for the fathers who have gathered to express their joy as husbands, they watch as the wives and the husbands embrace each other. Having no knowledge, the spouses grow taller and, like youths, rest within the chambers of their new partners. Within their new dwellings, they strive to become vigorous guides who love all kinds and cultivate desire as the wondrous demigods do by way of the favoring grace of the lords of ample wealth. With longing stored up within their hearts, the lords of splendor serve as a twofold guard, who as friends are welcome to enter the abode of the noble soul Aryaman. They rejoice in their dwelling place, appearing in manifested mortal embodiments, and become as heroic sons with riches. As the lords of splendor, they enjoy the place where the manifested bodies drink, and even remove the spiteful tree stump standing in their path. Serving as wonderworkers, lords of luster, they bring delight for themselves and others, and control where they go, choosing which abodes of the sages they will enter to worship.

## CONVERSION

*Bhuta Loka* represents the region above the underworld where a gene from a one-celled bacterium moved to another bacterial cell, starting the process of conversion. In molecular biology and genetics, the conversion takes place only if the recipient bacterium is in a state of competence, which might occur in nature and sometimes induced in a laboratory. As part of the transformation, the genetic material passes through the intervening medium, and uptake is completely dependent on the recipient bacterium.

According to *Rig-Veda* 10:41, the divine carriage serving the trinity comes pick them up; and converted through libations. Serving as the ultimate carriage, worthy of sacrifice, it called upon with pure hymns amid the first flush of morning light dawn by the enhanced demigods the *Nāsatyas*. They mount the carriage, to which horses harnessed, and begin their travels early, the carriage laden with its freight of balm to serve heroes, who with sacrifice and worship visit all, even the poor clans. The honorable priest Adhvaryu brings meath to support and strengthen the clans, a kindly priest serving as friend of the household. Pour libations, the sages approach the twin demigod Aśvins, serving them meath.

According to *Rig-Veda* 10:42, as an archer, Indra shoots his arrows afar to offer laudation. Sages serving as singers rest beside the mythical juice. As lovers, they wake Indra to come and draw soma from the plants, like milking a cow. Indra wastes no time in granting riches to the heroes from a vessel filled to the brim with treasure. He brings his messenger Maghavan to serve as the bounteous giver, who quickens to join forces with the active intelligence Śakra, who is fortunate to revive eternal wisdom. With such wisdom, Maghavan and Śakra find the wealth hidden by their foes in battle, Indra standing together with the manifested bodies, entering the fray with those who bring gifts, serving as a hero. By pouring out soma, he makes them his comrades, seeking more than friendship.

Those with plenteous food express the plants quickly to acquire the treasured soma, so early in the morning they may march swiftly with their weapons to overpower their foes and slay the tyrant. Maghavan joins them when needed, and before long the foes tremble and bow to all the noble glorious ones. With the fierce godly thunderbolt, they intimidate many, driving their foes away into the distance. Indra provides corn and cattle as the divine singers pray to gain spiritual strength and riches. Indra, the swallower of strong rich libations, brings a great boon of potent soma to serve to them. The messenger does not restrict the delivery of this bounty and even brings much wealth unto those who press the plants to produce soma. Maghavan and Indra fight superiorly to win the advantage, like a gambler stacks up chips when is on a winning streak. The devotees, celestial-natured, overwhelmed with riches, do not hold back their treasure. Much invoked, they eradicate famine and subdue the evil who ones want to steal all their grain and cattle. Allied, first in rank, Indra and Maghavan take from the princes their possessions. The perishable noble Bṛhaspati come to protect them from sinners from the rear, from above, and from below. Lord Indra, as a friend among friends, comes from the front and from the center to guard their space and provide them with room to grow and gain their freedom.

In perfect unison, all yearning to sing hymns, the troops sing forth with songs of praise for Indra, light of heaven, embrace him as their lord like wives embrace their husbands. The worshippers accept the help he provides as he directs their spirits, which never stray, nor pin their hopes on those who are much invoked. They sit as wonderfully as a king upon the sacred grass and drink the soma, paying no mind to indigence and deprivation. Indra turns away and lets Maghavan manage such situations, regulating the dominion filled with precious wealth. Indra himself moves along with the seven rivers, flowing with the water and moving along their downward course to increase their vitality and vigor, like potent steer and birds, which rest in the trees with colorful leaves. Indra flows along with the gladdening soma, which fills bowls.

With splendor, Indra's face glows with mighty power, and his worshippers, the noble Āryans, see it shining in the heavens, serving the eternal light. As a gambler piles up his winnings, Maghavan sweeps up whatever has gained in the glorious fight. No one prior had the ability to perform this mighty deed. Maghavan, when he comes, turns toward the manifested tribes, witnessed by the steer, and takes notice of the people's songs of praise. The manifested embodiments whose libations of soma delight Śakra, given him the means to vanquish the foes.

All the streams of soma come together and flow unto Indra, flowing like water in the river, or rivulets in a lake. In the place of sacrifice, sages exalt their might, as the rain swells the corn and sends moisture back to heaven. Sūrya, like a furious bull, is the one who causes these floods. The daughters of the worthy lord Sūrya, through Maghavan, now find the light to offer oblation and soma, which promptly pours out as a gift. This causes their intelligence to sharpen as they come forth with the light. Like cows pouring out sacrificial milk, they welcomed by the moon, the Red God, which shines brightly with its refulgent rays, causing the lord of the heroes to glow with the sheen of heaven. Among invoked, the lords eradicate all famine and evil by providing a store of grain and cattle, allied as those of highest rank, with princes obtaining possessions by their own effort. The perishable body *Bṛhaspati* comes to protect them all from sinners coming from the rear, from above, and from below. Indra comes from the front and the center, serving as a friend among friends, vouchsafing the space and providing freedom.

According to *Rig-Veda* 10:44, as sovereign, Indra comes to the celebration, bringing the holy law to serve the overcomers. The conquering forces, with great steer whose power knows no limit, all seated firmly within their embodiments, with passive hands, support the king by grasping the thunder as they walk the path, serving Indra as the lord of humanity. They handle and support the strong steeds, all blessed with mighty powers, according to the divine will, to increase in power and wield the thunder, gathering it into their arms to bring to the banquet and share it.

The steer, like the bull, with might and vigor, rushes forward in love toward the vat. It gathers its energy, which it has amassed by itself, benefit, to the head of the wise, with precious treasures meant for those who pray and offer gifts as worshippers. Serving with art, the lord, as such, sits on the holy grass with his vessels inviolate as the law commands. Since the earliest invocation, the gods have won a glory that can never surpassed. Those who are unable to ascend with the ship of sacrifice sink down in desolation, trembling with alarm. Such is the case for the others, the evilhearted, whose horses, difficult to harness, have yoked. Here the advance force stands near to offer gifts, by whom work that brings a reward done. The lord fixes the plains and mountains as they shake.

The sky lord Dyaus thunders forth, making the midair region quake, separating the two conflicting worlds: heaven and earth. He sings loudly, joyfully drinking potent soma. He bears the deftly fashioned goad with which the messenger Maghavan stops the strikers in their path and breaks their hooves, offering libation until they are well satisfied. Maghavan partakes of the juice, partakes of the worship, and much invoked, eradicates all famine and evil, bringing a store of grain and cattle. The high-ranking allied princes obtain possessions by way of their own effort.

According to *Rig-Veda* 10:45, as part of the order of the sacred dominion, Agni, the first time he emerged from heaven, sprang to life. The second time, the united godly power Jātavedas and the immortal soul (Paramatman) appeared manifested in the waters, later to appear as the eternal living spirit (Atman), which kindles as the Pious One. The god Agni, in service to the three powers in three stations, in divided form, comes to serve in many places. The supreme powers prevail with secret names, knowing the source from which they come. The living spirit in manifested forms, in the sea, flowing with the water, become illuminated souls floating in the river, viewing the light from the heavenly sky shield. There they stand in the third-highest region, like steers watching as they embrace the waters. Agni roars out like the father of the sky Dyaus, sometimes with thunder licking the ground, where the plants flicker. Once he is born, he looks around, enkindled with the splendor of heaven and earth, springing forth in glory to gather up riches, the rouser of thoughts among the guardians of the soma.

Amid the waters, a good Son of Strength, as a king, appears before the morning light enkindled. With a shining embryo, the germ of the world, the ensign of all creation, he comes to life filled with blessings from earth and heaven. Even solid rocks split open when the five tribes pass over the earth to bring a sacrifice to Agni, who presents to mortals the immortal eternal flame, establishing them as holy and wise, willing to serve as his envoys. The waves, amid the red smoke, lift the embodiments above as they struggle to reach the heavens accompanied with a radiant luster. They appear as gold and, when looked upon, become refulgent, beaming with imperishable life and glory. Agni, serving as the vital power, once prolific, makes the father of the sky Dyaus immortal. Even today Agni serves as the eternal flame, which with its lovely powers produces a cake, by mixed with butter, which brings further fortune. With bliss, the bounty bestowed by the godly powers among most newborns and youths. Agni endows these with his share of glory, appearing in every song of praise sung forth for purposes of enrichment. The heavenly body Sūrya, with his preeminent son the sun, and its children's children, that is, the constellations and the moon, passing each day in prayer and worship, win all the treasure worth wishing for. Allied with the eager ones, who crave riches, they come to a stable filled with cattle.

Serving as the keeper of the soma, Vaishvanara, lauded by Agni, manifests as noble universal souls (rishis). The rishis come to invoke the benign deities serving earth and heaven, asking them to bring wealth to support the heroes' children. They established as a vital force, givers of wealth, who guard the manifested bodies serving as transitory mortal servants.

According to *Rig-Veda* 10:46, the Great Priest, who knows the clouds and how they were born, accepts the others seated in the lap of the water. In worship, they seek like lost creatures who in the footsteps of the divine, now coming to serve as the wise patron Bhrigu, with yearning in their hearts. They pursue those who forage where the floodwaters are deep, such as cows. As he performs such labor, the solar deity Trita serves among his offspring the Vibhiavas, who are born in their own houses and, as youths, fully bestowed with joy. They attain central point brightness that, through homage and yearning, makes them lighthearted as compared to other priests. They come to serve as the oblation-bearers, leaders of rites, and purifiers, envoys who make sacrifices and still advance the foolish, who brought forward to meet with the never-bewildered victor, song inspirer, and fort destroyer. Unshaven youth with golden bears, they serve as coursers gleaming with wealth, firmly maintaining their place in the house of Trita, home to all law-abiding flying insects such as bees. They depart to serve as champions of the tribes, collecting other heroes without compulsion. They come with the eternal flame to purify every house and make it a home to move in. Using their shining eternal power, hiding in the smoke, they produce white beeswax, which increases their strength, as they sit in the woods and stir up the winds to produce soma.

Serving with the tongue of eternal flame, the youths bear away with songs of praise. Carefully, they preside over earthly operations, serving as radiant embodiments who, like lighthearted priests, are the chiefs of the sacrifice. Agni in the form of the eternal flame serves both heaven and earth, provoking the waters to appear as the manifested creative power Tvaṣṭṛ. With might, the patron Bhrigu serves as the divine Mātariśvan, who fashions the godly priests (rishis) and entreats them to serve as holy souls. It is through ferocious fire that Agni, the creator, and oblation-bearer, brings life to the noble souls who laud him, offer sacrifices to him, and serve as righteous warriors who implement the divine covenant.

CHAPTER 20

# Exalted Dominion

THE EXALTED DOMINION REPRESENTS OUTER SPACE, WHICH LIES within the celestial region, where the lofty ones have their abodes, from which they regulate the manifested illusion, through which they serve the kingdom as an exalted dominion (Vaishnavism). This exalted dominion created by the supreme trinity Vishnu, Brahma, and Shiva, who create, protect, and transform the illusory material world. This trinity supported by the primordial power, Shakti, goddess of creative power, who serves as an equal and partner to Vishnu, manifested to serve as the goddess of material wealth Lakshmi. Whenever the world threatened with evil, chaos, or destructive forces, Vishnu descends as an incarnation to restore the cosmic order and protect the ten primary incarnations who are his avatars. These come to protect eternal wisdom and the absolute truth. As revered supreme beings, they impose traditional Vaishnavism to regulate the exalted illusory material world through faith (Parama Padam), which accompanied by specially made sacrifices (Nitya Vibhūti) generating sacred ash. This dominion is located right below the region where the power of essence separates into three kinds of purity (*guṇas*). It is also where the highest cosmic substance, comprised of matter, passes through a fully luminous state to become higher than the purest state of existence (sattva). According to traditional Vaishnavism, this cosmic substance exceeds the eternal, the mythical, and even the transcendental aspects of the material universe (Lila Vibhūti), which distinguished from true *vibhūti*, or divine wealth and glory. This highest of all states is beyond all those differentiated spheres representing nothing else. Those spheres served by the demigods, who stand guard as righteous warriors or the fearsome giant *Dvarapalaka.* They often armed with weapons, such as a mace (*gada*), which they use to protect the absolute truth (*Vaikuṇṭha*) unveiled. They serve in the golden palaces filled with hanging gardens that grow fragrant fruits and flowers. This coincides with the constellation Capricorn within the celestial region, from where Lord Vishnu watches the activities of the cosmic hosts (Maruts) serving the cosmic region, and from where Indra, as the lord of treasure, seizes the right to manage all civilizations that serve the holy powers.

## ABOVE GROUND (PRITHVI)

It represents the place where herds of animals and civilized people, always longing for treasure, vouchsafed by the mighty powers, and given magnificent riches. According to *Rig-Veda* 10:47, such wealth guarded by a fully armed protector who springs from the four seas and propped up to stay above the ground, which filled with treasures. Burdened with the great bounty, civilized people, with praises and glory unto the gods, receive resplendent riches. Among the godly powers who serve the heights, the widths, and the depths, the civilized people, from the dry bases, serve with wealth and widen their foundation by singing songs along with the famed sanctified souls (rishis) presenting as noble souls (Brahmans). After conquering foemen, the Brahmans appear victorious, increasing in strength, serving as the heroes of all confirmed powers and as most useful sages. They attract eternal wealth, by serving the sky lord Dyaus, with sanctified souls as the shield. They observe as Lord Indra crushes mighty forts with resplendent riches and slaying the evil powers. Filled with wealth, horses pull their carriages. Strengthened, in the hundreds of thousands, they serve as happy troops, like sages.

Winning internal light, along with resplendent riches, the Saptarishis manifest as perishable Bṛhaspati. They approach the messengers of Agni, the envoy Aṅgirases, and received with loud homage. Craving for loving-kindness, they go forth with powerful desire to serve Indra. Generating heartily vibrations, they utter through their immortal living spirits for

Indra to grant a boon for the creations for which they were praying. They establish for themselves a large space at the metaphysical center point between heaven and earth.

According to *Rig-Veda* 10:48, Indra, first gaining possession of all the required precious gear, brings wealth for every creation, which they gather up like fathers and happily offer them as gifts to the legendary sage Atharvan, who serves as Agni's legendary envoy. With firm support from Indra, Atharvan brings forth the solar god Trita to support the sky lord Dyaus and comes to serve each creation with mighty rites. Opening the stalls of all kinds of steeds, Atharvan, Trita, and Dyaus bring the creative power Tvaṣṭṛ to forge an iron thunderbolt, using the intellectual power of Mātariśvan and Dadhyac. The heavenly power Sūrya, with an intolerably bright light, with plasma creates a celestial body, the sun, which awakens all the creations, who come to recollect past happenings and, with honor, seek to experience the future. Through Indra's indestructible bolt, winning the herd of cattle, steeds, and all kinds of animals, plus an ample store of precious metals, thousands awaken to come with full support to serve as worshippers. In time they provided soma to make them all loud and glad enough to win the wealth. However, none ever wins Indra's wealth at any time, although they toil to do so until death. Only the holy tribe of *Puru,* who are the friends of Indra, suffer no harm. They breathe loudly and come in fury, two by two, when Indra brings his thunderbolt to the fray to threaten any challengers. He strikes them all down with his deadly weapon and stands firm as he speaks. As a special personality, *Sapya Nami* provides enjoyment and joins as a friend searching for godly creations. Indra gives him with arrows for the fight, which makes him worthy of producing songs of praise. Bringing soma to serve to herders, and second coming forth to fight with sharpened horns, *Sapya Nami* stands shackled within the demons' broad region. In any fight, the statutes of the god Rudra never violated, nor is the power of nature (Vasu) or the noble Ādityas. They are all established forever as auspicious, unconquered, and invincible, the vigorous ones who serve the holy tribe of the Purus.

According to *Rig-Veda* 10:49, the enriched singers singing holy hymns strengthened and wealthy, going on to offer sacrifices and win each fight against those who worship not. In heaven, within the waters, and on the earth, they establish a link with the godly powers. They worship Indra, in whose name they serve, so that he will come. Taken unto the godhead with swift vigor, they mount the carriage pulled by two bays, which speed along the divine paths, accompanied by the fierce thunderbolt of strength. Delivering deadly blows for their sake, Indra smites the Transformer, Kavi, for the sake of those he loves, the Atka, whom he guards well with the help of Kutsa. Brandishing darts of death, the gods initiate an attack upon the evil Śuṣṇa, so the noble Āryans need not call upon the name of the sky lord Dyaus to defeat their foes. The defeated Smadibha, Tugra, and Vetasus are handed over as prey to the fatherly helper Kutsa.

Indra, as a worthy king, comes to rule over the worshippers and gives them inviolable gifts to live in harmony, for example, Taoism (Tuji), also giving up the family peacock Mṛgaya as prey to Srutarvan so he will forever the divine law and keep it intact. Like arrows (*āyu*), drawing onward for the sake of the cause, bending his bow (*veta*) in his hands (*savya*), with the mighty power Padgrbhi, Indra delivers the lofty carriage to Navavāstva, filled with devotees, to crush and kill the evil Dāsas. As the Vṛtra-slayer, Indra kills the fiends, then straightway proceeds to the region's farthest edge, bringing illumination to broaden the minds of his worshippers. Traveling onward with might, he borne by fleet-footed dappled horses, all worshipping the sun, which is stronger than the pantheon of Nabus. Indra slays the seven tribes and glorified as mighty by the *Yadu* and *Turvaga* tribes, who bring one another low with their strength, turning the mighty ninety-nine with their skills and power. The bull crosses over all the streams that flow along the ground and seek the seven rivers, where they hope to establish the domain of the gods on the holy ground, gifted with great wisdom that spreads abroad with the floods.

During the war, the manifested embodiments fight, on their way to success. Indra, sitting among the cows, observes as they provide white milk without any godly support, not even from the creative force Tvaṣṭṛ. By themselves, they deposit the milk, much longed for, in their udders, along with savory essence (meath), mixing the milk with soma. Indra's messenger Maghavan, truly bounteous, speeds with his godly power to support the divine creations. The pious noble soul glorifies them all and, exploiting them, comes to serve as the lord of the bay coursers, strong and self-resplendent.

According to *Rig-Veda* 10:50, the mighty one's drink soma loudly and with joy, and they share it with all those they have created, providing strength to conquer powerful enemies in war, win fame, and then with vigor revere heaven and earth. Their active friends, lauded, serving as noble souls, glorified as heroes and as lords of the brave, whose bodies are delighted to be fighting against evil on the ground or against demons in the water. Those who wilt supported by Indra, who enables them to strive and win both bliss and riches. Those whom Indra urges forward, endow them with divine valor to fight in the war, go to water their fields. Those who offer sacrifices to the mighty Indra, with libations and prayers, to fight join the cast of heroes on the earth, singing the noblest songs of worship to the lord of all people. They offer their sacrifices to the Highest One, who toils for them and knows better, providing them with protection. The Everlasting One gives them the ability to succeed, along with libations to endow them with strength. All these libations become effectual, serve artfully by themselves, providing supporter to the sons of the mighty powers. In this way, the embodiments esteemed as offering the best sacrifices permitted to help to create the holy text, prayers, and exalted speech. With flowing soma, they pray to the sages and pour forth with gifts of opulence and wealth. They come forward with their eternal spirits to follow the path of bliss, and in their wild joy, the effuse the mythical juice into soma.

According to *Rig-Veda* 10:51, the god Soma by himself covers the warriors with his firmness, enfolded them within immortal living spirit, which enters the waters serving as the deity Jātavedas, who observed by Agni when forming divine creations in sundry places. The godly power seen appearing in places, creating many who clearly have divine form. Wherever Jātavedas lies, he makes that which is around him sacred, such as wood or firestone, which leads others to the eternal law (Varuna) and eternal love (Mitra). In places Agni, as deity Jātavedas, come to seek the hidden spots among the roots of plants that grow in standing waters. Serving as death, Yama makes of his existence a godly wondrous splendor that brings tenfold effulgence to these secret dwelling places. Yama takes the fear out of sacrificial worship and, with the eternal law (Varuna), engages with the godly powers to bring strength to all who lie within these places. As pious living beings perform their worship in honor of Agni, the eternal flame, Agni waits, prepared to remove gloom that dwells among the embodiments. Yama and Varuna make pathways leading toward the godly powers to make it easy for the worshippers to bear their oblations with a kindly spirit. As elder brothers, Yama and Varuna select the embodiment who will lead and determine the path to travel. With the eternal law, terror cast far away, with the living beings fleeing like wild bulls.

Jātavedas, appearing as an archer with a bow, gives life to dormant powers, thus using his divine power, not wasting it, and in so doing, deploys his arrows that ever cause injury. So, those who are noble born acquire kindly spirits to bear with the gods and offer them oblations granting them the first oblations. Later, the entire team shares with the rootless souls to create plants that live in the water, wishing them long lives. The messenger of Agni, according to divine will, orders the entire force to share, offering presents to the gods that they may serve the four regions of the world.

According to *Rig-Veda* 10:52, the godly powers elect a priest, who must sit with them and instruct them in how to share their portion with others and tell them by what path to bring their oblations. The cosmic hosts (Maruts) and celestial twin Aśvins, as demigods, come each day to do their duty as the *adhvaryus* who manifest in bodies as Brahmans, hiding their immortal souls in the woods. They offer their oblations as priests serving either the life force (prana) or the god of death Yama. God-appointed honor and trust is a matter of life and death.

Each day that passes, the godly powers select one priest as their oblation-bearer. Agni ordains the worship in five ways. With three or seven passes through Indra's arms, the thunder consigned in all battles to gain victory. All the deities, three hundred thirty-nine of them, serve and honor the eternal flame strewn upon the sacred grass and anointed with butter, where the priest seated as the invoker of the gods.

## IMMORTAL SOUL

According to *Rig-Veda* 10:53, the immortal universal soul, as a female spirit, fills all the clouds with cosmic vapor that comes down in the form of water, either rain, hail, snow, or ice. These immortal female souls are beautiful, called *apsaras*, they remain ever youthful and elegant, and are superb at the art of dancing. They are often recognized as cohorts of color so as the males can differentiate one from the other. They appear in two prominent forms: celestial souls (*nymphs*) and cosmic spirits *virgin aid*. The celestial soul serves as the unmanifested mother of the universe, *Laukika,* and the young cosmic daughter appears embodied as the living spirit *Daivika.* They manifest as thirty-four mighty powers (divinities, deities, and demigods, ten of which are the most famous, for example, the one who controls the heart, *Urvaśī,* and the one who controls the mind, *Menakā.* They jointly control passion, *Rambhā,* which is the one who controls the vibrations used to produce beautiful music (*Tilottama.*) Further, the power who controls the smallest and finest particles (*Ghritachi*) serving as the spiritual mother.

When the apsaras dance to the music made by the male spirits of nature, usually in the palaces of the godly powers, to entertain and sometimes seduce the male gods, the ethereal souls inhabit the skies and often depicted in flight, serving as godly powers comparable to seraphim, or angels. Apsaras may change their shape at will. They are the spirits behind the performing arts and are associated with fertility rites.

According to *Rig-Veda* 10:54, through the powers of the apsaras, the messenger Maghavan harnesses Indra's powers from the surrounding heaven and earth, which he uses to invoke and provide aid to the devotees pursued by the Dāsas. Maghavan helps to quell the evil powers save many hopeless races and tribes by strengthening the bodies of manifested creations and bringing the mighty powers to help the creations by creating illusions in the battle to make it impossible to tell who a friend is and who is a foe. This way, the noble souls (rishis) come to comprehend the powers of greatness. When bound together within embodiments, they generate progeny. At the same time, the mother gives birth to the living things, and the father endures such new creations. From the four supreme powers of nature, noble and mighty steer that may never injured are created. All this is surely known to the messenger Maghavan, who performs great works. All divine treasures are in his sole possession, manifested and remaining hidden. Maghavan defers, having no longings himself and blessed in the art of giving. Maghavan is the one who provides things with both light and the sweet blends of soma and amrit, which are both essential to creations. Indra, with hymns, welcome Maghavan, and strengthens by word transformed them to serves as a votary or as the monk (*Bṛhaduktha)*.

According to *Rig-Veda* 10:55, the monk *Bṛhaduktha,* with vigor, brings heaven and earth close to each other by invoking the votary with a secret name—*Maghavan*. who makes all bright creations serving as the children of men. With this secret name, all that is far away comes closer. The five prevailing tribes, all of whom are loved, now receive the external light and eternal love that was made before the region between heaven and earth was created and between all the godly powers in their proper seasons increased sevenfold with thirty-four lights, looking around themselves and serving as one light of one color, all driven in their diverse ways. The first of the lights to appear is that of dawn, which shines forth to increase the great Asuras, who are of a matchless nature, the spirit or the ghost. The one who is the father is high above, with other kin below them. The light of dawn wakens the earth, separating the old creation from the new creation as regulated by the young body, the moon, which emerges from its slumber to circle the earth, running courses, the old creations beholding God's highest form of greatness and wisdom, that is, the sun. The young who died yesterday live today as the Redbird, Agni, who with his strength continues to serve as the great hero (the sun) who is strong and knows the truth but has no nest in which to dwell, so he is never idle. Agni wins the war and gives he wealth they desire. Through the thunder, gain manly vigor and the skills to smite the evil power Vṛtra. Some, through the mighty Indra, come forth to follow the gods, the course of the law, obeying the divine order. Strong, and performing works with their companions, they all mark a rapid victory as curse-averting heroes polishing their skills. After drafts of soma, they come from the far heaven, the father of the sky Dyaus being their indestructible weapon.

According to *Rig-Veda* 10:56, they combine one light with another over yonder and then enter as three united in one body. They welcome the godly powers in the sublime astral body, which is born of a virgin, and afforded the blessing of self-protection. Steadfast, they establish themselves as if they were in heaven with their own mighty god, with eternal light serving as their supporter. Strong steeds with their art go yearning as virgin aid with vigor, happily ascending to heaven with praises, flying happily to the gods, making an easy passage according to the first and faithful statutes. Part of their grandeur, their fathers have also gained: The gods have mental power seated within them. They embrace all energy within themselves, which, issuing forth, passes again into their bodies. They stride through all the regions with victorious might, reestablishing the old law. Their bodies encompass all things in existence stream forth with offspring of many forms. In these two ways have the sons established their place as Asuras who find the light. By this action, as fathers, they set their heritage on earth, their offspring as a thread continuously spinning out.

As a ship sails across the billowy waves, so Bṛhaduktha travels through the regions of the air with blessings, passing through toil and troubles. Bṛhaduktha brings his seed with glory and places it here and in the realms beyond.

According to *Rig-Veda* 10:57, Indra ensures the fathers and their offspring do not leave their path and indeed follow where pressed soma offered as a sacrifice. He also ensures no malignity dwells nearby. The fathers and their offspring given twisted thread to spin before offering a perfect sacrifice to the gods. The living spirit now joins with the fathers to drink holy soma as the departed sires once did. The living spirit now accompanied with eternal wisdom, eternal energy, and eternal flame, so it may behold the direct light from the sun. Serving with the fathers, heavenly folk once again given living spirits, which support those who live with Soma and stay with their progeny in service to the law.

According to *Rig-Veda* 10:58, the living spirits that end up going far away in death (Yama) come to serve as the sons of the godly powers the Vivasvans. And when they return, they stay and remain in service. They serve from the four restricted corners of earth, the four quarters of the world, from deep unto the billowy sea to on high with the flashing beams of light. They flow with the waters to support the plants, and even go as far away as the sun, where they visit the dawn. The living spirit rises to the lofty mountain heights and goes among all that lives and moves. The spirit goes to distant realms beyond any kin and to all that is and ever will be. After traveling everywhere yet again, it returns to live and sojourn here.

According to *Rig-Veda* 10:59, the life force (prana) as breath is renewed and carried forward in two manifested forms, that is, physical embodiments, which act as vehicles, with the second immortal embodied spirit acting as the skillful driver. When a physical embodiment falls, then the immortal living sprit with quickened vigor seeks another embodiment. The living spirit residing within the invisible astral body, as the goddess Nirrti, departs and travels to a distant sacred place as a psalm filled with eternal wealth and plenty food to perform many deeds that bring glory as a singer brings delight. The astral body as the goddess Nirrti further departs and travels to distant places to defeat foes, performing acts of valor while traveling from heaven to earth, over the hills and across the lowlands. Still performing deeds that, like a singer, bring delight Nirrti departs yet again and travels to still distant places, not giving up. Becoming prey unto death, she seeks the god Soma by looking upon the rising sun. From experience, such as passing into old age, she becomes kind and benevolent, thus allowing her to depart a fourth time and travel far to reach the goddess of the universal soul *Asuniti*, whose astral body is within the universal soul; thus, the astral body gains more days to live as an invisible power. She permitted to look upon the sunlight, which strengthens the astral body with the eternal flame and returns it to Asuniti as breath, life force (prana), also providing vigor and physical strength for purposes of enjoyment of life.

Asuniti, seeing upon the sun rising, with favor blesses the astral body and restores its vital spiritual powers. Provided from heaven, the celestial powers, along with the cosmic powers, all located in the midair region, restored. They receive soma once again to give them support. The patron Pūṣan shows them the path of peace and comfort. With blessings from both worlds (heaven and earth), the young mother *Subandhu*, with the everlasting law, uproots iniquity and shame and sweeps it away: no sin, no sorrow. She clears all trouble for the new creations, giving them health and medicine that sent down from heaven to wander alone on the manifested holy ground located above the earth. Indra drives *Usinarani's* wagon, pulled by oxen, uprooting shame and inequity and sweeping them away: no more sin, sorrow, or trouble.

According to *Rig-Veda* 10:60, with glorify from the mighty gods, *Asamati*, coming from the sky, appears as a brave lord with a radiant embodiment. With only a spear in his hand and no other weapon, he overthrows the strong buffalo rider *Bhagiratha*, declaring victory in the tribal war. King *Iksvaku* comes to flourish manifested as the first incarnation, that is, the cosmic man Manu, and appears bright, rich, and dazzling to serve the five tribes already established and in service to Indra, also supporting the matchless prince *Rathaprosthas*. King *Iksvaku* sees Agastya as a demigod serving the Aśvins, his sister's sons. Agastya is a new ruler who brings no gifts. He serves as the mother and the father to bring forth life using his exotic power. With leather straps, he binds his chariot, yoking it to make it secure for transporting the immortal living spirit, injuring himself against death.

With the holy ground held fast, the monarchs of the woods come to the exotic power Subandhu, who carries the living spirit in water, *Yarna*, to delivered to the sons of godly powers the Vivasvans. The wind blowing down from on high sends heat from the sun, as the mother pours out her milk without pain or grief. Propitious hands contain all healing balms, which means the whole action performed with a gentle touch.

## PROVOCATION

According to *Rig-Veda* 10:61, the twin demigod Aśvins, in the heat of battle, utter a mighty prayer to the noble tribe of Paktha, who come to rescue the Aśvins as their parents and to assail one of the seven noble sages, Hotar, who serves Agni. The ancient sage Cyavāna, with all the necessary ingredients, makes the altar ready, where the sweet-voiced sage *Tūrvayāṇa* pours oblations to fertilize the ground with a flood of water. With his oblations, as swift as thought, hurried, he eagerly welcomes the prayers offered. With arrows in his hand, the mighty power forces all his servants to obey. He calls on the demigod Aśvins, sons of the sky lord Dyaus, representing creation on the holy ground, asking that dark pigment added to the newborn red ones. He enjoys the sacrifice that made by the new power all, contented with nutrition, not failing to deliver on any expectation. Remember, if the fire that burns for the people not tended to by day, then by night the naked evil force the rakshasas will come, withholding Agni's eternal flame and nutritious food, thus preventing the rite performed so no one will be born with the power to overcome these mighty enemies.

The *Navagvas* come speedily, uttering praises, performing a suitable rite to win the friendship of young women. They approach the doubly strong stable keeper, throwing the mead less milk to the meteors (compressed cosmic stones) before anyone may shake it to get to the living spirit. Becoming fast friends, they accept the genuine seed as a bounty from the sacred cow *Sabardughā,* which like a milk cow yields a bright heritage, afterward noticing that they missed the fact that the cow was in a joyful mood. They address the speaker as matchless singers filled with natural powers (Vasu), which bring food along with all other possessions. Their followers having remained in multifarious places, they desire to slay the son of the resistless foe *(Nṛṣad)*, who found hidden amid the treasure of *Śuṣṇa*, who served by multiple offspring. With effulgence, in threefold dwellings, sits the immortal living spirit, enjoying the light of heaven, supported by the god Agni as his envoy *Jātavedas*.

Guileless priests offer holy worship to Indra, whom they laud, asking him to serve them through the resplendently glorious half-mortal Nāsatyas. Blithe, bounteous, the priests offer man like sacrifice, honored among the prevailing manifested living beings to offer nourishment. They praised and honored by the ordained king, serving as sages. They speed over water to serve as the bridge between the two worlds, heaven, and earth, connected with flowing waters. The evil force stirred up as the eminent sage Kakṣīvān, who serves Agni, and t *Kakṣīvān's* steeds move swiftly, the fellies turning and moving the chariot onward, reaching the relative *Vaitarana,* who sacrifices the milk cow *Sabardhu*, which never had calves.

Once Kakṣīvān reaches eternal law (Varuna) and eternal love (Mitra), he establishes safe shelters. These regulated by the noble Ādityas, who appear as the manifested noble soul Aryaman. As the princes of heaven, the Ādityas establish themselves near to relatives, turning their thought process toward showing kindness as they speak. With their speech, they establish the tightest form of bond with their offspring, successively producing their own kin, and establish a place for the godly powers to dwell with full strength, thus being twice born. The firstborn, as the son of order, as the first milk-bearing animals, milk themselves to feed the tribes who are their friendly envoys, borne on two paths, that of the refulgent lord of the eternal flame and that of the god of eternal love.

When the newborn babes spring up, erect, with their mother's support, they become strong and blessed. Then the milk cows go forth to seek other damsels to milk them for the good of every other living being, including males. The wealthy lord learns to appreciate their sacrifice for others, helping to create mighty grown-ups, all filled with supreme virtue (Aśvaghna). Even Indra notices their ample riches and supreme virtues. He sends thunder to protect the wealthy noble souls, guarding them as unmenacing princes. As the lord of the tawny coursers, Indra goes forth as a pair of kings, speeding, loud, to win the war and seek the booty with praises to please the singers serving the dearest sages, supporting them by leading them forth and then bringing them back safely. Now for this noble god's support and comfort, they sing with easy voices, imploring that he supports their offspring and their fleet of coursers so they may win with glory.

The priests, winning friends, with loud adoration accept virtue as a branching road opened for everyone who as a singer of a noble race glorifies Indra with hymns and homage. Indra blesses the free-flowing waters with his godly power and fully enriched with prayers and praises, opens the path for the milk cow to attain supreme virtue (Aśvaghna). It is all up to living beings to receive godly merit through their worship, with one accord asking for full protection. Those who are undeceivable explorers and go no other way gain vigor.

According to *Rig-Veda* 10:62, adored through the sacrifice, Indra wins friends. Agni provides the eternal flame. Jointly, through a divine messenger, Indra and Agni bring about the first manifested cosmic body, Manu, who serves as a wise father with a mother, the sacred cow, which in a year, by way of the eternal law, is cleaved to the prophet (Vala). Lengthening the life span of living beings, Manu welcomed by all as the son of the wisest living beings. He raised by the sun and comes to experience heaven as a father. Indra and Agni spread the eternal law broadly across the earth, serving as the mother who issues forth with progeny in all directions, all regulated by the divine messenger who come to support the wisest son, Manu. As relatives, they establish their dwelling place and speak pleasant words from the embodiments given to them, serving as prophets (rishis), representing the children of the gods. They dignified as the high Brahman who worship the messenger Aṅgiras. Distinguished by their various forms, the rishis deeply moved and respected as sons of Aṅgiras, who sprang to life from Agni. Distinguished by his form, springing out of the sky shield as the noblest soul, Aṅgiras given a bounty by the godly powers. Indra and his associated priests clear the stable of steeds and cattle and give them to Aṅgiras as a thousandfold gift. With their eight marked embodiments, the Manus are renowned among the gods. Manu's sons multiply as the corn grows in spring, and he provided a bounteous gift, including one thousand cattle and one hundred steeds. No one attains to the cosmic body; it is only through Manu's grasp that one may reach the heights of heaven.

With sacrificial food (*sāvarnya*) flowing amply in a flood, the two devotees Yadu and Tugra given the freedom to serve together with a great store of cattle. The most liberal Manu blessed to serve as the chief of earthly power, whose bounty comes to rival that of the heavenly power. May the gods let Manu's life be long as the un-wearying *Savarṇi* come to live and prosper.

According to *Rig-Veda* 10:63, coming from far away, the Savarni assume kinship with the generations of Vivasvans and the dearly loved Manu. The gods who sit upon the sacred grass bless the Puranic king Yayāti. Worthy of obeisance, adoration, and sacrifice, the Savarni are all named after godly powers and were born from water, as the children of the godly mother Aditi were born from the earth. They call to and listen to their mother and rejoice addressed as her children, like the Ādityas, for whom the mother pours forth water rich in balm. The sky lord, infinite and as firm as cosmic rocks, as well as soft, served sweet milk as the god Dyaus, made strong by laudation, holds the bull with his might. Looking on, the Manus, serving as the Ādityas, never slumber, and with their desire they attain immortality, becoming like gods. Borne by refulgent embodiments, sinless, they robe themselves with serpents for their own welfare as they ascend to the heights of heaven. They come to bless great kings who, never having assailed, come to sacrifice, and build their mansions in the sky. With adoration and with mighty hymns, the sons of Mother Aditi invited to offer laudation and respect to gods of Manu, the mighty ones, and prepare a sacrifice to bear them through trouble to contentment. The Manus, with seven priests, kindle a fire to offer the first oblation with their hearts and souls, asking that all vouchsafed in the name of the Ādityas. Free of fear, they come provide shelter, asking that they provided a good and easily followed path to happiness. Like the wise deities, their dominion spread across the world. They think all about that which moves and that which moves not. Protected from all sin, both uncommitted and committed, they preserve us, even today, from all sin to provide happiness.

In battle, Indra, swift to hear, invokes the other holy hosts of heaven, Agni, Mitra, and Varuna. To banish the grief that arises from association with the material world, the holy hosts of the earth, Dyaus, Bhaga, the Maruts, and Prithvi, provide happiness on earth, which is incomparable to the happiness of heaven. This secured by Aditi, who defends earth like a well-oared boat filled with dense dark matter, preventing both water and sunlight from getting through and freeing herself from defect. Only with divine will may anything ascend from the dark matter to seek happiness. All those who seek help blessed by the holy ones, who guard them and protect them from injury. With fruitful invocation, they call to the gods, who through their grace grant them happiness. The gods keep them free of all disease and, with their sacrifices, keep them safe from the enmity of the wicked and malicious. Keeping them far away from all hatred, the gods provide them with ample shelter for their survival. Untouched by any evil, every mortal thrives and, following the law, procreates in exchange for good guidance. The noble Ādityas lead them safely through all pain and grief to happiness. They guard them in battle with their grace, serving as the cosmic hosts (Maruts), and help them win the wealth. As heroes, they appear as conquerors. Like the warrior god Indra, they set out with the morning light when dawn breaks. With blessings, they arise in search of happiness, following the vouchsafed paths like desert tracts, blessed with water and with light in battle. Blessings upon the wombs bring forth male children, whom the Maruts bless so they will gain wealth. The goddess of fortune, Lakshmi, who brings abundant riches, comes from a distant pathway, where she dwells under the gods' protection. Through the thoughtful sage, the son of Plati, the godly mother Aditi, and all the Ādityas (noble souls) make them rich. As immortals, they, like the heavenly folk (*gaya*), extolled and ascend to heaven.

## SPIRITUAL WARFARE

According to *Rig-Veda* 10:64, the gods, hearing their names praised and recorded in sacrifice, through their gracious nature, provide bliss to those who come out as hosts to lend their aid. With divine will and internal thoughts, they exert their power among the manifested bodies, who yearn for love and fly to all the regions of the world. They can find no other comforter who is able to soothe their longings and give them what they hope for, so they fixed on serving the gods. They sing forth to Narāśaṁsa and to Pūṣan to reveal themselves, representing Agni, along with the gods of the sun and the moon, in the form of he who serves death, Yama, in heaven and on earth, and he who serves the sun, Trita, creating morning light (dawn) and the evening light (dusk), with both serving day and night as the twin Aśvins. They all extolled as sages, given all praise by the singers. These voices singing hymns invoke the perishable Bṛhaspati, the powerful dragon that lives at the bottom of the ocean (Aja-Ekapād), and the swift Rkvans, asking them to hear them and listen unto their calls amid the deep, where large fish such as ahi listen to Mother Aditi. At birth, the dexterous embodiment Dakṣa makes a vow, as summoned by the king, to Mitra and Varuna.

With his course unchecked, and with chariots, Aryaman comes to the various tribes served by the seven priests. Like vigorous coursers, they listen to the cry, hear the invocation, and speed on their way to serve the winners of thousands. Having won mead, and they gather up the great wealth. In every race, they bring the ancient power Purandhi, accompanied by the wind (Vayu) as the breath that yokes the steeds together, and create a friendship through Pūṣan, singing songs of praise. Of one mind, with one thought, they attend the sacrifice, urged by the goddess of rain, Savitar, who grants them her favor. The twenty-one wandering rivers, flooding over, reach the ground to serve the forests on the mountains. Agni provides aid to the archer Lord Kṛśānu, along with holistic wellness to Tisya, who serves those who meet at the gathering place, while the god of the wind, Vayu, blows forcefully to create mighty waves within the mighty river Indus. The goddesses Sarasvatī and Sarayu flood Mother Earth, animating all with the promise that water will bring them riches and, with unguent, create the manifested material world, combining nature (prakriti) and creation (purusha). The godly mother Aditi calls upon the mother of origination, Brhaddiva; the father of creation, Tvaṣṭṛ; and other goddesses, serving as young girls. She calls upon manifested cosmic planetary bodies such as the *Ṛbhukṣans, Vāja, Bhaga, and Rathaspati,* who all come with sweet speech to serve as wonderworkers who work hard to guard all creations, including planetary bodies. They are pleasant to look upon within the dwelling, both rich in food and blessed with favor, appearing as the cosmic hosts the Maruts, Rudra's sons. They famed among the people for the wealth they bring from the animal kingdom, including steeds and cattle, which serve as sacred food. In thought, the Maruts, serving the heavenly powers Indra and Agni, along with eternal love (*Mitra*) and the eternal law (*Varuna*), appear animated, growing and swelling like milk cows. As a sacrifice, they provide milk and go further to carry off the mythical sound falling on the embodiments. The Maruts, never recollecting this relationship, meet next at pivotal point, where Mother Aditi confirms their brotherhood. The mothers of heaven and earth, those mighty goddesses, make a worthy sacrifice to rescue the race of the gods. They support and uphold both gods and humankind, whereas the fathers pour out the copious streams. This invocation wins over the all-good perishable godly power Bṛhaspati and, as desired, causes the highly praised goddess of devotion, Aramati, to appear. Then meath pressed out by stones, and the divine voices of the sages' ring t loud, singing hymns. Thus, those skilled in song, according to their sense of duty, desiring riches, yearn for such treasure. They serve as priestly singers, and with hymns and praises they are content to serve as celestial people. Throughout this thoughtful process, they send praises to he who has attained the central position, Plati; the firmament, Aaiti; and the noble Ādityas—all three serving as the offspring of Mother Aditi. They are all blessed with riches and immortality. As heavenly beings, they extolled in their yearning to enter the place of bounty, Gaya.

According to *Rig-Veda* 10:65, the celestial godly powers Agni, Indra, Mitra, and Varuna, with consent, come to join the cosmic godly powers Aryaman, Vayu, Pūṣan, and Sarasvatī, deciding with the terrestrial godly powers the Ādityas, the Maruts, Vishnu, Soma, Dyaus, Rudra, and Aditi to support the perishable divine force, Bṛhaspati, who is regulated by the imperishable force, Brahmaṇaspati. Indra and Agni serve as the lords of warriors to overpower that which envelops, such as the serpent or the dragon, which appear within the dwelling place of the Asuras. All heavenly powers come quickly with blended soma and the eternal flame, pouring forth with power in their greatness to fill the mighty firmament. Skilled in the law, they rise with the hymns of praise, these strengtheners of law, unassailed, in majesty. With their wondrous bounty, like kindly friends, they send gifts to the watery sea to make it great. With their might, both in heaven and on earth, they cover the holy ground (Prithvi) as the lords of light, creating the lustrous spheres within the firmament located between heaven and earth. Their fleet-footed steeds make their masters glad, appearing as royal gods, praised as the most bountiful living beings. They bring gifts of eternal love (Mitra) and eternal law (Varuna), serving as the lords of all manifested bodies with individual living spirits, never failing those who worship them. The manifested embodiment, like a statue, shines on high through the everlasting law, whose places of refuge are the heavens and earth. The cow that yields milk goes her appointed way as the leader of holy rites. Speaking aloud, the eternal law (Varuna) and eternal love (Mitra) come to serve the oblation-givers the Vivasvans, who serve the mighty gods. The god with a tongue of ferocious fire, Agni, dwells in heaven, establishing the eternal force reflected at the seat of law. He props up the heavens and then brings along the god who comes as soothing cosmic vapor, Indra, to restore calm with his might, generating fair weather for making the sacrifice.

According to *Rig-Veda* 10:66, born in ancient times, serving as parent to those who dwell within the same mansion, Prithvi serves the holy ground in the home of the law. She is bound by her vow to the sky lord Dyaus, who brings forth rain as a lubricant to create manifested physical powers such as steer to serve the law (Varuna). On the ground, as in the manifested heavens, mighty deities serve as Parjanya, deity of rain, thunder, and lightning, who come to fertilize the ground. The deity Vāta, in his normal state, protects the body, bestows enthusiasm, and supports exhalation and inhalation, which account for the body's urges. Indra maintains proper function of the seven fundamental principles needed to support the basic structure of the manifested body. These include breath (Vayu), the eternal law (Varuna), eternal love (Mitra), the noble soul Aryaman, the godly mother Aditi, and her offspring the Ādityas, who cover solid dark matter, that is, the unmanifested universe (earth). In the middle ground, Prithvi filled with flowing water and is host to heaven, serving as the home of the supreme power of causation Rudra, from where the creative life force

Tvaṣṭṛ manifests. By joining with Vayu, Rudra appears as the sanctified cosmic body Ṛbhu. They all appear as the celestial priest Hotar and the cosmic demigods serving as the morning light (for happiness) and the evening light, hoping to obtain eternal wealth while sleeping.

The perishable embodiment of wisdom, Bṛhaspati, comes as the destroyer of foes and, as a friend of Indra, provides soma. And as a friend, he generates a prayer to support domesticated animals, such as the female cow providing milk and the male horse providing vitality. He comes to support the plants and the trees in the forest, with water coming down from the hills. Very bounteous, he serves as a godhead mounted in heaven, appearing as the sun, which spreads the righteous law, through the noble Aryaman, across the land. As twin demigods, the Aśvins preserve *Bhujyu* and *Śyāva*, the animated sons of *Vadhrmati*, from distress. They bring mythological flying palaces as self-moving aerial bodies, serving as a seat or throne for Vimada, their chariots carrying their occupants through the air. To provide a consort, Kamadyu, the Aśvins return with Viśvaka to replace the lost Viṣṇāpū. For the thunder, the lightning's daughter Aja-Ekapād, of heaven, is the bearer of the holy river Indus. Aja-Ekapād makes the waters of the rivers flow into the sea. Hearing this through the gods' mouths, the goddess Sarasvatī gives them all the ears, together with Purandhi, to hear holy thoughts. With his holy thoughts, Purandhi, like many gods, knows the eternal law and, like Manu, is holy, a boon-givers, a favorer, a finder of light and of heaven, with gracious love enough to accept songs, prayers, and hymns. Immortal gods such as Vasiṣṭha, lauded, are set high above all other beings. May they this day grant us wide space and freedom: ye gods, preserve us evermore with blessings.

## NOBLE SIRE

According to *Rig-Veda* 10:67, holy, sublime, with seven heads, Āyasa springs from the eternal law and serves as a friend to all manifested mortal embodiments. The instruments of Āyasa engender the fourth hymn that presented to laud Indra, thinking aright by praising the eternal order to the Asuras, the sons of the sky god Dyaus, the messenger Aṅgirases holding rank as first honored noble sages according to the holy statutes. Girded by his friends, who cry with swanlike voices, Āyasa bursts through the stony barrier walls of the prison. At the same time, the perishable Bṛhaspati appears as a spike in thunder to support the cattle and utters praises and sing songs as he finds such creations. Āyasa and Bṛhaspati drive the steads that stand in invisible bonds. Bṛhaspati, seeking light amid the darkness, drives forth the bright cows of three colors: black, brown, and white. They cleave the hideouts, and at the western castle, they cut off three heavily built water buffaloes (bovines). The perishable Bṛhaspati discovered, while the father, the sky lord Dyaus, thunders to bring the morning light (dawn) to the ground (Prithvi). Prithvi, as the mother, accepts the lightning that comes along with the sunrays. With one hand, roaring Indra cleaves through Vala to serve as guardian of the cattle.

Seeking the milky draft, with his comrades shining with sweat, Indra takes the stolen cattle away and leaves the demon Paṇis weeping. With brightness as a faithful friend, winner of booty, Indra takes the cows to those who come to milk them. Bṛhaspati, along with wild boars, strong and mighty, sweating in the heat, now gains a new possession, having longed to own animals, his faithful spirit and his hymns inspiring the shepherds to come serve him. The freed radiant cows, avoiding one another, serve as self-yoked comrades, representing the perishable Bṛhaspati. In assembly, with auspicious praises, the shepherds exalt him, roaring like lions, and after every fight from which he emerges as the heroic conqueror, they rejoice in his strength. When they have won every sort of booty, they feel they are ready to go to heaven and enter the loftiest mansions. They see their manifested embodiments praised as the perishable godly body of Bṛhaspati, who brings within his mouth the light from sundry places. In the traditional manner, Bṛhaspati fulfills their prayers for vitality and vigor, along with aid from his humble living spirit. This causes all foes to be turned and driven backward, thus allowing the perishable body to appear as a producer, like the immortal Indra, and with his mighty strength, cleave in half the head of the demon Arbuda and the watery fish monster ahi, and set free the seven rivers serving the holy ground between heaven and earth that is protected by the imperishable gods.

According to *Rig-Veda* 10:68, like flying birds that keep watch, splashing in the water, Bṛhaspati, with his voice, brings thunder and rain clouds. This causes streamlets to burst from the mountains and begin flowing with the sound of hymns. The son of the messenger Aṅgirases comes to meet the cattle, as the patron of the holy ground Bhaga brings along the noble soul Aryaman as friends of manifested embodiments. Decked spouses, they race to motivate the coursers. Bṛhaspati, having won barley from the mountains, now scatters it from winnowing baskets. The vigorous, wandering cows, aiding the pious in their blameless forms, come in desire, colored by the rays of the sun. As essence, they come to bedew those seated in the holy order, who have the power to cast from heaven a flaming meteor to alight on the ground. With such a cosmic rock, Bṛhaspati forces the cattle down through a fissure in the earth filled with water. From the midair region, light forth to drive off the prevailing darkness. A howling wind blows, grasping at the clouds (Vala) gathered to serve Bṛhaspati, causing the cattle to fly like lilies from the river. Fiery lightning cleaves through the disparaging cloud (Vala) like a weapon, consuming it like a cat swallowing its teeth, with the red cows freed from their stalls by the forces of evil.

With their secret names uttered by the lowing cattle, *Bhaga* and *Aryaman,* discovering that they are in a cave, drive themselves as bright cattle out of the mountain, making the truth become apparent like a hatchling bird, with revelation, breaks through its eggshell. They look around their rock prison with sweetness, as one who spots a fish in shallow water. After cleaving through the rock clamorously, Bṛhaspati comes forth like a bowl carved from a piece of wood, thereafter, finding the fire, the light of heaven, creating the lucid rays of morning, forcing out the darkness. From a joint, Bṛhaspati takes the marrow as the spirit within a cloud (Vala), to bring out the glorious power from within cattle. Among trees stripped of their leaves in winter, Vala, as the glorified power within cattle, mourns for what Bṛhaspati has taken. His work never done, and he is never equaled, living where the sun and moon alternately ascend. Like a dark steed adorned with pearls, which the fathers have used to decorate the heavens with constellations, Vala is responsible for the light in daytime and for darkness at night. When Bṛhaspati cleaves the rock and finds the cattle, he comes to offer the Vala homage as the god who thunders out too many, which as a result causes Bṛhaspati to distribute the cattle and horses to the manifested heroes.

## IMPERISHABLE FORCE

According to *Rig-Veda* 10:69, one auspicious aspect of Agni, as an imperishable power, in addition to providing fire, is that he serves as peasant *Vadhryasva*, to whom he provides guidance when they make their first visit to the ancient kingdom of Sumitra, where they are honored by the princess as the wisest ones. They pour butter onto sacred wood to enkindle a fire that crackles and shines, producing bright light. It is the butter that makes the fire grow strong. Butter, as a fatty food, widely distributed as a bomb that floats within the streams, shining forth like the sun. With a new face, the auspicious Agni, enkindled as the ancient soul Manu, brings along Sumitra to create a rich shine. The two of them accept the songs that serve as strengthening food, and in glory they accept it as the offering of old, allowing the powers of Vadhryasva to enkindled.

Within their guarded homes, the manifested bodies protected by an invisible divine bond, the splendid guard also serving their relatives, protecting them from any enmity. The hero Cyavāna nominated by Sumitra to overcome his past and given the honor of serving as both relative of *Vadhryaiva* and bold hero, having won all treasures buried within the plains and the mountains. Cyavāna quashes any hatred against devotees coming from the Dāsas or the poised souls (Āryans). With the support of Agni, Cyavāna appointed to serve as a righteous warrior who fights long in battle. Agni stands tall over the oxen, which serve the thousands of heifers. They come all decked with devices, serving as manifested imperishable creations. Splendidly bright, they pour forth with shining devotion, appearing before the *Sumitras*, serving the godly power Jātavedas, who at once begins pouring out a ceaseless flow (*Sabardhuk*) that lights up the manifested bodies, enriching them to serve as guardians of the pious Sumitras, who serve Jātavedas and are the relatives of Vadhryasva. They declare divine grandeur when human tribes (Manus) draw near with supplication, gaining strength from these divine conquerors. As a father bears his son, the god Agni bears in his lap the relative Vadhryasva, who comes to serve as a son. As the youngest god, having enjoyed this new source of fuel, he vanquishes those who are old, even though they are mighty. Vadhryasva evermore vanquishes his foes, along with the heroes who come to press the soma. Lords of the bright rays, they burned up in battle by subduing even the mightiest of the foemen. Agni, with Vadhryasva, in the face of the serpent or the dragon, if he not invoked with homage, allows the enemy to assail Vadhryasva, whether the foes be strangers or relatives.

According to *Rig-Veda* 10:70, Agni enjoys it when a fuel-based, fat-filled ladle used to pour out libation. As the relative rises above the earth to worship the godly powers, even when the days are bright and filled with beauty, those who go before the gods come with steeds of various shapes

(*Narasarhsa*). With godlike speed, they offer viands and pay homage so they may guide on the path of order. Manifested embodiments, loud, with constant oblations, pray to Agni, who comes to perform the envoy's duty. With their lightly rolling carriage and their best draft horses, they present themselves to the gods, who seated with the holy priest Hotar. The delight of sitting with the gods causes them to spread out transversely. Filled with fragrance, the sacred grass, friendly in spirit, calls to the willing gods to choose a chief. They come from far away, with a far-reaching height, springing the heavens apart to accommodate the wide girth of the earth. Tearing open the doors, they win over any heavenly embodiment that comes forth within this shrine, such as the morning light (dawn) or the evening light (dusk). Serving as daughters of heaven, the skillful goddesses come seated. In their auspiciously wide laps, these willing women, with a willing spirit, provide a seat for the gods, whom they allow to stand like stone that struck to enkindle fire. In attendance is the godly mother Aditi, who gives birth to the friendly essence (purusha) and to nature (prakriti). These two serve as the chief priests who are the source of creation, supported by divine worship and blessed in skills to win riches for all.

On the great lawn of heavenly grass, Purusha and Prakriti give birth to three goddesses, Iḷā, Sarasvatī, and Mahi, who are all seated and prepared to create the material world. They generate drops of soma, which fall at their feet and, like oil, invoke the eternal flame. The goddess Prakriti tastes the sacrifice from the god Purusha, which presented to give birth to the creative god Tvaṣṭṛ, who makes everything beautiful and perfect. Through the companion Agni, the envoy Aṅgirases willingly come to serve as wealthy one who give away all their possessions. Those who know granted by the assembly of gods a binding cord to bring together all the deities serving as lords of the wood. Calling out, they present with seasonal oblations, remaining gracious in honoring heaven and earth. Agni brings with him the eternal law, Varuna, to provide help from heaven, along with Indra, who brings the cosmic hosts the Maruts from the midair region. As all the holy ones seated on the sacred grass, they rejoice with the immortal gods, forging the ultimate union between them by worshipping the ending (*svāhā*).

According to *Rig-Veda* 10:71, when perishable bodies such as Bṛhaspati sent out as speech (*vāk*), the first and earliest utterance of all that is excellent and spotless, representing the treasure within him, they disclose their personal affections. Like corn flour through a sieve, this forces a wise spirit appear to create a different language, which friends recognize as a mark of friendship. With their speech, they retain the blessed sign as it was first imprinted. With traces of speech (*vāk*), they follow the trail of sacrifice and find the living spirit harbored among the noble souls (rishis). The living spirit brought forth to deal in many places, serving through the seven singers, who make the living spirit produce resounding tones in concert. The one body who is ever able to trace the source of speech is the goddess Vāk, who hears each body as it has never heard before, with Vāk showing her beauty to others as a well-dressed woman shows herself to her husband. As individual living spirits, one is a laggard, its friendship dull, but they never urge anyone to commit valorous deeds. Such a spirit wanders on in profitless illusion, where its voice heard yet yields neither fruit nor blossom. No part of speech ever abandons its dear friend who knows the truth of their friendship. Even when in vain, it still listens and hears, even when not knowing the path of righteous action. Unequal in the quickness of their spirit, they endow friends with eyes to see and with ears to hear. look like containers reach the mouth or come up to the shoulders of others, appearing as pools of water fit to bathe in. When friendly Brahmans, upon impulse, make a sacrifice together with their heart aligned, they leave one far behind in his attainments, and leave others to wander elsewhere. Those living beings who neither step back nor move forward never preparers libations for the Brahmans and never attain the right level of speech. In a sinful fashion, they spun out like spinsters with their threads of ignorance. All joyful friends come in triumph, having conquered as an assembly. As blame averter and food providers, they are prepared food fit for them and their deeds of valor. Those who constantly attend the task of reciting verses and singing holy psalms (*Śakvarī*), established in the midair region, used to gauge the measure of the holy Brahmans and tell the lore, as another Brahman lays out the rules of sacrifice.

According to *Rig-Veda* 10:72, skillfully singing a tune, the Brahmans proclaim the generations of the gods, with no one able to see the vibrations they use to generate the hymns that, along with chanting, usher in a future age. As imperishable powers, the Brahmans are welcome to appear as blacksmiths, who in a blast furnace, smelting metal, demonstrate existence springing out of nonexistence just as nonexistence sprang up during the early ages of divine power. Appearing thereafter in different regions, they all spring from nonexistence to serve as the productive power Shakti, who brings the life force (prana), consisting of five types of wind (Vayu), and establishes the different regions forming the holy ground (Prithvi), which was all born out of dark matter (Mother Earth). This holy ground (Prithvi) served by Mother Aditi, who produces dexterous children, the Dakṣa, which brought forward as her offspring, along with a daughter. After Mother Aditi, they blessed to share immortal life, yonder coming close as if hugging one another, as they stand like godly powers, appearing as dancers who create with their feet a thick cloud of dust that rises, creating the innovative solution *yatis*, which causes all existing things to grow.

The Dakṣa bring along the heavenly illuminous body Sūrya, who moves forward from the earth, lying hidden beneath the sea. Eight offspring from Mother Aditi spring to life, with seven going to meet the gods, leaving far behind the eighth, *Martanda*. The seven offspring, after meeting with gods, become imperishable, and the eighth, *Martanda*, left to serve with a perishable embodiment. She comes to grow on the perishable holy ground.

According to *Rig-Veda* 10:73, the mighty powers born with victorious valor, exulting, strong, full of pride and courage, appear as the demigods who, as the cosmic hosts the Maruts, strengthened when their mother, Pṛśni, wife of the lord of creation Prajāpati, produces them as heroes. They come stirring up the water to create rapids, which keep evil far away from Mother Pṛśni, who remains seated as she exalted with the god Indra. As if to encompass the footed darkness, near at hand, Pṛśni and Prajāpati come forth with their children. High on their feet, they go on their way to gain in strength and vigor. Like the carnivorous dog with its forelimbs stronger than its hind limbs, they stand erect as filiform mammals of the family *Hyaenidae*. As scavengers, holding dead animals in their mouths, they turn to the Aśvins at once to offer them a sacrifice and attain friendship with the twin Nāsatyas. With one thousand treasures in their possession, they serve Aśvins and thereby come to serve as heroes who gladly give their riches in exchange for the race that rests on the holy order. With their friends, they hasten to reach their goal of meeting Indra through the magic power of the sky god Dyaus. They cast away the gloomy mist and the darkness by bringing the morning light (dawn) and the evening light (dusk), serving as affiliates of the goddess (Uṣas) before attacked by Indra. With beloved friends on high, they come with an assurance of heart, like the war loving Namuci, which smite the Dāsas, robbing them of their magic and giving it to the noble souls (rishis). On the modest, pleasant pathways leading directly godward, they seek the name of the divine who has completely fulfilled his obligation, serving as the boldest one: Indra—and his great might.

When the gods are joyful, the roots of the trees directed upward. Sweet soma juice flows, making everyone happy, by casting an iron ring to secure the rope that lies deep within the water. Then attached to the udder, which is aboveground, fastened in such a way that the milk pours out from the herbage. When the offspring of the coursers called, they bring mighty power. By means of their bodyguards, the Manus, they produce soma and remain in their houses: whence spring comes is known only to Indra. Like birds with beautiful wings, such as the peacock, *Priyamedha*, as an imploring rishi, comes near to Indra to dispel the darkness and fulfill the vision, thus delivering up those who snared in his trap.

According to *Rig-Veda* 10:74, the noble ones on earth and in heaven come to appear as coursers who have triumphed in the contest, or those who, now famous, have gloriously won the prize. They kiss the ground and with glory-seeking spirits call upon the godly powers to send them up to heaven, where the gods look upon them with happiness and favor fortune and, with heavenly kindness, give them their bounties, singing the song of immortality for those who long for treasures in their full perfection. After completing prayers and sacrifices, they bestowed with wealth, left wanting for nothing. Now they extolled for having performed deeds for Indra. They burst through the stall, freeing the cattle, both those that still provide milk and those that are barren, great and lofty, their many offspring streaming past. *Sacivan*, who never hesitates to fight the foe, with assistance from Indra, wins over the Ṛbhukṣans. Through the singing of hymns, the messenger Maghavan upheld as kind friend bringing the thunder to provide the manifested embodiments with rich food. Both old and young triumph through the power of Indra, who enters as the Vṛtra-slayer, in so doing appearing as the mighty lord of conquest.

## ESSENCE

According to *Rig-Veda* 10:75, the divine souls, as the singers regulating the cosmic soul, moves from its place to tell of the incomparable grandeur flowing within the holy river. They come forward like a trinity, passing through the mighty Indus, which serves all seven streams that flow upon the earth. Varuna, the power of eternal law, cuts the channels for them to flow forward. Following the course of the Indus, the divine souls run on to win the race. With speed, they pass over the precipitous ridges of the earth. With skill, as lords and leaders, they agitate the water to create floods, which roar when rising above the ground and moving upward to the heavens, all working vigorously to create a flash of light. Floods of rain fall with the thunder from the clouds. The Indus River rushes on, bellowing like a bull. Milk-producing mother cows and their calves move into the Indus and other rivers, roaring as they run. The warrior king, with wings, in time comes with his army to the forefront of these swift streams. With favor, the five holy rivers the *Gangā, Yamunā, Sutudri, Paruṣṇī,* and *Sarasvatī,* along with other rivers, the Asikni, Vitasta, Marudvrdha, Ārjīkīya, and *Susoma,* come to hear their call. First, with the *zealous Trishtama,* they flow forth carrying moisture (*Rasā),* memory *(Susartu*), and mercy *(Svetya*). With that, the *Kubha, Indus,* and *Mehatnu* cover the surrounding areas, each seeking a course through the regions of *Krum*u and *Gomati.* Whitely gleaming, flashing in their mightiness, the rivers move along with their great volume of water, passing through the realms. The most active among them, the holy river Indus, unrestrained, is like a dappled mare, beautiful. Rich with good steeds, the Indus travels along with carriages, carts, and robes, rich in gold, nobly fashioned, rich in wealth. This is all blessed by the goddess *Silamavati* and the young *Urnavati,* who vest themselves with stores of riches, wearing sweet costumes. Indus yokes their carriage, which rolls lightly, drawn by steeds, and with that they win booty in this fight. They all praise its power, mighty and unrestrained, and its independent glory, roaring as it runs.

According to *Rig-Veda* 10:76, grasping power and strength, the warrior king and his army begin with the morning light, bedewed to serve the celestial cosmic hosts the Maruts, who supported by the powers of heaven and earth. The Maruts appear day and night in every hall of sacrifice, waiting to blessed with their first spring of mythical juice. The most excellent among all the pressed soma produced by using the compressed cosmic stone (meteor), which grasped like a handheld tool. This form of soma enables the valorous ones to subdue their foes, and with might the fleet-footed coursers speed along with ample wealth. The soma pressed with stone (meteors), as in olden times, removes any defects and brings prosperity to manifested embodiments. At the time of sacrifice, they perform holy rites for the creative power Tvaṣṭṛ, who makes soma blended with milk bright in hue. Tvaṣṭṛ drives treacherous demons far away from the embodiments and keeps Nirrti far off by banishing extreme poverty. The soma pours forth richly for the troops, the heroic sons who bear compressed stones as they march along in song to visit the gods. The one who is mightier than the heroes of heaven, Vibhvan, finishes the task to reach far, being skillful, clever, and capable of pervading the solid manifested masculine body of Ṛbhu. Vibhvan moves more rapidly than the wind (Vayu) and able to seize the soma juice even better than Agni, who provides juice through food and with the vibrations generated by the singing of hymns. Stirred by the glorious stones, soma pressed out with song that reaches up to heaven. Where drawn forth, the power of essence transforms nonexistence into existence, for which Vibhvan longs by sending his voice around at a speed to rivalry that of sound. The stones press out the soma. Fast borne and eager for the spoils, Vibhvan drains the sap to fill the beaker, exhaust the udder's store, and with purifying oblations takes it with his lips. The newborn is most skillful in their work, learning even to press soma to serve to Indra to drink. Even though all have a fair in the heavenly race, the first fill a beak with this treasure served by the worshippers on earth.

According to *Rig-Veda* 10:77, Ṛbhu, along with his company, comes from the clouds to serve as a wise liberal. With his sweet voice, he makes sacrifices and, meriting such, worshipped and honored as the good priest *Martiti*. Youths with hand-fashioned ornaments travel for nights to join with the noble band of cosmic hosts (Maruts). Serving as sons of the sky lord Dyaus, they driven onward like stags, and as they grow, they become strong like the sons of Aditi. Serving as pillars, they extend outward, forming their own mass as they travel away from the clouds to form star constellations, which serve in the pantheon of the heavenly body Sūrya. Like mighty heroes desirous of glory, they are gallant as they nearly destroy the wicked, sending them deep into the waters. They cause turbulence to loosen the solid matter from the earth to create the holy ground (Prithvi), where they appear to offer sacrifices and approach living things to feed them with nourishing viands and to unite all who dwell there. Like horses fastened to the chariot poles, they bring luminous beams of splendor, creating the morning light (dawn). Like bright raptors (falcons), they hover when urged forward, scattering rain all around. Serving as the punishers of wicked men, they come forth from the distance as the cosmic hosts (Maruts) with a great treasury of possessions. Knowing Mother Nature (Vasu), they create boons that, even from afar, drive back the enemies, especially those who hate newly manifested noble souls. Those who are engaged in the final duty perform the rites and offer oblation to worship the cosmic hosts (Maruts). Blessed as heroes, full of the wealth life has to offer, drinking the gods' mythical juice, soma, they present themselves to make sacrifices to the adored ones, bringing good fortune to the noble Ādityas and speeding forth to help and protect, offering praises along with sacrifices and worship.

According to *Rig-Veda* 10:78, the skillful singers, with hymns and lofty thoughts, offer sacrifices to the gods, asking them to be fair in their dealings with kings so they may serve, brightly adorned, as spotless gallant leaders of the people. The singers bring fire to the gods, including the flashing eternal flame, and with chains of pure gold around their chests, binding them, they blast like a tempest, making the self-moving embodiments call out to them to swiftly lend their aid. As the best of all foreknowers, with excellence, they guide the guardians of the soma to follow the law. They travel like gales of wind, and as the Shakers of all, in their effulgence, with their tongues they receive the essence of the mightily burning fire, the eternal flame, by which they turn manifested bodies into righteous warriors clad in armor, like the most bounteous givers offering prayers as the fathers. Like the spokes of a wheels united in one nave, ever victorious, they come like youthful suitors and as heavenly heroes, shedding their precious balm, raising their voices and chanting psalms as singers. Fleet of foot, they travel like the noblest steeds, longing to obtain the prize like bounteous charioteers. Like waters speeding on with their precipitous floods, organized by the messenger Aṅgirases, they bring *sāman* hymns borne from the stream and, like compressed stones, become princes, serving forever like the crushed stones whose pieces become part of the soil to manifest as the sons of a beautiful mother serving as a great host who marches along in splendor. As the rays of dawn, serving as visitors at the place of sacrifice, they shine with ornaments, eager as bright. Within rivers they hasten on, glittering with their spears, coming from far away to measure out the distance between the gods and sending happiness that makes all wealthy, the singers prospering the Maruts. With noble thoughts, praise, and friendship, they, from days of old, have vouchsafed living things.

According to *Rig-Veda* 10:79, immortals appear among all the mortal tribes. Beholding a great mighty power, they open their mouths with their tongues, using their jaws, and when they clamp their jaws together, they devour that which they insatiably chew and then swallow. They turn their eyes away from this hidden insatiability to eat the food that fuels them.

With reverence within their embodiments, and with their hands upraised, they quickly bring their food to their mouths. Seeking, as if secreted in their mother's bosom like children, they creep through the widespread bushes. Once they find the glowing flame, they produce hot food by digging deep within the sanctuary of the earth, making it ready to eat. With the holy law, they tell infants upon birth to devour both earth and heaven as their ultimate parents. Unlike others, who come to accept Agni as the godhead who provides the best wisdom to the manifested body, they just receive food. They offer as gifts their oil and butter to support Agni and, with one thousand eyes, look closely upon the divine path. From within, they agree to commit no sin, including treason, against the godly powers. Even in ignorance, they seek the godly powers. Whether they are playing or not playing, their golden-hued toothless mouths help them to cut up their food. They use the same knife spared from becoming victims. Born in wood, yoked with horses, they rush in all directions, holding invisible reins that glitter. The wellborn friend of nature (Vasu) carves up food to give them to eat to increase their strength and make them prosperous.

According to *Rig-Veda* 10:80, Agni decks out both heaven and earth, filling the two regions with fertile females teamed up with heroes. Agni bestows an armada of prizewinning coursers upon the famed heroes with a firm duty to take the eternal fire things and bless things such as wood, which feeds the eternal flame and keeps it active within these two great worlds served by Agni. The flame induces every single soul to join the battle and fight along with Agni, tearing the foes to pieces. Agni, with the rejoicing embodiments, praised with limbs and follows the water to burn out the attacker *Jarutha*. This spares the great sage Atri, who lives in a fiery cave, and makes the noble ruler *Nrmedha* rich with children, who now serve as troops. Agni grants wealth to the heroes serving as shepherds, allowing them to win, also giving them one thousand cattle and oblations so they may rise to serve in heaven and follow the eternal law regulated by the heavenly body Varuna.

With songs of praise, the rishis call on the heroes worsted in the fray. Birds that fly around the region, as well as the thousand cattle, call on Agni. Races of humans at birth come to pay homage to Agni, who spring from an adored ancestral line, the Nahuṣas. Anointed with holy oil, they enter Agni's pasture to serve the *Gandharvan* path of law and order. *Ṛbhu* fabricates a prayer for Agni, and with mighty hymns calls on the most youthful god to come and protect the singers, who win by worshipping Agni and go on to acquire a great many possessions.

## DIVINE LINEAGE

According to *Rig-Veda* 10:81, the heavenly priest Hotar, along with noble earthly priests (rishis) as archetypal heavenly bodies, sits down, representing the Creator, to establish a divine lineage to regulate the earthly region. Hotar and the rishis visit all the divine creations serving as heroes who seek high positions while serving the holy ground (Prithvi). This all takes place in a spot where ultimate reality, *Visvakarma*, can see the dark matter of the earth and where an immortal soul may endowed with heavenly energy. Ultimate reality, *Visvakarma*, serves the immortal souls with their eyes and their mouths open, their limbs all facing upward, with wings and feet on each side of their bodies. He serves as the ultimate reality responsible for creating the differentiated universe, with its two halves, heaven, and earth, being part of the one. Wherever trees grow, he used their wood to fashion the ground, with the earth below and with heaven and its illuminating power above. The thoughtful living beings inquire about the powers of the immortal soul upon which all creation established. Ultimate reality (*Visvakarm*a) teaches the creations as friends. They all have a sacrificial nature, being most blessed and exalted. As part of their worship, they bring oblation to honor *Visvakarma*, the Creator of both earth and heaven. Others live in folly, seeking to become rich and liberal patrons. They invoked each day to provide aid with their labor, learning from Vāk, the goddess of speech, and generating thoughts to please Ultimate Reality. They learn all invocations that bring bliss and aid to those whose work as righteous souls.

According to *Rig-Veda* 10:82, immortals, through their fatherly vision, come to see through their eyes and acquire wisdom along with an eternal universal soul, as created by the heavenly powers that made the two worlds, submerged at the eastern end, which is firmly fastened, allowing heaven and earth to coexist, and become elongated. Visvakarma, with creative mind, along with the mighty powers of causation, comes to serve as the Maker of existence and nonexistence, the disposer of all that is of lofty essence or the individual living spirit. With the presence of the individual living spirit, the mighty powers offer eternal joy by generating rich drops of amrit, with its value being beyond that of soma, which served to the Saptarishis, who serve as the seven holy souls (rishis). Since they made to be the disposers of mortal embodiments subject to death, they know all about the existing races, who serve all things through the gods or deities who spread happiness and seek information. Old holy souls (rishis), with troops, as singers, offer sacrifices and treasures to those who come from the lower region, the underworld, but in the distance, they are near to all that has made, ready to serve all things in existence.

Those who prevailed before the earth and heaven even existed live as the evil powers the Asuras and as noble souls (Ādityas). They survived previously as the primeval germ that existed in the godly waters, where all the gods were seen together. The waters received the primeval germ that the gods, gathered, were fed. The germ rested upon the navel of the unborn, abiding among all existing things. No one can find or define the power that produced these creatures, which keep rising among all, wrapped in clouds of mist, with lips that stammer, as hymn chanters who wander and remain discontented.

According to *Rig-Veda* 10:83, after the first destructive bolt appeared from heaven, breeding all creatures, and conquering the celestial godhead, *Manyu* appeared, who, like the original devotees the Āryans, comes to convert the prevailing earthly devotees (*Dāsas*) and make them become like celestial imperishable embodiments, with support from Indra. To serve as many cosmic embodiments, *Manyu* joined with the Godhead to create sanctified bodies such as Hotar, Varuna, and Jātavedas, who serve the tribes of humanity, their lineage established as they are worshipped in the image of their celestial father, Manyu. Accordant with their passion, they fully protected and guarded by Manyu, so they, his offspring, may become mightier than the mighty. They enthusiastically chase after those who would be their allies, who will fight against the foemen and slay the evil power Vṛtra and the evil sky lord Dyaus, who rules such evil powers, in exchange for all kinds of material wealth and treasure. With their sanctified bodies, they are unsurpassed in vigor, becoming fierce killers of their foes, and they achieve self-existence, shared by both perishable and imperishable manifested embodiments. They are victorious because of their exceptional strength in battle. The departed godheads left behind a portion of their eternal wisdom, which now used to seek the ultimate mighty power. A feeble man now may attain by himself power and vigor to serve like the first cosmic embodiment, Manu, and by orchestrating his own advancement, become victorious and attain mighty powers to support others, such as the wielders of the thunder, whom they think of as friends, to slay the evil sky lord Dyaus, holding in their right hands their weapons of attack to slay a multitude of foemen and, in their left hands, carrying essence (meath) to offer to all to promote peace and tranquility.

According to *Rig-Veda* 10:84, the newborn Manyu supported with gifts provided by the cosmic hosts (Maruts). The Maruts brave and impetuous, bursting with eternal flame, exulting in their pointed arrows or other sharpened weapons. Like flashing fire, they appear to invoke the newborn Manyu, who as the army's leader achieves victory by slaying foes and distributing their possessions among other creations. With vigor, Manyu scatters those who dislike serving as evil powers. Then Manyu, overcome by his assailants, break the foemen, slays them and crushes them so they will never again drain him of vigor. Thus, a mighty soul is born who makes them subjects.

Alone, but with worshippers, the mighty soul sharpens the individual living spirits who are ready to fight in battle as a clan. With his aid, perfect splendor uplifted to conquer with a glorious shout. Unyielding, the god Indra brings victory with Manyu, setting the two of them up as sovereign rulers. With individual names, as victors, they jointly sing praises that spring from their hearts. The twin demigods, with power, bring a destructive bolt of thunder to conquer the highest of the mighty ones by subduing them, as the friendly Manyu, filled with inner spirit, much invoked, shocks those engaged in the battle. The eternal law, Varuna, along with the cosmic body Manyu, receives the wealth from both sides as the gatherer. The enemy-stricken spirits, overwhelmed with terror, skulk away, defeated.

## CEREMONY

According to *Rig-Veda* 10:85, the ultimate truth unveiled when holy ground (Prithvi), serving as part of the earth, sustained as part of the heavenly power Sūrya, regulated by the eternal law (Varuna) and eternal love (Mitra). Further, secured by the moon, Prithvi provides the mythical juice soma, holding in place both heaven and earth. The strong noble souls the Ādityas, serving the holy ground and the night sky filled with constellations of stars, are at the center of the region. While trying to find their place, the manifested imperishable Brahmans, who know all about the taste of soma, secured within shelters and guarded by hymns, hollering out to protect the *Bṛhati* with soma. The godly powers stand and listen to the cosmic showers that bring compressed stones (meteors) from the cosmic region. The Brahmans come to dwell on holy ground (Prithvi), where the godly powers serving as guardians come near, surging, with soma. With the celestial wind (Vayu) covering years of life, the celebratory spiritual *Raibhi* and *Narasamsi* verses exposed. The Brahmans all appear in lovely robes with the heavenly body Sūrya, along with his component star constellations (*gāthā*), all the Brahmans adorned and looking as if they are thinking, reclining on pillows on the couch. With the powers of embrocation, they see through the treasury of earth and heaven. The heavenly body Sūrya notices that the holy ground between the poles filled with craters. All decked out in *Kurira* (headdresses), the demigod Aśvins, as the leading pair, train all those wooed with soma to come and bind the brides and grooms. The goddess Savitar, serving the living spirit, brings the wedding embodiment, her carriage drawn by bright steeds, approaching the home of her husband, the heavenly the lord Sūrya. Well positioned, the steeds kept in place, singing the verses of the holy *sāman* hymn. All chariots and carriages with two wheels pass through the tremulous path in the sky, which filled with clean air, both their wheels fastened. They all proceed onward to the Lord, mounted with a spirit-fashioned embodiment. The bridegroom Sūrya and the goddess Savitar start to move along with the groomsmen (Maghā) and the bride said (*Naksharta*), soon arriving as a wedding procession (*Arjuris*) with a plan to welcome the bride as the holy ground. In their three-wheeled chariot with two seats, the demigod Aśvins, as wooers, provide support to Sūrya, the bridegroom. Then, all the gods agree to the proposal made by Pūṣan as son of the elected father. Two lords of luster come wooing to one chariot, Sūrya's, that stands for the perishable Brahmans, who commanded by the seasons, knowing all about Sūrya, who comes in a chariot with two wheels, while keeping one concealed—the one with the highest truths among those who are skilled and learned. The deity Sūrya, accompanied by eternal love (Mitra) and eternal law (Varuna), makes the right oblation and, of his own power, brings the twin Aśvins in close to move in succession.

Like playing children, the Aśvins go around the place of sacrifice, one of the two beholding all existing things, the other ordering the seasons to be born afresh, with a new and eternal ensign of days, before coming in the morning with orders for the individual godly portion. The celestial moon prolongs the days of existence and mounts itself in all shapes, golden hued, like two strong wheels, fashioned as the bride said *Kimsuka* and *Salmali*, with light rolling, bound for the world, bringing to Sūrya immortal life to make for a happy wedding journey. This causes the bride and her husband rise, and with loud hymns they pay homage to the home of her father, *Visvavasu*. Hence, *Visvavasu*, with reverence, seeks a willing aid virgin who, with her husband, will lead the bride straight along the thornless paths whereon other people travel to witness the wooing. Both Aryaman and Bhaga lead all to attend the perfect godly union of the wife and husband.

Now, Varuna, with the most blessed earthly goddess Savitar, who is bound to the seat of the law to serve the world through virtuous action, giving up on all who are uninjured, comes to free the law from the bridle. Hence, and not thence, Savitar sets them free but softly restrains them, blessing the bounteous female with fortune and with her sons. The messenger Pūṣan takes his hand and hence conducts the activities of the twin demigod Aśvins as they transport the ceremonial procession to the house, where the bride is to be the household's lover speak as a lady to the people gathered there. Happy and prosperous with children, the bride is vigilant to rule the household in this homeland. The female body and the male body are thus closely united, full of years, addressed as a divine union. The bride takes on hues of blue and red, seeking friends to whom to cling, and driven off. The relatives of this bride and her husband thrive, quickly forming bonds. They give the woolen robe away, dealing in treasure through the Brahman priests. Thus, the female friend as a villain attends to serve her lord. The husband, unlovely in nature, has a body that glistens in the company of this wicked fiend. The husband at times wraps his limbs within the garment of his wife. Her people, who follow her resplendent train, once again allow the holy gods to bear them to the place from whence they came. Let not the highway thieves who lie in ambush find the wedded pair; let the wedded pair escape the danger; and let foes depart. Signs of good fortune mark the bride, who comes to all so they may look upon her and wish her prosperity, and then return home pungent, bitter, their arrows filled with poisoned barbs, rendering them unfit for use.

The Brahman who knows Sūrya well is worthy of the bride's garment. Sūrya decks her head in fringe, and then takes the triply parted robe, beholds the hues, and dons it to purify the Brahman. He instructs the bride to take the groom's hand for happy fortune, which may reach old age with him as her husband. The godly powers Aryaman, Bhaga, Savitar, and Purandhi given household mistresses. Pūṣan sends them on as most auspicious sharers of pleasure, the demigods with loving arms welcoming all with love in their embrace. The nuptial train escorted by Sūrya in the lead, heading to the bride's home, where she in return serves her the husband, according to the eternal flame (Agni), with progeny. Then Agni presents the bride with splendor and an amply long life to serve her lord—one hundred autumns to live.

They first obtain soma; next, she takes the Gandharvan as her lord and goes home. Her third husband, Agni, now one born of woman, is also the fourth. From soma to Gandharva, and from Gandharva to the eternal flame, the living spirit bestowed upon the husband to give his wife both riches and sons, plus a dwelling place on the holy ground. Each reaches the full span of human life, with sons and grandsons who sport and play, rejoicing in their own abode.

The godly father Prajāpati brings forth all children as Aryaman, adored till old age. Auspiciously, they enter the house to serve as the husband's children, who bring a blessing to the manifested bipeds and quadrupeds. With no evil in his eyes, and with no intention to become a slayer, the divine husband brings wealth to cattle, radiant, as gentle-hearted creatures who love the gods. Delightful, bearing heroes, they come along with blessings from the bounteous Indra to support the bride with a blessed fortune in sons. Indra vouchsafes the wife's first ten sons and makes a husband of the eleventh man. The husband's father and the husband's mother both bear full sway over the sister of the lord, and the brothers, as the supreme rulers of the universal soul, through the water join their hearts to manifest as *Mātariśvan, Dhātar,* and *Destri.* They together form a close trinity to serve the dynamic universe.

CHAPTER 21

# Terrestrial Dominion

THE PLANET EARTH IS IN THE TERRESTRIAL REGION, WHERE FROM the holy ground it brings forth light to dispel the darkness from the region known as the subterranean or the chthonic home. The concept of a subterranean domain found in every religion, a vital part of the burial ceremony, reinforced by tradition. Coming out of such a domain, life appears zombie like, going on to form its own tribe, which prevails as part of the unenhanced dark matter. These beings appear as will-less and speechless and go on to become supernaturally reanimated beings who join with others to hold together, but they resemble the walking dead. They considered the mythological undead, corporeal revenants created through the reanimation of corpses. They found in the horror and fantasy genres.

The dead bodies reanimated by various methods, most commonly coming from the primitive world, where they prevail for a long time and perceived as uncivilized, the primitive spirit residing within dark matter. Such beings considered as part of a certain primitive cultural group (such as nomads) or revenants of primitive nature, like the wild creatures that prevailed in the past. Alternatively, they admired and romanticized as noble savages, idiomatically or figuratively personified as "barbarians," that is, individuals who are brutal, cruel, warlike, insensitive, or evil.

Mythologies incorporate the concept of the soul of the deceased making its own journey with the dead, needing to taken across a defining obstacle to reach its eternal destination. Imagery depicting such a journey found in both ancient and modern art.

## NOMADS

According to *Rig-Veda* 10:86, Indra passes by all as an ill-willed friend who knows no way of finding either soma or the spiritual path walked to achieve awakening. The supreme god Indra, instead of injuring such nomadic brutes (*Vrsakapi*), lets them want and meet up with those who hunt like boar before biting the innocent embodiment. Supreme Indra, serving as the noble soul, covers all the holy ground to protect these brutes as their friend, although they spoil all beautiful things and all joy. Making music using the *kapi*, a musical instrument, they woo, but they fall to pieces with the sinner's portion. There is no woman of wealth or delight who will offer them love. None with passion offers her beauty, like a lord's embrace.

All in search of motherly love, they quickly win over the mother, resting their heads upon her breast. With both hips trembling, they take her lovely hands and arms, braid her hair in plaits, and admire her ample hips, serving as the hero's wife. As sons of the godly mother, the cosmic hosts (Maruts), friends of the supreme queen, come to Indra to ask him to serve the matron who attends the feast of sacrifice to honor the mother of the heroes. With rites of ordination, the supreme queen offers a eulogy to *Indrani,* the most fortunate among women whose consort will die at time in the future. She serves *Indrani*, not because she enjoys being friends with a brut, *Vrishakap*i, but because she wishes to offer pure water to reach the gods. The wealthy brute Vrishakapi, blessed with sons and consorts, seeks the divine will to cause the bulls to eat of the oblation he offers, hoping it will affect them significantly. In numbers of fifteen, bullocks prepare to devour all the fat, thereafter, to fill Indra's belly full of food. For the bulls with pointed horns, bellowing loudly among the sweet herd, the fat goes to their hearts, and they tend to pour it out like a drink.

Indra watches as the brute slays a wild animal and dresses it with a newly made pan and knife, then loads it onto his wooden wagon. Indra observes both the Dāsas and the Āryans, who, looking over them all, selects the wise one who drinks the simple votary's soma and goes to the desert plains with a steep descent to gauge how long it is before they go to the houses that are houses and look for the home of the brute. They bring the twin demigods, who bring happiness as they go along their way, following the path that leads them to sleep. The noble Indra travels upward, where the noisome beast Vrsakapi troubles the innocent daughters of Manu, who as the largest, most authoritative person among the Parsu, has helped from birth a score of unadorned children with his portion verily blessed, though the ones who devoured cause him grief.

## WICKED SPIRIT

According to *Rig-Veda* 10:87, the most famous friends of the brutes live in shelters. As supernatural "man-eaters" (rakshasas), they come to appear in human form, or as Asuras with sharpened teeth, performing rites to attain the protection, both day and night, of the eternal flame, Agni. With teeth of iron, they enkindle the eternal flame and go on to attack the mighty power Jātavedas, like demons foolishly grabbing the one whom the god adores. With slit tongues, they feed upon raw flesh, using the teeth of both their upper and lower jaws to either enkindle or destroy. They roam around in the air, appearing as kings. Using their jaws, they assail wicked spirits. To perform sacrifices, they bend to pass through divine shafts, using the eternal fire to whet their stones, producing song as if passing by a whetstone. Once the mighty power Jātavedas pierces the heart of the evil power *Yātudhāna*, causing him to lift his arms, he continues the attack, piercing through Yātudhāna's skin. Simultaneously, Agni, with fire, destroys his darts, consuming them all. Jātavedas now allows the flesh-seeker to inspect his injured body. Now Agni can see, as can Jātavedas, that not one demon still stands, or roams, or flies on the paths in the midair region. He sharpens his arrow as an archer would to tear the evil spirit to pieces. Jātavedas seizes their spears before striking them down. Agni spots them before the carrion-eating kites can devour the noble power. Jātavedas tells Agni whosoever attacks a demon, who grasps one identified as having one eye, given him as an ill-gotten gain. Glancing around keenly, Jātavedas guards the sacrifice made by the sages and pass it on to his superior to be carrying ahead and given to Mother Nature (Vasu). Let not the fiends, beholders of humankind, harm the burning rakshasas or slay them, but look upon the fiends amid men as man-beholders.

Jātavedas breaks each of their extremities into three pieces, demolishing their ribs with flame, and from the root Agni destroys the triply evil power

Yātudhāna. Agni, further, puts three nooses around the demon, who with falsehood comes to injure the holy order. Loudly roaring with flames, Jātavedas crushes the demon and casts him down before the singers and the worship leaders, whom Agni, supports, who look at the hoof, as the armed demon, in front of the celestial priest Atharvan, burned up for having ruined the truth with his falsehood. Agni, to this day, curses those who uttered false words or used heated words while serving as worshippers, the arrows flying speedily toward the insulting angry spirits, such as the evil Yātudhānas, and piercing them through the heart. With fervent heat, the flaming arrow exterminates demons and destroy the fiends. The gods adore the blaze they create to destroy these insatiable monsters. To this day, the gods will destroy all evildoers who speak curses, blasting them with fire. Let arrows pierce the liar in his vital parts and may the net of the *Visvavedas* enclose all the *Yātudhānas*. The fiend who smears himself with the flesh of cattle, the flesh of horses, or the flesh of human beings, or who steals milk from the cow, is torn apart by Agni in his fiery fury, enabling the cow to give milk each year with no *Yātudhān*a ever tasting it.

When the gods can, they swamp the Yātudhānas with beestings, which, with the eternal flame, pierce through to the vitals. Mother Aditi kills the evildoers serving as fiends by giving them poison to drink, and the goddess Savitar kills them by denying them any share of plants or herbs. Agni, from olden days, has slain the demons, so the evil rakshasas may never overcome in any fight. He burns up the foolish flesh-devourers, ensuring none of them escape from the heavenly arrow. Agni guards his worshippers from above and below and protects them from behind and in the front with the fiercest flames, never wasting any, all of them glowing with fervent heat, consuming the sinner. From the rear, from the front, from below, and from above, the king—Agni—protects the sages with wisdom and guards them as eternal friends. Immortal Agni guards the mortal sages as they set up a fort in victory. Sages descended from a heroic lineage day by day, destroy their treacherous foes, burning them with divine poison, turning against the treacherous rakshasas. Agni with a sharp glowing lance armed with licks of flame burns the Kimīdins and Yātudhānas, while the sages sing hymns. The ever-vigilant Agni shoots his flaming arrows in all directions to break the strength of the Yātudhānas and the vigor of the rakshasas.

According to *Rig-Veda* 10:88, the godly powers, knowing their celestial nature as mighty powers, spread out to face the new world (Prithvi). They elect to sustain themselves by drinking soma as a sacrifice, which grants immortality, which offered by the heavens-pervading fire, Agni serving the heavenly body Sūrya, swallows everything concealed in darkness. Agni was born generating bright rays that make apparent everything that prevails on the holy ground (Prithvi). The mighty powers, as divinities and deities from the heavens and earth, serving the holy ground, provide life through the plant kingdom, supported by the free-flowing waters. Inspired by gods and adored by the divine will, with the lauded eternal flame (Agni), the plants spread across the earth with luster from heaven and the midair region. The earliest priests, whom all the gods accepted anointed with butter or oil, with which Agni caused all things fly, generating all kinds of motion among the godly power Jātavedas. Because of the eternal flame, the godly powers come to stand at the head of the world, serving in refulgent splendor. The priests send forth with hymns, songs, and praises that fill the earth below and the heavens above, serving the Creator with their worship. The head of the world, after the nighttime, brings the morning light, which springs up and rises to invoke the priests. Knowing the wondrous godly powers, with honor, kindled with greatness, the priests behold, seated in the heavens, the refulgent heavenly body Sūrya. With resonant hymns, all the gods guard the manifested embodiments who offer oblation to Agni. At first the hymns bring other godly powers into being, but then oblation engenders Agni.

With their sacrifice, the gods guard the embodiments, the heavens prevailing in the water on the ground (Prithvi), which water supported by both earth and heaven. Agni, generating all the other godly powers and offering his support to all creatures, appears as a hot, bright glow coming from the ground (Prithvi), urged forward amid the grandeur of earth to the laud the gods in heaven, with Agni providing both worlds strength and vigor. He appears in a threefold essence as ripe plants, serving as every form of nature. The godly powers, with due worship, set into motion the heavenly body Sūrya and the great mother Aditi, along with their offspring the Ādityas, who serve as the twin demigod Aśvins, who spring up to serve human beings and all creatures. For all the life in the world, the gods make Agni to be the days' bright banner, Vaishvanara, which spreads out amid the radiant mornings, followed by bright light to unveil the darkness. The mighty powers, holy and wise, manifested as divinities, deities, and demigods all engendered by Agni, never touched by age. They are the Vaishvanara.

The imperishable powers manifest within the constellation with the most ancient of stars, the holy one that wanders forever, lofty and strong, serving as the protective lord of manifested mortal embodiments, including all human beings. The sage with holy verses calls upon the imperishable Vaishvanara, who, beaming forever, pass both heaven and earth, bringing greatness to the earth below and the heavens above. Each moving creature travels on these two paths, between the father (heaven) and the mother (earth), which unite for those who are born for the journey. The living spirit, standing next to all things in existence, hastens, arresting in its fiery splendor and majesty.

The Aśvins know when to speak together, with one of the two serving as the upper, and the other serving as the lower, leading rites, helping to gather the assembly. They make a joint announcement, knowing how fires make up the shining sun, how dawns there are, and how, through the power of water, noble sages speak to the gods. Serving as twin demigods, as father, and mother, fair-winged, they appear in the morning, where Mātariśvan and the embodied Brahma dwell. They approach and make sacrifices, sitting below the heavenly priest Hotar and extolling the heroic god Indra who, with mighty force, as one of the supreme powers of causation, covers the space between the ground and the sky to serve as the upholder of the all-surpassing floods and the great rivers.

CHAPTER 22

# Perpetual Dominion

THE PERPETUAL (EVERLASTING) DOMINION SURROUNDED BY STAR constellations, which perceived as representing mythological creatures. This dominion is located right below the manifested terrestrial dominion and above the unmanifested underworld. It is a region occupied by manifested mortal embodiments, which are related to the godly powers through their beliefs, mythologies, faith, and experience. Interestingly, when observed throughout the year, the constellations as gradually shifting to the west, confirming the earth's orbital movement around the sun. During summer, viewers looking up into space at night see the constellations appearing in a different place from that which they occupy during the winter. The perpetual dominion holds the constellations that represent the supreme powers of causation, which, all-knowing, come to appear as invisible omnipotent embodiments, having eyes, faces, arms, feet, and wings. They come to serve from all directions among newly manifested material world (Virāj), dwelling with living creatures, seeking to reach the pinnacle of prosperity, displayed as the four-faced (north, south, east, and west) god Brahma, as well as the four-armed goddess (northeast, northwest, southeast, and southwest)—again, covering every direction, appearing as heavenly gods above and as earthly goddesses below.

## COMPLEX CONCEPT

According to *Rig-Veda* 10:89, an embodiment reaching in all directions generates vibrations, which transform into oscillations, which creates speech (*vāk*), which as which represents the supreme powers of causation, that is, the chief godly powers Indra, Varuna, Agni, et al., who help to direct the individual living spirit, serving in every part of the vast universe. All creation starts by spreading from the navel of ultimate reality, from the umbilical cord connecting the golden embryo. The golden embryo, which emanates with divine nature (*Prakriti*), serves as the cosmic being *Purusha Sukta* and merges with the creative force *Tvaṣṭṛ*, serving the creator *Vishwakarma*, who as the first epithet gives birth to a visible primordial force (Shakti) namely, the trinity of *Indra, Sūrya, and Agni*, who serve, respectively, as the Creator, the Protector, and the Sustainer. The monolithic body Brahma manifests and intertwines with the mighty powers, joining with the ancient immortal power *Vastospati*, who combines all the five great elements of nature, striking a balance between human and material. They all come to serve as the imperishable *Brahmaṇaspat*i and worshipped with divine prayers by devoted mortal noble souls, *Brahman*, and as the perishable body *Bṛhaspati,* who in his vastness serves the immortal living spirit embodied in the mortal. All these gods appear as different mythical figures, including planetary bodies, and form a council depending on the stage of existence.

During the last phase of existence, the creative force Tvaṣṭṛ, emerges and perceived as the invisible ancient holy priest Hotar,. This invisible creative power is responsible for the creation of the heavenly esoteric region, including holy ground (*Prithvi*), located below the esoteric region and above the earth. Thus, the holy ground filled with embodiments, with limbs and wings, help to pass through the process of physical evolution. Each advancement is supported by visible or physical evolution, (*Sarvamedha),* coming to manifest as a physical body, (*Purusha Sukta*), represented as a pair of supreme deities, namely, *Vishnu* and his partner goddess, *Lakshmi,* who, as *Puruṣhottama,* are considered as supreme beings serving as the ultimate power in the universe (i.e., the *Vaishnavismas)*. They are blessed with the attributes of speech (*Vachaspathy*); they serve as perishable embodiments (*Bṛhaspati)*; and they are pictured as the noble power (*Prajāpati*) and the evil power (*Rudrasiva*), each having its own kind of embodiment. These embodiments came into existence long before the five great elements of nature (earth, sky, water, light, air), serving in different forms as the universal soul. The universal soul separated into individual living spirits, which, once manifested, appear as individual holy spirits, serving as male (Ṛṣi) and as female (*Śilpi*). The male and female each focus upon defined name, form, and qualities, and jointly they represent Supreme Being, never looked upon as different deities.

The five great tributes include *Sadyojāta*, who controls individual desire, happiness, and sadness, and brings in perfect balance, (*Ahaṃkāra*) Such balance attained by way of solitude or through a practice that surpasses that conventionally.

The second of the five tributes *Vāmadeva*, attained by being acquainted with the special powers of the sun (*turīya*). This provides superior power to heal, both mentally and physically, accomplished through practicing a mantra (*Parāliṅga*), which through red blood serves as unmatched force that can transform all the great elements of nature and enable them to rise into the cosmos from the north (*Tejasa*). This brings the vital force, represented by an indescribably bright light.

The third is the power of infinite knowledge, (*Aghora)*, who brings eternal wisdom The *Jñāna Śaktī,* functions as the consort of nature (*prakriti*). It acquire *Parā Śaktī*, who brings enlightenment (*Buddhi rūpa*). Infinite knowledge invoked by way of the ancient mantras (*Pūrṇagiri Pīṭha*) and the new mantras (*Banaliṅgam*).

The fourth, (*Tatpuruṣa*), represents the east, *Ānānda Śaktī*, who dictates the ultimate structure within the individual living spirit prevailing on the infinite ground (*Prithvi*) as part of earth (*tattva*), making difficult to focus while facing east (*Svambhuva liṅga*), as upon the birth of the living spirit, *Ānānda Śaktī* departs to merge with the universal soul.

The fifth, (*Īśāna*), represents the power of space and time, *Citta Śaktī*, that controls absolute truth, leads to the discovery of *Brahma Randra*, the face of essence, responsible through mantras for existence and nonexistence or cosmology (*ākāśa*),.

Depending upon ancestry and heritage (*gotra*), the embodiment manifests as the archetypal immortal embodiment (*Manu*) a survivor of the great flood, who ultimately is honored as the father of the human race, ready to face the newly created material world, (*Virā)j,* which is subject to illusion (*Maya*), which is created as a distortion of the senses, to dispelled it requires spinal cord be aligned in a straight position to allow the spiritual energy to reach beyond the physical body (*Śilpy*), along with an understanding of the fundamentals of the vibrations that create singing and speech, which transforms one's ability (Viswajna) to behold the image of the holy spirit Vishwakarma, as accomplished by holy sages (rishis).

The cosmic body, purusha, served through the conscience, which evolves over time, after passing through in covenant with the universal soul (*Paramatman*). The conscience, after passing through a mystic sacrifice, ends up separating the individual living spirit (*Atman*) from the shackles of physical embodiment. Once fully purified of residual memories, the conscience, now free, comes to guide the manifested individual embodiment. This requires possession of the indestructible power of essence, meath, which, without form, becomes all-pervasive. It swiftly expands to cause even Indra to spread out like a wheel in never-ending motion. Ever active, indestructible, Indra travels with the eternal light to dispel the black darkness.

The cosmic conscience, with holy prayer, ceaseless and matchless, now filled with new worship, further increasing the space between earth and heaven. It well marked and backed by other living creatures, which never fail to serve as the friends of Indra. With songs, it sends forth an unceasing flow, like water traveling from the surface of the earth to reach the depths of the ocean. Indra's carriage securely fixed on both sides, the wheels bound by an axle. He roused by drafts of soma, rushing onward. Like a Shaker, impetuous, great, and strong, he arms himself with arrows and drives through forests filled with trees and no bushes that bear any likeness to soma plants. The heavenly mythical fluid that flows for all is something that nothing on earth can equal, from the firmament to the mountain ranges.

When heightened in his outrage, Indra shatters even the strongest firmament, breaking it into pieces. Like an ax fells a tree, he slays the evil power Vṛtra and breaks down his strongholds, even those dug out from the rivers. By cleaving the mountains, he creates a pitcher to bring out any hidden water. This brings forth the animals to serve as companions. The wise Indra, punisher of guilt, smites the sinner by cutting off his limbs. He does the same to those living beings who injure others, acting as comrade to the eternal law (*Varuna*) and eternal love (*Mitra*). Any who break their agreements with these gods led to live evil lives or serve as foes. Those who injure the powers of the trinity Varuna, Mitra, and Aryaman met by a furious bull of a fiery color, which brings them an early death.

The sovereign lord of the earth and heaven, Indra causes the waters to run over the mountains. Serving as the lord of prosperity, he supports the sages who invoke him, and sets up shelters for them. Their effort over days and nights increase the vast firmament and supports even the flooding of the oceans. Indra, like wind, moving faster than the rivers, extends the firmament and blesses it to make the ground holy, served by the herald of morning light, his insatiable arrows flying fast to pierce through the compressed cosmic stones (meteors), launched with the hottest blaze, far from heaven, which creates the illusion of heavenly support. Verily, it is the reflective light of the moon that passes over the mountains and through the tall trees, coming to fall upon plants.

Yearning with eternal love, Indra, for the first time, approaches as long-awaited, creating the connection between the two worlds, with water flowing between them. With his vindictive darts, Indra shoots the demons, outraged, and whatever fiends that lie upon the ground, filling creation with these lower souls, like cattle in the place of immolation. Those who are antagonistic toward the noble union (*ogaṇa*) targeted by Indra, who uses his mighty power to bring inner illumination and remove the blinding darkness from among the foemen, showing them that that which shines at night can bring bright light and dispel the darkness.

Plentiful libations, with singing and holy prayers of rejoicing, offered by noble souls (rishis). Hearing such loving invocation, Indra delivers to all who praise him, allowing them to partake of his favors that bring profit to all. Singing with love, the godly *Viśvāmitras* in the daylight win over Indra and his envoy Maghavan as the best hero in the fight, who gathers up the spoils and, as a strong listener, provides aid in battle to those who slay Vṛtra to win riches.

## CONSCIOUSNESS

According to *Rig-Veda* 10:90, the cosmic conscience manifests as *Puruṣa*, which becomes aware of its surroundings by way of its thousand heads, thousand eyes, and thousand feet. All-pervasive, from every direction of the earth, Puruṣa comes to fill any space larger than ten fingers wide. This is all observed by the lord of immortality, who allows Puruṣa to grow greater as it consumes food. Puruṣa is mighty in greatness as compared to all other creatures; its manifested body is one-fourth their size and has three-quarters' life. Even manifested with three-quarters' life, Puruṣa's consciousness, again one-quarter the size, strides out in all directions over the newly manifested world, Virāj. The manifested embodiment Puruṣa itself is alive to serve as the sun, which starts by spreading its illumination from the east to the west, covering all the newly manifested holy ground, representing the terrestrial bodies including Earth. Puruṣa, along with the godly powers, prepares to make a sacrifice by bringing lubricant as an offering, springing up as the holy gift giver, as nature (prakriti) creates the seasons of autumn and summer, which impact the kingdom of wood and vegetation. Holy grass, created in the earliest times, supports all noble souls, sadhus, rishis, and deities, which they observe as a great general sacrifice. They gather up the dripping fat that gives birth to the creatures of the air, which support the earthly animal kingdom, both wild animals and tame ones. With this great sacrifice, they sing hymns (*Ṛcas)* and further raise their voices to sing *sāman* hymns, from which mantras *(Yajus)* are born, which produce spells and charms, which support the transformation of wild animals into domesticated animals such as horses and cattle, all with two rows of teeth, and give birth to other kinds such as goats and sheep. Each creation represents a divided portion of the godly Puruṣa and depending on what and how portions each creation given, they develop mouths; limbs such as arms; thighs; and feet. The highest portion endows with mouths the moral Brahmans. Those with both arms and wings represent the next-highest level as righteous warriors (*Rājanya*). The next highest possess thighs and legs, using their legs to move around and perform their obligatory responsibilities *(Vaiśya*), and the lowest level possess feet (śūdra), which connect the embodiment with the ground.

The cosmic conscience, Puruṣa, blessed with a mind (the moon), vision (the sun), eternal flame (Agni), breath (Indra), and life force (Vayu). The purusha serves as the navel located within the midair region forming the sky shield, which fashioned as the head to represent the heavenly body, with the feet of the earthly body representing the holy ground. Together, this represents the true manifested mortal embodiment serving all the regions of the material world. The material world held together with seven fence posts, serving as the supreme powers of causation (mighty powers), which serve all three regions: the celestial (closer to heaven), the terrestrial (closer to earth), and the cosmic, which is the middle esoteric region. These twenty-one layers of causation are all regulated by the eternal flame of Sūrya, who offers all sacrifices performed for his sake to complex cosmic consciousness, Puruṣa, as the victim of the godly powers make sacrifice to save those who subjected to the earliest holy ordinances. The mighty powers serving as one attain the heights of heaven, where the seed (*puruṣa*) of the material world (Virāj) comes to serve in the old dwelling as the goddess Sādhyas.

According to *Rig-Veda* 10:91, walking briskly to the dwelling place of Iḷā, sages engage in worship and sing hymns to become awakened and to become familiar with the holy sage Hotar. First, they enkindled the house, offering choice oblation, then as beaming trusty friends with eternal love, they offer their altruistic souls to the lord of all. Excellent in glory, guests in every house, they find in every tree a swift-winged bird resting. They reject no living being as a friend and welcome any and every tribe that comes to dwell. Most sages with insight are skillful with divine powers. Agni, all-knowing and wise, and Vasu serve as a group of the eight elemental gods, the Aṣṭavasu. This includes the five great elements of nature (earth, fire, wind, water, and sky) and three cosmic phenomena (the sun, the moon, and the constellations). Together they bring all good things from heaven above to the earth below.

Knowing well, Iḷā, located centrally on the earth, and Agni (fire) both occupy the place filled with emollient and marked with the coming dawn, which brings with it the spotless source of light, Sūrya, producing lightning with glory and bringing the dark rain clouds. Thus, cosmic vapor fills the dawn, with many-hued water drops loosening to wander, providing moisture to serve plants and trees. The ceramist makes the containers used for cooking the food to feed the creations that have mouths. All the seeds of plants receive the warmth provided by Agni that needed to bring the life force. In the same vein, the trees and plants require the eternal flame to reproduce. With the divine will, they speed along, urged on by the wind, swiftly picking up food. With the ever-burning blaze, they consume food like men in chariots, while Agni works on all sides.

Appearing as the priest Hotar, Agni fills the assembly of fully awakened souls with knowledge. Serving as the chief controller of thoughts, nothing less than divine, he selects the sages who offer sacrificial offerings to great and small alike. As the arranger, Agni elects those who remain attached to their priest at the sacred gathering. Living beings sprinkle grass clippings, offering them as sacrificial gifts to the piously inclined as a form of entertainment. It is the herald's task and the cleanser's duty, as leaders, to serve the pious kindler. Such become directors who minister to the priests and recognize Brahma as the lord and head of their homes. When humans presented with the eternal flame from the immortal Agni, it offered with their sacrificial gifts to the messenger Adhvaryu, who called upon as the godly power of Hotar to attend the sacrifice. Singing hymns in concert with holy words, he hears the songs of praise and then offers eulogies to those eager for wealth. They first to receive this wealth go the place where it is polished and refined to please to the Strengthener, Jātavedas. With this new eulogy, Jātavedas and Adhvaryu then go forth to speak to the Ancient One, who loves to hear their individual voices, which touch his heart and makes it stir with eternal love—like a well-dressed matron clinging to her lord, who is duly set apart by horses, bulls, oxen, barren cows, and rams.

Agni, as the Disposer, offers up a sprinkling of sweet soma that comes from his divine heart. This brings forth a hymn into his mouth, as he pours the offering of soma into a cup. With oil in a ladle, he vouchsafes the wealth and strength of the heroes, lofty, praised by men, and full of splendor.

## HOLY HERALD

According to *Rig-Veda* 10:92, heavenly bodies appear as the holy herald, serving as the lord charioteer and the priest of the manifested tribes. Refulgent, as overnights guest, they blaze the plants dry by snatching up the ones that are green. Only the strong and holy among these heralds reach up to heaven. Like Agni, they serve as noble souls, chiefs who supported with rich drink offered in sacrifice. They caress and kiss the grandson of the Red God, who comes as a swift ray of light, serving as the household priest. They discriminate against those who are mean, miserly, or envious, serving as offshoots of branches, which consumed. When the terrific flame reaches them from the world of the immortal ones, only then do they remember to extol like the heavenly folk do.

The sky lord Dyaus, who supports the law, widely worshipped upon the earth, and with devotion, meets with the highest praise from the trinity of Varuna, Indra, and Mitra. Of one accord and with holy might, Savitar and Bhaga move forward with the roaming Rudra, who floods over with mighty obedience, Aramati, then runs *parijman*, moving around in this vast domain.

Bellowing loudly, Dyaus bedews all things within, straightaway supporting Rudra and the Maruts, who visit all living things and as home dwellers, like falcons, serve with the Asuras and the trinity of Varuna, Mitra, and Aryaman. All these looks upon the living things, like Indra, the swiftly moving godly power. With Indra they find enjoyment. They toil in the beauty of the light, moving in the same way the Strong One moves. The singers who make up the assembly forged according to their friend Indra with his thunderbolt. Even the sun's bay coursers lie in check as each one fears the mightiest of all the powers: Indra.

Unhindered, from the air's vault, they thunder forth day by day with loud triumphant voices, breathing like the fearsome bull. With humble adoration, they sing songs of praise to brave ad mighty ruler Rudra. Along with the eager Maruts, they travel their designated course, coming from heaven as bright auspicious ones, serving as strong guards. They spread abroad as the bull (Bṛhaspati) with their brother Soma, serving humankind with their fame. The noble prophet Atharvan first makes sacrifices to ensure that Bhrigu esteemed among the gods before coming to serve the earth and heaven with his abundant seed, the four heavenly embodiments Narāśaṁsa, Yama, Aditi, and Tvaṣṭṛ and the four earthly embodiments the Ṛbhukṣaṇs, Rodasī, the Maruts, and Vishnu), whom he claims with merit and praise. They give the embodiments to serve as sages from afar and to control the yearning calls from the dragon deep in the water. Like the sun and moon, these embodiments serve heaven and, thoughtfully, in turn, serve the ground and all that is observable beneath the sky shield.

Dear to all gods, Pūṣan guards the way to allow the child of the waters to move through the wind (Vayu) and seek success. Lauded with blissful songs, Vayu is the breath for all. The twin demigod Aśvins, prompt to hear, hear this as travel on their way. With hymns of praise, they sing to those who crowned as lords among the fearless tribes of the Self-Resplendent One. They praise night's youthful lord of benevolence, who is without a foe, moving freely among all the celestial females. By reason of their birth, the noble envoys the Aṅgirases are the first to sing out to welcome the compressed cosmic stones (meteors), which raised up in sacrifice, beheld in their exceeding vastness, sharp like an ax, obtained in battle in this beauteous place.

According to *Rig-Veda* 10:93, the Aṅgirases, mighty in strength, extending into heaven and across the earth, stronger than any foe, forever guard the two worlds evermore, like young beauties, each receiving the sacrifices made by mortal embodiments to honor the godly powers, most widely known for bestowing happiness. They come to serve as the rulers overall, with great sovereign godly power. They possess all majesty, making sacrifices to serve others in joy such as the immortal kings Parijman, Mitra, Aryaman, and Varuna, and the heavenly power Rudra, who found among the trinity of perishable embodiments the Maruts, Bhaga, and Pūṣaṇa. They also come into the dwelling serving as lords of spiritual wealth and are partakers of the clouds' cosmic vapor, covering both the sun and the moon, as well as the place where the great dragon lives, deep within the ocean, settling upon the waters. The splendorous Aśvins are both set free, along with Mitra and Varuna, into the land of woe, a desert, speeding their way to a place of opulence. The opulence enables the twin Aśvins to be gracious unto all, including the heavenly *Rudras; Bhaga, Rathaspati, Parijman, Ṛbhu, and Vāja*; and with the lords of all wealth, the *Ṛbhukṣaṇas*. Together they prompt the worshippers with strong drink to create a fleet of bay steeds, to approach not the perishable bodies, but the imperishable bodies, to make a sacrifice. Their sacred song is unassailable like that of the goddess Savitar, who is unharmed and, as lauded, provides the perishable bodies a place among the wealthy imperishable princes. In their carriage pulled by steeds, the Aśvins receive guidance from Indra, who takes the reins to control the carriage carrying the perishable manifested souls, granting them with lofty fame, which extends to all humankind. The steeds with their strength win the wealth. In victory, Indra speaks as a friend guarding the warriors and forever helps humans to attain wisdom and prosper amid nature (Vasu). So, they strengthen their singing of hymns and take the bright path established by the immortal sun, reconciling themselves with mortal beings (humanity). Thus, like carpenters, they yoke their horses, never displaced, the chariot seat once again laden with wealth and bright with gold. Lightly, they move toward the piercing end, before the heroes in rank for the fight. They sing to the manifested body *Duḥśīma Pṛthavāna,* asking him to serve the imperishable Vena, with the poised perishable embodiment Rama serving as a noble king. They touch the five hundred subtle points on the body to invoke all the famed gods along their way to eternal love with seventy-seven kinds of heavenly heritage, in forms and shapes, which at once display their patronymic heritage. Then *Tānva,* as the descendant of holy ground (Prithvi), acknowledges the presence of *Pārthya* through his illusionary descendants, the *Māyava.*

According to *Rig-Veda* 10:94, as consumers of soma, the illusionary descendants the Māyava speak out loudly, allowing others to speak loud to the cosmic bodies (meteors), which come filled with rich soma juice. Like the stones of the mountains, they are united to represent Indra and his swift power, who comes with the sounds of praise to speak out as one hundred thousand men, who cry aloud with their green-tinted faces. As the pious stones, they bombarded with piousness as they set about their task to stand before the heavenly priest Hotar, who comes to taste the food they offer. They find the savory essence (meath) and speak loudly like well-pastured bellowing bulls, preparing a meal as they hum and utter. After drinking the strong exhilarating drink, they devour a branch of the red-colored tree to show Lord Indra how they found the meath. As courageous ones, they dance with their sisters and embrace them as they reach the ground with a ringing sound. They send forth eagles from the earth, which cry when passing through the sky's vault, flying aloft to heaven. Dancing with a dark impulse downward, they fix a place for the stone, where it sinks into the ground, like the splendid sun effused with the plentiful free-flowing stream. Like strong ones, they draw all their strength like bulls harnessed together, bearing the chariot poles.

After they have bellowed, panted, and swallowed their food, snorting loudly, they rest like steeds. The ten workers with a tenfold girth yoked with ten straps and ten binding thongs, bearing ten reins, all singing the eternal praises of those who bear the ten chariot poles to which they yoked. These compressed stones with ten conductors, on their rapid course, travel round and round in a lovely revolution. They are the first to enjoy the milky fluid of the stalk, as the soma eaters are the first to drink the flowing soma, and kiss Indra's bay-colored steeds. After draining the stalk, they sit upon ox hide and then drink of Indra's essence (soma and meath), refined with strength, famed, as mighty as bulls. Because the stalk is strong, verily it does them no harm, and as refreshment it always satisfies. Fair and splendid, they bring wealth to those who sacrifice the compressed cosmic stones, which they find delightful.

Deeply bored into, but not pierced through with holes, the compressed stones, not loosened, never weary and are exempt from death. As eternal bodies moving in sundry ways, unthrusting, full of fatness, void of all desire, the Māyava, like fathers, verily, stand firm from age to age. Loving to rest, they not dissevered from their seat. Untouched by time, never lacking in green plants or green trees, they, with their voices, cause the heavens and the earth to hear the stones proclaim, at which time they disjoined, and with ringing sounds, the Māyava move forward and drink the balm. Like tillers of the ground, they sow seeds and mix the soma, neither devouring it nor diminishing the supply. They raised their voices high for the juice. For sacrifice, they strike Mother Earth (Prithvi) though they dance thereon. With loose divine thought, they effuse the sap, and let the stones, which they honor, be disjoined and become their consorts. They stay with the fierce-souled mother and reason for a while together. Such thoughts, while yet unspoken in days gone by, have never brought comfort.

## LEGENDARY ENTITY

According to *Rig-Veda* 10:95, a legendary celestial entity associated with the illuminated body Sūrya and the cosmic dawn, Uṣas, with their son Ilā, comes from the middle region to serve as a pious king, representing the ancestral tribe the Purūravas. They set out at first light from their ancestral tribal dwelling place with the wind and return from a shaft of light that is difficult to capture, sending their glorious tremor forth like a swift steed to win hundreds of cattle. The cowards, as singers, complain like a lamb in trouble as the lightning seems to flash, giving the father and husband riches so he will emerge from his dwelling as if a lover whom he craves for is nearby. He seeks the home where his lover found pleasure in his embrace, accepting her lord day and night. Thrice in the daytime, they embrace as divine consorts, though coldly, and she receives his fond caresses.

The Purūravas tribe desires the full yield as if it were a king, admiring the bodies of the hero, along with those of the aid virgin Sujirni, Sreni, Sumne-api, Charanyu, Granthini, and Hradecaksus. Red-blooded, they hasten forth with the bright ones, and in emulation low like milk cows. When they were born, all the aid virgin sat down together, serving like rivers, nurturing freely with kindness. Then, the godly Purūravas rose to fight in the mighty battle, mortals wooed by the sky lord Dyaus, embraced by the heavenly nymphs, who laid aside their attire and, like a scared snake, fled like chariot horses. Where the mortals are in terror of their embodiments being touch since the immortal ones love to consort with those who are mortal, the nymphs, like swans, allow them to see the beauty of their bodies. In their play, they bite like horses and nibble each other, flashing brilliantly like lightning striking the water and bringing forth delicious presents.

Now from the flood is born a strong young planet that controls the heart, Uruvasi, and prolongs life so it lasts forever. At birth, Uruvasi makes the nymphs drink milk from the ground, which vouchsafes them to this day. When no one is available to hear when a child is born, the Purūravas seek their fathers. When the child is first known, spouses grieve and weep, becoming divided. With his eternal flame shining, Agni consoles the parents as their tears fall, not knowing himself how to weep as he cares for them as blessed souls. He shines, sending forth his fire before going home again, not allowing any fool to win.

As the lovers flee far away, they seek never to return, making a bed for themselves in the bosom of extinction, where the fierce rapacious wolves devour all evil. They, like the Purūravas, are imperishable, neither dying nor vanishing. Nor do they let the evil-omened wolves consume them. As with women, there can be no lasting friendship. With the hearts of hyenas, they become women among men, but with their shape altered. They sojourn through four autumns, spending the nights among the wolves, content to have but one taste of butter, which also satisfies the eternal flame. With the best love, the strong young planet Uruvasi extends out to meet with breath, the air that fills the measureless region.

Let the gift brought by the pious ones heal any heart that is troubled. Thus, the godly power speaks and comes to serve the son of Iḷā, who verily banishes death from such subjects, and as the son of godly powers serves them with oblation, moreover, coming to enjoy and rejoice within the heavenly Svarga Loka.

According to *Rig-Veda* 10:96, from the great synod, loud, the divine will comes from both heaven and earth to serve as two bay steeds, which after taking a strong drink of sweet soma, become a warrior god who pours forth with eternal fuel, the drops of yellow nectar (amrit) falling, with the amrit supporting the singers whose songs enter the material world, which in this form is tinted gold. In concert, they sing unto the golden-hued place, driving onward like bay steeds to the seat of heaven. Indra, their ally in strength, like the tawny steeds the Aśvins, brings with him milk-bearing creatures, all content, enjoying the yellow drops of immortality (amrit). When Indra comes with his thunderbolts of iron, which are gold in color, he gives off a yellow hue, radiant energy invoked by his arms, which equips the Aśvins with bright strong teeth, able to destroy in their tawny rage. Indra sets fast all hues with his lovely rays, all laid upon the sky with his golden thunderbolt, which spreads out to all in the race. The iron thunderbolt, with a yellow flash, smites down deep into the water, where the ahi prevails, coming with one thousand flames that bear the tawny hued Aśvins. With praises, the old creation sacrificed, the oldest pleasure coming to with Indra, all golden-haired, to become part of a divine song of praise that welcomes in the perfect golden hue as a gift from birth. The two dear bays bring Indra's carriage, all thunder-armed, joyous to meet him with laudation and soma filled. Libations flow for those who love Indra, who brings the golden-hued soma mixed with golden-hued amrit, which flows to gratify individual wishes. With the yellow amrit, he urges the swift bays to become stronger and speed on, even if their longing for the golden drops has not been satisfied.

Taking a quick draft, the soma drinker becomes polished like the undead warrior, the Iron One with a yellow beard and yellow hair, serving as the lord of the tawny coursers, the one who formed the lord of the fleet-footed chargers, who guides the bay steeds safely through all distress. At time their yellow-colored jaws open like ladles to drink and thereby acquire strength to stir all that tinted yellow. While the mixing bowl stands, the tawny steeds, after groomed, drink of the strong sweet soma juice that they love. These dear ones they in the home of heaven and earth, served by the lord of the bay steeds, neighing like horses for food. Then, as per their greatest wish, they seized upon in their might and, as the Beloved One, gain a high station in life, all because they comprehend the mighty wealth hidden between earth and heaven. They come to accept that they will be singing hymns forever, repeatedly, to uncover the evil bodies of the Asuras and make them visible to the bright golden sun in the beloved home of the cows.

Let the eager wishes of the folk bring Indra as the delightful golden visitor in his carriage. May he be pleased with sacrifices in the place wherein the ten fingers toil, and at the feast, where he offered a drink of meath as it was before. The lord of the bay's drinks especially of the gladdening libation offered him, who as the Mighty One pours down meath-rich soma upon the heroes.

According to *Rig-Veda* 10:97, over time, plants as savory herbs sprang up. As in the previous three ages, these served by the godly powers, their brown hue declaring that they are seven years older with one hundred powers, and who like mothers have one hundred homes, with a growth potential of one thousand, with one thousand powers to rid of disease those who have long suffered. Be glad and joyful living among the plants, both those that blossom and those that bear fruit, as plants lead to success like a horse wins a race. Plants, in their own names, come to speak like their mothers, the goddesses, who help them manifested as steed and cattle, which come in their embodiments and win back their very selves.

In homes, including mansions, the holy fig tree serves as a sustainable tree, which like the innards of cattle know only how to serve living creations. There are those who know how to store special herbs and keep them on hand, such as physician sages, who serve among the crowd of men as the kings who come to serve as fiend-slayers and chasers of disease. A combination of herbs and rich soma provides nourishment and strengthening power to steeds, as well as provides strength to all manifested bodies so they may become whole again. The healing virtues of the stalks of the plants flowing forth in the stream cause even cattle to win stores of wealth, which enables them to save their vital breath. They serve as relievers in their mother's name, and hence called the restorers, floating in the rivers, helping the birds with wings to fly, and keeping far away from whatever brings disease. The climb over all the fences like thieves, to steal the cattle and bring them all into the fold. Driven forth from the structure of such herbs, they produce whatever remedy needed to restore power or any strength that has vanished. Even while they are holding these herbs in their hands, the spirit of disease departs so those afflicted can seize upon life.

Plants, because of their structure, member by member, joint by joint, drive away disease like strong arbiters. With the spirit of disease gone, they fly like birds, such as the blue jay or kingfisher, impetuously, at the speed of wind, and vanish together in the storm. By helping everyone and helping each other, they reach everyone, all in accord, and give the eternal speech to invoke all. Both fruitful and fruitless plants, including those with blossoms and those that are blossomless, urged onward by the perishable godly power Bṛhaspati to release others from pain and grief. This releases the curse of epidemic and banishes woe, enforced by the eternal law, Varuna, who frees all concerned from the god of death, Yama, and from all sins and offenses committed against the gods, before descending from the sky. Once invoked, they fly to holy ground, establishing space for themselves away from evil and other manifested bodies where life pervades. The plants, among which soma is the king, planted in their one hundred forms. The most excellent plant prompt the wish that is sweet to the heart. Of all the herbs, whose king is soma, which spread over the material world urged onward by the perishable Bṛhaspati, who combines all virtues in this one plant. Unharmed, he digs them up unharmed to serve to living things. No malady thereafter attacks any biped or quadruped who drinks of the soma.

All plants those who hear this speech, and those who have departed and are now far away, come to assemble to receive the healing power extracted from the herb. With Soma as their sovereign lord, the plants hold a colloquy by saying to the king that they saved from death as the Brahmans have cured after having taken the soma. Most excellent of all is the divine will where the plant given vassals and the trees are subject to the power of the man who seeks to injure them.

According to *Rig-Veda* 10:98, Mitra, Varuna, and Pūṣan come from the celestial region in response to the oblations from Bṛhaspati, while from the cosmic region the Maruts, Vasu, and the Ādityas bring Parjanya, pouring out raindrops upon Śantanu. The godly powers send the speedy envoy Devapi, full of eternal wisdom, to address the assembly and cause their lips to speak the brilliant language that comes from the mouth of Bṛhaspati. This deposited as lucid speech, filling them with vigor and freeing them from weakness. Thereby, with the rainfall, Śantanu brings essence (meath) from heaven to share among all. These sweet drops descend with the godhead Indra, who sets down one thousand wagons next to the heavenly priest Hotar, who has the task to duly worship and serve with oblation Devapi, eternal wisdom. Knowing the gods' will, Devapi, through the holy sage (rishi), reaches the son of Rstisena, who sits with Hotar, who has been down from the heavens to serve upon the loftiest summit, bringing the celestial waters to fill the oceans with rainwater. Gathered in the greatest ocean, the waters stand obstructed by the deities on the ground. From where it buried deep, the deity Arstisena frees the water, which rushes out from the gaping clefts, moving onward with eternal wisdom (Devapi).

As chief priest, Hotar has the duty of choosing the rain (Śantanu) and eternal wisdom (Devapi) and, with them, beseeching the gracious Bṛhaspati to vouchsafe them, their voices reaching the godly powers as they win the waters. Agni, with Devapi and Arstisena, comes to serve the mortal embodiments kindled in glory and to joyfully bring all the gods together, all of them urging the sender of the rain, Parjanya. All ancient noble souls (rishis), singing, approach the gods who are invoked during sacrificial rites. They come with wagonloads to participate in the solemn rite on behalf of the lord of the red horses. The ninety-nine thousand wagonloads are all offered in worship of Agni, serving as the hero, with an increasing number of nobles, who when stimulated send rain from heaven. After given these ninety-nine thousand wagonloads, both Agni and Indra become as bulls to allocate portions. Knowing the paths that the deities duly travel, they set up Aulana in the middle region, who is also known as Agni, to drive the foes far away, chasing away trouble, maladies, and wicked demons. From the air, from the ocean, and from the lofty heavens, he sends a mighty flood of water down upon the earth.

## OVERPOWERING

According to *Rig-Veda* 10:99, Agni is the Splendid One, loud voiced, far striding, well knowing of the urge of all to exalt him with praises, which will persuade the mighty power to emerge, fashioned like a slaying thunderbolt. With the cosmic vapor traveling to the ends of the earth and reaching the underworld, overpower the demonic Asura with his magical devices (*saptathas*), Agni comes with his companions. They find a most auspicious path that could use to bring down the heaven's light. During the battle, they travel this auspicious path to win. Full of willingness, they seize the gated castles that filled with treasure, all of it unattended, and butcher the lustful demons. Fighting for the spoils of war, they roam among those who are guileful and wealthy, moving along with the stream, where they manifest as footless and come to join the team of steeds to pull the carriage. They pour forth a flood of butter, beholding the unsolicited wealth. They come as blameless, all having had their dwellings confiscated, and bring along the balanced (*vamra*) food. In concert, they leave the couples weeping and unsheltered.

The lord of the dwelling first subdues the demon that appears with a loud roar. This is the six-eyed and triple-headed deity Trita, who made stronger, ready to strike down the boar with his shaft, the boar having a sharp pointed tusk as strong as iron. They raise themselves on high as they released their arrows against the guileful and oppressive foemen. The strong, glorious, manly shattered forts Nabus overpowers Dyaus, ruler of the sky. Like a cloud that rains upon the pasture, he finds a way for all to dwell in safety, even when the hawk comes to grab soma from their hands with its talons of iron and turns to slay the ruler Dyaus.

With potent friends, the mighty power, as the Splendid One, arises to restore the good name of Kutsa, who leads the lauded singer Kavi and delivers the noble souls to the Alaskan island of Atka to save them from becoming victims and so they may serve as heroes. Mighty forces with godly power come to love the wondrous human beings by giving them the eternal law, Varuna, whose works are magic and who becomes known to those who are still young as the guardian of the seasons—and who kills the four-footed dragon Araru without mercy. With loud sounds, the powerful Agni, as *hamro* dharma, bursts out as Auśija Ṛjiśvan, with mighty aid from the association of the Pipru, who are devotees. Saints provide him with pressed soma, which also given to the singers to seize the forts and, with skill, subdue the evil power. So, they swiftly vanquish the evil power Asura and come to exalted. Small creatures such as ants (*vamraka*) come along with the mighty Indra to restore the balance of power and bring tranquility, supplicated with blessings to providing food, strength, and happy dwelling places.

According to *Rig-Veda* 10:100, the goddess Savitar, serving with Indra, hears the twin demigod Aśvins ask for godly protection, especially as drinkers of the gladdening soma juice. Like the envoy Maghavan, they ask for freedom and complete happiness. While passing through, they make a swift offering, seeing that they could potentially entrapped, at time they bring along the wind, Vayu. As drinkers of pure soma, they come roaring for a draft of shining milk, with Savitar being the goddess to whom each makes a sacrifice, asking for full lives and to live aright, as they pour out the soma and, with simple hearts, wait upon the godly powers to provide them with freedom and complete happiness. Indra is ever more gracious unto all who bring him soma, so much so that he considers providing the manifested mortal bodies with complete happiness.

In their asking for freedom and complete happiness, Indra looks at such manifested mortal bodies as they sing their songs and ask for the strength to meet with the perishable body Bṛhaspati, who has the power to lengthen their life spans. Like the first manifested cosmic body, Manu, Bṛhaspati, with divine intervention, serves as the sire, whereas Indra, in his celestial form, comes as a singer to the house of the eternal flame, Agni, where he serves as a prudent heavenly sage. Serving amid the council of the gods, with fair sacrifices, those nearest, although not often, secretly sin against Agni, openly provoking him, but not against divine nature (Vasu).

When one becomes worn and alien in shape, Savitar removes the malaise, and uses the mountains to keep the embodiment far away from the place where the compressed stones (meteors) shed essence and ring forth loudly for Mother Nature (Vasu). The compressed stones stand erect, averting all enmity, and stay far away in the remotest regions, serving as guards who adore the heavenly goddess, Savitar. They eat of fat to gain the strength to tend to the animals in the pasture and to serve in the seat of the eternal law. They provide medicine to the singers and fill them with living spirit, among all loved creations. Indra takes good care of those who pour the juice and offer libations to fill the heavenly udder. The wondrous living spirit, filled with inner illumination, tremulant, serves as a host and saves the pious votaries from decay, sending them on the straightest path to gain possession of the best of all the cattle.

According to *Rig-Veda* 10:101, with an awakened mind, as a friend, Agni kindles who dwell together at dawn, as the courser Dadhikrā and the god Indra come down to help. With pleasant hymns, they spin out songs and praises while building a ship with oars equipped for transport. Prepared with their implements, they make all things ready, and with the sacrifice, they let their friends go forward. They lay on the yokes and fasten well the traces: formed is the furrow. They sow the seed within the soil, singing songs, and find plenty of fruit-bearing plants. They approach the ripened grain with a sickle. Wise, according to the gods' desire, they skillfully bind the traces fast and lay the yokes on either side. They arrange the buckets in their place and securely fasten the straps. The well pours forth in a copious stream, fair-flowing; this is the well that never fails. They pour the water from the well into pails, to which strong straps are fastened, unfailing. Refreshing their horses, they win the prize before they equip their chariot, fraught with their happy fortune. From the well with the stone wheel, they fill their wooden buckets to take water to the heroes to drink. Using the trough for armor, they prepare the cow stall, allowing the cows to drink while they repair their many coats of armor. Building iron forts to protect themselves from all assailants, they let not their pitcher's leak.

For help, the toilers turn to the heavenly minds of the holy gods, who long for sacrifices. To pour forth with milk, even the stately cow seeks a pasture that yields a thousand streams, the water pouring like golden juice into the wooden vessels. With stone axes, all in a fashion, Dadhikrā, Agni, and Indra encircle the chariot poles with a tenfold girdle, attaching the poles to the horse-driven carriage. Between the two poles the cart horse walks, pressed close, and with its chariot moves like the doubly wedded who lie in the woods as the sovereigns of the forest.

Creating a well without digging, Indra provides his devotees with happiness, for sport urging them, as the giver of delight, to increase in strength. They quickly oblige, bringing priests to give aid and provide soma, as Indra does for the son of Mother *Nistigri*.

According to *Rig-Veda* 10:102, Indra boldly speeds along in his carriage that moves in all directions, offering favor to those who fight against the raiders of wealth. Like the wind, he travels so swiftly that he and his chariot look like a loosened woman's robe, streaming forth to win a cartload of great worth. The charioteer Indra, with the female *Mudgalani*, shoots darts, which allows him to heap up the spoils of war. Indra casts his thunderbolt at his assailants, the weapon that kills both Dāsa and Ārya, with Maghavan slaughtering all whom he encounters, keeping the foes far away. The bull joyfully drinks water from the lake and comes with a shattering horn whenever he encounters an opponent. Swiftly, with vigorous strength, eager for glory, he stretches his forelimbs gladly to emerge triumphant. Indra and Maghavan fight close to the bull, making thunder and pouring down with rain until the fight is over. The male Mudgala wins the contest, with well-pastured animals in the hundreds of thousands.

In hope of victory, the bull harnessed as the leader *Kesi*, who shouts and urges his comrades to run swiftly with the cart behind them. Lifting his heels, presses close upon the female *Mudgalani.* Skillfully stretched forward toward the chariot poles, the bull guided thereto and then firmly yoked by Indra vouchsafed as the lord of cows, who with favor and his mighty steps makes the buffalo run onward. Touched by the goad, the shaggy beast goes nobly, bound to the pole, yoked by a thong of leather. Performing deeds of might for the others, Indra and Maghavan look upon the cows, gaining strength and vigor. They look upon the mace, as the bull's companion, now lying midway on the field of battle. Mudgala at this point wins one hundred thousand cattle for himself. Far away are the evil ones who beheld the bull yoked and given food and water.

Reaching beyond the post, Mudgala and Mudgalani given directions. Like one forsaken, Mudgalani finds her husband, and teems as if her breasts are full and flowing with milk. In a swiftly racing chariot, they conquer all and become rich with gains in battle. Indra marks the spot with his eyes whereon all of life rests. The divine bull drives the other bulls, who droop, still winning the race despite his weakling friends.

## LIBERAL MUNIFICENCE

According to *Rig-Veda* 10:103, with eyes that close not, bellowing, the hero whom Indra subdued at once becomes one of liberal munificence serving one hundred armies. Roaring loudly, ever watchful, victorious, bold, hard to overthrow, as the rouser of battle, Indra appears with arrows in his hand as a conquering warrior, who now vanquishes any in combat, ruler over those who carry shafts and quivers. Indra with his band is a foe conqueror, a strong-armed the soma drinker, who with his mighty bow shoots well-placed arrows. The perishable embodiment Bṛhaspati flies with Indra in his chariot, the two of them known as slayers of demons, driving off foemen. They arrive as protectors of the carriage, well-known destroyers, victors in battle, breakers of armies. Conspicuous by their strength, they are firm, foremost among fighters, mighty, fierce, victorious, and all-subduing, coming as the sons of conquest, passing as manifested bodies and heroes, mounted in their conquering carriage pulled by winner animals. Indra, cleaver of stalls, winner of all kinds of animals, armed with thunder, quells any army and, with might, destroys it.

Bṛhaspati and Indra as brothers, who are quick themselves, serving as heroes, showing zeal and courage. Piercing the cow stalls with unsurpassed vigor, the pitiless heroes, wild with anger, victors in the fight, unshaken and resistless, protect their armies in battle. Indra comes to guide the perishable Bṛhaspati so he may precede as the resistless one, making sacrifices of soma and allowing the banded Maruts to march in front of the heavenly hosts to conquer and demolish. Serving as the most potent hosts, Maruts guide the noble Ādityas, uplifting them like the mighty gods Indra and Varuna, and other similar noble powers who come shouting to conquer the high-minded evil Asuras, thereby causing the world to tremble.

The messenger Maghavan sent up with his weapons to excite the spirits of the opposing heroes, urging himself on upon his mighty steed, appearing as a Vṛtra-slayer, his carriage in a tumult as it goes upward. Indra, with his flags, aids to gather up the arrows of the victorious army. The brave men of war, to prevail in the battle, ask the gods out the outset to protect them. Bewildering the senses of the foemen, the victors seize their bodies as they depart, the most authoritative force, Apvā, ready to attack and, with the eternal flame, set fire to the hearts of their foes, who reside in utter darkness in the underworld, the supernatural world of the dead located below the world of the living. Advancing, the noble souls, as heroes, win the day, with Indra exceedingly mighty, whom none may wound or injure.

According to *Rig-Veda* 10:104, the soma flows for those who are invoked to break the shackles of the material world, offered as a sacrifice by the twin coursers who stream with song, or like the mighty singers who come imploring Indra, drinking of the soma like the lords of the tawny horses, the Aśvins, who have been washed in the waters and fully filled. Indra, after hearing the loud sound of the stones used to press the soma and enhance it with rapture, makes a strong draft to offer to the bull, while the bay steeds carry it forward with delight to Indra. Singing hymns, the singers feel the powerful soma as it reaches their inner spirits, with help from Indra, who serves with dexterity. Obtaining life, zealous, the singers, in order according to their skill and power, manifest as living bodies in the house where they share in the sacred banquet. By their standing and singing praises, Indra brings them a store of children. Moving in all directions, the twin demigod Aśvins, serving as tawny coursers, who are firm, splendid, and blessed to be with people to obtain aid for their salvation, praise Indra through their excellency. The lords of the bays come with their two bay horses, offering prayer and seeking to drink the juice of soma. They offer a sacrifice to become skilled in holy rites and in the arts that give them a thousand powers to subdue their foes. They accepted with praise by the messenger Maghavan and offered hymns and a drink of soma. Their songs approach the irresistible Indra. With adorations from the singers, Maghavan shows them how to receive bliss from the godhead, and in turn the worshippers' become devotees of Indra, who rules the seven lovely rivers, untroubled, divine, rending forts that do not move, flowing with the ocean that does move, and with the ninety-nine flowing streams of water serving as rivers. Because of a curse, the mighty waters cannot free the singers; only resistless Indra can, who watches and guards them, and evermore comes to cherish the noble bodies who quell Vṛtra to win heroic power and praise. Indra, with songs of worship, comes to invoke the evil Vṛtra, quelling him, which provides the singers with both the room and the freedom to establish the *Galra* empire, which includes an alien species, or a collective thereof, known as the sharp-edged Marmora, who have conquered armies. As an auspicious hero, Maghavan serves as Indra's best hero in the fight, where there are spoils gathered. Maghavan listens, gives aid in battle, and slays Vṛtra, thereby winning riches.

According to *Rig-Veda* 10:105, when the powers of nature (Vasu) wither, and along with them their love, nature is expressed through new channels, it causes soma to fill the streams. Two well-harnessed bay steeds start out in pursuit as birds with long tail feathers. They give power by the lord Indra to serve heaven and earth, appearing as some weary hairy person. In fear, propelled forward with their skills, they move like sinners, especially when the mighty one has prepared himself for victory. Indra, along with these steeds, drives round, until meeting up with the one who worships, the pair, who inhales and moves along his way, borne onward by the long-maned steeds, who stretch themselves as there were food. The ones at the helm, with jaws to defend themselves, sing mighty songs for the lofty ones. Appearing as a hero, fashioned with strength, the skillful Mātariśvan comes with power and might, letting loose his bolt of lightning, which at once pierces through the vitals of the sky lord Dyaus, thus easily eliminating the atmosphere (ether). With an uninjured jaw, serving according to divine will, Mātariśvan grinds away his sins with song to conquer the individual living spirit who sings no hymns and is not easily pleased with prayerless sacrifice. When a threefold flame burning high, resting on the poles of sacrifice, the living spirits come in their self-illuminated ship, bearing glory in their speckled cup. Flawless, they scoop up the soma and pour it all into the divine repository. In the hundreds, the immortal gods sing to their good friend Sumitra, as well as to the ruler of the seven tribes, *Durmitra*, who with praises comes in time to help when Dyaus has fallen, with the hopeless, holiest Kutsa, as the darling son, surviving.

According to *Rig-Veda* 10:106, the twin demigods, learning to hold the loom, become skillful weavers. They weave garments and unite everyone together to awaken and spread the food around on days with lovely weather. Like two bulls, they plow and move along in the tracks, eager as guests to attend the banquet. Glorious envoys they, from the midpoint, like bulls, approach the place where there is water to drink. Like the two pinions of a bird, connected, as two choice animals, they seek to worship with a bright fire. Like a votary with vows, they enkindled and, as roamers, offer sacrifices in many a spot. As kinsmen, such as the two sons of one father, strong in their splendor, come like kings to the conquest, appearing as rays of enjoyment, being fed by the lords, who feed them and then listen to the pleasant call of the well-fed ones as they move toward eternal love (*Mitra*) and the eternal law (*Varuna*). The two divine bestowers of happiness, voracious, possessors of infinite wealth and happiness, like two plump horses with fodder, abide in the firmament. Two uncastrated sheep (rams) provide them with nourishment in the form of sacrificial food, which cherished with oblations. Like two mad elephants, by bending their forequarters and smiting and destroying the foe's son *Nitosa*, and cherishing two bright waterborne gems, they are victorious, which renders their decaying mortal bodies immortal, free of decay. The fierce demigod Aśvins, like two powerful heroes, quick to move, in their perishable mortal embodiments cross over the waters to reach their destination, appearing extremely strong, as bright Ṛbhu, with his chariot, reaches his destination, moving as swiftly as the wind, which pervades every place as it dispenses riches. With their bellies full of soma, like two saucepans, they preserve their wealth destroy enemies and those armed with hatchets. They move like two birds with characteristics like those of the moon, flying to attain whatever is on their minds and bringing success by creating two laudable living beings, one male and the other female, who approach for the sacrifice. Like giants, they find firm ground to stand on, and in the depths, with their feet, they cross over to shallow water. Their embodiments attend their orders, serving with two wondrous directives: to enjoy and to share. They bring honey like worker bees and come to hide that which opens downward. With increasing laudation, they gain vigor by humming a song, which carries in the air along with ripened essence (meath). Filled with glory, the noble rishis the *Bhutamsa* all come to support the longings of the twin *Aśvins*.

According to *Rig-Veda* 10:107, the Aśvins manifest great bounties as the whole the world is set free from darkness. A great light comes to vouchsafe all, like fathers following the path and, as a reward, going on high to heaven, where they abide with the reward givers, to whom they give their steeds in exchange for the privilege of dwelling forever with the rays of the sun. Those who give pure gold blessed with eternal life. They wear robes on their bodies and prolong their lives with soma. As for the misers who refuse to make sacrifices to satisfy the gods, such living beings, with dread, their hands outstretched, presented with their gifts. They dishonor humankind who offer oblation, just as the streaming wind (Vayu) finds no guardian and only superficial knowledge with no depth (*arka*).

Satisfied with their gifts, the misers make donation to the seven rivers. First, they invited to visit the chief of the hamlet, the ruler of the people who is the first, to introduce them to the guardian. They call upon noble moral souls (*Rishis, Brahma*, and *Sāma*), as the chanter leads them in worship. The brightly shining gods in three forms are known first by those who bestow upon them a sacrificial gift, such as a horse or a bullock, or better yet pure gold, as the resistors. As a reward, they given food to support both their lives and their spirits. Those who are wise become guardians in exchange for the armor of a righteous warrior. Liberal, they die not, neither are they ruined: as liberal ones, they suffer neither harm nor trouble.

The universe offers the light of heaven as the sacrificial reward to the first among others, and thus the liberal ones given a fragrant dwelling place and a bride in fair apparel. These liberal ones obtain their drafts of liquor and conquer those who, unprovoked, assail them. They decked like a fleet of steeds, or like the bounteous giver, just as a aid virgin adorns herself and waits to meet such liberals to make a home with them in the lake filled with lotus blossoms as in the gods' palaces. Adorned, and with splendid steeds, the liberal is given a good draft to deliver to others. Lightly rolling, they move as embodied guardians who come to assist the gods, these liberal men who conquer their foes in combat.

According to *Rig-Veda* 10:108, the third mythological creature to appear is the female dog (*Saramā)*, which as an embodied guardian comes to serve the noble moral souls and righteous warriors. *Saramā* taken to a path that leads far into the distance, where the demons have stored up ample wealth, such as stolen cows, located behind the river (*Rasā* all wealth sought out by *Saramā*. She comes well-armed and will not let the cows taken without a fight. The cows are well hidden in a rocky chamber. *Saramā*, threatened by the might of godhead Indra, by the fire of Agni, and by the messenger Aṅgirases, who work according to divine will, seeks to recover the cows from the miser Paṇis, who keeps them as part of a bargain and lives in fear that they will cross the waters of the river (*Rasā*). Paṇis knows that the cows are safe from *Saramā*, but still he punishes those who sent out as envoys into the river, which flows deep with water.

At low tide, Paṇis keeps an eye out for Saramā, who flies with the Blessed One to the ends of the heavens, determined not to lose the cattle without a fight. *Saramā's* sharp pointed horns serve as warlike weapons. Even when wicked bodies like the miserly (*Paṇis*) use divine will, they do not become arrow-proof, as their words make them weak and unable to master the winding path to *Bṛhaspati*. In no case will the divine will pave the path with rocks such as those in the treasure chamber full of other precious things, such as cows and horses. The bargaining *Paṇis*, serving as a watchful guard, in vain approaches the lonely station where rishis come fully inspirited with soma, as do the un-wearying Aṅgirases and Navagvas the heavenly priests.

When the cattle stall opened, this forces *Paṇis* to make a wish, his words unspoken. Even then, *Saramā,* according to divine will, forced by celestial might to make such a journey. Do not turn your back on the sisters who, as blessed ones, bring cattle along with blessings. By forming a brotherhood or sisterhood, the messengers of both Indra and Agni become trepidatious. Saramā seems to long for such domesticated animals, especially when they take far away by misers (Paṇis) The cattle lowing, come forth to receive the holy law as commanded by Bṛhaspati and by the mighty rishis who, thanks to the noble sages, find them cattle hidden behind the cosmic stones.

CHAPTER 23

# Holy Order Dominion

HOLY ORDERS ORDAIN THEIR POSTULANTS WITH SACRAMENTS and rites, supported by divine power, to educate living beings and guide them so they may comprehend, and then lead other creations to manage and serve the congregation of worshippers, with the aim of sharing absolute truth. In this way, living things may live in the material world in peace and tranquility.

Each holy order has seven special sacraments that the individual must personally experience to become a part of this grand cosmic network. Once they join in with the others and focus upon prayer and meditation, they witness the host of light (Sūrya), ascends, placing his divine power into the center (i.e., the heart). So, through consciousness, an embodiment stabilized in the material world and learns to raise living spirits with higher vibrations to acquire ultimate wisdom and learn to live in the turbulent world with inner peace and tranquility.

## PROGRESSION

According to *Rig-Veda* 10:109, first, the boundless water as the sea, and then a fierce-glowing fire as the land, pass on their genes to create a strong messenger growing within its mother, Mātariśvan, the bliss bestower, who comes along to create food for the firstborn, who then go on to serve in the holy order. Exclaiming in exasperation, this messenger comes to serve as the holy sage Brahma. Beholding the soma, and without reluctance, the messenger and Brahma make restitution with the spouse of the reigning monarch. They invite eternal love (Mitra) and the eternal law (Varuna), along with the eternal flame, Agni, to serve as the heavenly priest Hotar, who takes the hand of the crying mother Aditi. Holding her hand, Hotar pledges to be her consort and to stay as a Brahman, but not to be the herald or support the kingdom as its ruler. This consort, along with older godly powers serving the heavenly region with the well-known seven supreme powers of causation, manifests as a moral noble soul (rishi). He sits down in ascetic devotion, serving the ominous Brahman wife, who led home and planted within the material world, mayhem ruling her life. The consort, who conduct his life as the celibate *Brahmacari*, consistent with the ominous Brahman, as per the holy order, becomes engaged in duty as a member of the perishable embodiment Bṛhaspati, who himself is a consort. The two find a ladle that used to serve powerful soma to the gods, and they use it to restore the ominous Brahman woman as the mother, returning her to her male partner, where again she may serve as a female. The king keeps his promise to restore her as the wedded wife, aided by the gods, and free her from sin. Then all come to share the fullness of the holy ground and thereby hold greater sway.

According to *Rig-Veda* 10:110, on this day, the enkindled godly power Jātavedas observes a bright light, which ushers in the sapient one of eternal love, Mitra, who predicts the coming of the demigod Tanūnapāt as a fair-tongued envoy. Jātavedas and Mitra bring a sweet essence with them, moving toward the path to set things up according to the holy order. Making themselves pleasing enough to convey the offering to heaven, exalting the other gods with their holy thoughts and hymns of praise, they offer worship. With Agni, who is deserving prayer and adoration, they come in accordance with Mother Nature, Vasu, as invokers. The youthful lord serving the godly powers offers the best sacrifices, which enable the gods to quickly take over and rule the sacred grass, scattering it eastward, placing their robes upon the ground, covering the earth, before dawn breaks to bring the morning light. The robes and the grass spread around, extending far, to create a fair place for the gods to bring peace and freedom.

The spacious doors of heaven opened wide as wives deck themselves beautifully for their husbands. From the lofty celestial region, all portals opened to receive the gods and provide them easy passage. Pouring out sweet holy dew at night and in the morning, each comes close seated at their respective station. The lofty celestial feminine powers decked with gold to enhance their radiant beauty. First, they bring two sweet-voiced celestial priests, who arrange a sacrifice for the male gods. Singing, they inspire all who have assembled, showing them the path illuminated by the sun rising in the east. The heavenly goddess Bhāratī comes quickly to offer worship to the earthly goddess Iḷā, who comes to show how to perform as a human. The heavenly power goddess *Sarasvati* follows these two, the skillful goddesses *Bhāratī* and *Iḷā*, showing them how to seat on the sacred grass. Skilled in sacrifice, the heavenly priest Hotar comes as the creative godly power who, since the time of his creation, has served the earth and the heavens, and now serves as the parents to each new creation. They all send forth their offerings, making themselves companions of the godly powers who are responsible for creating order and the seasons. Agni provides the eternal flame, Vanaspati brings sweet soma and essence, served along with refined butter (ghee). As soon as they are born, they make sacrifices and proceed to cater to the gods with an offering of sacred wisdom, according to the voice and the guidance of the true priest.

According to *Rig-Veda* 10:111, this brings forth sacred songs from the prudent singers, and even noble thoughts among human beings. Indra draws near, singing love songs to those whose deeds have made them true, strong heroes. With hymns, shown, from the seat of worship, the illuminated wise soul (Sūrya), appearing as a strong bull, offspring of the heifer. Amid the mighty bellowing, they all arise and rule all over the spacious region. Indra knows, verily, how to hear the singing of the victorious, who make a path to reach the heavenly power Sūrya. The offspring of the milk-bearing cow becomes the sovereign of heaven, primeval, matchless, and unshaken.

Praised by the heavenly messenger Aṅgiras, Indra destroys the works of the great watery monster extend into many regions, even pervading the foundation of truth, supported by holy ground or earth, which serves as the counterpart of heaven. Indra, knowing all libations, slays the evil power Śuṣṇa and comes to support the vast sky shield. With the illuminating power of the sun, he creates a set of invisible pillars connecting the earth with heaven. Serving as the Vṛtra-slayer, Indra sends down his immortal thunderbolt bolt, which falls upon Vṛtra and destroys the magic of the godless one. By rubbing his thunderbolt to polish it, he divests them of their might.

The bold assailant serving as the messenger Maghavan conquers with his arms and, as an attendant, brings the morning light from Sūrya, whose rays reveal the wealth of color hidden behind the stars of heaven (constellations), which can be approached by one who is nearby. This remains hidden and is known to no one other than those who have departed and gone with the first waters that sent back to heaven. Now Indra causes these waters to flow forth in spring, establishing the ground as their holy foundation. These waters become the midway point serving the free-flowing rivers that soon swallow the dragon and rapidly set themselves in motion, loose and reveling in their much-longed-for freedom. Excited, running without resting, yearning together, they speed along like the large river Indus, with the power to destroy forts in their praise of and love for Indra. The water reaches the terrestrial treasure, which can reach only with songs full of joy coming from within the individual dwelling that holds the immortal universal soul, (*Paramatman*).

According to *Rig-Veda* 10:112, Indra drinks soma early in the morning as the first draft and, with a divine plea and libation, goes on to rejoice in the heroes who have slain the foes. Then, through divine will, he loudly tells all about the mighty powers at work and invites them to come to explore and exploit the manifested material world and its treasures. Indra tells the heroes they have each provided with a physical embodiment and with noble thoughts, which thoughts become swifter after drinking soma. This drink turns the bay steeds into stallions, and with such embodiments, they sound out with their cornets, bringing delight to their bodies, which are all decked out in the fairest colors, creating a golden splendor. Adorned by Indra, they herewith invite their friends to seated, as joyful and grand, in the festively decorated transports, not only traveling between two great worlds, but also coming to comprehend their relationship.

Indra and his dear harnessed bay horses take them to their dwelling, where he loves the food, they serve him the pressed soma juice, celebrating at the joyous banquet. Ever drinking, instigating battles with foemen, they are all prompted to continue the mighty flow of abundant food and drink. They find an old cup of soma given to them by Indra, which they fill like a beaker, mixing the soma with the meath used to worship the ancient sage Śatakratu, then passing the beaker around to all the deities. With delight from all sides, amid the entertainment, the people see Indra calling to the Mighty Power with libations, provided the richest of the meath to drink, where therefore he finds very pleasant. Indra declares all ancient deeds as mighty acts, which first accomplished to overcome wrath and loosen the ground to establish the mountains, so milk-bearing animals could find a safe place to reside on the newly created ground (Prithvi) covering the surface of the earth. The lord of heavenly hosts, amid such bands of mountain ranges, seated as the greatest sage (rishi) among all sages. Nothing is done, not even far away, without the great, wondrous messenger Maghavan, who sings hymns, keep his eyes on the goal, and implores the friend of the friends, who is also the lord of treasures, to serve as the mighty righteous warrior, strong in truth, who fights the battle to give all their share of undivided riches.

## GODLY POWERS

According to *Rig-Veda* 10:113, both heaven and earth, in accordance with all the godly powers, graciously encouraged by the mighty powers, including those with the godly nature, to come with vigor and show forth by drinking soma with His Divine Majesty and the godly powers. The mighty powers bring refined soma with exceedingly strong amrit. The majesty of the supreme being Vishnu extolled and lauded as he presses the stalk of the soma plant to cause meath to flow forth, increasing the perception and sensitivity of the messenger Maghavan. The messenger of Indra, smitten, follows the gods' directive to produce warlike weapons and, in so doing, win praise. In a simple singular form, Maghavan takes on a peerless quality as he shows the cosmic hosts the Maruts how to fight with the dragon Vṛtra. With cosmic power, they get a chance to fight against Vṛtra and summarily commended by the powerful majestic Mighty One.

Soon, things spring to life, forcing the heroes in their tranquility to anticipate war. First, the rock is cleft to let concurrent streams of water flow forth, and then with skillful art the vault of the heavens established within the dynamic universe. The Mighty One possesses the all-surpassing primordial supreme powers of causation, who with force establish the dynamic universe, splitting heaven and earth apart. With impetuosity, the Mighty One hurls down his iron thunderbolt, joyfully representing himself to the established eternal law, Varuna, and eternal love, Mitra, to serve the worshippers. Then Varuna and Mitra send the mighty power Indra. Wrathful, as fierce as a storm, loud of voice, with speed, the Mighty One decides with his strength to take charge of the evil power Vṛtra and determines the time to hold the waters back, which will cause darkness everywhere. In the first of these heroic acts, the three gods strive together with their mighty power to cause a deep darkness to fall upon those slain. With the victory, Indra wins the right to be the first invoked, and then all the godly powers extolled with eloquence, inspired by drafts of soma, for their deeds of manly might. The godhead Agni eats dry food quietly as the evil Vṛtra, the dragon disfigured by Indra's deadly dart.

Proclaiming of the many friendships he has made among the singers, who are skillful with their eloquent songs, Indra subdues Dhuni and Cumuri, two sites where criminal atrocities were committed against noble souls, and moves on to Dabhīti so the faithful will allow their spirits to experience manifold riches, such as noble horses, all remembering to whom they address their songs. Making this an easy path to take to bypass all trouble and find a new day, Indra creates the stepping-stones to a broader, longer life.

According to *Rig-Veda* 10:114, two perfect hot springs exist in the threefold regions served by the demigod Mātariśvan, who comes with his craving for milk that the gods of heaven provide. The gods know well, by way of the *sāman* hymns they sing, that the bearded priests from the holy order come from far away with the three auspicious goddesses the Nirrtis. The sages, who know well, trace the First produced the mysterious chambers as a far-off dwelling place for the Youthful One, who is well shaped, with four braided locks, brightened with oil. Two birds of mighty power seated near the auspicious goddess, from whom the deities receive their portion. One of these birds passes into the sea of air and hence looks around to view the universal world. With a simple heart, he beholds it from a spot close to where his mother kisses him, and he returns her kiss. With fair wings, though only one in nature, wise singers shape, with songs, figures. While they attend the sacrifice, they determine the meter as the standard measurement of length, which is equal to twelve chalices filled with soma. They establish the gross, one hundred forty-four, as another standard of measurement.

Having disposed of the sacrifice, the seven thoughtful sages send their chariot forward with hymns (*sāmans*) and, with fourteen others, lead the procession onward with their voices. In this way they declare the passage (*apnana*) whereby the first fifteen drafts of soma taken to the one thousand vast places that easily accessed. Contained within the mighty thousand places, they spread out in the form of speech (*vāk*) as far as their prayers extended. Once the sages learn the concept of units of measurement and learn to it apply, they gain, through the application of speech (*vāk*), the aim of all manifested spirits and objects. These ministering priests identified as the eight heroes who track the two bay steeds of Indra, which yoked to the chariot pole where the coursers that traveled to the farthest limits of the earth once stood. When their driver settled in his home, he receives the meath allotted for their efforts.

According to *Rig-Veda* 10:115, verily wondrous is the tender youngling's growth who never draws nigh to drink of the milk from its mother. When there is no udder, mothers bear their young and assign them a great errand so they will grow strong. Then Agni with eternal his flame bestows upon them a name, at which time they gather up the trees with their consuming teeth. Skilled in fair sacrifice, armed with a destructive impetuous tongue, he is like a bull that snorts in the mead. Praise him as a god who, like a bird, rests upon a tree, scattering drops of soma and pouring it forth in a flood, speaking aloud with flames from his lips as a priest broadening the pathway, like one of high command. Everlasting, he is the one who, striding far to burn the winds, uninterrupted, never overcome. Approached by warriors eager to fight, the heroic god Trita guiding him to fulfill his wish to serve as a friend to the best among the conquerors, the Kaṇvas, who defeat their foes everywhere. Agni guards the singers and guards the princes as well, granting his gracious help to those who offer aid to the princes. The Divine maintains the paternal character Supitrya, who swiftly follows to make himself like the mightiest of all godly powers, Jātavedas, who is prepared to provide aid, surely giving a boon even within arid land inhabited by wild creatures. Noble Agni, with mortal princes, comes lauded. Excellent as conquering chiefs, they, with strength, serve the manifested mortal bodies as friends well-disposed and true to the law, even in heaven, where majesty surpasses humankind.

Victorious Upastutas, as the Son of Strength, with a most potent voice, admires the blessed brave sons who extol and lengthen the days of existence. Agni, with the sons of the noble soul *Vrstihavya*, who like the rishis invoke Upastutas, guards and protects the singers and the princes. With the powers of causation, Vaṣaṭ comes crying and with his hands uplifted in glory.

According to *Rig-Veda* 10:116, the mighty power of soma grants vigor to the strongest one, who smites the evil power Vṛtra after drinking to invoke physical strength, riches, and eternal wisdom. The richest soma mixed with meath and poured out for Indra to drink. He drinks it as food, the juice stirring him into action, this drink that chosen from the flowing soma. This libation makes the spirit joyful and in turn brings blessings for prosperity. With the gladdening heavenly soma, Indra effused with delight for humankind, rejoicing in that which gives them the greatest freedom to conquer their foes. Their victory causes Indra to become impetuous and make his bull doubly mighty, which with poured soma comes to serve as two bay coursers. The soma pressed with milk, then mixed with essence presented in a glut, allowing Indra evermore to manage the thunderbolt and dash down the foes, destroying them. Famous for their sharp weapons and for their ability to withhold, the strong manifested embodiments urge the Mighty One to become victorious over the demons. With great strength and conquest, Indra goes and meets their foes, tearing them apart in battle. This causes his fame and glory to extend afar, as the firm archer with strength drives the foemen beyond the mountain range. Growing stronger in might as he conquers, Indra never defeated, with his body continuing to increase in strength and size. Because of this, presented with oblation and accepted as the sovereign ruler, free from anger.

The worshippers drink the pressed soma and eat the ripen fruit with Indra, attending to the meeting as they eat. With oblations, they approach the divine to please him with the food made ready and served with soma. With entertainment, the seekers receive their rewards, and as part of their sacrifice they send forth with sweet speech towards the godheads Indra and Agni. This comes in the form of hymns or vibrations, which along speed like a boat passing through water. Even after this, the worshippers find that the gods keep moving around like fountains, bestowing riches and eternal wisdom.

According to *Rig-Veda* 10:117, the godly powers do not ordain hunger or death: they bring death in various forms to the well-fed man. Those rich with open minds and eternal wisdom never die, but they do waste away because they find no one to whom to give such wisdom. A man with food in his storehouse, when seeing a miserable needy beggar begging for bread to eat, gives him, but he does so with his heart hardened against the beggar. Even as an old man, he finds no comfort in living, so he wastes away. Bounteous are those who give unto the beggar or the feeble one who comes to them seeking food. They succeed like rishis in battle; instead of shooting, they shout out to save, and this makes them friends in the future for any who are troubled. No friend who comes to them begging for food turned away to go home, not even a stranger, whom they also support. Let the rich satisfy the poor implorer and turn their eyes toward the longer pathway. Riches now come one after the other, like the wheels ever rolling to move the carts.

For the foolish man who wins food with his fruitless labor, his food speaks the truth and sets up his ruin. One who fails to feed a trusted friend has no man to love him. Guilty are all who eat with no partakers. The plowshare and the plowing are what makes the food that feeds, and with cut feet as the plow follows the path. Better to speak than to be silent. The wise man (Brahman) gives not to a liberal friend without values. With one foot, one cannot outrun the biped, and the two-footed one catches the one who is three-footed. Four-footed creatures come when bipeds call them; then they stand and look at the place where they meet with the five-footed ones. Although their hands are alike, their labor differs. The yield of the mother milk cow is unequalled. Twins even differ in their strength and vigor: the two, even though they are relatives, differ in their bounties.

According to *Rig-Veda* 10:118, among all, the refulgent flame, after slaying the devouring fiend, comes to appear as the eternal flame, a bright ruler with its own abode. Springing up like the sun, worshipped with offerings of mothers' milk, as well as with butter, which brings near the bright light that is close to the flame. Its shine travels far with songs of adoration, with which it is honored, the initiating flame, Agni, bringing gifts such as ladles dripping with balm to brighten their expressions. Agni is honored with gifts of honey, which he takes into his mouth to serve as a balm with oil, wherewith he brings forth a refulgent wealth of bright light.

Praised by hymns, kindled with oblation, as the bearer to the mortals, Agni calls upon other immortal godly powers as lord of the house, whom none deceives. His fire burns the evil rakshasas with its unconquerable flame as the shining guardian of the eternal law, Varuna. So, with his glowing face, Agni burns the fierce female friends, shining among humankind as the oblation-bearer, with hymns serving the best worshippers among humankind, such as the sages.

## DOMESTICATED ANIMALS

According to *Rig-Veda* 10:119, with the power of hymns, Agni can even enhance the animal kingdom, enabling the mother cow to produce milk and the vigorous horse to perform physical work, as well as readying other animals to serve humankind as domesticated animals. Until they have received soma, they behave like a violent gusty wind. After drinking drafts of soma, they gain the knowledge to serve as fleet-footed steeds that come to draw a carriage or chariot and, with the right set of skills, to pull seated chariots. They come to serve with their hearts, singing the right hymns and vibrating in such a way to reach other animals such as mother cows, which low to locate their darling calves. With no motes in their eyes, the animals cultivate union in tribes, as human beings do, coming to establish new generations.

The heaven and the earth themselves do not grow, whereas the spacious ground (Prithvi) surpasses them both in grandeur, able to become part of either heaven or earth. In moment, the godly powers serving the ground can smite the ground in wrath, with one of the flanks ascending to the sky, and the other trailing below to the underworld. The greatest of the mighty ones come to lift the whole firmament for the worshippers who make oblation to enter the abode of the gods.

According to *Rig-Veda* 10:120, the best and the highest among the mighty gods spring out from another world, bringing splendor and valor. As soon as they settle, they overcome foemen, striking them down. To grow in might and strength, with ample vigor they gain support from the devotees the Dāsas, who are eager to win. Both the breathing and the breathless sing praises at the banquet and make oblations. At all times they concentrate to improve their mental acuity, offering worship twice or thrice a day and, with their assistants, developing a blend that is sweeter than sweet, which wins them the essence in battle. They win the riches, at every banquet serving as joyful sages. With mighty power, and bold and firm, they are not malignant Yātudhānas and do not harm others. They proudly put their trust in the battles and behold great wealth as the prize of combat. With their words, they impel weapons onward, and with prayer they sharpen their vitality. Worthy of praises, skillfully shaped, most energetic, they appear as the solar deity Trita Āptya, who with his might destroys the seven evil powers and subdues many more deemed to be their equals. In the house with divine protection, they stand guard and bestow wealth upon the higher female (mother) and the lower female (daughter). Thus, they establish two wandering mothers who commit many deeds to be completed as two females, Brhaddiva, the foremost winner of light. With repeated prayers, they provide added strength to Indra, who by himself rules the great self-illuminating fold of cattle and calves, throwing open the stall doors to let in the light. Thus, Brhaddiva comes to serve as the great legendry source of eternal wisdom, with Atharvan representing Indra as himself. As spotless sisters, Brhaddiva serve as mothers to support Atharvan with their power, exalting him and impelling him to move onward into the perpetual dominion.

According to *Rig-Veda* 10:121, in the beginning, the golden embryo Hiranyagarbha arose as the only lord of all creation. He fixed and held up the earth and the heavens, providing spiritual life force and physical vigor, both regulated by the divine commandments. He acknowledged by the ruling supreme powers of causation, who regulate immortal and mortal life with shades regulated by the lord of death. Serving as the sole ruler, Hiranyagarbha controls the mortal embodiments prevailing within the differentiated universe. He breathes and slumbers, representing the lord of living things, including animals and human beings. The godly powers regulating all creation adore him and are pleased to receive sacrifices and oblations. It is the godly powers who establish imperishable mighty nature (prakriti), which includes snow-covered mountain ranges, and fill the ground with moisture and humidity, which comes from the heavenly region as cosmic vapor (*rasa*), coming into the arms of the mortal embodiments as a gift from the gods. With this arrangement, those in heaven become the strong partners of those on earth, which is steadfast, creating the sphere of the sky vault filled with illumination, all supported by the midair region, which the godly powers adore because it can be measured.

Oblation and sacrifice offered by two kinds of armies, immortal and mortal, who look embattled, their spirits vibrating. Above them is the rising sun, generating bright shining rays and providing the mighty waters that come in time, bringing the universal germ, all supported by the eternal flame, Agni, who springs forth from the universal soul, Paramatman, to prevail as the individual living spirit, Atman, thus turning living spirits into living beings.

The mighty powers survey the floods, which contain the productive force, ready to generate sacrifice and worship. As the god of gods, no one there besides him to harm, who is the begetter of the law, which is as sure as the creator of the heavens, who brings forth the great clear waters. The godly father Prajāpati is the only who comprehends all created things, and only he grants one's heart's desire when he invoked with his store of riches.

According to *Rig-Veda* 10:122, Indra, with mighty praise, lovely as a pleasant guest, whom all welcome as the priest, serving as head of the household, brings strength to the heroes, along with all-sustaining riches. Agni graciously, with song, passing through, accepts those who know every ordinance. Covered in holy oil, he goes through the course of prayer and, with his godly powers, bestows gifts upon them according to the holy law. As an immortal power wandering around the seven rivers, Agni gives liberal pious worshippers eternal wealth so they may serve as his brave sons. With this they are ready to serve him, welcoming him, who comes with the eternal flame to serve the seven living beings who offer oblations as their first act of worship. Strong like the great chief priest, they offer the emblem of sacrifice, the oil-anointed bull representing Agni. Then they sent godly strength, which is freely given them to serve as the first messengers with the skills to drink their fully. They invited, through the grace of *Anirta*, as votāries to the house of the cosmic hosts the Maruts. The adored saint Bhrigu gives them the light and, in glory, brings them the milk of the seething cow, the all-sustaining food. Serving the Wise One, they come to worship, dropping oil into fire, thus generating three lightning bolts, all working to support the eternal law, as they encircle their homes with wisdom and sacrifice. Flushing with the morning light, they appointed as divine messengers, and as such shown reverence. With godly power, strengthened for work to glorify Agni, they produce pure butter for sacrifice. Arrangers of the council, they sing as the sons of the oldest revered rishi *Vasisistha*, and called upon to serve the Potent One, who maintains eternal wisdom and allows them to grow among the mortal embodiments, whose sacrifices preserve all with godly blessings forevermore.

According to *Rig-Veda* 10:123, trust, love, desire, and wishes, all together, are born as light, Vena, which comes riding in on the air, driven in a chariot pulled by a bullock, which also transports the godly mother Pṛśni. With hymns, singers embrace them as infants coming from heavenly region, where the waters and the sunlight mingle. The trusted light Vena drawn up like waves from the ocean, filling the air with mist, returning, brightly shining, from aloft, the summit, where the hosts sing in glory to honor their common birthplace. Many, lowing, stand with their mothers amid their jointly owned dwellings as the darling daughters. Ascending to the lofty height of the holy order, the bands of singers sip the sweet nectar (amrit), knowing the sages are yearning to meet with the higher power. They come nigh to hear the bellowing of the wild bull. They perform sacrifices to reach the river that appears as the male spirits of nature, the Gandharva, and the female spirits of nature, the *apsaras*, hoping to find where the immortal waters flow. The apsaras, female nymphs, sweetly smiling, sublimely support the heavenly region. In their friend's dwelling, as friends, they wander with trust, love, desire, and wishes and with the light, Vena, who rests on the golden pinion. They gaze on with longing in their spirits, as a strong-winged bird mounts skyward like an envoy with wings of gold (Varuna).

Like a bird that faces death, the Yama go straight home to heaven, mounted on the heavenly Gandharva, with many-colored pointed weapons, attired in sweet raiment, their beautiful astral bodies looking for the bright white light that appears as a pleasant spark emerging from the ground near the ocean. Looking with a vulture's eye toward the lustrous heavens, they enjoy the bright splendor of the constellation, which appear glorious in the lowest region.

## UNDERWORLD—PROFUSION

According to *Rig-Veda* 10:124, the universal soul (God), as the immortal Agni, with sacrifices, serves the seven rivers and five divisions of land. As a threefold godly power (trinity), he goes to serve within the lower terrestrial region. As the oblation-bearer, he arrives by way of a secret pathways and proceeds along in darkness to reach the underworld, below the ground, to find where those who were once gracious have deserted to, becoming ungracious, leaving their own friends to seek kinship among strangers. As a guest, Agni finds that the underworld is absent the rule of law and therefore order the gracious ones to bid farewell to the great god in contempt. They take their shares, complaining that they have waited years, serving within the same platform as Indra, Agni, Varuna, and Soma, who serve the kingdom of truth, not the kingdom of falsehood.

With the lovely light of heaven, through the radiant air, Indra, Agni, Varuna, and Soma spread across the region to slaughter any evil threat from the Vṛtra. They use soma and oblation to serve as noble sages who, with heavenly wisdom, work with the ruler of eternal law, Varuna, to cause the waters to flow and bring prosperity without violence. Like womenfolk set on fire, they create colors and wait upon their admirer, the loftiest power, who with vigor dwells in triumph as the Godhead. Once the people elect their ruler, they turn away in hatred from Vṛtra, whom they call Swan, an abhorrent companion, to move on in friendship in the celestial waters. The poets look upon Indra and sing hymns as they approach, the verses containing eight syllables per foot, or quarter verse (*Anustup*).

According to *Rig-Veda* 10:125, the heavenly immortal Rudras, along with nature (Vasu), traveling with the godly powers the Ādityas, wanders, holding aloft the power of eternal law (Varuna), the power of eternal love (Mitra), and the gods Indra and Agni, bringing in the twin demigod Aśvins. By drinking the highly cherished soma, they sustained, with the support of the trinity Tvaṣṭṛ, Pūṣan, and Bhaga, who loaded with wealth and enthusiastically pour out soma as an offering of worship and oblation. Like the godly mothers, most thoughtful, they first serve those who gather to worship, and then share the treasures with the godly powers established in other places, with homes, who come to eat the food that fed to them. They all abide—each man who sees them breaching also hears the word spoken by the universal soul (God), whom they do not know as an individual, all of them living alongside the universal soul. All hear the truth as declared by the universal, verily by God, who utter his word through the godly powers, who are like the manifested mortal embodiments serving as individual living beings. These created by the universal soul (God) in love, and as exceedingly mighty, they come to serve as sages (rishis) and as manifested noble souls (Brahmans).

As the universal soul, God bends like a bow to serve as the solar wind Rudra, who strikes and slays those who hate devotion. The universal soul rouses the manifested moral embodiments as a group, ordering them in ranks to serve in battle, and as individuals, the living spirit, Atman, penetrates all regions, including earth and heaven. As part of the universal soul (God), they all appear at the summit of the world, serving the heavenly father, who has his home in the free-flowing waters, filling bodies of water such as lakes and oceans. God, as the universal soul, extends over all existing creatures, who even yonder to heaven touch God's forehead and come to breathe with strong breath, which like the wind creates a tempest, while the universal soul holds all existence together, even that beyond the wide earth and beyond the heavens, serving in mighty grandeur.

According to *Rig-Veda* 10:126, no peril and no distress, according to the godly powers, may affect the mortal humans, led by the trinity of Aryaman, Mitra, and Varuna, who, of one accord, with power beyond that of their foes, do everything they desire, serving as one. They guard the mortal embodiments from soreness and distress, leading them to safety, away from their foes. Varuna, Mitra, and Aryaman each come today to help, serving as the best leaders and the best deliverers, leading the mortals to safety. They gather round and guard each mortal as dear, keeping them away from their foes. The noble Ādityas come along with Rudra from the celestial region, with the cosmic hosts the Maruts, along with Indra and Agni, who call for prosperity. Like kings, they lead the mortals to safety. Even today they come to help the humans get past all trouble and stay far away from their foes.

Varuna, Mitra, and Aryaman, along with the Ādityas, set up vast defensive shelters that are impenetrable by the enemies. As the holy ones, they, along with nature (Vasu), freed the embodiments from the desire for material ornaments (*gaud*), which shackle their feet, also free them from trouble and affliction, which lengthens their life spans.

According to *Rig-Veda* 10:127, with their eyes, serving as the goddess of night, they look forth and approach a spot that they may fill with immortal glory, without waste, vast in both height and depth as the goddess of night conquers the darkness with her light. The goddess sets up the dawn and the dusk as two sisters in one place, where darkness will vanish with the coming of the light. Granting favor during the dark of night, the goddess's pathway used by those who come like birds to nest within a tree. Similarly, other inhabitants of this seek their homes, away from all that walks and all that flies, even the falcons that hunt for prey and keep the she-wolf and the he-wolf (*Urmya*) away. They keep thieves away by making a place that is difficult to pass through, asking the goddess to stay nigh and deck the dark in rich hues. The morning light cancels the darkness like a debt. The universal soul brings animals after nightfall, which serve as the children of heaven, where with laudation they serve as conquerors.

According to *Rig-Veda* 10:128, those who dwell within the four regions bend and bow before the universal soul, asking him to guard them so that they may win the battle and thereby allow Agni to win glory, also asking that Agni enkindle their bodies and make them strong for combat. With all the gods on their side in battle, the cosmic hosts the Maruts lead the trinity of Indra, Vishnu, and Agni, who come to serve the midair region and cause the wind to blow upon those who favored, according to divine will. The godly powers grant them riches and bless them and, with invocation, come to assist the universal soul (God). Foremost in the fight, the universal soul invoked as brave, uninjured heroes, who cause that which exists in their minds as intention accomplished. The guiltless universal soul, without transgression, comes to unite all the godly powers and bless them all. The six divine powers thus stretch out as they granted freedom and equipped with power to serve like the manifested mortal heroes. They protect the embodiments, preventing them from losing any children and preventing their foes from benefiting from the powerful soma, which they drink to baffle their wrathful adversaries, while Agni stands guard as their infallible protector. Let the foes turn back and seek their homes and let them watch as their homes ruined.

The lord of the world, the Creator of creators, the savior God, serving as the universal soul, overcomes the foemen. The godly perishable body Bṛhaspati comes along with the twin demigod Aśvins, who provide shelter to all who have made sacrifices. Much invoked and fully fed, like the great bull, the Aśvins come to vouchsafe, and providing all with a wide net of protection. Indra, as the lord of the bay coursers, flies fast so that the children will neither harmed nor fall prey to others. The foemen stay far away, thanks to the protection provided by Indra and Agni, who drive them off. The trinity of Vasu, the Ādityas, and Rudra revered as far-reaching mighty thinkers who serve as sovereign lords.

According to *Rig-Veda* 10:129, in the beginning there was nothing but the dormant universe consisting of dark matter. There was neither nonexistence nor existence: there was no realm of air to cover the ground or provide shelter. There was water filling the fathomless depths, but there was no death. Nor was there immortality. There was no sign of light separating the day from the night, but there was One Thing, the universal soul (God), which breathed by its own nature. Apart from this, there was nothing whatsoever. There was darkness, which even concealed the universal soul (God). Also hidden within darkness was the divine will. This created chaos as there was only a formless void. Then, by the great power of the eternal fire, Agni, the next component rose to serve as the primordial power that, as part of the immortal universal soul, appeared to represent the individual living spirit. Once manifested, the individual living spirit began searching to create living things with hearts and minds with a desire to discover their kinship through the power of essence (meath), which turned the nonexistent into existent, creating a transverse line and turning what was below, that is, dark matter, into the illuminated region above, thus turning dark matter into energy, producing light, as demonstrated by Albert Einstein's equation ($E = mc^2$). This generate primordial force Shakti that serves the dynamic universe, and provides all with the realization, verily the knowledge, of whence they were born. But they cannot declare from whence came the supreme powers of causation, serving as the godly powers, which later come to be known as the creators of the different worlds and the different dominions. No one knows whence the universal soul (God) first came into being, or when creation formed, or when the eye formed that beholds this world, God being he who verily knows this, or know's not.

According to *Rig-Veda* 10:130, threads spun out from all directions, with the sacrifice that stretched by the hundred sacred souls serving as the fathers, but with only one being the Creator. This way, like the weaver, the fathers come to sit amid the distortion and shout as they weave forth and weave back. A manifested mortal body extends, and as it unbinds, the vault of heaven spins out. With pegs fastened to the seat of worship, the manifested bodies sing hymns (*sāmans*), moving like weaving shuttles. They rule the order, and the shuttle, like wooden fenders, producing vibrations or hymns, and like butter, these turn into chants, which with recitation are offered to the universal soul (God) and to godly powers such as deities who pray and worship, singing the first holy hymn (Gāyatrī), before they are conjoined with Agni and the goddess Savitar. They jointly combine to produce brilliant hymns in meter aid when they drink soma, it creates aid within them a craving to regulate the planetary system (*Anustup*). Then, through combining the perishable body Bṛhaspati with the holy voice (*Brhati*), they help to establish the material world, *Virāj*. This new world regulated by the eternal law (*Varuna*) and eternal love (*Mitra*), who jointly serve as the solar deity *Triṣṭup,* who day by day helps individuals experience the inner light (*Jagatī*).

As part of the blessing, Indra enters to provide the embodiments with inner illumination. This connects them with physical enlightenment to help the manifested mortal embodiments rise and seek to join with the holy soul (rishis). With ancient sacrifices, they come to honor their ancestral fathers; thus their minds, instead of their brains, envision the sacrificial worship and transform vibrations into oscillations, producing hymns sung in verses, used as part of the ritual, all measured by the seven godlike powers (rishis), who view the ancient path and take up the reins to drive the individual embodiments forward like chariot drivers.

## ALLIANCE/CONQUERORS

According to *Rig-Veda* 10:131, by first driving all enemies away far to the west, the western mighty conquerors join with the eastern mighty conquerors to drive off the northern foes and then drive off the southern foe. They build wide shelters to support the fields full of barley and reap the ripe corn, preparing it as food instead of offering it in worship. The manifested mortal embodiments, in the sacred seasons, come with more than one animal to receive honor at the assembly. With herds of cows and horses, sages strengthened and form a friendship with the mighty power Indra. The twin demigod Aśvins, serving as the lords of splendor, drink full drafts of soma and come to aid Indra. Working with material wealth, Maya Danava, they are reborn as Namuci, an Asura. Serving as parents, the two Aśvins and Indra, through their wondrous powers and wisdom, when all have drunk the draft that gladdens and refreshes through the powers of Sarasvatī, come to referred as Maghavan, the envoy of Indra. Serving with strength, which provides rich assistance, and by possessing all graciousness, they disperse among their foes and provide their charges with safety and vigor. Bestowing his favor with holy, blessed loving-kindness, Indra, as the good protector, drives off all those who hate the noble souls.

According to *Rig-Veda* 10:132, the god of the sky, Dyaus, lauded with material wealth, standing above the earth, comes to watch the heavenly gods Mitra and Varuna, with strength, bless the twin Aśvins to serve the worshippers. In this way, the Aśvins are honored, blessed with sustaining power to go help the manifested bodies, forming bonds of friendship with them and subduing the fiends. They seek to win previous material wealth from the sky lord Dyaus, which they hope to use to try to win the battle, with Mitra bringing love and friendship, increasing their riches, which they distribute, knowing this pipeline of treasure cut off.

Asura, also born of heaven, now serving as the god of the sky Dyaus, while traveling among the mortals, who are all contented, forbearing in their anger, commits a sin to bring about the demise of the great hero Śakapūta, who flees to the home of his dear friend to avoid slain. As steeds, Asura and Dyaus come down to seek the favor of Mother Aditi, making an offering to her, their dear bodies, as part of the worship, filled with wisdom as the pour out purified water upon the earth, its having purified in heaven with love and kindness. Sitting right below her, they wash her in rays of heavenly light. The twin demigods, seated with the lord of wealth and the god of the sky Dyaus, mount up the chariot pole and fly into the forest to save the disheartened Nrmedha and Sumedha tribes, coming to save them from woe.

According to *Rig-Veda* 10:133, Indra, singing at the top of his voice, sets down his chariot at the foremost place that gives him the most room for a fight. Then he begins the war with a shock, which allows the foes to bear up through the experience with great encouragement instead of fear. Let the weak bowstrings of the feeble enemy's break. Thus, the dragon destroyed and sent down into the rivers or deep into earth. Indra, as the foeless one, well considers each choice, drawing all the folk close and to behold the invisible bowstrings of the feeble enemy's break. He destroys all those who are malign and all other enemies by design, casting his thunderbolt at the foes and smiting them dead, thereafter liberally giving to others the ultimate bounty of wealth. Both robbers and demons watch Indra and aim to kill him, but Indra tramples them beneath his feet, outperforming them in his skill and with his weapons, causing them to scatter.

Indra comes to assail all embodiments, whether stranger or kin, and take them down with his vast heavenly strength. All Indra's close friends cling together as he leads them beyond pain and grief, following the path of the holy law. Indra grants their wishes, according to the longings they express in song. The great milk-bearing animals, with exhaustless udders, pour out milk that runs in a thousand streams.

According to *Rig-Veda* 10:134, by morning the cows have filled all the rivers on earth with the heavenly gift from the Mighty Power, the great king of the world, and the goddesses who come forth as the Blessed Mother bring the life force. This helps to lessen mortals' stubbornness, through the loving heart of the Blessed Mother, who tears through those who are wicked, trampling them beneath her feet as they seek their ultimate objective. The Blessed Mother, who brings forth the life force, able to slay any foe and wipe out even their great armies. Indra, through the powers of the heavenly ruler Śakra, first comes to shake down the wicked, and then together with the heavenly noble soul Śatakratu, the shakes them all down, distributing their wealth among the thousands, whom he also provides with soma.

From all directions, drops of sweat fall, creating flashes of lightning. Let all malevolence die like one blade of the holy grass (darbha) that covers the ground. The god serving as the great counselor uses the darbha primarily for cleaning hollow horns (shofars) or conch shells to draw the attention of his messenger Maghavan, who neither offends nor is ever obstinate, to follow his commands from the holy texts that clasped shut and clutched in his arms.

According to *Rig-Veda* 10:135, the god of death, Yama, hiding in a tree, clothed with leaves, drinking water just like mortal beings, representing the godly powers, comes to serve as the father, the head of the house, which he attends with love like the ancient sires. The universal soul (God) looks on reluctantly, cherishing men of old age, those who tread on the path of evil and those who even he desires will come again. Yama, through his power, even though he sees not the child, doe see the new embodiment with old embodiment moving like a wheelless embodiment. Fashioned mentally as one pole turning in many directions, they grow from childhood, thereafter, rolling with the sages to come to understand the hymns (*sāmans*). They follow closely, as if lying together on a ship, not even knowing who their father is or who the one is who made the embodiment of the child. They roll away and on any given day declared dead. At the funeral, a gift placed so that straightway it will appear at the point of the flame. From the depths, with a passageway extending from the front, they go out to the place where Yama dwells. This called the home of the gods, where singers play flutes and sing glorious songs honoring the heavenly power Rudra as they drink soma from a cup.

According to *Rig-Veda* 10:136, the heavenly eternal flame brings heat, and earthly water brings moisture. Together, they fill the sky with ambient illumination, which looks like long hair, the loose locks making a circle. The universal soul (God), serving as a manifested individual spirit, appears as a holy body (*munis*) in soiled garments, creating a yellow hue as he follows the swift wind and goes on his course, his generosity already gone as he stands before the unified group (*munihood*). He beholds natural individual spirits pressed into astral bodies and nothing more. As the winds, he becomes mortal embodiments serving as saints (*munis*), remaining associated with his holy work. He looks upon all the various physical embodiments, which he created, and monitors them as they fly off to cover the regions. The physical body (Vata), along with the wind (Vayu), creates the saint (*muni*), who impelled join the eastern and western regions, including the oceans, as his home. Treading a path among trees and vegetation, the saints pass by the woody living things that are male (*Gandharvas*) and those with long curls that are female (*apsaras*). Know their wish to have him as a sweet friend, he churns the wind (Vayu) into the life force and pounds hard to bend the wood and loosen the curls.

## RENOVATION

According to *Rig-Veda* 10:137, the immortal universal soul (God) rises once more to transform the living beings he has created into humble servants to give new life to all who hate sin. To help in this effort, he brings along two of the great elements of nature: first, the blowing wind, and second, the water that flows freely in the holy river, coming from a distant land to provide energy. Both works to purify and to banish disease. The wind creates the atmosphere that blows away all kinds of disease; the water serves as a purifier, as a healer, or as medicine. Both, as envoys of the universal soul (the immortal God), come nigh as a pair to provide mortals with rest and keep them safe, also blessing them with strength, which drives away any malady that may weaken them. Serving from the cosmic region as demigods, the Maruts appear as a band to deliver all things needed to provide healing power, which drives evil powers away and serves as a bomb or medicine to cure physical pain. The Maruts use their tongues to produce voice, with which they direct and lead the tenfold digits branching off the hands and feet. They proceed to stroke these gently, while they chase evil powers away, air and water serving as support.

## RESTORATION

According to *Rig-Veda* 10:138, all those allied in friendship with Indra come to serve as the priests, reminding the mortals of the holy law, which controls them from limb to limb, in order to protect them from the evil power Vṛtra, while the cosmic hosts (Maruts) bestow the morning light, which causes the waters to flow freely, and chastise dragons with the noble Kutsa, who sends forth productive powers able to cleave the hills and drive forth the animals to come and drink of the pleasant essence (meath). With divine power surpassing that of the mighty powers, Kutsa passes through vegetation and the trees, supported by the shining sun and singing hymns that spring from the holy law. In the middle of the sun's heavenly path, he unyokes the carriage carrying the imperishable noble soul Ārya, who properly matched against the perishable soul Dam as his foe. Serving as an associate of the king, protected by Indra, Ṛjiśvan, in a manifested body, appears along with Indra to overthrow the strong forts, conjuring up the evil Asuras, who rule over the region of Pipru. Ṛjiśvan boldly casts down these forts, which no one had ever assailed: unwearied, he destroys the treasure stores of the godless. With the sun and the moon, he takes the wealth from the stronghold and, uttering praises and singing songs, destroys the foes with flashing darts. Armed with resistless weapons, and with vast powers to cleave, Indra as the Vṛtra-slayer awakens with his darts to deal out wounds. The bright morning light and the dusky evening light, serving as Uṣas, sends a warning with the slaughtering bolt from Indra, who goes upon his way, leaving his chariot there. The heavenly power the father sun, by setting the order with the moon, hears his felly fall out.

According to *Rig-Veda* 10:139, golden-haired, the sun goddess Savitar, with bright sunbeams, rises from the east. She brings luster in the form of eternal energy, which she uses to survey all existence. The wise herder Pūṣan comes as a guard. Sitting in their position on high, they look upon the far-spreading rich pastures extending from the eastern limit to the western limit, the root of all wealth. They gather up treasures. Savitar looks upon the immortal universal soul (God), whom she comes to serve in every form and image, monitored by his eternal law, Varuna, who stands in the battle to save the spoils and serve like Indra. By sacrificing the natural elements water and wind, they manifest as perishable bodies, male (Gandharva) and female (*apsaras*), who drink soma before they approach the godly powers the Visvavasu. From this, they come to realize eternal wisdom, also understanding that by serving Indra, they can realize the presence of the invisible immortal universal soul, which as the individual living spirit, keeps coming and passing through the enclosures that cover all beings who look upon the heavenly power, all served by the mighty Sūrya, the father of all illumination, who provided direct light from the sun, reflective light from the moon, and sprightly light from the constellations of stars. These are all worshipped with songs and hymns by the supreme powers of causation, the Visvavasu, who serve within the midair region.

The immortal universal soul (God) represented by the heavenly bodies who understand what is right, who can separate truth from falsehood, and who know the absolute truth that inspires noble thoughts, which measured by one's praise. Even in a flood, these heavenly bodies seek and find booty, the seekers throwing the doors of the cow pen wide open, allowing manifested perishable bodies to create soma by turning water into milk extract to bring out the nectar (amrit). Then they come to serve Indra, who knows well all the evil powers (dragons).

According to *Rig-Veda* 10:140, Agni, serving as the life power, famous, rich in wealth, and with a mighty blaze, comes as beams of light to enlighten the holy sages, just by passing on his bright light, which strengthens worshipper as food does. With a brilliant, purified, perfect sheen, they levitate amid the light, to visit both mother and daughter, providing aid to those who, as sons, join earth and heaven, serving as the Son of Strength, Jātavedas. They rejoice with gracious hymns and songs, treasuring types of strengthening food, to serve those noble born and provide them with help.

As the ruler of living things, Agni spreads forth, providing wealth that comes from the immortal universal soul (God). Shining with beauty, fair to look upon, he, as the divine, leads all to conquer in power. The wise ones, who make sacrifices with their great riches, under control, blessed with an award of goods and plenteous food and given wealth as they conquer all. Those who come before Agni to vouchsafe their welfare, see Agni as strong and holy, visible to all as godlike. They are born with ears to hear, and like the most famous ones of their generation, they magnified when they sing songs of praise.

According to *Rig-Veda* 10:141, Agni speaks with a gracious mind and, as the enriched head of the house, comes to serve with the art and skill to be the giver of wealth. The trinity of Aryaman, Bhaga, and Bṛhaspati vouchsafe wealth and, as perishable godly powers, give their gifts to the goddess Sūnṛtā, the granter of wealth. The king or the ruler brings soma to aid the God, Agni. The trinity are welcomed with songs and hymns, which invites the cosmic trinity of the Ādityas, Vishnu, and Sūrya, who ask the Brahman priests to join with the perishable Bṛhaspati to serve the heavenly trinity of Indra, Vayu, and Bṛhaspati, singing godly hymns swift to invoke them, who form the council of the people, ready to serve as benevolent. They all urge Aryaman to send gifts to the imperishable Indra, and the perishable Bṛhaspati, and Vata, Vishnu, and Sarasvatī, who all come riding in on strong coursers. Agni with his fires strengthens prayer and sacrifice, urging givers to bestow their wealth to the gods as a form of aid and service.

According to *Rig-Veda* 10:142, Agni, the singer who has no kin, as the Son of Strength, creates the blessed shelter that guarded by the trinity who keep the destructive lightning far away from creations who, at birth, seek food even in the floodwaters. Agni as a comrade wins over all living things and their coursers, which sing victoriously and, by themselves, advance like shepherds, the ones who guard the herds. Agni, with his godlike nature, spares the stones while gathering up the brushwood from tracts like desert among the cornlands. He stirs no one to wrath with his mighty arrow. Over the hills and through the valleys, he goes devouring like an army in search of booty. Like a barber shaves a beard, Agni shaves the surface of earth, fanning his flame with the wind as it blows. The divine lines become apparent as he approaches the single course with chariots, at which point he makes his arms splendid, advancing across the land and through that which lies beneath the ground. He lets his strength, as burning flames, fly upward, generating energy. While generating waste, the energy fills the gap in creation, which widens. He bends over, vigorously polishing, while nature, Vasu, sits beside him near the waters that fill the great reservoir, building a home for the free-flowing streams to form a body of water such as a lake or deep sea. The water finds another path where creations can walk thereon. On his way, flowing along, the holy grass darbha springs up like ponds filled with lotus blossoms, which serve as the mansions of the floodwaters.

## FLYING HORSE

According to *Rig-Veda* 10:143, Atri, the Vedic sage who belongs to the seven sages (Saptarishis), attained eternal freedom to serve like a flying horse. Fully restored with youth and strength, his reincarnated living spirit comes to serve as the universal soul (God). Once freed, Atri returns the newborns to the earth, where they grow. He moves as if tied firmly. His embodied soul appears as a godly power, as unsoiled matter, which commonly taken up as dirt to form the mortal embodiments. As heroes embodiment with a most wondrous power as the Vedic sage Atri, who strives to win with fair songs; and then as heroes of the sky, they produce hymns of praise that shall never cease, as they seek and noticed by the bounteous demigod Aśvins with oblation and eternal love. As heroes in the fight, they come to a safe and ample room. The demigod Aśvins, as the fire element Jupiter, appear as Sagittarius (Bhujyu), coming from the ocean to settle at the end of the terrestrial region, with their wings establishing the cosmos as the planet Jupiter. With joy, the Nāsatyas, serving the most liberal godly planet, also serve as the lords of all treasure, creating a long and narrow strip full of fresh water in the ground to fill a well from which to serve water to the heroes.

According to *Rig-Veda* 10:144, Atri, as the sage worn with age, freed and comes as a flying horse to achieve his goal of restoring the youth, giving them strength and a renewed embodiment, Kakṣīvān. Freed like a flying horse, they appear as newborns to serve the ground (Prithvi), their embodiments already having made from loose soil tied into a firm knot. They now appear as a godly body, one unsoiled by dust or grime, which otherwise binds to physical embodiments. As heroes, most present with wondrous power like that of the sage Atri, who strives to win with fair songs, and serve as the heroes of the sky, singing hymns of praise that never cease. They claim to noticed as bounteous gods who come to serve the celestial demigods, who serve with oblation, the Aśvins serving with love. These heroes, in the fight, create ample room for shelter and ensure safety by tossing Sagittarius (Bhujyu) from the oceanic end of the region, where he represented as half man and half horse—a centaur—carrying a bow and arrow. They appear as archangels, Nāsatyas in molecular structure, with four rings representing carbon, along with many hormones, alkaloids, and vitamins, which in the form of wings provide them nigh with the strength to win. Archangels, like demigods, bring joy like the most liberal of godly powers. Lords of all treasure, they mark the places full of fresh water and come to swell like heroes.

## REVOLUTION

According to *Rig-Veda* 10:145, the goddess of the vegetation, *(Sapatnibadhanam)*, serves as herbs providing different forms of power: effectual power, auspicious power, strong power, silent power, victorious power, and vanquishing power. The forms of vegetation that, according to *Rig-Veda* 10:146, grow wild in the forest gradually vanish from sight and reappear as a swollen screaming membrane forming large wings, which used like drums to produce a high-pitched buzz. They appear as flying grasshoppers or cicadas, which sound like tinkling bells. Yonder where the cattle graze, they build their dwelling places and manifest in the evening, before night, and appear as a lady of the forest who is free to wander. Some call to the animals, and others fall on trees and plants, where they end up setting up their fancy dwellings in the woods, where they make screaming sounds. The goddess never slays unless approached by some murderous enemy. The living beings eat savory fruit and then take rest at their will and praise the goddess with a sweet-scented balm, which is the mother of all sylvan things, where they store their food.

According to *Rig-Veda* 10:147, Indra trusts first in performing divine wrathful deeds, before acting to eliminate the evil power Vṛtra, who may be performing work to profit noble souls. No one knows when the two world halves, heaven above and earth below, fell short to cause a trembling force like thunder. Using magical power, the Blameless One did not shred the evil power with a heart that longs for fame. The gods elect heroes to battle against those who prey, endowing them with divine powers in response to their sacrifices worthy of renown. The universal soul (God), much invoked, takes pleasure in those princes who come with wealth to serve as exalters, for example, the envoy Maghavan. At the council, when the rite succeeds, the princes sing hymns to provide strength and distribute the riches among the sons and progeny. The manifested embodiments serving as humans find delight in the well-protected eternal wealth that provides them with care and joyous drafts. This, with oblations, brings strong powers such as Maghavan, and the heroes, swiftly winning the fight, treated. Now for the whole band, Maghavan with his loud voice makes ample room and, with his might, grants riches provided by the eternal law, Varuna, and by eternal love, Mitra, along with the wondrous food dispenser.

According to *Rig-Veda* 10:148, after they have pressed soma, and with loud voices, the heroes serve Indra as the most valorous one to win the booty. This brings prosperity, which each desire, and under Indra's protection, the heroes conquer those who are born sublime. They blessed, by Indra to serve as heroes. With the power of the heavenly father Sūrya, they overcome the lower race the Dāsas, then bring forth the soma that lay hidden in the water. With votary's hymns for those who crave for the rishis' prayer, the singers come to drink the mythical juice with delight and eat the sweet food offered to all the chariot riders. With holy prayers to Indra, they sing for strength e granted to manifested human beings, those ready to serve as heroes, with one mind to keep all the holy singers safe as their devotees and form friendships among them. They listen to the celebrity demigod Pṛthi, who as a rishi calls upon the heroic strength of Indra, lauded by the loving hymns of pearly heaven (Venya), who, rich in lubricant, comes to serve the ferocious power Agni, who comes rolling in like a torrent.

According to *Rig-Veda* 10:149, the goddess Savitar comes to fix the earth, bind it with bands, and prop it up without any support so it becomes steadfast in heaven. Savitar, as a restless courser, exploited by air and water, which are bound as if no foot has trodden over them. Well-knowing, Savitar, as a child of the water, fixed as an ocean, overflows her limits. Thence springs the world from that uprisen region, and hence the powers of heaven spread out and expand to serve the broad surface of the earth. Then, with a full crowd of immortal embodiments, this and other realms later come to serve as high and holy.

First, verily, Savitar, as a child of the water, appears as a strong-pinioned eagle, to obey the divine immortal law. As holy warriors, like steeds, Savitar and the eagle serve their village, providing milk to cows for their young. A manifested human being, as a man to his wife, lets Savitar come down from heaven as a bearer, serving as the lord of blessing. Savitar, with the envoy Aṅgiras Hiranvastupa, calls this a big achievement: so, she worshipped and lauded in exchange for her favor and watched as the stalk of plant soma.

According to *Rig-Veda* 10:150, the universal soul (God), the bearer of oblations, through the art of fire, appears as a trinity of godly powers, namely, the Ādityas, the Rudras, and Vasu, who appear according to their favor to show themselves to the manifested bodies, joyfully accepted the sacrifices and the hymns that are to other kindled gods. Being invoke by way of called, they exhibit their grace like the lord of blessing Jātavedas. This brings herewith the god of eternal law, Varuna, and the god of eternal love, Mitra, who both come with grace to show themselves before Agni, who appears in the image of the high priest Hotar, serving the godly powers as a noble soul (rishi), enkindled with eternal flame among living beings in the mortal world. Agni is invoked to win ample wealth; he kindly disposes of all winnings to the five noble tribes, *Atri, Bhāradvāja, Gavisthira, Kaṇva, and Trasadasyu.* They all come to help in the fight, calling upon the household priest *Vasiṣṭha*, themselves serving as household priests who come to win grace.

According to *Rig-Veda* 10:151, with eternal faith and oblation offered up to Agni, and by celebrating with praises, worshippers taken to the heights of happiness. Because of their faith, they given blessings, along with divine words spoken by the universal soul (God). The deities, who maintain their faith amid the evil powers the Asuras, utter their desires to the liberal worshippers to have their wishes come true. Guarded by the wind (Vayu), the gods and the manifested liberal worshippers who offer selfless sacrifices draw near to eternal faith to win the yearnings of their hearts, and opulence, by way of their faith. They practice eternal faith in the early morning, at noonday, and at sunset endowed with immortal powers.

According to *Rig-Veda* 10:152, an immortal governor with art and skills, as a wondrous destroyer of the foe, remains a friend. Even after death, such a being helps others to overcome and brings bliss. As a warrior, a fiend-slayer, beings of this sort accompany Indra to drink soma. The lord of the clan comes like a bull and goes ahead to bring peace, first driving the evil rakshasas and other foes far away. They even smash Vṛtra's jaws to pieces, before Indra comes as the Vṛtra-slayer, to quell the foeman's wrath, which threatens noble souls. Indra even beats away foes who challenge those who seek to do any injury, sending them down to endless darkness in the underworld. Indra and the warriors baffle the foemen's plans and ward off any strikes of their weapons, which otherwise could conquer the noble worshippers. By given shelter, the warriors made safe from those with furious wrath, staying far away from their murderous darts.

According to *Rig-Veda* 10:153, the immortal governor, swaying about, come at birth, then nigh to Indra, as the active ones who share in Indra's great heroic might. Based upon their strength and victorious power, they are strong indeed as they serve the Mighty One. They support Indra in his Vṛtra-slaying art and his spreading of the firmament as the holy ground (Prithvi), which with its might holds up the heavens. Indra bears in his arms the whetted weapon the thunderbolt, along with which comes heavenly lightning. Indra, with preeminent art, serves over all creatures and mighty powers to pervade every place.

According to *Rig-Veda* 10:154, Indra brings purified soma, along with sacrificial oil, for those who are looking for meath to flow forth. He even helps those who are ready to depart, with an invincible passion to advance to heaven, and those who show great passion to live longer as heroes, to fight in war and boldly cast their lives away. These given a thousandfold reward. Those who allowed to depart to serve as the first followers of the eternal law given pure holy strength. The god of death, Yama, in favor moves on. Indra lets him depart because he is skilled in a thousand ways. He enlists the sages to protect him, as the sun protects the heavenly souls (rishis). He even provides Yama with support so he can leave to go and serve the eternal law, Varuna.

## SANCTUARY / SACRED HILL

According to *Rig-Veda* 10:155, even the one-eyed, limping, flying old witch (*Arayi)* protected by the divine power *(Prakriti*) and supported by the invisible noble soul (*Sirimbitha.*) Ever screeching, *Arayi* frightens away any who come to the holy place. In this divine sanctuary, goddesses as mothers protect the unborn seed/embryo from any who would seek to destroy it. The manifested immortal power Brahmaṇaspti, with sharp horns like the heavenly Brahman bull, comes to drive *Arayi* extremely far away, leaving her to float on a log without anyone to guide her to the river's edge. The bull seizes her in its hideous jaws and will not let go. When *Arayi* befouled with stains and spots from the bull's jaws, the beast hastens onward, all its enemies slain, disappearing like froth and foam. The manifested noble souls led about like sacred cows and duly carried round raised up in glory by the eternal flame and the other godly powers who had come to protect them from getting killed.

According to *Rig-Veda* 10:156, with songs and speed, the eternal flame, Agni, goes forth like a fleet courser in the race and wins all. The eternal flame, as a dart, comes to save cattle and horses and thereby bring wealth. Agni brings vast wealth by helping to secure horses and cows, like grease in the socket to get the wheel to turn. Agni further gives birth to the illuminated bodies, including the sun, the moon, and the constellations of stars, all mounted up in the sky, bestowing light upon living beings. With the eternal flame serving to provide people with light, the best, the dearest, and the wealthiest seated in the shrine, watching the singers provided with extended life spans.

According to *Rig-Veda* 10:157, Indra and all other godly powers provide aid to allow the existing worlds to dominate. With personal sacrifice, with their bodies, and through their offspring, the warriors now come to help Indra, who, together with the noble Ādityas, rallies together a band of demigods, the Maruts, serving as cosmic hosts. The Maruts, with Indra, serve as the protectors of manifested bodies. These godly powers seek to slaughter the evil Asuras but guard their godlike nature to serve the noble souls, such as the Ādityas, using the illumination of the sun, and other mighty powers whom they look upon for vigor.

According to *Rig-Veda* 10:158, the godly pantheon of Sūrya comes to guard both the upper stratum (heaven) and the lower stratum (the earth), thereby allowing the firmament (Vata) to be established among planetary terrestrial bodies, all created by Agni with his flame, who offers one hundred libations to protect the solar goddess Savitar from failing to illuminate. Savitar gives mortal embodiments the ability to see Parvata, providing them with the eyes to survey the newly created world and distinguish the things within it. Now, within the godly pantheon of Sūrya, everyone looks upon the sun with the eyes to see it clearly.

According to *Rig-Veda* 10:159, knowing the *plasmic* body the sun as the conqueror mounted high up in the sky, the universal soul made happy. God also observes victorious primordial powers serving as the arbiters *Śaci and Paulomī*, who use their submissive powers to guide their sons who serve as foe-slayers. The ruling queen and her daughters serve with a song of triumph, offering the best of oblation to Indra, who thus grows glorious and most high, making the offer that the gods will get rid of all the rival wives. Once these destroyed, the queen will become the sole spouse of the conquering king. Then the universal soul will seize the wealth of the other spouses to give to the weaker daughters. The primeval immortal universal soul becomes the powerful Shakti, who comes to subdue the rival wives and, as conqueror, uphold an imperial sway over the heroes and the regular folk.

According to *Rig-Veda* 10:160, the primeval immortal universal soul becomes the powerful Shakti, who with a taste of strong soma, enriched with viands, unyokes the horses from their chariot and sets them free to serve as flying chargers. Shakti sheds soma for all those who are ready. Once they fully effused with pressed soma, they sing resonant songs and hymns to invite Indra, who is pleased with the libation and comes to those who know all about the mythical juice. Whosoever devoted to God fully effused with a yearning heart and spirit.

Indra will never give away the sacred cow: for him, the cow made famous by the soma. Indra looks with loving favor upon the mortal embodiments and, like a rich man, pours out soma for the gods. The envoy Maghavan comes with bended arm to provide support. He slays the people who hate devotion. They call on him, desirous of goods and the spoils, such as cattle and horses. Indra, with divine love and favor, presents himself when invoked for the welfare for all.

According to *Rig-Veda* 10:161, any grasping demon that, with oblation, has ever possessed the universal soul (God), as the unknown, and has declined to eat is set free by Indra or Agni, from this day forward allowed to depart, even though such a demon may have been brought very near to death. The universal soul comes to snatch such creatures from the lap of destruction, granting them a life span of one hundred autumns with hundred-eyed oblation. The hundred autumns to live by the universal soul and Indra for a hundred more years so that the demon souls led to safety to faraway shores, protected from all misfortune. While gaining in strength through those hundred autumns, they live through one hundred springs and one hundred winters too. Though Indra, Agni, Bṛhaspati, and Savitar may grant a life span of one hundred autumns, they also may grant far more than one hundred years, so the living spirit may rescued and made ready to return as a renewed youth. Whole in members, the universal soul (God) finds the divine sight to serve all life.

According to *Rig-Veda* 10:162, yielding up prayers to slay the evil rakshasas, the warriors drive toward the godhead to protect the woman in labor and drive off the flesh eaters before they can attack the mother and the fruit of her womb. Answering the prayers, the gods arrive before the evil power moves to destroy the embryo, thus preventing the babe from birth killed. The gods further drive the rakshasas into another region, where they cut off their legs. Then the rakshasas lie down between the married couple, attempting to penetrate their bodies as they lick their wounds, and the gods exterminate them. What remains is the progeny, taking on the form of brother or lover, leaving it to the lords to destroy anything that, through sleep or darkness, comes to deceive and lie down to destroy the progeny. Such an intruder exterminated.

According to *Rig-Veda* 10:163, the universal soul drives any malady away from the nostrils, the eyes, the ears, the chin, the head, the brain, and the tongue. Then he drives all maladies away from the neck ligaments, the neck itself, the breastbone, the spine, the shoulders, and the upper and lower arms. Next, he drives all maladies away from the intestines, the rectum, the heart, the kidneys, the liver, and the spleen. After this, God drives any malady away from the thighs, the kneecaps, the heels, the tops of the feet, the hips, the stomach, and the groin. From the rejected regions, including the hair, the nails, the toes, and the joints, God drives all malady away.

According to *Rig-Veda* 10:164, from the command center of his mind, the universal soul looks upon annihilation, Avaunt, from afar, hence knowing the manifold powers of the mind, then brings a happy boon to the elected godly powers the Vaivasvata, also giving them the blessing of divine bliss, which enables them to see the new world and, with their minds, also see the many places within the newly established material world,

Virāj, located on holy ground (Prithvi). Those who addressed by name are associated with blame, by implication committing sins, whether in state of wakefulness or while sleeping. Because of their hateful acts, all evil doers subjected to the eternal flame of Agni, who brings Brahmaṇaspati from a distant place, along with the immortal Indra, to judge their all wrongful and unjust deeds. The powers of the envoy Aṅgirases prevent these foes from troubling the manifested mortal embodiments, who prevail even to this day, freed from sin and guilt. Any ill thoughts that visit the embodiments, when either awake or sleeping, seized upon by the Aṅgirases. The evil powers hate the noble powers, so the Aṅgirases seize the evil powers who hate the noble souls.

According to *Rig-Veda* 10:165, the godly powers, like doves, dive deep in search Avaunt, the envoy of annihilation, hoping to send him far away. Manifested perishable bodies sing hymns and make their atonement, be they quadrupeds or bipeds. Auspicious like the dove, a harmless bird, they sent by the godly powers to a safe dwelling place. Agni, serving as a sage, is pleased with the oblation borne by the wide-winged eagle that, holding an arrow, settles beside the fireplace, on the hearth, to distract the manifested quadrupeds and bipeds and ensure their welfare, protecting them from those looking to harm them. The screeching of the owl is ineffective when the eagle seated beside the fire or next to calm waters, where doves like to settle. The owl sent as a devoted envoy to death, Yama, who bars against all grief and trouble. Flying forth with holy verses, the dove causes all to rejoice in the food and cattle brought to them. Then, swiftly, the dove flies away, leaving the embodiments without vigor.

## MONARCH

According to *Rig-Veda* 10:166, among peers, the dove arrives as a rival conqueror, appearing as a sovereign ruler in service to the animal kingdom. The universal soul (God) appears as the slayer of rivals, protecting Indra, who remains unwounded and unhurt among the enemies of the noble souls, whom he vanquishes by trampling them beneath his feet. Verily, the universal soul binds the two ends of the bow with the bowstring. Pressed down like humankind to serve as the lord of speech, the universal soul comes as a conqueror with almighty power. He has mastered all their thoughts. Like a council performing holy work, having gained the highest level of strength in war, the enemies with all their skills come in peace to God's feet, where they trampled. They speak from beneath God's feet, where *Sapatnanāśanam* appears, along with tailless amphibians such as frogs with short, squat bodies, smooth moist skin, and long hind legs that allow them to leap from the water with a croak.

According to *Rig-Veda* 10:167, taking with them traces of earth, and in a hurry with the wind, the gods come to the assembly as dames in a wind-powered chariot. In power and glory, they come crashing down as they go forth with voices of thunder, painting the regions red as if touching heaven. As they move from the ground, all the dust scatters. Thus, born with embodiments, they come to serve as attendants, and they speed forth with God to create the universe as its monarchs, on the holy ground traveling the paths of the midair region. Immediately they all come to rest or slumber. Holy and earliest-born, friends of the water, from where they spring and travel from region to region, thus creating embryos, the germs of the world manifest as individual living spirits and appear as the vital spirits serving as envoys of God. They move, ever inclined to do so by way of divine will, which heard as the voice of God, who assumes all shapes, ever invisible, and is adorned with oblation.

CHAPTER 24

# Underworld Dominion

THE UNDERWORLD IS THE DOMAIN OF THE EVIL SPIRIT, MADE UP of elements from embodied living beings, who after death remain active and come to manifest as skeletons that once belonged to those who killed both humans and beasts. Such spirits come to the innate domain called the underworld. Death appears as a gray fog. Alongside those of flesh and blood who killed, they devoured and converted into usable strength, able to grow and become more powerful as those who once killed.

## SAPIENT SOULS

According to *Rig-Veda* 10:169, the wind blows upon domesticated animals such as cows, helping them to heal as they eat herbage that filled with vigorous mythical juice. They drink water, rich in life, and eat fatty food. Moving on their feet, they serving as the gracious power Rudra, created in assorted colors or else being single-hued, all of them named by the eternal flame, Agni, who as the envoy Aṅgiras produces passion to vouchsafe them. Under the protection of the great Parjanya, they offered up to the gods to them provide with bodies of various forms. They are all well-known as the source of soma. Because of this, Indra supports such livestock, providing them with full streams of milk to feed their plenteous offspring. The all-bestowing Prajāpati, of one mind, serves as the godly power who also serves as the father to all kinds of livestock. He is the one who provides cattle with offspring, which bear other manifested powers.

According to *Rig-Veda* 10:170, Prajāpati bestowed with bright godly powers. He drinks glorious soma mixed with milk to become essence (meath), and with this sacrifice provided with immortal life, the wind urging the breath in people, which allows them to guard their offspring well. Well-nourished with food, Prajāpati comes to shine over land. Radiant, as the high truth, cherished, best at winning strength, Prajāpati serves with eternal truth, based upon the statutes of the law and the covenant with the heavens. Prajāpati rises with the light, serving as the killer of the evil power Vṛtra and other enemies, even while the sky lord Dyaus serves to slay the ignoble Asuras and other foes.

All-conquering, winner of riches, exalted and highly lauded as the best of all lights, including the supreme direct light, reflective light, and ambient light, all of which are radiant, the mighty Sūrya comes as the sun, which provides unfailing victory and strength everywhere. Beaming forth with splendor, the divine light dwells in the lustrous realm of heaven. By this light, all things in existence brought together, possessed by the all-effecting God.

According to *Rig-Veda* 10:171, Indra brings pressed soma for Iṭa, the power of the liturgical language Pali, who comes to protect individual embodiments who hear the divine call, which borne through skin. With a swift-moving head, the righteous warrior seeks his home among the soma pourers. The manifested mortal embodiment Venya, as a devotee of Indra, encounters *Āstrabudhna*, who many times was set free by Indra, but he keeps coming from the east with the sun, to serve along with it as it moves toward the west, against the will of the gods.

According to *Rig-Veda* 10:172, with all beauty, the embryo appears with the individual living spirit to fill the udders of the cows so they may follow on the path. This brings kind and noble thoughts, most liberal, rousing with hymns the righteous warrior who praised among the bounteous ones. The embryo tied with an umbilical cord, serving to nourish it and, with liberal bounty, to offer sacrifice. The coming of the morning light drives away the sister's gloom through its excellence, which makes it easy to retrace her path.

According to *Rig-Veda* 10:174, warriors offer to join in the fight, where Indra, victorious, serves as the imperishable embodiment Brahmaṇaspati, which allows him to attain royal sway. Subduing the rivals and subduing all malignities, Indra stands up to the menacing man, which causes living things to become angry. The godly powers Soma and Savitar use all the elements of nature to aid Indra, who conquers the foes and becomes the king. Offering oblation to Indra, Soma and Savitar become more glorious, highest among the gods, and hence now, verily, are rival less. The victorious slayer, with royal sway, comes to rule living beings as their sovereign.

According to *Rig-Veda* 10:175, the goddess Savitar, a celestial power, comes through the shafts of compressed cosmic stones (meteorites). By bringing the eternal law, she drives away calamity and malevolence, serving like medicine to harness the bull by herself, bringing its physical power to the upper region, filled with compressed stones, as the bull serves as the father. Savitar looks down with pride, commanding that the manifested embodiments pour out soma and serve it as milk from the mother.

According to *Rig-Veda* 10:176, with praises, Savitar serve Ṛbhu by providing him offspring, who upon arrival perform mighty deeds. Provided with all forms of support, the offspring come to enjoy the ground (Prithvi), where a mother cow brings forth the universal soul (God) with song, also bringing the divine will, which appears as the godly power Jātavedas. Jātavedas at once distributes heavenly gifts, serving as a god-devoted priest who moves forward to offer a sacrifice. Riding along a path in a chariot, he glows, the path known only to him. Agni comes to rescue from distress those among the race of immortals, mighty in strength, who have transformed by the universal soul (God) and now represented as the individual spirit residing within the mortal embodiment that lives on the earth as a perishable body. According to *Rig-Veda* 10:177, these perishable bodies appear as the sapient Māyābheda, beheld as heart and mind, adorned like a bird with mighty magic power and etymological roots that comes to the world as the departed spirit *Saṃhitā* and appearing as the divine Āditya, as well as the not so divine Asura, who constantly battle, each hoping to overrule the others.

The departed *Saṃhitās* follow the eternal law, Varuna, and appear as devotees (devas) or as individuals following the malevolent beings who appear as the source of wrath and unrest, the *Dānavas*. The imperishable spirits the Gandharans, serving as sages, observe every departed living spirit (*Saṃhitā*) as the source of wrath and unrest. Prevailing in the depths of the ocean, they seek the location of the wisdom disposers, where rays from the pantheon of Sūrya bring light. These rays light up the individual living spirit, which appears as a feathered friend in flight, its speech bearing a likeness to the sounds of the living spirit, serving in the womb, pronounced as the astral body, the seat of sacrifice. The imperishable living spirits the Gandharans thus cherish such radiant brightness from heaven. As the rishis, act like herders they never reveal their pathways whether approaching or departing. Whether as clothed embodiments or embodied souls, they gather in a diffusive splendor, continually traveling within the three worlds.

According to *Rig-Veda* 10:178, the One, the Almighty, as commissioned by the godly powers, conquerors all manifested embodiments. Ever triumphant, swift, flying into battle with unbroken fellies, the mythical coiled creation Tārkṣya, as per his divine calling, unravels and offers up gifts to the godheads to help them ascend with strong embodiments, like a ship seeking a safe harbor. The two wide worlds, broad, deep, and extending far, are safe when left with Indra, who, with might, pervades the newly established material world created as five landmasses surrounded by water. All this supported by the heavenly pantheon of Sūrya and his luster, who, with the free-flowing waters and their strength, wins over hundreds of thousands, nonable to avoid him, including the young ones with their mothers, who repel no lover.

According to *Rig-Veda* 10:179, the five landmasses now lift themselves up and looked upon by the invisible godheads who created the seasons. When ready, those of Virāj offer oblation in preparation of meeting the invisible, immortal Indra, who travels along with manifested illuminations, having traveled more than half his journey with friends, who sit around waiting amid their storehouses and serving as the lords of their clans, wandering chieftains among the tribes. Dressed fancily with the eternal flame, their udders are full of fresh soma, which they offer Indra to drink. With this libation and with curd, Indra offers them his with favor, honoring their mighty deeds with his thunder.

According to *Rig-Veda* 10:180, much invoked, Indra helps to subdue the foemen, displaying his might and bounty. In his right hand, Indra brings treasures. He has the skills to create rivers filled with riches. In his other hand is the dreaded wild beast that roams in the mountains. The godly powers approach afar, having whetted their weapons so the blades are sharp enough to slice through the foes, who scattered and who hate noble souls. Mighty Indra springs forth as the strongest being, exercising his lordship over the tribes as they drive off the unfriendly folk, making room for the godly souls to travel freely.

According to *Rig-Veda* 10:181, the first hermit, Vasishta, accepts the godly soul Rathantara as his master, who admires the radiant trinity Dhātar, Savitar, and Vishnu, who come to teach numerology, the study of the significance of numbers, that is, the divine relationship between any given number and its coinciding events, practiced by the paranormal Saprathas and pure essence, Pratah. The sages (rishis) lying remote and hidden among the loftiest regions discover the eternal power of essence (meath), prevailing within the trinity of Dhātar, Savitar, and Vishnu as the radiant powers served by ferocious fire or the pantheon of Sūrya. Such illumination thus illuminates the holy ground, with Bṛhati being the ruling power a descendant of Agni. Appearing as the envoy Aṅgiras, the manifested immortal powers represented as the seven great sages or rishis (Saptarishis), including the sage Manu (Manvantara) and his eternal mother, Atri, along with other with powers of eternal wisdom, including Vashishtha, Vishvamitra, Gautama, Jamadagni, and Kashyapa. They are all referred to as Bhāradvāja, who through their mental power have visualized the earliest pathway, through Yajus, to reach the godly powers who descended from the radiant trinity of Dhātar, Savitar, and Vishnu, all coming from the pantheon of Sūrya, from whom holy sages serving as prophets receive the ultimate truth (dharma).

## CREATION

According to *Rig-Veda* 10:183, the unmanifested immortal living spirit of the universal soul (God) springs forth with passion as an individual who hence developed offspring, who spread and had their own offspring, bestowed with riches and eternal wisdom, and craving the children of the water as embryos. The universal soul, with his heart and mind, saw himself in the form of a pondering soul seeking in time to have a physical body that might be fruitful. The physical body comes as a youthful woman, who rises to meet with the universal soul to have offspring such as plants and herbs, all existing as part of the universal soul to increase in number deposited with the germ of the living spirit. Thus, creating progeny on the earth all genders, sons and daughters, who will prosper hereafter.

According to *Rig-Veda* 10:184, the universal soul (God), in the form of a germ with its protector, Vishnu, is safe in the womb and, with the help of the creative power Tvaṣṭṛ, is duly shaped into its ultimate form, as the father

Prajāpati infuses the water, which in a stream comes to serve the upholder Dhātar, bringing the germ to be laid. Agni, through his envoy Aṅgiras, sends his daughter the inactive living spirit Sinīvālī to set the germ. The goddess Sarasvatī crowned, her germ like lotuses flourish with no need for soil. The twin demigod Aśvins rub together gold sticks and, with the wear and tear, invoke the germ that comes to be born in the tenth month.

According to *Rig-Veda* 10:185, by way of the great unassailable heavenly favor, the godly trinity of Varuna, Mitra, and Aryaman, neither at home nor abroad, look for the strange pathways walked by the powerful evil-minded foe. Mother Aditi bestows eternal light, which allows her sons to find their way without any favor. According to *Rig-Veda* 10:186, Agni, from far away, sends brilliantly shining rays across the wasteland (dark matter), with vibrations like a prayer to help all the folk so they may bear up as their history, in the form of residual memories, with their adversaries revealed. A bull with a brightly gleaming flame utterly consumes the fiends, so their residual memories as adversaries must borne as well. Those who look with the proper perspective able to view and comprehend all things in existence and bear up against current foes as past adversaries borne up against. Splendid Agni, born in the farthest region, the interstellar region, helps them to bear up against their foes.

According to *Rig-Veda* 10:187, the godly power Jātavedas now sends forth the vigorous steed from his position seated on the sacred grass. The universal soul (God) raises up a lofty eulogy for Jātavedas, who brings the rain and joins with the noble sages to form a band of heroes. With flames, Jātavedas carries an oblation to the gods to offer in sacrifice. According to *Rig-Veda* 10:188, Jātavedas with his vigorous steed raises up the lofty eulogy to support the rain, which with flames carries and promotes the sacrifice. According to *Rig-Veda* 10:189, the spotted bull thus comes and sits in the east before its mother, having made as the king to advance and serve as the heavenly father. Expiring, he draws his life force as breath and, along with his mother, moves along the lucid spheres. The bull, like the sun, shines throughout all the sky, generating vibrations and creating songs to bestow upon the individual living spirit, which as a bird comes to be ruled by the supreme powers of causation covering all three realms, with thirty mighty powers serving as divinities, deities, and demigods, bringing the morning light (dawn) and the evening light (dusk), thus creating day and night.

According to *Rig-Veda* 10:190, with kindled fervor, from the heights, eternal law and absolute truth are born. Hence falls the night, which produces billowy waves in the seas, which raises the water level in the oceans. From the same billows, the ocean flooded, which years afterward produces that which ordained as day and night, regulated by Dhātar, the Great Creator, as the lord over all manifested embodiments, who close his eyes to form the direct light (the sun) and the reflective light (the moon). In the same manner, the Creator forms heaven and earth, its regions served by air and light.

According to *Rig-Veda* 10:191, the eternal flame, Agni, gathers up all that is precious for his friends, and brings his friends all treasures and skills that are enkindle with libation in the assembly place. He speaks to them: "Let your minds be of one accord." As the ancient gods unanimously sit down in their appointed places among the assembly, they are of one mind, meaning they are united in thought. A common purpose, the universal soul (God), laid before all manifested mortal embodiments worshipped and given general oblation. The same be they all to seek a resolution, and their minds working in accord. United be the thoughts of all, so that all may happily agree and be involuted.

# Conclusion

In conclusion, the universe in the beginning had two aspects, one dormant and the other dynamic. All creations belong to the dynamic universe, subjected to supreme powers of causation who generate the universal soul responsible for essence, which regulates existence and nonexistence, thereby giving birth to physical evolution, spiritual involution, and ultimate truth. With this evolution, physical bodies manifested and subjected to enhancement, thus creating the physical world, including the material world that we all live in. The next stage is involution, where the subtle or nonphysical aspects of the manifestations enhanced, these aspects becoming an integral part of the physical evolution of the manifested physical bodies. The third stage is spiritual evolution, where the eternal universal soul, in the form of essence, comes to regulate the existence of manifested physical and nonphysical bodies. This establishes the duration of life and its quality, both of which are determined by the divine will, which appears in the form of individual knowledge, which includes consciousness, intellect, eternal wisdom, and understanding of absolute truth. The divine will remains secret until an individual embodiment makes the commitment to seek it and unveil the hidden knowledge of everything about the Creator, creations, and the powers of the universal soul, who becomes an integral part of the embodiment serving as the individual living spirt regulating the embodiment and influencing its life.

In the Vedas, there are seven or eight supreme powers of causation, which as mighty powers manifest as visible (perishable) and nonvisible (imperishable), personified as divinities, deities, and demigods. They prevail throughout the universe and in time become an integral part of life, bringing changes, and creating specific environments and circumstances. They all function as a monolith; however, each power behaves differently and thus makes a different impact on individual embodiments. The mighty powers commonly addressed with assigned names to differentiate the great elements of nature, that is, earth, fire, air, water, and space, all of which transform to become classical elements or the ether, serving as the individual living spirit. In addition to ether, there are three sources of illumination: the sun, the moon, and the constellations of stars. Whereas the sun provides direct light, the moon provides reflective light and constellations provide nimble light.

The dynamic universe itself divided into three major segments, including heaven, the illuminated region above; earth, the dark matter below; and the middle esoteric region, where matter and energy constantly interact to bring about changes. The illuminated heaven above consists of seven celestial regions that all cover the illuminated region, which keeps rising, and below these are the seven cosmic regions, which also rise to fill the gap, thereby creating and modifying the solar system. Right below this is the terrestrial region, composed of seven manifested worlds and seven unmanifested worlds.

Within the terrestrial region is a stable platform called holy ground (Prithvi), which established as the place where the supreme powers of causation come to reside, operating as the invisible immortal universal soul, which appears in two forms: imperishable and perishable. Both forms are subject to the divine covenants of Varuna (eternal law) and Mitra (eternal love), who provide the vital imperishable powers that needed by all perishable creations to survive in the material world (Virāj). The perishable body may be enhanced to become an imperishable embodiment, and from the state of imperishability, embodiments can even be enhanced to become immortal by way of understanding the cycle of life and death, which persists beyond one lifetime and into the epochs (yugas), where one knows the past and also envisions the future to help the creations enter the holy order and be ordained by way of sacraments and rites, by which the divine power educates the creations that come from the earth and those that come from the underworld. In a simple, the invoked divine power guides such embodiments so they may comprehend the material world and through the holy order so they may serve the congregation of worshippers with the aim of sharing the absolute truth, which allows all living things to live in the material world in peace and tranquility. Each holy order consists of seven special sacraments that individual required to undergo personally to become a part of the grand cosmic network. They join with the others and focus on prayer and meditation to witness the host of the light Sūrya, who ascends, placing his divine power into the center of their heart so they become humble and gain the focus to cultivate and organize their minds. Through the powers of consciousness, the mortal embodiment stabilized within the material world and, through raising the living spirit by way of higher vibrations, acquires ultimate eternal wisdom, thereby learning to live in the turbulent world with inner peace and tranquility. Such wisdom expressed in the *Rig-Veda* comes very gradually to lead a devotee to comprehending eternal truth, at a pace where first consciousness itself helps transform the individual mind and heart so they may work together to comprehend the material world and thus unveil the absolute truth, thereby acquiring inner peace and tranquility.

# Reference

## Vedic gods and goddesses

**Primordial Power (*Trinity*)**

Primordial power (***Shakti)*** that prevailed before the creation of universe regulates triple deity includes ***Vishnu, Brahma*** and ***Shiva***. The trinity as the supreme being creates, protects, and transforms the universe. In benevolent aspects, **Vishnu** depicted as an omniscient being sleeping on the coils of the serpent (who represents time) floating in the primeval ocean of milk with his consort, **Lakshmi.** Whenever the world threatened with evil, chaos, and destructive forces, godhead Vishnu descends in the form of an avatar *(incarnation)* to restore the cosmic order.

**Sky God (Dyaus)**

*Dyauṣ* refer to daylight-sky god which appears with ground thus combining 'heaven' and 'earth' most defining paternal role as *Dyauṣ* and *Prithv*i. They bring with morning dawn and evening dusk (*Uṣas)*. Their offspring include fire (*Agni*), rain and thunder (*Parjanya*), noble rulers (*Ādityas)*, cosmic host (*Maruts),* and messengers (*Angirases*). The twain (*Ashvin*) meaning grandson or offspring of *Dyauṣ* appear as a black stallion studded with pearls in a simile with the night sky. Separation of *Dyauṣ* and *Prithvi* lead to the myth of f Godhead *(Indra*)

**Godhead Superior (Indra)**

The main god of the Rigveda, often depicted as a warrior god which is superior to any other godly power. It is associated with the sky, lightning, weather, thunder, storms, rains, river flows. Indra celebrated for its powers, and as the one who killed the great evil power who obstructed human prosperity and happiness. Indra rules over the much-sought realm of demigods (*Devas)*

**Godhead ferocious Fire (Agni)**

In the classical cosmology Agni as fire is one of the five inert impermanent elements of nature which along with space, water, air and earth in five combining to form to manifest and empirically present the divine nature (*Prakriti*). It conceptualized to exist at three levels, on earth as fire, in the atmosphere as lightning, and in the sky as the sun.

**Mythical Drink (Soma)**

The Soma as the mythical primeval drink that used by godly powers. It is a fermented juice drink which the godly powers as well as the ancient priests (*brahmanas)* consumed while performing rituals to go beyond the material world. It is an elixir, its consumption not only healed illness but also brought great inner awakening. Soma also personified with God of sacrifices. In mythology, the gods gained their immortality by drinking Soma. This drink since ancient times considered as deity or divine beverage which help living being to come closer to the primordial force.

**Godly Solar Wind (Rudra)**

It appears by making loud sound, personified as 'the roarer/howler'. Rudra praised as the 'mightiest of the mighty' power which eradicates problems by pulling roots. Rudra can mean 'the most frightening one'. Lod Śiva considered to have evolved from Rudra, sometimes appear as Maruts.

**Dual pair (Varuna/Mitra)**

Varuna as the deity, is associated sky, which later join with seas to brings justice and truth. Said to be the son from one of the seven ancient sages Varuna rides crocodile with a weapon as noose, rope loop. As the guardian deity, he serves as the father of the Vedic sage (*Vasishtha).* Varuna found in Japanese Buddhist mythology as *Suiten.* Mitra is mostly indistinguishable from Varuna, together with as pair Mitra-Varuna. represents an apotropaic application of "friend"] to the otherwise frightening and dangerous Varuna."

**Ribhus**

The evolved over time to appear as three male artisans whose abilities and austerities make them into divinities Their individual names were Ribhu Vaja and Vibhvan they were collectively called er, skillful, inventive, prudent", cognate Ribhus are depicted in some legends of the Vedic literature as three sons of the goddess of morning light Ribhus are born in human form who then bring their innovation to earth, remain humble and kind. This makes some gods angry and the Ribhus are refused entry back to heaven. Other gods intervene and make the inventive Ribhus immortal. They revered in ancient Hindu texts as sages, as stars, or rays of the sun.

**Goddesses**

The goddess not referred to in Rigveda is *Saraswati.* She is the goddess of learning, music, and art. *Saraswat*i often depicted as a beautiful woman, wearing white clothes, and seated on a lotus flower. Another Rigveda goddess is Apsaras. She is the goddess of beauty, grace, and charm. *Apsaras* often depicted as beautiful women with long flowing hair. *Aditi* and *Aryani* are two other Rigvedic goddesses. *Aditi i*s the goddess of space and time, and Aryani is the goddess of love and fertility.

Printed in the United States
by Baker & Taylor Publisher Services